D0452809

COORDINATED SCIENCE SECOND EDITION

Physics

Mary Jones, Geoff Jones & Phillip Marchington

PUBLISHED BY THE PRESS SYNDICATE OF THE UNIVERSITY OF CAMBRIDGE
The Pitt Building, Trumpington Street, Cambridge CB2 1RP, United Kingdom

CAMBRIDGE UNIVERSITY PRESS
The Edinburgh Building, Cambridge CB2 2RU, United Kingdom
40 West 20th Street, New York, NY 10011-4211, USA
10 Stamford Road, Oakleigh, Melbourne 3166, Australia

First published 1993
Second edition 1997

Printed in the United Kingdom at the University Press, Cambridge

A catalogue record for this book is available from the British Library

ISBN 0 521 59982 2 ✓

Prepared for the publishers by Stenton Associates

Cover photograph: Fibre optics, Adam Hart-Davis/Science Photo Library

CONTENTS

HOW TO USE THIS BOOK

The material is organised into main **subject areas**. Each has its own colour key which is shown on the contents list on page 3 and on the contents lists appearing at the beginning of each subject area.

Core text is material suitable for students of a wide ability range. However, not all of the core text will be suitable for all syllabuses and teachers should be aware of this.

Investigations which the authors have found to be particularly useful or enjoyable have been chosen. The instructions are detailed enough to be followed by most students without further help. However, instructions for drawing up results tables and graphs have been deliberately omitted in several cases, so that the student's ability to do this can be assessed.
In some places measurements are shown as fractions rather than decimals. This has been done deliberately to make it easier for students to understand.

33 CONTROLLING HEAT FLOW

Insulators slow down the transfer of energy from hot to cold bodies.

Fins are used for cooling by radiation

Most animals are poikilothermic. This means that their body temperature is the same as their surroundings. If it is hot, they are hot. If it is cold, they are cold.
Reptiles are poikilothermic. If the air temperature is high, their body temperature is also high. This makes their metabolic reactions take place at a faster rate. They are more active. It is thought that the large fins on the backs of dinosaurs like *Dimetrodon* might have helped them to warm up quickly in the morning. If they stood sideways on to the sun, the large area of the fin would absorb radiated heat. This would raise their body temperature, and make them more active. Butterflies do this, too. On a cool day, a butterfly will rest with its wings outstretched, at right angles to the sun's rays. This warms its body and makes it more active. Large fins can also be used to *lose* heat by convection, conduction and radiation. *Dimetrodon's* fin might have been used for this on hot days. It would have stood end on to the sun's rays. Air-cooled engines also have fins. Heat is lost from the large surface area of the fins into the air.

Fig. 33.1 *Dimetrodon*. The large fin is believed to have been useful in controlling body temperature. Energy would be absorbed as radiation, or lost by radiation and convection in the air.

Insulation saves energy

Mammals and birds are **homeothermic** animals. They can keep their body temperature high, even when outside temperatures are low. They use food to generate heat inside their bodies. This uses a lot of food, so homeothermic animals need to make sure that they do not lose too much of this heat. As it is, they have to eat a lot more food than poikilothermic animals. It is important to save as much as internal energy as possible so as not to waste food which might be difficult to obtain.

Layers of fat or blubber around the animal's body act as insulators. They slow down loss of heat energy. Fur and feathers are also good insulators. Thick layers of fur trap air, which is a very poor conductor of heat. In cold weather, animals and birds may fluff up their fur or feathers. This traps even more air, and increases the insulation. Humans do not have much fur! We make up for it by wearing clothing. Wool is a good insulator because wool fibres trap air. Woollen clothing stops the heat generated inside your body from escaping. Cotton is not such a good insulator because the fibres don't trap much air. Cotton is good to wear in summer when you actually want to *lose* heat from your body. If you really want to keep warm, many thin layers of clothes are better than one or two thick ones. Air is trapped between each layer. The more layers, the better the insulation.

Fig. 33.2 The thick layer of fat, and the fur which traps air, insulates the polar bear.

INVESTIGATION 33.1

Penguins

Penguins living in very cold regions around the Antarctic often huddle together to keep warm. Using test tubes full of water to represent penguins, design an experiment to find out if huddling together helps penguins to retain their body heat.

86

Apparatus Lists for the investigations will be found on pages 240–242. These lists also include other notes for teachers, such as particular safety points or ways in which the investigation might be slightly altered or extended. These notes should be read before attempting any experiments.

Small objects lose their internal energy faster than large ones

Fig. 33.3 How surface area changes with volume.

This block has sides of 1 cm. What is its surface area? What is its volume?

This block has sides of 5 cm. What is its surface area? What is its volume?

Which block has the greatest ratio of surface area to volume? What can you say about the way in which this ratio changes as things get bigger?

Energy is lost through surfaces. The larger the surface area, the faster the rate of energy loss.

A small animal has a larger surface area for its size than a big animal. A polar bear, for example has a very large volume. It also has a large surface area. But most of a polar bear is 'inside'. Its volume is large compared to its surface area. A shrew has a very small volume. It also has a small surface area. But a lot of a shrew is 'outside'. A shrew's surface area is large compared to its volume. Both polar bears and shrews are homeothermic animals. They generate heat inside their bodies. A polar bear is much bigger than a shrew, so it generates a lot more heat. And not very much of this heat escapes from the polar bear, because its surface area is small compared to its volume. But the small shrew generates much less heat. And a lot of this heat escapes from its relatively large surface area.

So small animals have problems keeping warm. They lose heat quickly through their relatively large surface area. A shrew has to eat its own weight in food every day, just to generate enough heat to keep warm. A polar bear can manage by just eating one seal every few days.

Human babies have large surface areas compared to their volumes. They lose heat easily. Small babies must be wrapped up well in cold temperatures.

Vacuum flasks reduce heat flow between the contents and the air

A vacuum flask is made of two containers inside one another, and separated by a vacuum. (There is usually another covering on the outside, to make it stronger and to look attractive.) The surfaces of both containers are shiny. They are made from glass or stainless steel.

These shiny surfaces reduce energy transfer by radiation. The vacuum between them prevents heat loss by conduction. (Remember – conduction only happens through materials.) A small amount of energy is conducted up the sides of the inner wall. This is kept as small as possible by making the sides of the walls very thin.

So if hot coffee is put into a vacuum flask, it is difficult for heat to be transferred from the coffee to the air. The coffee stays hot. If liquid nitrogen at −196 °C is put into a vacuum flask, it is difficult for heat to be transferred from the air into the liquid nitrogen. The liquid nitrogen stays cold. Vacuum flasks are just as good at keeping things cold as keeping things hot. A flask of ice-cold orange juice will stay cold for a long time, even on a hot day.

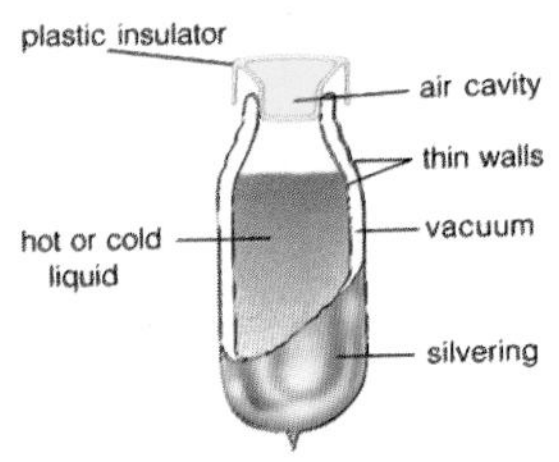

Fig. 33.4 A vacuum flask, with its outer covering removed.

Heat pumps reverse the normal direction of heat flow

Heat normally flows from objects with a high temperature to objects with lower temperatures. But heat pumps can make heat flow the other way.

Even cold water at 3 °C has a lot of energy in it. If the water was made even cooler, some of this energy could be taken from it. This is what a heat pump does. It cools down substances that we might already think of as 'cold'. The energy taken from the substance can be used for heating. For example, the water in the river Thames, in England, provides heat energy for heating the Festival Hall in London. Heat pumps take energy from the cold water, making it even colder. Enough energy is obtained from the water to heat the whole building. The heat pump uses power to take the heat from the water. But for every 100 W of electricity it uses, it can produce 300 W of heat.

EXTENSION

DID YOU KNOW?

Ten people dancing generate more heat than a gas fire. Even at a winter party, you will probably need to open a few windows!

Questions

1 Explain why:
- a Thin people tend to feel the cold more than fat people.
- b It is important for old people to eat well in winter.
- c Homeothermic animals need to eat far more than poikilothermic animals of similar size.
- d Supermarkets usually display frozen goods in chest freezers rather than upright freezers. (Clue – think what happens when the door is opened.)
- e Several layers of thin clothes will keep you warmer than two layers of thick ones.
- f Large penguins are found at the South Pole and smaller ones are found further away.

87

Extension text is material which only more able students need to consider. It includes such things as rearranging formulae, performing calculations, or understanding more difficult concepts. However, there is no sharp dividing line between core and extension material and individual teachers may well disagree with us in particular instances. Weaker students may be able to cope with some of the extension material if sufficiently motivated.

Questions are included in most topics. They range widely, from relatively simple structured questions, through comprehensions, to open-ended questions requiring considerable planning, and perhaps further research by the student.
In addition, each subject area ends with a range of structured questions relating to all the topics within it. Teachers should be able to find questions to suit students of a wide ability range.
Answers to numerical questions will be found on pages 243–244.

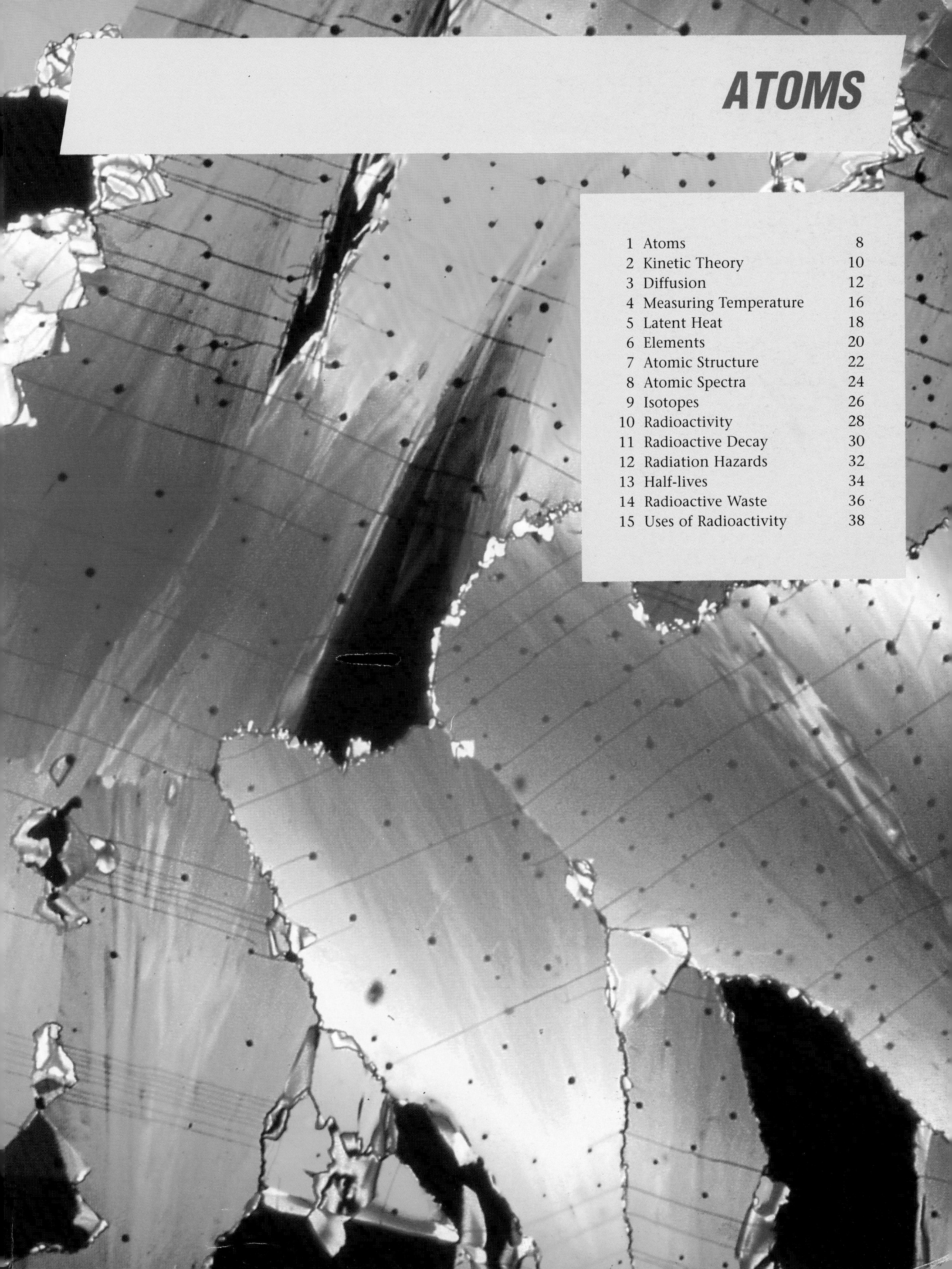

ATOMS

1 ATOMS *All material is made from tiny particles, called atoms.*

All substances are made of atoms

Everything that you see around you is made out of tiny particles called **atoms**. This page, the ink on it, you and your chair are all made of atoms. Atoms are remarkably small. The head of a pin contains about 60 000 000 000 000 000 000 atoms. It is difficult to imagine anything quite so small as an atom. The ancient Greeks believed that nothing smaller than an atom could exist, so they gave them the name 'atomos', meaning 'indivisible'. Atoms sometimes exist singly, and sometimes in groups. These groups of atoms are also known as **molecules**.

The way substances behave suggests that they are made of tiny particles

Atoms are far too small to be seen. Yet we know they must be there, because of the way that substances behave.

Crystals of many materials have regular shapes. The crystals of a particular substance always have the same shape. One explanation for this is that crystals are built up of tiny particles, put together in a regular way. These tiny particles are atoms.

Fig. 1.1 Sodium chloride (salt) crystals. The actual size of the biggest crystal in this enlarged photograph is about 0.3 mm across.

A crystal such as the one in the photograph contains millions upon millions of atoms. If a small piece is chipped away from a salt crystal, for example, the piece is still salt. Even the very smallest, microscopic piece you can chip away is still salt.

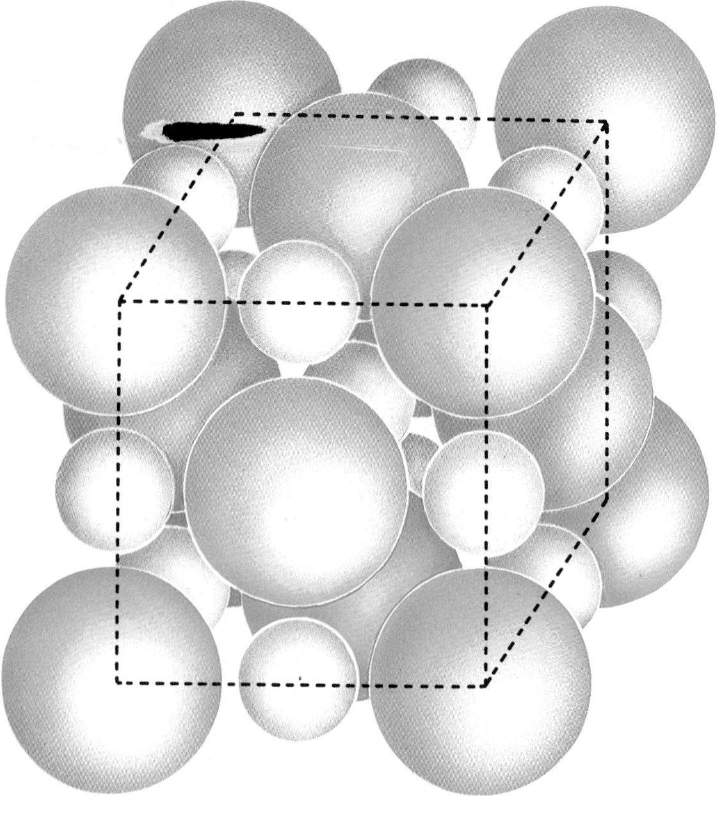

Fig. 1.2 A salt crystal. Sodium chloride crystals are cube-shaped. This is because they are made of particles which are arranged in a regular, cubic pattern. The diagram shows the particles in a very, very tiny piece of sodium chloride.

DID YOU KNOW?

If you divided a single drop of water so that everyone in the world had an equal share, everyone would still get about one million million molecules.

Brownian motion is evidence for the existence of particles

In 1827, an Oxford scientist, Robert Brown, was studying pollen grains through a microscope. The pollen grains were in liquid, and Brown was surprised to see that the movement was jerky. Other scientists became interested in Brown's observations. Many suggestions were made to try to explain them. Some people thought that the pollen might be moving of its own accord. Others suggested that it was being knocked around by something invisible in the liquid in which it was floating.

You can see this effect with the apparatus in Figure 1.4, using smoke grains instead of pollen grains. No-one could possibly imagine that smoke grains are alive. The jerky movement can best be explained by imagining tiny air molecules around the smoke grains, bumping into them. This knocks the smoke grains around in jerky movements. The air molecules are much too small to be seen. They must be moving around very quickly.

This jerky movement of the pollen grains or smoke grains is called **Brownian motion**, after Robert Brown. It is strong evidence that all substances are made up of molecules, in constant motion, and much too small to be seen.

Fig. 1.3 Brownian motion. Small particles like smoke particles seem to move randomly, constantly changing direction.

INVESTIGATION 1.1

Using a smoke cell to see Brownian motion

A smoke cell is a small glass container in which you can trap smoke grains, and then watch them through a microscope.

1 Make sure that you understand the smoke cell apparatus. The smoke cell itself (see Figure 1.4) should be clean, because light must be able to shine through the sides of it. The light comes from a small bulb. It is focused onto the smoke cell through a cylindrical glass lens.

2 Set up a microscope.

3 Now trap some smoke in the smoke cell, in the following way. Set light to one end of a waxed paper straw. If you hold the burning straw at an angle, you can make the smoke pour out of the lower end and into the smoke cell. Quickly place a cover slip over the smoke in the smoke cell.

4 Put the smoke cell apparatus on the stage of the microscope. Switch on the light. Focus on the contents of the smoke cell.

You should be able to see small specks of light dancing around. These are the smoke grains. They look bright because the light reflects off them.

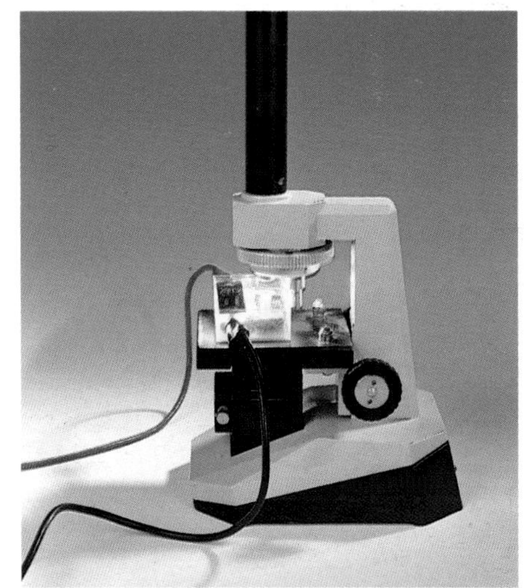

Fig. 1.5 Using a smoke cell

Fig. 1.4 The smoke cell apparatus

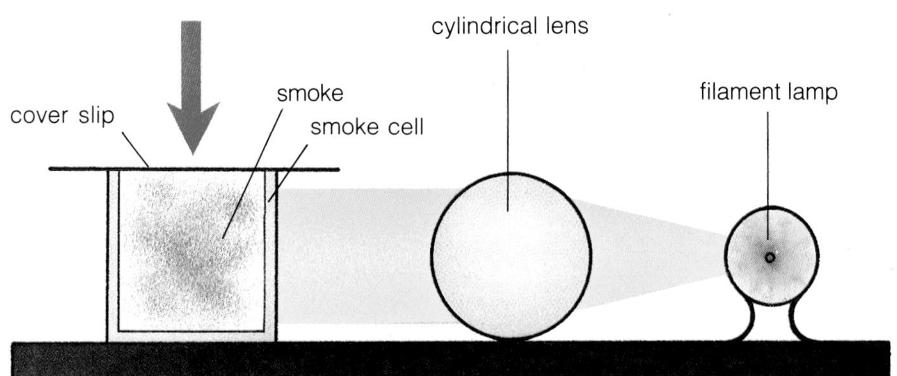

Questions

1 a What can you see in the smoke cell?

b What is in the cell which cannot be seen?

2 Why are the smoke grains dancing around?

3 What is the name for this movement?

2 KINETIC THEORY

All material is made from small moving particles called atoms. Materials can be solid, liquid or gaseous, depending on the arrangement and freedom of movement of these particles.

There are three states of matter

All material is made from tiny particles. These particles are constantly moving. The kinetic theory uses this idea of tiny moving particles to explain the different forms that material can take. 'Kinetic' means 'to do with movement'.

The three states of matter are solid, liquid and gas.

DID YOU KNOW?

At very low temperatures, gases can form 'super-fluids'. Liquid helium flows *up* the sides of a beaker at –272 °C.

The first state - solid

In this state, matter tends to keep its shape. If it is squashed or stretched enough, it will change shape slightly. Usually, any change in volume is too small to be noticed. The particles are not moving around, although they are vibrating very slightly. Normally they vibrate about fixed positions. If a solid is heated the particles start to vibrate more.

Fig. 2.1a

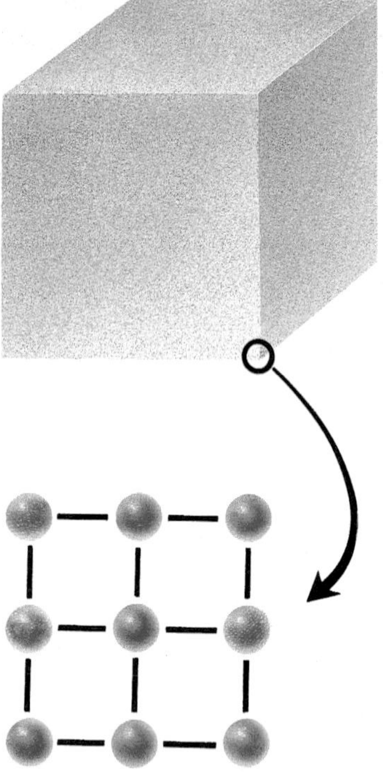

The particles are fixed in position. The forces between particles are strong. The particles cannot move past each other. They are close together.

The second state - liquid

In this state matter will flow. It will take up the shape of any container it is put in. The liquid normally fills a container from the bottom up. It has a fixed volume. If the liquid is squeezed it will change shape, but the volume hardly changes at all. The particles, like those in a solid, are vibrating. However, in a liquid the particles are free to move around each other. If a liquid is heated, the particles move faster.

Fig. 2.1b

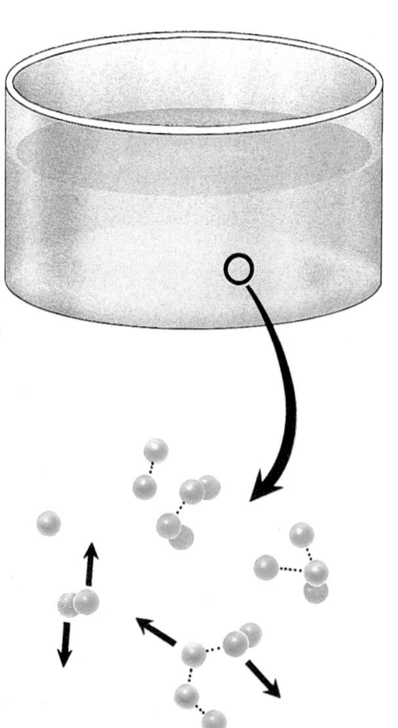

The particles can move past each other. They are joined together in small groups. They are not as close together as in a solid. The forces between the particles are not so strong.

The third state - gas

In this state matter will take up the shape of a container and fill it. The volume of the gas depends on the size of its container. If the gas is squashed it will change both volume and shape. The particles are free to move around, and do not often meet each other. The particles whizz around very quickly. If heated they move even faster.

Fig. 2.1c

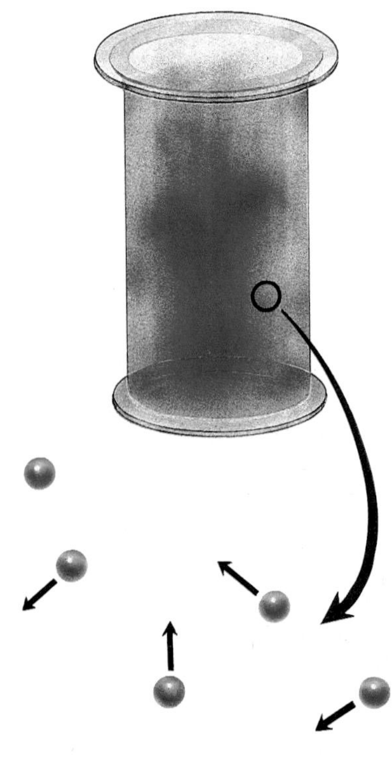

There are hardly any forces between the particles. They are a long way apart. The particles are moving quickly and so they spread out. If squashed, they move closer together.

A model for the kinetic theory

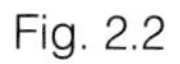

A platform is attached to an electric motor. The motor vibrates the platform up and down. The speed of the vibrations can be controlled.

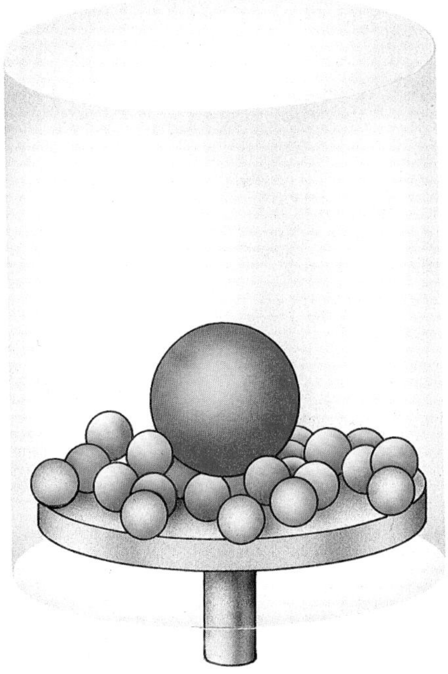

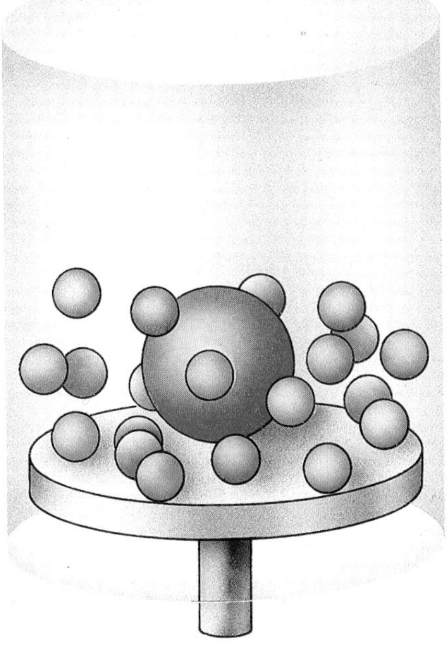

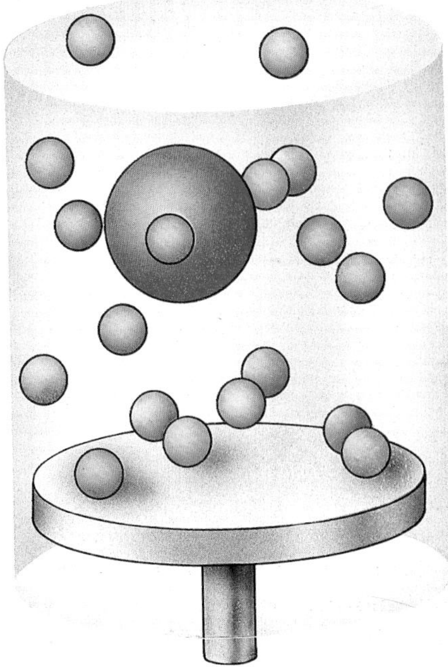

Fig. 2.2

When the platform is still the small balls are like the particles in a solid. They are in fixed positions. If a larger ball is placed on the small ones, it sits on top of them as it would on a solid.

If the platform is made to vibrate gently, the small balls vibrate. But they still stay in the same place. This is what happens when a solid warms up. The particles vibrate, but stay in the same place.

If the platform vibrates faster, the balls start to move faster. It is as though the solid is being heated. When the balls begin to bounce above the level of the platform they are behaving like the particles in a liquid. Now the larger ball is surrounded by the smaller ones. It is as though it has 'sunk' into the liquid.

If the platform vibrates very fast, the balls fly around the whole container. They bounce off the walls. Now they are behaving like the particles in a gas. The large ball is knocked about by the small balls. It is behaving like the smoke grains in the smoke cell experiment.

In this model the average speed of the balls depends on the speed of vibration of the motor. In a substance, the average speed of the particles depends on the temperature. The temperature of a material indicates how quickly the particles are moving.

DID YOU KNOW?

If a gas is heated to a very high temperature, the molecules and then the atoms break apart. At tens of thousands of degrees Celsius, a plasma is formed. The Sun is a plasma. A fluorescent tube contains a plasma.

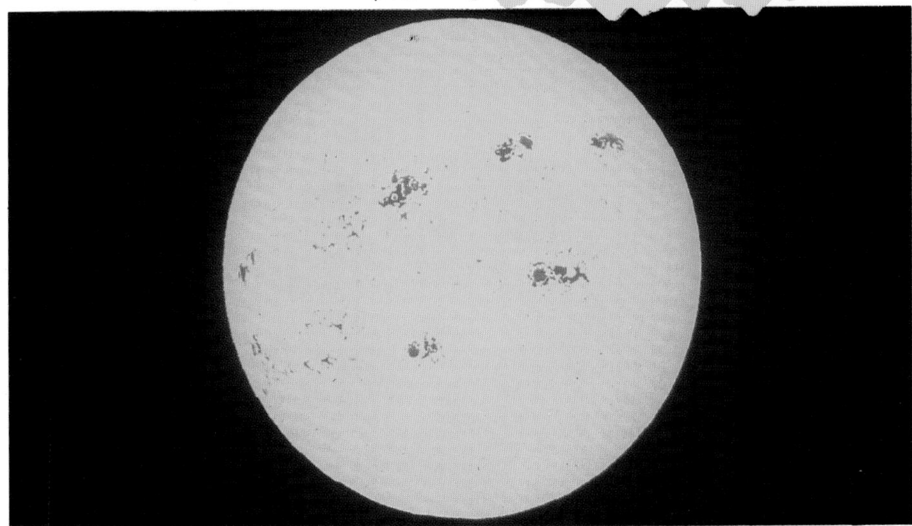

Fig. 2.3 The Sun is a ball of plasma. The red and blue patches are sunspots.

Questions

1 a Name the three states of matter.

b Describe the arrangement and behaviour of particles in each of the three states.

c For each of these three states, give one example of a substance which is normally in this state at room temperature.

3 DIFFUSION

Diffusion is the spreading out of particles. It provides further evidence for the kinetic theory.

Moving particles spread around

A smell will slowly spread across a room. We can explain this by imagining that the smell is made of moving particles of a smelly substance. The molecules move around, filling the room. This movement is called **diffusion**. Diffusion can be defined as *the movement of particles from a place where there is a high concentration of them, to a place where there is a lower concentration of them.* Diffusion tends to spread the particles out evenly.

You can watch diffusion happening if you use a substance, such as potassium permanganate, which has coloured particles. If a crystal of potassium permanganate is carefully dropped into a beaker of water, it dissolves. The particles in the crystal separate from each other and slowly move through the water. The colour only spreads slowly. The particles keep bumping into the water molecules. They do not travel in straight lines. Eventually the colour fills the whole beaker, but this takes a very long time.

Diffusion happens faster in gases than in liquids

In a gas the molecules are not so close together as in a liquid. If a coloured gas is mixed with a clear one, the colour spreads. This happens faster than in a liquid, because fewer particles get in the way. You can watch this happening with bromine, as it diffuses through air. Bromine is a brown gas. It covers about 2 cm in 100 s. If it diffuses into a vacuum, it goes even faster, because there are no particles to get in the way. It then travels 20 km in 100 s!

Fig. 3.1 Potassium permanganate diffusing in water. A crystal has just been dropped into the gas jar on the left. The potassium permanganate has been diffusing for about 30 minutes in the centre jar, and for 24 hours in the jar on the right.

Fig. 3.2 An experiment showing the diffusion of bromine gas. On the left, the two gas jars are separated by a glass lid. The lower one contains bromine, and the upper one contains air. On the right, the lid has been removed. The bromine and air diffuse into one another.

Questions

1 Using examples, and diagrams if they help, explain how each of the following supports the idea that everything is made up of particles:

a Brownian motion

b crystal structure

c diffusion

INVESTIGATION 3.1

How quickly do scent particles move?

If a bottle of perfume is opened, the smell spreads across a room. Design an experiment to find out how quickly the smell spreads from a particular type of perfume.

You will need to consider how you will decide when the scent has reached a particular part of the room. Would the same group of experimenters always get the same results? Would you get the same results in a different room? Or in the same room on a different day? Try to take these problems into account when you design your experiment.

Get your experiment checked, and then carry it out. Record your results in the way you think best. Discuss what your results suggest to you about the speed at which scent particles (molecules) move.

INVESTIGATION 3.2

Diffusion of two gases

This experiment will be demonstrated for you, as the liquids used should not be touched.

A piece of cotton wool is soaked in hydrochloric acid. A second piece of cotton wool is soaked in ammonia solution. The two pieces of cotton wool are pushed into the ends of a long glass tube. Rubber bungs are then pushed in, to seal the ends of the tube.

The hydrochloric acid gives off hydrogen chloride gas. The ammonia solution gives off ammonia gas. (Both of these gases smell very unpleasant, and should not be breathed in in large quantities.)

Fig. 3.3 Diffusion of two gases

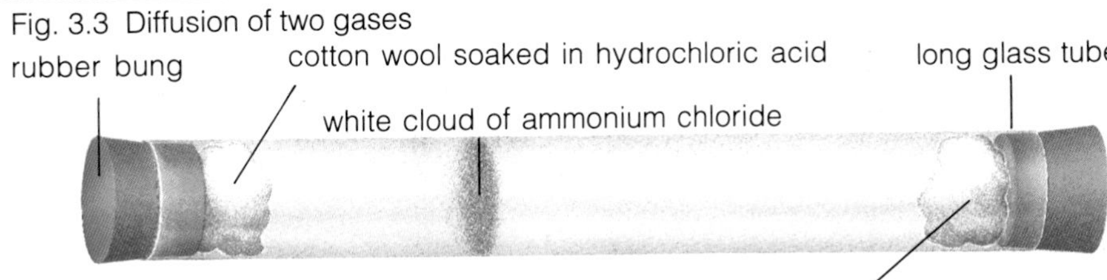

Questions

1 Hydrogen chloride and ammonia react together to form a white substance called ammonium chloride. Nearest which end of the tube does the ammonium chloride form?

2 How had the two gases travelled along the tube?

3 Which gas travelled faster?

4 The molecules of ammonia are smaller and lighter than the molecules of hydrogen chloride. What does this experiment suggest about how the size and mass of its molecules might affect the speed of diffusion of a gas?

5 If this experiment could be repeated at a higher temperature, would you expect it to take a longer or shorter time for the ammonium chloride to form? Explain your answer.

INVESTIGATION 3.3

How small are potassium permanganate particles?

1 Measure 10 cm^3 of water into a test tube. Add a few crystals of potassium permanganate and stir to dissolve.

2 Using a syringe, take exactly 1 cm^3 of this solution and put it into a second tube. Add 9 cm^3 of water to this tube, to make the total up to 10 cm^3. You have diluted the original solution by 10 times. Put your two solutions side by side in a test tube rack.

3 Now dilute the second solution by 10 times, by taking exactly 1 cm^3 of it, and adding it to 9 cm^3 of water in a third tube. Add this tube to the row in the test tube rack.

4 Continue diluting the solution by 10 times, until you have a tube in which you can only just see the colour.

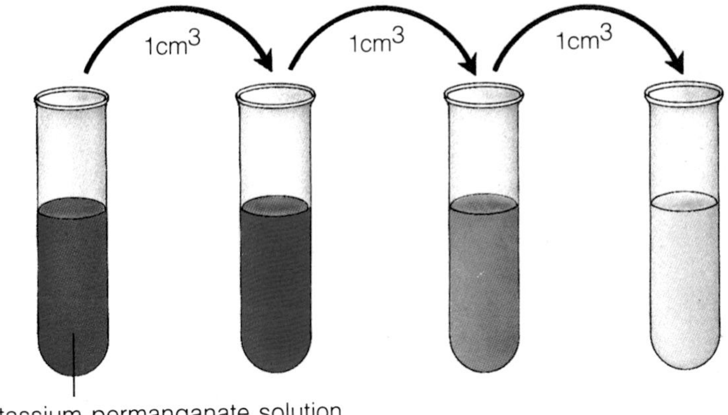

Fig. 3.4 Making serial dilutions of a potassium permanganate solution

Questions

Think about the number of potassium permanganate particles in each of your tubes. You began with a lot of particles in your first tube – all the ones that were in the crystals that you added to the water. You mixed them thoroughly into the water, and then took **one tenth** of them out to put into the second tube. So the second tube contained only one tenth as many potassium permanganate particles as the first one.

1 How many times fewer particles are there in the third tube than in the first tube?

2 How many times fewer particles are there in the last tube than in the first tube?

3 In your last, very faintly coloured tube the colour is still evenly spread through the water. So there must still be at least a few thousand potassium permanganate particles there. If you imagine that there are a thousand potassium permanganate particles in this tube, can you work out how many there must have been in the first tube? (You need to do some multiplications by 10 – lots of them.)

4 What does this experiment tell you about the size of potassium permanganate particles?

Questions

1 A petri dish was filled with agar jelly, in which some starch solution was dissolved. Two holes were cut in the agar jelly. Water was put into one hole. A solution of amylase was put into the other hole. Amylase is an enzyme which digests starch. It changes starch into sugar.

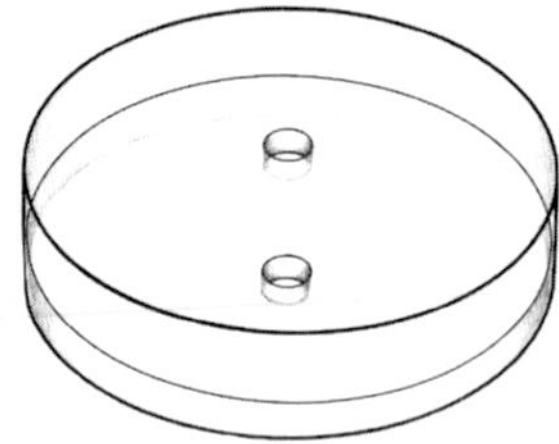

After a day, iodine solution was poured over the agar jelly in the dish. Iodine solution turns blue-black when in contact with starch. It does not change colour when in contact with sugar. The results are shown below.

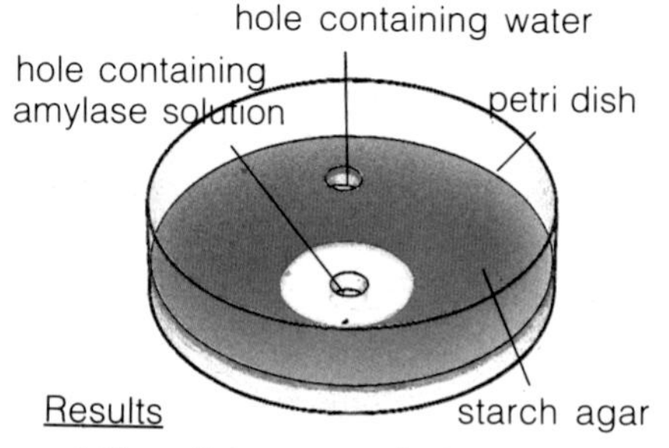

Results

a Why did most of the agar jelly turn blue-black when iodine solution was poured over it?

b Why did the part of the jelly around the hole which contained amylase solution not turn black?

c The area which did not turn blue-black was roughly circular in shape. Explain why. Use the word 'diffusion' in your answer.

d Why do you think that water was put into one of the holes in this experiment?

2 Divide part of a page in your book into three columns, headed solid, liquid and gas. Copy each of the following words and statements into the correct column. Some of them may belong in more than one column.

a water at room temperature
b salt at room temperature
c oxygen at room temperature
d made up of particles
e particles vibrate
f particles move around freely, a long way apart
g particles vibrate slightly, and are held together tightly
h particles held together, but move around each other freely
i fills a container from the bottom
j completely fills a container
k does not spread out in a container
l particles move faster when heated
m particles move much closer together when squashed

3 Explain the following:

a If you grow a salt crystal it will be cube-shaped.

b A solution of potassium permanganate can be diluted many times, and still look purple.

c If ammonia solution is spilt in a corner of a laboratory, the people nearest it will smell it several seconds before the people in the opposite corner.

d Pollen grains floating on water appear to be jigging around if seen through a microscope.

e A copper sulphate crystal dissolves in water to form a blue solution. This happens faster in warm water than in cold water.

Gases get in and out of living things by diffusion

air
water
carbon dioxide
oxygen
Amoeba

Diffusion is a very important process for living things. Oxygen diffuses from your lungs into your blood. Carbon dioxide diffuses from your blood into your lungs. Figure 3.5 shows how oxygen and carbon dioxide move in and out of a single-celled organism called *Amoeba*.

Fig. 3.5 Gas exchange in *Amoeba*. The *Amoeba's* cell uses oxygen in respiration. As the oxygen near to it is used up, this produces a low concentration of oxygen. The oxygen concentration in the air is greater so oxygen diffuses from the air into the *Amoeba*.
The *Amoeba* produces carbon dioxide in respiration. This produces a high concentration of carbon dioxide near the *Amoeba*. The concentration of carbon dioxide diffuses from the *Amoeba* into the air.

Question

Read the following passage carefully. Use the diagrams to help you to understand the description. Then answer the questions, giving as much scientific detail in your answers as you can.

The manufacture of a transistor

Diffusion is a process of great importance in the manufacture and operation of electronic components, such as transistors. A transistor is an electronic switch. It is used to control the flow of electrons in a circuit.

A transistor is formed from a silicon crystal, in which there is a small percentage of atoms of other substances. These other atoms alter the electrical properties of the crystal. The other atoms are added to particular regions of the silicon, so that these regions have different properties. These regions are known as n-type and p-type semiconductors.

Transistors need to be very small so that they can respond to changes quickly. There are several ways of making them.

This is one method.

First, a wafer of n-type silicon is heated in oxygen. The oxygen forms a layer of silicon oxide on the surface of the silicon. Chemicals are then used to etch away the oxide in a small area, of diameter a. In this area, the pure silicon is exposed. This is called an n-type semi-conductor.

Next, the silicon wafer is placed in a hot boron atomosphere. The boron atoms cannot penetrate the silicon oxide layer, but they can diffuse into the exposed silicon. They enter the surface and spread a little way under the silicon oxide layer. Wherever the boron enters the silicon, a p-type semiconductor is formed. The p-type semiconductor has a diameter a little larger than a.

Now the silicon wafer is heated in oxygen again to cover it completely with an oxide layer. A new area, of diameter b, is etched in the oxide. The wafer is then exposed to hot phosphorus gas. Phosphorus atoms diffuse into the exposed surface, but not through the silicon oxide. Where the phosphorus atoms enter the silicon, an n-type semiconductor is formed. The phosphorus atoms spread a little way under the oxide layer.

The junctions between the n-type and p-type semiconductors are very important if the transistor is to work well. By making them like this, the junctions are protected underneath a layer of silicon oxide.

Finally, electrical contacts are made by depositing metallic vapour on certain parts of the transistor and heating it. So now the whole transistor is covered and protected by either an oxide layer or the electrical contacts. This prevents impurity atoms in the air from diffusing into the junctions and spoiling the transistor.

Fig. 3.6

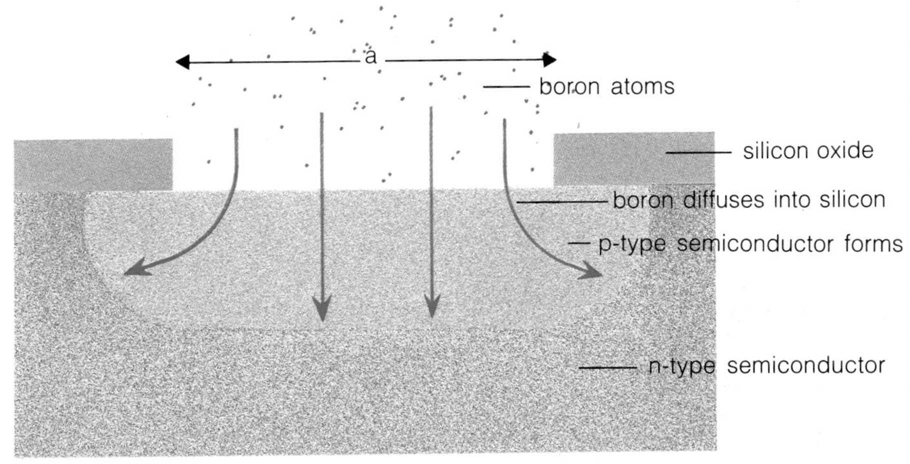

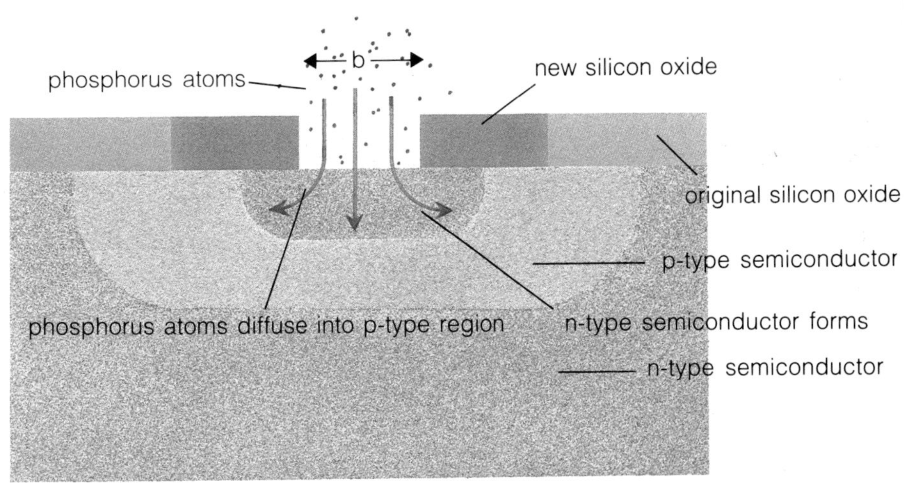

Questions

1 Why is it a good idea to make transistors small?

2 a How is a layer of silicon oxide made to form on the surface of the silicon wafer?

b Explain how this layer helps in the next stage of the process.

3 Why are the new semiconductor regions bigger than the exposed areas on the silicon wafer?

4 The higher the temperature while the boron is entering the silicon wafer, the bigger the diameter of the p-type semiconductor region. Why?

5 What use is the oxide layer in the completed transistor?

4 MEASURING TEMPERATURE

Temperature is a measure of the average speed of movement of the particles in a substance. The faster they are moving, the higher the temperature.

The human sense of temperature is not very reliable

We have nerve endings in our skin which sense temperature. These send messages to the brain. The brain uses these messages to decide whether whatever is touching our skin is hot, warm or cold. But this is not a very accurate sense. It tends to *compare* temperatures rather than measure them. If you have been outside on a very cold winter's day, you may feel really warm when you go into a room. But that same room, at the same temperature, would feel cool to you if you had just been outside in hot sunshine.

Temperatures can be measured by comparing them with fixed points

Temperatures are measured by comparing them with fixed points. The two fixed points most often used are the melting and boiling points of pure water. On the **Celsius** scale of temperature, the lower fixed point is the melting point of pure ice at normal atmospheric pressure. This is called **0 °C**. The upper fixed point is the boiling point of pure water. This is **100 °C**. The gap in between these two fixed points is divided into 100 equal intervals, or **degrees**. If the temperature of something is 50 °Celsius, then it is halfway between the temperature of melting ice and boiling water. This temperature scale is called Celsius after the Swedish scientist who invented it. But it is sometimes also called centigrade, because it uses 100 intervals between the melting and boiling points of water.

Liquid-in-glass thermometers use the expansion of liquid to measure temperature

The diagram shows the sort of thermometer you use in a laboratory. As the liquid inside gets hotter it takes up more room. The liquid moves up the narrow capillary tube. Because the tube is extremely narrow, a small change of temperature makes the liquid move a long way up the tube. The walls of the bulb are very thin, so that heat goes through quickly. The walls of the stem are thicker, so that they are strong.

Fig. 4.1a A liquid-in-glass laboratory thermometer

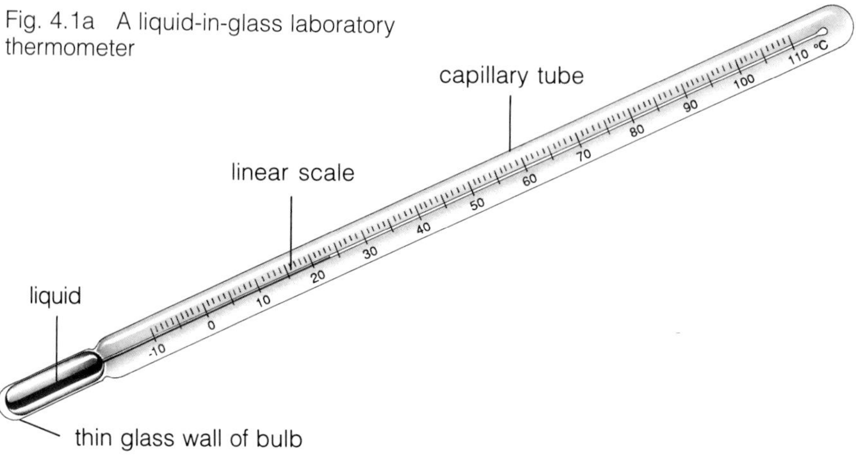

Fig. 4.1b A clinical thermometer

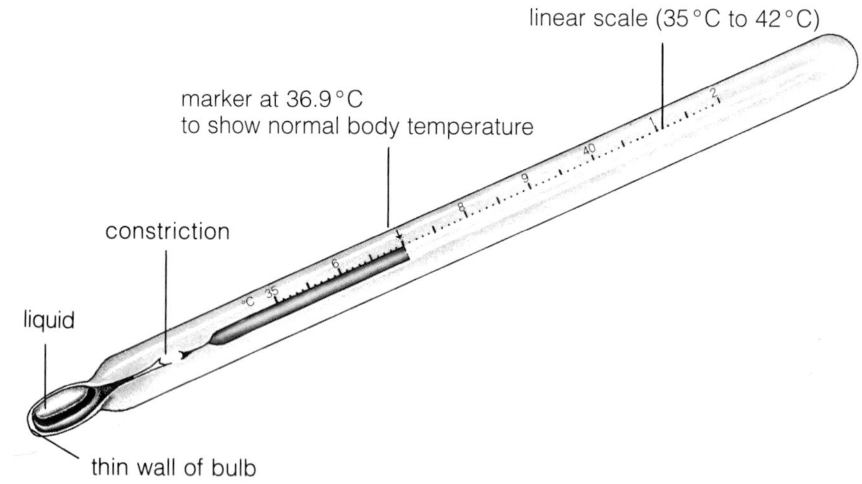

Clinical thermometers are used for measuring human temperature

The clinical thermometer is also a liquid-in-glass thermometer. It has a constriction in the capillary tube. As the temperature rises, the liquid is forced past the constriction. When the thermometer cools, the liquid does not go back into the bulb. This means that a temperature can be measured in the mouth, and the thermometer taken out to be read. The reading stays the same until the liquid is shaken down past the constriction. This must be done before it is used again.

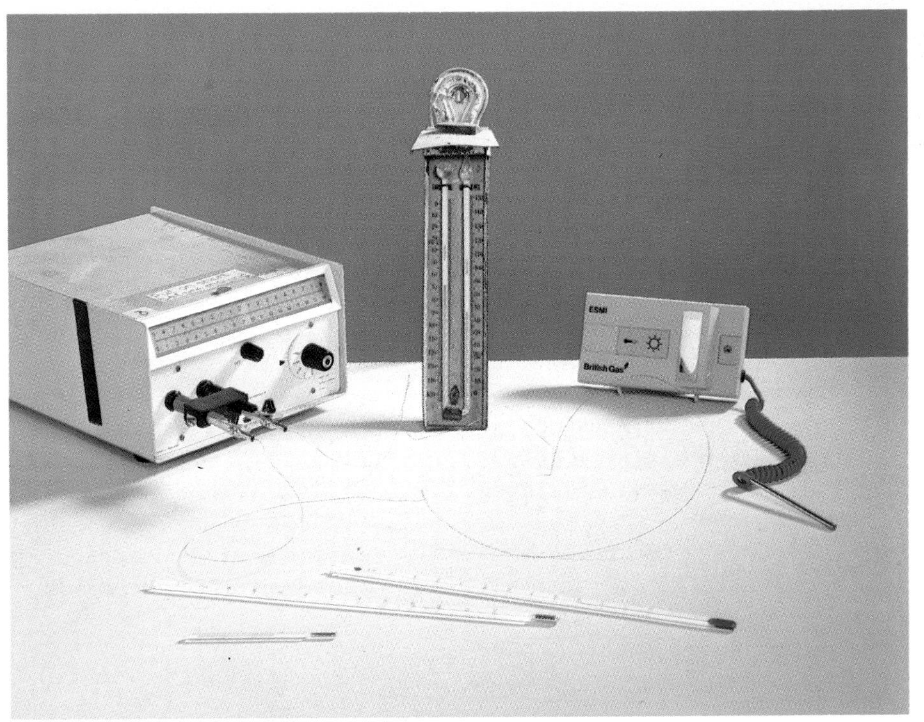

Fig. 4.2 A variety of thermometers. At the back left is a galvanometer and thermocouple. The wires connected to the galvanometer are joined to a different type of wire – you can see two junctions, where they are twisted together. These junctions are **thermocouples**. They produce a voltage when heated, which gives a reading on the galvanometer. One of the junctions is put in melting ice to provide a reference reading for 0 °C, while the other is used to measure the temperature you want to know. Thermocouples give accurate readings, work at higher temperatures than many other types of thermometer, and can be used to take temperatures of very small things. The other thermometers, moving clockwise from the galvanometer, are: a maximum/minimum thermometer; an electronic digital thermometer; a thermometer containing alcohol; one containing mercury; and a clinical thermometer.

Questions

1 Think carefully about this one! You may come up with some surprising answers. You might like to check them by experiment afterwards – but you will need be very observant.

a When the bulb of a thermometer is suddenly placed in a hot liquid, which part of the thermometer gets hot first?

b Which part of the thermometer will expand first?

c What happens if the bulb increases in volume, but the liquid in the thermometer does not?

d What happens to the 'reading' on the thermometer at the moment it is placed in the hot liquid?

2 Why is a thermometer a better measure of temperature than your skin?

3 Two liquids often used in thermometers are mercury and alcohol.

Some of their properties are listed in the table below.

a You have been asked to choose a liquid to put in a thermometer. Which of the properties in the table are relevant to your choice?

b For each of the following uses, say which of the two liquids you would prefer to have in your thermometer. In each case, give reasons for your choice.

i measuring the temperature of a stew.

ii measuring body temperature.

iii measuring the temperature at the South Pole.

iv for general laboratory use.

v to check the temperature inside a fridge.

vi to check the temperature inside a freezer.

	mercury	*alcohol*
boiling point	365 °C	78.5 °C
freezing point	–39 °C	–117 °C
colour	silver	clear, but can be dyed
cost	expensive	cheap
conducts heat	well	not so well
toxicity	poisonous	not poisonous in small amounts
metal or not	metal	non-metal
conducts electricity	well	an insulator
flammability	nonflammable	flammable
density	high	low
surface tension	high	not so high
degree of expansion when heated	average	large

4 The kelvin scale of temperature is used for many scientific calculations and measurements. Each kelvin is the same size as 1 °C. But the 'starting points' are different. The kelvin scale begins at a much lower temperature than the Celsius scale. 0 K is –273 °C. (Notice that there is no ° when writing temperatures in the kelvin scale.)

What is the melting point of ice in kelvin?

EXTENSION

DID YOU KNOW?

The lowest temperature that is possible is called absolute zero. This is –273 degrees Celsius or 0 K (see Q4).

5 LATENT HEAT

When water changes from a liquid into a gas, a lot of energy is used. This overcomes the attractive forces between the molecules, and rearranges them. This energy is called latent heat.

A lot of energy is used to change water from a liquid to a gas

Imagine that you have a beaker of pure water with a thermometer in it. You heat the water with a Bunsen burner. The temperature increases.

What is actually happening to the water molecules in your beaker? They are moving faster and faster as you heat them. This is why the temperature increases.

But when the temperature gets to 100 °C, something different starts to happen. Now the heat from the Bunsen burner, instead of making the molecules move faster, is used to break the attractive forces between them. The water molecules become free. They fly off into the air. The water boils.

All the time that the water is boiling, your thermometer goes on reading 100 °C. All the heat energy from the Bunsen burner is being used to break the attractive forces between the water molecules. The temperature stays constant. It is as though you are pouring heat energy into the water, and it just disappears! When you heat something, you expect its temperature to increase. But when liquid water is turning into gas, its temperature does not increase. The heat energy becomes 'hidden' in the water. Another word for 'hidden' is 'latent'. We call this 'disappearing' heat energy **latent heat**. A fuller name for it is **latent heat of vaporisation**.

Water evaporates well below boiling point

Imagine that it has been raining. Puddles have formed. It stops raining, and the sun begins to shine. After a few hours, the puddles have disappeared. The water in them has evaporated.

But the water in the puddles has certainly not boiled! Water can evaporate at temperatures well below boiling point.

In a puddle of water, the water molecules are moving around randomly. Some have more energy than others and move faster. At the surface of the water, the most energetic particles will have enough energy to be able to break away from the other water molecules. They will escape into the air. The temperature of the puddle of water is related to the average speed of movement of the water molecules in it. If the faster moving molecules escape, then the average speed of movement of the particles goes down. So the temperature of the water decreases.

So liquid water can become a gas without boiling. This is called **evaporation**. Evaporation is not the same as boiling. Boiling takes place *throughout* a liquid. All the particles are so hot that they have enough energy to break away from one another. Evaporation takes place at the *surface* of the liquid, at temperatures well below boiling point. Only the most energetic particles can break away from the others.

EXTENSION

When water evaporates, it cools things down

When you get out of a swimming pool or your bath, you may feel cold. But you would not feel cold if you were dry. It is the water evaporating from your body which cools you down. The water evaporates as the most energetic water molecules escape from the others. This lowers the average temperature of the water on your skin. The water cools, and so does your skin. Moreover, the change from a liquid to a gas takes energy. If the water happens to be sitting on your skin when it does this, it will take heat energy from your skin. So your skin feels cooler.

We and some other mammals, use this fact to cool our bodies. Human cells work best at a temperature of 37 °C. In hot weather, or when we exercise, the body temperature may go above this. Sweat glands in the skin produce a watery liquid which lies on the skin surface. The water in the sweat evaporates. As it does so, it takes heat energy from the skin. This cools the skin down.

Plants may use a similar method to cool their leaves. In hot climates, it would be all too easy for a plant's leaves to get so hot that the cells would be damaged. But if it has plenty of water, a plant can keep itself cool. Water is allowed to evaporate from its leaves. It evaporates through small holes on the underside of the leaves, called **stomata**. As the water evaporates, it takes heat energy from the leaf cells, and cools them down.

Fig. 5.1 Huge quantities of water evaporate from rain forests. The evaporation helps to keep the plants cool.

INVESTIGATION 5.1

The effect of evaporation on temperature

You need to get fully organised with this experiment before you begin, because once the tubes have cotton wool on them you need to start taking temperatures straight away. Ideally, each tube should have its cotton wool put on at exactly the same time. Draw a results chart before you start.

1 Fill five boiling tubes with tap water, leaving room for a bung to go in.

Support all five tubes in clamps on a retort stand.

2 Surround one of the tubes with dry cotton wool. Surround another with cotton wool soaked in warm water. Surround a third with cotton wool soaked in cold water. Surround the fourth one with cotton wool soaked in ethanol. Leave the fifth one with no covering.

3 Put the bungs with thermometers into each tube, and immediately take the temperature of each. This is Time 0. Take the temperatures every 2 min for at least 20 min. Carry on for longer if you have time.

4 Record your results in the way you think best. A line graph is a good idea.

Questions

1 Why were all five tubes supported in clamps, rather than lying on the bench or being held in your hand?

2 Which tube cooled most slowly? Try to explain why.

3 Which tube cooled fastest? Explain why.

4 Was there much difference between the rate of cooling of the tube with cold wet cotton wool and the tube with warm wet cotton wool? If so, can you explain this?

5 Do you think that your experiment gave a fair comparison between the five tubes? How could you have improved it?

Refrigerators use evaporation to produce cooling

When a liquid evaporates it takes in energy and cools its surroundings. When the gas condenses back to a liquid, the latent heat is released. This is used to take heat from inside a fridge, and release it outside.

A liquid which evaporates easily is used. Liquids which evaporate easily are called **volatile** liquids. The liquid used in most fridges is a type of CFC called 'Freon'. The liquid evaporates in the coils around the ice box or cold plate inside the fridge. This causes cooling. The gas formed is pumped away. It is pressurised in the condenser on the back of the fridge. Here the gas condenses back into a liquid. As it condenses it releases the heat energy it has taken in. So heat energy has been taken from inside the fridge, and released outside it. Because the pump is working hard to push the liquid around, more energy is released from the back of the fridge than is taken from inside it. If you leave the fridge door open, the pump will be working very hard. So your kitchen will eventually become hotter!

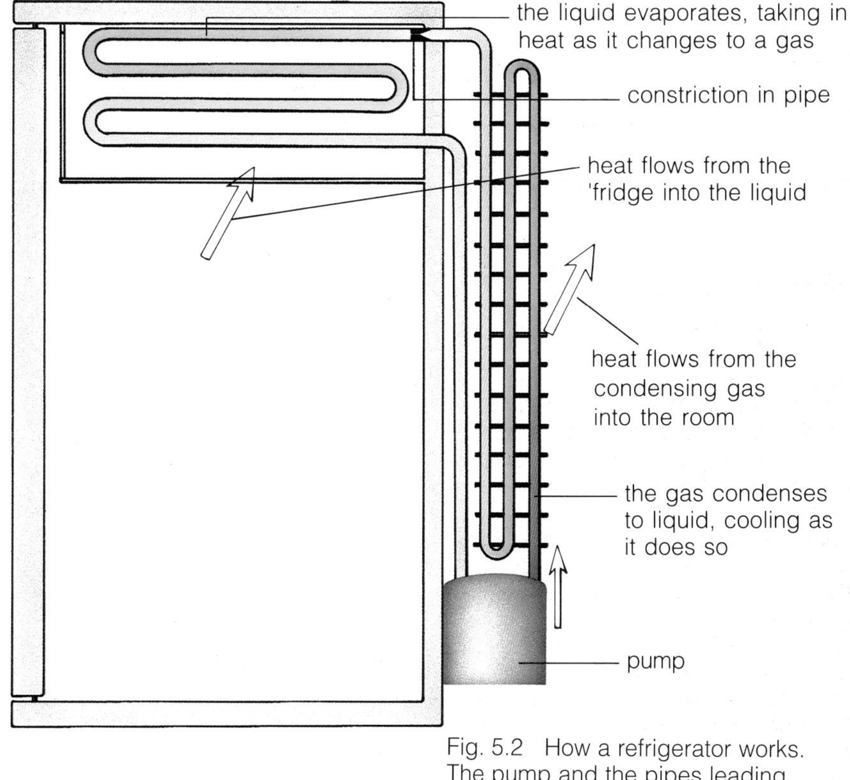

Fig. 5.2 How a refrigerator works. The pump and the pipes leading from it (the condenser) are at the back of the 'fridge. Can you suggest why there is a constriction in the pipe carrying the liquid from the condenser into the coils around the ice box?

EXTENSION

Questions

1 Why does the temperature of boiling water not change, even if you continue heating it?

2 a Explain what is meant by **latent heat of vaporisation**.

b When you are going to have an injection, you will probably have ethanol put on to your skin to kill any germs. The ethanol quickly disappears and your skin feels cold. Why is this?

c Explain how mammals and plants use the latent heat of vaporisation of water to cool themselves.

3 Someone has fallen into a river on a cold day. You manage to get them on to the bank. They are still conscious and breathing, but exhausted. What should you do next, and why?

6 ELEMENTS

An element is a substance made of atoms which all contain the same number of protons.

There are over 100 different kinds of atom

Over 100 different kinds of atoms exist. They are different from each other because they do not have the same numbers of protons, neutrons and electrons.

Atoms with the same number of protons as each other behave in the same way chemically. Atoms with different numbers of protons behave differently. There are about 90 naturally occurring types of atoms. The remainder are made by humans.

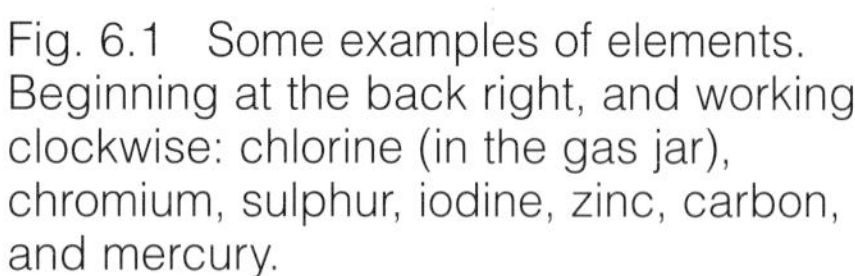

Fig. 6.1 Some examples of elements. Beginning at the back right, and working clockwise: chlorine (in the gas jar), chromium, sulphur, iodine, zinc, carbon, and mercury.

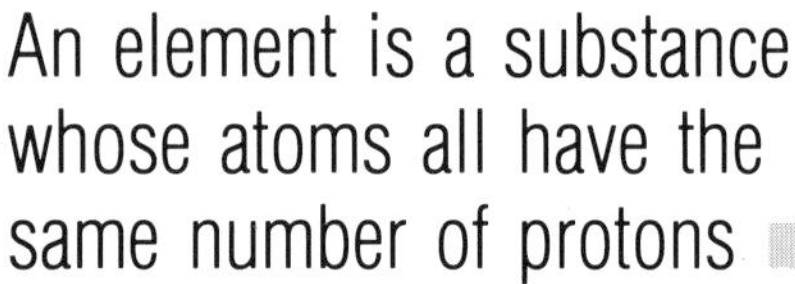

An element is a substance whose atoms all have the same number of protons

A substance made from atoms which all have the same number of protons is called an **element**. As there are about 90 naturally occurring kinds of atoms, there are about 90 naturally occurring elements. Each element has its own symbol. Hydrogen, for example, has the symbol **H**. Helium has the symbol **He**.

The atomic number of an element is the number of protons in each atom

The number of protons an atom contains is called its **atomic number**. All the atoms of an element contain the same number of protons so they all have the same atomic number. The element with the smallest number of protons is hydrogen. It has just one proton, so its atomic number is one. Helium has two protons, so its atomic number is two.

You sometimes need to write the atomic number of an element when you write its symbol. You show it like this: $_{1}\mathbf{H}$. This shows that the atomic number of hydrogen is one. Helium has the atomic number two so it is written $_{2}\mathbf{He}$.

Fig. 6.2 A hydrogen atom.

Atomic number = number of protons = 1

Mass number = number of protons + number of neutrons = 1

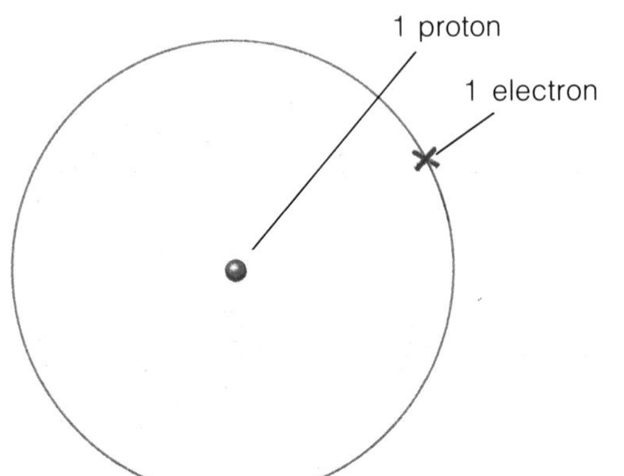

Fig. 6.3 A helium atom.

Atomic number = number of protons = 2

Mass number = number of protons + number of neutrons = 4

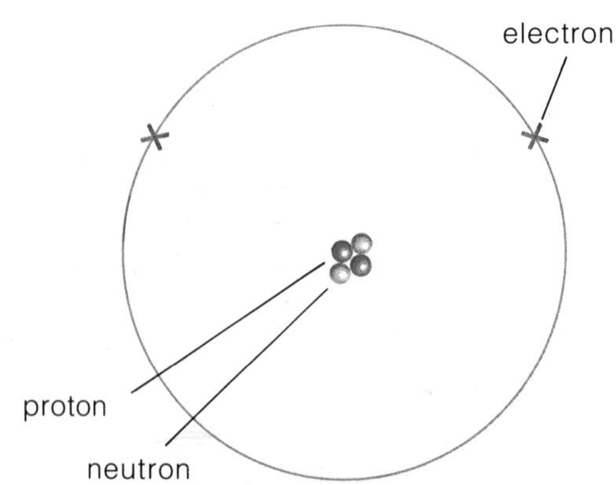

The mass number of an atom is the total number of protons and neutrons it contains

The **mass number** of an atom is the total number of 'heavy' particles that it contains. If you look at the table on page 22, you will see that the 'heavy' particles are neutrons and protons. A hydrogen atom contains just one proton, one electron and no neutrons, so its mass number is one. It is the smallest atom.

The next largest atom is the **helium** atom. A helium atom contains two protons, two neutrons and two electrons. As it has two protons, its atomic number is two. It has four 'heavy' particles – two protons and two neutrons – so its mass number is four.

If you want to show the mass number of an element, you write it like this: ^{1}**H** or ^{4}**He**.

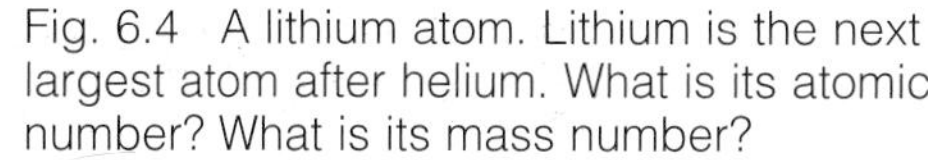

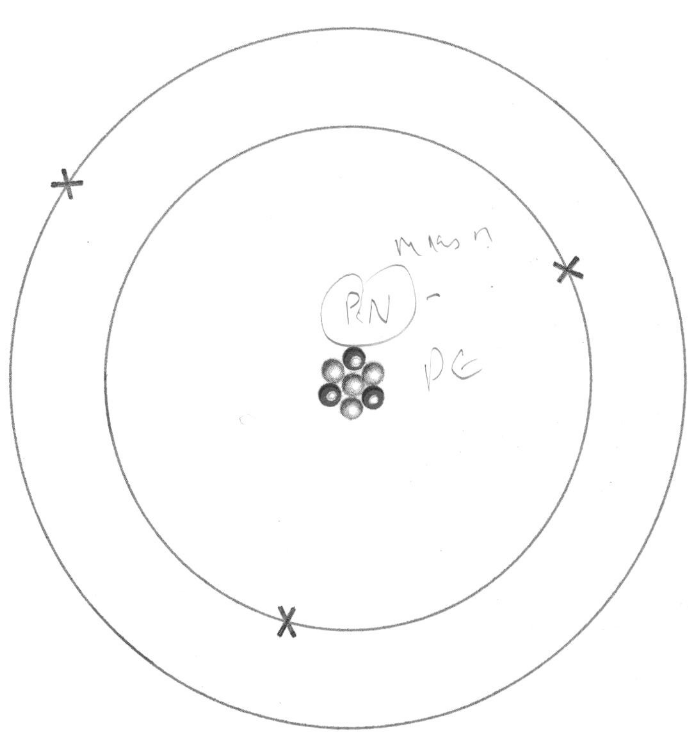

Fig. 6.4 A lithium atom. Lithium is the next largest atom after helium. What is its atomic number? What is its mass number?

Fig. 6.5 Using symbols to show atomic number and mass number.

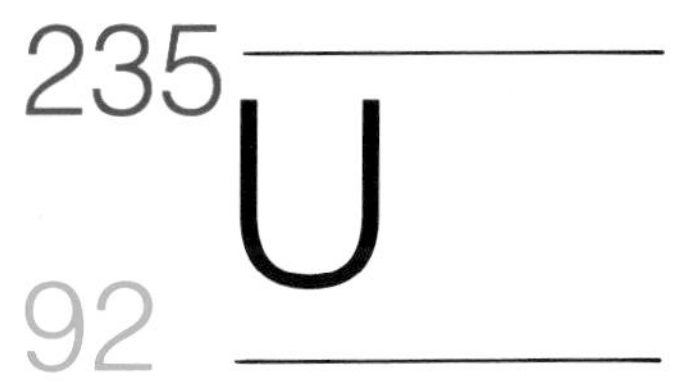

This is the mass number. It tells you the total number of protons and neutrons in one atom of the element.

This is the atomic number. It tells you how many protons there are in one atom of the element.

Questions

1 What is an element? Give three examples of elements.

2 a What is meant by the term atomic number?

b What is the atomic number of:
i hydrogen
ii lithium
iii uranium?

c What is meant by the term mass number?

d For each of the following examples, give (a) the atomic number and (b) the mass number:
i $^{35}_{17}Cl$ **ii** $^{12}_{6}C$ **iii** $^{14}_{6}C$ **iv** $^{16}_{8}O$

3 Copy and complete the following table.

Mass number	20	40			28
Atomic number	10			13	
Number of neutrons		22			
Symbol	Ne	Ar	$^{24}_{12}Mg$	$^{27}_{13}Al$	$^{28}_{14}Si$

7 ATOMIC STRUCTURE

Atoms themselves are made up of even smaller particles. The most important of these are protons, neutrons and electrons.

Atoms contain protons, neutrons and electrons

Fig. 7.1 An atom

Atoms are made up of even smaller particles. There is a **nucleus** in the centre of each atom. The nucleus can contain **protons** and **neutrons**. Around the nucleus is the rest of the atom, where **electrons** are most likely to be found. Protons and neutrons have about the same mass. Electrons are about 2000 times lighter.

Protons have a small positive electrical charge. Electrons have an equal but opposite (negative) charge. The number of protons and electrons in an atom are exactly equal, so the two equal and opposite charges cancel out. Atoms have no overall charge.

Protons, neutrons and electrons

Particle	*Relative mass*	*Relative charge*
proton	1	+1
neutron	1	0
electron	1/2000	-1

Questions

1 If an atom has 10 protons, how many electrons does it have?
2 Which particle in an atom carries a positive charge?
3 Which particle in an atom carries a negative charge?

DID YOU KNOW?

Although atoms are made from electrons, protons and neutrons, these are not the fundamental building blocks of the atom. There are at least 37 of these fundamental particles. There are many kinds of leptons, quarks, antiquarks, photons, gravitons, bosons and gluons. Some of these particles have not actually been detected yet, but physicists think they must exist because of the way that atoms behave.

The history of atomic structure

The Ancient Greeks were the first people to think of matter as being made of tiny particles. They imagined these particles to be like solid balls and this idea of the atom remained until the early 1900s. Around this time, evidence emerged that atoms contained at least two kinds of matter, some of it with a positive charge and some with a negative charge. A new model of the atom was suggested – a ball of positively charged 'dough' in which negatively charged electrons were dotted around like currants.

Fig. 7.2a The ancient Greeks imagined that atoms were like solid balls.

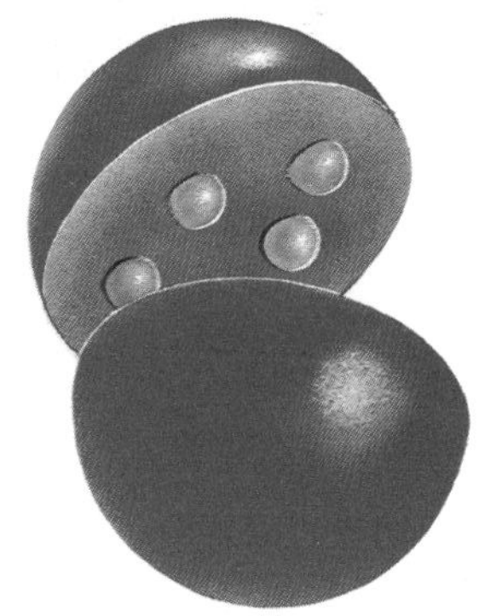

Fig. 7.2b Around 90 years ago it was suggested that an atom was rather like a plum pudding.

The Rutherford experiment

Ernest Rutherford was born in New Zealand in 1871. He won a Nobel Prize in 1908 for work on radioactivity. While continuing this work in Manchester, England, he made a discovery which he, and all other scientists at the time, found quite amazing.

He and two colleagues, Geiger and Marsden, were carrying out an experiment in which they shot alpha particles at a very thin piece of gold foil, in a vacuum. The apparatus is shown in Figure 7.3a.

Most of the alpha particles went straight through (A), some went through but changed direction slightly (B) and an even smaller number actually bounced back (C).

This suggested to Rutherford that the atom must be mainly space, and that the positive charge was not spread around, but in the centre. There was a positively charged central core, made of particles called protons, with the negatively charged electrons around the outside. He put forward this new model of the atom in 1911, and the modern view of the atom is still very similar.

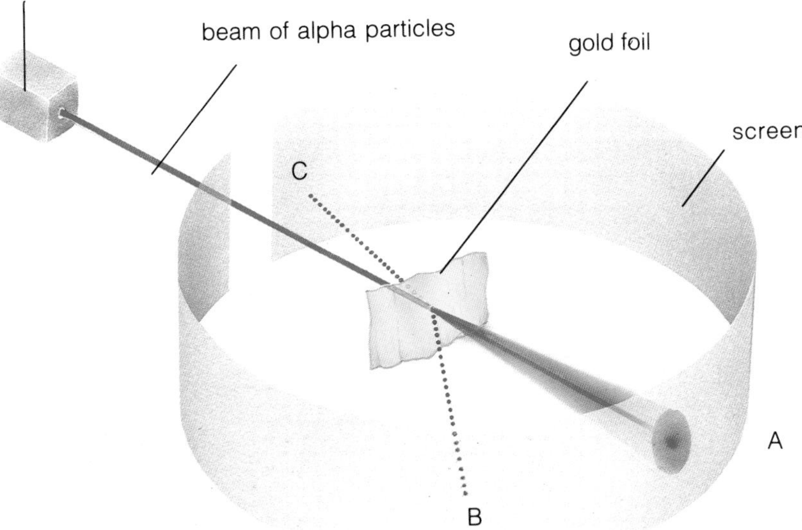

Fig. 7.3a Rutherford's experiment. The entire apparatus was enclosed in a vacuum chamber. Why do you think this was necessary?

Fig. 7.3b Particles can pass through the gold because most of an atom is space.

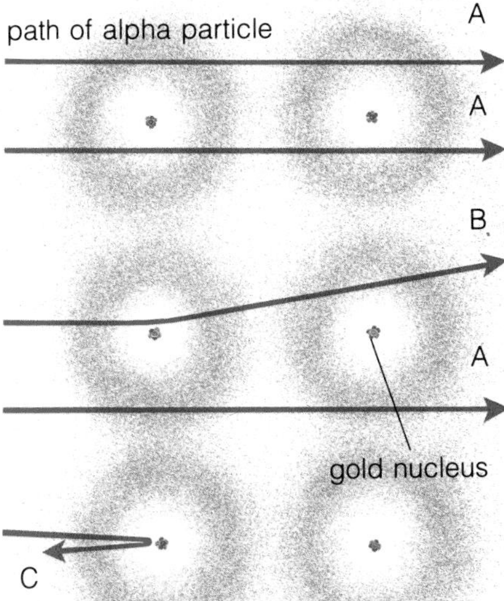

Rutherford was astonished at these results. He wrote: 'It was quite the most incredible event that ever happened to me in my life. It was as incredible as if you fired a 15-inch shell at a piece of tissue paper and it came back and hit you. On consideration, I realised that this scattering backwards must be the results of a single collision, and when I made calculations I saw that it was impossible to get anything of that order of magnitude unless you took a system in which the greater part of the mass of the atom was concentrated in a minute nucleus.'

8 ATOMIC SPECTRA

The electrons in an atom are arranged in orbits. Movement of electrons between these orbits may result in the absorption or emission of light.

Heating atoms can make them emit light

Figure 8.1 shows how the structure of a sodium atom can change. The elctrons are arranged in shells around the nucleus. This diagram shows the atom changing from its **lowest energy state**. This is the state in which the arrangement of electrons is most stable.

If the atom is heated, the heat energy may allow an electron to move out into a higher orbit than normal. We can say that the electron has been 'excited'. This is an unstable situation. The electron very quickly returns to its normal orbit. But as it does so it releases the extra energy it has been given. This energy is given out as light.

Fig. 8.1a An atom can be excited by heating, or by light of a particular colour.

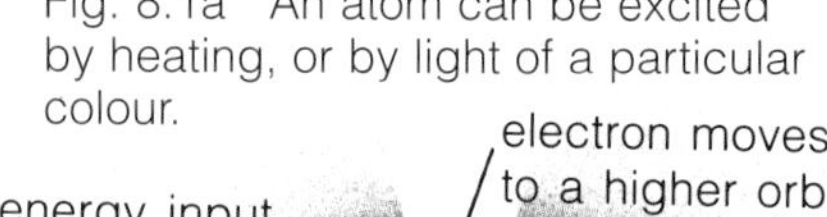

A particular energy change produces a particular colour of light

When an electron falls between two particular orbits in a particular kind of atom, the energy given out is always the same. The colour of the light given out, or **emitted**, depends on these energy changes. So whenever an electron falls between the same two orbits in a particular kind of atom, the same colour of light is emitted.

Figure 8.2 shows the colours of light emitted by a sodium when it is heated. This is called the **line emission spectrum** of sodium. Notice that there are several coloured lines. Each line represents an energy change in the atom. The two yellow lines are the strongest. This is the yellow light that comes from sodium street lamps. You can also see this colour if you hold a small amount of a sodium compound in a blue Bunsen burner flame.

Fig. 8.2 Sodium emission spectrum. The colours produced by excited sodium atoms can be separated into lines. The emission spectrum is produced when the atoms release energy.

Fig. 8.1b An excited atom releases the extra energy as light.

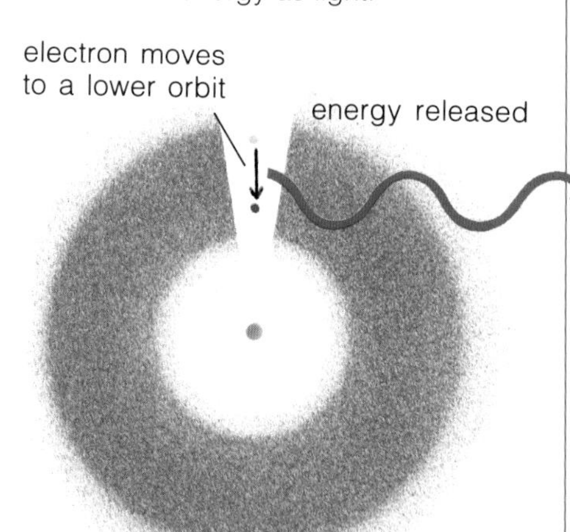

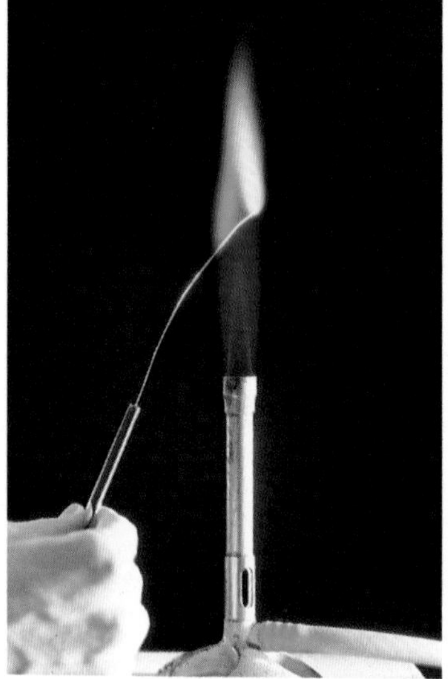

Fig. 8.3 Sodium chloride in a Bunsen burner flame emits a yellow light which is the same as that seen in sodium street lamps.

EXTENSION

The light from stars gives us information about them

Stars are a long way off. Light from our own Sun, 150 million km away, takes $8\frac{1}{2}$ minutes to reach us. Light from the next nearest star, Proxima Centauri, takes over four years! When you look at the North Star, the light entering your eye has taken 700 years to arrive. You are seeing the star as it was 700 years ago.

It is very unlikely that anyone will ever be able to go to a star. But we can learn a lot from their light.

You have seen how atoms can **emit** light if they are given particular sorts of energy. This process also happens in reverse. Atoms can **absorb** light, if it is of the particular colour that makes these energy changes happen. The energy of the light is used to excite the electrons in the atom. Each kind of atom can absorb particular colours of light.

If we look at the light from a particular star, we can find which colours are missing from its spectrum. Figure 8.4 shows an example from the Sun. This is called an **absorption spectrum**. The colours are missing because particular atoms in the Sun have absorbed them. So we can work out which kinds of atom are present in the Sun.

Space is not as empty as many people think. If we look at the light from a more distant star, the light may have passed through clouds of gas deep in space. These gas clouds, known as **nebulas**, might only have ten hydrogen atoms in every 1 cm^3. But the clouds are enormous, so the overall number of atoms can be large. As well as single atoms, the gas clouds contain more complex groups of atoms. These can absorb colours from the starlight. In 1937, the atom pair CN was discovered out in space, from an absorption spectrum.

Hydrogen clouds around a nebula can absorb all the ultraviolet light from a star. The gas cannot absorb all this energy for ever, and much of it is released again as particular colours.

The study of spectra is called spectroscopy. Spectroscopy can tell us about the atoms in space, which we will never be able to reach. It is the energy changes within the atom that enable us to identify them.

Fig. 8.4 The Sun's absorption spectrum. The dark lines represent 'missing' colours. These tell us which atoms are present in the Sun.

DID YOU KNOW?

Helium was identified in the Sun, using spectroscopy, *before* it was discovered on Earth.

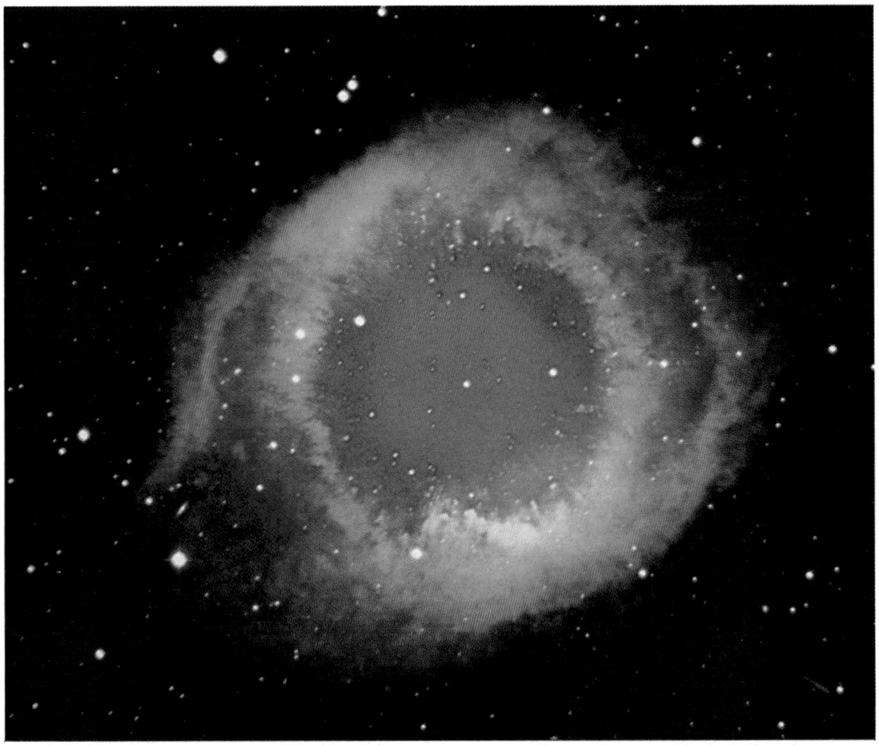

Fig. 8.5 A gas cloud, or nebula. This is the Helix planetary nebula photographed from Australia. It is 38 million million km across. In the centre is a white dwarf star. The blue-green parts contain mostly oxygen and nitrogen. The pink parts contain hydrogen.

Questions

1 Explain why some kinds of atoms give out light when they are heated.

2 a What is an absorption spectrum?
  b How can absorption spectra give us information about distant stars and galaxies?

EXTENSION

9 ISOTOPES

Isotopes are atoms of the same element, but with different numbers of neutrons.

Isotopes of an element have the same atomic number, but different mass numbers

All atoms with the same number of protons belong to the same element. They behave in exactly the same way in chemical reactions. As well as having the same number of protons, they also have the same number of electrons. For example, all hydrogen atoms have one proton and one electron. The atomic number is one.

Most hydrogen atoms have no neutrons so the mass number is one. But about one hydrogen atom in 10 000 is heavier than this. It has a neutron in its nucleus. This form of hydrogen still has one proton. It still has an atomic number of one. It is chemically identical to the most common form. It occupies the same place in the Periodic Table. For this reason it is called an **isotope** of hydrogen. ('Isotope' means 'same place'.) This isotope is sometimes called **deuterium**. Hydrogen and deuterium are both isotopes of hydrogen. They have the same atomic number, but different mass numbers. A deuterium atom is heavier than a hydrogen atom, because of its extra neutron.

Fig. 9.1a A hydrogen atom

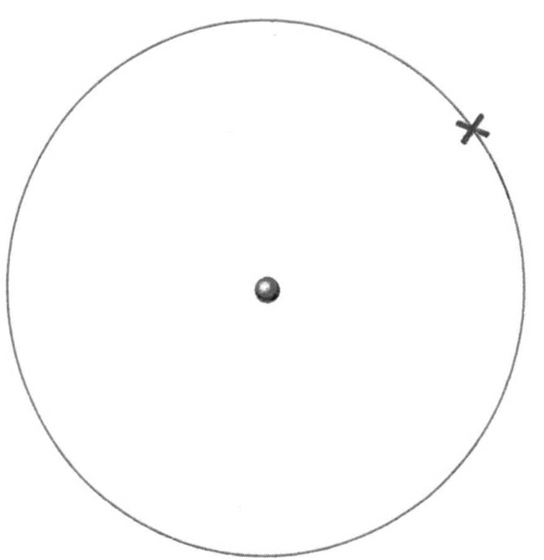

Fig. 9.1b A deuterium atom

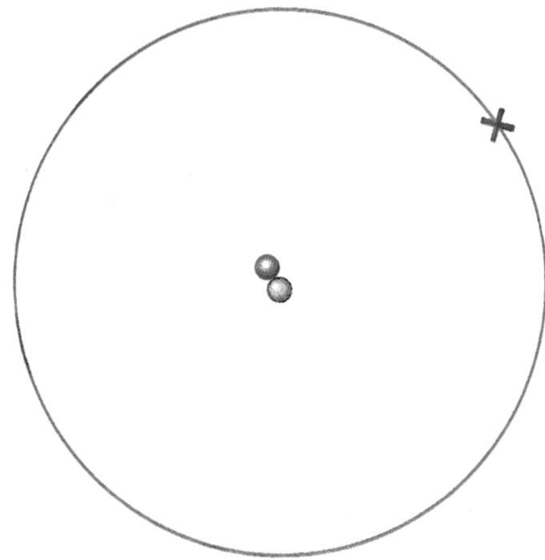

Carbon also has isotopes

Hydrogen is not the only element to have isotopes. Many elements have isotopes. Carbon has several isotopes. The 'normal' carbon atom has six protons and six neutrons. It has a mass number of 12, and its symbol is ^{12}C. It is called carbon twelve. Another isotope has eight neutrons. It still has six protons, or it would not be carbon. Its mass number is 14 and its symbol is ^{14}C. It is called carbon fourteen.

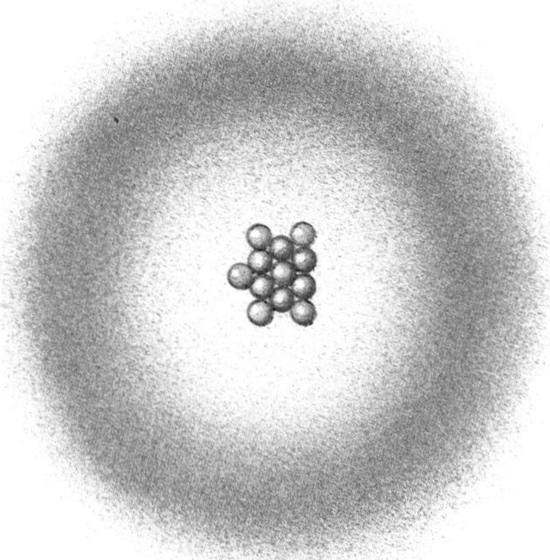

Fig. 9.2a A carbon 12 atom has 6 protons and 6 neutrons.

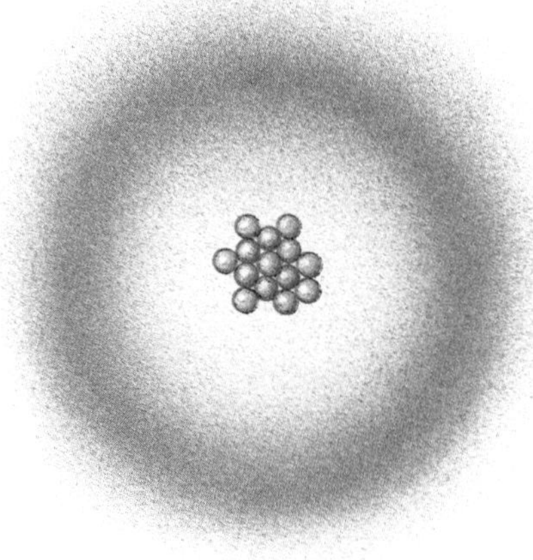

Fig. 9.2b A carbon 14 atom has 6 protons and 8 neutrons.

EXTENSION

Relative atomic masses are used for the masses of atoms

A single atom of hydrogen has a mass of 0.00000000000000000000000017g. This is a rather clumsy number to use. Instead of using grams, we compare the masses of atoms to the mass of a single atom of carbon 12. Carbon 12 has a mass of 12 atomic mass units. A hydrogen atom has a mass one twelfth of this. The atomic mass of hydrogen is one. The atomic mass of carbon 14 is 14 atomic mass units. Chromium has a mass which is twice that of carbon 12. Its atomic mass is 24.

Mass number is the atomic mass of a particular isotope of an element

When we talk about the atomic mass of an element, we can mean two things. We might mean the atomic mass of a particular isotope of that element. Or we might mean the average atomic mass of all the isotopes present in a particular sample of that element.

Take the element carbon, for example. The commonest isotope of carbon has six protons and six neutrons. We can say that its mass number is 12. Mass number refers to the atomic mass of a particular isotope of an element. If you say 'the mass number of carbon is 12', you really mean 'the mass number of the commonest isotope of carbon is 12'.

Relative atomic mass is an average for the different isotopes

In a sample of carbon, there will be atoms with different mass numbers. If you took 100 carbon atoms, you would probably find that 99 of them were carbon 12 atoms. One of them would probably be a carbon 13 atom. If you sorted through millions of carbon atoms, you might find a carbon 14 atom.

So if you found the *average* mass of a random sample of 100 carbon atoms, it would be a little bigger than 12. The few heavier atoms would make the average mass about 12.01. This average mass number of a random sample of an element, taking into account the different isotopes in it, is called the **relative atomic mass.** Because the relative atomic mass of an element is an average, it is often not a whole number.

Chlorine, for example, has two common isotopes. They are chlorine 35 and chlorine 37. In a sample of chlorine, there are nearly three times as many chlorine 35 atoms as chlorine 37 atoms. This makes the average mass of the atoms 35.5. The relative atomic mass, or A_r, of chlorine is 35.5.

Table 9.1 Some relative atomic masses

element	*relative atomic mass (A_r)*	*most common isotope*	*percentage occurrence*
chlorine	35.5	^{35}Cl	75
barium	137.34	^{138}Ba	72
germanium	72.69	^{74}Ge	36.5
mercury	200.5	^{202}Hg	30
strontium	87.62	^{88}Sr	82.6
thallium	204.3	^{205}Tl	70.5

DID YOU KNOW?

Two elements share the record for the highest number of known isotopes. Both xenon and caesium have 36.

Questions

1 a What do all isotopes of a particular element have in common?

b How do isotopes of a particular element differ from each other?

2 Three isotopes of magnesium are ^{24}Mg, ^{25}Mg and ^{26}Mg.

a Use a copy of the Periodic Table to find the atomic number of magnesium.

b Every magnesium atom has the same number of protons. What is this number?

c What is the total number of protons and neutrons in a ^{24}Mg atom?

d How many neutrons are there in a ^{26}Mg atom?

e The relative atomic mass of magnesium is 24.3. Why is this not a whole number?

f Which is the most common isotope of magnesium?

3 In 1000 thallium atoms, there are 705 atoms of ^{205}Tl.

a What is the total number of neutrons and protons in these 705 thallium atoms?

b The remaining 295 atoms are ^{203}Tl atoms. What is the total number of neutrons and protons in these 295 thallium atoms?

c What is the average number of protons and neutrons in the 1000 thallium atoms?

d What is the A_r (relative atomic mass) of thallium?

4 Natural copper contains two isotopes ^{63}Cu and ^{65}Cu. The atomic number of copper is 29.

a How many protons are there in a copper atom?

b How many neutrons are there in each of the two isotopes of copper?

c In naturally occurring copper, 69% of the atoms are ^{63}Cu, and the remainder are ^{65}Cu. What is the relative atomic mass of copper?

10 RADIOACTIVITY

Many isotopes are radioactive. The radiation they give off can cause ionisation. The three types of ionising radiation are alpha, beta and gamma radiation.

Some isotopes produce ionising radiation

'Radiation' is something which is sent out, or 'radiated' from an object. Many isotopes produce radiation. The type of radiation they produce is **ionising radiation**.

Towards the end of the nineteenth century, a French scientist, Becquerel, discovered that uranium gave out radiation. The radiation blackened a photographic plate. Marie Curie, a Polish scientist married to a Frenchman, read about Becquerel's experiments. She did experiments of her own, and in 1898 discovered radioactive isotopes in pitchblende ore. By 1902, with the help of her husband, she had isolated radioactive isotopes of the elements radium and polonium. In 1903, Marie Curie, her husband Pierre, and Becquerel were awarded a Nobel Prize. Marie was awarded a second Nobel prize, for Chemistry, in 1911. But she paid highly for her fame. In 1934 she died as a result of her prolonged exposure to ionising radiation.

Unstable isotopes tend to be radioactive

Isotopes may be stable or unstable. Stable isotopes stay as they are. Carbon 12 is an example of a stable isotope. Unstable isotopes tend to change. When an atom of an unstable isotope changes it gives out ionising radiation. Carbon 14 is an example of an unstable isotope. An element or isotope which gives off radiation is said to be **radioactive**. Carbon 14 is a **radioactive isotope** of carbon, or **radioisotope**.

A radioisotope can also be called a **radionuclide**. A stable isotope can be made unstable by hitting it with neutrons.

stable	*unstable (radioactive)*
carbon 12	carbon 14
gold 197	gold 198
lead 208	lead 198

Table 10.1 Stable and unstable isotopes

Radiation can be detected because it causes ionisation

Humans have no sense which can detect ionising radiation. We must use instruments to detect it. Ionising radiation ionises atoms. As the radiation passes through material it removes electrons from atoms, producing ions. Ions, unlike atoms, have a charge. If we can detect this charge we can detect ionising radiation.

Fig. 10.1 shows a **Geiger–Müller** tube. When ionising radiation enters the tube it ionises the argon gas. The electrons from the argon atoms go to the anode. The positive argon ions go to the cathode. This causes a tiny current to flow in the circuit. The current is amplified and detected on a counter.

Another way of detecting radiation is with **photographic film**. If radiation falls on a film, and the film is developed, it appears dark. Care must be taken not to allow any light to fall on to the film before it is developed.

Fig. 10.1 A Geiger–Müller tube

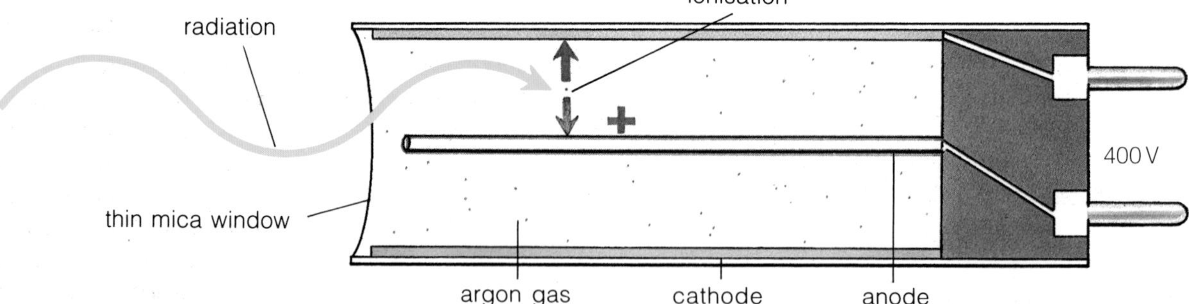

INVESTIGATION 10.1

Investigating the radiation levels from a gamma source

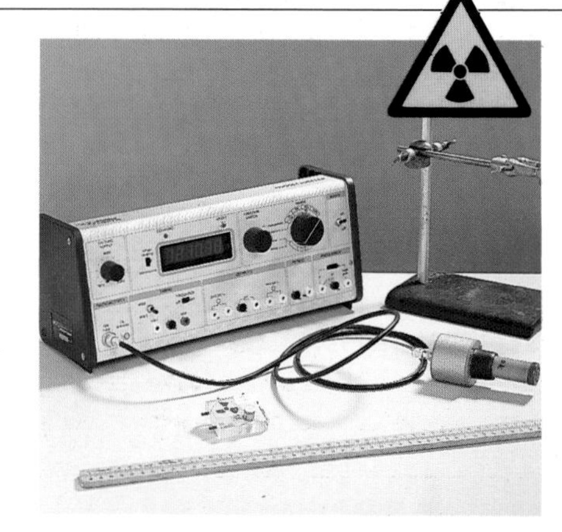

The photograph shows some apparatus which could be used to find out how the radiation from a gamma source varies with distance from the source.

Design an experiment to find out the answer to this problem, using some or all of the apparatus in the photograph. You will not be able to do the experiment yourself, but your teacher may demonstrate it to you.

Think about:

what you would measure

how you would measure it

how you would present your results.

Write down your ideas fully, so that someone could follow your instructions without having to ask you for any more help.

Alpha, beta and gamma radiation

There are three different types of ionising radiation which can be emitted by radioactive isotopes.

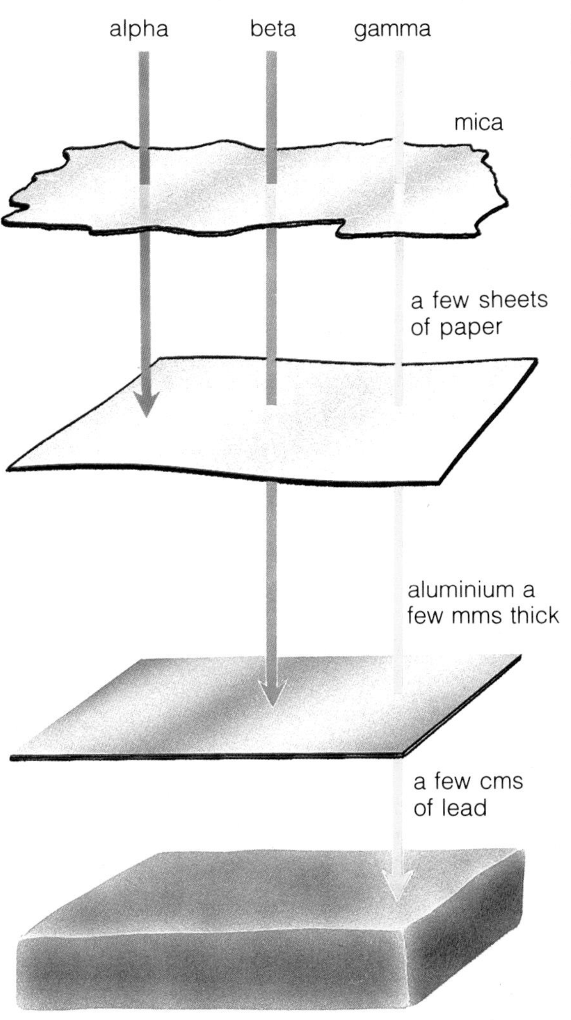

Fig. 10.2 The penetrating properties of ionising radiation.

Alpha radiation is made up of fast moving helium nuclei. The helium nuclei are called alpha particles. The particles have a positive charge. Alpha particles change direction if they pass through an electric or magnetic field. They are said to be **deflected** by the field. Alpha particles are quite easily stopped by thin materials. Even air will stop them. If you hold a Geiger–Müller tube more than a few centimetres from an alpha source, you will not be able to detect the radiation. It is stopped by the air.

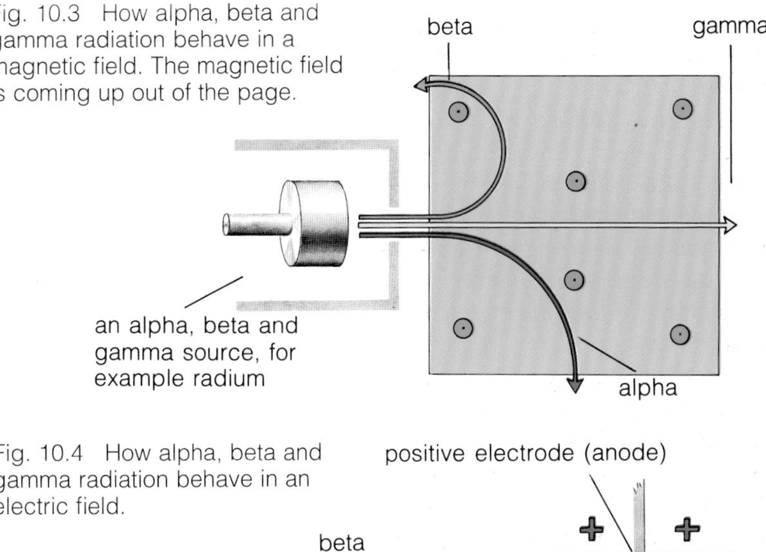

Fig. 10.3 How alpha, beta and gamma radiation behave in a magnetic field. The magnetic field is coming up out of the page.

Fig. 10.4 How alpha, beta and gamma radiation behave in an electric field.

positive electrode (anode)
beta
gamma
alpha
an alpha, beta and gamma source, for example radium
negative electrode (cathode)

Beta radiation is made up of electrons moving at high speed. The electrons are called **beta particles**. They have a negative charge. Like alpha particles, they are deflected by electric and magnetic fields. But because they have a negative charge instead of a positive charge, they are deflected in the opposite direction. Beta particles are not stopped as easily as alpha particles. Beta particles can travel several metres in air.

Gamma radiation is not a stream of particles. It is a form of electromagnetic radiation. Gamma radiation does not carry a charge, so it is not deflected by electric or magnetic fields. Gamma radiation has very high energy. It can travel a very long way in air, and can even pass through several centimetres of lead or an even thicker piece of concrete.

INVESTIGATION 10.2

The effect of radiation on living organisms

You will be given some normal barley seeds, and some barley seeds which have been exposed to radiation. Barley seeds take about 7 to 10 days to germinate. Over the next few days, they will grow to a height of several centimetres.

Design an experiment, using these two types of barley seeds, to find out how radiation affects barley seeds. Write up your method in detail. (Don't forget to take timing into account, as the barley seeds may take longer to germinate and grow than you think.) Get your design checked by your teacher before you carry out your experiment.

Record your results in the way you think is best. Discuss what your results suggest to you about the way in which radiation affects barley seeds. How accurate do you think your results are? How would you improve your experiment if you could do it again?

11 RADIOACTIVE DECAY

No-one can tell exactly when an individual atom will decay. The decay of one atom to form another can be shown by nuclear equations.

Atoms produce radiation when their nuclei change

A radioactive atom is an unstable atom. Atoms must have the correct balance of neutrons and protons to be stable. Small atoms have similar numbers of neutrons and protons. The heaviest atoms have about 50% more neutrons than protons. No atom with more than 83 protons is stable. In an unstable atom, changes happen in the nucleus to make it more stable. These changes cause radiation and energy to be released.

For example, carbon 14 emits beta radiation. The nucleus of a carbon 14 atom contains six protons and eight neutrons. This is unstable. Sooner or later, one of the neutrons changes to a proton and an electron. The electron is emitted from the atom as a beta particle. But is the atom still a carbon atom? It now has seven protons in its nucleus. The element with seven protons in each of its atoms is **nitrogen**. So the carbon atom has become a nitrogen atom!

This process of changing from one element to another while emitting radiation is called **radioactive decay**. The nucleus you start with is called the **parent nuclide** and the product of the decay is the **daughter nuclide**. Nitrogen is stable because it has seven protons and seven neutrons, so the radioactive decay of carbon 14 stops at nitrogen. Figure 11.3 shows some more examples.

Fig. 11.1 Carbon 14 decay. One of the neutrons in the carbon atom changes to a proton and an electron. The electron is emitted as a beta particle.

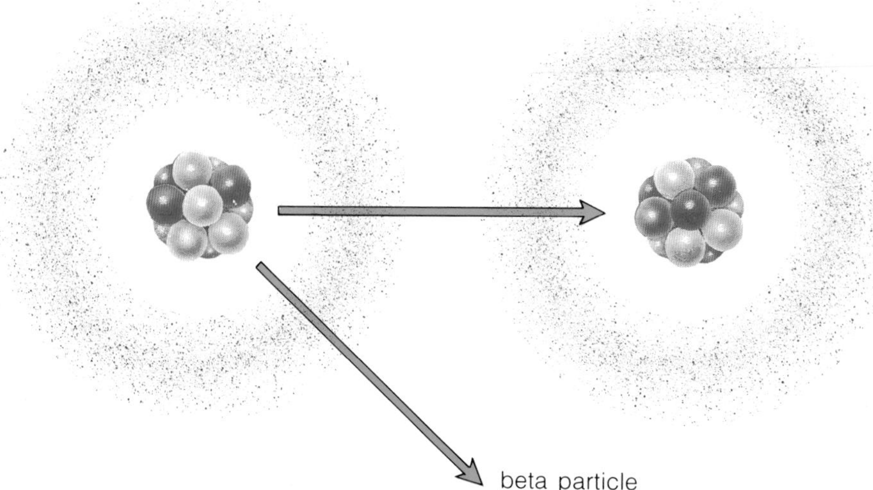

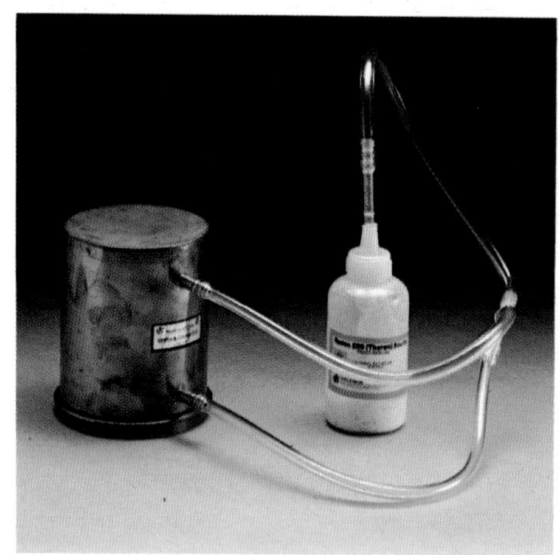

Fig. 11.2 Apparatus for measuring radioactive decay of radon gas. Squeezing the plastic container pushes the gas into the closed ionisation chamber, on the left. This has a central brass electrode, connected to a 16 volt supply. As the radon decays, it emits alpha particles, which produce a small current. A very sensitive ammeter measures this current, which depends on the number of radon atoms in the chamber. As the radon decays, the current drops, so a graph of current against time produces a decay curve.

Fig. 11.3 Radioactive decay of uranium. A uranium 238 atom decays to thorium 234. In the process it gives off two neutrons and two protons, which form an alpha particle.

Thorium 234 is not stable, either. It goes through 13 more decays, in which 7 alpha particles and 6 beta particles (electrons) are lost. Eventually, lead 206 is produced, which is stable and does not undergo radioactive decay.

All 14 steps make up the **radioactive decay series** for uranium 238. Material does not just vanish during radioactive decay. If you start with a sample of uranium 238 it will gradually change into other atoms.

Uranium 238 atom, containing 92 protons and 146 neutrons

an alpha particle

Thorium 234 atom, with 90 protons and 144 neutrons

7 alpha particles are lost

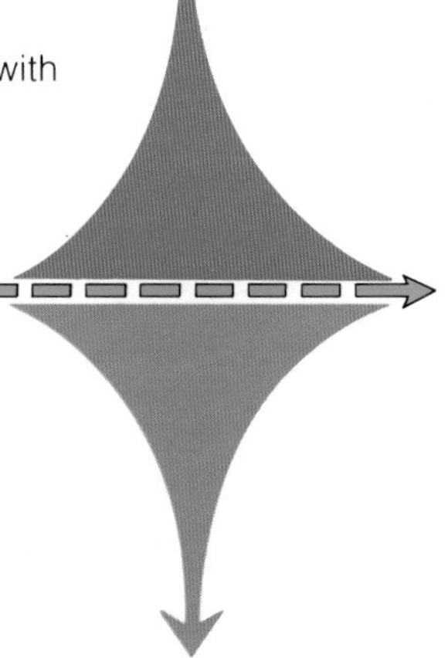

6 beta particles are lost

a lead 206 atom, with 82 protons and 124 neutrons

Radioactive decay is a random process

The atoms of radioactive isotopes are unstable. Sooner or later they will decay, giving off radiation as they do so. This is a random process, and we cannot tell exactly when any particular atom will decay. But in a lump of radioactive material, there are millions upon millions of atoms. Some will decay quickly, and others will take longer. The **activity** of the material tells you how quickly the atoms are decaying.

Activity is measured in **becquerels**. If one atom decays every second then the activity is one becquerel (1 Bq). You can calculate the activity by finding the number of decays per second.

$$\text{activity} = \frac{\text{number of decays}}{\text{time taken in seconds}}$$

Remember that the activity tells you how often, on average, the atoms are turning into other atoms. Changing the physical conditions, for example temperature, will not change the activity. Changing the chemical conditions, for example pH, will not change the activity. This is particularly important when radioactive material is used in the body to diagnose different conditions (see Topic 15). Whatever the physical and chemical conditions inside the body, the activity of the sample will behave in a predictable way.

What *will* change the activity is the amount of radioactive material you have. The more atoms there are, the more likely it is that some will decay. In 1 kg of uranium 238, approximately 12 million atoms will decay to thorium 234 every second. The activity would be 12 MBq (Figure 11.4).

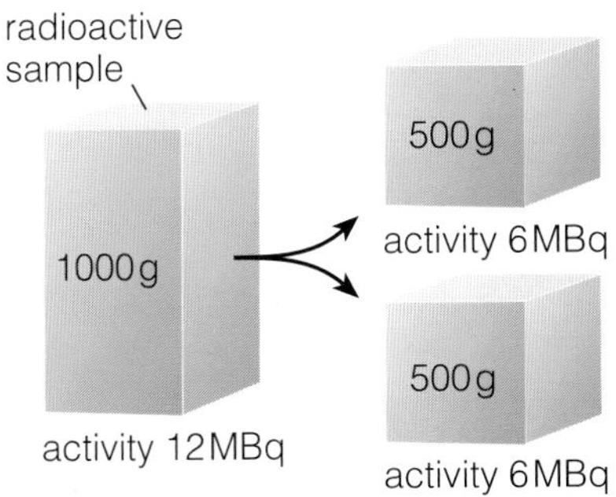

Fig. 11.4 The count from a radioactive sample depends on what isotope is in the sample, and how many atoms the sample contains.

EXTENSION

Nuclear equations show what happens in a decay

The decay shown in Figure 11.3 can be represented by an equation:

$$^{238}_{92}\text{U} \longrightarrow {}^{234}_{90}\text{Th} + {}^{4}_{2}\text{He}$$

(nucleon number: top; proton number: bottom)

For each atom:

- The top number is the total number of **nucleons** (particles in the nucleus). As this is the number of protons and neutrons, it is the same as the **mass number**. In nuclear equations it is called the **nucleon** number.
- The bottom number is the number of protons. It is the same as the atomic number and is called the **proton** number.
- The number of particles in the nucleus less the number of protons must equal the number of neutrons so:
  number of neutrons = nucleon number – proton number

example: The thorium atom has 234 nucleons and 90 protons so it has 234 – 90 =144 neutrons.

In nuclear equations, the nucleon numbers and proton numbers on each side of the equation must be the same – the equation must be **balanced**. In this equation, the uranium atom loses 4 nucleons in the form of an alpha particle. This is a helium nucleus and has 2 neutrons and 2 protons. So the nucleon number goes down to 234 and the proton number goes down to 90 – a thorium atom. Checking the top and bottom numbers on each side of the equation: 238 = 234 + 4 and 92 = 90 + 2, so the equation is balanced.

In beta particle decay, an electron leaves the nucleus. A neutron changes into a proton (Figure 11.5), so the nucleon number stays the same but the proton number goes up. So, for beta decay, we just increase the proton number by one for each beta particle emitted. The decay of carbon to nitrogen is shown by this equation. We balance the top and bottom by saying that the proton number of the electron is –1.

$$^{14}_{6}\text{C} \longrightarrow {}^{14}_{7}\text{N} + {}^{0}_{-1}\text{e}$$

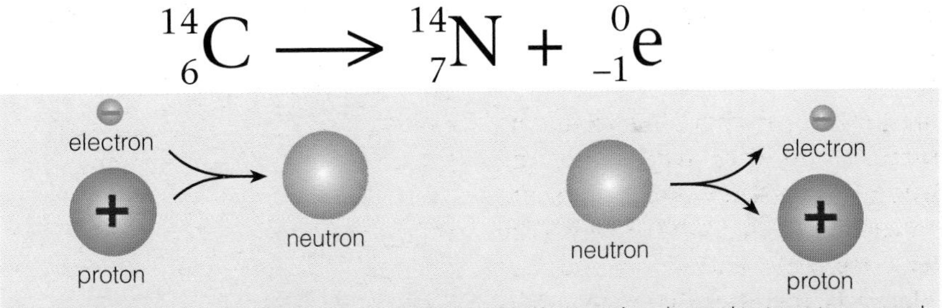

Fig. 11.5 Think of a neutron as a proton that has gained an electron to cancel its positive charge. Then you can see that if an electron is ejected from the nucleus of an atom, a neutron has changed into a proton.

- Gamma rays don't contain any particles, so they don't appear in a nuclear equation. All that happens is that the radioactive nucleus gives out some energy. For example, nickel 60 produces gamma rays.

$$^{60}_{28}\text{Ni} \longrightarrow {}^{60}_{28}\text{Ni}$$

higher energy ⟶ lower energy + gamma radiation

Question

1 For each atom listed below, calculate the number of neutrons. Plot a graph of number of neutrons against number of protons. What pattern do you notice for the proton/neutron balance for these stable atoms? How would the graph look if the numbers of protons and neutrons were always equal?

	C	Si	Ca	Fe	Y	Rh	I	Tm	Bi
mass number	12	28	40	56	89	103	127	169	209
atomic number	6	14	20	26	39	45	53	69	83

12 RADIATION HAZARDS

Radiation is all around us. Large doses of radiation can be very harmful to living things.

Everyone is constantly exposed to radiation

Radiation is all around you. Most is produced by natural substances, such as rocks. Some is made by humans. The normal level of radiation to which we are all exposed is called background radiation. Figure 12.2 shows the most important sources to which we are exposed.

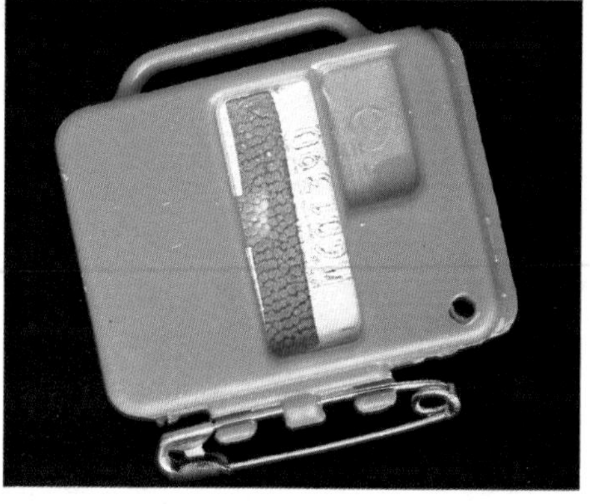

Fig. 12.1 A film badge contains photographic film. If the wearer is exposed to radiation, it will affect the film. The badges are collected regularly, and the film is developed, to check if the wearer is being exposed to radiation.

Fig. 12.2 The main sources of radiation in the United Kingdom. About 87% of the radiation to which people are exposed is from natural sources.

The air we breathe in contains small amounts of radioactive isotopes. These produce radiation in our lungs. All types of food also contain radioactive isotopes. The main one is potassium 40.

Radioactive radon gas enters buildings from the ground. It gets trapped inside the building. So radiation levels from radon are much higher indoors than outside.

Many building materials contain radioactive isotopes which emit gamma radiation.

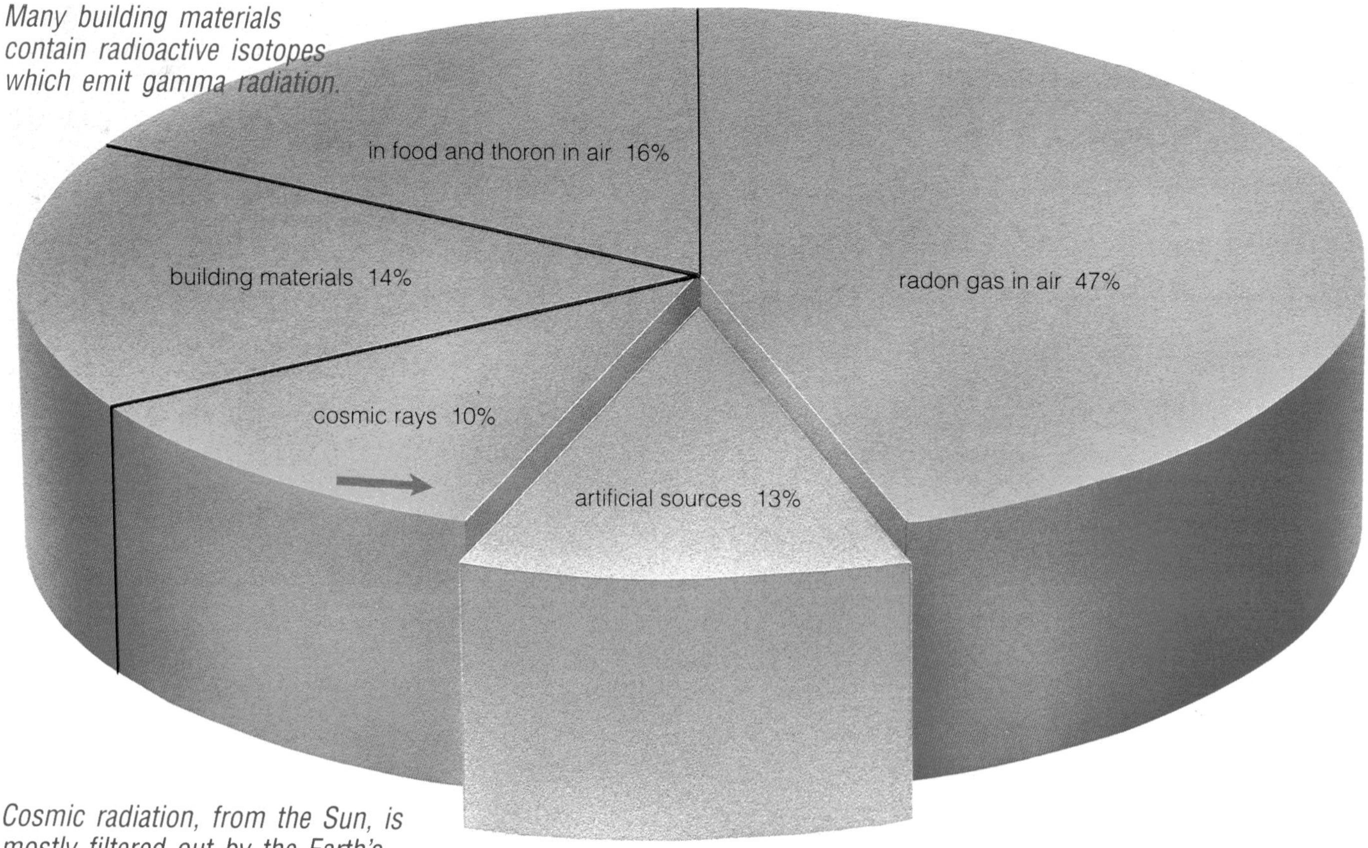

in food and thoron in air 16%

building materials 14%

radon gas in air 47%

cosmic rays 10%

artificial sources 13%

Cosmic radiation, from the Sun, is mostly filtered out by the Earth's atmosphere before it reaches the ground. Travellers in aeroplanes are exposed to much more cosmic radiation than people on the ground.

By far the largest human-made contribution is from X rays and other medical uses. Only 1 % is from sources such as nuclear waste, or accidents such as at Chernobyl.

Large doses of radiation can be harmful

Radiation damages living things because it damages the molecules in their cells. Alpha, beta and gamma radiation are all ionising radiations. They knock electrons away from atoms. This changes the way in which the atoms behave, and so changes the structure and behaviour of molecules in cells. If an organism receives a large dose of radiation, then a great many molecules may be damaged. This affects all sorts of processes going on in the body, and the person feels very ill. This is called **radiation sickness**.

The skin is also badly damaged with **radiation burns**.

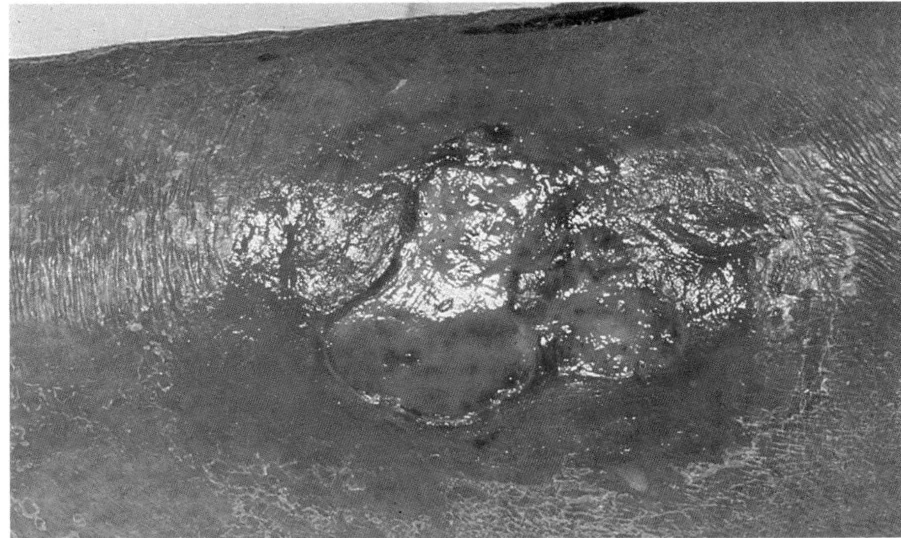

Fig. 12.3 This ulcer was caused by a high dose of radiation. The radiation has killed the skin cells. Eventually, the cells surrounding the ulcer will divide to form new ones, making a new layer of skin over the wound.

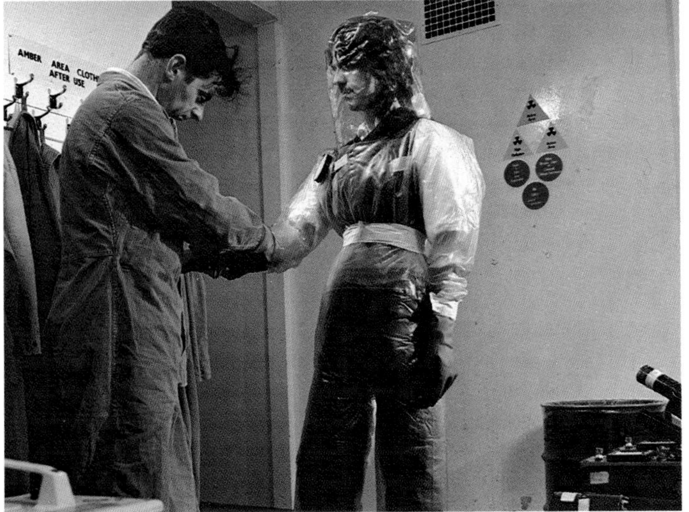

Fig. 12.4 A worker wearing protective clothing to protect his body from radiation.

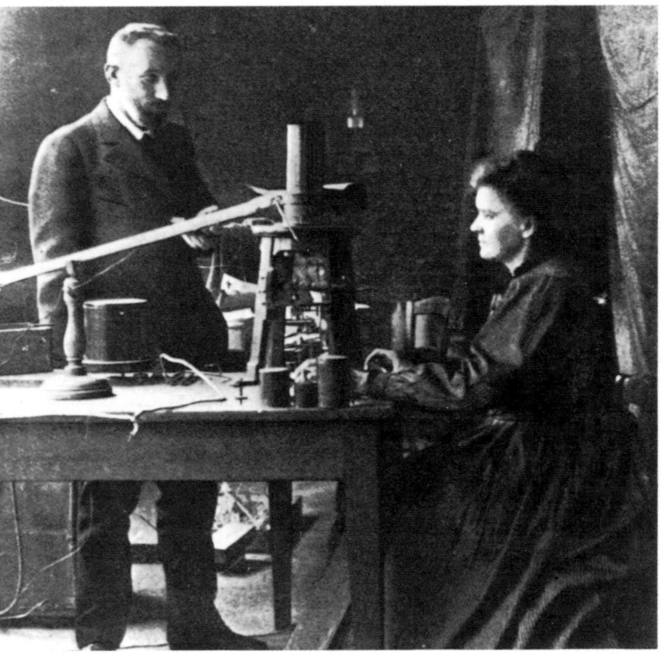

Fig. 12.5 Marie Curie was born in Poland in 1867. She worked on uranium, radium and radioactivity. The old unit of radioactivity, the curie, is named after her. 1 curie = 37 000 million becquerels (37 GBq).

Radiation can cause cancer

One very important molecule found in every cell is **DNA**. DNA is the chemical which carries inherited information from one generation to another. It is the DNA in your cells which gives instructions for everything which your cells do. If the DNA in a cell is damaged, then the cell may begin to behave very differently from normal. It is said to have **mutated**.

Radiation can cause mutations in cells by damaging the DNA. Sometimes this is not harmful. But sometimes the mutations cause the cell to divide uncontrollably. This may develop into **cancer**. Sometimes, the cancer does not develop until many years after exposure to the harmful radiation.

Questions

1 **a** What is meant by the term 'background radiation'?

b Make a list of the main causes of background radiation.

c Where does most background radiation come from?

2 Give three ways in which someone's dosage of radiation might be made higher than average.

3 Alpha particles are heavy. They are quickly stopped by air, or by skin. Gamma rays, though, can pass easily through most materials.

a If an alpha source and a gamma source were held 20 cm from your hand, which would be the more dangerous to you?

b If you swallowed an alpha source and a gamma source, which would be the more dangerous to you? Explain why.

13 HALF-LIVES

The large number of atoms involved in radioactive decay means that we can predict how fast decay will take place in a particular isotope.

The half-life of a radioactive isotope is the time taken for half of it to decay

The more unstable an isotope is, the more its atoms are likely to decay. If you have a sample of carbon 14, the atoms will stay around much longer than if you had a sample of the metal polonium 212. If you have 10g of carbon 14 and watch it for 5600 years, you will find that you have only 5g left. The other half would have decayed to nitrogen. Polonium 212 takes 0.00000003 seconds for half of it to decay. The activity of a 10g polonium 212 sample would be much higher than that of a 10g carbon 14 sample.

The time taken for half of a particular radioactive isotope to decay is always the same. This is called its **half-life**.

The activity tells you how quickly the atoms are decaying, so a high activity means a short half-life. A sample of a more stable isotope has a lower activity and a longer half-life. Since the activity is not affected by physical and chemical changes, the half-life does not change either.

A half-life curve shows how the activity falls with time

A plot of activity against time falls quickly at first and then slows down. With fewer unstable atoms, the activity is less. This type of curve is called an **exponential curve**. After one half-life, half the atoms have not decayed. After two half-lives, one quarter of the original number of atoms is left.

Some half-lives

Thorium 232	13 900 000 000 years
Uranium 238	4510 000 000 years
Potassium 40	1260 000 000 years
Uranium 235	713 000 000 years
Radium 226	1622 years
Cobalt 60	5.26 years
Iodine 131	8.07 days
Radon 222	3.82 days

Working out half-lives

If the half-life of a radioactive substance is short, you can time how long it takes until half of it has decayed. For a less active isotope it isn't practical to wait for half its lifetime. It would take about 23 years for the activity of a sample of radium 226 to fall by just 1 per cent! You could start by plotting the beginning of a curve like Figure 13.1, and then predict when half of the isotope would have decayed. An even better way is to measure the activity and amount of isotope, from which it is possible to calculate the half-life. After allowing for the number of atoms, a greater activity means a shorter half-life.

INVESTIGATION 13.1

Using cubes to simulate radioactive decay

You will need at least 100 cubes, with one face different from the other five faces.

1 Draw a results chart.
2 Scatter the cubes on the bench top. Take away all the cubes which fall with the different face uppermost. These are the ones which have decayed. Record the number remaining.
3 Keep repeating this process, removing the 'decayed' cubes each time. Keep going until you run out of cubes.
4 Plot a graph of the number of cubes (y axis) against the number of throws (x axis). Join the points to make a smooth curve.

Questions

1 What can you say about the shape of the graph?
2 How many throws does it take before you remove half the cubes?
3 How many throws does it take to remove the next half?
4 What is the 'half-life' for this decay, measured in number of throws?

Fig. 13.1 A half-life curve. The half-life in this example is 25 seconds. Every 25 seconds, the amount of the radioactive material falls by one-half. This will also reduce the count rate by one-half every 25 seconds.

The radioactive material decays into another material.

In this example, the count rate has been adjusted to allow for the background count. Unless the background level is found and taken from the results, the curve would not be quite this shape. This shape of curve is called an exponential curve.

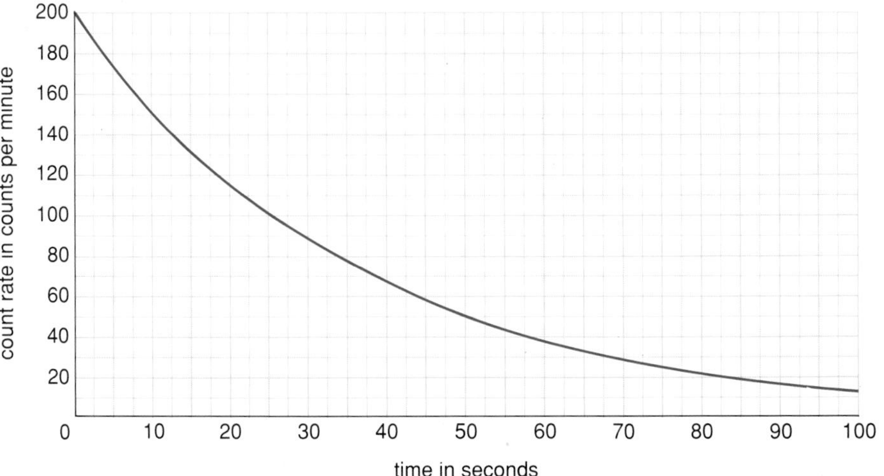

Radioactivity in rocks can be used to calculate the age of the Earth or samples of rock

Uranium 238, uranium 235 and thorium 232 are all found naturally on Earth. They each decay through a number of stages called a **radioactive decay series**. For all three isotopes the series ends in forms of lead that are stable. The half-lives of the daughter nuclei formed are all much shorter than the half-life of the isotope that started the series. The half-lives of uranium and thorium control the time taken to decay to lead. By measuring the amounts of these isotopes and lead in samples of rock, you can calculate the time for which the isotopes have been decaying. If the alpha particles from the decay have been trapped in the rock as helium, then the relative amounts of uranium and helium can be used as the basis of this calculation. Another useful isotope with a long half-life is potassium 40. The amount of this isotope is compared to the amount of stable argon 40 trapped as a gas. From these and other measurements, the age of the Earth has been estimated at 4500 000 000 years. Measurements of meteorites and samples of rocks from the Moon give about the same age for the rest of the solar system.

Questions

Read the following passage and then answer the questions that follow.

Radon gas in the home

Radon gas is a naturally occurring radioactive gas. It is formed during the radioactive decay of natural material and has little to do with the nuclear industry. Most soil and rock contains some uranium. Uranium decays over a long period of time and one of the products of this decay is radium. Radium decays to radon gas, releasing alpha particles. As the half-life of uranium is very large, uranium acts as a 'reservoir', constantly topping up the radon levels. The half life of radon is 3.825 days.

The main source of radon in houses is from the ground. Brick and stone (especially granite) do contain uranium but don't generate much radon gas. Where there are no buildings, the radon from the ground disperses into the atmosphere, but in houses it can collect and concentrate. The levels of radon in the home are affected by many factors. The type of soil or rock in the ground affects the amount of radon produced. Radon levels are generally higher in south-west England but there are other 'hot-spots', such as parts of Northamptonshire and Scotland. This does not mean that all houses in these regions have high levels of radon, because it can vary from one house to the next. Houses also tend to draw more air (containing radon) in from the ground as warm air escapes from the top of the house, through chimneys and upstairs vents. So open upstairs windows can bring in more radon than they let out.

Radon is dangerous if we inhale the radioactive decay products. Some of these products have very short half-lives and could increase the risk of lung cancer. Smoking is still the biggest cause of lung cancer, but in the USA it is thought that radon may cause 20000 lung cancer deaths a year.

The activity of a radioactive source is measured in becquerels. Radon gas concentrations are measured in becquerels per cubic metre, or Bq/m^3. Most houses have levels of around 20 Bq/m^3. A lifetime exposure to levels of 200 Bq/m^3 increases the risk of cancer by a factor of ten, and this is the **action level** at which a householder should do something about radon. The National Radiological Protection Board will take measurements in homes at risk using plastic sensors. These are left in place for 3 months and then analysed to work out the average levels of radon gas. Peak readings are of no use since it is the long-term exposure that is important in assessing the risks.

If levels are high they can be reduced by preventing radon getting in. This can be done by sealing floors or by pressurising the whole house with a small air pump. Fitting small vents in downstairs windows encourages fresh air to come from outside, and not through the floor. The best method is to ventilate the ground under the floor. A hole or **sump** is created if the house has solid floors and the air (and radon with it) is extracted by a pump.

1 What is meant by the term 'half-life'? How long is the half-life of uranium?

2 Name the two nuclei that are formed when radium decays.

3 a Complete the nuclear decay equations.

$${}^{226}_{?}Ra \longrightarrow {}^{?}_{86}Rn + {}^{4}_{2}He$$

$${}^{?}_{86}Rn \longrightarrow {}^{218}_{?}Po + {}^{4}_{2}He$$

$${}^{234}_{90}Th \longrightarrow {}^{234}_{91}Pa + {}^{?}_{?}?$$

b What is the other decay product from thorium?

c Why is this product less dangerous in the lungs than the product formed from radon?

4 A room measures 2 m by 3 m by 2.5 m.

a What is the volume of the room?

b Assuming average radon levels, what would be the total radon activity in the room?

5 In a sealed room with an activity of 800 Bq/m^3, how long would it take until radon activity fell to the action level?

6 The half-lives of some of the radon decay products are less than that of radon. What does that tell you about the activity of these products? Your friend says that if they don't last as long, they can't be as dangerous. Do you agree or disagree with this statement? Give your reasons.

14 RADIOACTIVE WASTE

Radioactive material can stay radioactive for a long time and must be disposed of carefully.

Nuclear power stations produce less waste than coal-fired power stations

A nuclear power station uses the energy released in nuclear reactions to generate electricity. (You can read more about this in Topic 89.) In one year a nuclear reactor produces around 20 tonnes of waste. About 50 000 tonnes of uranium have to be mined to make the fuel. To generate the same amount of electricity by burning coal would need 2 million tonnes of coal. A coal-fired power station produces up to 120 000 tonnes of ash, 200 000 tonnes of sulphur dioxide, 7 million tonnes of carbon dioxide and releases more radioactivity than the nuclear power station does.

Although there is not much waste from the nuclear power station, this waste is radioactive. Radioactive (nuclear) waste is also produced by nuclear reactors in other industries. Nuclear waste can be grouped into three classes.

Low-level waste comes from nuclear reactors in power stations, and also hospitals and industry. Most nuclear waste is low-level waste. It isn't very radioactive and the products have short half-lives, so it can just be buried in the ground. Only 1% of the radioactivity from nuclear waste is from low-level waste. A lot of it is paper or cloth so it is often burnt (in sealed containers!) to reduce its size. Liquids can be diluted and released into the sea.

Intermediate-level waste usually contains reactor parts and chemicals, and material contaminated by a reactor or from the reprocessing ('recycling') of nuclear fuel. The radioactivity must be contained so the waste is often covered in concrete. If the material has a long half-life it must be buried deep underground.

High-level waste is mainly liquid from fuel reprocessing. This is very radioactive and contains isotopes with long half-lives. As well as shielding, the waste needs to be cooled, because the radioactive decay releases energy. High-level waste can be **vitrified** by trapping it in special types of glass. It is then sealed in stainless steel tanks and can be stored deep underground. Most of the radioactivity from nuclear waste comes from high-level waste, although it only accounts for 3% of the volume.

Fig 14.1 High-level liquid waste is converted into solid glass blocks by a process called vitrification.

Fig 14.2 Spent fuel is transported in flasks which have walls one foot thick and are capable of withstanding the severest of accidents.

Spent fuel can be buried or reprocessed

When nuclear fuel is removed from a power station it is held in storage under water. Most of the radioactivity produced in the reactor stays in the fuel. Water helps trap the radiation and keep the fuel rods cool. The rods are stored in this way for up to 40 years. Some of the material will have to be stored for thousands of years. To be safe it will have to be buried very deep in areas where there is no danger of earthquakes or other natural disasters.

The fuel rods contain a lot of material that can be used again. In Europe the fuel is **reprocessed**. A large amount of uranium (96% or more) and a small amount of plutonium can be recovered. To do this, the fuel is dissolved in nitric acid and the uranium and plutonium are separated out from the waste material. This still leaves a small amount of high-level waste to be disposed of.

One possibility of reducing the time for which nuclear waste will have to be stored is to change the isotopes with long half-lives into shorter-lived ones. This is called **transmutation**. By bombarding the waste with neutrons from a reactor, isotopes can be converted to different ones. For example, iodine 129 has a half-life of 20 million years and can be converted to stable xenon.

Fig 14.3 Chernobyl nuclear reactor after the explosion of 26 April 1986. More than 6 tonnes of nuclear material was released.

Fig 14.4 Chernobyl in 1991. A large concrete shelter or sarcophagus constructed during 1986 in an attempt to contain radiation and seal the plant. This is the darker part of the structure in the centre of the picture.

Nuclear accidents can happen

In 1986 an experiment at the nuclear power station at Chernobyl, in the Ukraine, went wrong. An explosion blew open the reactor and released radiation into the atmosphere. Over 6 tonnes of nuclear material escaped. The world-wide release of radiation may have been as high as 10 000 000 000 000 000 000 Bq.

Radiation absorbed by the body can cause damage. The **dose** is the energy absorbed per kilogram of body mass. A dose of 1 gray or 1 Gy means each kilogram has absorbed 1 joule of energy. As some types of radiation are absorbed more than others the dose is multiplied by a 'quality factor'. This number is 1 for beta and gamma radiation, and 20 for alpha radiation. The dose multiplied by the quality factor produces the **dose equivalent**, which is measured in sieverts (Sv).

The background radiation to which we are all exposed, on average, is 2 mSv per year. Doses of 3 Sv (1500 times the average background radiation) will cause radiation burns to the skin. Radiation workers have to keep their dose levels low as effects can build up with time. A weekly dose of 1 mSv might be considered safe. Clean-up workers at Chernobyl received an average dose of 170 mSv. 134 workers received doses high enough to give **acute radiation sickness** and 28 died.

A large amount of radioactive iodine 131 was released in the Chernobyl accident. Food chains were contaminated. Iodine collects in the thyroid gland and young children are particularly affected. For the people living near Chernobyl, thyroid radiation doses reached several sieverts in some cases. Already, 800 thyroid cancer cases have been reported and it is expected that this may reach a few thousand.

Eventually, the remaining reactors at Chernobyl will be shut down. The damaged reactor still holds 200 tonnes of nuclear fuel and its ten-year-old protective covering of concrete still contains 700 000 000 000 000 000 Bq of activity.

EXTENSION

15 USES OF RADIOACTIVITY

Despite its dangers, radioactivity has many uses.

Cancer cells can be killed by radiation

Radiation can kill living cells because it ionises molecules inside them. Cancer cells can be killed in this way. Cobalt 60 is often used. It produces gamma rays which can penetrate deep inside the body. For skin cancers, phosphorus 32 or strontium 90 may be used instead. These produce beta radiation. The dose of radiation has to be carefully controlled. Otherwise the radiation could do more damage than help.

Patients undergoing radiation treatment often feel ill, because the radiation also damages other cells.

Fig. 15.1 A patient receiving radiotherapy treatment using a linear accelerator.

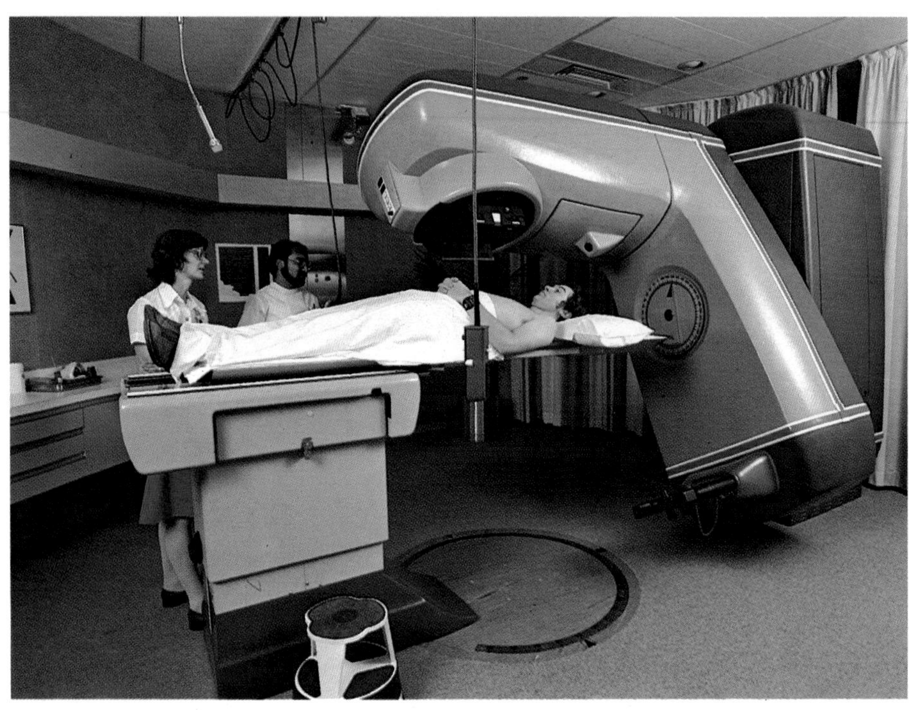

Radiation can be used to sterilise surgical instruments

Gamma rays are often used to kill bacteria and viruses on dressings, syringes, and other medical equipment. This is called **sterilisation**. Sterilisation means killing all living things. These items used to be sterilised using very high temperatures, or steam. Gamma radiation is a more convenient and more effective method.

Radioactive tracers show what happens during biological processes

Inside a living organism, a radioactive isotope of a particular substance behaves in just the same way as the normal isotope. So, if a plant is given carbon 14, for example, it will use it in exactly the same way as it always uses carbon 12. But the carbon 14 produces beta radiation. By measuring the radioactivity in different areas of the plant, the path taken by the carbon atoms can be followed.

In a similar way radioactive iodine can be used to check that a person's thyroid gland is working properly. The thyroid gland uses iodine. If a person is given a tablet containing iodine 131, the thyroid takes it up as though it was normal iodine. The amount of radioactivity emitted by the thyroid gland can then show how much iodine has been taken up.

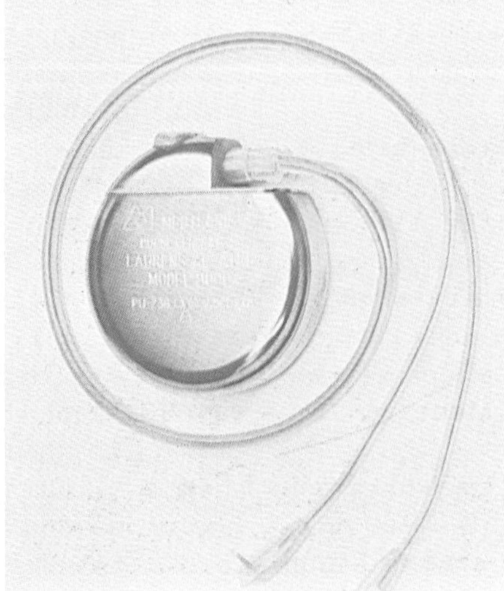

Radiation can provide energy

When an atom decays it gives out energy. This energy can be used to provide electricity. **Nuclear batteries** use this process. A nuclear battery lasts for a very long time. Nuclear batteries are often used to power heart pacemakers. The heat energy produced by radioactivity can be used to generate electricity on a very large scale. In a **nuclear reactor** special nuclear reactions are encouraged that release large amounts of energy.

Fig. 15.2 This pacemaker can be inserted into a human heart whose own pacemaker is faulty. It emits regular pulses, which stimulate the heart to contract rhythmically. If powered by a nuclear battery, rather than a conventional one, it can run for much longer before the battery needs to be replaced.

Radiation can be used to check the thickness of metal sheets

Gamma radiation is used to make sure that steel sheets are made to the correct thickness. Figure 15.3 shows how this is done. The steel is pressed between rollers to produce a sheet of a particular thickness. A source of gamma radiation is then positioned on one side of the steel sheet. A detector is positioned opposite it, with the steel in between. Gamma radiation can pass through steel, but the thicker the steel the less radiation gets through. If the sheet comes through thicker than usual, the radiation picked up by the detector falls. This causes the pressure on the roller to be increased, until the radiation detected increases to its normal level. What do you think happens if the detector picks up *more* radiation than usual? A similar method can be used to check the thickness of sheets of paper. This time, though, alpha radiation is used.

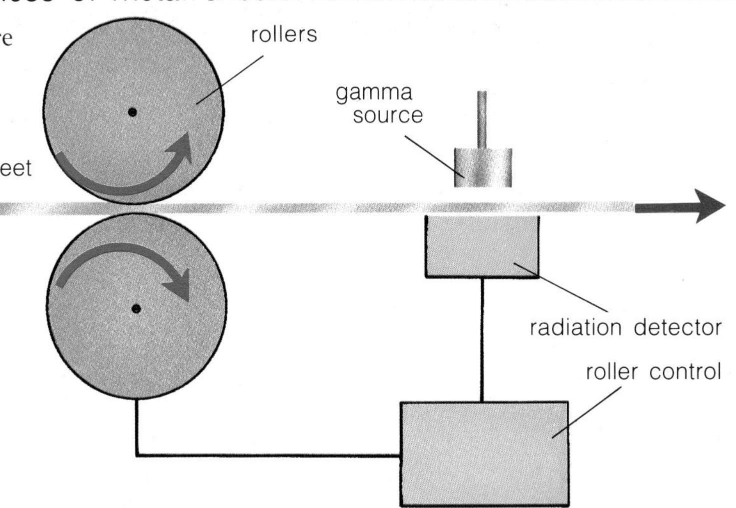

Fig. 15.3 Using radiation to check metal sheet thickness.

Questions

1 a How can radioactivity help in the treatment of cancer?

b Why do you think that gamma radiation is used to treat cancers inside the body, but beta radiation is used to treat skin cancers?

2 a What is meant by sterilisation?

b Why do you think it is important that surgical dressings should be sterilised?

c Why is gamma radiation, not beta radiation, used for sterilising dressings?

3 Why are nuclear batteries, rather than ordinary batteries, used to power heart pacemakers?

Radiocarbon dating

Air contains 0.04 % carbon dioxide. Most of the carbon atoms in the carbon dioxide are carbon 12 atoms. But a small proportion are carbon 14 atoms. These carbon 14 atoms decay to nitrogen, emitting beta particles. But new carbon 14 atoms are always being produced by the action of cosmic rays. So the amount of carbon 14 atoms in the carbon dioxide in the air stays the same.

When plants photosynthesise they take in carbon dioxide from the air. The carbon atoms become part of molecules in the plant. The carbon 14 atoms in these molecules slowly decay to nitrogen. But, unlike the carbon 14 in the air, they will not be replaced. So the amount of carbon 14 in the plant gradually falls.

Many things might happen to the plant. It might be eaten by an animal. It might be made into material such as cotton or linen. It might form coal. But whatever happens the carbon 14 in it gradually decays. After 5600 years there will only be half as many carbon 14 atoms as there were when they first entered the plant from the air.

So, by finding out how much carbon 14 there is in an object, we can work out how long ago the plant from which it was made was alive. The less carbon 14 compared with carbon 12, the older the object is.

Fig. 15.4 Part of the Turin shroud. This ancient piece of cloth shows marks which some people believe to have been made by Christ's body after crucifixion. In this detail, you can see the image of hands, and a mark which could have been made by a nail. In 1988 three small pieces of the shroud were dated using the radio-carbon technique. Three different laboratories all showed the shroud to be about 500–600 years old. Although this shows that it cannot really have been Christ's shroud, the way in which the marks were made is still a mystery.

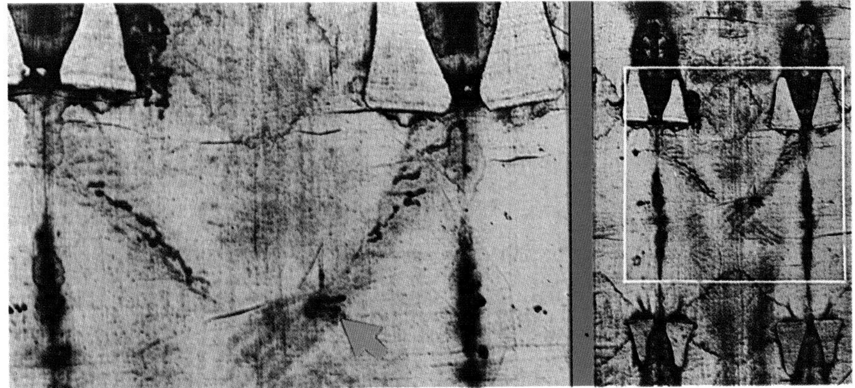

EXTENSION

4 ^{14}C makes up about $\frac{1}{10\,000\,000}$ of the carbon in the air.
The half-life of ^{14}C is 5600 years.

a In what substance is carbon present in the air?

b Which is the commonest isotope of carbon?

c ^{14}C is constantly decaying. So why does the amount of ^{14}C in the air not decrease?

d Carbon is taken in by plants. In what substance is the carbon? What is the process by which the plants take it in?

e What happens to the amount of ^{14}C in a plant, or in something made from the plant, as time goes by?

f The amount of ^{14}C in a piece of linen is analysed. It is found to make up $\frac{1}{20\,000\,000}$ of the carbon in the cloth. How old is the cloth?

EXTENSION

Questions

1 a Name the three types of radiation emitted by radioisotopes.

b Which is negatively charged?

c Which is made up of positively charged helium nuclei?

d Which can penetrate the farthest in air?

e All three types are ionising radiation. What does this mean?

2 Film badges are worn by people who may be exposed to radiation.

a Why do they wear the badges?

b Why must no light be allowed to fall on the badges?

3 Find out what pitchblende ore is and where it comes from.

4 To measure engine wear an engine is run with piston rings that have been made radioactive by bombarding them with neutrons in a nuclear reactor. Radioactive material goes into the oil when the rings wear against the sides of the cylinders. The radioactivity in the oil is used to estimate the amount of metal that has worn off the rings. Why is it important to know the half-life of the radioisotope in the piston rings?

5 The level of radiation from a radioactive source was measured for just over one minute. The results are shown below.

Time (s)	0	10	20	30	40	50	60	70
Level of radioactivity	112	103	109	111	116	117	109	107

a What causes the change in the readings?

b What was the average reading?

c When the source was removed from the room, the average count fell by 80 counts. If the source has a half-life of two years, estimate the count (with the source back in the room) in six years' time.

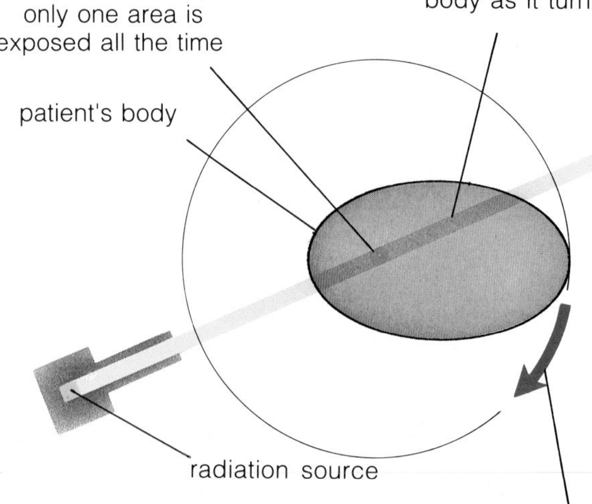

6 The diagram above shows how gamma rays may be used to kill cancer cells.

a Why are gamma rays used, rather than alpha or beta radiation?

b During treatment the person is rotated in a circle with the tumour at the centre. Why is this done?

7 The table shows the radiation count from a source over a period of 40 min.

Time (min)	0	5	10	15	20	25	30	35	40
Count	152	115	87	66	50	38	29	22	17

a Plot a line graph to show these results.

b What is the time taken for the count to drop from 110 to 55 counts?

c What is the time taken for the count to drop from 80 to 40 counts?

d What is the half-life of this radioactive element?

e How long would it take for the count to reach 10 counts?

EXTENSION

8 The energy from nuclear reactions is used in power stations. Uranium 235 is encouraged to split into two similar-sized nuclei by bombarding it with neutrons. One possible reaction is:

$$^{235}_{92}U + ^{1}_{0}n \longrightarrow ^{141}_{56}Ba + ^{92}_{36}Kr + 3^{1}_{0}n$$

Neutrons are released, which could go on to start other reactions. If one of the daughter nuclei was barium 144 and the other was krypton 90, what difference would this make? (Hint: rewrite the equation, putting in the values that you know and recalculate the nucleon and proton numbers – how many neutrons are released now?)

9 Cobalt 60 is commonly used as a source of gamma rays for medical and industrial uses. It can be used for imaging, thickness measurements and killing cells in cancer treatment. It decays to nickel by beta particle emission and the nickel nucleus then releases gamma radiation. Write a nuclear equation for this decay.

10 A Geiger–Müller tube was used to measure the radiation at different distances from a source emitting alpha and gamma radiation. As the Geiger–Müller tube was gradually moved away from the source, it was found that the level of radiation fell very rapidly over the first few centimetres. After that, the radiation fell more slowly. Why was this?

11 Smoke detectors contain radioactive Americium 241, which is an alpha and gamma source with a half-life of 460 years. If the distance travelled by the alpha particles is decreased significantly, the smoke detector is activated.

a Why is an isotope with a long half-life used in smoke detectors?

b What is the approximate range of alpha particles in air?

c What effect would the presence of smoke particles have on this range? What does this do to the smoke detector?

12 A manufacturer intends to check that cereal packets are full to the top as they pass down a conveyor belt. If you were provided with a selection of radioactive sources and a detector, how could you do this?

FORCES

16 FORCES

The most simple forces are pushes and pulls. If we push or pull on an object, it often moves. Sometimes the force makes the shape of the object change.

There are many different types of force

A force can start an object moving. It can also slow down or speed up a moving object. A force can change the shape of an object. Sometimes a force seems to be doing nothing. This might be because it is cancelling out the effects of another force.

There are many types of force. They include elastic, magnetic, electrostatic, compressive, tensile, gravitational, turning, squashing, squeezing, twisting, stretching... you can probably think of many more. Often, these are just different names for the same thing. A compressive force is a squashing force. A tensile force is a stretching force.

Fig. 16.1 A pile driver uses gravitational force to pull the large mass downwards.

Large electric currents in superconductors levitate the disc with magnetic forces.

Forces are measured in newtons

To measure forces we use a newton meter. This is a spring and a scale. A large force stretches the spring. The scale is calibrated in **newtons**. The newton, N, is the unit of force. It is named after Sir Isaac Newton.

INVESTIGATION 16.1

Measuring the extension of a spring

1 Read through the experiment and design a results chart.
2 Set up the apparatus as shown in the diagram. Measure the length of the spring. Add a load of 1 N to the spring. Measure how much longer the spring now is. You should record by how much the spring has **stretched** – not its actual length.
3 Repeat the measurements, increasing the load a little each time.
4 Plot your results as a line graph. Put 'load' on the horizontal axis, and 'extension' – how much the spring has stretched – on the vertical axis.

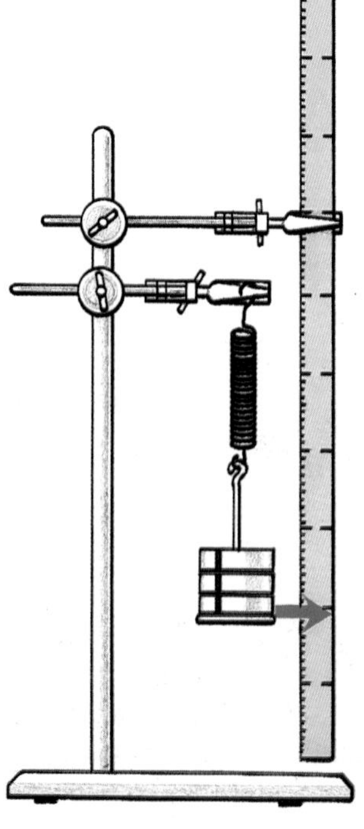

Fig. 16.2

You may have loaded your spring so much that it became permanently stretched. If you did this, your graph will change shape at this point. The point where this happens is called the **elastic limit** of the spring.

Questions

1 What is the shape of your graph?
2 If your spring extended by 25 mm, what force was being applied to it?
3 If the load on your spring is doubled, what happens to the extension?
4 If you reached the elastic limit of your spring, at what load did this happen?
5 What would happen if the spring in a newton meter went beyond its elastic limit? How is this prevented in a newton meter?

Forces change the way things move

Sir Isaac Newton spent a lot of time thinking about forces. He stated some important laws about them.

Newton's First Law says that **an object keeps on going as it is, unless an unbalanced force acts on it.**

This helps to describe what a force is. A force is something that changes the way in which something moves. The force will either speed it up or slow it down.

Imagine a book on a table. If you give it a push, it starts moving. Newton's First Law says that when you stop pushing, the book will keep on going – unless it is acted on by an unbalanced force. You know that when you stop pushing, the book very quickly stops moving.

So there must be an unbalanced force acting on it!

What exactly is an **'unbalanced force'**? Think about a seesaw. If the people on either side push down with the same force, they cancel one another out. The seesaw is balanced and it does not move. The two forces are balanced. But if one person is heavier then the forces are unbalanced. In Figure 16.3 there is an unbalanced force of 50 N. This moves the seesaw down at one end. So if an unbalanced force acts on a stationary object it will start moving. If *all* the forces acting on a moving object are balanced it will keep on moving.

Fig. 16.3 Unbalanced forces. The right-hand end of the seesaw will move downwards.

Friction slows things down

Now think about the book on the table again. When it slides across the table the unbalanced force is friction. The surface of the book and table are not perfectly smooth. The two surfaces catch on one another, and stop the book moving.

Does this mean that if the surfaces were perfectly smooth the book would keep on going for ever? Newton's First Law says that it would. But the book also has to push the air aside as it moves. Air resistance is another frictional force, and it will slow the book down. But if you were out in space and you pushed the book away from you, it really would go on moving away from you for ever. There is no surface and no air to slow it down.

One force always produces a reaction to itself

If a book is placed on a table, the force of its weight acts downwards. So why does it not *move* downwards? A simple answer would be that the table gets in the way!

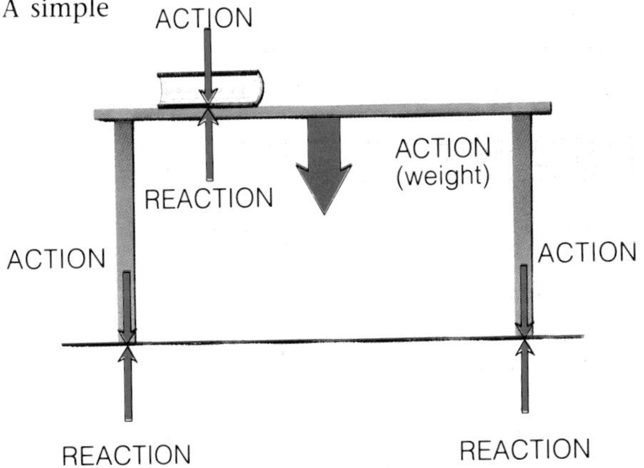

Fig. 16.4

Newton's Third Law states that if one body pushes on a second body, the second body pushes back on the first with the same force. **For every action there is an equal and opposite reaction.** If the book pushes down on the table, the table pushes up on the book. The push of the table on the book balances the weight of the book, so the book does not move. The table rests on the Earth. It pushes down with a force due to its own weight, and the book. The Earth pushes back with an equal and opposite force. So the table stays where it is.

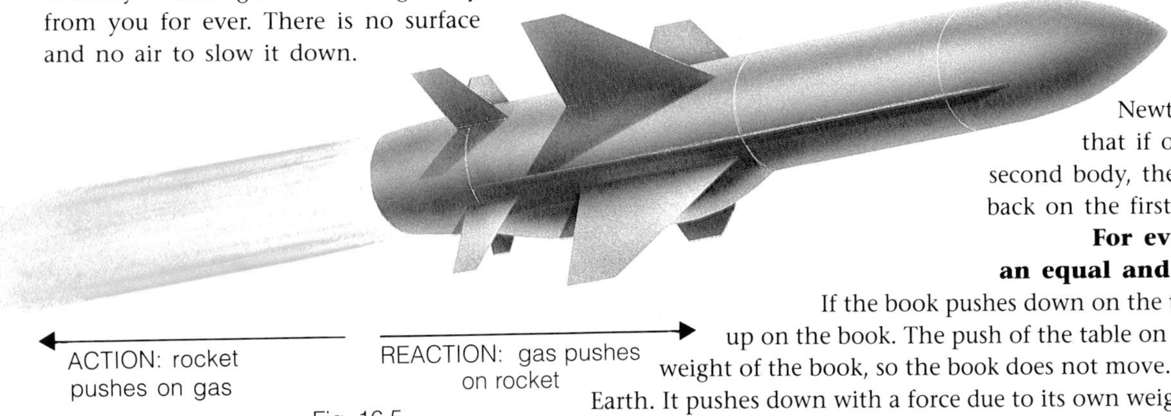

ACTION: rocket pushes on gas

REACTION: gas pushes on rocket

Fig. 16.5

Forces can cause objects to change shape

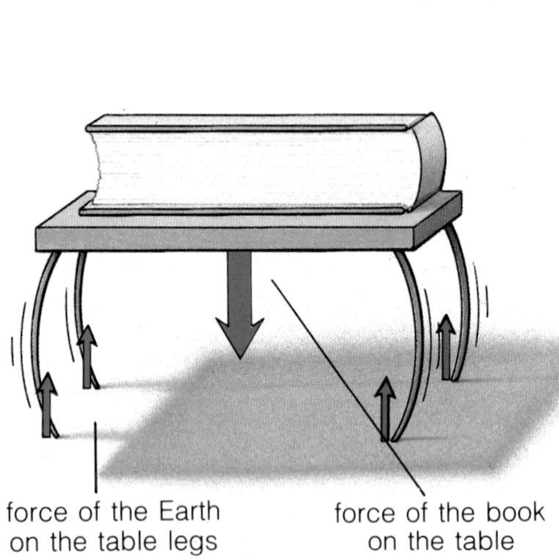

Fig. 16.6 Even when forces are balanced, things can happen

Fig. 16.7 Balanced forces squashing a balloon

Balanced forces will not make an object move – but they might make it change shape. Think of the book on the table again. The book and the table stay where they are, because the push of the book on the table is balanced by the push of the Earth on the table. But the table is 'squashed' between the force of the book pushing down on it, and the force of the Earth pushing up on it. This could change the shape of the table. If the book were very heavy, and the table legs very thin, they could bend. You can see this happening when you squeeze a balloon. If you push hard on either side of a balloon, the forces of each hand are balanced. The balloon does not go anywhere (unless you suddenly let go!) but it does change shape.

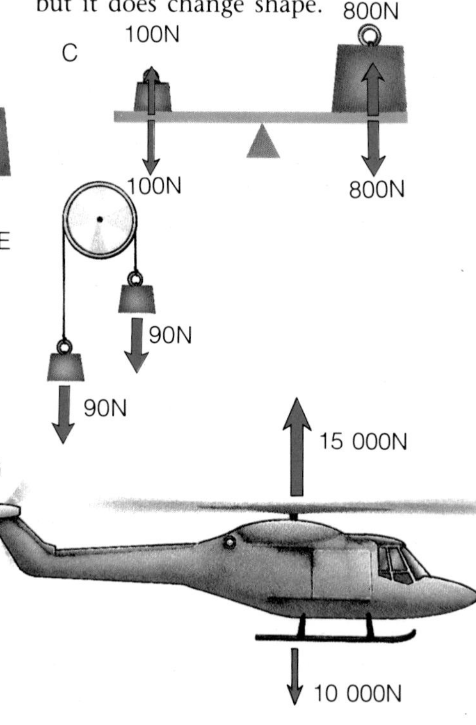

Questions

1 If an object is not moving, then either no forces are acting on it at all (which is unlikely), or all the forces acting on it are balanced. For each of the diagrams shown:

a Say whether the forces are balanced or unbalanced

b Describe any 'missing' forces

c If the forces are unbalanced, say how big the resulting force is

2 A spring is stretched from 2.5 cm to 5 cm when it is loaded with a weight of 5 N.

a What would be the new length of the spring if a weight of 2 N was added to the 5 N weight?

b Can you make a sensible prediction for the length of the spring if a weight of 100 N was hung on it?

3 A body builder uses a chest expander. It has five springs. It takes 300 N to pull one spring out by 20 cm.

a What force is needed to pull all five springs out by 20 cm?

b How hard will the body builder have to pull to extend all five springs by 40 cm?

4 The weight of a car produces a downward force of 10 000 N. This pushes each of the four springs in its suspension down by 20 cm. If five adults get into the car, the downwards force increases by 4000 N. If the force is shared equally by the four springs, how much more will they be pushed down?

5 A set of bathroom weighing scales contain a spring. As the top is pushed down, the movement of the spring turns a pointer on the scale.

a When person A stands on the scales, they depress the top by 10 mm. Person B weighs 2/3 as much as person A. By how much would person B depress the top of the scales?

b What would happen if 10 people, all weighing the same as person A, balanced on the top of the scales?

6 An aircraft in flight has four forces acting on it. They are weight, lift, thrust and drag.

a Draw a diagram with arrows showing these forces.

b Which forces must balance each other?

EXTENSION

17 GRAVITY, MASS AND WEIGHT

Gravity attracts objects towards each other, producing a force called weight. Weight and mass are not the same.

Mass is one way of measuring how much of something there is

Mass is a quantity of matter. The mass of an object tells you how much of it there is. Mass is measured by finding out the force needed to change the way the object moves. The greater the force needed, then the greater the mass of the object.

If you push on a book, it moves faster than if you push with the same force on a car. This is because the car has more mass than the book. If you had two identical tins, one containing lead and the other full of feathers, you could find out which was which by pushing them. The lead-filled tin has more mass, so you need more force to move it. We can say that the car and the lead-filled tin are more 'reluctant' to move than the book and the tin of feathers. We call this reluctance to move **inertia**. The larger the mass of an object, the larger its inertia.

Moving objects have inertia, too. A moving object needs force to make it stop. A moving car has more inertia than a moving book. It needs more force to make it stop.

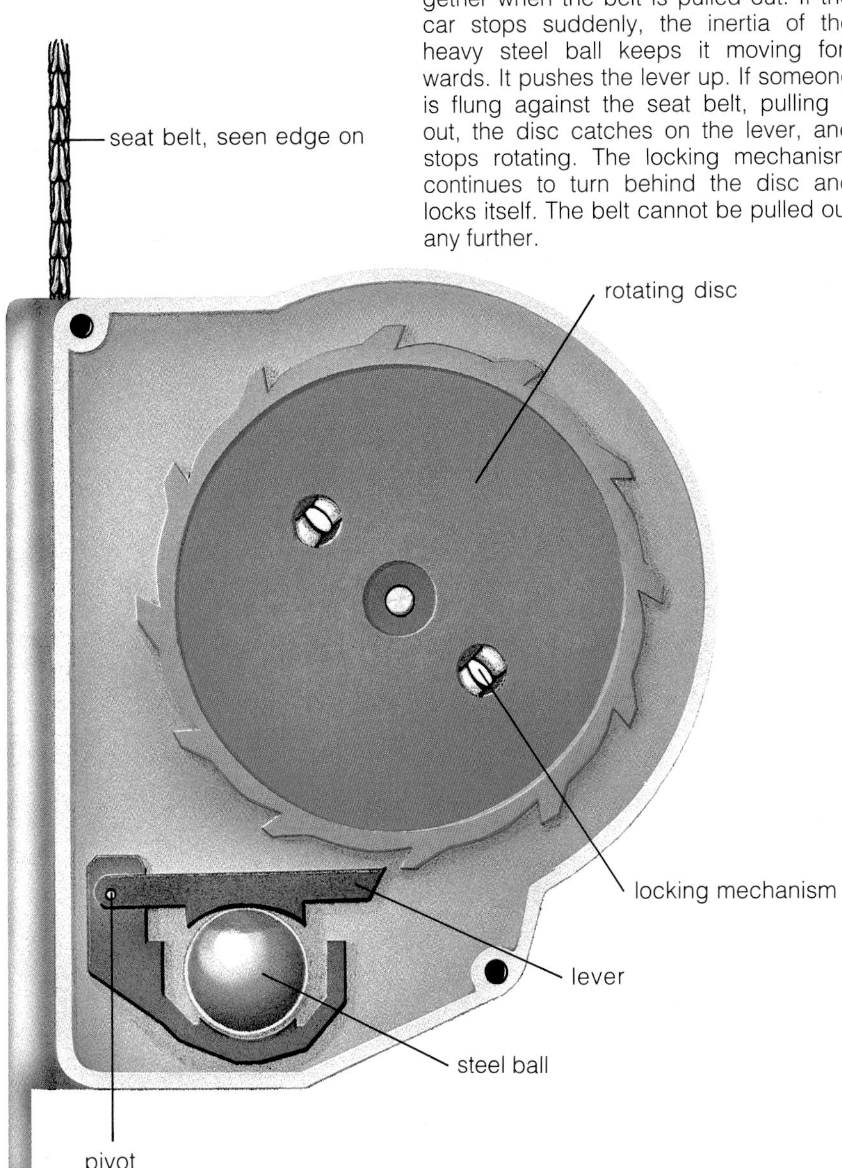

Fig. 17.1 An inertia reel seat belt; the locking mechanism and disc rotate together when the belt is pulled out. If the car stops suddenly, the inertia of the heavy steel ball keeps it moving forwards. It pushes the lever up. If someone is flung against the seat belt, pulling it out, the disc catches on the lever, and stops rotating. The locking mechanism continues to turn behind the disc and locks itself. The belt cannot be pulled out any further.

Mass is measured in kilograms

The kilogram (1000 g) is the usual scientific unit of mass. The standard kilogram is the mass of a particular cylinder of platinum-iridium alloy kept near Paris in France. All masses that are measured are compared (usually rather indirectly) with this.

Large masses are measured in **tonnes** (t). One tonne is 1000 kg.

Questions

1 a When a car stops suddenly, you appear to be 'thrown' forwards. What actually happens, in terms of mass, forces and inertia?

b If children who are not wearing seat belts sit in the back space in an estate car, what will happen to them if the car is suddenly knocked forwards? Why?

2 If a car suddenly speeds away from traffic lights, it exerts a backwards force on the road. Why does the road not move backwards?

DID YOU KNOW?

The kilogram was meant to be the mass of 1000 cm^3 of pure water at 4 °C. But a slight mistake meant that the kilogram was actually the mass of 1000.028 cm^3 of water! This is not good enough for scientists, so a standard cylinder had to be made instead. (What is important about water at 4 °C?)

Weight is a force

A mass is pulled down towards the Earth. This is because all mass is attracted together. The force which pulls masses together is called **gravity**. Normally, the force is too small to notice. But with a mass as big as the Earth, the force becomes quite large.

You are attracted towards the Earth, and the Earth is attracted towards you, with the same force. But the Earth has a much greater mass, and much greater inertia, than you have. If you jump up in the air, you and the Earth pull on each other with the same force. But the Earth is much more reluctant to move than you are, because it has more mass. So the Earth does not seem to come up to you – you drop down to the Earth.

A large mass is pulled towards the Earth more than a small one. So we can compare masses by measuring the force that pulls them down. The size of the force pulling an object towards the Earth is called its **weight**. Like all forces it is measured in newtons.

Weight = mass x g

A kilogram mass is pulled towards the Earth by a force of 9.81 N. So the weight of 1 kg is 9.81 N.

9.81 is very close to 10. To make calculations much easier, we can use 10 instead of 9.81 most of the time. We say that the strength of gravity (on Earth) is 10 newtons per kg, or 10 N/kg. The strength of gravity is given the symbol g. So, on Earth, g is 10 N/kg.

The apparent weight of an object is **the force it exerts on its support**.

The weight of a book is the force it exerts on the table it is resting on, or the force it exerts on the spring balance it is hanging from. If the book has a mass of 2 kg, gravity pulls down with a force of 10 N per kg. So the total force of the book on the table is 2 x 10 N, which is 20 N.

So, if you know the mass of an object, you can find its weight by multiplying its mass in kilograms by g. **Weight = mass x g.**

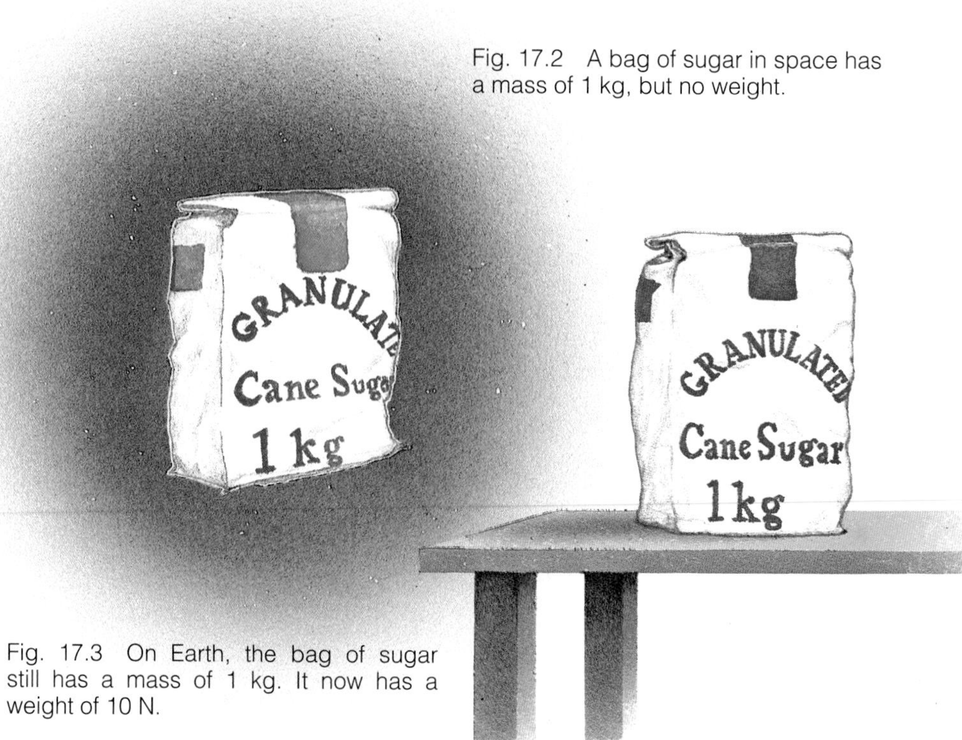

Fig. 17.2 A bag of sugar in space has a mass of 1 kg, but no weight.

Fig. 17.3 On Earth, the bag of sugar still has a mass of 1 kg. It now has a weight of 10 N.

If the scale of a balance is in kg, you are not weighing things – you are massing them

What happens when you weigh something? If you are measuring the force due to gravity on an object, then you are measuring its weight. You are weighing it. A spring balance does this. Its scale is in newtons.

But if you use a lever arm balance, you are comparing the force pulling on the object's mass with the force pulling on a known mass. You are measuring the mass of your object. The scale will be in kilograms. You can easily multiply the mass in kilograms by 9.81 to find the weight in newtons. Many balances have scales where this has already been done.

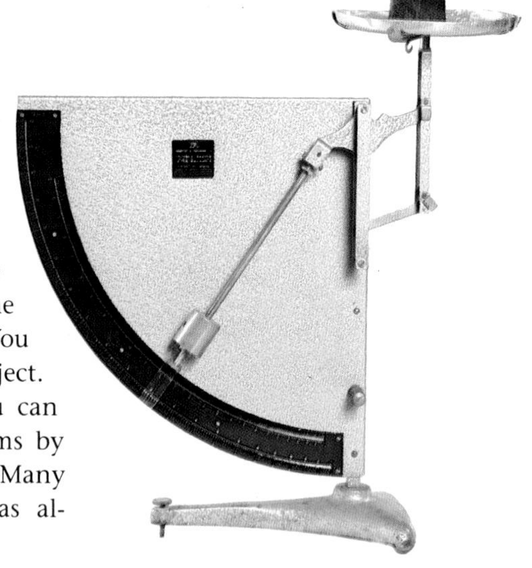

Fig. 17.4 A lever arm balance. Gravity acting on the mass on the pan produces a force which rotates the arm clockwise, while gravity acting on the mass near the pointer produces a force which rotates the arm counterclockwise. If gravity was different – say on the Moon – it would be different for both masses, so the reading would be the same as on Earth. So a lever arm balance measures mass, rather than weight.

Gravity is not the same everywhere

Gravity is not the same all over the Earth's surface. The accepted value for the force due to gravity is 9.81 newtons per kilogram of mass. But this varies, depending where you are.

On the Moon the pull downwards is much less than on the Earth. This is because the Moon is many times smaller than the Earth. The force due to gravity on the Moon is one-sixth that on the Earth. The force of gravity on the Moon is 1.67 newtons per kilogram. So the weight of a 1 kg mass on the Moon is 1.67 N.

Weightless objects still have mass

Out in space you would be weightless. You are too far from the Earth, or any other large body, to be pulled towards it by gravity.

You would be able to pick up a very heavy object – because the object would not be heavy! It would have no weight because there would be no gravity. You could hold it up with no effort at all. But both you and the object would still have mass. And you would both have inertia. To start a 1000 kg mass moving through space, you would still have to push very hard. It would only begin to move very slowly. No matter where it is, a 1000 kg mass has a mass of 1000 kg. Because it has a large mass, its inertia is large too. Even out in space, if the mass was moving towards you fast, it could still crush you against your spacecraft. It has a lot of inertia so it would take a lot of force to stop it moving.

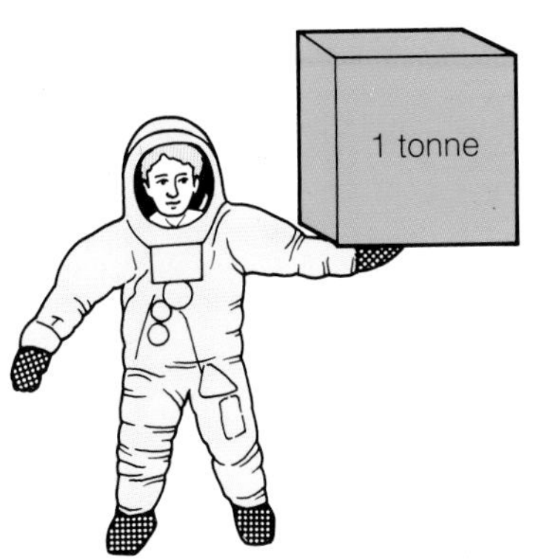

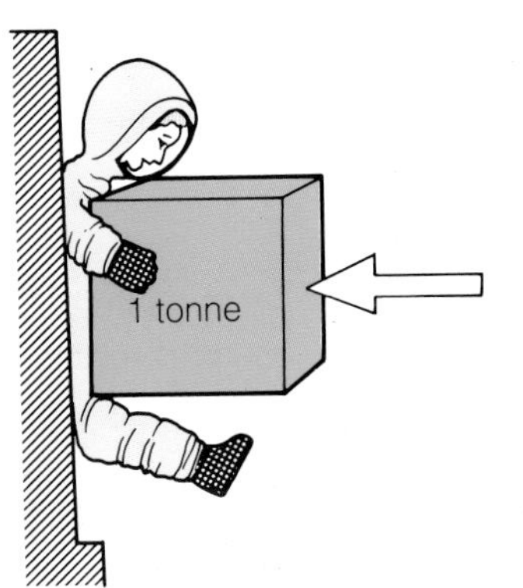

EXTENSION

Gravity produces acceleration

There are two ways of thinking about gravity. So far, we have thought about it as causing a force on an object, which we call its weight. The force of gravity acting on a 1 kg mass produces a force of 9.81 N, which is the object's weight.

But gravity can also pull on an object and make it move. The force of gravity starts the object moving, and makes it go it faster and faster. Gravity causes the object to **accelerate**. The acceleration which gravity causes is 9.81 m/s^2.

So we can either think of gravity as causing weight, or causing acceleration.

Summary

A lot of very important ideas have been covered in these last few pages. Learn and try to understand them!

An unbalanced force changes the motion of an object.

Every force has an equal and opposite reaction.

Mass is a quantity of matter measured in kg.

Mass has inertia.

Inertia is the reluctance of an object to have its motion changed. Inertia increases with mass.

Gravity acts on mass and gives it weight.

Weight is a force and is measured in newtons.

Weight is found by multiplying the local gravitational field strength (g) by the mass of the object:
weight = m x g.

Questions

1 On Earth, the force of gravity is about 10 N/kg.
Complete the following table.

Mass (kg)	*Weight (N)*
1	10
2	
4.6	
	85

2 An empty space shuttle has a mass of 68 t. It can carry a cargo of 29 t.

a What is the total mass of the full shuttle in kilograms?

b What is the weight of the shuttle before launching?

c What force, or **thrust**, would the rockets have to provide to just balance this weight?

d Draw a diagram showing all the forces acting on the space shuttle at take-off.

3 The force due to gravity is given the symbol g. On Earth g is about 10 N/kg. To find the weight of an object, you multiply its mass in kilograms by g. So on Earth the weight of an object is found by multiplying its mass in kilograms by 10.

Complete the following table:

Place	*Object*	*Mass*	*Local value of g*	*Weight*
Earth	1 kg mass	1 kg	10 N/kg	
Jupiter	1 kg mass			24.9 N
Earth	bag of coal			250 N
Sun	bag of sugar	1 kg	274 N/kg	
Moon	car	2000 kg	1.67 N/kg	

EXTENSION

18 CENTRES OF GRAVITY

All objects have a point at which we can consider all their mass to be located. The position of this point affects the stability of the object.

We can say that gravity acts at a single point

The weight of an object is the force due to gravity, when the object is at rest.

Imagine a stone resting on the ground. It is pulled down towards the Earth by gravity. We can think of the stone as many particles, all pulled towards the Earth by many little forces. We can also think of a single force pulling the stone down. This single force acts on the **centre of gravity** or **centre of mass** of the stone.

All objects can be thought of as behaving as though all their mass is concentrated at a single point. If the object is supported under that point, it will balance.

Fig. 18.1a Gravity acts on all the particles in a stone, pulling it down.

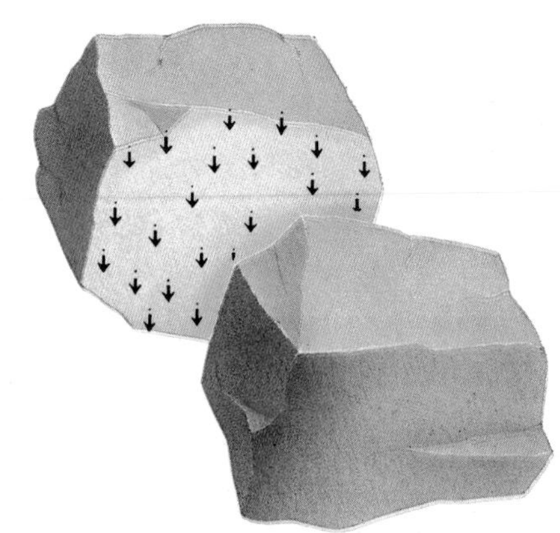

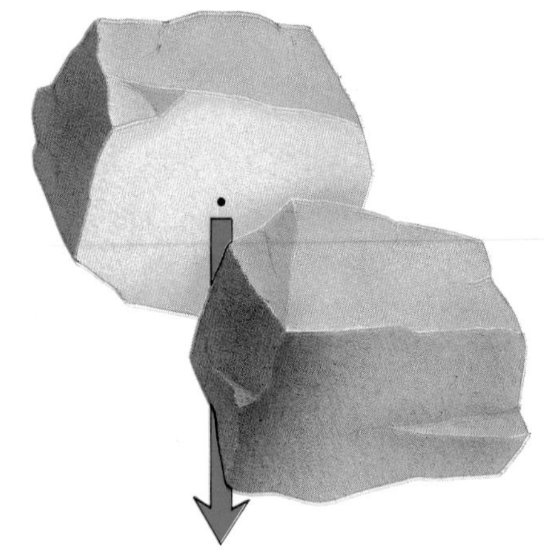

Fig. 18.1b All the individual forces can be represented by a single force.

INVESTIGATION 18.1

Finding centres of gravity

If you support an object under its centre of gravity, it balances. Half of its weight tries to topple it one way. The other half tries to topple it the other way. The two forces cancel one another. The same thing happens if it is hung so that the centre of gravity is directly below the support. We can use this to find the centre of gravity of an object.

1 Take your first shape. Hang it from a pin as shown in the diagram.

Fig. 18.2a

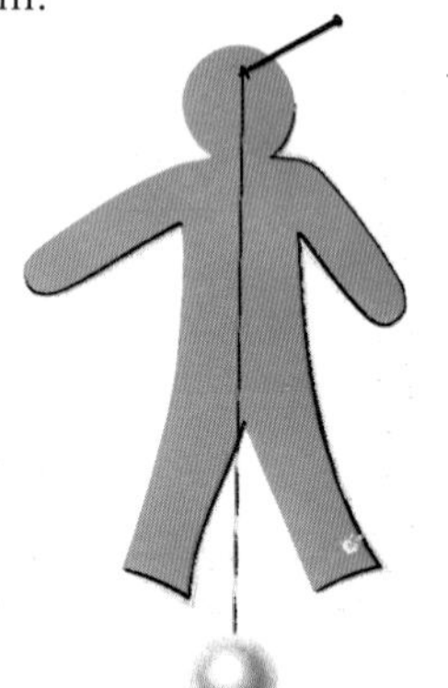

b

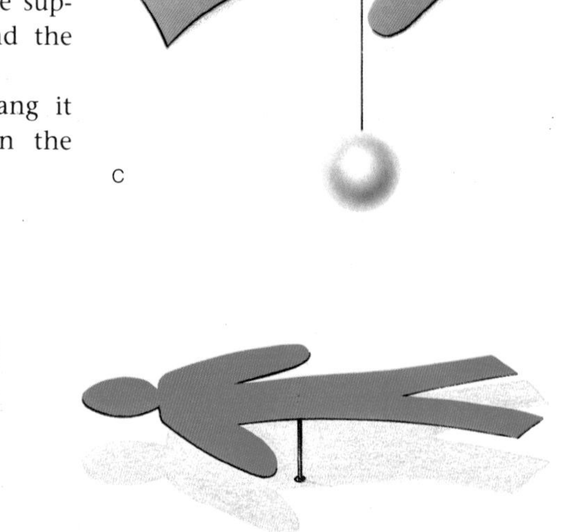

c

2 Now hang a thread, with a weight on the end, from the same pin. The thread will hang vertically downwards. Wait until the shape and the thread come to rest.

3 The thread is now passing through the centre of gravity of your shape. Draw this line down your object.

4 Now hang your object from the same pin, but in a different position. Again, the vertical line of the thread passes through the centre of gravity of your object. Draw the line on it.

The point at which the two lines cross is the centre of gravity of the object. But it is probably a good idea to repeat with the object in different positions, to improve your accuracy.

5 You can check that you really have found the centre of gravity by trying to balance your object on the point of a pin at exactly the point you have marked.

The centre of gravity does not always lie inside an object

The centre of gravity of a ruler is in the middle of it. The centre of gravity of a sphere is at its centre. But the centre of gravity of some objects is *outside* them. A boomerang is a good example of an object whose centre of gravity is not inside it. Figure 18.3a shows where it is. You could certainly not support the boomerang at this point! But the boomerang does behave as though all its mass was concentrated at this point. When the boomerang spins, it spins about its centre of gravity.

Fig. 18.3a The centre of gravity of a boomerang lies outside its shape. It rotates about this point when thrown.

b When thrown, the two spheres of the bolas spin about their centre of gravity, which is halfway along the rope which joins them.

If two equal masses are attached to each other by a string, and thrown through the air, they spin round the central point of the string. This is how a South American bolas works. The centre of gravity of the two masses is half way between them. If one mass is larger than the other, then the centre of gravity is nearer to the larger one.

The Earth and the Sun are rather like the two masses joined by a string. Gravitational attraction stops them flying apart. The Sun is 330 000 times the mass of the Earth. The centre of mass of the Earth-Sun system is very close to the centre of the Sun. The Sun and Earth orbit around this point. The orbit is the path of one body in space around another. (This path is an ellipse.)

Many stars also orbit around each other in pairs. A pair of stars like this is called a **binary system**. The two stars often appear to be very close together. The centre of mass of the binary system lies somewhere between the two stars. The two stars rotate about this point. Some binary stars take centuries to complete one orbit! Some orbit very fast.

The way in which the stars move can tell us how far apart the stars are, and how heavy they are. Sometimes a star may seem to be 'wobbling' around in space. This gives astronomers a clue that there is another undiscovered star nearby, spinning around with it.

c Binary stars. The two stars of a binary star system orbit around their centre of mass.

The position of the centre of gravity helps us to balance an object

An object is balanced when its centre of gravity and its point of support lie on a vertical line. The forces on each side are balanced. The object is in **equilibrium**. There are two possible ways of balancing the object. The supporting point can be placed either *above* or *below* the centre of gravity. One of these is much easier to find than the other. Which is the tricky one?

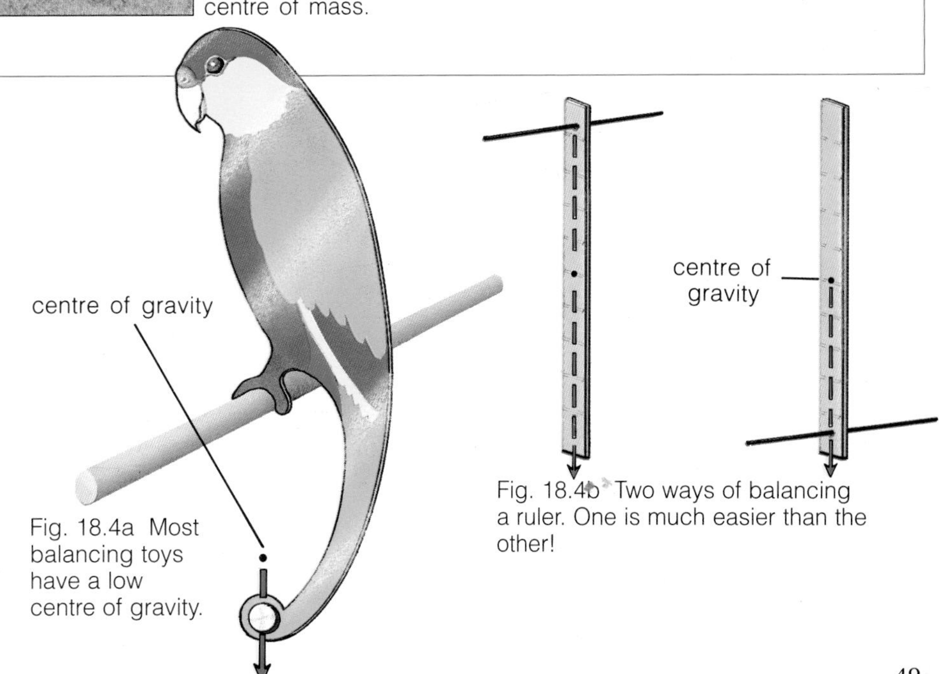

Fig. 18.4a Most balancing toys have a low centre of gravity.

Fig. 18.4b Two ways of balancing a ruler. One is much easier than the other!

19 EQUILIBRIUM

An object is said to be in equilibrium when all the forces acting on it are balanced. There are three types of equilibrium – stable, unstable and neutral.

There are three types of equilibrium

If you tried to balance a cone like the one in the diagrams, you could find three different positions in which it would stay. Two are quite easy. One is so difficult as to be almost impossible!

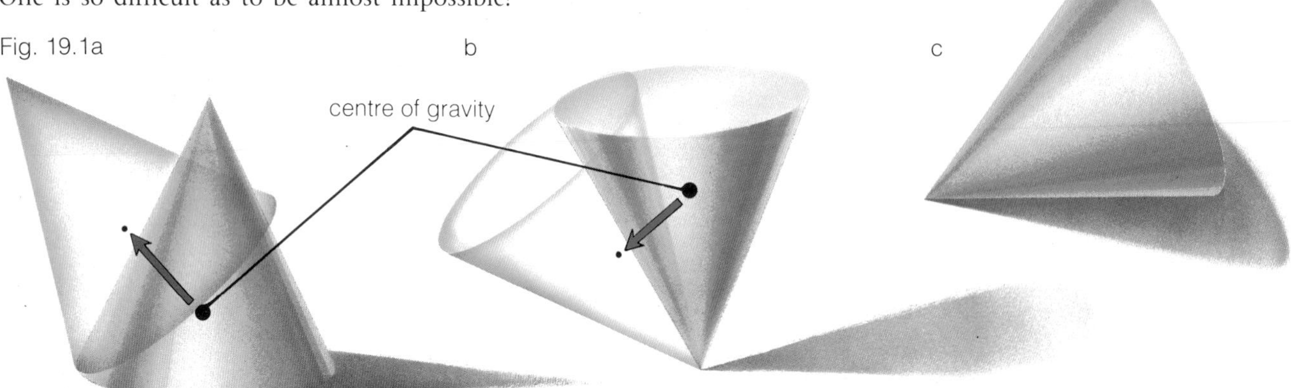

This cone is in a position of **stable equilibrium**. If you tried to push it over you would *raise* its centre of gravity. It is as though you are lifting the cone. When you let it go it falls back to where it was.

This cone is in a position of **unstable equilibrium**. If you tilt it you will *lower* its centre of gravity. When you let go it carries on falling. Even the slightest tilt will make it fall.

This cone is in a position of **neutral equilibrium**. If you tilt it the centre of gravity is still at the same height as it was before. In neutral equilibrium, a push does not change the height of the centre of gravity. When you push the cone it just stays in its new position.

d

A ball on a horizontal table is in neutral equilibrium all the time. This is because, however it rolls, its centre of gravity stays at the *same height*. It will only become unstable or stable if you change the shape of the surface on which it is resting. (See question 1 below.)

Stable objects have a low centre of gravity

An object is stable if its centre of gravity lies above its base. An object is unstable when its centre of gravity lies outside its base. In other words, an object is unstable if a line drawn between its centre of gravity and the centre of the Earth does not pass through its base.

A stable object becomes unstable when it has been tilted so far that any more tilt starts to lower the centre of gravity. The critical point is reached when the centre of gravity is vertically above the edge of the base.

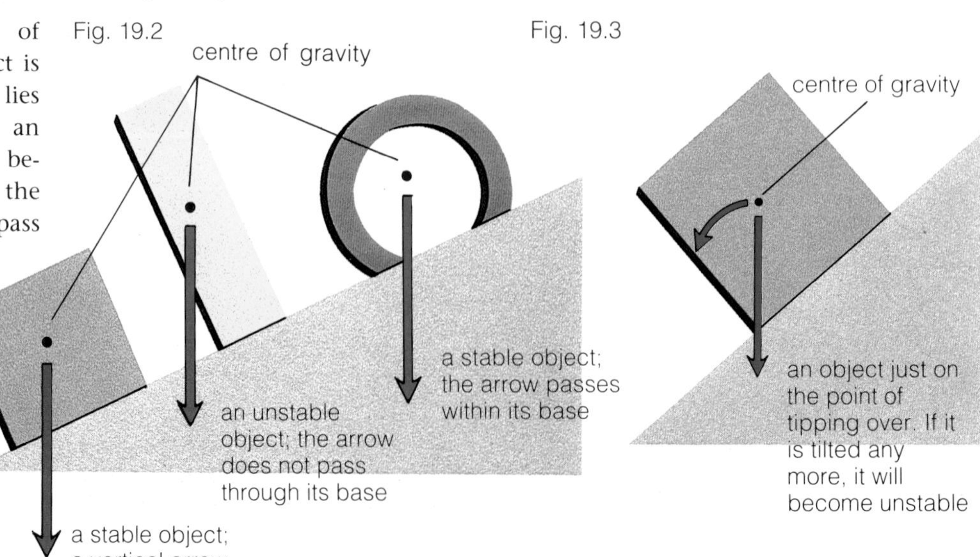

There are two ways of making an object more stable. One way is to *lower its centre of gravity*. Racing cars have very low centres of gravity, so that they are less likely to roll over even when cornering at high speeds.

The other way is to *make the base of the object wider*. Racing cars have very wide bases with the wheels far apart from each other.

So even if the car tips, the centre of gravity still lies above its base, and it is unlikely to turn over.

Fig. 19.4 A low centre of gravity and wide wheelbase prevents a racing car from turning over as it corners at speed.

INVESTIGATION 19.1

Equilibrium in animals

You will be provided with some plasticine and cocktail sticks. Use them to make models of animals, and to answer the following questions. Plan your investigation carefully before you begin. Make diagrams of your models. Describe how you make your measurements of stability, and the evidence you have for each of your answers.

1 Are two legs more stable than one leg?

2 Are two legs more stable than four legs?

3 Which is more stable – a hippopotamus or a giraffe?

4 How could a giraffe make itself more stable?

Fig. 19.5 Tractors are designed with low centres of gravity, as they may have to work on steep slopes.

Questions

1 The diagrams show a ball bearing on a smooth surface. In which case is the ball bearing:

a in neutral equilibrium?
b in stable equilibrium?
c in unstable equilibrium?

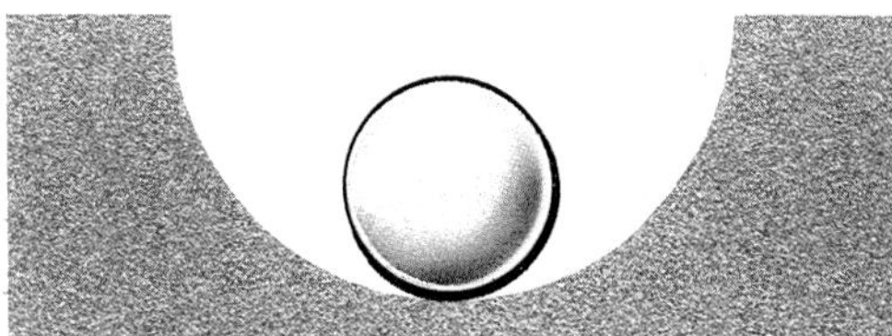

2 A boat has a high mast and sails. The force of the wind on the sails could turn the boat over.

a Where should the centre of gravity be to make the boat as stable as possible?
b How does a heavy keel help stability?

EXTENSION

3 The diagram shows a double decker bus on a slope. At what angle will the bus become unstable?

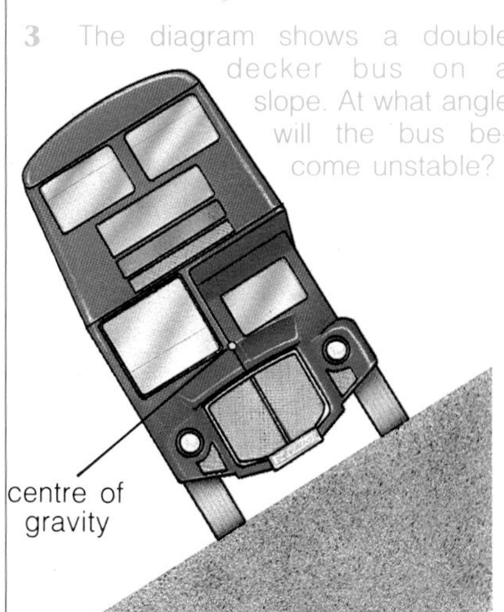

4 a Some fast boats have keel fins. Find out about these. What are their advantages?

b Fish have fins. Find out about the different functions of the fins of fish. Do fins help with stability? What else do fish use their fins for?

20 FLOATING AND SINKING

When something is placed in water its weight is reduced. The object experiences an upthrust from the water. If the weight is reduced enough, the object floats.

An object displaces fluid

When you climb into a bath the water level rises. You **displace** some water. The volume of water you displace is the same as your volume.

You may have used this method to measure the volume of complicated shapes.

If you put a stone into water it weighs less than it does in air. If you collect and weigh the water which the stone displaces, you will find that its weight is the same as the lost weight of the stone. If the stone weighs less then something must be lifting it up. The lifting force comes from the water and is called **upthrust**.

The force of the upthrust is the same as the weight of the water displaced.

This was discovered by Archimedes more than 2000 years ago.

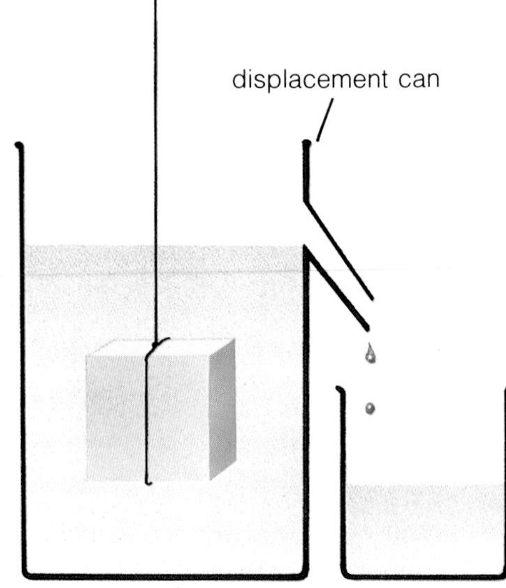

an object displaces a volume of water equal to its own volume

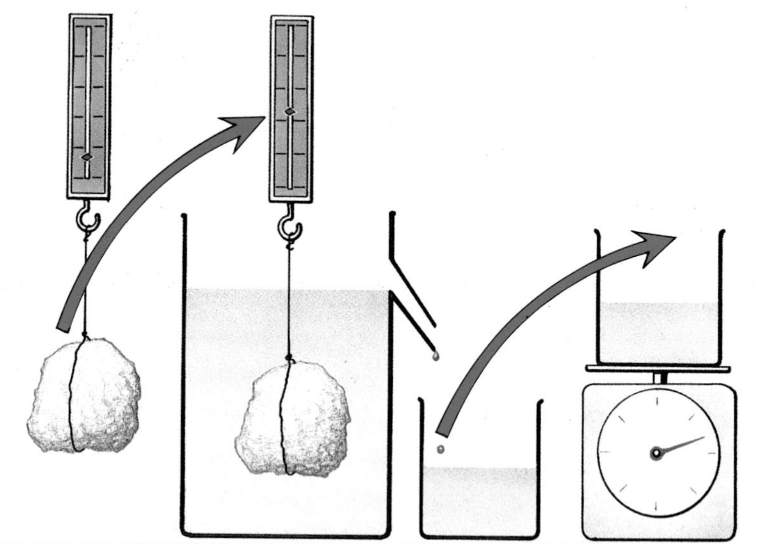

Fig. 20.1 The force of upthrust is the same as the weight of water displaced.

Any liquid or gas produces upthrust

It is not only water which produces upthrust. Any liquid or gas will do it. For example, the upthrust of air keeps a hot air balloon up. The balloon displaces a volume of air equal to its own volume. The air displaced is *colder* than the hot air inside the balloon. A certain volume of cold air is heavier than the same volume of hot air. So the air displaced is *heavier* than the air in the balloon. And, remember, the force of the upthrust produced is the same as the weight of air displaced. So the force of the upthrust is greater than the weight of the balloon. There is enough extra force to lift not only the balloon, but also the passengers and their basket.

Fig. 20.2 Hot air displaces cold air in a balloon, producing upthrust. This upthrust is balanced by the weight of the balloon.

Why does water produce upthrust?

When an object is immersed in water the water pushes in on it. This force is called water pressure. Water pressure is greater the deeper you go. So the water pressure on the bottom of an object is greater than the water pressure on the top. This tends to push the object upwards.

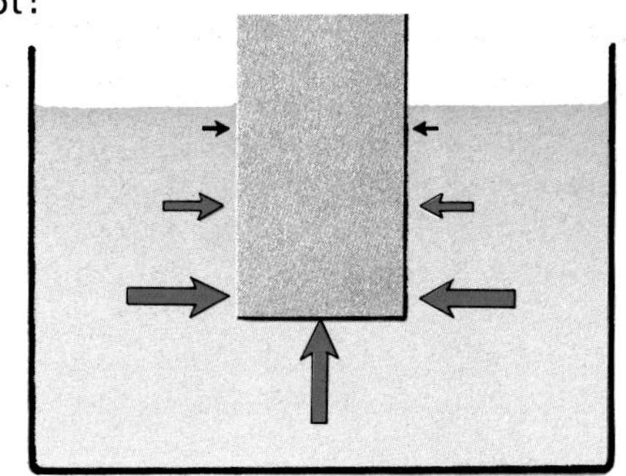

Fig. 20.3 Upthrust. The sizes of the arrows represent the sizes of the forces. The difference between the water pressure on the bottom and top of an object results in an overall upwards force, called upthrust.

EXTENSION

Does it float or sink?

Block A is floating. The upthrust of the water must be balancing the weight of the block. So the weight of water displaced must equal the weight of the block.

Not all the block is under water. The volume of water displaced is less than the volume of the block. But the weight of water displaced equals the weight of the block. So equal volumes of block and water cannot weigh the same. The block would be lighter. We say that the **density** of the block is less than the density of water.

A

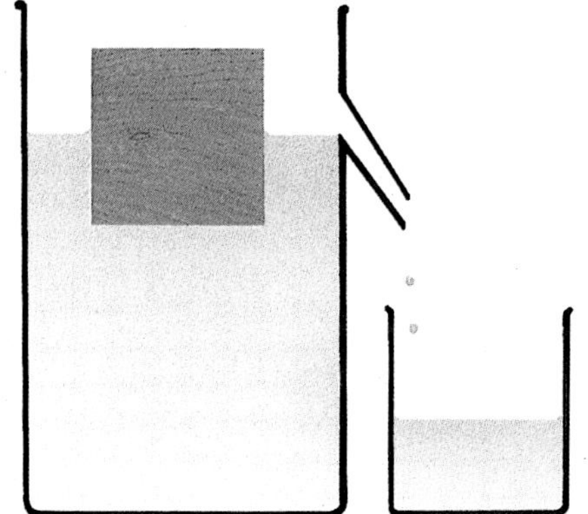

B

Block B is just floating. The upthrust of the water must be just balancing the weight of the block. So the weight of water displaced must equal the weight of the block.

All of the block is under water. The volume of water displaced is the same as the volume of the block. So both weight and volume of the block and the displaced water are equal. The density of the block and the water are the same.

Block C has sunk. The upthrust from the water is not enough to make the block float. So the weight of the displaced water must be less than the weight of the block.

So equal volumes of water and the block do not weigh the same. The block is denser than water.

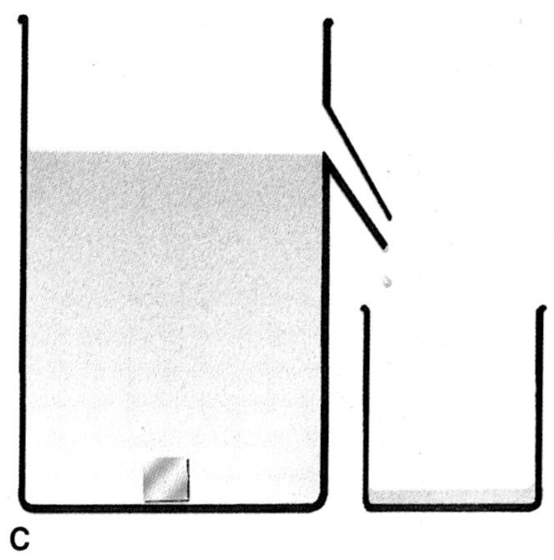

C

DID YOU KNOW?

The first people to cross the Atlantic Ocean in a hot-air balloon were Richard Branson and Per Lindstrand, in July 1987. At the time, the balloon was the largest ever flown, with a capacity of 65 000 m^3.

Density is the mass of a certain volume of a substance

Density is a way of comparing the masses of equal volumes of materials. It is meaningless to say that lead is heavier than feathers. It is more correct to say that a certain volume of lead is heavier than the same volume of feathers. We can say that lead has a greater density than feathers.

If an object has the same density as water, it just floats. If its density is less than water, it floats well. If its density is greater than water, it sinks.

EXTENSION

Questions

1 A balloon weighs 2000 N. It is filled with 5000 N of helium and it displaces 10 000 N of air.
  - **a** What is the upthrust on the balloon?
  - **b** What load could the balloon carry?

2 A block of copper is weighed in air, hydrogen, water and salt water. Which would give:
  - **a** the highest reading?
  - **b** the lowest reading?
  - **c** If the copper block was massed in air, hydrogen, water and salt water, what would be the result?

21 DENSITY

Density is mass per unit volume. It can be measured in g/cm³ or kg/m³.

Density is the mass per unit volume

The density of something is the mass of a particular volume of it.

One cubic centimetre of water has a mass of one gram. So the density of water is one gram per cubic centimetre. In shorthand this is 1 g/cm³.

Densities can also be written in terms of metres and kilograms. One cubic metre of water has a mass of 1000 kilograms. The density of water can therefore be written as 1000 kg/m³.

Mass = volume x density

If you know the volume and density of a substance, you can work out its mass. For example, the density of sand is 1600 kg/m³. If you ordered 3 m³ of sand, you would get:

mass = volume x density
= 3 m³ x 1600 kg/m³
= 4800 kg

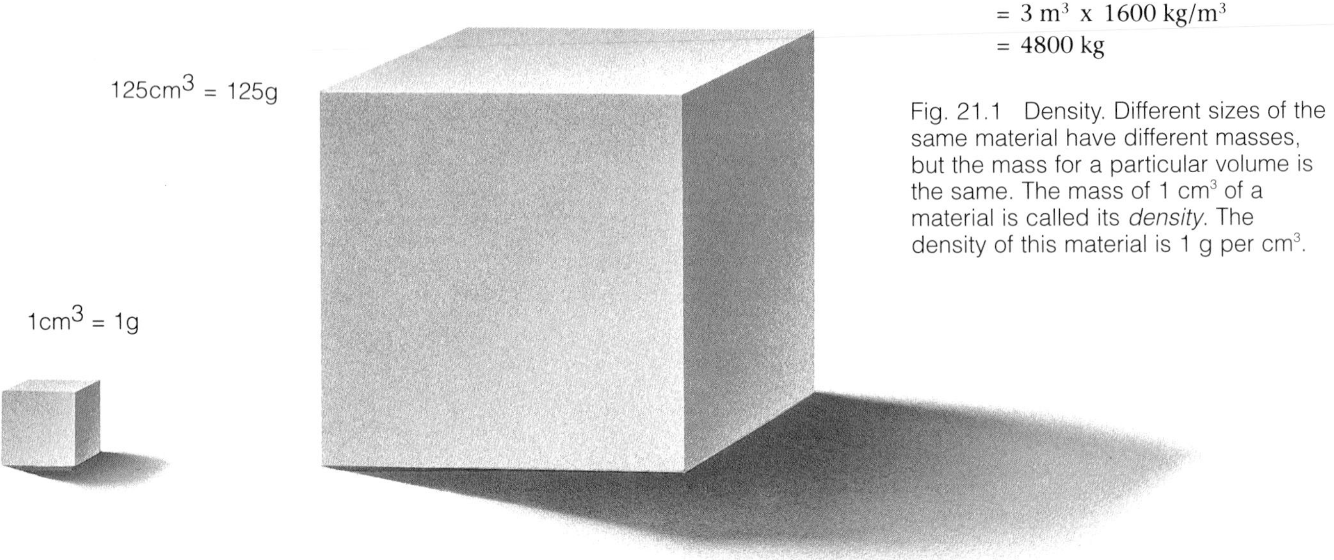

Fig. 21.1 Density. Different sizes of the same material have different masses, but the mass for a particular volume is the same. The mass of 1 cm³ of a material is called its *density*. The density of this material is 1 g per cm³.

Rearrange the formula to find volume or density

The formula can be rearranged:

mass = volume x density

volume = $\frac{\text{mass}}{\text{density}}$

density = $\frac{\text{mass}}{\text{volume}}$

For example, the density of 22 carat gold is 17.5 g/cm³. The density of 9 carat gold is 11.3 g/cm³.

If you have a piece of gold jewellery, you can find out whether it is 22 carat or 9 carat by weighing it, and finding its volume. If it weighs 5 g, and has a volume of 0.286 cm³, then:

$$\text{density} = \frac{\text{mass}}{\text{volume}} = \frac{5\text{ g}}{0.286\text{ cm}^3} = 17.48\text{ g/cm}^3$$

So it must be 22 carat gold.

Archimedes used this method to find out if the King's jeweller had made a crown out of pure gold. Pure gold has a density of 19.3 g/cm³. So a 386 g crown should have a volume of $\frac{386\text{ g}}{19.3\text{ g/cm}^3}$

This works out as 20 cm³.

When the crown was put into water, it should displace 20 cm³ of water. This should make it weigh 20 g less in water than in air. But it did not. Archimedes proved that the gold had been mixed with cheaper metal.

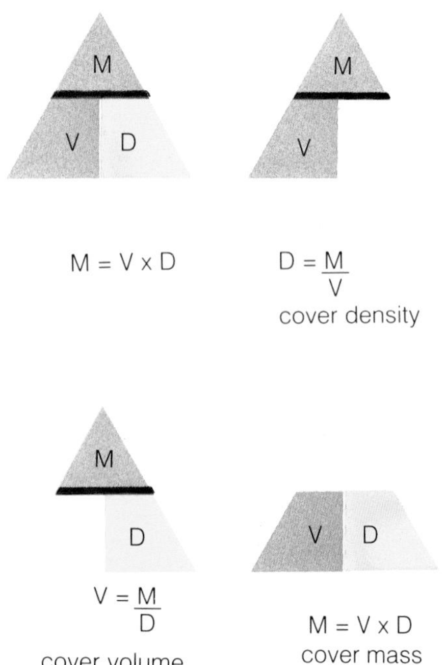

Fig. 21.2 A formula triangle can be used to rearrange a formula. If you cover up the quantity you want to find, the arrangement for the other two is shown.

EXTENSION

INVESTIGATION 21.1

Finding the density of an object

You are going to find out the volume of an object by measuring the volume of water it displaces. If you also measure its mass, you can calculate its density.

1 Choose an object, and a beaker large enough for it to fit into easily.

2 Tie a thread around the object. Weigh it. Calculate its mass. Remember:

weight = mass x g

or mass = $\frac{\text{weight}}{g}$ g is 10 N/kg

3 Either: *If you have a displacement can available:*

Fill the displacement can. Put your object into it, until it is completely immersed. Catch all the water which overflows, and measure its volume.

Or: *If you have a beaker:*

Fill the beaker with water until it overflows, using a measuring cylinder. Record the volume of water it took to fill your beaker. Immerse the object in the beaker, letting the water that it displaces overflow. Measure how much water is left in the beaker. Work out how much water the object displaced.

4 Record the volume of your object.

5 Calculate the density of your object by using the formula:

density = $\frac{\text{mass in grams}}{\text{volume in cm}^3}$

6 Suspend the object from the thread again. Measure its weight when it is immersed in water.

Questions

1 What weight has the object lost in water, compared with its weight in air?

2 What weight of water must have been displaced?

3 What mass would this water have?(Use the formula in step **2**.)

4 What volume would this mass of water have? (The volume of 1 g of water is 1 cm^3.)

5 Does this volume agree with the volume you measured in step **3**?

6 Suggest any possible causes of error in this experiment. How could you improve its accuracy?

INVESTIGATION 21.2

Finding the density of sand

1 Measure out 200 g of dry sand. Find out, and record, the volume of your dry sand.

2 Calculate the density of your dry sand.

3 Measure out 200 g of water. Find out, and record, the volume of your water.

4 Add the sand to the water. Stir, and allow to settle. Then measure and record the volume of the sand and water together.

5 The volume of sand and water together will be less than the two separate volumes added together. Why is this?

6 Work out the actual volume of the sand particles.

7 Calculate the density of sand if it contains no air spaces.

8 Glass is made by heating sand, so that the particles fuse together. The density of glass is around 2.5 g/cm^3. Can you link this information to the results you have obtained in this experiment?

Questions

1 Marble has a density of 2.7 g/cm^3. What is the mass of 200 cm^3 of marble?

2 The density of butter is 0.9 g/cm^3. What is the volume of 800 g of butter?

3 A cast iron pair of kitchen scales has a volume of 500 cm^3 and weighs 3.5 kg.

a What is the density of cast iron?

b If the scales had been made in mild steel, which has a density of 7.9 g/cm^3, how much heavier or lighter would they be?

4 Milk has a density of 1.03 g/cm^3. One pint is the same as 568 cm^3. How much heavier is a pint of milk than a pint of water?

5 A floating buoy weighs 2000 N. When its cable snaps, it drifts away, but stays at the same height in the water.

a What weight of water must the buoy displace?

b If g is 10 N/kg, what mass of water does the buoy displace?

c If the density of water is 1000 kg/m^3, what is the volume of the water displaced by the buoy?

6 Coal has a density of 4.0 g/cm^3. Paraffin has a density of 0.8 g/cm^3. A piece of coal is lowered into paraffin. Its weight is reduced by 1 N. Assume that g = 10 N/kg.

a What mass of paraffin is displaced?

b What volume of paraffin is displaced?

c What is the volume of the piece of coal?

d What is the mass of the piece of coal?

EXTENSION

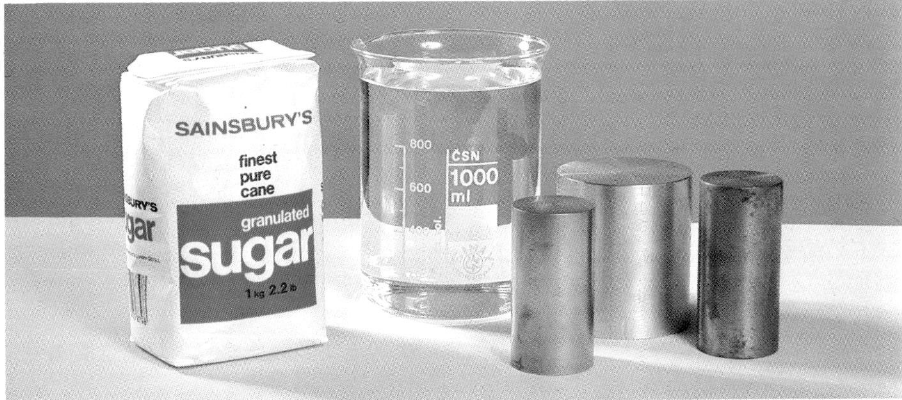

Fig. 21.3 1 kg masses of different substances. From left, they are sugar, water, brass, aluminium and steel. Which has the greatest density? Which has the lowest density?

Some animals use water to support their bodies

It is fairly obvious that a large animal is heavier than a small one! But you may not realise just how great an increase in weight is caused by quite a small increase in size. Imagine a cube-shaped animal. If it is 1 cm wide in each direction, it has a volume of 1 cm^3. If its density is 1 g/cm^3, then it weighs 1 g. Now imagine the animal doubling its size. It now measures 2 cm in each direction. Its volume is now 2x2x2 = 8 cm^3. So it now weighs 8 g. So, if an animal doubles its size, it becomes eight times heavier. To support its weight, its legs would need to have an area eight times larger! This works up to a point. If you think of the relative size of the legs of a mouse and the legs of a rhinoceros you can see that legs do get relatively larger in bigger animals. But *very* big animals would need legs so big that they could not move them.

The biggest animal which has ever lived on Earth is the blue whale. It may have a mass of over 100 t. It would be impossible for it to live on land. But in water, the water it displaces reduces its weight. The water helps to support it. It can manage with quite a small skeleton for its size. If a blue whale gets stranded on a beach, it dies, because its body weight crushes its ribs and stops the lungs working.

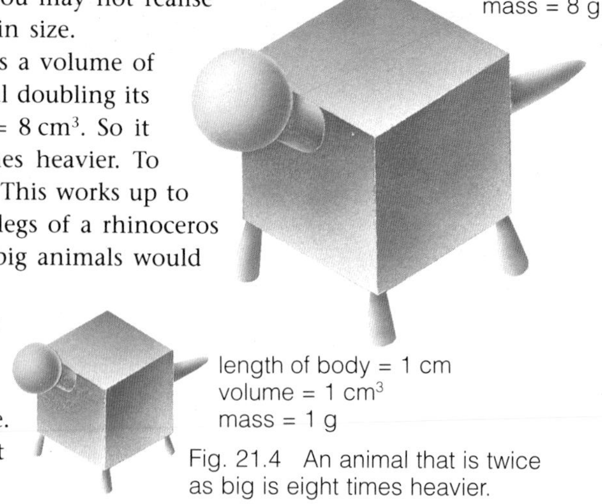

length of body = 2 cm
volume = 8 cm^3
mass = 8 g

length of body = 1 cm
volume = 1 cm^3
mass = 1 g

Fig. 21.4 An animal that is twice as big is eight times heavier.

Fish and submarines can alter their density

Fish and submarines have a similar problem. They need to be able to stay at a particular depth in the water, without using unnecessary energy.

If the density of a fish is more than the density of water, it will sink. If it is less than the density of water, it will float. To float at a particular depth in the sea, a fish must be able to control its density. Most fish have a **swim bladder**. The swim bladder contains air. The more air there is in the swim bladder, the lower the density of the fish. If the fish tends to sink, it can add a little more air to its swim bladder until it is the same density as the water. The fish then has **neutral buoyancy**. It will neither sink nor rise in the water. Since the density of water changes with temperature, depth and saltiness, fish are always making small adjustments to keep their position in the water. The air needed comes either from their gut, or from their blood through capillaries. Submarines work on the same principle. They have **ballast tanks**. Compressed air is blown into the tanks to make the average density of the submarine less. This makes the submarine go up. To make it sink, air is released from the tanks.

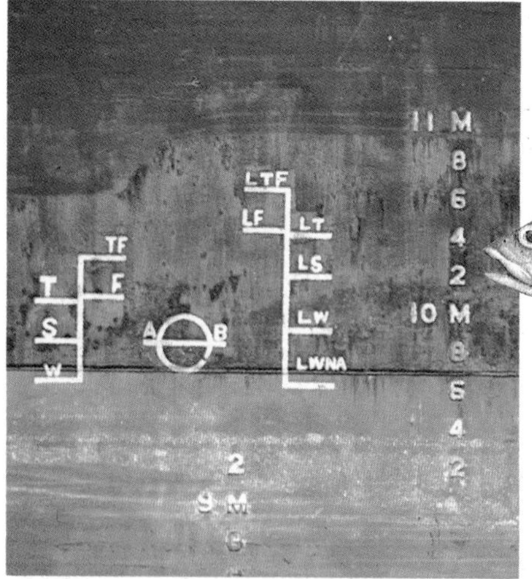

Fig. 21.5 Plimsoll lines. These lines on the side of a ship show the level at which it may safely lie in the water. The line AB, across the central disc, shows the standard position. The lines on the left show safe levels in different circumstances. TF stands for tropical fresh water, F for fresh water, T for tropical, S for summer and W for winter. Can you explain their relative positions?

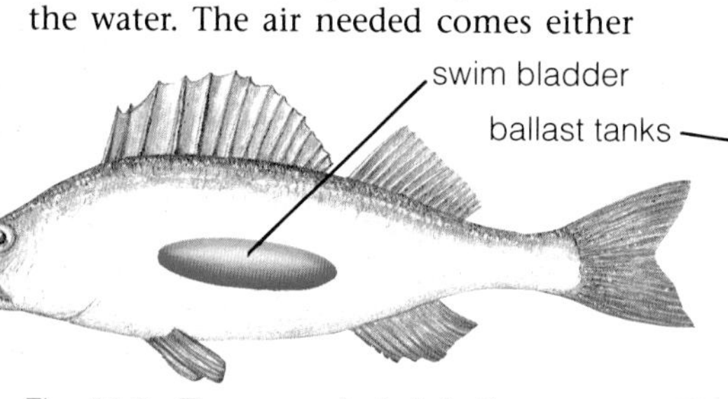

Fig. 21.6 The amount of air in the swim bladder controls the average density of the fish.

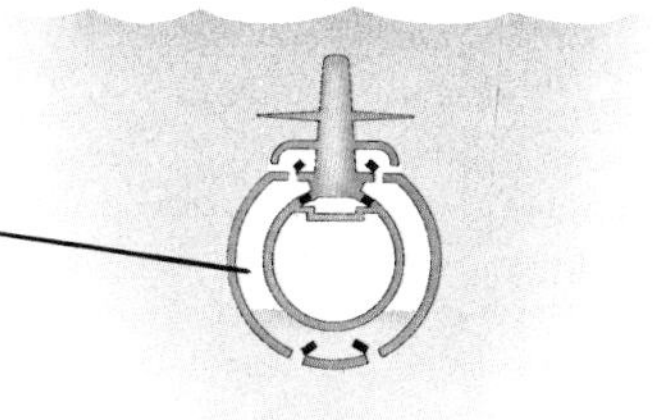

Fig. 21.7 The amount of air in the ballast tanks controls the average density of the submarine.

Ships float because their average density is less than water

Steel is denser than water. A lump of steel sinks in water. But a steel ship contains a lot of air. Its average density is less than water. So a steel ship floats.

A ship displaces water. The weight of the displaced water gives the amount of weight that can be supported. To take more weight, more water must be displaced. This means that the ship sits lower in the water. In the early days of shipping, owners were often tempted to put too much cargo on ships. This made the ships float so low in the water that they were likely to sink. Now, to show the safe maximum load, a Plimsoll line is marked on the side of a ship. This was enforced in England by act of Parliament in 1785. The marks show the safe water level. They are different for summer and winter, and for fresh and salt water. This is because the density of water changes with temperature and saltiness.

22 FIELDS

Some forces act only when objects are in contact. Others can act at a distance. A field is a region in which one object can exert a force on another, even when they are not in contact.

There are forces resulting from contact and forces acting at a distance

There are two types of force that we meet in everyday life. One type comes from contact with something. When you push on a door, the surface of your hand and the surface of the door touch. The door pushes back on you just as hard as you push on it. The force only seems to act when your hand touches the door. This sort of force results from contact. The other type of force does not need any contact. If you jump up in the air, there is no contact between you and the Earth. But a force acts on you. The attraction between you and the Earth is still there. The force of gravity still acts even when there is no contact.

A field is a region in space

The force of gravity acts between you and the Earth, even when you and the Earth are not in contact. There is a certain region all around the Earth, stretching out into space, where gravity acts on objects, pulling them towards the Earth. This region is called the Earth's **gravitational field**. In science, a field is a space where one object can exert a force on another object without touching it.

Fig. 22.1 Contact and non contact forces. A force acts between the electromagnet and the iron scrap even if they are not in contact. But the large force between the two cars only acts when they are in contact.

There are three main types of field

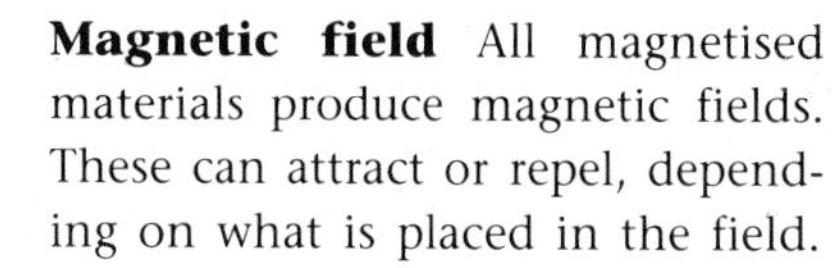

There are three types of field that you are likely to meet.

1 **Gravitational field** In a gravitational field, matter is attracted to other matter. All matter produces a gravitational field. But only very large masses, such as the Earth, have strong gravitational fields which produce large forces.

2 **Magnetic field** All magnetised materials produce magnetic fields. These can attract or repel, depending on what is placed in the field.

3 **Electric field** All charged objects produce electric fields. Like magnetic fields, these can attract or repel, depending on what is placed in the field.

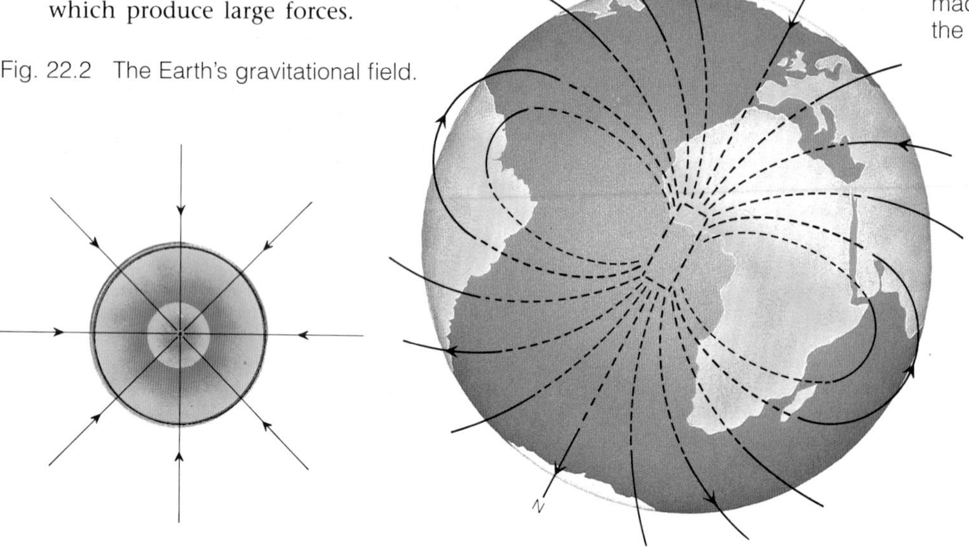

Fig. 22.2 The Earth's gravitational field.

Fig. 22.3 The Earth's magnetic field.

Fig. 22.4 This girl is touching the dome of a van de Graaff generator. The pattern made by her hair suggests the pattern of the electric field around her head.

Fig. 22.5 This magnetically levitated linear railroad car (MLV-002) is suspended in a magnetic and a gravitational field. The forces from each field cancel each other and the train floats above the track.

23 MAGNETS

Magnets can attract or repel one another. Permanent magnets keep their magnetism. Magnetism results from small magnetic regions called domains.

The pole of a magnet is where the magnetism is strongest

A magnet always has two poles. These are the points where the magnetism is strongest. The two poles are always different. If the magnet is freely suspended, it will swing until one end points towards the North Pole of the Earth. This end of the magnet is the **north seeking pole**, or **north pole** of the magnet. The other pole is the **south pole**, which points towards the South Pole of the Earth.

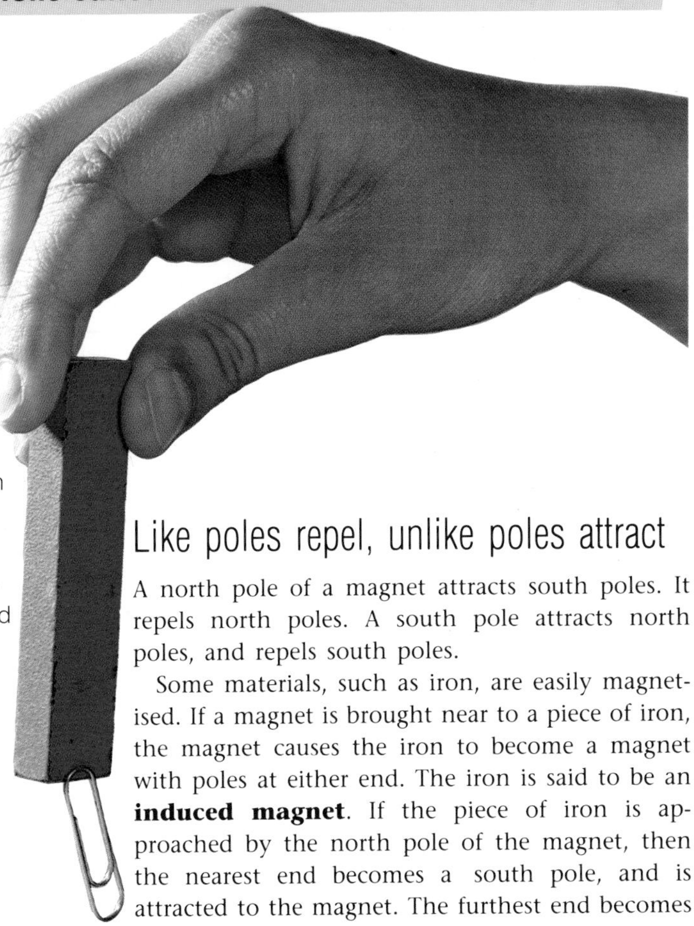

Fig. 23.1 A magnet attracts a paper clip. The magnet induces magnetism in the paper clip. The end of the paper clip nearest to the magnet's north pole becomes a south pole. The north and south poles are attracted to each other – which is why the paper clip is attracted to the magnet.

Fig. 23.2a Opposite poles attract

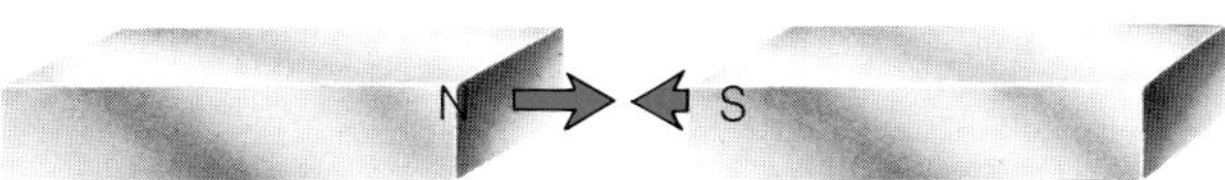

Fig. 23.2b Like poles repel

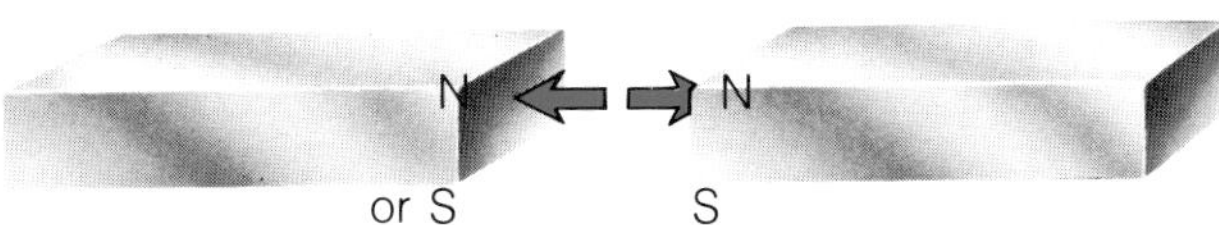

Fig. 23.3 A magnet induces magnetism in a piece of iron.

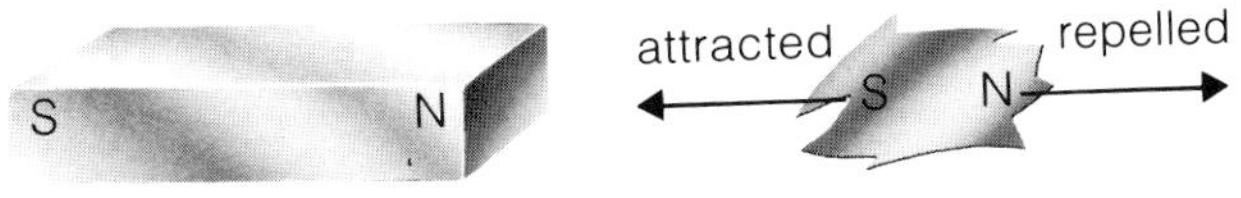

S N attracted S N repelled

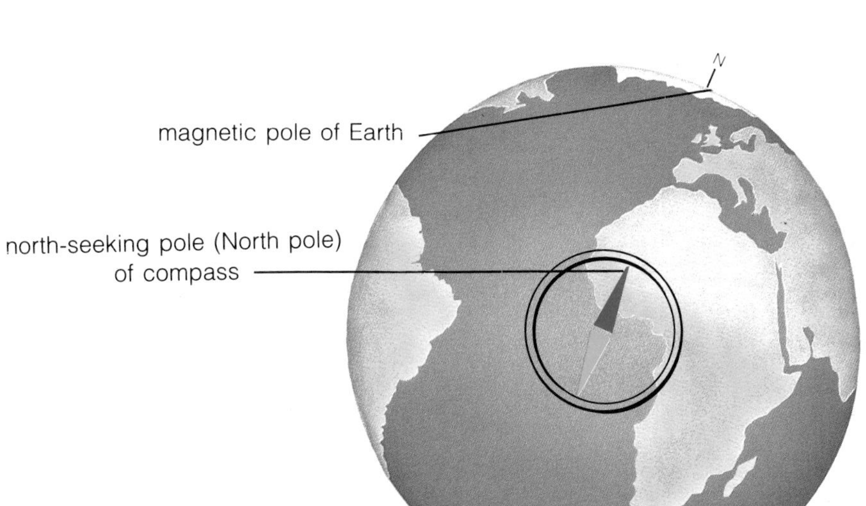

Fig. 23.4 The north pole of a compass needle points towards the North Pole of the Earth.

Like poles repel, unlike poles attract

A north pole of a magnet attracts south poles. It repels north poles. A south pole attracts north poles, and repels south poles.

Some materials, such as iron, are easily magnetised. If a magnet is brought near to a piece of iron, the magnet causes the iron to become a magnet with poles at either end. The iron is said to be an **induced magnet**. If the piece of iron is approached by the north pole of the magnet, then the nearest end becomes a south pole, and is attracted to the magnet. The furthest end becomes a north pole.

Iron is a **magnetic** material. This means that it can be made into a magnet. You can find out if a material is magnetic by seeing if it is attracted to a magnet. But this does not prove that it is a magnet! To find out if a piece of iron is a magnet, you must try approaching it with both ends of a magnet. If one of your magnet's poles *repels* the piece of iron, then the piece of iron is a magnet. If it is only a weak magnet, though, this repulsion can be very hard to detect.

A compass needle is a magnet

A compass needle is a small magnet. It is supported so that it can swing round freely. Its north pole points towards the North Pole of the Earth.

If a compass needle is put near a magnet, its north pole will point towards the south pole of the magnet. What does this tell you about the North Pole of the Earth?

INVESTIGATION 23.1

Plotting magnetic fields

The space around a magnet in which it can affect other objects is called its **magnetic field**.

1. Put a bar magnet on a sheet of paper, and draw round it. Label the N and S poles.
2. Leave the bar magnet in position on the paper. Place a plotting compass near one end. Note which way the needle is pointing. Mark a dot on the paper against the plotting compass to show the direction that it points in. Move the compass forward so that the back end of the needle points at the spot you have just marked. Mark a new spot on the paper against the edge of the plotting compass to show the direction that it points in now.
3. Repeat this until the compass reaches the edge of the paper or the magnet. Draw a smooth line to join all the points. Mark arrows on the line to show the direction of the force on the compass.
4. Repeat 2 and 3 at several positions around the bar magnet.
5. Try the same thing with different combinations of magnets. You could try two bar magnets with their N and S poles facing; two bar magnets with their N poles facing; two bar magnets lying side by side; a bar magnet and a block of iron.

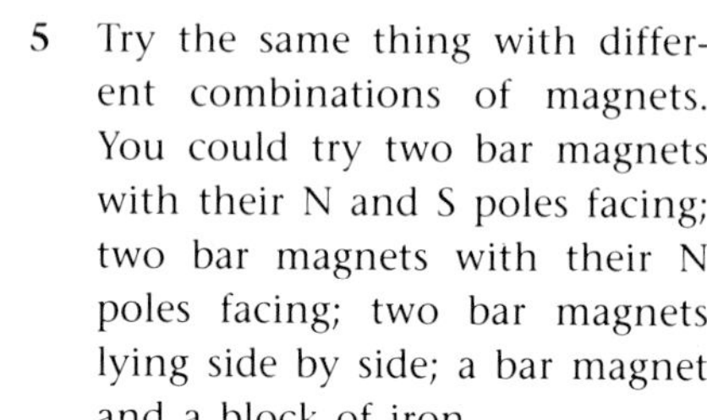

Fig. 23.5 Plotting field lines. The direction of the compass needle is drawn for several positions around the magnet.

INVESTIGATION 23.2

Comparing the strength and permanence of iron and steel magnets

1. Take a strong bar magnet. Use it to pick up a piece of iron wire, and a piece of steel wire. The iron and steel pieces should be of the same size.
2. Hold the magnet so that the iron and steel touch a heap of iron filings. Lift the magnet. Which picks up the most iron filings – the iron or the steel?
3. Carefully detach the iron and steel from the magnet, and put them near the iron filings again. Do either of them still pick up any iron fillings? Have either of them kept their magnetism?
4. Take fresh, unmagnetised pieces of iron and steel. Magnetise each of them by stroking with a strong magnet in one direction only. Make sure that you do it fairly. Design a way to find out:
   - **a** which is the most strongly magnetised
   - **b** which keeps its magnetism best and then carry out experiments to find out.

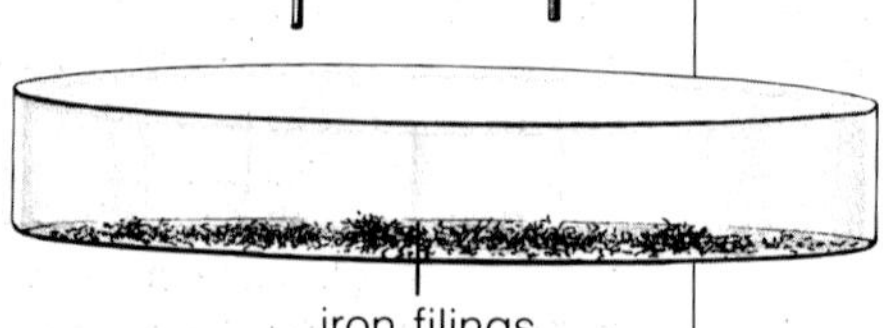

Fig. 23.6 Comparing iron and steel magnets

Questions

1. You are given a piece of thread and three iron rods. Two of the rods are magnetised. How can you find out which of the rods is not magnetised?
2. How can you show the magnetic field pattern around a magnet?
3. A heap of scrap metal contains iron, steel, nickel, zinc, copper, aluminium and some tin cans. Find out which of these could be removed using a magnet.
4. Explain the difference between a magnetic material and a magnet.

Fig. 23.7 Iron filings on a piece of card over a bar magnet. The pattern they make shows the field lines around the magnet.

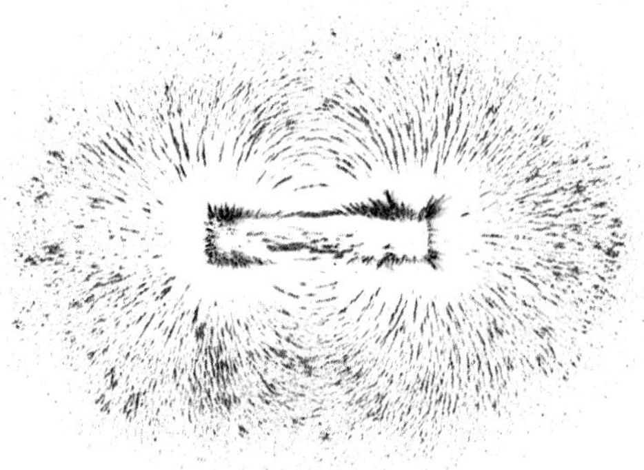

The magnetic field is the space around a magnet in which it can affect other objects

Every magnet has a space around it in which it can affect some objects. This space is called its **magnetic field**.

You cannot see a magnetic field. But you can show its effects. If you scatter iron filings on a piece of paper, and place it over a bar magnet, each iron filing acts like a tiny compass needle. Figure 23.7 shows the patterns they make.

It helps to imagine the magnetic field of a magnet as a series of **field lines**.

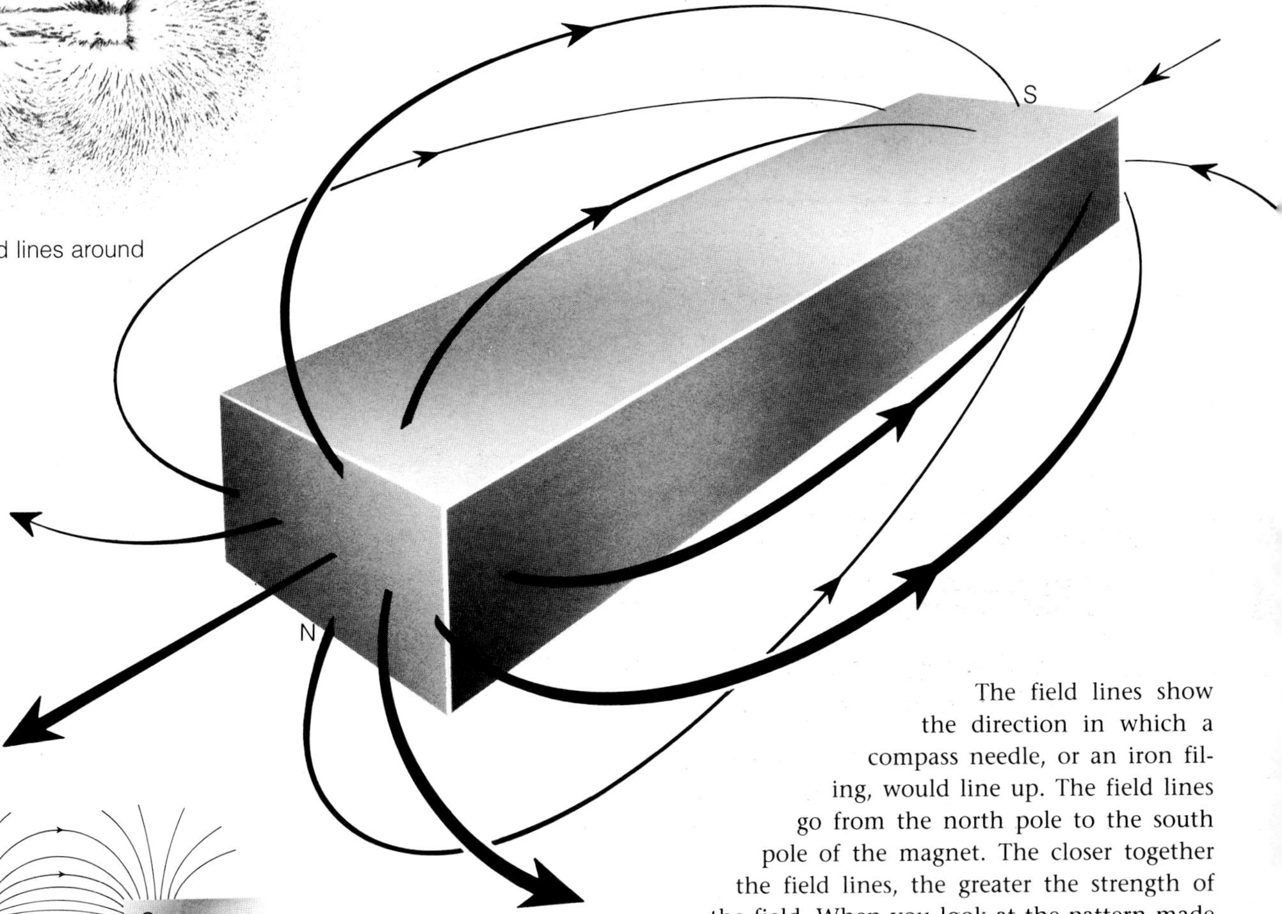

Fig. 23.8 Field lines around a bar magnet

The field lines show the direction in which a compass needle, or an iron filing, would line up. The field lines go from the north pole to the south pole of the magnet. The closer together the field lines, the greater the strength of the field. When you look at the pattern made by the iron filings you can see the direction of the field lines. Remember, though, that you are only looking at a small part of the field. It actually extends right around the magnet, in three dimensions.

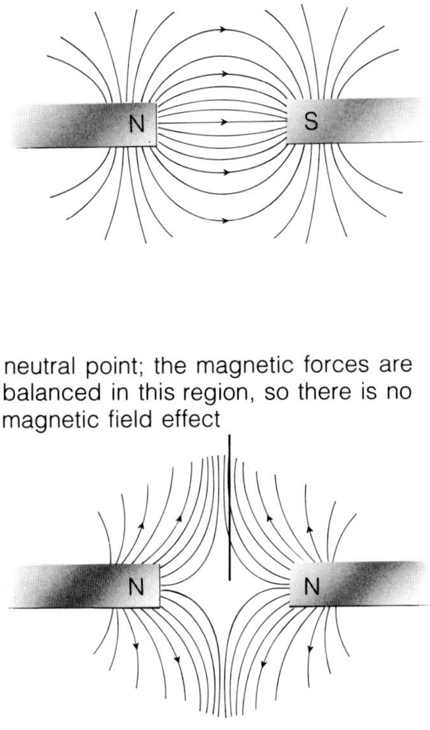

neutral point; the magnetic forces are balanced in this region, so there is no magnetic field effect

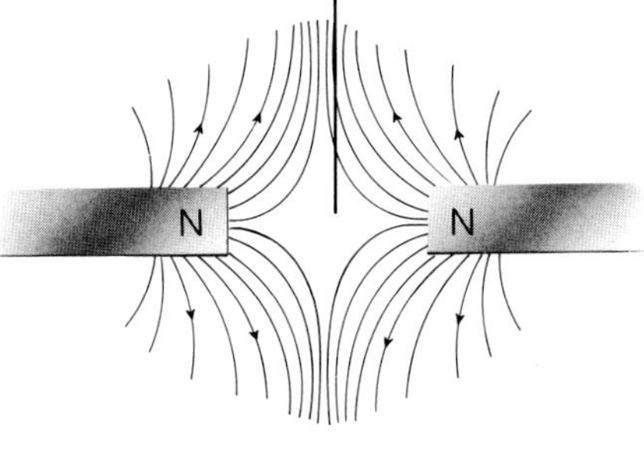

Fig. 23.9 Magnetic field lines between two bar magnets

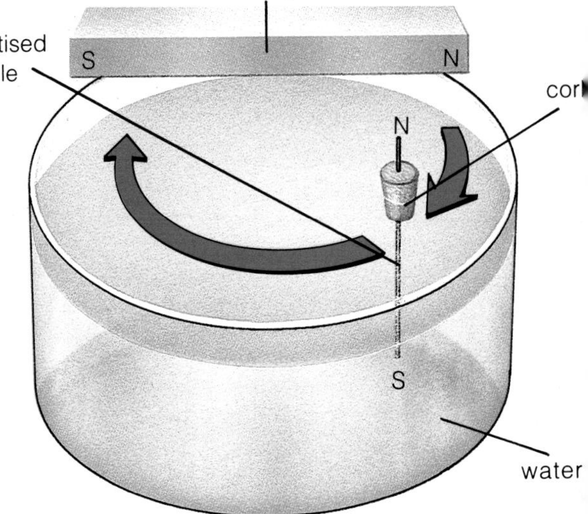

Fig. 23.10 Field lines show the direction in which a north pole would move. You can show this by setting up this apparatus. If the needle is long enough, the south pole is too low in the water to be affected by the magnet. The north pole moves along a curved path from the north to the south pole of the bar magnet.

The Earth behaves like a giant magnet

The Earth is like an enormous magnet. Its North Pole is actually a magnetic south pole – the north poles of magnets are attracted towards it. Its South Pole is a magnetic north pole – the south poles of magnets are attracted towards it.

The field lines of the Earth's magnetic field extend far out into space.

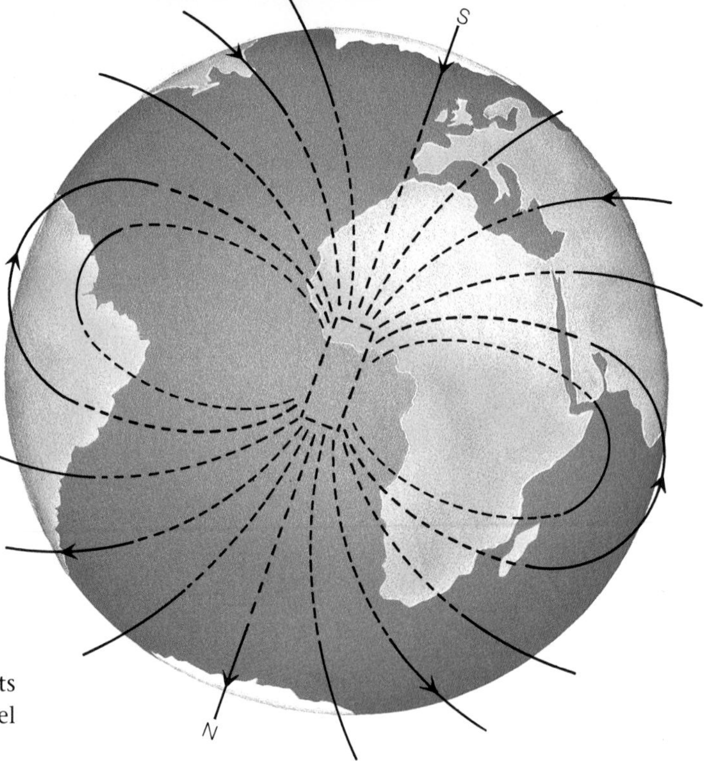

Fig. 23.11 The Earth's magnetic field. The Earth behaves like a giant bar magnet, with a south-seeking pole at the North Pole, and a north-seeking pole at the South Pole. In fact, the poles of the magnet are not exactly at the geographical North and South poles, but just a few degrees away.

Magnetism is caused by domains

A magnetic material is made up of tiny magnetic regions, or **domains**. These regions are about 20 millionths of a metre in size.

An electron spinning round the nucleus of an atom produces a tiny magnetic field. In the domain of a magnet, the spinning electrons are lined up in a way that lines up their magnetic fields. This produces a tiny magnetic region in the material.

If the material is unmagnetised, the domains point in lots of different directions. The different field directions cancel each other out so there is no overall magnetic effect.

If the unmagnetised material is put into a magnetic field, the domains which are pointing in the same direction as the magnetic field grow bigger. They gradually 'take over' the piece of material, until all the domains have fields pointing in the same direction as the magnetic field. The material has now become a magnet.

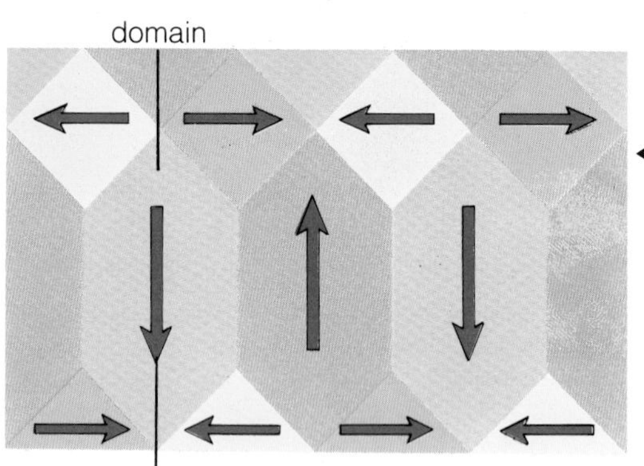

Fig. 23.12 Magnetising a substance changes the size of some of the domains. In an unmagnetised sample of iron, the domains' magnetic fields point in all directions. When the iron is magnetised, the domains in the direction of the outside field get bigger, at the expense of the domains not in the same direction.

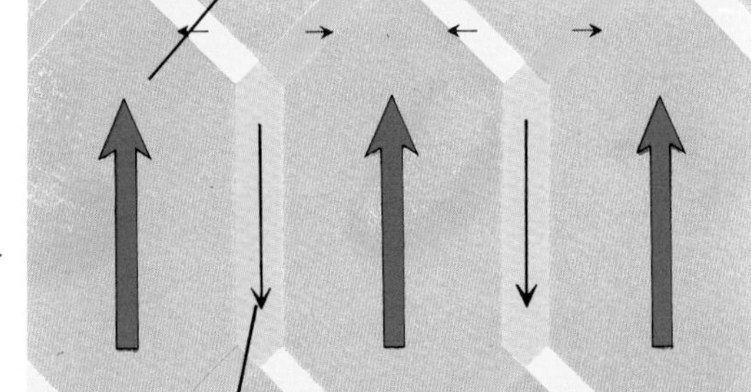

Iron is easier to magnetise than steel

When a magnet is held close to iron filings, each iron filing becomes a tiny magnet. Its domains easily change position. But as soon as the magnet is taken away, the filings lose their magnetism. Its domains do not stay in their new position.

We say that iron is a **soft** magnetic material. It is easy to magnetise and makes a strong magnet, but it easily loses its magnetism. This is useful if you want a magnet that you can switch on and off. This type of magnet is called a **temporary magnet**. Soft magnetic materials are used in electromagnets.

Paper-clips are made of steel. If you stroke a paper-clip in one direction with the pole of a magnet, you can make its domains line up, so that it becomes a magnet. When you take the magnet away, the paper-clip stays magnetised. We say that steel is a **hard** magnetic material. Once its domains are lined up, they stay lined up. The steel becomes a **permanent magnet**. Permanent magnets are used in door catches, motors, cassette and video tape and for computer discs. But even so-called permanent magnets can be demagnetised. Anything which can knock domains out of alignment can demagnetise a magnet. Dropping or hitting or heating the magnet can remove the magnetism. So can exposure to a strong magnetic field.

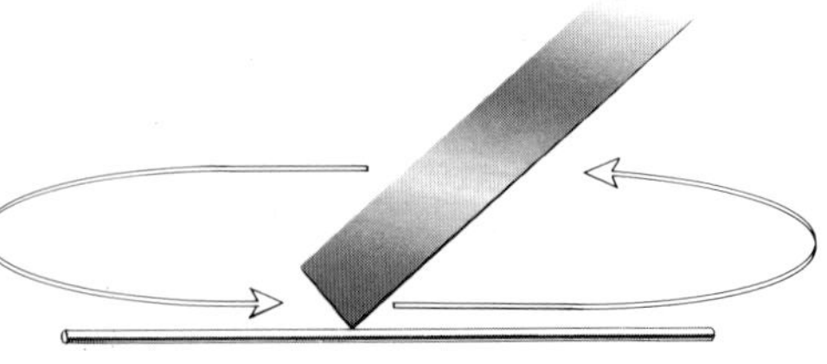

24 ELECTRIC FIELDS

Atoms contain electrons and protons. If these are separated, a charge results. This charge can be positive or negative.

Some materials can be given an electric charge

Atoms contain electrons and protons. If the number of protons equals the number of electrons, the atom is uncharged.

If you rub two materials together, it is possible that electrons might be rubbed off one and on to the other. The electrons and protons in each material are now no longer balanced. One material has extra electrons and the other is missing some electrons. The materials become **charged**. The Greeks discovered this in the 6th century B.C. When a piece of amber is rubbed, it becomes charged. It attracts dust and small pieces of paper. The Greek word for amber is 'elektron'. We now call the charge **static** (stationary) **electricity**.

Some charged objects, such as perspex and polythene, attract one another. But two pieces of charged polythene repel each other. This is because there are two kinds of charge. If the charges are the same, they repel each other. If the two charges are different, they attract each other.

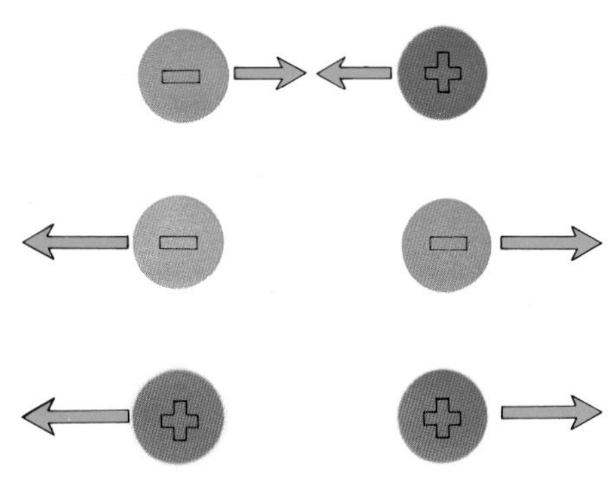

Fig. 24.1 Like charges repel. Unlike charges attract.

Like charges repel, unlike charges attract.

Extra electrons produce a negative charge; too few electrons produce a positive charge

If a polythene or amber rod is rubbed with a cloth, electrons are transferred from the cloth to the rod. The rod now has extra electrons. Electrons have a negative charge, so the rod has an overall **negative** charge. The cloth now has too few electrons and too many protons. Protons have a positive charge, so the cloth has an overall **positive** charge.

Rubbing the rod has not produced the charge. The energy used in rubbing has only separated the positive and negative charges already in the atoms.

If a perspex rod is rubbed with wool, it loses electrons to the wool. The perspex rod becomes positively charged. The wool becomes negatively charged.

Charged materials may attract other objects

If either a positively or negatively charged rod is brought close to tiny pieces of foil, the foil is attracted to the rod. But if they touch the rod, they acquire the same charge as the rod, and are repelled.

Before touching, when the charged rod is brought close, a charge separation is **induced** in the foil. If the rod is negatively charged, for example, it has extra electrons. These repel electrons in the foil, which move away from its surface. The part of the foil nearest to the rod becomes positively charged, and is attracted towards the rod.

But when the foil touches the rod, some of the extra electrons from the rod jump on to the foil. Now the foil is negatively charged too. So it is repelled from the rod.

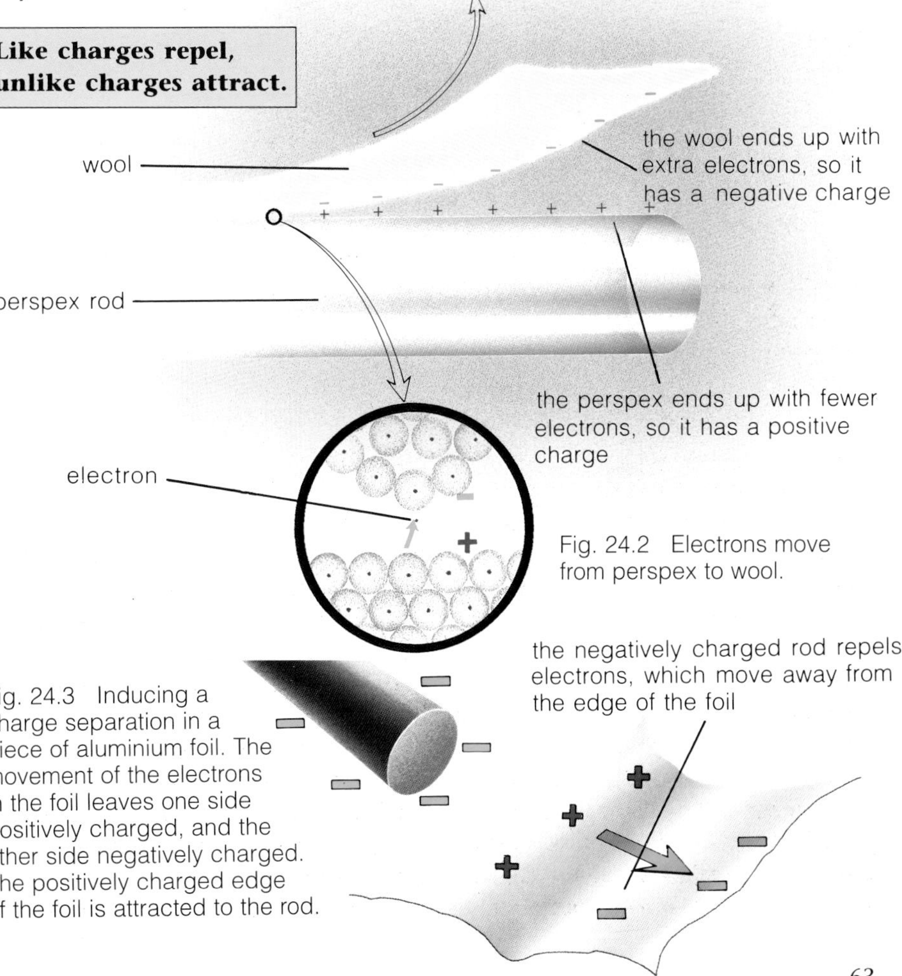

Fig. 24.2 Electrons move from perspex to wool.

Fig. 24.3 Inducing a charge separation in a piece of aluminium foil. The movement of the electrons in the foil leaves one side positively charged, and the other side negatively charged. The positively charged edge of the foil is attracted to the rod.

Static electricity stays where it is, until discharged

When two materials are rubbed together and become charged, electrons are transferred from one to the other. If the material does not conduct electricity, the charge stays where it is. A material which does not conduct electricity is called an **insulator**. If the charge stays where it is, it is called static electricity. Static means 'not moving'.

If you walk around on a nylon carpet, electrons can be rubbed off the carpet on to you. You can build up quite a large negative charge of static electricity. But you do not realise it, because the charge stays where it is. If you now touch a metal post connected to the ground, the electrons can escape. The metal post is a **conductor**. It will let the electrons rush away from you into the ground. And you can certainly feel that! You get a small electric shock. The escape of the charge from your body is called a **discharge**. You can get a similar effect when you pull off a nylon jumper. The crackling sound you may hear is a discharge of static electricity. As the charge on an object increases, its **voltage** rises. A high voltage can make the charge jump to the ground or to the nearest conductor connected to the ground – which could be you. An object can be discharged by connecting it to the ground. If the object is negatively charged then the extra electrons flow to the ground. A positively charged object is discharged as electrons flow onto it.

Fig. 24.4 Lightning is a violent discharge of static electricity. Some buildings have a pointed lightning conductor on the top, which is connected to the ground by a thick copper strap. The charged cloud attracts an opposite charge to the point. Charge is transferred at the point. This helps to reduce the chance of a strike. If lightning does strike, it passes down the strap and not through the building.

The most impressive static discharge that you are likely to see is lightning. A static charge builds up in thunderclouds. It is discharged to the ground, often through a large building or tall tree. A lightning flash usually consists of several static discharges one after another. The temperature inside the flash can be 30 000 °C.

In operating theatres, great care is taken to ensure that static charges cannot build up. This is because anaesthetics can release explosive vapours. What could happen, and why, if charges build up?

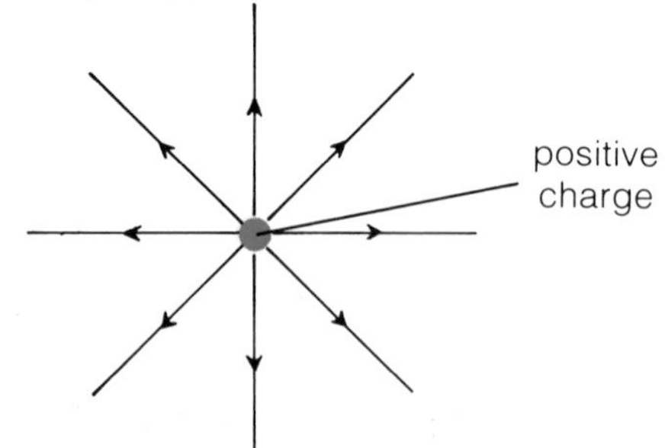

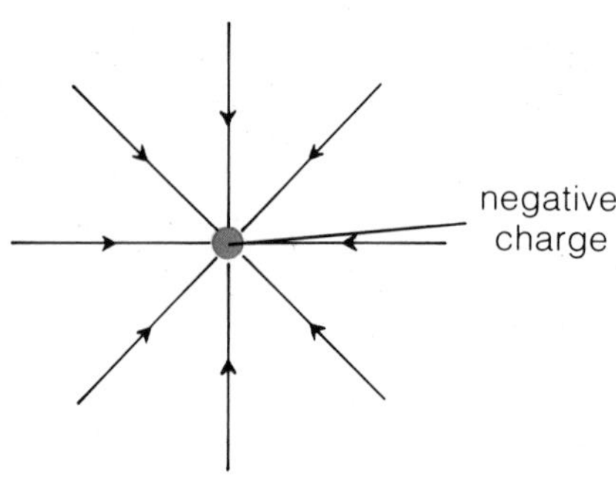

Fig. 24.5 Electric field lines

Charged objects produce electric fields

Like magnets, charged objects can affect other objects without coming into contact with them. A charged rod can attract or repel other rods without coming into contact with them. The space around a charged object in which it can affect other objects is called its **electric field.**

As with magnetic fields, field lines around charged objects can be drawn to show the direction of the force. Arrows are drawn on the field lines to show the direction in which the force would act on a positively charged object.

25 MORE ABOUT STATIC

Opposite charges can be used to make particles stick where you want them to.

A photocopier uses a static charge to transfer an image to the page

When a page to be copied is placed on the top of a copier, it is lit by a lamp. A lens focuses the image of the page onto a rotating **drum**. The drum is covered with a light-sensitive or **photoconductive** layer, which is charged with static electricity. Where light hits the surface, the photoconductive layer conducts electricity and the charge flows away. Charge is left behind in places corresponding to the black parts of the original page. As the drum moves round, a copy of the black parts of the page is left as a charged pattern on the drum. Black **toner** dust is then applied to the drum. The toner is given a charge opposite to that of the charge on the drum, so the toner is attracted to those parts of the drum that are still charged. A black powder image of the page forms on the drum.

To print this image, a sheet of paper is rolled over the drum. The paper picks up a dusty copy of the original image. The paper then passes between heated rollers that melt or **fuse** the black toner onto the surface of the paper.

The copier can be made to enlarge or reduce the size of the image by changing the position of the lens.

Laser and similar computer printers use the same principles. The computer forms an image of the page directly on the drum. A laser or other bright light is used to light up an image straight from the computer onto the drum.

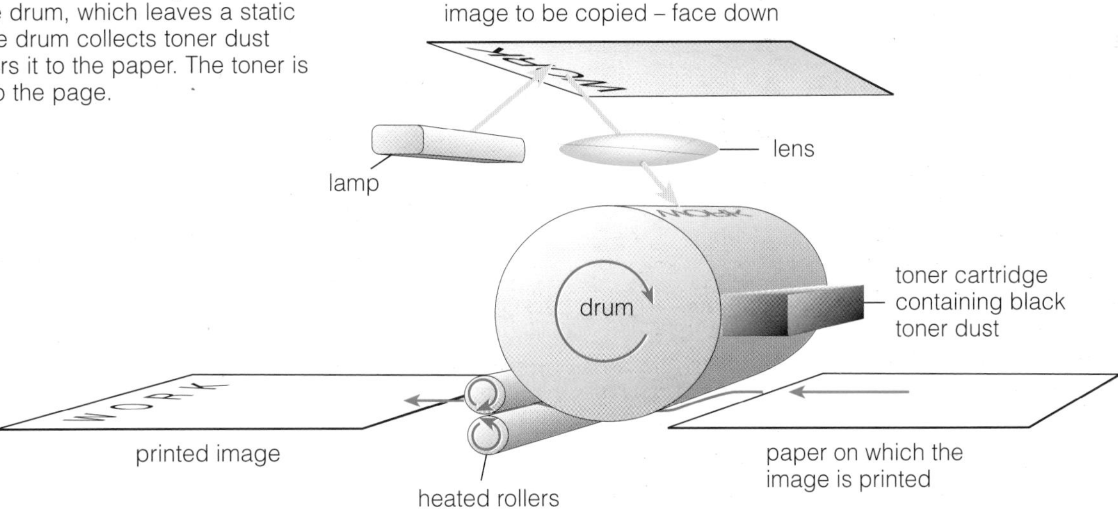

Fig. 25.1 The basics of photocopying or xerography.
The lamp transfers an image of the page to the drum, which leaves a static charge. The drum collects toner dust and transfers it to the paper. The toner is melted onto the page.

Fig. 25.2 Changing a computer card. The strap prevents damage to the chips by static charges.

Electronic components can be damaged by static

Most computer chips are sensitive to static electricity. As you move around and brush against surfaces, a static charge can build up. Nylon carpets in particular are very good at giving people static charges. The charge that builds up can generate a voltage of thousands of volts. A computer chip may be destroyed if you touch it before removing any charge on you.

You can make sure that all the charge flows away first by wearing a conducting band connected to the ground. You have **earthed** yourself. You will then be at the same voltage as the chip and the computer, if that is earthed as well. If you have gained a positive charge, it is cancelled by electrons flowing up to you from the Earth.

Fig. 25.3 When an aircraft is refuelled, the plane must first be earthed so there is no chance of a static discharge igniting the fuel. The earthing wire here is attached to the nosewheel.

DID YOU KNOW?

The inside of your television screen is being hit by a stream of electrons fired from the back of the set. The accelerating voltage might be 25 000 volts.

A dangerous static charge is prevented from building up because the inside of the screen is coated with a conducting layer.

Powders and liquids flowing in pipes can cause static charge problems

The plastic pipe from a vacuum cleaner can collect charge as all the air and dust particles rush through it. You can see small hairs and fluff sticking to the outside of the pipe, attracted by this charge. The charge builds up because the pipe is an insulator and is not earthed. This can be a problem with industrial powders flowing in pipes, as a large static charge may build up on the pipes. Powders mixed with air can make explosive mixtures. For example, a cloud of custard powder would burn very quickly if ignited by a spark produced from a static discharge.

When pipes are carrying fuels, it is vital that a charge cannot jump between a nozzle and a fuel tank. If everything is conducting and earthed, sparks can be prevented. Aircraft and racing car filling systems are usually electrically connected to the vehicle before any pumping of fuel starts.

Ordinary car filler pipes and petrol pump hoses have to be carefully designed to make sure that any charge can safely leak away and not build up. It is not possible to rely on people attaching a connector to their cars before filling up. A series of petrol station fires in Germany, involving a particular make of car, are thought to have been caused by static buildup on the pipework near to the filler cap, which was isolated from the rest of the car by plastic.

With the increased use of plastics in cars, it is more likely that charge could build up somewhere. It is recommended that hoses, tyres and garage forecourts should be conducting. This ensures that the car and fuel pipe are at the same voltage.

Fig. 25.4 A racing car being refuelled.

Question

1 Formula One racing regulations state that:

- All fuel system fittings should be metal.
- The car must be earthed before refuelling begins.
- All metal parts of the refuelling system as far back as the supply tank must be connected to earth as well.

Why is this?

The Van de Graaff generator

The Van de Graaff generator is a machine for producing large charges. A motor or handle drives a rubber belt around two rollers. The friction between the rollers and the belt charges the belt. The action of the points collects charge. If electrons are *repelled* from the points to the outside of the dome it becomes negatively charged. If electrons are *attracted* to the points from the dome, the dome becomes positively charged. Van de Graaff generators can be designed to produce either negatively or positively charged domes.

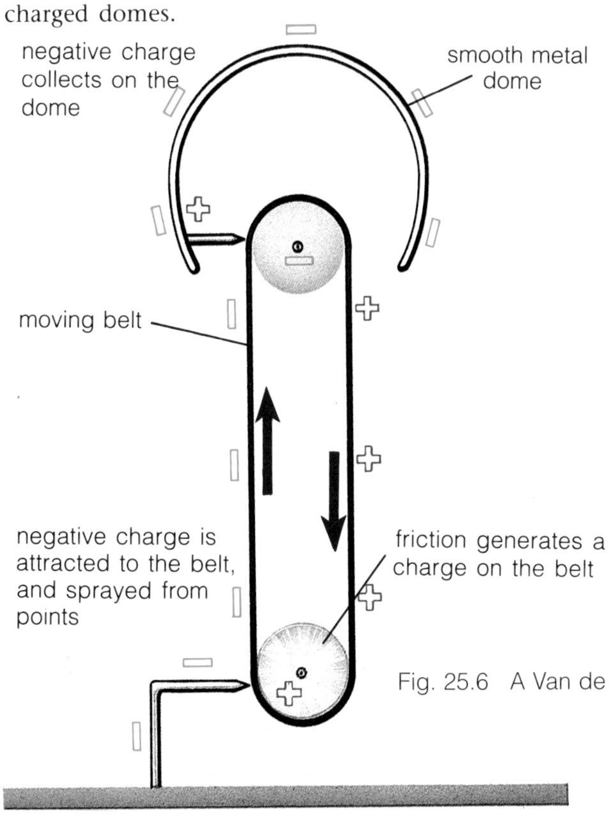

negative charge collects on the dome
smooth metal dome
moving belt
negative charge is attracted to the belt, and sprayed from points
friction generates a charge on the belt

Fig. 25.6 A Van de Graaff generator

Fig. 25.7 The car body is charged to attract paint from this sprayer. This gives a much more even coating than other methods of painting, and the paint reaches all parts of the car's surface. Great care has to be taken to keep dust particles out of the air around the car, or they too will be attracted on to its charged surface.

unit providing high voltage between wires and plates
vibrator shakes the wires to dislodge any dust from them
vibrator shakes the plates to dislodge the dust
dust falls from the plates into this hopper
negatively charged wires
positively charged plate

Fig. 25.8 A power station dust extractor. In a coal-burning power station, the waste gases contain a lot of dust and ash. Around 30 tonnes of this flue dust may be produced each hour. The flue gases are passed through a **precipitator** to remove the dust. As the gas passes through the negatively charged wires, it picks up a negative charge itself. The charged dust particles are then attracted to the positively charged plate. The dust collects on the plate, and can be collected and taken away. 99% of the dust in the flue gases can be removed like this, before the gases are released into the atmosphere.

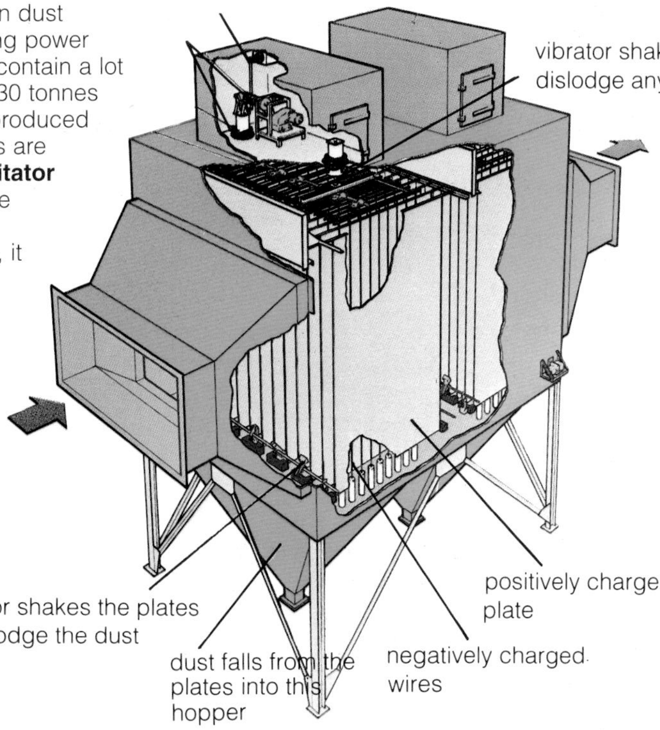

Questions

1 a How would you charge a piece of polythene with static electricity?
  b Explain how the polythene becomes charged, in terms of electrons.
  c How does a charged perspex rod attract a small piece of foil?

2 If you slide out of a car seat on a dry day, you can get an electric shock when you touch the car bodywork. If you hold on to the bodywork as you slide out, this does not happen. Why is this?

Questions

1 Which block has the greatest unbalanced force?

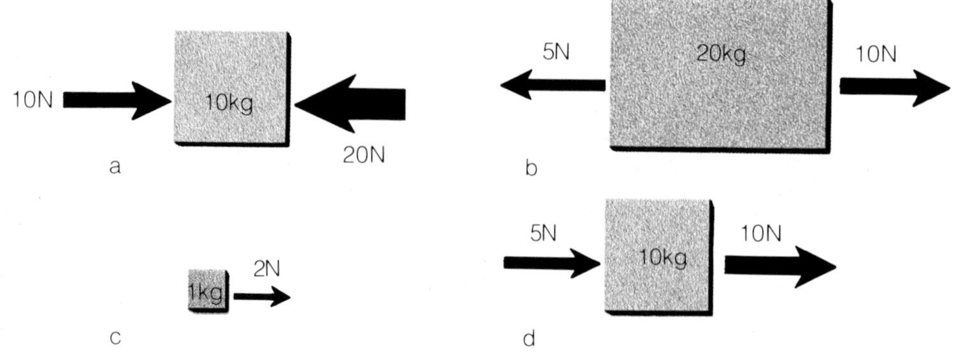

2 A sky diver with a mass of 65 kg falls through the air. As the diver goes faster, air resistance increases. Eventually a steady velocity is reached.

a What force must the air resistance exert?

b Draw a diagram showing all the forces acting on the sky diver.

3 Draw all the force-reaction pairs of force and reaction for someone standing on a pair of stepladders. There are at least four.

4 a On the surface of the Earth, the gravitational field strength is 10 N/kg. Explain what this means.

b On the Moon, a 10 kg mass has a weight of 16.7 N. What is the gravitational field strength on the Moon?

c Which has the greater weight – a 1.8 kg mass on Earth, or a 10 kg mass on the Moon?

d Which of the masses in part **c** would do more damage if it were thrown at you?

EXTENSION

5 The diagram shows an 'executive toy'.

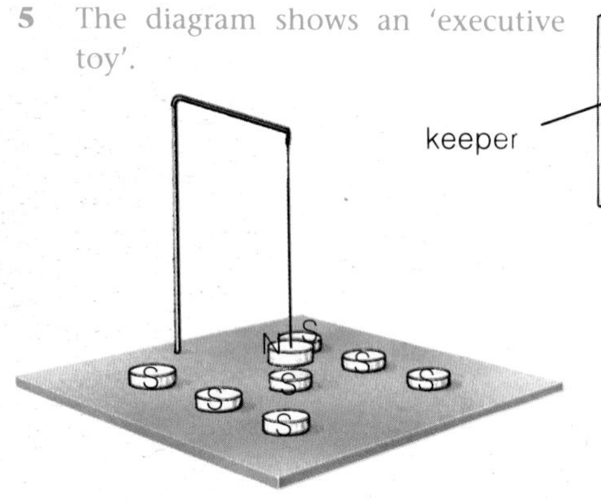

If the pendulum is swung, how will it move? Why?

6 A magnet left on its own slowly loses its magnetism. At each pole, the atomic magnets repel one another. Eventually, some change direction.

To prevent this happening, keepers are used. Keepers are made of iron, and are not permanently magnetised. Two keepers are used for two bar magnets. The diagram shows the arrangement used.

keeper

S N

N S

Complete the diagram, by labelling two North poles and two South poles. Some of them may be induced poles.

7 The diagram shows the apparatus used in an experiment. The surface was tilted, and the angle measured at which the block on the surface began to slip. Different surfaces were tested.

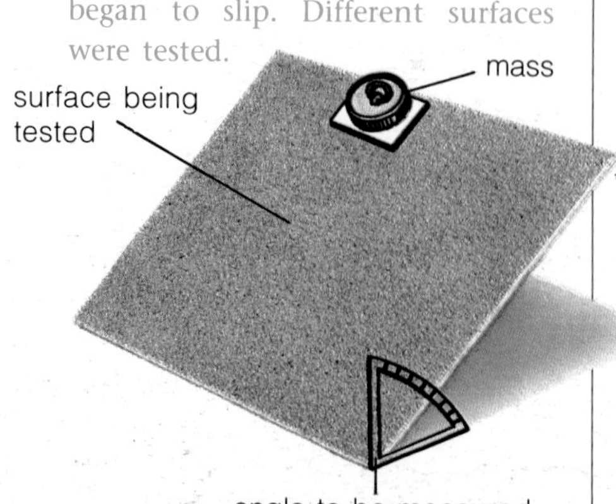

7 The results are shown below:

Surface material	*Angle at which block began to slip*
glass	9°
ceramic tile	10°
polished metal	11°
cushioned vinyl	16°
polished wood	16°
unpolished wood	20°
cork	25°
carpet	30°

a Which material gave the most grip?

b Which material would you choose for making the surface of a children's slide? Give your reasons.

c Which material would be best to cover the floor in a hospital corridor? Give your reasons.

d Ceramic tiles are often used on steps, or around swimming pools. What precautions must be taken in the design of these tiles?

e What is the force which prevents the block from slipping down the slope?

f What is the force which pulls the block down the slope?

EXTENSION

8 The diagram shows a section through a ship. The total volume of the ship is 1000 m³. The total mass of the ship and its load is 400 000 kg.

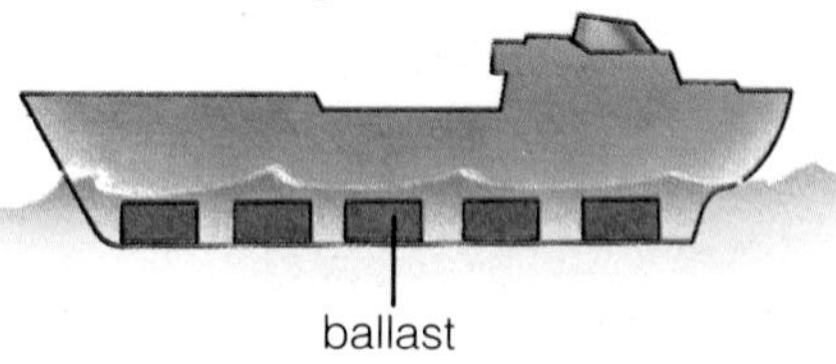

ballast

a What is the weight of the ship and its load?

b What upthrust must be provided by the water to keep the ship afloat?

c What is the average density of the ship?

d Why is the ballast carried in the bottom of the ship?

e If the ship sails in salt water, would it need more or less ballast than if it was in fresh water? Explain your answer.

f If the ship sails in warm water, would it need more or less ballast than if it was in cold water? Explain your answer.

ENERGY

26 ENERGY

We cannot do anything without energy. When something happens, energy is transferred. Energy is not used up, but is passed on to something else, or changed into a different form.

Fig. 26.1 Nuclear energy is released in the explosion of an atomic bomb. Into what forms of energy is it transferred?

Things happen when energy is transferred

Energy is needed in order to do things. Nothing happens without energy. Nothing happens, either, when energy is just stored. Things only happen when energy is **transferred**. The energy may be transferred from one object to another. Or it may be transferred from one form into another. When energy is transferred, things happen.

For example, petrol contains chemical energy. If the petrol remains in a car's fuel tank, nothing happens. But when the chemical energy is converted to thermal (heat) energy in the car's engine, movement occurs.

Most things that happen involve many different energy transfers. Each transfer causes something to change. Usually, the energy ends up in the surroundings. This usually means that there is a small temperature rise in the surroundings.

Internal energy is energy in a substance

In everyday speech, we often talk about 'heat energy' in an object. A hot object has 'heat energy'. However, a better term for the energy in an object is **internal energy**.

Energy transfers in firing a cannonball

Kinetic (movement) energy of a match is converted to internal energy in chemicals in the match head. This ignites them. The chemical energy is released as heat.

The heat raises the internal energy of the wick. The wick ignites. Chemical energy in the wick is released as heat.

The heat raises the internal energy of the gunpowder. The gunpowder burns very rapidly. Its chemical energy is released as heat. This raises the internal energy of gas molecules in the gun barrel. Their kinetic energy increases. The gas expands rapidly.

As the gas expands, the internal energy of the gas is transferred to kinetic energy in the cannon ball.

If you lift something and let it go it falls. The higher you lift it the harder it hits the ground when it drops. Lifting something gives it gravitational energy.

As the cannon ball rises, it gains gravitational energy, but loses kinetic energy.

At the highest point of its path, the cannon ball has maximum gravitational energy. For a split second it is vertically motionless. It has lost kinetic energy.

As the cannon ball falls, it loses gravitational energy and gains kinetic energy.

When the cannon ball lands, it has lost all its gravitational energy. On impact, its kinetic energy is converted to heat energy. The heat warms the ball, the air and ground.

Fig. 26.2

Mechanical energy has two main forms

Potential energy is stored energy. Something which has a store of energy has potential energy. A raised pendulum has potential energy. **Gravitational energy** is potential energy.

As the pendulum falls, it loses its potential energy. The potential energy changes to kinetic energy. At the bottom of the swing, it has lost all the extra potential energy it had at the top of its swing. As it rises up the other side, it gains potential energy again.

Eventually, the pendulum slows down and stops. All the potential energy has been lost to the air. The energy has been spread out into the surroundings.

Kinetic energy is energy of motion. A swinging pendulum has kinetic energy. It has most kinetic energy at the bottom of its swing. This is when it is going at its fastest. As it rises up the other side, the kinetic energy is converted back to potential energy. At the top point of its swing the kinetic energy is zero.

As the pendulum swings, air molecules bounce off it. The air molecules gain energy. The pendulum loses energy. After each swing, the pendulum rises a little less.

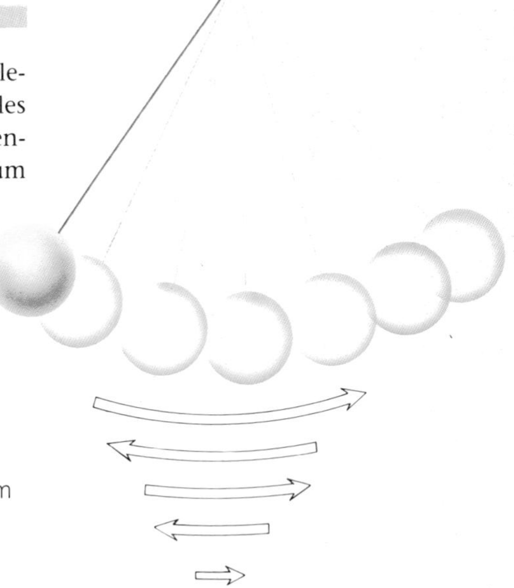

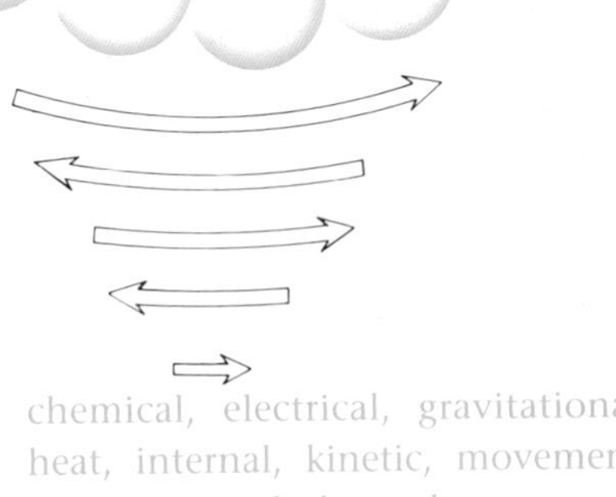

Fig. 26.3 At the top of its swing, a pendulum bob has zero kinetic energy and high potential energy. At the bottom of its swing it has high kinetic energy and low potential energy.

Questions

1 List all the energy transfers involved in firing a cannon ball.

2 A pendulum is set swinging in a vacuum. Will it continue to swing forever? Explain your answer.

3 Here is a list of some forms of energy:

chemical, electrical, gravitational, heat, internal, kinetic, movement, nuclear, sound, thermal.

a Which forms are similar, or the same?

b Describe six possible energy transfers that can be useful, giving the form that the energy starts with and how it ends up.

27 ENERGY AND WORK

Energy enables something to do work. Both energy and work are measured in joules.

Work is done when a force moves an object

It takes energy to drag a block up a slope. If people pull a block up a slope, the energy comes from food in their bodies. This energy is chemical potential energy. Some of the chemical energy is changed to gravitational potential energy as the block is raised higher.

As the block is moved, a force is applied to it. We say that **work** has been done. This is the scientific use of the word 'work'. Work is done only if a **force** is **moving** an object.

Fig. 27.1 Work is done in pulling a block up a slope.

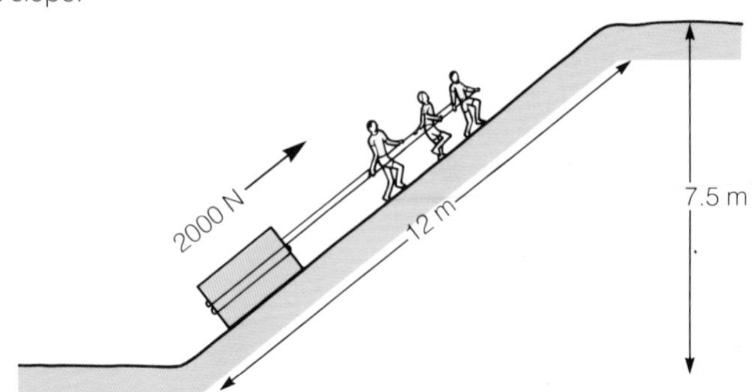

Work is a transfer of energy, and is measured in joules

It is easy to calculate how much work is done.

work done = force applied x distance moved in the direction of the force

In Figure 27.1, the force being used is 2000 N. The block has been pulled a distance of 12 m. So the work done is 2000 N x 12 m, which is 24 000 newton-metres.

'Newton-metres' are usually called **joules**. So the work done in pulling the block up the slope is 24 000 joules. The symbol for joules is **J**.

Note that the equation

work done = force applied x distance moved in the direction of the force

is often written as

$W = F \times d$ or $W = Fd$

Unfortunately, this can sometimes cause confusion, because W is also the unit of power, the watt. You must be careful not to confuse these two uses of the symbol W. (There is more about power in Topic 28.)

DID YOU KNOW?

Mass can be thought of as a form of energy. Einstein's famous equation, $E = mc^2$ means energy = mass x constant^2. The constant is a very large number. According to this equation, a 1 kg mass is actually 90 000 000 000 000 000 J.

Gravitational energy = mass x *g* x height

When the block reaches the top of the slope, it has gained gravitational energy. If it is pushed off, it falls back down and loses this energy.

Fig. 27.2

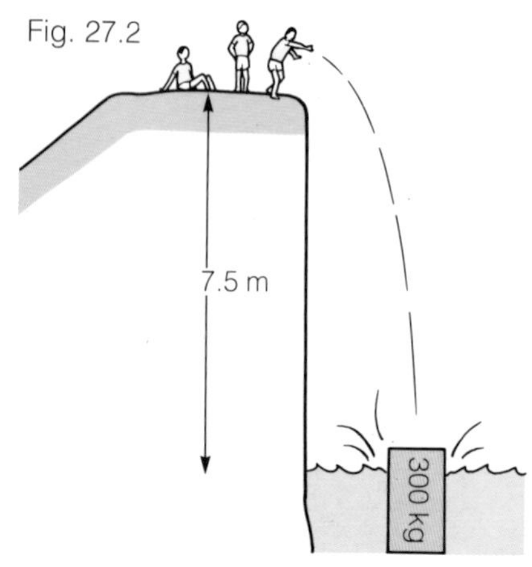

If the block weighs 300 kg, the force pulling down on it – its weight – is 300 kg x 10 N/kg. This is 3000 N.

The block falls 7.5 m. So the energy transferred is:

force x distance

3000 N x 7.5 m = 22 500 J

Notice that the amount of gravitational energy the block has is nothing to do with how it got to the top of the cliff. It might have been pulled up the slope by people, or it might have been lifted straight up by a crane. It makes no difference. The gravitational energy of the block depends only on its weight and how high up it is. Gravitational energy = mass x *g* x height.

Not all energy produces useful work

If you look back, you will see that the work done by the people who dragged the block up the slope was 24 000 J. But the gravitational energy that the block gained was only 22 500 J. 1500 J seems to have gone missing somewhere.

The block is pulled up the slope against a **gravitational** force and against a **frictional** force. The work done against gravity is not wasted. It becomes gravitational energy in the block. It can be released again when the block falls off the cliff.

The work done against friction is wasted. It is lost to the surroundings. The surroundings will be a little warmer after the people have pulled the block up the slope. This energy is very difficult to get back again.

EXTENSION

Energy transfer always involves some wastage

Whenever energy is transferred, some is wasted. When a block is pulled up a slope, friction causes energy to be lost as heat. The energy does not disappear. It is transferred to the surroundings.

Eventually, all the energy from most energy transfers ends up in the surroundings. It usually warms up the surroundings. This might be useful, but often this is just wasted energy.

> **DID YOU KNOW?**
> All the food you eat in one day has about the same energy as 1/3 dm^3 of petrol.

Fig. 27.3 Energy transfers in pulling a block

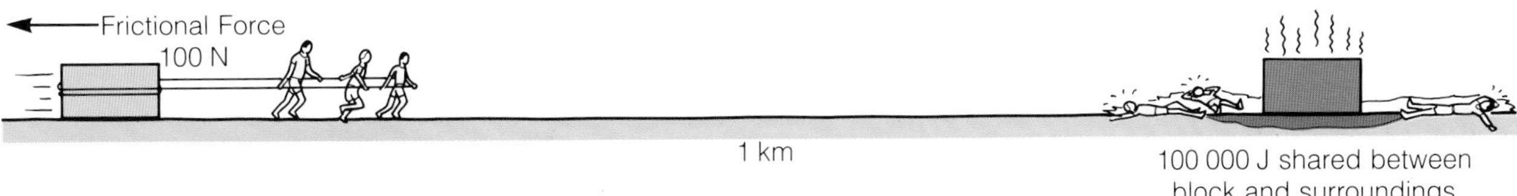

Energy never disappears

Most energy transfers 'lose' energy. But the energy does not disappear. The energy goes into the surroundings.

> **Energy is never created or destroyed.** It is just transferred from one form to another. This is the **principle of the conservation of energy**.

As energy transfers continue, the energy ends up as heat in the surroundings. The 'surroundings' include the whole universe. This is enormous, so we hardly notice the temperature rise. The energy is effectively 'lost' to us.

Combustion transfers chemical energy into heat

Sometimes, we actually *want* a lot of energy to be released to the surroundings. A fire transfers chemical energy to internal energy (heat) in the fire and surroundings. A tiny fraction is used to raise the potential energy of the smoke particles as they go up the chimney. Since heat is what we want from the fire, we do not think of this as a wasteful energy transfer.

Muscles transfer chemical energy to work and heat

Muscles transfer chemical energy into work. Muscle cells contain a substance called glycogen. Glycogen contains chemical energy. When the muscle does work the glycogen is broken down to glucose. The chemical energy in the glucose is transferred to work in the muscle fibres. This actually involves many different energy transfers between different molecules in the muscle.

At each of these different energy transfers, some energy goes into the surroundings as heat. This is why you get hot when you exercise vigorously. Your body has special regulatory mechanisms to make sure you do not get too hot.

Fig. 27.4 Energy transfers in a coal fire

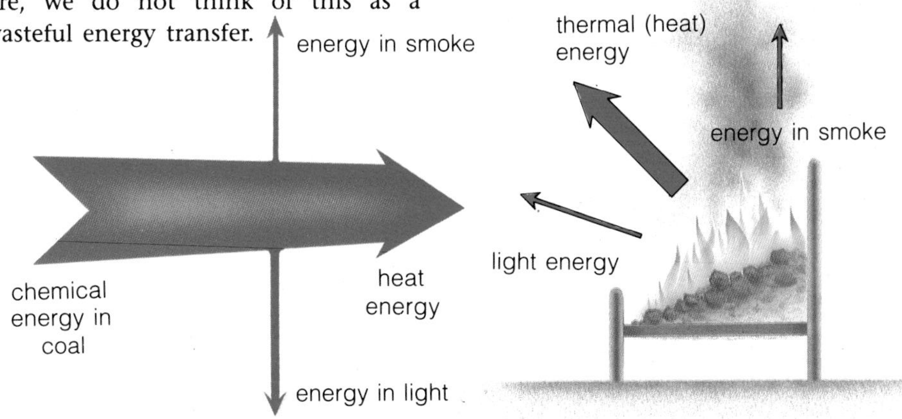

Questions

1 A block is dragged up a slope for 12 m. 1500 J is wasted in dragging this block against a frictional force. What is the size of this force? (Remember work = force x distance).

2 Draw a diagram to show all the energy transfers in lighting a gas fire using matches.

3 a If you weigh 60 kg, what force is required to lift you?
b If you run upstairs, and arrive 2.5 m higher than you started, how much gravitational energy have you gained?
c Estimate how much energy you think you would have used to get there.
d Where has a lot of the energy gone?

EXTENSION

4 A steam engine transfers 2 % of its heat into useful work. How much energy would be wasted if a steam-powered crane lifted a 200 kg block by 3 m?

5 A builder drops his sandwich from the top of a 300 m tower.
a The sandwich weighs 100 g. How much energy does it lose when it falls?
b Where does this energy go?
c The sandwich contains 200 000 J of energy. If the builder weighs 70 kg is it worth the builder climbing down to get the sandwich?

28 POWER

Power is the rate of doing work. Power is measured in watts. A powerful system is one which is producing a lot of energy, or which does so in a short time.

Power tells you how quickly energy is transferred

Imagine a weight-lifter lifting a 400 kg mass. With enough levers or pulleys, anyone could lift this. But it would be a slow process. The weight-lifter can do it quickly.

The energy required to lift 4 000 N by 2.5 m is 10 000 J. This is less than half the chemical energy in 1 g of peanuts! So the amount of energy used by the weight-lifter is not large. But he does transfer the energy from himself to the 400 kg mass very quickly. He might take 1 s or 2 s to transfer the energy.

If you lifted the 400 kg mass with pulleys, it would take about 10 s to lift it. The same energy would be transferred, but much more slowly. So we say that the weight-lifter is more powerful. Power tells us how quickly energy is transferred.

$$\text{Power} = \frac{\text{work done in joules}}{\text{time taken in seconds}}$$

$$\text{or} \quad \frac{\text{energy transferred in joules}}{\text{time taken in seconds}}$$

The units of power are joules per second, or **watts**. The symbol for watts is **W**. So 1 W is the same as 1 J/s.

The weight-lifter transfers 10 000 J in 2 s. So his power output is:

$$\frac{10\,000\text{ J}}{2\text{s}} = 5000\text{ W}$$

This is a very high power output. No-one could keep up this power output for very long!

Power is still sometimes measured in **horsepower**. A horse transfers about 750 J of energy per second. This is a power output of 750 W. So one horsepower is 750 W.

Fig. 28.1

Power must not be confused with energy

A 500 000 000 W or 500 MW (megawatt) power station produces 500 million J of energy every second. This is electrical energy transferred through heat from chemical energy in the fuel. This is a lot of energy per second! This energy output would heat 1400 kg of water to boiling point every second. So a power station is suitably named. It is very powerful.

A 100 000 000 000 W or 100 GW (gigawatt) laser system is 200 times more powerful than a power station. The laser flash lasts only 0.001 millionths of a second. The total energy transferred, however, is very small. It is about 100 J. This would raise the temperature of a teaspoon of water to boiling point! Yet, because the energy transfer is concentrated into such a short time, we say that the laser system is very powerful. Very powerful systems, like this laser system, often rely on short bursts of energy. They cannot run continuously.

Racing cars are much more powerful than normal cars. They can transfer energy very quickly. The racing car transfers chemical energy from its fuel at a much faster rate. So it uses up fuel more quickly than a normal car. For example, 40 cm^3 of petrol might take a small car 1 km. The same amount of fuel would probably take a racing car about 100 m!

Fig. 28.2 Didcot Power Station has four 500 MW coal-burning generators. It also has four 25 MW gas turbines, which are sometimes used to meet a sudden extra demand on its electricity production.

Sprinters need to transfer energy quickly for a short time

Sprinting and long distance running make very different demands on an athlete. Sprinters need to be more powerful than long distance runners.

A sprinter trains his or her muscles to deliver a very quick burst of energy. In a top class 100 m race, the runners may transfer chemical energy to kinetic energy at a rate of almost 1500 W. They cannot keep this up for long. Some of the very best sprinters can only produce this sort of power output for the first 60 m or so.

A long distance runner needs to train muscles to transfer energy over a very long period of time. The power output is much lower, but takes place over a longer time. The total amount of energy transferred by a marathon runner is much greater than that transferred by a sprinter.

INVESTIGATION 28.1

Calculating power output

$$\text{Power} = \frac{\text{energy transferred}}{\text{time taken}} = \frac{\text{force x distance}}{\text{time taken}}$$

If you move a force through a distance and find the time that it takes you, you can calculate your power output.

Pedalling an exercise bicycle

Use a newton meter to measure the force that you exert. (Hook a newton meter to the pedal and pull at right angles to the crank until it is moving.) Measure the length of the pedal crank in metres. Pedal hard for one minute, and count the number of turns that you complete.

> Force used = F newtons
>
> Distance moved = circumference of circle x number of turns = $2\pi r$ x number of turns
>
> Energy transferred = force used x distance moved = F newtons x $2\pi r$ x number of turns
>
> So power output = F newtons x $2\pi r$ x number of turns/time taken in seconds

Running upstairs

Find your weight in newtons. Measure the vertical height of the stairs. Run up the stairs as fast as you can. Time yourself in seconds.

> Energy transferred = force used x distance moved = your weight in newtons x height of stairs in metres
>
> Power output = your weight x height of stairs/time taken in seconds

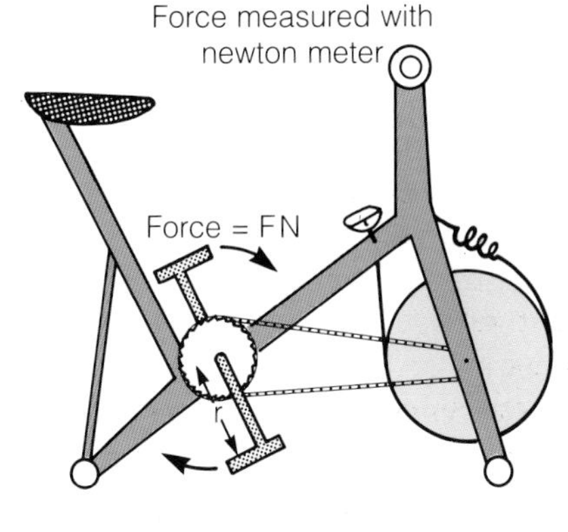

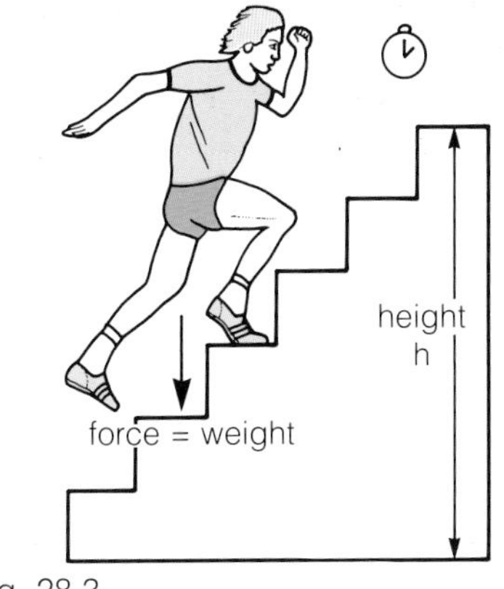

Fig. 28.3

Questions

1 Student A pedalled an exercise bicycle against a force of 100 N for 2 min. During this time the pedals turned 100 times. The pedals were 20 cm long.
Student B ran upstairs. She weighed 60 kg. She climbed 5 m in 10 s.
   a Who was the more powerful?
   b Who would be able to keep up this rate of energy transfer the longest?

2 A builder carries 24 bricks to the top of a 3 m wall. Each brick weighs 25 N.
   a How much energy is transferred to the bricks?
   b In what form is this energy after transfer?
   c If the builder weighs 800 N, and takes 15 s, calculate the power that he delivers.
   A motor driven conveyor is an alternative way of carrying the bricks to the top of the wall. The conveyor produces 1000 W of useful output.
   d How long would it take the conveyor to lift the bricks?
   e Which is the better way of lifting the bricks? Why?

3 A litre of petrol contains 35 000 000 J. If a car travels at a speed of 25 m/s, 1 dm^3 of petrol lasts 13 min.
   a What power output does this represent?
   b In 13 min, the car travels 20 km. If all the chemical energy is transferred, what force pushes against the car?

EXTENSION

29 HEAT

Heat is thermal energy as it is being transferred. If objects are heated, they gain internal energy. This can change their temperature, or the arrangement of their particles.

Heat flows from hot bodies to cold ones

A pan of cold water on a hot cooker hob gets hotter. Because the hob is hotter than the pan, energy is transferred from the hob to the pan. The energy being transferred from the hob to the pan is **heat energy**. Heat energy flows from hot bodies to cold ones.

Strictly speaking, we can only use the term 'heat' for energy *as it is being transferred*. The energy *in* the hot cooker hob is not heat energy. A better name for it is **thermal energy** or **internal energy**. The hot cooker hob has higher internal energy than the cold water. Heat flows from bodies with high internal energy to bodies with lower internal energy.

Fig. 29.1 Heating water on an electric hob. Heat energy flows from the rings, through the pan, and into the water.

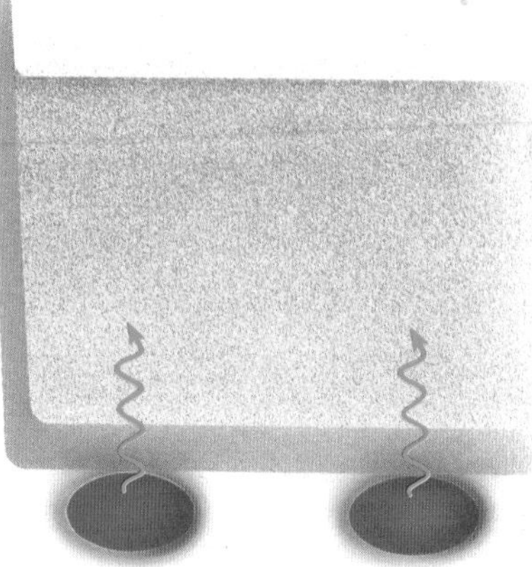

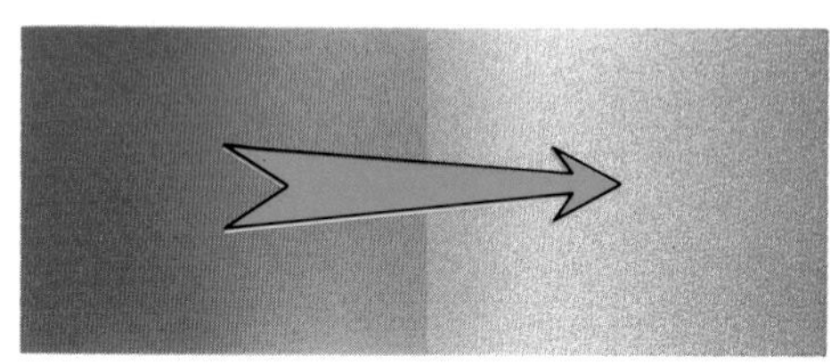

Heat energy flows from hot areas to colder ones.

Heating does not always increase temperature

Temperature is a measure of the speed of movement of the particles in a substance. The higher the kinetic energy of these particles, the higher the temperature. When heat flows into a substance, it may **increase the kinetic energy** of the particles. The temperature goes up. This is what we expect to happen. When we heat something, we expect it to get hotter.

But this is not always the case. Heat flowing into a substance may just **change the arrangement of the particles**. Instead of increasing their kinetic energy, it increases their potential energy. The particles get further away from each other. This is what happens to water at 100 °C. The particles fly away from each other and the water boils. It changes state from a liquid to a gas. While this is happening, the temperature of the water does not change. The heat energy flowing into it does not raise its temperature. It changes its state. This heat energy is called **latent heat**.

So when heat energy flows into a substance, it may increase its temperature, or change the arrangement of its particles, or both. Both of these changes involve a change in the internal energy of the substance. Heating a substance always raises its internal energy.

Temperature and internal energy are not the same

Temperature is related to internal energy. If the temperature of a substance increases, its internal energy increases. But temperature and internal energy are not the same. A hot spark has a higher temperature than a cup of tea. The individual particles in a hot spark have a higher internal energy than the individual particles in a cup of hot tea. But there are *more* particles in the cup of tea. Although each particle in the tea has a lower energy than the particles in the spark, the *total* energy in the cup of tea is greater. So although the temperature of the spark is greater than the cup of tea, the total internal energy of the cup of tea is greater than the spark.

Fig. 29.2 Although the temperature of the sparkler is greater than the tea, the total internal energy of the tea is greater than that of the sparkler.

Measuring changes in internal energy

Heating can cause a rise in temperature. The more particles there are to heat, the more energy is needed to produce the same change in temperature.

For example, it takes 4.2 J of energy to raise the temperature of 1 g of pure water by 1 °C. To raise twice as much water by this amount takes twice as much energy. So it takes 8.4 J of energy to raise the temperature of 2 g of pure water by 1 °C.

The energy needed to raise 1 g of a substance by 1 °C is called the **specific heat capacity** of that substance. The specific heat capacity of water is 4.2 J/g °C.

Specific heat capacities can be measured using the apparatus shown in Figure 29.3. Energy is transferred to the substance in the form of an electric current.

For example, it is found that 4550 J are needed to raise the temperature of 1 kg of aluminium by 5 °C.

The specific heat capacity of aluminium is the number of joules needed to raise 1 g of it by 1 °C.

So the specific heat capacity of

$$\text{aluminium} = \frac{4500\ \text{J}}{5\ ^\circ\text{C} \times 1000\ \text{g}} = \mathbf{0.91\ J/g\ ^\circ C}$$

Fig. 29.3 Measuring specific heat capacity. To measure the electrical energy being transferred to the block, you can use a joule meter. If you do not have one, you need to measure the voltage (usually 6 V or 12 V) and the current (in amperes).
Energy used = voltage x current x time in seconds.

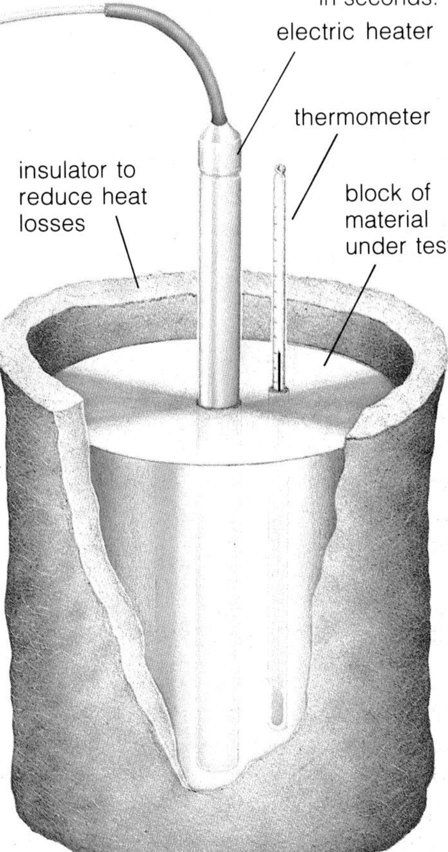

Water has a high specific heat capacity

The specific heat capacity of water is 4.2 J/g °C. This is a high value. It means that a lot of heat energy is needed to produce even a small temperature rise. This makes water a very useful substance for animals and plants. Your body is mostly water (65-70 %). So you have a high specific heat capacity. Large amounts of heat must flow into or out of your body before your temperature changes. This helps you to keep your body temperature constant.

Large bodies of water, such as lakes and the sea, do not change temperature rapidly. You have probably noticed how cold the sea is around Britain, even in summer! Large amounts of heat energy must flow into the sea before its temperature changes much. This makes life easier for the animals and plants which live in water. They do not have to cope with rapid temperature changes.

Questions

1 a An electric storage radiator contains 100 kg of blocks. The specific heat capacity of the blocks is 0.8 J/g °C. How much energy is needed to heat the blocks from 10 °C to 70 °C?

b It takes 3 h for the radiator to cool down to 10 °C again. Does it give out more or less heat than a 1 kW electric fire over this time?

2 In a heating experiment, energy was transferred to 10 kg of water at a power of 42 W. The initial temperature of the water was 10 °C. The results were as follows.

Time (s)	100	200	300	400	500	600
Temp. (°C)	10.1	10.2	10.3	10.4	10.5	10.6

a What is the total temperature rise during the experiment?

b What is the total energy supplied during the experiment?

c What is the specific heat capacity of the water?

3 The specific heat capacity of water is 4.2 J/g °C. The specific heat capacity of concrete is 0.8 J/g °C.

a What mass of water will store 2.52 kJ for a 60 °C rise in temperature?
(Use the equation:
energy = mass x specific heat capacity x temp. rise)

b What mass of concrete will store the same amount of energy under the same conditions?

c The density of water is 1 g/cm^3. The density of concrete is 2.5 g/cm^3.
What volume of concrete would store the same energy as 100 cm^3 of water?

d Is this the reason that concrete and not water is used in storage radiators? Explain your answer.

DID YOU KNOW?

The scientist, James Prescott Joule did many experiments to find out how work caused heating. He is said to have measured the temperature change between the top and bottom of a waterfall on his honeymoon! Joule's experiments show that heat is a form of energy. The unit of energy is named after him.

30 ENERGY STORES

Stored energy is potential energy. Most of our stored energy comes from the Sun.

The Sun provides most of our energy

Sunlight falls on the Earth with a power of nearly 1 kW per square metre. Very little of this energy is used directly by humans. After a series of energy transfers, and perhaps millions of years, it appears in a form that we can store and conveniently transport. After all these transfers, much of this energy is wasted and appears as heat in the surroundings.

Fig. 30.1 Almost all energy on Earth originates from the Sun. Some of this energy becomes stored in forms which we can use.

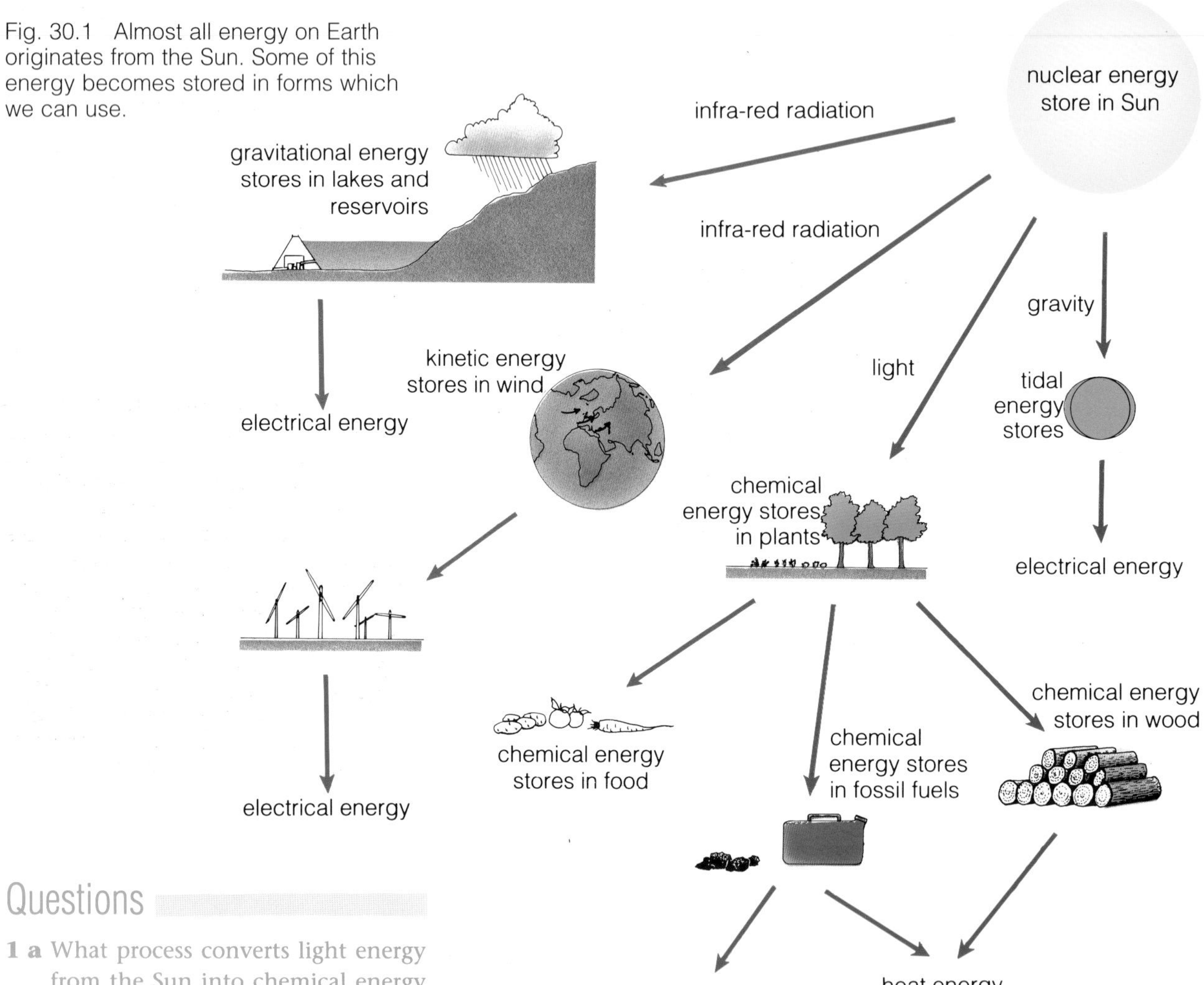

Questions

1 a What process converts light energy from the Sun into chemical energy stores?

b Explain how infra-red radiation from the Sun provides gravitational energy stores in lakes and reservoirs.

c Name one important source of electrical energy which is not included in this diagram.

d What type of chemical reaction converts chemical energy in fossil fuels into heat energy?

DID YOU KNOW?

There is more energy reaching Earth in 10 days of sunlight than in all the fossil fuels on Earth.

Human-made energy stores

Springs and weights can store energy. The weights in a grandfather clock or the spring in a clockwork motor store energy. The work they do is running the clock. A pile driver uses the stored gravitational energy in the weight to drive the piles into the ground. Piles are metal rods used to support building foundations and prevent earth collapsing.

Batteries store chemical energy. This is transferred into electrical energy when a current flows.

An electric central heating radiator has a core of special bricks. These are heated at night when electricity is cheap. Electrical energy is transferred to internal (heat) energy in the bricks. The energy is released throughout the day. In gas or oil central heating, the heat energy is stored in water and pumped around the house.

The Earth also stores energy like this. Rocks contain heat energy. This is called geothermal energy. Geothermal energy can be transferred to water pumped to the rocks. The hot water or steam produced is then pumped away to where it is needed.

Fig 30.2 Part of the Joint European Torus (JET) research torus, shown here under construction. The large flywheels store kinetic energy for later release.

Fig. 30.3a Batteries store chemical energy, which is transferred into electrical energy when a current flows.

Fig. 30.3b The large mass of a pile driver stores gravitational potential energy at the top of its tower.

DID YOU KNOW?

JET, the Joint European Torus, is situated at Culham, near Oxford, in England. It is used for research into fusion power. To start the nuclear reactions required, a very large power input is needed. The National Grid cannot supply the amount needed, so electricity is used to provide energy to set large flywheels spinning. These can take in energy over a long period of time, and store it. The flywheels can then release this energy over a very short period of time, in a huge burst.

Questions

1 When you drink a glass of milk it gives you energy.

  a How did the energy get into the milk? Show all the energy transfers.

  b One argument for vegetarianism is that vegetarians make better use of the Sun's energy falling on to the Earth. Is this true? Explain your answer.

EXTENSION

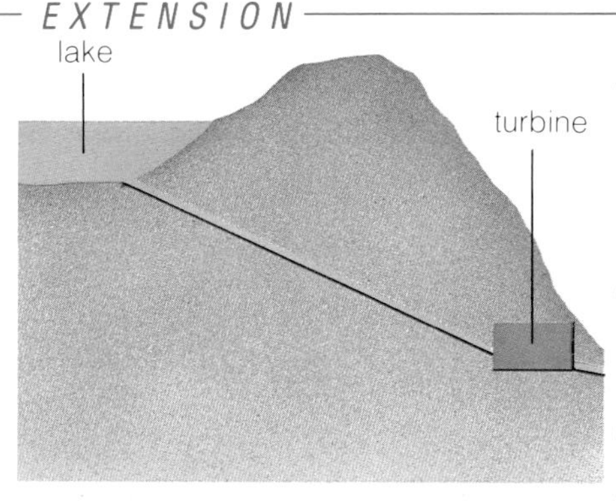

2 A turbine is rather like a propeller. Water pushing past it turns the turbine. This movement can be used to generate electricity.

  a A turbine is 200 m below a lake. How much gravitational energy does each kilogram of water lose as it falls down to the turbine?

  b Where does this energy go? Show all the energy transfers.

  c If 12 500 kg of water fall through the pipe every second, what is the total energy transfer per second?

  d What power (rate of work) does the system produce?

  e Is this the same as the amount of electrical power that could be produced?

  f Where else might some of the energy go?

31 EFFICIENCY

The efficiency of a system describes how good it is at carrying out an energy transfer without wasting energy.

Efficient systems transfer energy without waste

Nearly all energy transfers produce some heat. Unless heat is the required form of energy, this is wasted. The efficiency of a system tells us how much energy is wasted in a system. The efficiency of a system is defined as:

$$\text{efficiency} = \frac{\text{useful output energy}}{\text{total input energy}}$$

This is a ratio, so it has no units.

If a system wastes no energy at all then it has an efficiency of one. This is often multiplied by 100 to give a percentage.

$$\text{percentage efficiency} = \frac{\text{useful output energy}}{\text{total input energy}} \times 100$$

Calculating efficiency

A block is dragged up a slope with a force of 80 N. The block weighs 100 N. The slope is 20 m long and 10 m high.
Energy used = 80 N x 20 m = 1600 J.
Gravitational energy gained = 100 N x 10 m = 1000 J.
Energy 'wasted' = 1600 – 1000 = 600 J.

Notice that the *useful* output energy is 1000 J. But the total energy output is 1600 J.

$$\text{Efficiency} = \frac{1000\text{ J}}{1600\text{ J}} \times 100 = \mathbf{62.5\ \%}$$

So 37.5 % of the energy used in dragging the block up the slope is wasted.

Power stations are about 30 % efficient

An electric fire is very efficient at converting electric energy to heat energy. 1 kJ of electrical energy is converted to 1 kJ of heat energy every second. So an electric fire is 100 % efficient.

But the power station which produced the electricity is much less efficient. For every 100 J stored in the fuel used by the power station, only 30 J of electrical energy is produced. The power station is only 30 % efficient. So perhaps an electric fire is not so efficient after all! 70 % of the energy in the fuel used to produce the electricity to heat the fire is wasted at the power station.

Plants and animals are inefficient energy converters

Plants convert sunlight energy to chemical energy in carbohydrate molecules. The process by which they do this is called **photosynthesis**. Photosynthesis is only 1 % efficient. Only 1 % of the sunlight energy is converted to chemical energy in the plant.

If the plants are fed to sheep, only 10 % of the energy in the plant is converted to energy in the sheep. Sheep, like most animals, are about 10 % efficient in converting the energy in plants to energy in themselves. A lot of energy is lost as heat from the sheep's body.

If a human eats the sheep then only 10 % of the energy in the sheep is transferred to useful energy in the human. Humans are about 10 % efficient in converting the energy in their food into energy in themselves.

So, as a system for converting sunlight energy into useful work, food chains are not very efficient. Only a tiny fraction of the original energy in the sunlight ever reaches the animal at the end of the food chain. This is why food chains are usually quite short.

Fig. 31.1 Energy flows from the Sun, through plants, to animals.

EXTENSION

Questions

1 A light bulb transfers electrical energy to light energy. Electrical energy is transferred to internal energy in the light bulb filament. The tungsten filament reaches 2500 °C. In a light bulb using 100 W of power, only 20 J of light energy is produced per second. How efficient is the light bulb?

2 The newer type of light bulb, which contains a coiled up fluorescent tube, is more energy efficient. A 25 W new bulb produces the same output as an old-style 100 W bulb. How efficient is this type of light bulb?

EXTENSION

DID YOU KNOW?

If everyone in Britain replaced one light bulb in the house with an energy efficient light bulb, the energy saved would be enough to light the whole of Scotland.

Engines

A heat engine converts internal (heat) energy to useful work. Usually, the heat comes from burning a fuel. The earliest heat engine was the steam engine. The first steam engines were only 1 % efficient. A modern car petrol engine is about 20 % efficient. A diesel engine is 40 % efficient.

Heat engines usually have a lot of moving parts. So a lot of energy is lost because of friction. But even if friction could be completely eliminated, there is a limit on the engine's efficiency. The efficiency depends on the running temperature of the engine. The hotter the engine runs, the more efficient it will be. But the components of most engines cannot safely be heated to more than about 1100 °C. The maximum efficiency possible at this temperature is 75 %. Friction and other losses actually reduces this to between 25 % and 40 %.

A new type of engine, made of ceramics, has been built in Japan. This engine can be safely run at much higher temperatures than metal engines. It is much more efficient. It produces as much power from a 1600 cc engine as a normal 6000 cc engine.

Questions

1 An electric kettle uses 2.4 kW and runs for 100 s.

a If the water it heats gains 228 kJ in this time, how efficient is the kettle?

b Where has the wasted energy gone?

c The kettle is made from polished stainless steel. Would it be more or less efficient if it was made from dark blue plastic?

2 A gas fire has a power input of 6.6 kW. It provides 4 kW of room heating.

a How efficient is the gas fire?

b What energy transfers take place?

c In what form is the wasted energy?

d Where does the waste energy go?

e How does the efficiency of the gas fire compare with an electric fire?

f In answering question **e**, what other energy transfers need to be considered?

EXTENSION

3 A builder has two choices when he needs to lift bricks. He can pull them up himself using a pulley, or he can use an electric motor.

The diagrams show these two alternatives.

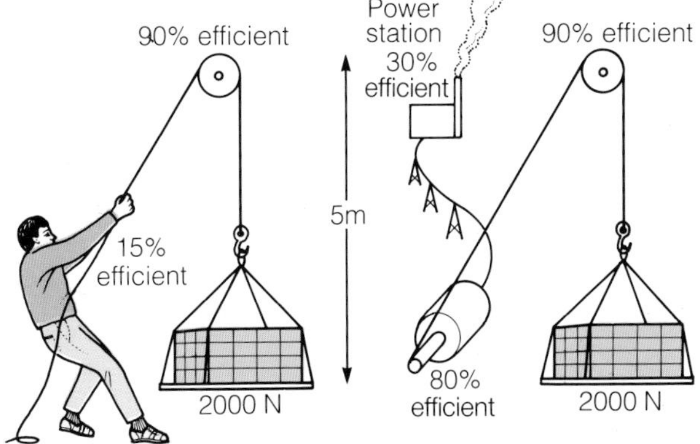

a What amount of chemical energy must the builder supply if he uses the pulley system to lift the bricks?

b What amount of electrical energy does the motor require from the power station to lift the bricks?

4 A food processor has a 400 W motor. A belt drives the blades around at 300 revolutions per minute. Each blade is 10 cm long.

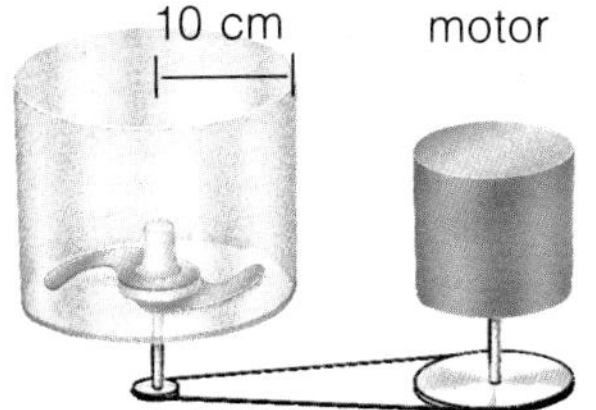

A food processor, with its outer casing removed.

a How many revolutions do the blades make in 1 s?

b How far does a blade travel in one second? (Circumference of a circle = $2\pi r$).

c If the motor and blade system is 75 % efficient, what is the useful work output?

d How much energy does the system transfer as useful work in 1 s?

e What force can the blade tips exert? (Energy = force x distance.)

f Why do food processors need safety switches?

5 A diesel electric train has a diesel engine that drives a generator that drives the electric motors which drive the wheels.

a If the diesel engine is 40 % efficient, the generator is 75 % efficient and the electric motor is 80 % efficient, estimate the maximum efficiency of the train.

b Draw a diagram to show the energy transfers in the train.

32 HEAT TRANSFER

Heat is thermal energy being transferred. It is transferred by three processes. Conduction transfers heat in all materials, convection transfers heat in fluids, and radiation needs no material at all.

Heat is transferred by conduction, convection and radiation

Heat energy can travel in three ways. **Conduction** transfers heat through any kind of material, although some materials are much better conductors than others. **Convection** transfers heat in liquids or gases. **Radiation** transfers heat even when no material is present at all. Heat from the Sun reaches us as radiation, which travels through space.

Metals are very good conductors of heat

Metals are made up of atoms which hold their electrons very loosely. Some of the electrons are free to move around the lattice structure. These electrons can carry the vibrational energy through the lattice more easily than phonons.

Mercury is a liquid so it ought to be a poor conductor of heat. But it is also a metal. The free electrons are able to carry the heat energy through the liquid. So mercury is actually a good heat conductor.

Another liquid metal – liquid sodium – is used as a heat conductor in nuclear power stations and some car engines. The valves in a car engine open and close to let gases in and out of the cylinders. The explosions in the cylinders make the valves very hot. Temperatures of around 700 °C are reached. It is important to stop the valves from overheating. In some cars the valve stems are hollow and contain sodium. When the valves get hot, the sodium melts. The molten sodium carries the heat away from the valve heads.

Conduction transfers heat through materials

Conduction happens in all materials. Conduction is a direct transfer of the vibrational energy of atoms.

In solids the atoms are rigidly held together. If some atoms start vibrating more than others, the vibration will be passed through the structure. Vibrational waves or 'phonons' pass the increased vibration through the material. If you heat one end of a rod, the energy is passed down the rod through the bonds between the particles.

In liquids the particles are further apart. So they do not conduct heat so easily. Most liquids are poor conductors of heat.

In gases the particles are very far apart. So gases are very poor conductors of heat.

Fig. 32.1 Vibrating atoms in one part of a material pass on their vibrations to atoms close to them. This is how heat is conducted.

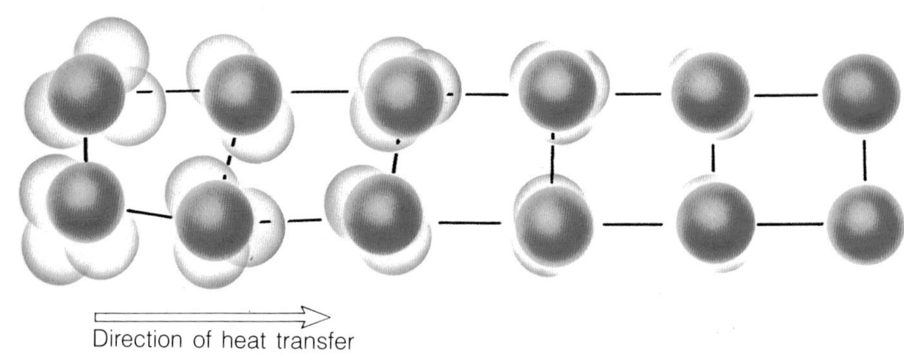

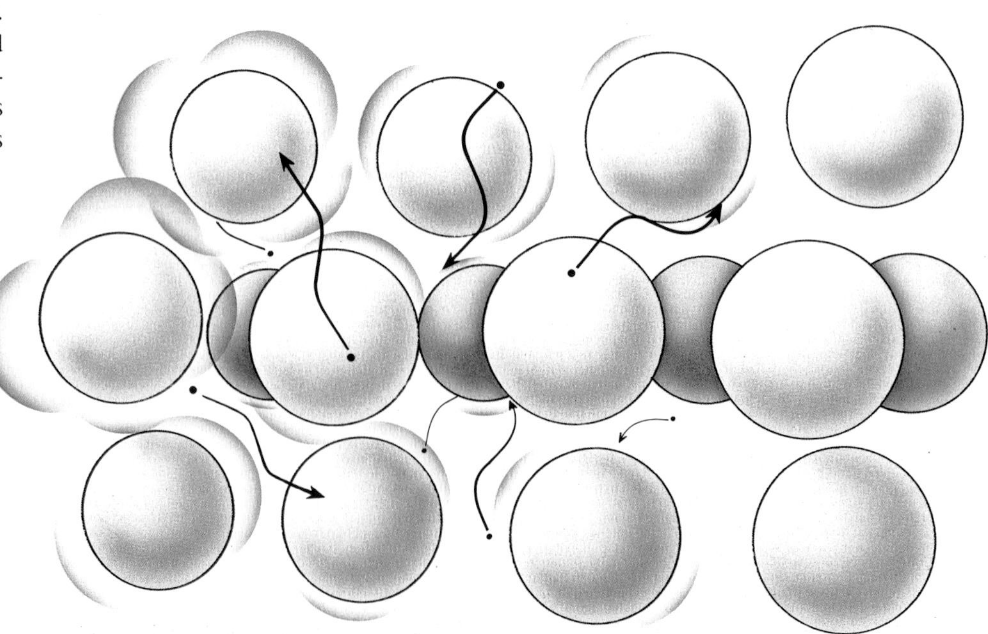

Fig 32.2 Metals contain freely-moving electrons, which transfer heat energy easily through the metal. At higher temperatures these electrons have more kinetic energy and move faster.

Substances which only conduct heat slowly are called insulators

Substances which are bad conductors of heat are called **insulators**. Materials which trap air inside themselves are good insulators. Air is a gas so it is a poor conductor of heat. Wood contains a lot of air, and is a good insulator. Fur is also a good insulator. Each hair contains trapped air. Fur can be made an even better insulator by raising the hairs on end, so that more air is trapped *between* the hairs.

The American space shuttle gets very hot as it travels quickly through the Earth's atmosphere. It is covered with special tiles which are good insulators. They stop the shuttle from overheating. You could heat one of these tiles with a blow lamp and pick it up straight away without burning yourself! Although the tile is very hot, it does not allow heat to travel from itself into your hand. It is a good insulator.

Convection transfers heat in fluids

If you drop a potassium permanganate crystal into a beaker of water, colour begins to spread into the water as the particles dissolve. If you heat the water, you can see the colour rise through the water.

Why does this happen? The heat energy transferred to the water increases the internal energy of the water and potassium permanganate particles. They get further away from each other. The water expands. This warmer water is now less dense than the colder water at the top of the beaker. So it rises upwards. People often say that 'heat rises'. This is not really true. The heat energy does not rise on its own. The *hot water* rises, and takes the energy with it.

So when one part of a fluid is hotter than another part, the hot part tends to move upwards. This movement is called **convection**. The currents produced are called **convection currents**. Convection currents circulate around the fluid. They spread the energy through the fluid. Fluids include liquids and gases.

Fig. 32.3 Convection transfers heat in fluids.

Winds are caused by convection currents

During the day, the land warms up more than the sea. This is because water has a high specific heat capacity. It takes a lot of heat to raise its temperature by only a small amount.

The warm air over the land rises. Cold air over the sea moves in to replace it. So during the day, breezes tend to blow from the sea on to the land.

At night the land cools down faster than the sea. The warmer air over the sea rises. Cold air over the land moves in to replace it. So during the night, breezes tend to blow from the land on to the sea.

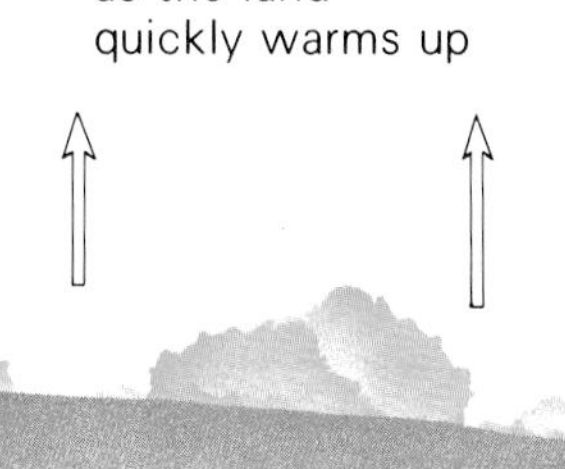

Fig. 32.4 During the day, sea breezes blow on to land.

This happens on a larger scale, too. The air near the equator heats up more than air near the poles. The hot air over the equator rises. Cooler air from the north and south moves in to replace it. This sets up air movements which cause winds.

Convection currents spread heat through a room

Central heating 'radiators' are badly named. They do not actually radiate much heat at all. They warm the air around them. This hot air rises. Cold air in the room moves towards the radiator to replace it. The radiator heats this cold air, so it rises. Convection currents are set up in the room, drawing cold air towards the 'radiator' and carrying warm air away from it.

Convection currents were used to ventilate mines. Air at the bottom of one shaft was heated. The hot air rose up the shaft. Cold air moved down another shaft and along the tunnels to replace the hot air.

Heat can be transferred as infra-red radiation

Changes in the internal energy of particles cause changes in the way in which atoms are arranged. These changes cause the atoms to emit energy in the form of **electromagnetic radiation**.

When an electric current flows through a lamp filament, it causes it to emit electromagnetic radiation. Some of this is high-energy radiation, which we see as light. But some of this radiation has a lower energy. It is called **infra-red radiation**. You cannot see infra-red radiation. But if it falls on to your skin it raises the temperature of your skin. Heat can be transferred by infra-red radiation. A filament lamp only produces 20 % of its energy as light. The remaining 80 % is infra-red radiation or heat. An electric fire produces even more of its energy as heat. Electric fires usually have a reflector behind the bars, to bounce the heat into the room.

Fig. 32.5 The element of an electric fire gets hot as an electric current flows through it, and produces infra-red radiation.

Black surfaces are the best radiators of heat

If two cans, one silver and one black, are filled with hot water, the black one will cool down faster than the silver one. This is because the black surface radiates heat away from the can faster than the silver surface. The best radiating surfaces are black.

A black surface looks black because it absorbs most of the light which falls on to it.

A lot of the light energy is radiated from the surface as heat, which you cannot see.

A good radiating surface also absorbs energy well. If you paint part of your hand black, and hold your hand in front of a fire, you will find that the black part feels hotter than the rest. The black part absorbs more heat.

Car radiators are used to keep the engine cool. They are painted black, so that they lose heat quickly. Kettles are usually made of shiny metal. This is so that they do not lose heat quickly.

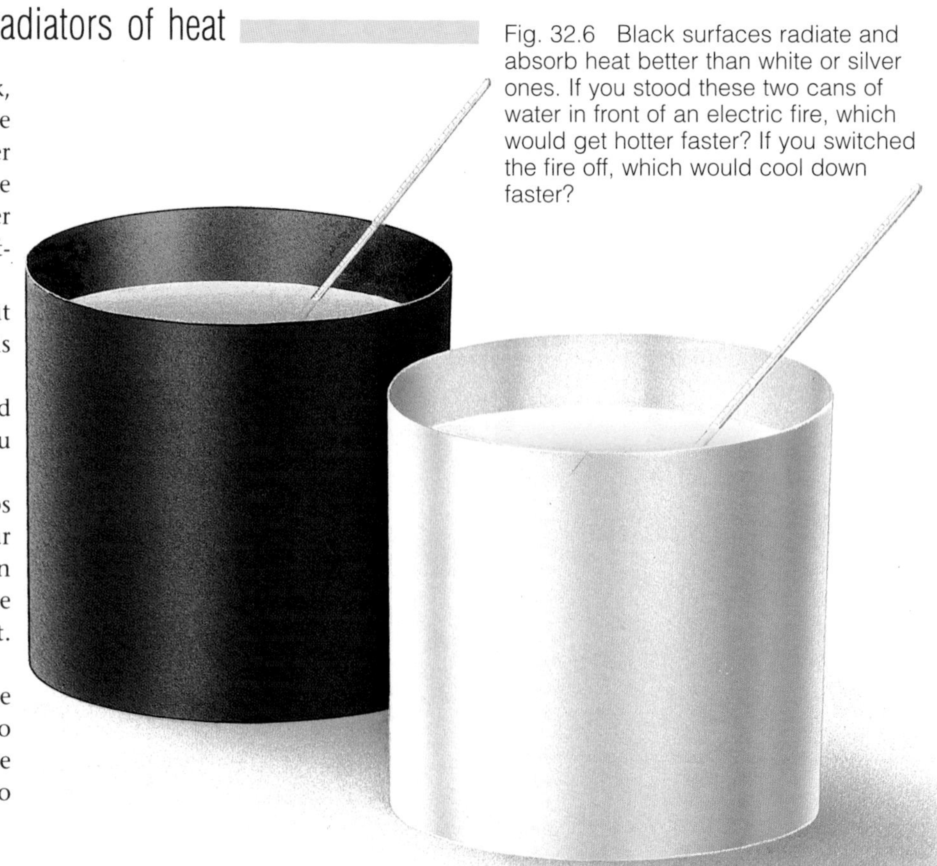

Fig. 32.6 Black surfaces radiate and absorb heat better than white or silver ones. If you stood these two cans of water in front of an electric fire, which would get hotter faster? If you switched the fire off, which would cool down faster?

Radiation travels in straight lines

Radiated heat travels in straight lines. If you sit facing a fire, the radiated heat from the fire warms your face. But your back will feel cold.

So radiation is not a good way of heating a whole room. It only heats those parts of the room which the radiation can reach in a straight line. Convection is a better way of heating a space.

Radiation does not need to travel through a material

Electromagnetic radiation does not need any material to travel through. It can pass through a vacuum. The energy we receive from the Sun is radiated to us.

Fig. 32.7 The woman's body is in thermal equilibrium with the surroundings. Her back is absorbing extra energy from the fire so it will have settled at a higher temperature than her front. The hot drink is losing more energy than it is absorbing from the room and is cooling down.

Everything radiates and absorbs at the same time

Objects radiate more energy as they get hotter. This energy is called **thermal radiation**. A paper clip heated in a Bunsen flame eventually radiates some energy that can be seen. As it gets hotter the colour changes and the metal starts to glow. It is also giving off a lot of energy that you can't see. Out of the flame it quickly cools. It is giving off more radiation than it is receiving from the room. When the temperature stops falling, the clip is absorbing as much energy from the room as it is radiating back. It has reached **thermal equilibrium** with its surroundings.

Questions

1 A central heating radiator is a thin aluminium or steel container full of hot water.

a Why does its surface feel hot to the touch?

b How does the radiator heat the air in contact with its surface?

c What happens to the hot air?

d Explain how the radiator heats the whole room.

e If you hold your hands in front of the radiator, without touching it, how are your hands heated?

f Why are radiators not painted matt black?

g Why are the inlet and outlet pipes of a radiator at the bottom, not the top?

h Why do radiators have a small outlet valve at the top?

2 An electric oven has heating elements in its walls, which release heat energy as electricity flows through them.

a Give the name of the process by which heat is transferred through the walls of the oven.

b Explain this process, in terms of the molecules in the oven walls. A diagram may help you to do this.

c How is the heat transferred from the walls of the oven into the air inside it?

d The inside surfaces of the oven walls are usually coloured black. Suggest why this is done.

e If you are cooking a dish which needs an especially high temperature, your recipe may tell you to put it on the top shelf of the oven. Why should you do this?

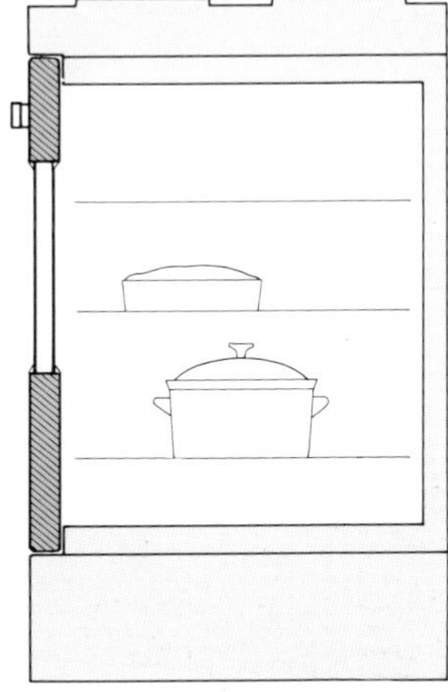

f The diagram shows a section through the door of the oven. It is double glazed – which means it is made of two sheets of glass with an air gap between them. Explain how the double glazing cuts down the amount of heat which is lost from the oven.

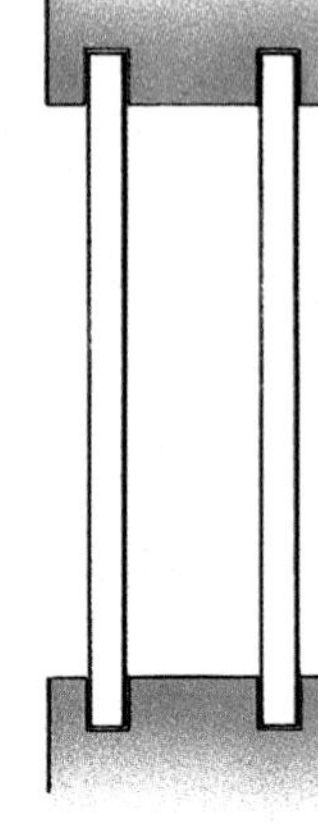

3 A crystal of potassium permanganate is dropped into a can of water.

a If the can was left alone, the colour from the crystal would gradually spread through the water. Name, and then briefly describe, the two processes which would cause this to happen.

b If the can was heated from below, convection currents would be produced in the water. Make a diagram to show the pattern of these currents. Explain why the currents make this pattern.

c Two of these cans were painted, one red and one black. They were then heated until the water in them was at 80 °C. Would you expect the water in the two cans to cool at the same rate? Explain your answer.

4 Explain why:

a Air is a poor conductor of heat.

b On a hot day, you may feel cooler if you wear white clothes than if you wear dark ones.

c It is more comfortable to stir a hot stew with a wooden spoon than with a metal one.

d Hot air balloons designed to travel very long distances are often coloured silver.

33 CONTROLLING HEAT FLOW

Insulators slow down the transfer of energy from hot to cold bodies.

Fins are used for cooling by radiation

Most animals are poikilothermic. This means that their body temperature is the same as their surroundings. If it is hot, they are hot. If it is cold, they are cold.

Reptiles are poikilothermic. If the air temperature is high, their body temperature is also high. This makes their metabolic reactions take place at a faster rate. They are more active. It is thought that the large fins on the backs of dinosaurs like *Dimetrodon* might have helped them to warm up quickly in the morning. If they stood sideways on to the sun, the large area of the fin would absorb radiated heat. This would raise their body temperature, and make them more active. Butterflies do this, too. On a cool day, a butterfly will rest with its wings outstretched, at right angles to the sun's rays. This warms its body and makes it more active. Large fins can also be used to *lose* heat by convection, conduction and radiation. *Dimetrodon's* fin might have been used for this on hot days. It would have stood end on to the sun's rays. Air-cooled engines also have fins. Heat is lost from the large surface area of the fins into the air.

Fig. 33.1 *Dimetrodon*. The large fin is believed to have been useful in controlling body temperature. Energy would be absorbed as radiation, or lost by radiation and convection in the air.

INVESTIGATION 33.1

Penguins

Penguins living in very cold regions around the Antarctic often huddle together to keep warm. Using test tubes full of water to represent penguins, design an experiment to find out if huddling together helps penguins to retain their body heat.

Insulation saves energy

Mammals and birds are **homeothermic** animals. They can keep their body temperature high, even when outside temperatures are low. They use food to generate heat inside their bodies. This uses a lot of food, so homeothermic animals need to make sure that they do not lose too much of this heat. As it is, they have to eat a lot more food than poikilothermic animals. It is important to save as much as internal energy as possible so as not to waste food which might be difficult to obtain.

Layers of fat or blubber around the animal's body act as insulators. They slow down loss of heat energy. Fur and feathers are also good insulators. Thick layers of fur trap air, which is a very poor conductor of heat. In cold weather, animals and birds may fluff up their fur or feathers. This traps even more air, and increases the insulation. Humans do not have much fur! We make up for it by wearing clothing. Wool is a good insulator because wool fibres trap air. Woollen clothing stops the heat generated inside your body from escaping. Cotton is not such a good insulator because the fibres don't trap much air. Cotton is good to wear in summer when you actually want to *lose* heat from your body. If you really want to keep warm, many thin layers of clothes are better than one or two thick ones. Air is trapped between each layer. The more layers, the better the insulation.

Fig. 33.2 The thick layer of fat, and the fur which traps air, insulates the polar bear.

Small objects lose their internal energy faster than large ones

Fig. 33.3 How surface area changes with volume.

This block has sides of 1 cm. What is its surface area? What is its volume?

This block has sides of 5 cm. What is its surface area? What is its volume?

Which block has the greatest ratio of surface area to volume? What can you say about the way in which this ratio changes as things get bigger?

Energy is lost through surfaces. The larger the surface area, the faster the rate of energy loss.

A small animal has a larger surface area for its size than a big animal. A polar bear, for example has a very large volume. It also has a large surface area. But most of a polar bear is 'inside . Its volume is large compared to its surface area. A shrew has a very small volume. It also has a small surface area. But a lot of a shrew is 'outside'. A shrew's surface area is large compared to its volume. Both polar bears and shrews are homeothermic animals. They generate heat inside their bodies. A polar bear is much bigger than a shrew, so it generates a lot more heat. And not very much of this heat escapes from the polar bear, because its surface area is small compared to its volume. But the small shrew generates much less heat. And a lot of this heat escapes from its relatively large surface area.

So small animals have problems keeping warm. They lose heat quickly through their relatively large surface area. A shrew has to eat its own weight in food every day, just to generate enough heat to keep warm. A polar bear can manage by just eating one seal every few days.

Human babies have large surface areas compared to their volumes. They lose heat easily. Small babies must be wrapped up well in cold temperatures.

Vacuum flasks reduce heat flow between the contents and the air

A vacuum flask is made of two containers inside one another, and separated by a vacuum. (There is usually another covering on the outside, to make it stronger and to look attractive.) The surfaces of both containers are shiny. They are made from glass or stainless steel.

These shiny surfaces reduce energy transfer by radiation. The vacuum between them prevents heat loss by conduction. (Remember – conduction only happens through materials.) A small amount of energy is conducted up the sides of the inner wall. This is kept as small as possible by making the sides of the walls very thin.

So if hot coffee is put into a vacuum flask, it is difficult for heat to be transferred from the coffee to the air. The coffee stays hot. If liquid nitrogen at −196 °C is put into a vacuum flask, it is difficult for heat to be transferred from the air into the liquid nitrogen. The liquid nitrogen stays cold. Vacuum flasks are just as good at keeping things cold as keeping things hot. A flask of ice-cold orange juice will stay cold for a long time, even on a hot day.

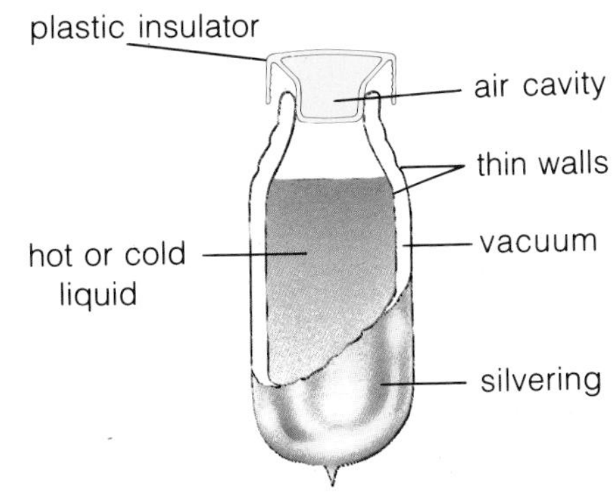

Fig. 33.4 A vacuum flask, with its outer covering removed.

Heat pumps reverse the normal direction of heat flow

Heat normally flows from objects with a high temperature to objects with lower temperatures. But heat pumps can make heat flow the other way.

Even cold water at 3 °C has a lot of energy in it. If the water was made even cooler, some of this energy could be taken from it. This is what a heat pump does. It cools down substances that we might already think of as 'cold'. The energy taken from the substance can be used for heating. For example, the water in the river Thames, in England, provides heat energy for heating the Festival Hall in London. Heat pumps take energy from the cold water, making it even colder. Enough energy is obtained from the water to heat the whole building. The heat pump uses power to take the heat from the water. But for every 100 W of electricity it uses, it can produce 300 W of heat.

EXTENSION

DID YOU KNOW?

Ten people dancing generate more heat than a gas fire. Even at a winter party, you will probably need to open a few windows!

Questions

1 Explain why:

a Thin people tend to feel the cold more than fat people.

b It is important for old people to eat well in winter.

c Homeothermic animals need to eat far more than poikilothermic animals of similar size.

d Supermarkets usually display frozen goods in chest freezers rather than upright freezers. (Clue – think what happens when the door is opened.)

e Several layers of thin clothes will keep you warmer than two layers of thick ones.

f Large penguins are found at the South Pole and smaller ones are found further away.

34 FRICTION

Whenever there is motion there is some friction, except in space. This means that all energy transfers involving movement produce some heat as well.

Friction is a force which results from surfaces in contact

The particles in materials often attract one another when the materials are in contact. So when one surface is dragged over another, work has to be done against this force of attraction. The energy transferred often causes heating. Rough materials have a larger frictional force than smooth ones. This is because the ridges and grooves on the surfaces catch on one another. There is also attraction between the particles.

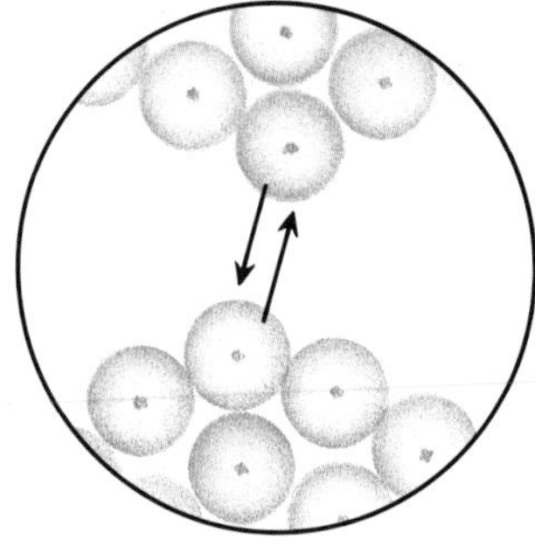

Fig. 34.1 Friction acts when surfaces move over one another.

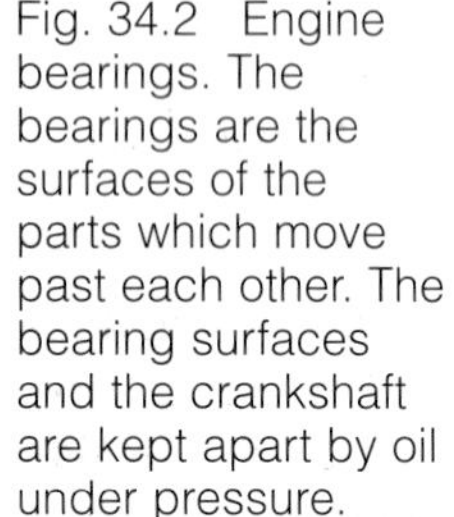

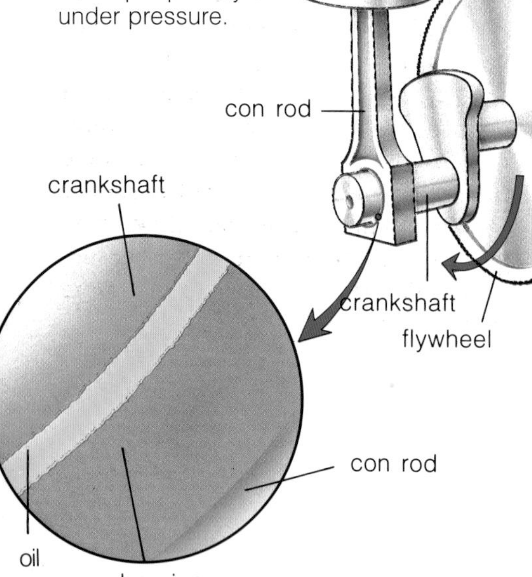

Fig. 34.2 Engine bearings. The bearings are the surfaces of the parts which move past each other. The bearing surfaces and the crankshaft are kept apart by oil under pressure.

Friction produces heat

When a match is dragged across the side of the matchbox, the friction between the match head and the rough surface raises the internal energy of the chemicals in the match head. This ignites them. The chemicals in the match head burn.

This is a useful heating effect. But often friction is a nuisance. It wastes energy and causes wear. In a car engine the moving parts are kept apart from each other by a layer of oil. The oil is a **lubricant**. A lubricant is a substance which reduces friction between two moving surfaces. As the piston moves up and down it causes the crankshaft to rotate inside the connecting rod (con rod). The con rod and crankshaft have oil between them to keep the surfaces separate and reduce friction. But, all the same, they will sometimes touch. So the con rod is lined with a **bearing** made of a soft alloy. If the moving surfaces make contact, the soft alloy will not damage the surface of the crankshaft. The soft bearing can be replaced if it wears out.

Braking systems make use of friction

A car braking system uses friction to slow down the rotation of the wheels. Asbestos-based pads or shoes push against metal discs. Friction between the pads and the discs slows down movement between them. It transfers the kinetic energy of the car to internal energy in the metal. If the car is travelling fast, the kinetic energy is very high. It could be as much as 1.5 MJ. So the amount of energy transferred is also very high. The discs can get very hot. Powerful cars and motorbikes have ventilated brake discs. This allows some of this energy to be lost to the air. This means that the kinetic energy of the moving car or motorbike can be transferred to thermal energy more quickly, without overheating the brakes. It is important that brake pads or shoes should not conduct heat to the brake mechanism. Heat can damage the brake mechanism and melt rubber or boil the fluid. The pads are made of asbestos, which is a good insulator. Some brakes are designed to be able to operate safely even when the discs are so hot that they are glowing!

DID YOU KNOW?

Manufacturers often quote the 'Cd' of a car. The Cd, or drag coefficient, shows how 'slippy' the *shape* is. A pea and a football are the same shape, so they have the same Cd. But the frictional force on a car also depends on its *size*. To know how much frictional force there is on a car, you need to know its size as well as its Cd. Some lorries have a Cd that is smaller than some cars!

Fluids can also cause friction

We often use liquids as lubricants. Liquids such as oil can reduce friction between solid surfaces. But liquids can also *cause* friction. 'Fluids' include gases and liquids. Anything moving through a fluid experiences fluid friction. The particles of the fluid have to be pushed aside by the moving object.

A fan can be used to blow air over a car to simulate the car moving through air. The layer of air next to the car is still. This is because the air molecules are attracted to the surface of the car. Further away from the car the air molecules move faster. So layers of air at different distances from the car are moving at different speeds. These layers have to slide over one another. The molecules in each layer attract one another. This produces friction between the layers.

You can see the same effect as water flows in a river. At the edge, there is friction between the water and the bank. In the centre, the water flows faster.

Fig. 34.3 To reduce air friction, it is important to have a smooth flow of air over the surface of a car. The unbroken stream of smoke shows how successfully this has been achieved.

Fig. 34.4 Friction in a river. Where the water flows near the bank it is slowed down. The water flows faster in the middle. The water in the middle flows past water near the edges, and friction acts between the flows of different speeds. This slows all of the water.

Air can be used as a lubricant

Instead of oil, air can be pumped between moving surfaces to reduce friction. This produces a very smooth bearing. A hovercraft moves on a cushion of air which keeps it above the surface over which it is moving. This reduces friction. But a lot of energy is required to 'levitate' the hovercraft. So not much energy is saved. The real benefit of this system is that the hovercraft can move over most surfaces.

Viscosity is internal friction in a fluid

In any moving fluid, there is friction between the layers which are moving at different speeds. This friction inside the fluid is called **viscosity**. Thick liquids, such as syrup, have high viscosity. We say that they are **viscous**. Thin liquids are less viscous. Low viscosity engine oils are more runny than some other oils. They still reduce the surface friction in the engine, but they cause less fluid friction than a thicker oil. This makes the car easier to get going in cold weather.

EXTENSION

At constant speed, force produced by a car's engine balances air resistance

When a car is travelling at a constant speed, the forces on the car balance. The force pushing the car forwards is the force provided by the engine. The force pushing the car backwards is air resistance. These forces are moving, so work is being done.

Imagine a car travelling at 160 km/h, with its engine supplying 44 kW of power. At this speed, the car travels about 44 m in a second. The engine supplies 44 kJ every second. So we can calculate the force provided by the engine as follows:

energy in joules = force in newtons x distance in metres

$$\text{so force in newtons} = \frac{\text{energy in joules}}{\text{distance in metres}}$$

$$\text{force} = \frac{44\ 000}{44} = 1000\,\text{N}$$

This is the forward force produced by the engine. It balances the air resistance on the car. So the air resistance is also 1000 N.

This frictional force on the car produces a lot of heating. 44 kJ of energy is transferred every second – a power of 44 kW. This is enough to raise 100 g of water to boiling point every second! The air and the car's body are warmed by this energy transfer.

Questions

1 a List as many examples as you can where friction is a nuisance and as many examples as you can where friction is useful.

b How do we try to increase or reduce friction in each case?

2 A match is struck with a force of 4 N. The distance that the match head moves across the box is 5 cm.

a How much energy is used in striking the match?

b If it takes 0.5 s to pull the match across the box, what power does it take to strike the match?

3 A manufacturer claims that his thinner oil will save petrol if used in your car.

a How can using oil save petrol?

b How would you test the manufacturer's claim?

35 PRESSURE

Pressure increases with applied force. If a force is concentrated on a small area, this produces a large pressure.

Pressure is force divided by area

If you push hard on a drawing pin, you can push the point into a wooden table top. If you pushed the pin when it was upside down, the point would go into you. Why?

Look at Figure 35.1. The *force* between your finger and the pin is nearly the *same* as the force between the pin and the table top. But the *area* over which this force acts is *different*. The force between your finger and the pin is spread all over the top of the drawing pin. This is quite a large area. But the force between the pin and the table is concentrated in the point of the pin. This is a much smaller area. When a force is spread over a large area, it produces a small **pressure**. If the same force is concentrated over a small area, it produces a larger pressure.

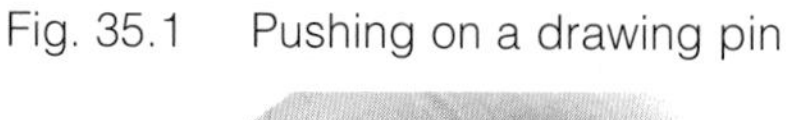
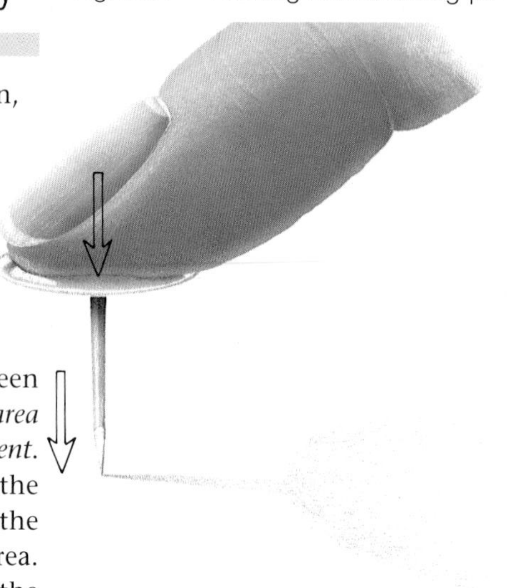

Fig. 35.1 Pushing on a drawing pin

Fig. 35.2 The surface area of the end of a brick is 60 cm^2. The surface area of the base of a brick is 200 cm^2. Each brick weighs 5 kg. What pressure is each of these bricks exerting on the ground?

> The pressure depends on the force applied, and the area over which this force is spread. **Pressure = force / area**
>
> Pressure is measured in **pascals (Pa)**. 1 pascal is a force of 1 N spread over an area of 1 m^2 (using the force acting at right angles to the surface).
>
> $$\text{Pressure in pascals} = \frac{\text{force in newtons}}{\text{area in m}^2}$$
>
> For example, if a force of 10 N is applied to an area of 0.1m^2, then the pressure is $\frac{10\text{ N}}{0.1\text{ m}^2} = 100$ Pa

If you squeeze a gas, it becomes squashed. Try squeezing a bicycle pump with your finger over the end. The plunger will go in a long way, as the gas particles squeeze closer together. If you try again with water in the pump instead of air, the plunger will not move much. If you squeeze a liquid, it hardly changes volume at all.

In a gas, the particles are far apart and can easily be pushed closer. In a liquid, the particles are already very close. Large forces are needed to push them even a little closer. Because the liquid is not squashed, most of the force at one end is passed on to the other. You can feel this with the bicycle pump. A large force on the bicycle pump full of water requires a strong thumb over the end! The water seems to push very hard on your thumb.

Fig. 35.3 Liquids such as water transmit forces from one place to another.

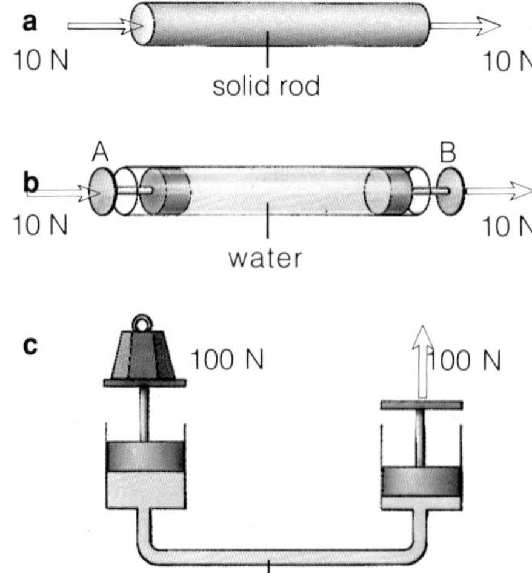

Pressure changes with the depth of a liquid. At the bottom of a swimming pool you can feel the extra weight of the water pushing on your eardrums. The extra weight of water above you increases the sideways pressure into your ears as well as onto your head. Pressure is the same in all directions at the same depth. This makes liquids and pipes a useful way of transmitting forces from one place to another.

Figure 35.3 shows water in a pipe. Piston A is pushing on the water, producing pressure. The water is not squashed and the pressure at the other end is the same. The pressure on piston B is the same as the pressure on A.

When you push on a liquid contained in a pipe, it is like pushing on a solid. The difference is that the liquid can transmit the force around corners. This is a really useful system of transmitting forces from one place to another. It is called a hydraulic system. 'Hydraulic' means 'to do with water'.

EXTENSION

Hydraulic systems can produce a greater force from the same pressure

You will remember that pressure depends on force and area.

Pressure = force / area

So Force = pressure x area

So if you exert a particular pressure on a *large* area, you will produce a *larger* force than if the same pressure was exerted on a small area. By changing the area that a liquid acts against, large forces can be produced. An example is in the braking system of a car.

In a car it is important to be able to stop quickly. Friction pads are pushed against moving discs or drums to slow the car down. The earliest type of car linked the pads to the brake pedal with cables and levers. But the best way to get forces to go round corners is to use hydraulics. A hydraulic system does not have complicated joints to wear out. The pistons in the calipers are larger than the piston in the master cylinder. The pressure in the pipes is the same. So the force on the pads is larger than the force on the pedal, because the pressure pushes on a larger area.

In use, friction can make the disc brake very hot. The fluid in the brake system is a special oil, not water. Can you suggest why this is?

Fig. 35.4 The hydraulic brake system of a car. A relatively small force exerted on the brake pedal produces a larger force on the brakes. The brake pads are pushed against the disc, causing a frictional force which stops the axle turning.

Fig 35.5 Forces are transferred around this digger through hydraulic pipes. The wide tyres help spread the load when driving on soft ground.

Air exerts pressure

The Earth is surrounded by a layer of air about 120 km deep. The air pushes in on objects at ground level with a pressure of 100 000 N/m^2. This is 100 000 pascals, or 100 kilopascals. A kilopascal, kPa for short, is 1000 pascals.

We are not crushed by this air pressure (atmospheric pressure) because the air inside us pushes outwards as hard as the air outside us pushes inwards. So we are not aware of the pressure at all.

As with a liquid, the pressure varies with depth. We tend to notice more that pressure decreases as you go up. You are already at the bottom of the atmosphere! Pressure changes can make your ears 'pop' when you fly.

Vacuum cleaners and lungs fill by lowering the air pressure inside them

Vacuum cleaners and lungs use air pressure to fill themselves with air. A vacuum cleaner works by removing some of the air inside itself. This reduces the air pressure inside it. So the air pressure outside is greater than the air pressure inside it. The air pressure outside the vacuum cleaner pushes air into it, taking bits of dirt with it.

When you breathe in, your rib and diaphragm muscles make the volume inside your chest larger. So the air inside you is spread over a larger space. This makes its pressure smaller. The air pressure outside you is now greater than the air pressure inside you. Just as with a vacuum cleaner, the air pressure outside you pushes air into your lungs.

Questions

1 Use what you know about pressure to explain the following.

a Snow shoes and skis stop you sinking into snow.

b A dam is always built with the base thicker than the top.

c Reindeer have broad feet.

d A brick wall should be built on a concrete foundation at least twice the width of the wall.

e Ice skates can do a great deal of damage to floor surfaces and to fingers.

2 a A person weighs 600 N. They are wearing shoes with a total area of 0.02 m^2. What pressure do they exert on the floor?

b If the same person wears stiletto heels, with an area of 0.00003 m^2, what pressure do they exert on the floor?

c What effect would this have on a wooden floor?

3 A brake master cylinder piston has an area of 1 cm^2. The piston in the brakes has an area of 4 cm^2. The master cylinder is pushed with a force of 600 N (see Figure 35.4).

a What is the pressure on the master cylinder piston?

b What is the pressure on the brake piston?

c What is the force applied to the brake pads?

EXTENSION

36 PRESSURE, VOLUME AND TEMPERATURE

Decreasing the volume of a gas increases its pressure and temperature.

Temperature changes with the speed of molecules

Atoms and molecules are always moving. As particles get hotter, they move faster. The temperature of a particular particle can tell us how quickly it is moving.

Look at Figure 36.1a. It shows a container full of gas. A piston seals the top. The piston does not drop down because the gas molecules keep hitting its surface and bouncing off. This produces a force on the piston. We say that the gas exerts a pressure on the piston.

You are surrounded by a mixture of gases called air. The molecules in the air produce **atmospheric pressure**. As you sit reading this book, millions of molecules are bouncing off your face with a velocity of about 3000 km/h. This produces the same force as a 100 kg mass resting on your face!

So why do you not feel it? The force is spread evenly all over your face. And there is an equal and opposite force pushing outwards from inside you to balance the atmospheric pressure. So you are not aware of it at all.

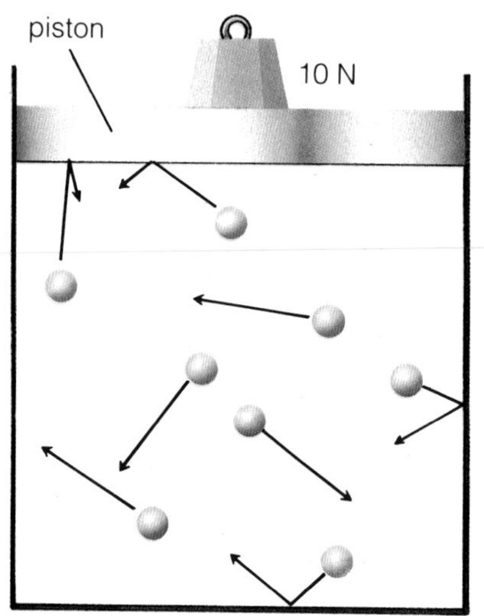

Fig. 36.1a Gas molecules bouncing against a surface produce a pressure.

EXTENSION

If the volume decreases, the pressure increases

If the piston in the diagram is pushed downwards, the gas particles have less room to move around in. The volume of the gas is decreased. But there are still the same number of particles. And they are still flying around and bumping into the piston. Because they have less space, they will hit the piston and the sides of the container more often than before. So they produce a greater force on the piston. The pressure is greater. The greater pressure produced by the gas is balanced by the greater force on the piston. This is why you have to push hard on the piston to push it downwards.

So an increase in pressure reduces the volume of a gas. A decrease in pressure increases the volume of a gas. For a fixed volume of gas, if pressure, P, is doubled then volume, V, will halve. This means that the volume multiplied by the pressure will always give the same number, as long as the temperature does not change.

initial pressure x initial volume
= final pressure x final volume
or $P \times V = \text{constant}$

This is called Boyle's Law.

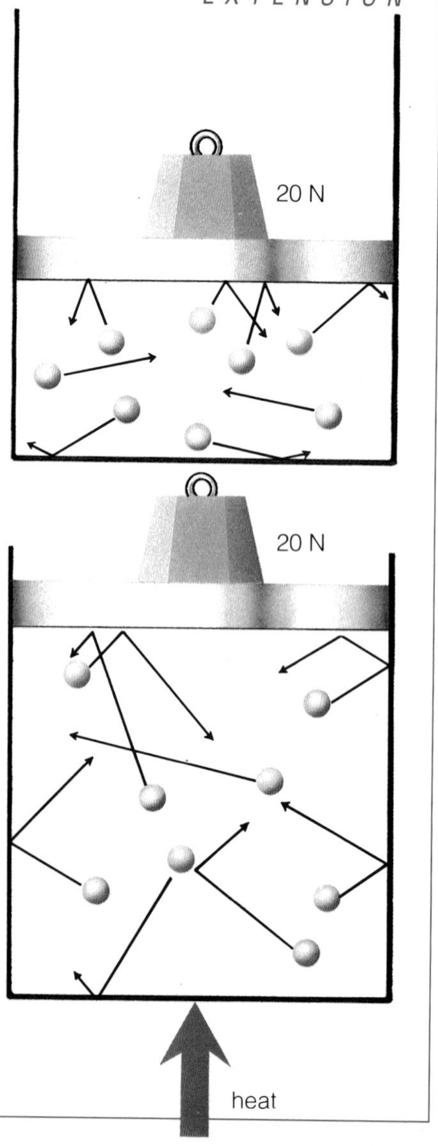

Fig. 36.1b If you squash the gas, the molecules hit the surfaces more often, producing a greater pressure.

Temperature changes volume or pressure

Imagine that the same container is now heated. The temperature rises. The gas particles move faster and faster. They hit the piston and sides of the container more often and harder. So the force on the piston increases. If you do not push down harder on it, the piston will move upwards. So now the gas has more room. Its volume has increased. Heating a gas can increase its volume.

But you could stop the piston moving upwards. You could push down harder on it. If you did this, the volume of the gas would not increase. But the pressure of the gas would be greater. So heating a gas can increase the pressure if the volume is restricted. Boyle's Law only applies if the temperature is fixed. Doubling the temperature (in kelvin) doubles the pressure if the volume is not allowed to change. At 0 K, a gas would have no pressure as its molecules are not moving.

$$\frac{P \times V}{T \text{ (in kelvin)}} = \text{constant}$$

Fig. 36.1c If you heat the gas, the molecules move faster, producing a greater pressure.

A manometer can measure gas pressure

A manometer is a tube with a U-bend. It contains a liquid. The container of gas with the pressure to be measured is attached to one end. The pressure of the gas pushes against the liquid in the tube. The height of liquid it can support is a measure of the gas pressure.

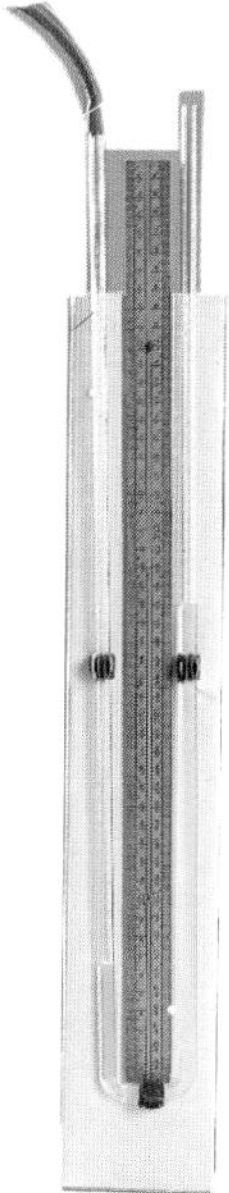

Fig. 36.2 A U-tube manometer measures the difference in pressure on the two ends of the liquid in the tube. A person blowing down one side of the tube causes the pressure on this side to increase, so the liquid moves round. The distance between the top of the liquid on the two sides gives a measure of pressure.

EXTENSION

Constant volume gas thermometers are very accurate

A manometer can also be used to measure temperature. It works because when a gas increases in temperature, its pressure rises. It can support a higher column of liquid.

The constant volume gas thermometer has a thin-walled glass container and a manometer. The glass container is full of gas. The manometer contains mercury. If the temperature rises, the pressure of the gas in the container increases. The mercury is kept at position B, so the volume of the gas cannot change. The height h is a measure of the pressure, and therefore the temperature of the gas. Constant volume gas thermometers are used when a very accurate temperature measurement is required.

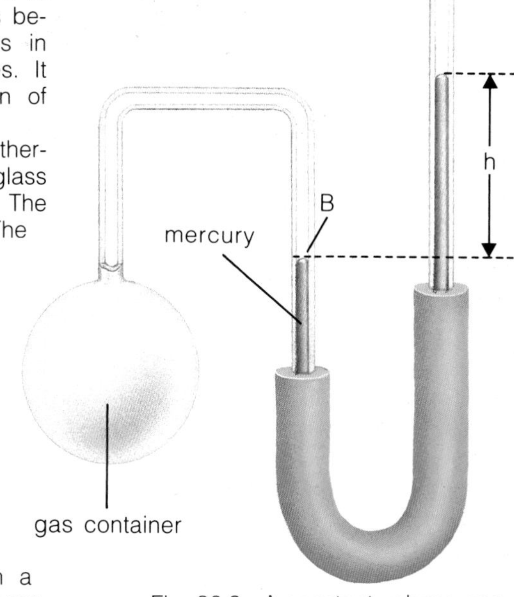

Fig. 36.3 A constant-volume gas thermometer

Calculating changes

You can use the pressure and volume equation to find what happens when pressure or volume changes. If you use the **suffix** 1 to represent initial or starting values and 2 to represent final or finishing values

then $P_1 \times V_1 = P_2 \times V_2$

By putting in the values you know, you can work out the answer. It is best to write everything out carefully so that you don't make any mistakes in substituting your numbers. In this example you have to work out which volumes to use as initial and final values.

A football contains $0.2\,m^3$ of air at one atmosphere pressure. An air pump adds another $0.3\,m^3$ of air. Assuming that the volume of the ball does not change, what is the new pressure in the ball?

For these problems you can use whatever units the question gives you. This is because P and V are on both sides of the equation. You don't have to convert atmospheres to pascals. (The same would apply if volume was in another unit such as litres.) Notice that $0.3\,m^3$ of air was **added**, so a total of $0.5\,m^3$ at 1 atm pressure in the pump and ball became $0.2\,m^3$ at the new pressure in the ball.

Write down what you know:

$P_1 = 1$ atm
$V_1 = 0.5\,m^3$
$V_2 = 0.2\,m^3$
$P_2 = ?$

Now put the numbers in:

$1\text{ atm} \times 0.5\,m^3 = P_2 \times 0.2\,m^3$

and so

$$P_2 = \frac{1\text{ atm} \times 0.5\,m^3}{0.2\,m^3} = 2.5\text{ atm}$$

So the new pressure is 2.5 atmospheres.

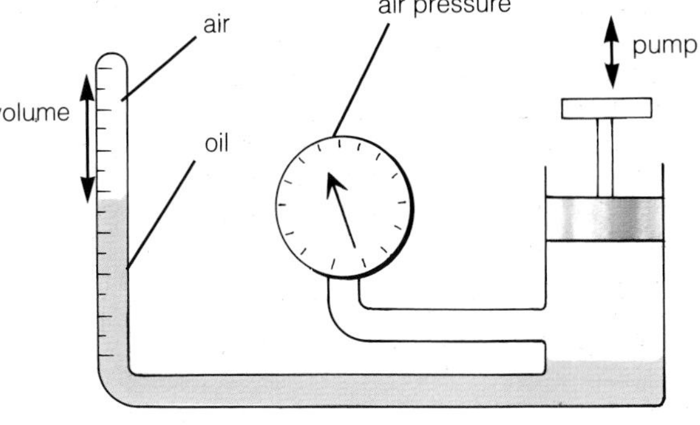

Fig 36.4 Apparatus to investigate the pressure and volume of a gas. As the pump varies the pressure, the volume of the enclosed gas can be measured.

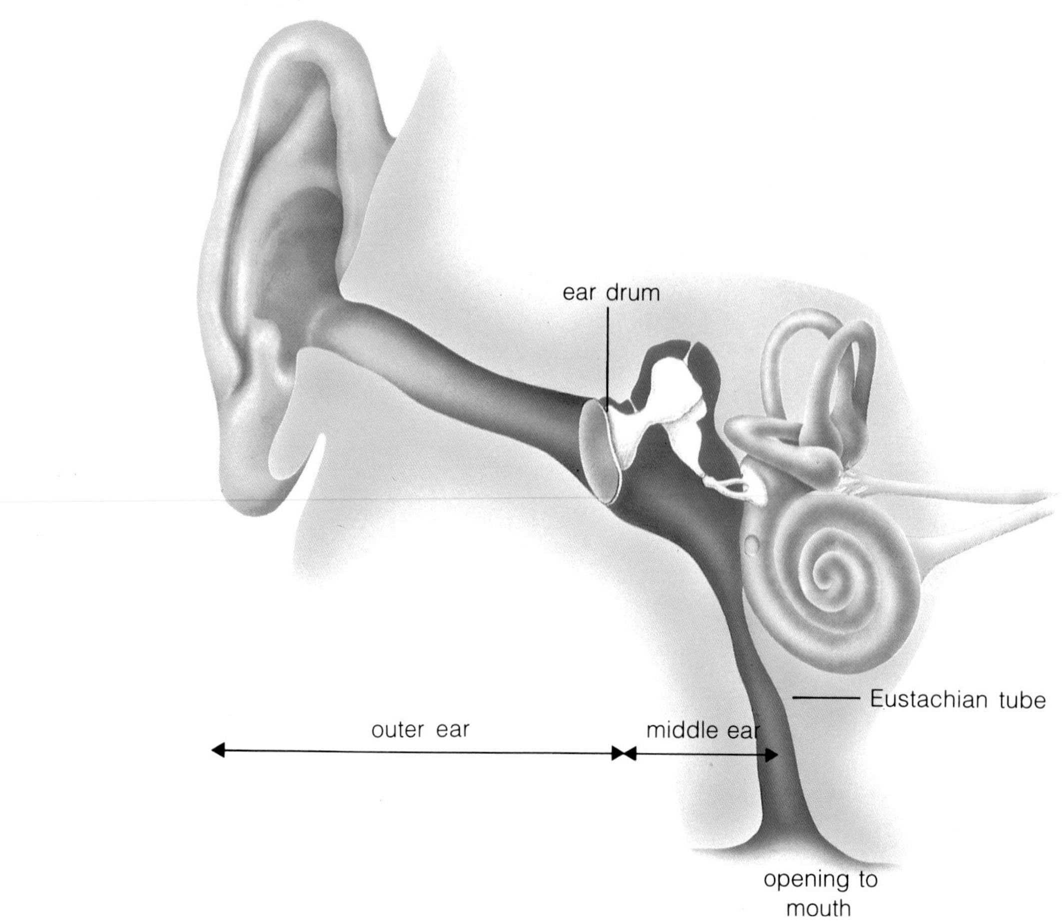

Questions

1 In an experiment the glass container of a gas thermometer was heated (see Figure 36.3). The pressure was measured at different temperatures. The manometer reading was converted to a pressure. The table shows the results.

Temperature (°C)	Pressure (kPa)
−30	89
−10	96
+10	103
+30	111
+50	118
+70	126
+90	133
+110	140

a Plot a graph of these results.
b What pressure would be read if the vessel was immersed in boiling water?
c Atmospheric pressure is 100 kPa. What temperature would the vessel have to be in order to produce this pressure?
d What could you dip the glass container into to make the levels on both sides of the manometer the same?

2 A bicycle pump has a volume of 150 cm^3. If you keep your thumb on the end and can squeeze the air down to 1 cm^3, what would the pressure be? Assume the pressure of the air starts at 100 kPa. If the hole at the end has an area of 0.0001 m^2, would you be able to keep your thumb over it? (Hint: calculate the force for this pressure.)

3 Figure 36.5 shows the structure of the human ear. Both the outer and middle ear are full of air. They are separated from each other by the eardrum. The Eustachian tube leads from the middle ear into the back of the mouth. Normally, the lower end of this tube is kept closed. It opens when you swallow or yawn. Under normal circumstances, the air pressure on both sides of the eardrum is the same.
a Imagine that you are taking off in an aeroplane. As you go higher, the air pressure gets less. What happens to the air pressure in your outer ear?
b If you do not swallow, what happens to the air pressure in your middle ear?
c What effect will this have on your eardrum?
d If you swallow hard, your ears may 'pop' and feel more comfortable again. What do you think happens when your ears 'pop'?

4 An oil can is connected to a vacuum pump and the air inside it removed. The surface area of the oil can is 0.4 m^2. Atmospheric pressure is 100 000 Pa.
a What is the total inwards force on the can?
b What mass is this equivalent to?
c What will happen to the can?
d Why does this not happen when the can is open to the air?

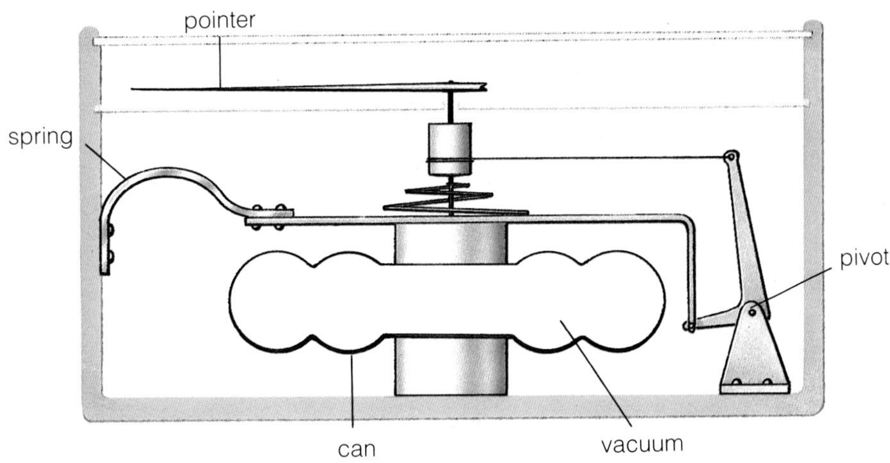

Fig. 36.7 An anaeroid barometer

5 An anaeroid barometer is used to measure pressure. 'Anaeroid' means 'without air'. The anaeroid barometer has a thin-walled metal can from which air has been removed. A strong spring prevents the can from collapsing.

a What will happen to the can if the air pressure gets greater?

b How will this affect the position of the pointer?

c Why is air pressure greater on the outside of the can than on the inside?

d A change in temperature has no effect on the position of the pointer. Why is this?

6 An aerosol can usually uses a propellant gas. The propellant is a gas at room temperature. The propellant is under pressure, so some of the propellant is liquid. As the contents are driven out, the pressure falls and more propellant evaporates, which keeps up the pressure. A company tries to market an environmentally friendly aerosol can that runs just on compressed air. The container must hold 125 ml of liquid product. In tests, the pressure in an unused can is 220 kPa and the pressure as the contents just run out is 110 kPa. What will the volume of the canister have to be?

7 A diver at a depth of 90 m releases a bubble of air of volume 1 mm^3. The pressure at this depth is 10 atmospheres. What is the volume of the bubble at the surface? Explain why divers should rise to the surface slowly.

8 A car airbag inflates quickly in an accident to protect the driver. You can get some idea of the forces involved by doing this calculation. You will have to assume that a canister blows up the bag with compressed air and not an explosive charge. The airbag has a volume of 60 litres. If it were only **just** inflated the bag would end up inflated to 100 kPa. If the canister has a volume of 0.1 litres, what is total volume of gas in the **inflated** system?
Calculate P x V for the inflated airbag system. All this gas was compressed in the canister.
What is the minimum pressure that the gases leaving the canister should have? If the surface area of the bag is 0.75 m^2, what is the initial force on the bag?

9 A bicycle tyre is inflated to 215 kPa at 20 °C. The bike is left in sunlight and the tyre heats up to 50 °C. Use the graph plotted from Question 1 in Topic 36 to estimate the new pressure in the tyre.

Questions

1 The diagram shows an experiment to measure the thermal conducting properties of materials.

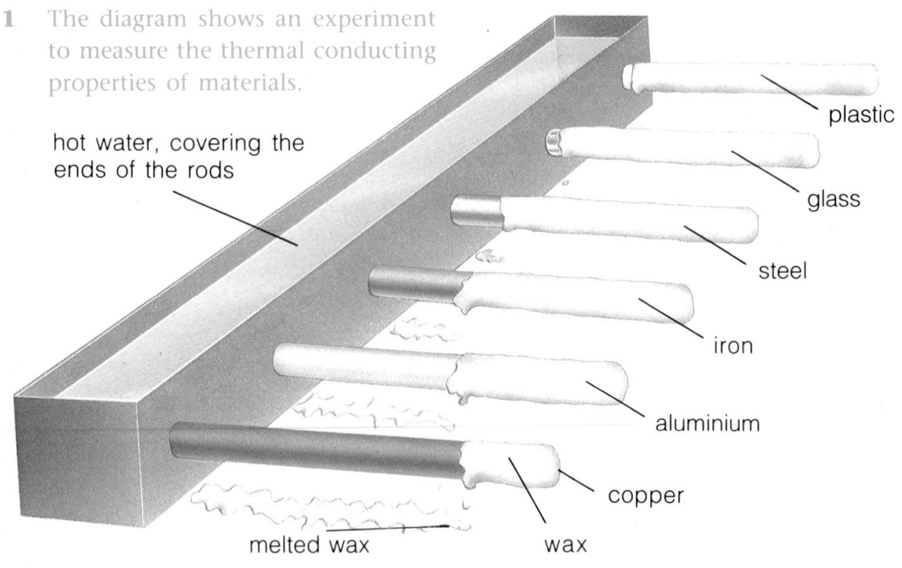

a Which material is the best conductor?

b Which material is the best insulator?

c Would food cook more quickly in a glass or an iron casserole dish?

d Is water more likely to freeze in a plastic or a copper pipe?

e Why do saucepans often have copper bases?

f Give two reasons why energy is saved if the lid is kept on a saucepan while it is being heated.

2 Two mugs, made from different materials, were filled with hot coffee and allowed to cool. The temperatures of the coffee in the mugs were noted at frequent intervals and cooling curves plotted as shown.

a What is the temperature of the coffee in mug A after 5 min?

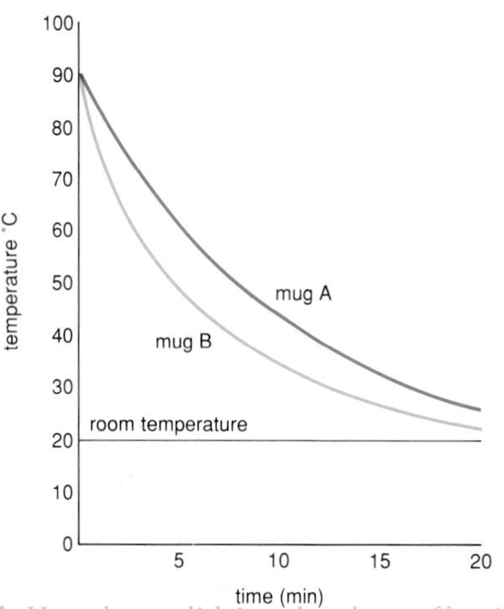

b How long did it take the coffee in mug B to reach 30 °C?

c What is the difference in temperature between the coffee in the mugs after 15 min?

d Which mug is made from the better insulating material?

e Give a reason for your answer to question **d**.

f What will be the final temperature of the coffee in both mugs?

EXTENSION

3 The diagram shows a solar panel. This is a metal box placed on a roof, facing the Sun. Water is circulated through the box by a pump. The box absorbs some of the Sun's radiation, and heats the water.

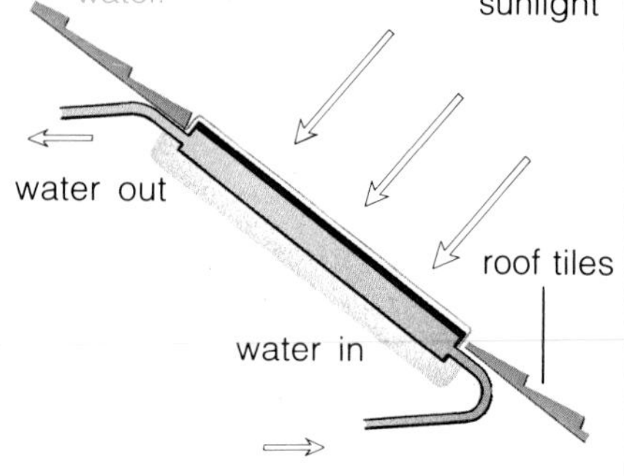

The histograms show the effect on the output temperature of covering the box in various ways.

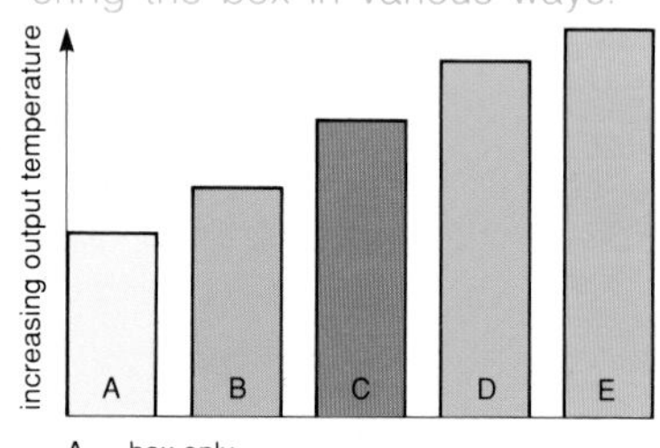

A — box only
B — box with cover
C — box with cover and black surface
D — box with cover, black surface and reduced flow of water
E — box with cover, black surface, with fins, and reduced flow of water

a For each of these coverings, suggest why the output changes as it does.

b What happens to radiation which is not absorbed by the water?

In the United Kingdom the average power of summer sunlight falling on a 1 m² panel is about 500 W. About 50 % of the energy falling on the panel goes to heat the water. A householder wants to install a panel which will have a useful power of 3 kW.

c How big should the panel be?

EXTENSION

4 A stone block is dragged along a level surface with a force of 1000 N.

a If the block is dragged for 100 m, how much energy has been used?

b What type of energy has the block gained?

c The same block is placed on rollers. It can now be moved with a force of 100 N. If the block is dragged for 100 m, how much energy is saved by using the rollers?

d A horse can move the block at a top speed of 5 m/s. One horsepower is 750 W. What frictional force is provided by the air?

5 A car travelling at 100 mph does an emergency stop, and comes to a halt without skidding. The moving car had a kinetic energy of 1 MJ.

a Where does this kinetic energy go when the car stops?

b If the total mass of the disc brakes is 16 kg, and they have a specific heat capacity of 500 J/kg°C, estimate how much hotter they will become as the car stops.

6 A car drives at an average speed of 30 mph against a frictional force of 130 N. In the car's lifetime, it travels 160 000 km.

a What energy is transferred working against the frictional force during the car's lifetime?

b If the average speed of the car is 55 mph, the frictional force is 460 N. How much more energy would be transferred at this average speed?

WAVES

37 VIBRATIONS

Many things vibrate when disturbed. Small objects tend to vibrate more quickly than large ones. The number of vibrations in one second is the frequency.

Frequency is the number of vibrations per second

If you twang a ruler against a desk, it vibrates or **oscillates**. A short ruler vibrates more quickly than a long one.

The **frequency** of vibration is the number of vibrations or oscillations in one second.

Frequency is measured in hertz. The abbreviation for hertz is **Hz**. A frequency of 1 Hz is one vibration per second. If the ruler vibrates 100 times in one second, the frequency is 100 Hz.

$$\text{Frequency in Hz} = \frac{\text{Number of oscillations or vibrations}}{\text{time taken in seconds}}$$

If the ruler vibrates 300 times in 2 s, the frequency is:

$$\frac{300}{2} = 150 \text{ Hz}$$

Fig. 37.1 The frequency at which a 'twanged' ruler oscillates depends on its length.

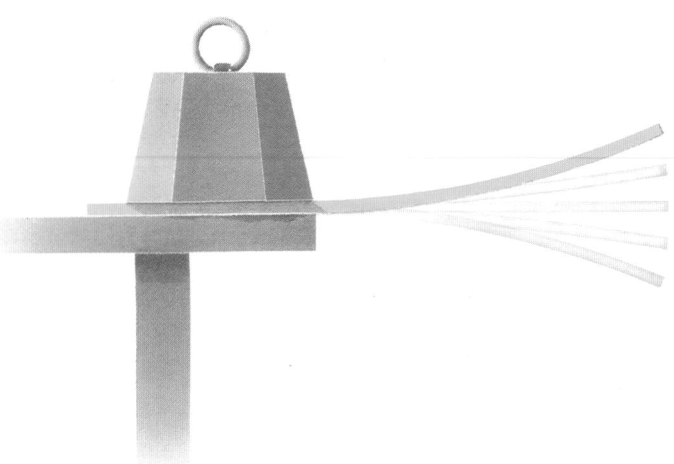

Period is the time taken for one oscillation

If a pendulum swings twice in 1 s, the frequency is 2 Hz. The time taken for one swing is $\frac{1}{2}$s. This is called the **period.** The period is the length of time it takes to make one oscillation. One oscillation is a swing from one side to the other and **back** to the starting position.

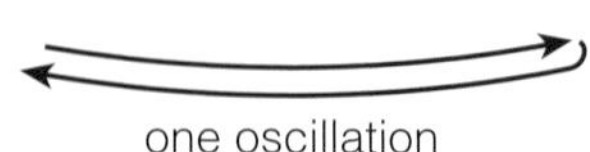

Vibrations can be used to indicate faults in machines

In a complex machine there are many sources of vibration. An engineer who knows what vibrations a machine should produce can predict a failure before it happens. If a study of the machine shows an unusual vibration developing, this could indicate a fault. Regular checks of vibration levels mean that servicing can be carried out less frequently. This wastes less time.

INVESTIGATION 37.1

Investigating a pendulum

1 Set up the apparatus as shown in the diagram. Investigate how the *length* of the string affects the *frequency* of oscillation. (The length of the string should be measured from the point of suspension to the centre of the bob.) Record your results fully. Look for a pattern in them.

2 Using the same apparatus, but with the ruler placed horizontally, investigate how the *size* of the oscillation affects the *frequency*.

Questions

1 A pendulum oscillates twice in one second. If the string is made four times as long, what will be the new frequency of oscillation?

2 What length of pendulum would you use to produce a frequency of 1 Hz?

3 Could you use this for timing something?

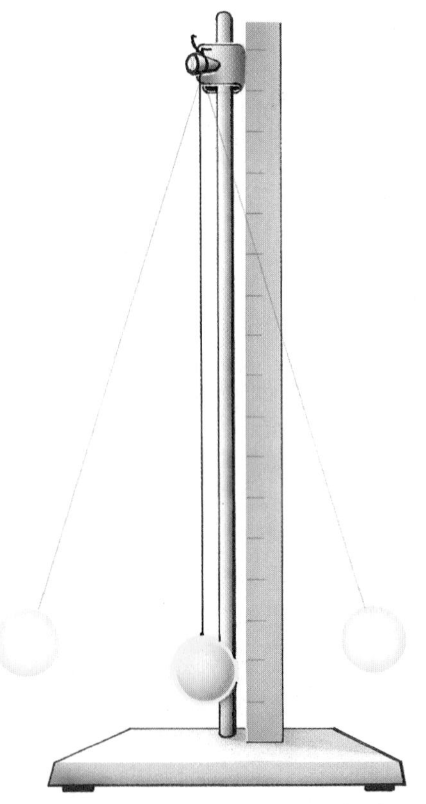

Fig. 37.2 Use this arrangement for Step 1. For Step 2, place the ruler horizontally.

Vibration causes settling

A pile of sand will quickly settle down if you shake what it stands on. When gravel is laid on driveways, it is made to settle by shaking it. You cannot simply shake the whole ground! Instead, a vibrating weight is dragged over the loose gravel. This flattens it, and causes the stones to fit tightly together.

Settling caused by vibration during transport can mean that packets filled in a factory never seem full when you open them at home. Cereal packets usually have an explanation of this written on them.

Vibrations are also used to make sure that concrete has no spaces in it. To make reinforced concrete, wet concrete is poured into moulds containing steel rods. It is important that the concrete should flow around all the rods. A vibrating rod is pushed into the concrete once it has been poured. The rod vibrates at 200 Hz. It is usually driven by a petrol engine, or compressed air. The vibration helps the concrete to flow around the rods.

Strong vibrations can cause damage

Vibrations can be used to break up objects. A hammer drill is used to drill holes in materials like brick, stone or concrete. The drill not only goes round, but also vibrates backwards and forwards at up to 700 Hz. These vibrations help to break up the material. The drill oscillates 14 times for each revolution. Pneumatic drills do not revolve at all. They rely only on vibration to break up the material.

Kidney stones are hard deposits which can build up inside a person's kidneys. They can be painful and dangerous and are sometimes removed by surgery. Another treatment is to direct ultrasonic (very fast) vibrations at them. This breaks up the stones into tiny pieces which can pass out of the kidney in the urine.

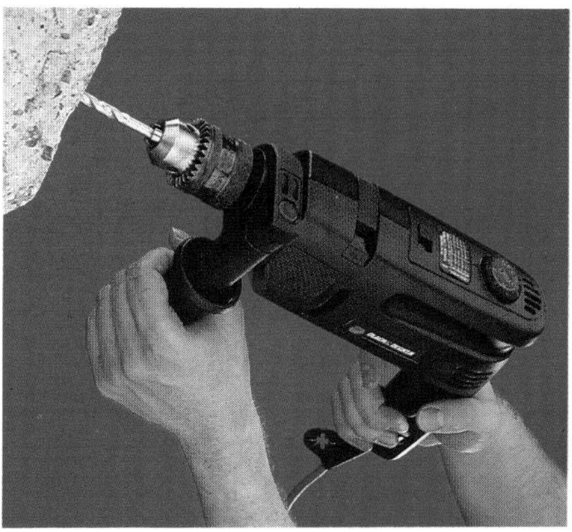

Fig. 37.3 A hammer drill rotates and vibrates backwards and forwards.

Fig. 37.4 Vibrations are used to help reinforced concrete to settle without leaving air gaps.

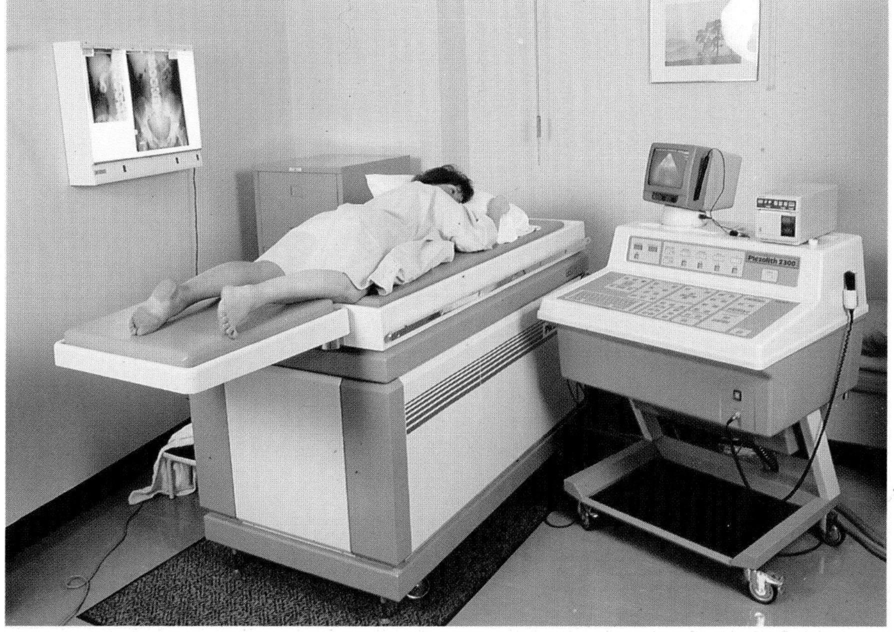

Fig. 37.5 A woman being treated for kidney stones, using ultrasound. At high sound intensities, ultrasound can be used to break up stones and weld plastic. At lower intensities, the vibrations can be used to shake dirt out of complex shapes like fine jewellery.

Questions

1 A tall factory chimney sways in the wind. It swings backwards and forwards eight times in 2 s.

a What is the frequency of oscillation in Hertz?

b What is the period of oscillation?

EXTENSION

2 The mains electricity delivered to a house in Britain has a frequency of 50 Hz.

a How many times does the electricity oscillate in 1 s?

b In America the frequency is 60 Hz. How much longer does one oscillation take in Britain than in America?

38 WAVES

A wave carries energy from one place to another. Waves can be mechanical or electromagnetic. A wave can be transverse or longitudinal.

A wave does not carry material with it

If a rope or 'Slinky' spring is shaken from side to side, a series of pulses travels down it. Each point on the rope moves up and down as a wave passes. A single wave pulse makes this easier to see.

The rope or spring is *not* carried along with the wave! After the wave has passed, the rope or spring is still there. What *is* being carried along is **energy**. Waves transfer energy from one place to another.

A wave in a rope or spring is a **mechanical wave**. Mechanical waves disturb material. The particles in the material oscillate to and fro. The oscillating particles transfer energy between themselves. The particles could be in a solid, liquid, or gas.

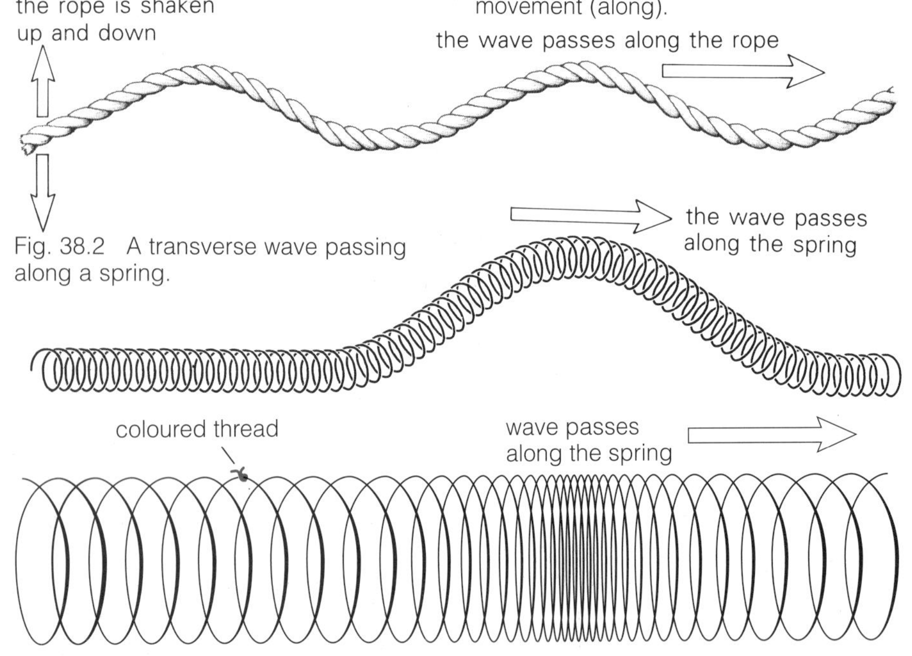

Fig. 38.1 A wave passing along a rope. The rope itself does not move along; only energy moves in the direction of the wave's travel. This is a transverse wave, in which the direction of oscillation (up and down) is at right angles to the direction of the wave's movement (along).

Fig. 38.2 A transverse wave passing along a spring.

Fig. 38.3 A single pulse passing along a spring. The spring as a whole does not move along, but individual coils move back and forth. This is a longitudinal wave, in which the direction of oscillation (back and forth) is in the same direction as the movement of the wave (along).

In a transverse wave, particles move at right angles to the wave

When you send a wave along a rope or spring, you are producing a **transverse wave**. The particles oscillate at right angles to the direction in which the wave is travelling. The wave is travelling *along* the rope, while the particles are moving *up and down*. As the wave passes, each particle moves away from its rest position and then back again. The particles do not move along in the direction of the wave.

In a longitudinal wave, the particles move in the same direction as the wave

If you push a 'Slinky' spring, you can make a single pulse travel along it. A small piece of brightly coloured string makes the movement of a single coil clearer. As the pulse passes, the coils oscillate backwards and forwards along the length of the spring. The coils return to their original position. A ripple passes down the spring, but the individual coils are left where they were in the first place. This is an example of a **longitudinal wave**. In a longitudinal wave the particles oscillate *along* the direction in which the wave is travelling.

Sound is a longitudinal wave

If you push a spring backwards and forwards, you can send a series of pulses down its length. In some parts of the spring the coils are closer together. These areas are **compressions**. As the coils oscillate, the compressions move along the spring. Again, a piece of coloured string may make it easier to see what is happening. Between the compressions are parts of the spring which are stretched out. These are called **rarefactions**.

Sound is a longitudinal wave. The compressions and rarefactions are regions of high and low pressure. A sound wave moves particles of materials, so it is a mechanical wave. Sound can only travel when there are particles which can be compressed and rarefied. So sound cannot pass through a vacuum. A sound wave is an example of a longitudinal, mechanical wave.

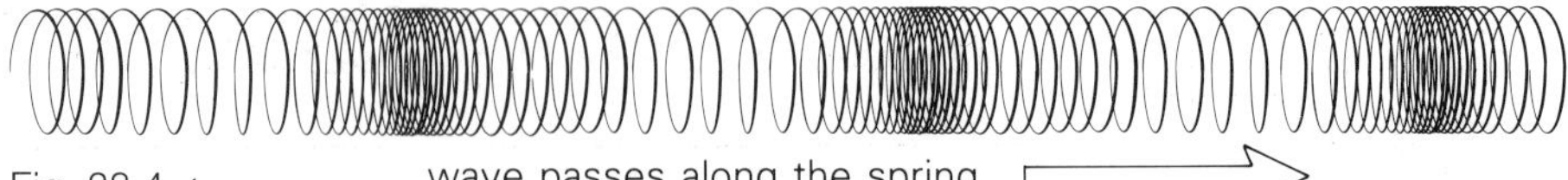

Fig. 38.4

Electromagnetic waves are not disturbances of particles

Not all waves are mechanical waves. An **electromagnetic wave** is not a disturbance of particles. It is varying electric and magnetic fields. It does not need any particles to pass the energy on. Electromagnetic waves travel more easily when there are no particles. Some examples of electromagnetic waves include X rays, gamma rays, microwaves, light waves and radio waves.

Measuring waves

If you took a photograph of a wave on a rope, or ripples spreading across a pond, it might look something like Figure 38.5. The centre line shows the undisturbed rope, or level of water in the pond. The top of the hump in the water or rope is called a **crest**. The bottom of a dip is a **trough**.

The distance between the peaks of two crests is the **wavelength** of the wave. The maximum distance that a particle moves away from the centre line is the **amplitude** of the wave. The amplitude is the height of a crest above the centre line.

The number of waves produced per second is called the **frequency**. If you shake your hand backwards and forwards twice per second, the frequency is 2 Hz. You are producing two waves in 1 s, so the wave frequency is 2 Hz.

These measurements also work for longitudinal waves. For these the wavelength is the distance between two compressions.

Fig. 38.5 Wavelength and amplitude of a transverse wave. Wavelength is the distance between two crests or two troughs. Amplitude is the height of a crest or depth of a trough from the rest position.

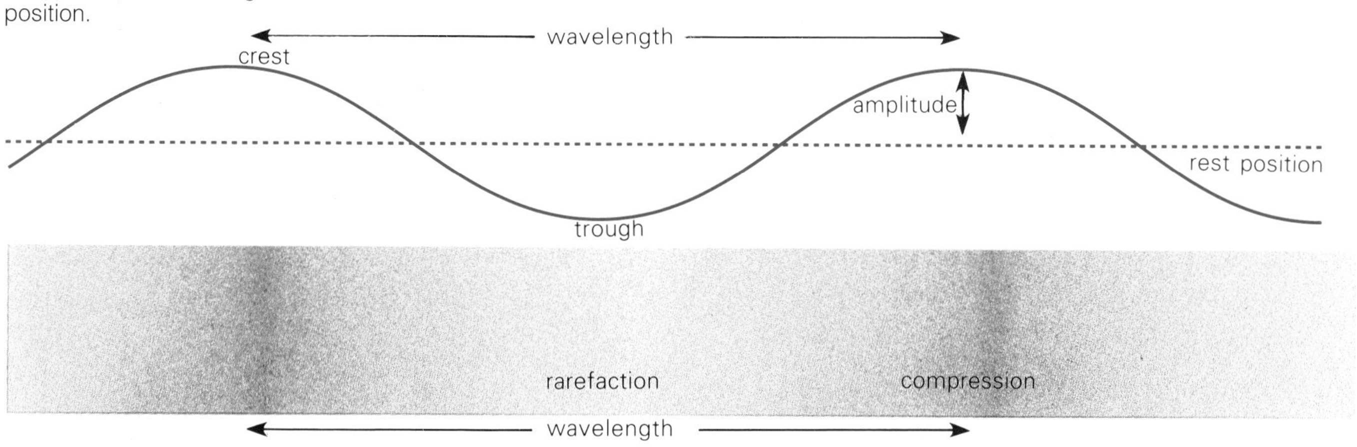

Fig. 38.6 Wavelength and amplitude of a longitudinal wave. Wavelength can be measured as the distance between the centre of two compressions. Amplitude is the maximum distance moved by a particle from its rest position.

INVESTIGATION 38.1

Standing waves

The apparatus shown in the photograph can be used to produce **standing waves**. If you adjust the frequency of the vibrations produced by the electromagnetic vibrator, you will find that you get especially large vibrations at some frequencies. A wave pattern is produced which does not travel down the string. This is called a standing wave.

A standing wave stores energy in the string. The wave travelling down the string is reflected at the end, and comes back. It combines with the wave from the vibrator to form the standing wave. Standing waves form on the strings of instruments, such as violins, when the string vibrates.

Fig. 38.7 Apparatus for investigating standing waves. This arrangement is using a power pack, which produces vibrations of 50 Hz. If you use a variable frequency oscillator instead, you can investigate the effects produced by many different frequencies.

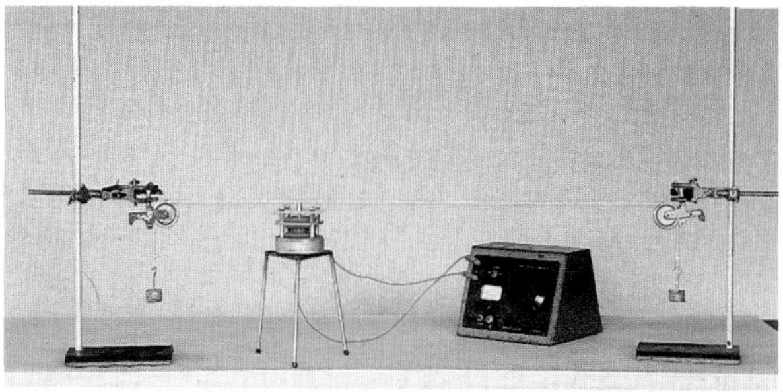

Try the following experiments with this apparatus.

1. Vary the frequency. At what frequencies are standing waves formed on a 1 m length of string? What do you notice about these frequencies?
2. Vary the length of the string. You could begin by trying a 0.5 m length of string. Find the frequencies which produce standing waves again. Can you see a pattern linking the frequencies which produce standing waves in the 1 m and 0.5 m lengths of string?
3. If you have time you could also experiment with different kinds of string, and different weights.

39 EARTHQUAKES AND TIDAL WAVES

The most destructive natural waves are caused by sudden movements of the Earth's crust.

Continents are moving over the Earth's surface

Although we think of the ground as being solid, it is really quite thin. The solid outer layer of the Earth, called the **crust**, floats on liquid rock. The thickness of the Earth's crust can be compared to a postage stamp stuck on the surface of a netball.

The thickest parts of the Earth's crust form the **continents**. The continents are moving around on the Earth's surface. You can imagine the continents as large 'stamps' or plates, sliding around on the surface of a netball. They move very slowly – perhaps a centimetre or so a year. Sometimes they run into each other. India has moved northwards and 'collided' with Asia. This has pushed up the Himalayas. This is still happening now, and the Himalayas are continuing to rise.

Fig. 39.1 Energy released at the focus of an earthquake, often many kilometres below the surface, travels out as body waves in all directions.

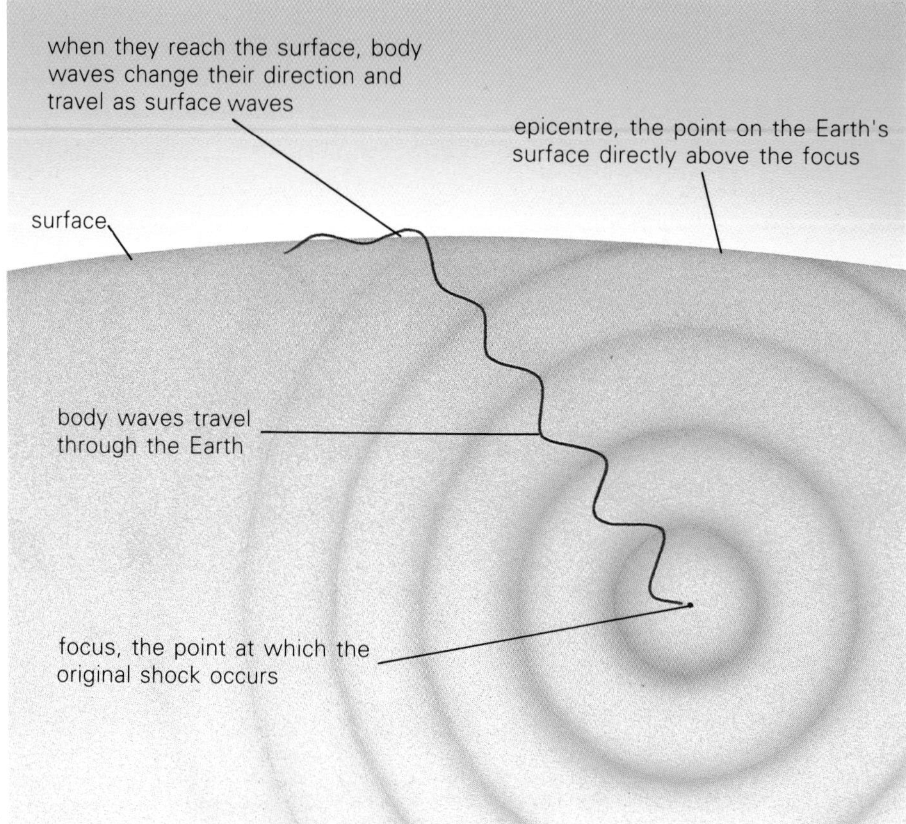

Earthquakes are caused when the crust moves suddenly

If parts of the Earth's crust are moving past one another, something has to give. Places where rock structures have broken apart and can slide past each other are called **faults**.

Movements of the Earth's crust are not smooth and steady. Usually, forces build up on either side of a fault until something suddenly gives. The sudden movement causes an **earthquake**. Many, but not all, earthquakes are caused when rocks suddenly slide past each other at a fault.

The place where the vibrations come from is called the **focus** of the earthquake. The focus of many earthquakes is near the surface of the Earth – often about 5 km underground. The point on the surface directly above the focus is called the **epicentre**. From the focus, shock waves spread out through the Earth. They are knows as **seismic waves**. There are two main types of seismic waves. Waves which pass through the deep layers of the Earth are called **body waves**. Waves travelling through the surface layers are called **surface waves**. The surface waves have a long wavelength and are called **L waves**. It is the surface waves which do the most damage.

DID YOU KNOW?

Los Angeles lies on a major fault called the San Andreas Fault, which stretches through California. It is predicted that one day an earthquake may occur here of magnitude 7.5. This is 15 times more intense than the Armenian earthquake.

Fig. 39.2 Poorly constructed houses were severely damaged in the Armenian earthquake in 1988.

Tidal waves may be produced by earthquakes

Fig. 39.3 The positions of earthquake epicentres are concentrated in certain parts of the world. These tend to be where different plates of the Earth's crust are moving past one another.

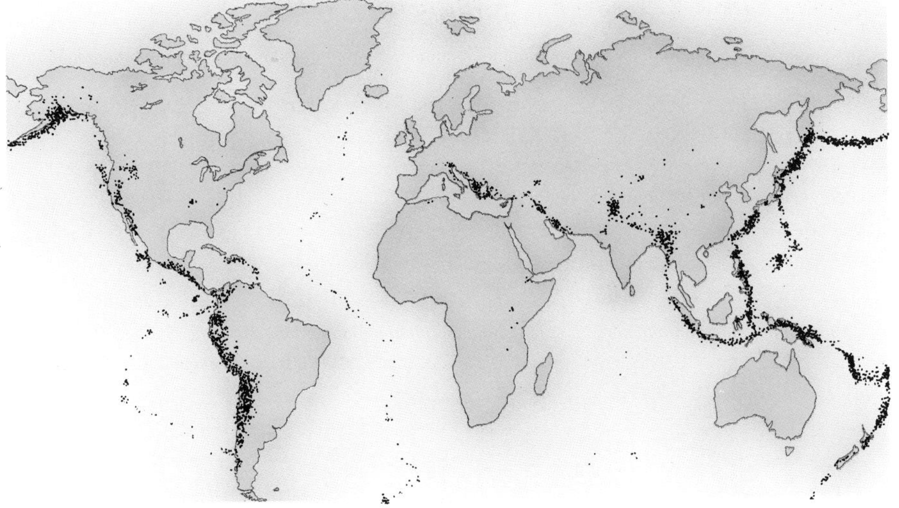

Fig. 39.4 A seismograph. Vibrations in the ground disturb the mechanism, producing a trace that records an earthquake.

Fig. 39.5 This shows the sea level changes as a tsunami passes.

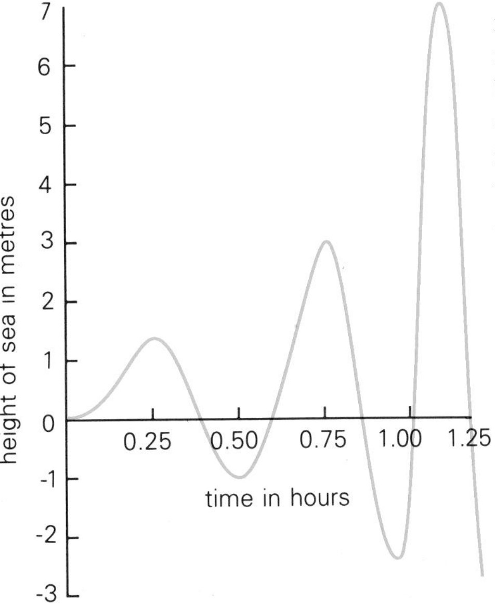

Tidal waves are nothing to do with the tide. They are produced by undersea earthquakes or other disturbances.

When a wave in the sea approaches land it runs into shallower water. This slows it down and makes it rise higher. The faster the wave is travelling, the higher it rises.

When the volcanic island of Krakatoa erupted in the Pacific Ocean in 1883, it caused waves about 1 m high to spread across the Pacific Ocean. A distance of 125 km separated each wave crest which moved at 500 km/h. As the waves approached the coasts of Java and Sumatra, they were slowed down in the shallower water. Like normal waves they rose higher – but these were no normal waves. They rose to a height of 30–40 m. 36000 people were killed.

Waves like this are called tidal waves or **tsunami**. A tsunami is a series of waves. The largest wave comes in the middle of the series. Each crest is followed by a trough. As the crests become larger, so the troughs become deeper. The troughs take the sea out farther and farther. It is as though the tide has gone out. This is why tsunami are known as tidal waves.

Questions

1 a What was the wavelength of the Krakatoa tsunami?

b What is the period of the tsunami shown in Figure 39.5? (Use the first two waves for your calculation.)

c Estimate the height of the second wave on this graph.

d How long after the first crest did the main wave hit the coast?

e As a tsunami approaches the coast, what form of energy does it lose?

f What form of energy does it gain?

g Describe what someone standing on a cliff top would see as a tsunami approached.

Earthquakes release huge amounts of energy

The energy released in a major earthquake is enormous. It has been estimated that the energy released in the famous 1906 earthquake in California was about the same as that produced by 100 000 atomic bombs. So it is not surprising that earthquakes can do huge amounts of damage.

The intensity of earthquakes is measured on the Richter scale. This was developed by Charles Richter in 1935. Low numbers indicate a weak earthquake. An increase of one unit on the scale means an increase in intensity of ×10. The highest value ever recorded was 8.9. This earthquake happened in Chile in 1960. Earthquakes measuring up to three on the Richter scale are not usually noticed except by scientific recording instruments. Around a value of five slight damage is caused. At a value of seven many buildings are destroyed. Above a value of eight waves can actually be seen moving over the surface of the ground.

DID YOU KNOW?

The Armenian earthquake in 1988 measured 6.9 on the Richter scale. Around 25 000 people lost their lives. There might have been fewer deaths if buildings had been better constructed.

40 THE STRUCTURE OF THE EARTH

The Earth is made up of several different layers. Evidence for this comes from the behaviour of earthquake waves.

The Earth's crust is like a thin skin

We think of the Earth under our feet as being a solid, unchanging structure. But this is not quite true. The Earth is not completely solid and it changes a great deal.

The outer layer of the Earth, on which we live, is called the **crust.** The crust is much thicker under the continents than under the oceans. Continental crust is between 25 and 40 km deep. Oceanic crust is between 5 and 10 km deep. These distances may sound quite large, but they are tiny compared with the size of the Earth. The radius of the Earth is about 6378 km, so the crust is just a very thin skin on the surface.

The thin oceanic crust is much denser than the thick continental crust.

Fig. 40.1 The structure of the Earth

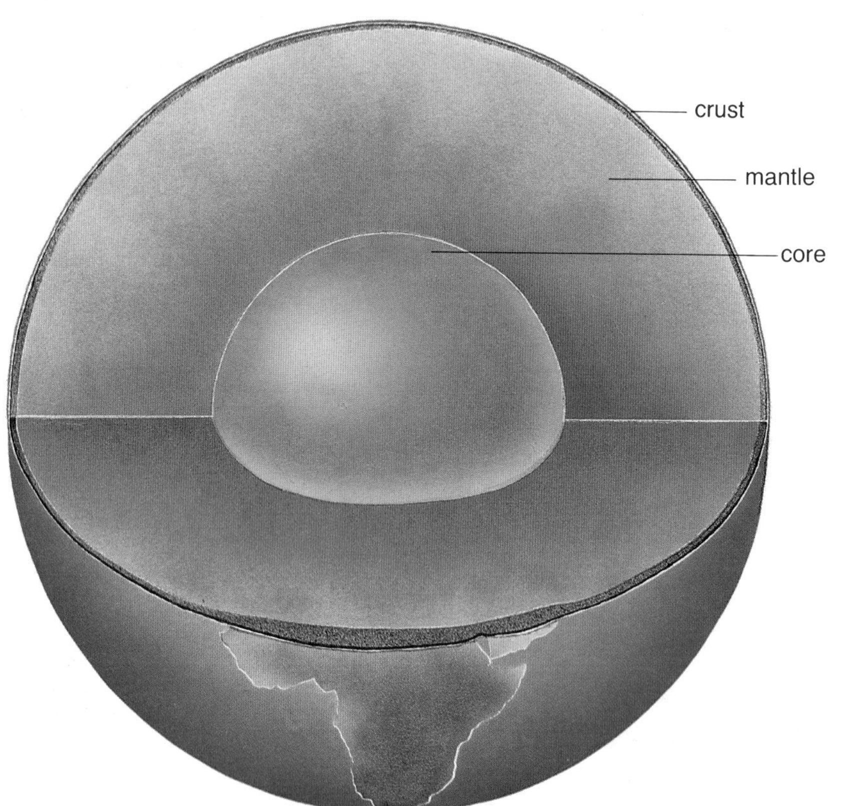

The mantle makes up most of the Earth

Beneath the crust, there is a very thick layer called the **mantle**. The mantle is about 2800 km thick. It is made up of rock containing a lot of iron. Together, the upper part of the mantle and the crust, are sometimes called the **lithosphere**.

The rocks in the mantle are very dense, because of the huge crushing forces of all the rocks above. They are also hot. Although the outer part of the mantle is fairly solid, the great forces can make it flow slowly. The rocks of the inner layers of the mantle are very hot, and they are partly liquid. This molten rock is called **magma**. Sometimes, this molten rock escapes through cracks in the crust. It is then called **lava**.

The core is partly liquid

The centre of the Earth is called the **core**. The core is about 6950 km in diameter. The inner part is solid, but the outer core is liquid. The core is mostly made up of iron and nickel. It is thought that the movements of the outer, liquid, core may be responsible for producing the Earth's magnetic field.

DID YOU KNOW?

Although the volume of the inner core is only 16% of the Earth's total volume, its mass makes up nearly 33% of the Earth's total mass. This is because the materials from which it is made are very dense.

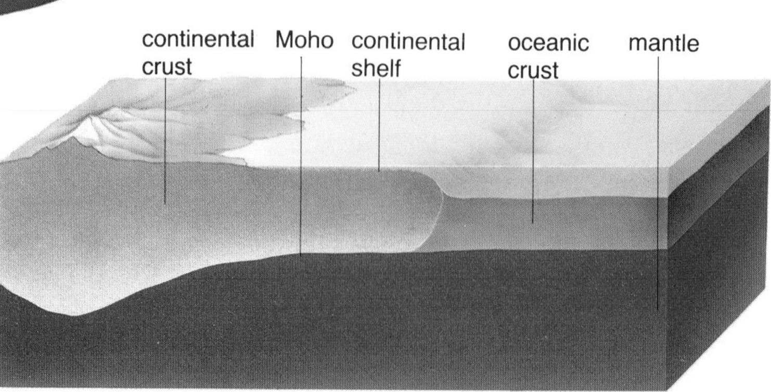

Fig. 40.2 Continental crust is a thick layer of relatively light rock, floating on the mantle. Oceanic crust is denser, and forms a thinner layer. The boundary between the crust and the mantle is called the Mohorovic discontinuity (Moho for short) after the Yugoslav geologist who discovered it.

The behaviour of earthquake waves gives clues about the structure of the Earth

No-one has been able to take samples from the inside of the Earth. Even the very deepest holes which have ever been made by humans only go into the crust. Everything we know about the inner layers of the Earth has been worked out indirectly.

Much of the evidence which suggests that the Earth is made up of layers comes from the study of **earthquake waves**. Earthquakes produce longitudinal waves and transverse waves. The longitudinal waves are called **P waves**. They are like sound waves. They produce alternating areas of compression and rarefaction in the material through which they travel. P waves travel very quickly. They are the fastest waves produced by an earthquake. This is why they are called P waves. The P stands for primary, because they are the first waves to be detected.

The transverse waves are called **S waves**. They travel like a wave in a rope which is shaken up and down. S waves travel more slowly than P waves. S stands for secondary, because these waves are not detected until after the P waves.

When an earthquake happens, P waves and S waves travel through the Earth. The waves are detected by **seismographs**. Seismographs pick up the P waves first, then the S waves. By comparing the time taken for the two different kinds of waves to reach a seismograph, scientists can work out where the earthquake happened.

But the P and S waves also give information about the inside of the Earth. For example, it is found that the waves suddenly begin to travel faster once they are about 25 to 40 km below the surface. This suggests that the density and composition of the rocks suddenly changes at this level. This change is called the **Mohorovic discontinuity**. It is at the boundary between the crust and the mantle.

Another change in the behaviour of the waves happens much deeper in the Earth. S waves cannot travel through the centre of the Earth at all. This suggests that it is at least partly liquid. So it is believed that there is a liquid outer core. P waves can travel through this region. The speed at which they travel suggests that the outer core is mostly made of iron.

Further evidence for the existence of a liquid, iron-containing outer core comes from studies of the Earth's magnetic field. In theory, the magnetic field could be produced by the movement of huge quantities of molten iron at this level in the Earth. What causes this movement is still a mystery. It is probably a combination of convection currents, caused by uneven heating of the Earth's interior, and forces set up by the rotation of the Earth.

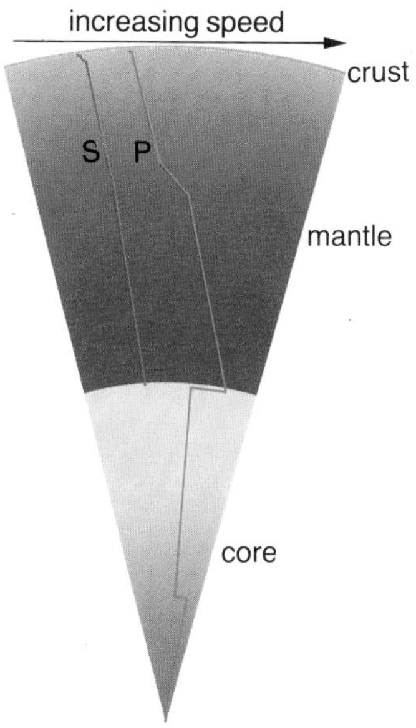

Fig. 40.3a P waves suddenly slow down about 3000 km below the surface and S waves stop completely. This indicates a change from solid mantle to liquid core at this depth.

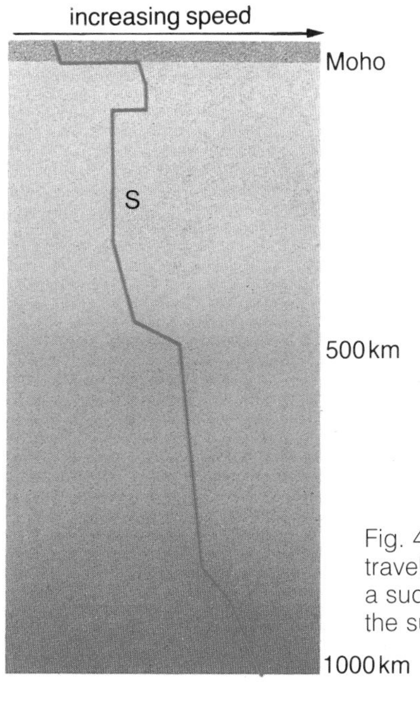

Fig. 40.3b A more detailed look at how S waves travel through the outer layers of the Earth shows a sudden increase in speed about 25–40 km below the surface. This is the Mohorovic discontinuity.

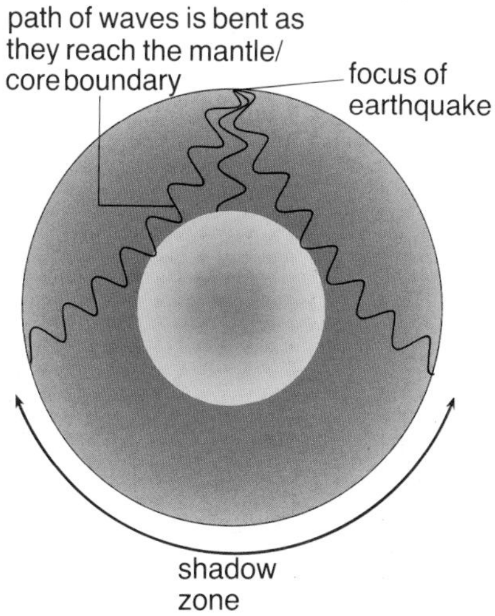

Fig. 40.4 S waves travelling outwards from the focus of an earthquake never reach the far side of the Earth. This **shadow zone** on the far side of the Earth is caused by the inability of the waves to travel through the liquid core.

DID YOU KNOW?

The world's deepest hole is in the Kola peninsula, in the USSR. It is 12 km deep, 0.2% of the way to the centre of the Earth.

Questions

1 The deepest mine in the world is a gold mine in South Africa. It goes 3582 m below the surface.

a Into which layer of the Earth does this mine penetrate?

b What fraction of the Earth's diameter has been crossed by this mine?

2 Summarise the evidence which suggests that the Earth is made up of several concentric layers.

EXTENSION

41 WAVE SPEED

Different types of waves travel at different speeds. Reflected waves are used by humans and other animals to locate objects and measure distances.

INVESTIGATION 41.1

Measuring the speed of sound in air

This experiment will be demonstrated for you, as a starting pistol can be dangerous.

1 Measure the length of your school field in metres, and record it. Mark the two points between which you have measured.

2 Send someone to one of your marked points with a starting pistol. A second person should stand at the other marked point, holding a stopwatch.

3 When everyone is ready, the starting pistol is fired. As soon as the person with the stop watch *sees the smoke* from the pistol, he or she starts the watch. When the person *hears the bang*, he or she stops the watch. Record the time between seeing the smoke and hearing the bang.

You will probably need to practice this a few times before you feel confident that you are getting it right. Collect three sets of reliable results.

Questions

1 Speed is the distance covered per second. In this case, the speed of sound is:

$$\frac{\text{distance travelled}}{\text{time taken}} \quad \text{or} \quad \frac{\text{length of field in metres}}{\text{time delay in seconds}}$$

Using an average of your three readings calculate the speed of sound in air.

2 You are assuming that you see the smoke from the pistol immediately.
Light travels one million times faster than sound. Is this assumption a reasonable one?

3 Does your reaction time in starting and stopping the watch produce a significant error in this experiment?

4 How could you reduce the errors in this experiment?

Sound can bounce off surfaces and cause echoes

If you shout at a wall from 340 m away, the sound takes 1 s to reach the wall. The sound reflects from the wall, and takes 1 s to return. So you hear the echo 2 s after you shouted.

The time it takes for an echo to return can be used to find how far away something is. This is how **sonar** works. A ship uses sonar to measure the depth of the seabed below it. Pulses of sound are sent downwards, and the time for them to return is measured. Sound travels at 1500 m/s in water, so the echoes return much sooner than in air. Fishing boats also use sonar to detect shoals of fish in the water below them.

Dolphins use a similar system for locating fish in murky water. They produce ultrasonic waves which bounce off the fish. This is called **echolocation**. Piranha fish use echolocation, and so do bats, rats and some birds. Ultrasonic waves are sound waves of a frequency too high for humans to hear.

You can use an ultrasonic 'tape measure' to measure the size of a room. It sends out ultrasonic waves which bounce off the walls. The time taken for the echo to return gives the distance to the reflecting surface. Some autofocusing cameras use the same method to find the distance between the camera and the object.

In air, over large distances, **radar** is used instead of sound waves. Radar uses the same method, but sound waves are replaced with radio waves. Radio waves travel at the speed of light which is 300 000 000 m/s. An echo from an object 300 km away would take 2 milliseconds (ms) to return.

(1ms is $\frac{1}{1000}$ s.)

Fig. 41.1

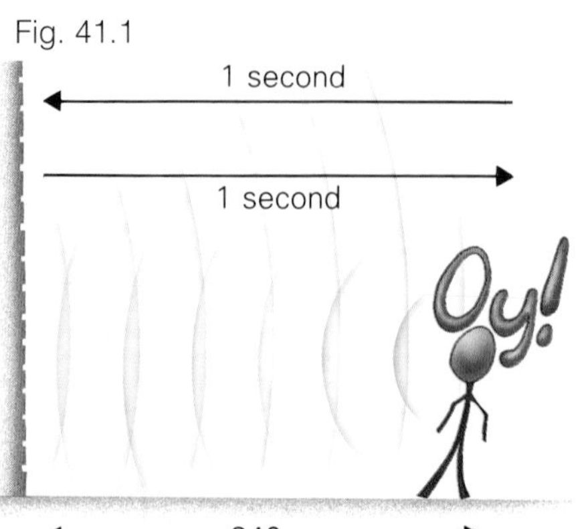

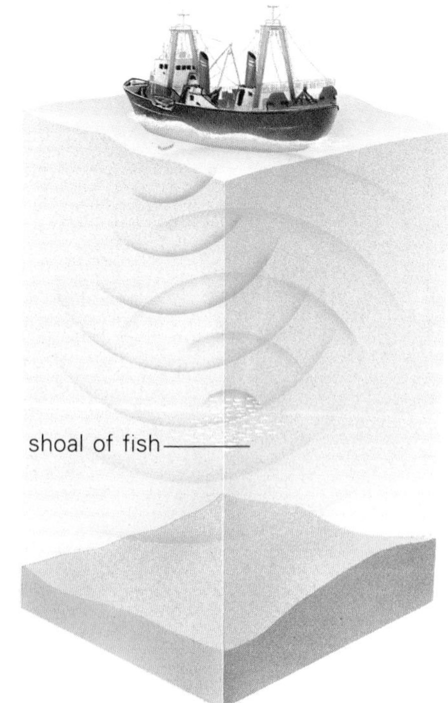

Fig. 41.2 A sonar system sends ultrasonic waves down into the water, and measures the time taken for the echo to return. Fishing boats can locate shoals of fish in this way.

Fig. 41.3 Bats navigate, and find food, by echolocation. They emit ultrasound squeaks, and pick up the echoes. This horseshoe bat has particularly large ears to pick up the returning vibrations. The closer an object is, the faster the sound bounces back to the bat.

Fig. 41.4 Air traffic control systems use radar. The tower emits radio waves, which travel at 300 000 000 m/s. They are reflected from aircraft, and picked up by receivers in the tower. The time taken for the signal to return can be used to calculate the distance of the aircraft. The signals are fed to a screen, which plots the aircraft's position.

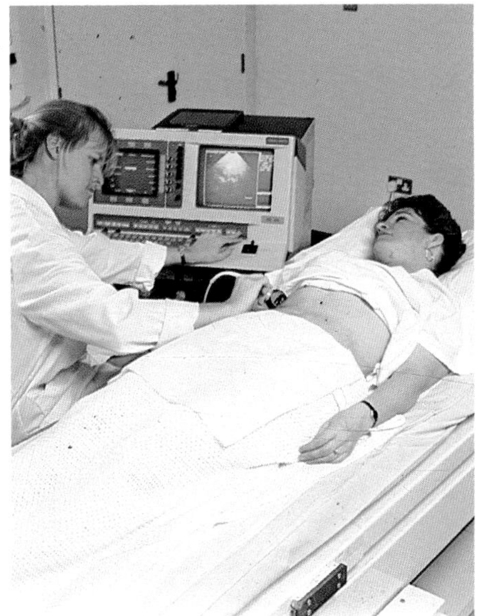

Fig 41.5 An ultrasound scanner beams sound waves into a person's body. Echoes are created when the sound meets a different surface, for example the stomach. The echoes can be used to give an image on a screen. This is thought to be much safer than using X rays to 'see' inside a person's body. Ultrasound scans are used to show the baby inside the uterus. Exactly the same scanning techniques can be used to detect faults in industrial products. A pipe can be tested for leaks by producing ultrasound inside it and seeing where it escapes.

Questions

1 Thunder and lightning occur at the same time. Lightning strikes 1 km away. If you see the flash immediately, how long do you have to wait before your hear the thunder? (Take the speed of sound as 333 m/s.)

2 a An ultrasonic tape measure in a room sends out a sound wave with a frequency of 40 kHz. A returning wave is detected 0.02 s later. How long is the room? (Assume that the speed of sound is 300 m/s.)

b In a second room, the measure reads 1.5 m. The estate agent thinks that the measure has broken. His scientific customer has another explanation. What might it be?

3 A light beam is bounced off the Moon. It returns 2.5 s later. If the velocity of light is 300 000 000 m/s, how far away is the Moon?

4 A dolphin produces ultrasonic waves. From his first pulse he receives a small echo $^{1}/_{100}$ s later, and another, larger, echo 1 s later. A second pulse from the dolphin produces echoes at $^{1}/_{100}$ s and 2 s later.

a What does this tell the dolphin about the fish and the killer whale?

b On both occasions the dolphin receives an echo at $^{1}/_{10}$ s. Where does this echo come from?

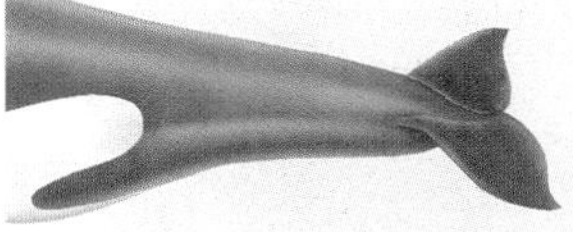

42 MORE ABOUT WAVE SPEED

Waves travel at different speeds in different materials. Some kinds of waves, such as sound waves, are also affected by temperature.

Waves travel at different speeds in different materials

The speed at which waves travel may be affected by the material through which they are travelling. Ocean waves, for example, travel faster in deep water than in shallow water. As a wave approaches shore, the water gets shallower. The wave slows in the shallow water and gets higher. Eventually the wave collapses and breaks.

The speed of sound is affected by temperature, the type of material through which it is moving, and the density of this material. The speed of sound in air is 331.46 m/s at 0 °C. When the air is warmer, sound travels faster. If you measure the speed of sound on a warm day, you should get an answer of around 340 m/s. The speed also rises as air density falls.

In water, the speed of sound is about 1500 m/s. In aluminium, sound waves travel at 6400 m/s. In steel, the speed is 6000 m/s.

Light travels much faster than this. Nothing travels faster than the speed of light. Light travels at 300 000 000 m/s in a vacuum.

Fig. 42.1 Ocean waves slow down as the water gets shallower. Their wavelength gets shorter, and their amplitude gets larger. Beyond a certain height, the top of the wave 'falls over', or breaks.

Fig. 42.2 Velocity = frequency x wavelength.
The velocity of something is the distance it travels per second. If the rod vibrates at a frequency of 5 Hz, it produces five ripples per second. If each ripple has a wavelength of 2 cm, these five ripples cover a distance of 5 x 2 = 10 cm. This is the distance covered per second = the velocity of the waves.
Velocity = f x λ.

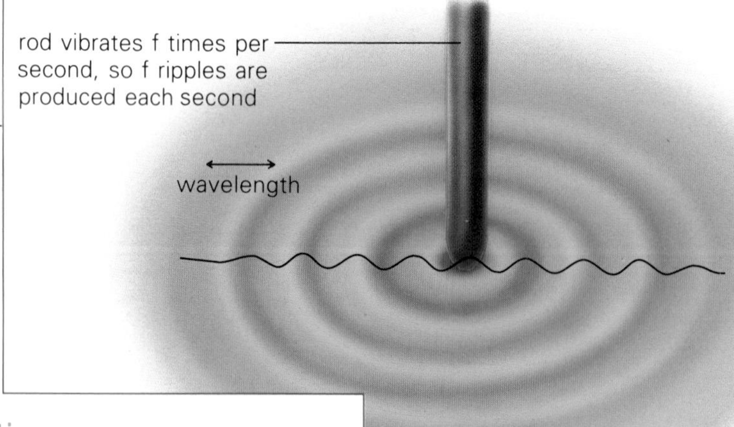

The wave equation

If a vibrating rod is dipped into a pond, ripples spread out from the rod across the surface.

If the frequency of vibration is **f**, then in 1 s there will have been f vibrations. Each vibration produces a ripple. In 1 s, f ripples will have been produced.

The distance between crests is the wavelength, λ. λ is a Greek letter called lambda.

So in 1 s, f ripples, each separated by distance λ, have spread out from the rod. The total distance covered is **f x λ**.

The distance covered in 1 s is the velocity of the wave. The velocity of a wave = frequency x wavelength.

$v = \mathbf{f} \times \lambda$.

If a sound wave of frequency 330 Hz has a wavelength of 1 m, the velocity is 330 Hz × 1 m = 330 m/s.

This wave equation applies to all waves.

What happens if a wave slows down? Velocity, v, gets smaller. Normally, frequency, f, does not change. This means that wavelength, λ must get smaller. So when a wave slows down its wavelength becomes smaller.

EXTENSION

Question

When people are working on a railway line, it is important that they should have as much warning as possible of an approaching train. If a team of workers was supplied with a microphone and detector, where should they place it to give the earliest warning?

Sonic booms are produced when aeroplanes break the sound barrier

Imagine Concorde travelling at the speed of sound. If the plane is at A, 660 m from the observer, the sound from the engines takes 2 s to reach him. One second later, both the sound and Concorde will reach point B, 330 m from the observer. The pressure waves from A and B will both take 1 s to reach the observer, and arrive together. The noise will be tremendous.

At speeds above the speed of sound, a cone of superimposed pressure waves reaches the ground.

All that sound energy arriving at once creates the 'sonic boom', which can break chimney pots and windows.

This problem has limited Concorde's flight routes. Many countries do not want Concorde to fly over them. Most of Concorde's flight paths lie over water to prevent damage and nuisance from sonic booms.

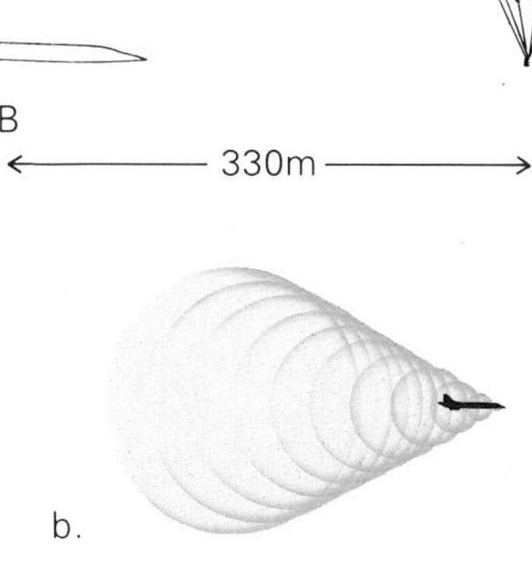

Fig. 42.3 A sonic boom is produced when an aircraft flies faster than the speed of sound. A plane flying very fast creates pressure waves at surfaces which hit the air, such as the nose and the wings. These pressure waves spread out in all directions at the speed of sound. If the plane is flying at the speed of sound, then the waves become concentrated at these points, and combine to produce a very loud noise.

If the plane is flying faster than sound, as shown in (b), then the pressure waves are left behind. As they spread outwards from the points at which they were formed along the plane's flightpath, they become concentrated at the edge of a cone. This reaches right down to the ground, where we hear a sonic boom.

INVESTIGATION 42.1

How is the speed of a wave affected by the depth of water through which it travels?

1 Read through the experiment, and draw up a suitable results chart.

2 Take a shallow rectangular tray and pour water into it to a depth of a few millimetres. Measure the length of the inside of the tray. Measure the depth of the water.

3 Raise one end of the tray 1 cm, and then gently drop it. Observe the ripple which moves across the water. Use a stopwatch to measure the time it takes to travel from one end to the other, and then back again. Repeat this several times, and work out an average reading.

4 Calculate the speed at which the ripple was travelling.

$$\text{Speed (cm/s)} = \frac{\text{distance travelled (twice length of tray, cm)}}{\text{average time taken (s)}}$$

5 Put more water into the tray, and measure the new depth. Repeat steps **3** and **4**.

6 Continue adding more water, and repeating steps **3** and **4**, until you have measurements for at least five different depths of water.

Questions

1 How does the depth of water affect the speed of the wave?

2 What would you expect to happen to the speed of an ocean wave as it approached the shore?

3 Is the wave that you produced a longitudinal wave or a transverse wave?

4 Do you think that your results are really accurate? Discuss any sources of error in your experiment.

Questions

1 a Complete the following table. MHz is short for megahertz, which is 1 000 000 Hz.

velocity m/s	*frequency*	*wavelength*	*radio station*
300 000 000	1089 kHz		Radio 1 MW
300 000 000		330 m	Radio 2 MW
	1215 kHz	247 m	Radio 3 MW
	198 kHz	1515 m	Radio 4 LW
	92.4 MHz		Radio 4 FM

b What do MW, LW and FM stand for?

2 A hi-fi manufacturer produces a system that can make sounds with frequencies between 20 Hz and 20 000 Hz.

a If the velocity of sound is 340 m/s what is the wavelength of the highest and lowest note?

b How many of each of these wavelengths would fit in a room 3.4 m long?

43 SOUND

Sound waves are longitudinal waves. They can be displayed on an oscilloscope. Human ears respond to sound waves of a wide range of frequencies.

An oscilloscope can display sound waves

A microphone is made of a diaphragm connected to a coil. Sound waves cause the diaphragm to vibrate and this vibrates the coil. The coil moves in a magnetic field which produces a changing voltage. (This is an **electromagnetic effect** – you will find much more about it in Topic 85.) The microphone changes sound energy to electrical energy.

The changing voltage caused by sound waves can be displayed on an **oscilloscope**. The oscilloscope shows the changing voltage on the vertical axis. The horizontal axis shows a change of time. Sound waves are longitudinal waves. But the wave on the oscilloscope looks like a transverse wave.

The distance between two crests on the screen shows the time taken for a complete oscillation. This is the **period** of the oscillation. The closer together the crests are, the shorter the period. A short period of oscillation means that the **frequency** is high. Remember – frequency is the number of oscillations in one second.

The height of a crest on the screen shows the **amplitude** of the oscillation. The greater the height of the crests, the greater the amplitude.

Fig. 43.1 A microphone converts sound waves into electrical signals.

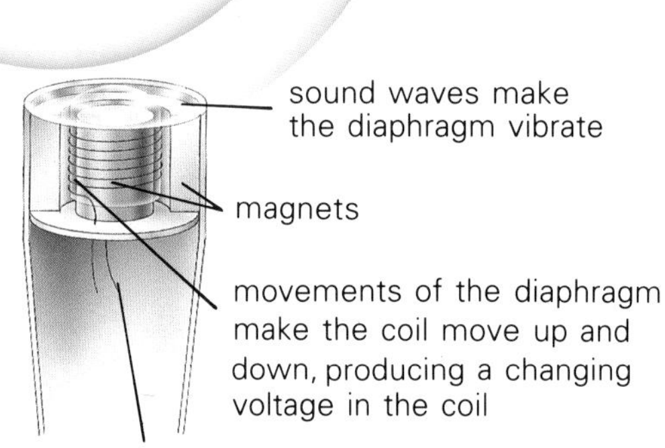

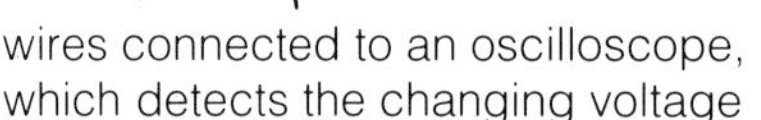

Fig. 43.2 An oscilloscope trace of a pure sound. The grid on the screen is often 1 cm squares. The **time base** setting tells you what time interval each division represents. If the time base is 1 sec/cm, then each large division represents a time of 1 second.
The vertical divisions show the voltage scale. At 1 V/cm each large square represents 1 V.

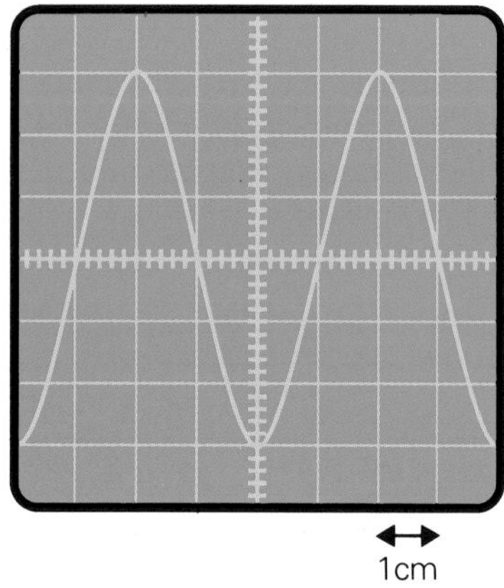

INVESTIGATION 43.1

Investigating oscilloscope traces of different types of sound

Set up a microphone connected to an oscilloscope. You will also need objects which can produce pure notes, such as tuning forks, a radio – and your voice! Make careful drawings of the traces on the oscilloscope screen produced by different types of notes.

INVESTIGATION 43.2

The range of human hearing

Use the apparatus shown in Figure 43.3. The oscillator produces an oscillating voltage which you can adjust with a dial. The oscillating voltage makes the loudspeaker vibrate, setting up sound waves in the air.

Fig. 43.3

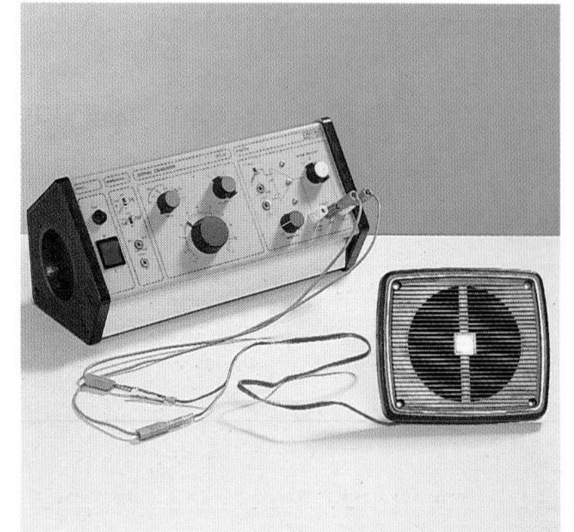

Find out answers to each of the following questions. In each case, you will need to take care that people are not 'cheating'! Devise a method of making sure that people do not say that they can hear a sound when they cannot.

1 What is the lowest frequency produced by your equipment which anyone can hear?

2 What is the highest frequency which anyone can hear?

3 At which frequency do most people find the sound is loudest?

4 Collect class results for the lowest and highest frequencies which people can hear. Draw a block graph to show these results.

5 Does age seem to make a difference to people's range of hearing?

Ears convert sound energy into electrical energy in nerves

A human ear has an **eardrum**, which behaves like the diaphragm on the microphone. Sound waves make the eardrum vibrate.

The vibrations of the eardrum set up vibrations in a chain of three small bones. The bones are arranged in a lever-like manner, so that the vibrations in the third bone, the stirrup, are greater than the vibrations set up in the eardrum. The bones **amplify** the vibrations.

The stirrup vibrates against a membrane on the outside of the **cochlea**. This is a coiled tube filled with fluid. The membrane makes the fluid vibrate. Inside it are cells which are sensitive to vibrations. They respond to the vibrations by setting up tiny electrical signals, which travel along the auditory nerve to the brain. The brain interprets these signals as sound.

Fig. 43.4 The human ear

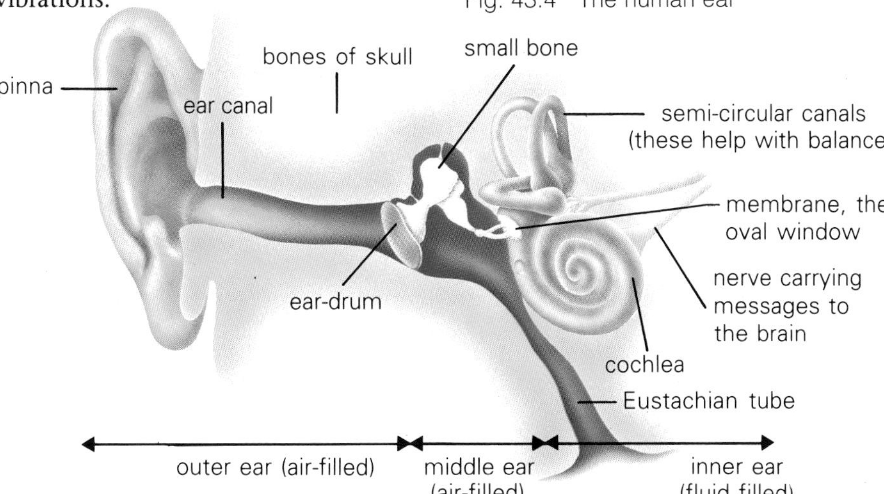

Deafness has many causes

Anything which stops the passage of vibrations through the eardrum into the cochlea, or which stops the sensitive cells from sending messages to the brain, will make you deaf.

A common cause of deafness is a build-up of **wax** in the outer ear. Wax is made by the ear to stop dust and bacteria entering it. But sometimes such a thick layer builds up that the eardrum cannot vibrate. This sort of deafness is easily cured by dissolving the wax. Because the deafness does not last long, it is called temporary deafness.

If any part of the ear that transmits the vibrations to the inner ear is damaged, this is called a **conductive** hearing loss.

The **eardrum** itself can be damaged by a blow to the head, by very loud sounds or by sudden pressure changes. Any of these can make a hole in the drum. Small tears in an eardrum can often heal themselves, but sometimes the damage is permanent.

Infections in the ear may cause damage to the three small bones. If these get jammed firmly together, vibrations cannot pass into the cochlea.

Conductive hearing loss reduces the amplitude of the vibrations reaching the inner ear. The hearing loss is similar across a range of frequencies. Some conductive loss can be treated by surgery or drugs.

Infections may also damage the cochlea or the auditory nerve. If the sensitive cells in the cochlea or the auditory nerve cells are damaged this is a **sensorineural** hearing loss. These cells cannot regrow and damage is permanent. Hearing loss is different at different frequencies and sound is **distorted** and reduced.

Long exposure to very loud sound can also cause this type of damage, especially at higher frequencies. People working in noisy environments should always wear ear protectors, or they may find that they become deaf as they get older. Portable hi-fi headphones may also cause damage. The sounds are produced very close to the eardrum, so it is easy to expose the ear to high sound levels for long periods of time.

Hearing aids amplify sound

A hearing aid is an electronic amplifier. It has a microphone which collects sound. The sound is amplified, and delivered to the ear by a small receiver, often worn inside the ear canal.

In deafness caused by damage to the eardrum or the small bones, hearing aids often produce very good hearing. But if the deafness is caused by damage to the cochlea, hearing aids may not be as successful. This is because the message sent to the brain by the cochlea is still not clear, even if the sound is loud. Sound may seem distorted, so that it is difficult to pick out important sounds like speech. Background noise is amplified as well, so the person may have problems in sorting out 'useful' noises from unwanted ones.

More advanced hearing aids are designed to amplify the sound selectively, to match more closely the hearing loss. In some cases, it is possible to connect a hearing aid to a **cochlea implant**. The implant is surgically placed inside the head and connects directly to the auditory nerves. It cannot reproduce the same amount of information as a normal ear, because it is not possible to connect up that many nerves. The deaf person can learn to interpret the sounds received. As the technology improves, more life-like hearing becomes possible.

Questions

1 What is meant by:
- **a** the period of an oscillation?
- **b** the frequency of an oscillation?
- **c** How does the sound of a high-frequency sound compare with the sound of a low-frequency sound?

2 Match each of these functions with a structure labelled on the diagram of the human ear in Figure 43.4
- **a** contains cells which convert vibrations in fluid into tiny electrical signals
- **b** vibrates when sound waves reach the ear
- **c** amplify the vibrations as they cross the middle ear
- **d** transmit the vibrations from the air in the middle ear to the liquid in the cochlea

44 LOUDNESS, PITCH AND QUALITY

Loudness, pitch and quality are terms we can use to describe the sounds we hear.

The loudness of a sound is related to its amplitude

The amplitude of a wave is the maximum distance that the vibrating particles move from their resting position. Sound waves are longitudinal waves, so the vibrating particles produce areas of compression and rarefaction. This causes pressure changes in the material through which the sound is moving. The further the particles move, the greater the pressure changes. So, in a sound wave, the amplitude can be measured by measuring the pressure changes which are produced.

Sound waves with a large amplitude tend to sound louder to us than ones with a small amplitude. But human ears are more sensitive to some frequencies than others, as you will have found out if you did Investigation 43.2. A sound of a frequency to which your ears are very sensitive will sound loud to you, even if its amplitude is quite small.

Fig. 44.1 People working in noisy environments must protect their ears from long-term damage.

Sound intensity is measured in W/m²

The **intensity** of a sound is the amount of energy passing through a square metre every second. It is measured in watts per square metre (W/m²). The intensity of a sound is related to its amplitude. If the amplitude doubles, the intensity is four times greater. Increasing the intensity of a sound increases its loudness. But this also depends on the sensitivity of the person hearing the sound.

EXTENSION

Loudness is measured in decibels

The loudness of a sound is often measured in decibels, written **dB**. The softest sound which human ears can hear is said to have a loudness of 0 dB. The sound of a jet aircraft 50 m away is about 10 000 000 000 000 times louder than this, or 10^{13} times louder. The aircraft is said to have a loudness of 130 dB.

A small change in the dB value of a sound represents a large change in its loudness. For example, a noise of 100dB sounds twice as loud as a noise of 90 dB.

Health Inspectors in Britain regularly measure noise levels in people's working environments. Excessive noise is not only unpleasant, but can make people work less safely, suffer stress, or suffer permanent damage to their ears. It is not enough just to measure the physical intensity of the sound, because our sensitivity is different to sounds of different frequencies. The meters the Inspectors use have electronic circuits which compensate for this changing sensitivity.

Table 44.1 Approximate sound levels of different sounds

Sound	*Sound level in dB*
Quiet countryside	25
People talking quietly	65
Vacuum cleaner 3 m away	70
Lorry 7 m away	90
Very noisy factory	100
Loud music in a disco	110
Jet aircraft 50 m away	130
Rifle firing near ear	160

DID YOU KNOW?

The lowest pitched orchestral instrument is the sub-contrabass clarinet, which can play C at 16.4 cycles/sec.

Pitch depends on frequency

The pitch of a note depends on its frequency. A note of high pitch has a high frequency. On an oscilloscope, a high pitched note has crests close together.

Humans can hear sounds with frequencies of between 20 Hz and 20 000 Hz. As you get older you become less sensitive to high frequencies. This usually begins in the late twenties or thirties, and gradually progresses throughout the rest of a person's life. It is caused by a degeneration of sensitive cells in the cochlea. These cells can also be damaged by exposure to loud noises. Loss of high frequency sensitivity can be a sign of hearing damage and not just old age. People do not normally notice it unless it becomes so bad that they can no longer hear speech.

Quality depends on the mixtures of frequencies in a sound

A tuning fork produces a note of a single frequency. This is a **pure** sound. With practice you can sing a note into a microphone which will produce a single frequency trace on an oscilloscope.

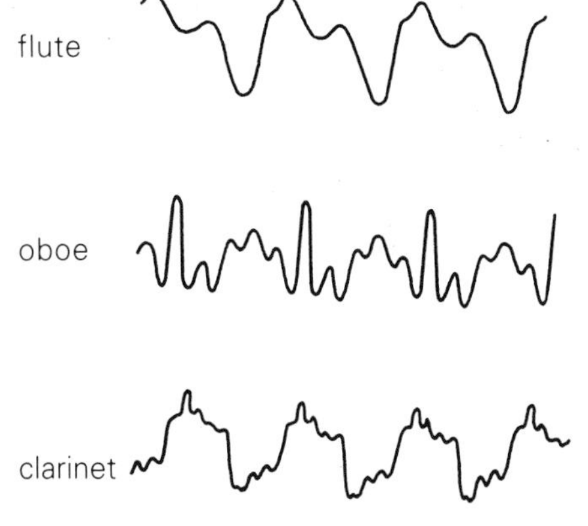

Fig. 44.2 Each type of musical instrument has its own distinctive sound pattern.

Most sounds, however, contain a mixture of frequencies. If the frequencies are simple multiples of each other they are called **harmonics**. Musical instruments tend to produce notes which consist of a basic, or **fundamental**, frequency and a number of harmonics. Our brains hear these sounds as 'musical'. If a sound contains a mixture of frequencies which are not related to each other, it does not sound musical. A sound with a large number of unrelated frequencies will just sound like 'noise'.

Room acoustics affect how different sounds appear

Sound is reflected from hard surfaces but is absorbed by soft ones. The sound in a gymnasium reflects off the walls and bounces back to the listener. The many echoes make a single clap last longer than the original sound. This is **reverberation**; the sound dies away gradually. If you want to talk or play music, the amount of reverberation is important. The **reverberation time** is the time taken for the sound intensity to fall to one millionth of its original value (a 60 dB drop). Reverberation gives sound 'life', and boosts the sound levels. But if the reverberation is too long, the sound may become confusing as different sounds overlap. For speech, a reverberation time of a second gives a good balance. For music, the reverberation time can be longer.

Polished stone surfaces reflect nearly all the sound that hits them. Heavy curtains and carpets can absorb most of the sound energy. With careful placing of the different materials in a room, the reverberation time can be controlled. If you have large, heavy curtains at home you may be able to experiment by comparing the sound of some music with them open and closed. You can experiment with a classroom that is empty and one that is full of quiet people. In a concert hall each person in the audience is a very good absorber. It can be difficult to arrange the seating so that the sound properties in rehearsal are not too different from when the hall is full. In a large enough room, the returning echo could arrive after the sound has finished. This would produce a noticeable echo and would be very confusing. Another problem is if there isn't enough sound coming from a particular direction. With careful design, reflecting materials can be used to fill in any 'gaps' (see Figure 49.5).

Fig. 44.4 A car being tested in a anechoic chamber.

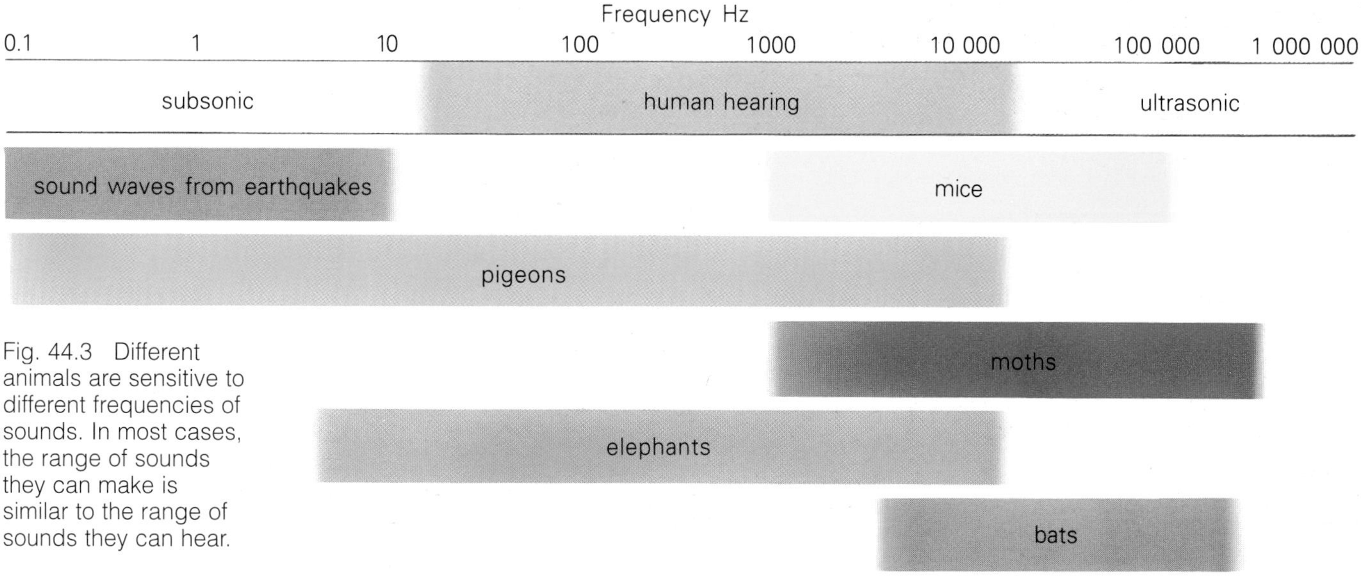

Frequency Hz

0.1 | 1 | 10 | 100 | 1000 | 10 000 | 100 000 | 1 000 000

subsonic | human hearing | ultrasonic

sound waves from earthquakes

mice

pigeons

moths

elephants

bats

Fig. 44.3 Different animals are sensitive to different frequencies of sounds. In most cases, the range of sounds they can make is similar to the range of sounds they can hear.

45 SOUND SYSTEMS

We often transfer information in the form of sound. Sound can be recorded on tape or records.

Sound is used for communication

Humans have always used sound for information transfer. Speech is an important way of communicating. Early societies used drums and other sound-producing objects to send sound over long distances.

Using sound for information transfer has its limitations. Sound is instantaneous – it happens and then stops. So if we want to store the signals, we must change them into something else which we can store. Another problem with sound is that the strength of a sound fades as it travels – so it can only be used over fairly short distances.

Both of these problems can be solved if the sound signal can be changed into another kind of signal, which can be stored. The stored signal can then be changed back into sound again whenever we want to hear it. This allows us to 'move' the sound from one place to another, and from one time to another. We can also amplify the sound if we wish.

A microphone is used to convert the sound to electrical signals. An electrical signal can be amplified or recorded. An amplifier takes the electrical signal and makes it larger or **amplifies** it. The amplified signal can then be converted back to a sound signal with a loudspeaker. This is how hearing aids, megaphones and public address (PA) systems work.

Advanced systems can filter and clean up the sounds before amplifying them.

Fig. 45.1 Alpenhorns can be used to transfer information over long distances. In mountainous regions, before modern methods of communication, this was one of the quickest methods of making contact with someone on the other side of the valley.

Fig. 45.2 A microphone, amplifier and loudspeaker can be used to produce a louder sound. The sound signals are converted into electrical signals and then back into sound signals again. The electrical signals change in just the same way as the sound signals. This is an example of an **analogue system**. It processes continuously changing signals.

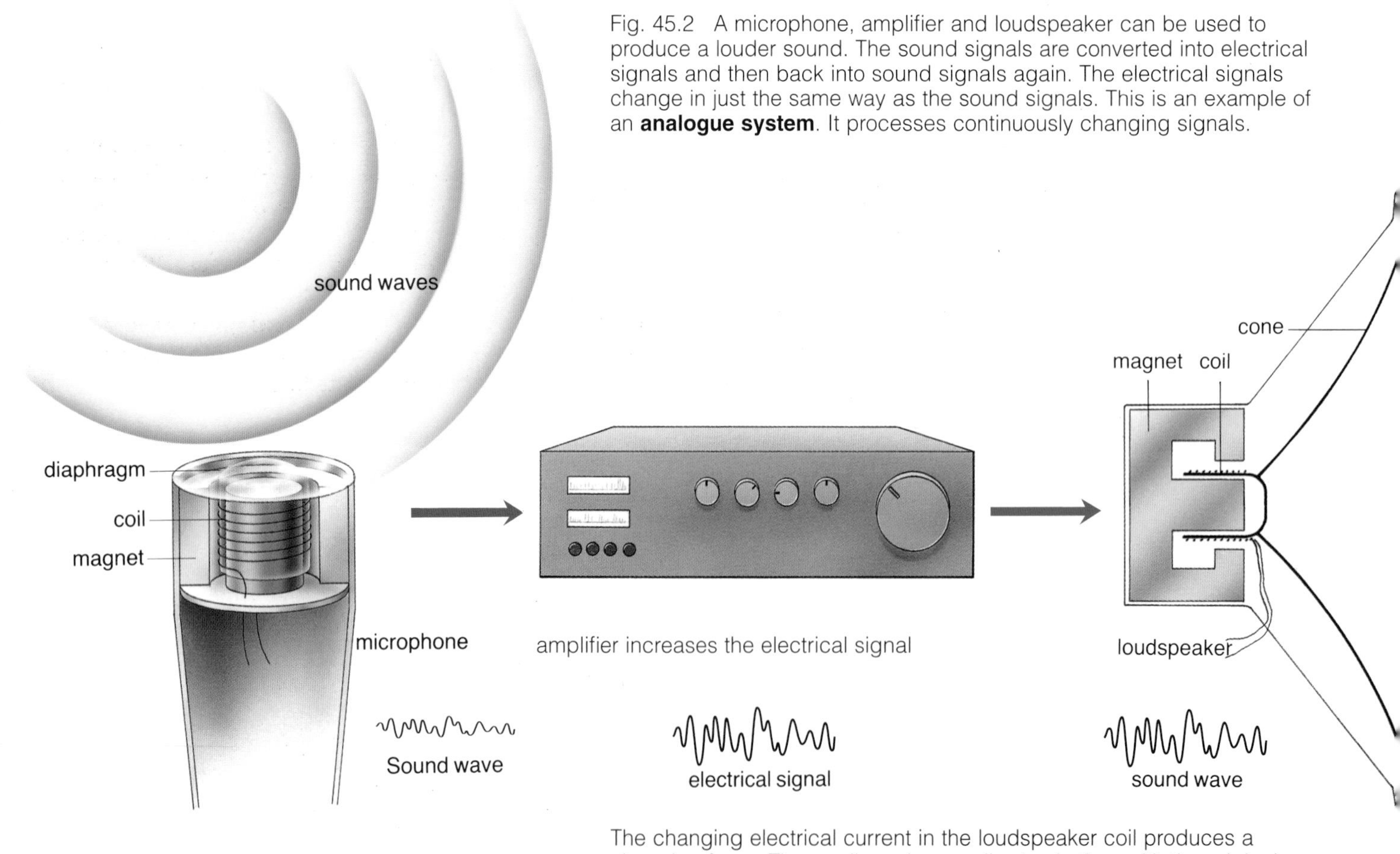

sound waves

diaphragm

coil

magnet

microphone

Sound wave

amplifier increases the electrical signal

electrical signal

cone

magnet coil

loudspeaker

sound wave

The changing electrical current in the loudspeaker coil produces a changing force. The cardboard cone vibrates in time with the original sound vibrations. These vibrations set the air vibrating. The original sound wave is reproduced.

INVESTIGATION 45.1

Building a loudspeaker

1 Cut a cardboard ring, as shown in the diagram. Join AB and BC to make a cone. Add a length of cardboard tube, to act as a coil-former.
2 Wind a coil on the former. Leave long ends.
3 Connect the two ends of the coil to an amplifier or a signal generator. If you put a 4 Ω resistor in series with the coil, this will prevent damage to the amplifier.
4 Hold one end of a bar magnet inside the coil. You should be able to produce a sound from your loudspeaker.

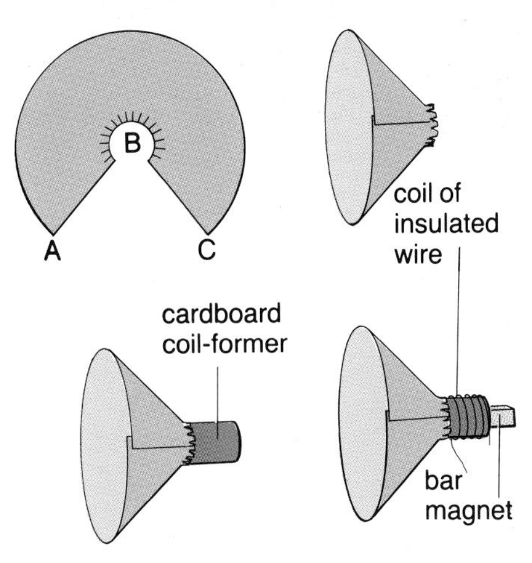

Fig. 45.3

Questions

1 Explain why a sound is produced when you change the current inside the coil.
2 Does your loudspeaker sound equally loud at all frequencies? Which is loudest?
3 Look carefully at a commercially produced loudspeaker. How is it similar to yours? What differences are there between the two loudspeakers?

Tapes store sound as magnetic fields

If a magnetic material is moved past an electromagnet, the magnetic material becomes magnetised. A changing current in the electromagnet will produce a changing magnetic field along the length of the material. This is how a tape or cassette recorder works.

To play back the tape, the tape is moved past a playback head. It moves at the same speed as when it was recorded. The changing magnetic field on the tape generates a changing a.c. signal in the coil as the tape moves past. The signal is then amplified, and passed into a loudspeaker to produce the sound.

The earliest magnetic recorders used iron wire to store the magnetic fields. Modern recorders use magnetic particles on a plastic backing tape. The cheapest tapes, called ferric tapes, use particles of iron oxide. Chrome tapes use chromium dioxide. Metal tapes use particles of iron.

The faster the tape moves past the heads, the better the quality of the recording. A cassette tape moves past the heads at 4.7 cm/s. This is quite slow, and it is difficult to eliminate background hiss. The Dolby® system reduces this noise by artificially boosting some frequencies during recording of quiet passages. When the tape is played back, the volume is reduced. This returns the boosted signal to its normal level, but cuts down the volume of the hiss.

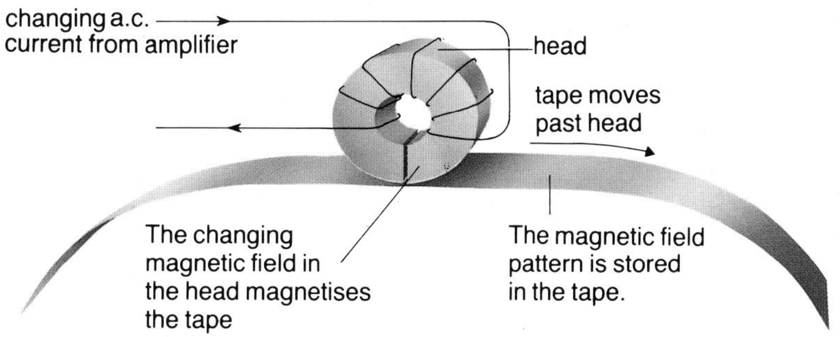

Fig. 45.4 Recording sound onto magnetic tape

Questions

1 Sound is produced by something vibrating. What vibrates to produce sound from the following instruments:
  a violin
  b guitar
  c flute
  d piano
  e drum?
2 Explain each of the following:
  a Sometimes young people can hear the squeaking of bats, but older people cannot.
  b It is recommended that no-one should be exposed to steady noise of more than 85 dB in their working environment.
  c High pitched notes show a trace with crests close together on an oscilloscope trace.
  d Hearing aids help people with deafness caused by damage to the bones in the middle ear, but are less help to people with damage to the cochlea.
  e Sound waves with a large amplitude often, but not always, sound louder to us than sound waves with a small amplitude.

3 Figure 43.2 shows an oscilloscope trace of a particular sound. The time base on an oscilloscope tells you the time scale for the trace. The time base was set at 1 ms/cm.
  a What is the period of the trace?
  b What is the frequency of the trace?
  c If this same trace was obtained with the time base set at 5 ms/cm, what would be the period of the trace?
  d What would be the frequency of this trace?

EXTENSION

46 ELECTROMAGNETIC WAVES

Electromagnetic radiation is a disturbance of electric and magnetic fields.

Electromagnetic waves can be grouped according to their wavelength

Energy changes in atoms or electrons may produce **electromagnetic waves**. These are disturbances of electric and magnetic fields. They travel as transverse waves.

The wavelength of electromagnetic waves determines how they behave. So it is useful to group electromagnetic waves according to their wavelength. Figure 46.1 shows these groups. This grouping is called the **electromagnetic spectrum**. Electromagnetic waves of a particular wavelength always have the same frequency in a particular material. Electromagnetic waves with short wavelengths have high frequency. Ones with long wavelengths have low frequency.

Electromagnetic waves are a form of energy. When they pass through a material, some of the energy they carry can be absorbed. This raises the internal energy of the material. The shorter the wavelength of the electromagnetic radiation, the more energy it carries.

All electromagnetic waves travel at the same speed in a vacuum. This speed is 300 000 000 m/s.

Table 46.1 The electromagnetic spectrum

Wavelength in metres	*Source*	*Detector*	*Uses*
10^{6} to 10^{-3} Radio waves	Electrons vibrated by electronic circuits, radio and TV transmitters, stars and galaxies including pulsars and quasars	Radio aerial	Communications – radio, television, telephone links, radar, cooking, astronomy
10^{-3} to 10^{-6} Infrared	'Hot' objects, especially the Sun	Electronic detectors, skin, special films	Heating, astronomy, thermography – taking temperature pictures
Visible light	The Sun, very hot objects	The eye, electronic detectors, photographic film	Seeing, photography, information transmission, photosynthesis, astronomy
10^{-6} to 10^{-9} Ultraviolet	The Sun, mercury vapour lamps, electric arcs	Fluorescence of chemicals, photographic film, tanning of skin, electronic detectors	Fluorescent lamps, crack detection, security marking, sterilizing food etc. astronomy
10^{-8} to 10^{-12} X rays	X ray tubes, stars, changes in electron energy	Photographic film, fluorescence of chemicals, Ionising effects, electronic detectors	Taking 'X rays' – radiography, astronomy, examining crystal structure, treating cancer, 'CAT scan'
10^{-12} and less Gamma rays	Radioactive materials, nuclear reactions	Geiger-Müller tube, photographic film, electronic detectors	Radiography, treating cancer, measuring thickness

Fig. 46.1 The electromagnetic spectrum

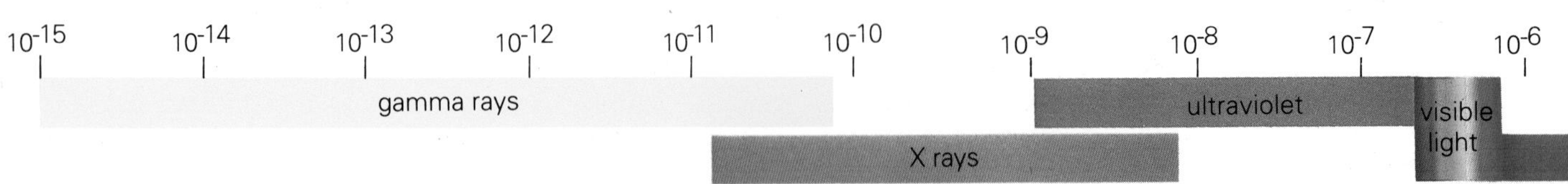

Radio waves have long wavelengths

Electromagnetic waves with wavelengths over 1 mm or so are called **radio waves**. Very short wavelength radio waves are known as **microwaves**.

Radio waves are produced by stars and galaxies. They are also produced by electrons vibrated by electronic circuits.

We use radio waves for communication. Telephone links between cities use microwaves. Communication to satellites is also by means of microwaves. Microwaves are used for cooking. A microwave oven produces electromagnetic waves with a wavelength of about 12 cm. These waves transmit energy to the food. Microwaves can be used to kill insects in grain stores. They are also used to kill bacteria in food, without heating the food so much that it spoils the flavour.

The wavelengths used for radar start in the microwave region of the electromagnetic spectrum and extend into the ultra high frequency radio waves. A short pulse is sent out which bounces back off any object which it hits. The time taken for the 'echo' to return can be used to calculate the distance of the object.

Terrestrial television broadcasts use UHF, or ultra high frequency, waves. Good quality sound broadcasts use VHF, or very high frequency, waves. The signals are sent by slightly altering the frequency of the waves, so this is known as frequency modulation, or FM. Long wavelength radio waves have a greater range in a straight line than short ones. However, short wavelength radio waves (shortwave) reflect off an upper layer of the atmosphere (see Topic 47). For this reason, very long range sound broadcasts (like the BBC World Service) can use shortwave radio. A great many television and radio broadcasts now use microwaves that are relayed by satellites.

When electromagnetic waves hit materials, they can set the electrons vibrating at the same frequency as the waves. This is how aerials detect radio waves. If the length of the aerial is matched to the frequency of the waves then the aerial will be some multiple of the wavelength. Many aerials have two branches. For an aerial on a car the body of the car counts as one of the branches. To receive radio (or television) waves this length is often set to a quarter of the expected wavelength. The aerial is described as a $^1/_4$ wave dipole.

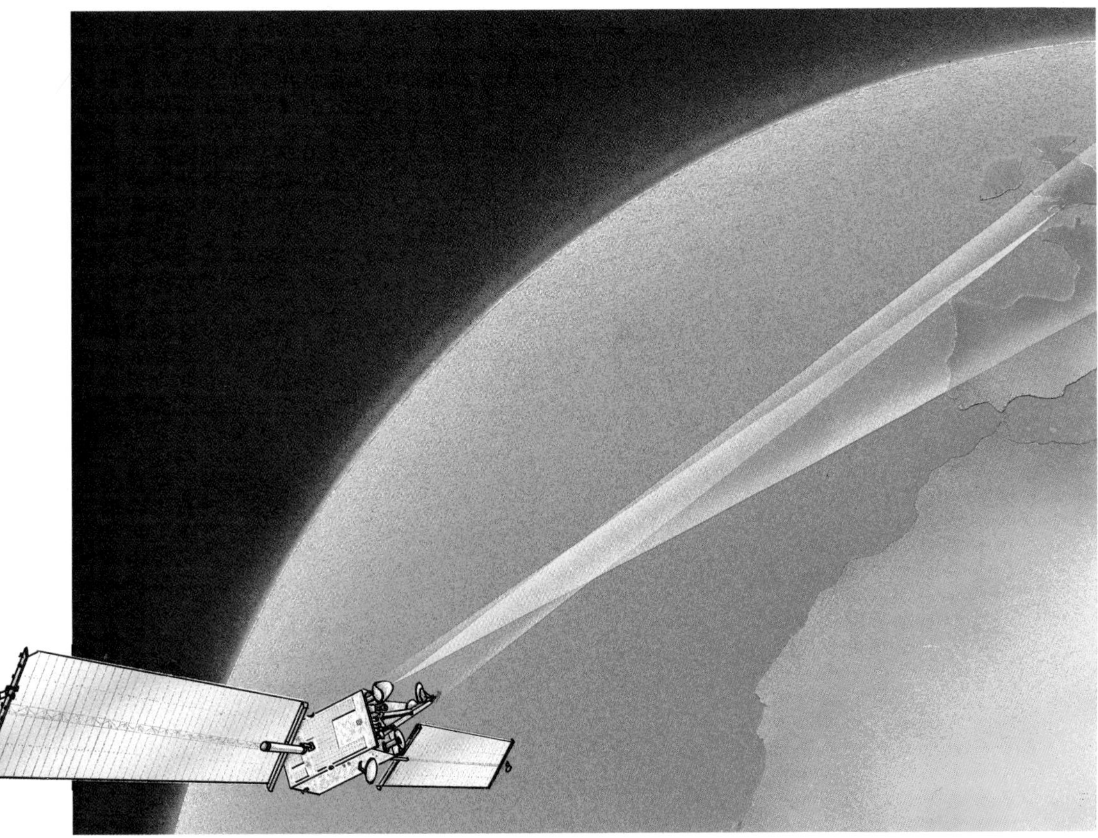

Fig. 46.2 A TV satellite broadcasts television pictures down to Earth from a stationary position 36 000 km above the Earth's surface. Pictures must first be transmitted up to the satellite. It is a relay station in the sky. The large solar panels provide the energy and can span half the width of a football pitch. The energy supply, control and transmission is all by electromagnetic radiation.

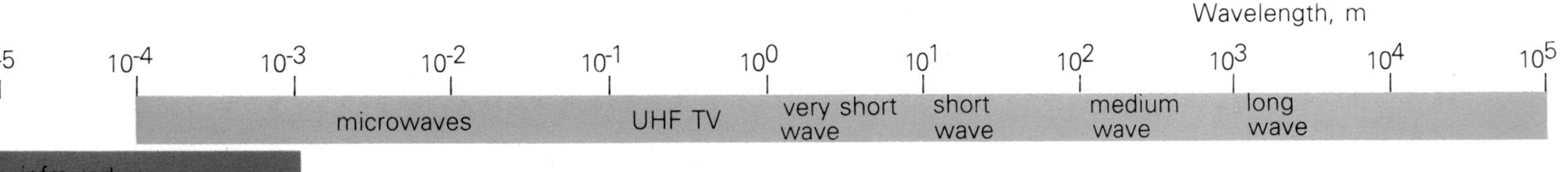

Infrared radiation is felt as heat

Electromagnetic radiation with wavelengths a little longer than that of red light is called **infrared radiation**. It is given off by hot objects. An electric lamp, for example, gives off radiation which we see as light, but also radiation with a wavelength of about $\frac{1}{1000}$ mm, which is infrared radiation. You give off infrared radiation, because you are quite hot! Your body gives off infrared radiation with a wavelength of $\frac{1}{10}$ mm to $\frac{1}{100}$ mm.

The human eye cannot detect infrared radiation, but you can feel it on your skin as warmth. The infrared is absorbed by skin, and the increase in internal energy of the skin is detected by temperature receptors. Some snakes have specially designed sense organs which make good use of this ability. They are situated in pits on either sides of their head, and they can use them to 'see' a warm object, such as a mouse, in the dark.

Infrared cameras can also 'see' hot objects. They collect and focus infrared rays just as an ordinary camera focuses light rays. They then convert the infrared rays to a visible image. These cameras can be used to find people buried in collapsed buildings. They can also be used to take pictures of buildings to find out where heat is being wasted. Infrared satellite pictures of the Earth are used in weather forecasting.

Infrared signals are also used in TV and hi-fi remote controls and for some cordless headphones, keyboards and printers. Infrared signals are also transmitted down fibre optic cables for telecommunications systems.

Light is electromagnetic radiation to which our eyes are sensitive

Light is just the same as all the other types of electromagnetic waves. But it is very important to us because our eyes happen to be sensitive to this particular range of wavelengths. Human eyes contain cells which respond to different wavelengths of light. Some react to red light, some to green, and some to blue light. This is why we can see colour.

Light will affect photographic film in a similar way to our eyes, so we can take pictures which are the same as our view of the world.

Sunlight contains a particular mixture of wavelengths of light. Artificial lighting is designed to give a similar mixture, which results in a 'natural' effect.

Questions

1 a What are meant by *electromagnetic waves*?

b What name is given to electromagnetic waves with each of the following wavelengths?

i 1 km
ii 1 cm
iii 1 μm (1/1000 mm)
iv 0.1 μm
v 0.0001 μm
vi 0.00000001 μm?

c For each of the types of waves in your answer to part **b**, briefly describe *one* source and *one* use.

d Which of the types of waves in your answer to part **b** carries

i the most energy?
ii the least energy?

2 Microwaves can be used in surveying. The time taken for them to travel between two points is used to calculate distance.

a A surveyor transmits microwaves to a second surveyor, whose receiver sends back the signal. The time between the transmission and reception of the signal by the first surveyor's equipment is 0.000033 s. How far apart are the two surveyors?

b It is known that this method is not completely accurate, and that an error of up to 40 mm might be expected over this distance. What is this as a percentage?

EXTENSION

Fig. 46.3 An infrared image of a house. The brightest parts of the picture show where most heat is being lost.

Fig. 46.4 Animals emit infrared radiation. This picture was taken with an infrared sensitive colour film.

Ultraviolet rays are produced by the Sun

Sunlight contains ultraviolet rays. We cannot see them, because human eyes cannot detect rays with such short wavelengths. But many insects can see ultraviolet light. Many flowers have petals with markings on them which reflect ultraviolet light. Insects can see these markings, which guide them to the nectar at the base of the flower.

Ultraviolet light falling on to human skin enables the skin to produce vitamin D. A lack of sunlight, combined with a lack of vitamin D in the diet, can cause a weakness in the bones, called rickets. In northern Russia, children are exposed to sunlamps for part of the day, to enable their skin to make vitamin D.

But too much ultraviolet light falling on to the skin can be harmful. It damages cells, giving you sunburn. It may even cause skin cancer. Skin cancer is now getting much commoner, as people who are not used to strong sunlight go on holidays to hot countries more often. Your skin can protect itself by making a pigment called **melanin**, which absorbs the ultraviolet rays. This is what happens when you tan. But it takes a while to happen, and until you have built up a deep tan you are in danger of damaging your skin if you expose it to strong ultraviolet radiation.

Ultraviolet radiation is produced by arc welders. An arc welder heats metal with an electric spark. The very hot atoms give out ultraviolet light. So a welder wears protective clothes, and also a dark green filter over his eyes. Eyes are easily damaged by ultraviolet light.

Ultraviolet light entering the Earth's upper atmosphere from the Sun is involved in the formation of the gas ozone. This absorbs a lot of the ultraviolet light reaching the Earth from the Sun. But chemicals such as chlorofluorocarbons, or CFCs, are damaging the ozone layer, so that more ultraviolet light can reach the Earth's surface. This could be dangerous to living things.

Some materials convert ultraviolet radiation into visible light

Inside a fluorescent lamp, electrical energy is converted into ultraviolet radiation. The inside of the tube in a lamp is coated with fluorescent powder. When the ultraviolet light hits this powder, it is absorbed by it. The atoms in the powder absorb some of the energy in the ultraviolet waves, and release it as visible light. This is called **fluorescence**.

Some washing powders contain chemicals which fluoresce. They absorb ultraviolet light in sunlight, and release it as visible light. So your white clothes look even brighter! At a disco an ultraviolet light source makes white clothing which has been washed in these powders glow in the dark.

'Invisible' ink fluoresces in ultraviolet light and is used for security marking. You can write your post code on an object like a video recorder. In normal light, the marking is not visible, but under an ultraviolet lamp the ink fluoresces and is clearly seen.

Fig. 46.5 An evening primrose flower photographed in ultraviolet light. This is how an insect might see it. Notice how the guide-lines show up clearly, directing the insect to the nectar in the base of the flower.

Fig. 46.6 Dark filters on the welder's goggles protect his eyes from electromagnetic radiation.

X rays can penetrate solids

X rays are produced by electrons that are slowed down very quickly. Electrons are accelerated by a voltage of 30 kV. They strike a metal target at 100 000 000 m/s. Some of their kinetic energy is converted into electromagnetic energy as they slow down.

As you can see from the chart on page 116, electromagnetic radiation with wavelengths between about 10^{-12} and 10^{-10} m may be classified either as gamma rays or as X rays. The rays themselves are no different. Whether they are called gamma rays or X rays depends on how they were produced.

X rays are high energy waves. They can be detected with photographic film. X rays can penetrate solids.

Different materials absorb different amounts of X ray radiation. X rays passing through an arm, for example, can pass easily through the skin and muscle, but not so easily through the bone. If you place your arm between an X ray source and a photographic film, you get a shadow picture of the bones in your arm. The film blackens where the X rays hit it, so the areas of skin and muscle show up black. Fewer X rays pass through the bones, so the areas of film behind the bones stay white.

X rays cause materials to fluoresce. If X rays hit a fluorescent screen, they cause the screen to emit visible light. So 'X rays' can also be taken by photographing the visible light emitted from a fluorescent screen which has been bombarded with X rays.

High energy X rays have high frequencies and low wavelengths. They can penetrate metal, and are used to inspect welds.

Fig. 46.7 X ray pictures of luggage can reveal their contents.

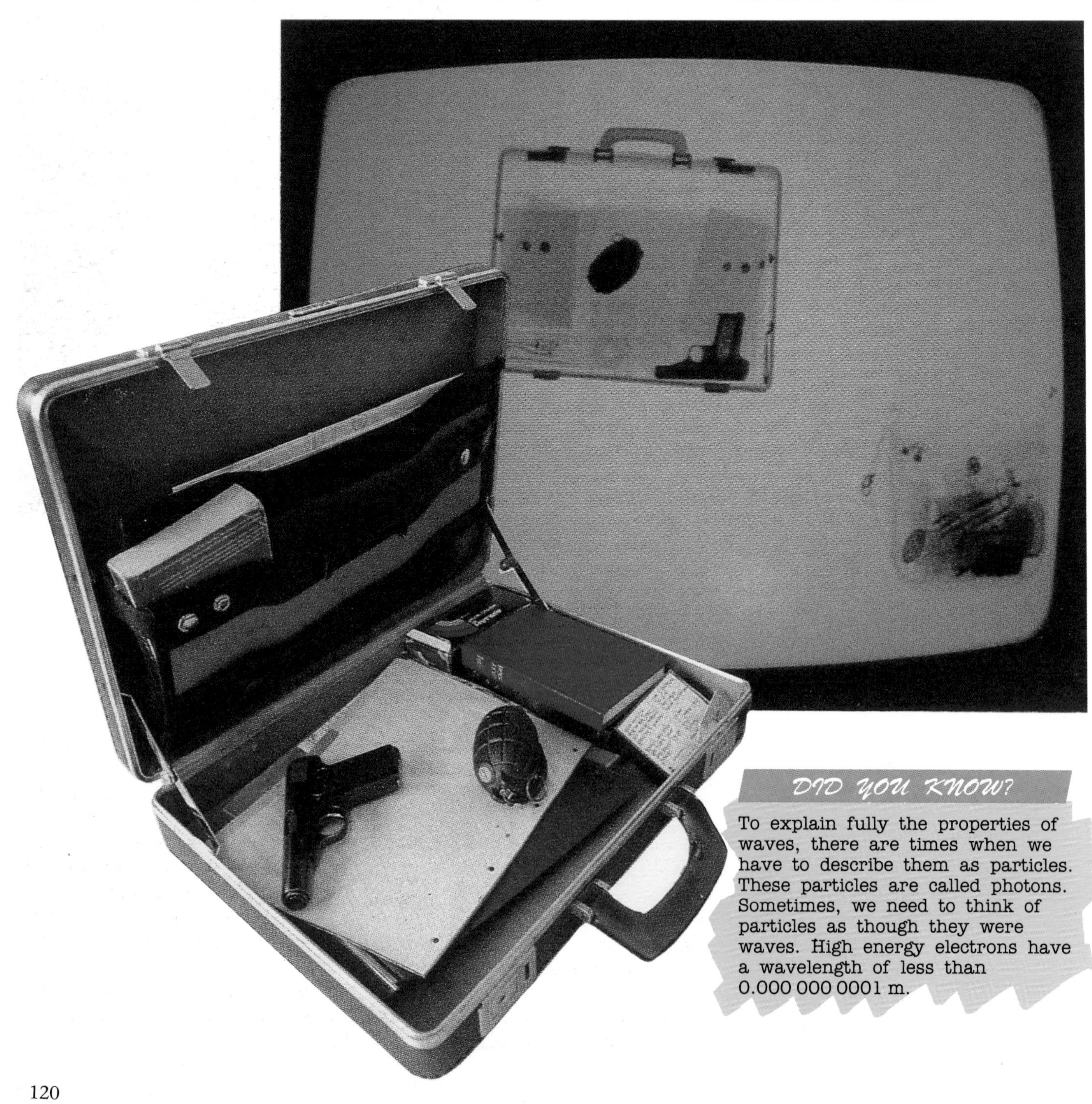

DID YOU KNOW?

To explain fully the properties of waves, there are times when we have to describe them as particles. These particles are called photons. Sometimes, we need to think of particles as though they were waves. High energy electrons have a wavelength of less than 0.000 000 0001 m.

Questions

1 Explain the following:

a You should always wear protective glasses when using a sunlamp.

b People with pale skin are more likely to get skin cancer than people with dark skin.

c X ray pictures show bones as light areas.

d Snakes can catch mice in the dark.

2 A fluorescent tube produces mainly ultra-violet radiation. A tube using 100 J of electrical energy per second produces 62 J of ultra-violet light, and 3 J of visible light.

a What is the visible light output power of the tube?

If the tube is coated with fluorescent powder, 20 J of visible light energy is produced from each 100 J of electrical energy.

b What is the visible light output power of the coated tube?

c What is the efficiency of the coated tube?

d How much more heat will the coated tube produce than the uncoated tube?

3 Iridium 192 is a gamma source. It has a half life of 74 days. An oil company uses iridium 192 to inspect the welds in a pipe line.

a Explain how iridium 192 could be used for inspecting welds.

b After a year of using the same iridium 192 sample, it is found that the film used needs to be exposed for much longer than before. Why is this?

c What happens to the intensity of the radiation from the iridium 192 after 370 days?

d How could this problem be prevented by the oil company?

4 A company decides to replace the lighting in its offices. In one office, the cost of running three normal light bulbs is £22.50 per year. A lighting consultant points out that fluorescent lighting would produce the same amount of light for only £5 a year.

a The manager finds this hard to believe. How would you explain to him why a fluorescent lamp saves so much money?

b If the company had 30 offices, how much money could they save in a year?

c If each fluorescent light cost £12 to install, how much money would they save in the first year by replacing all their normal lights with fluorescent lights?

d In houses, people tend only to use fluorescent lighting in the kitchen, if at all. Why is this?

EXTENSION

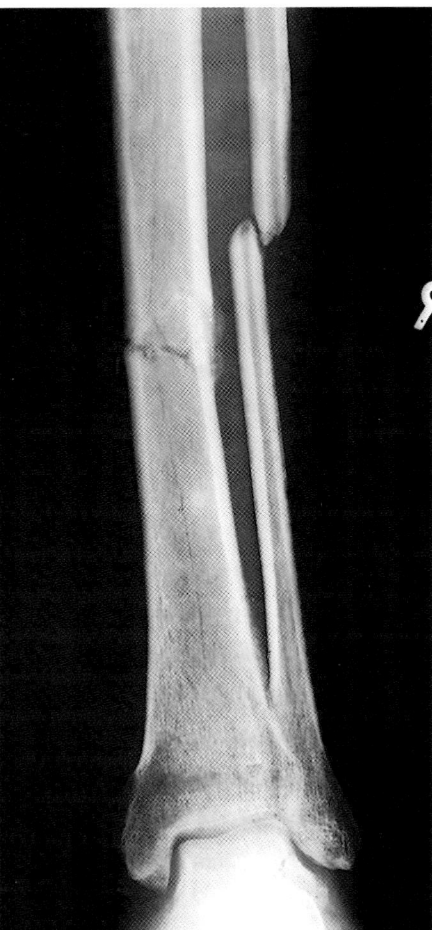

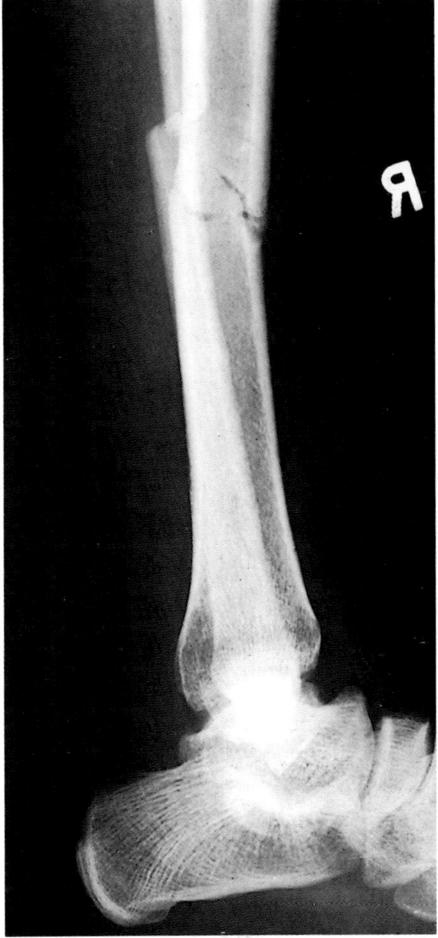

Fig. 46.8 An X ray produces a shadow picture of bones. Here, both the tibia and fibula in the lower leg are broken.

Gamma radiation has very short wavelengths

Electromagnetic waves with the shortest wavelengths and the highest frequencies are called **gamma rays**. Gamma rays are produced by changes in the nuclei of atoms. They carry very large amounts of energy – at least 10 million times more energy than light rays.

Gamma rays are used for measuring thicknesses of metal sheets, and for sterilising medical materials and instruments. The most common industrial sources of gamma rays are iridium 192 and cobalt 90. Gamma rays are harmful to living things because they cause ionisation in their cells. This can cause mutations in the cells. High doses of gamma radiation kill cells. With careful control they can be used to kill cancer cells.

Gamma rays can be detected using a Geiger-Müller tube, or photographic film.

47 MORE ABOUT RADIO WAVES

Radio signals are electromagnetic waves

Only 20 years after the first telephone conversation, the Italian scientist Marconi sent a radio signal across a distance of 12 miles. To begin with, signals were sent, like telegraph signals, as a series of pulses. The pulses, however, were of electromagnetic waves passing through the air, and not electrical signals passing along wires. So the system was called 'wireless'.

A radio signal is sent out as a **carrier wave**, on which information about a sound signal is superimposed. There are two ways in which the sound information can be added to the carrier wave. The sound signal can change the **amplitude** of the carrier wave. This method is called **amplitude modulation** or **AM**. Alternatively the sound signal can change the **frequency** of the carrier wave. This is called **frequency modulation** or **FM**.

The modulated radio waves are generated by the oscillation of electrons in wires. This produces an electromagnetic disturbance, or radio wave, which spreads out from the transmitter aerial. The radio waves travel at the speed of light, and can be picked up by a receiver. The receiver sorts out the superimposed sound signal from the carrier wave. This is called **demodulation**.

Fig. 47.1 A radio wave can carry information either as changes in frequency (FM) or as changes in amplitude (AM).

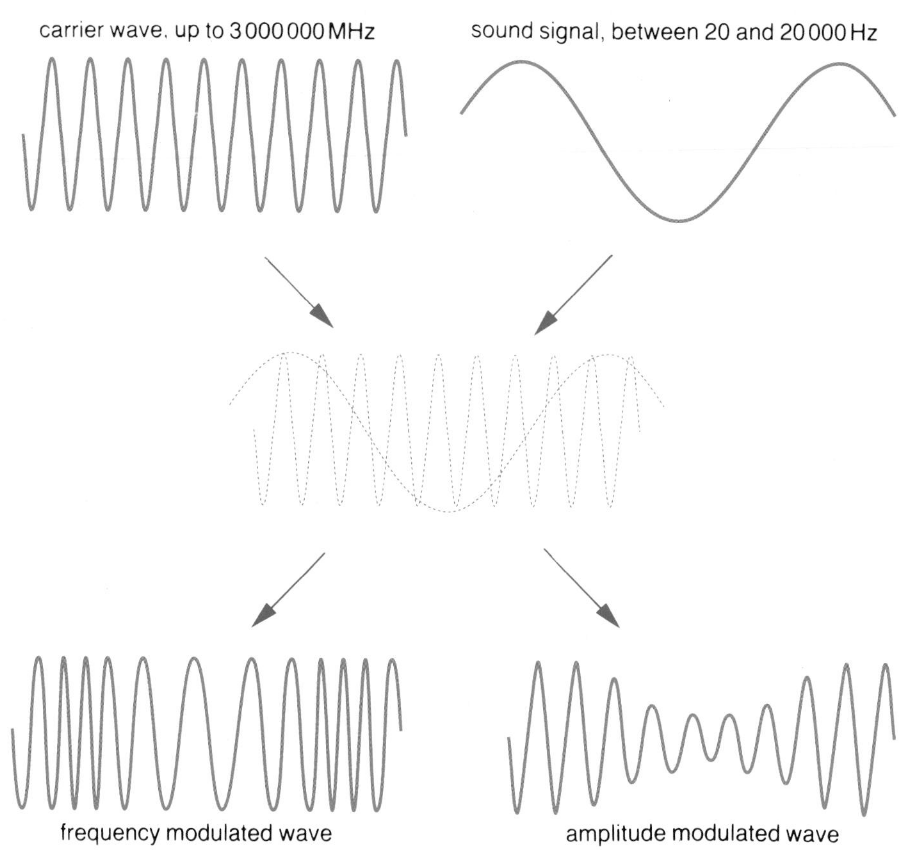

DID YOU KNOW?

Although we can hear sounds between 20 and 20 000 Hz, a conversation needs a range of only 3100 Hz. An optical fibre can carry only 250 music channels, but the restricted range of frequencies used in speech means the same optical fibre can carry 2000 telephone channels.

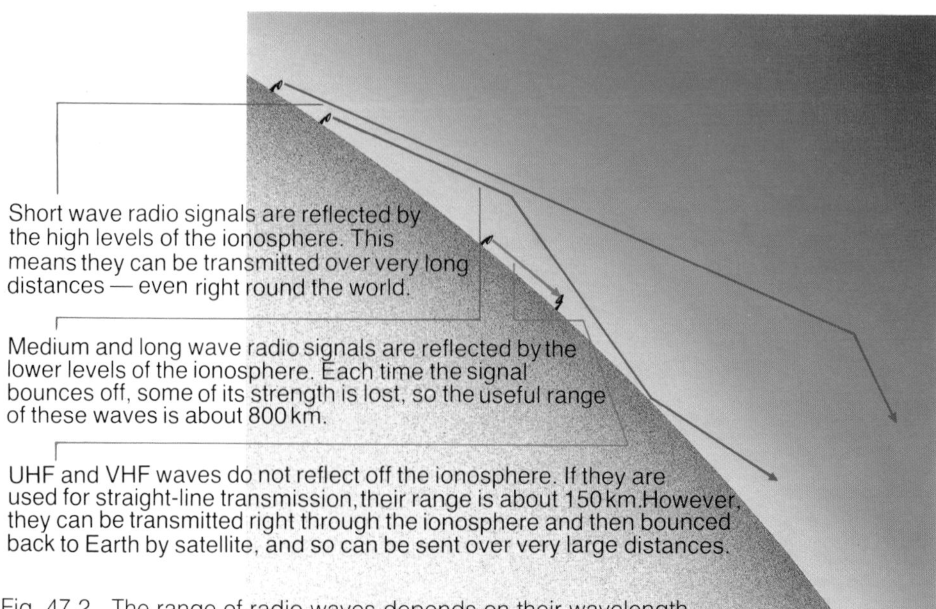

Fig. 47.2 The range of radio waves depends on their wavelength.

Fig. 47.3 Telecom Tower, London (189 m high) is a microwave relay tower. It can handle over 150 000 telephone messages and over 40 TV channels at the same time.

Fig. 47.4 Telephone conversations are broadcast in straight lines from one relay tower to the next. Away from London's tall buildings, microwave relay towers are much smaller.

Fig. 47.5 To cover large distances, to cross oceans for example, the easiest straight line transmission is up to a geostationary satellite and back down to Earth. Satellite ground stations have large dish antennae.

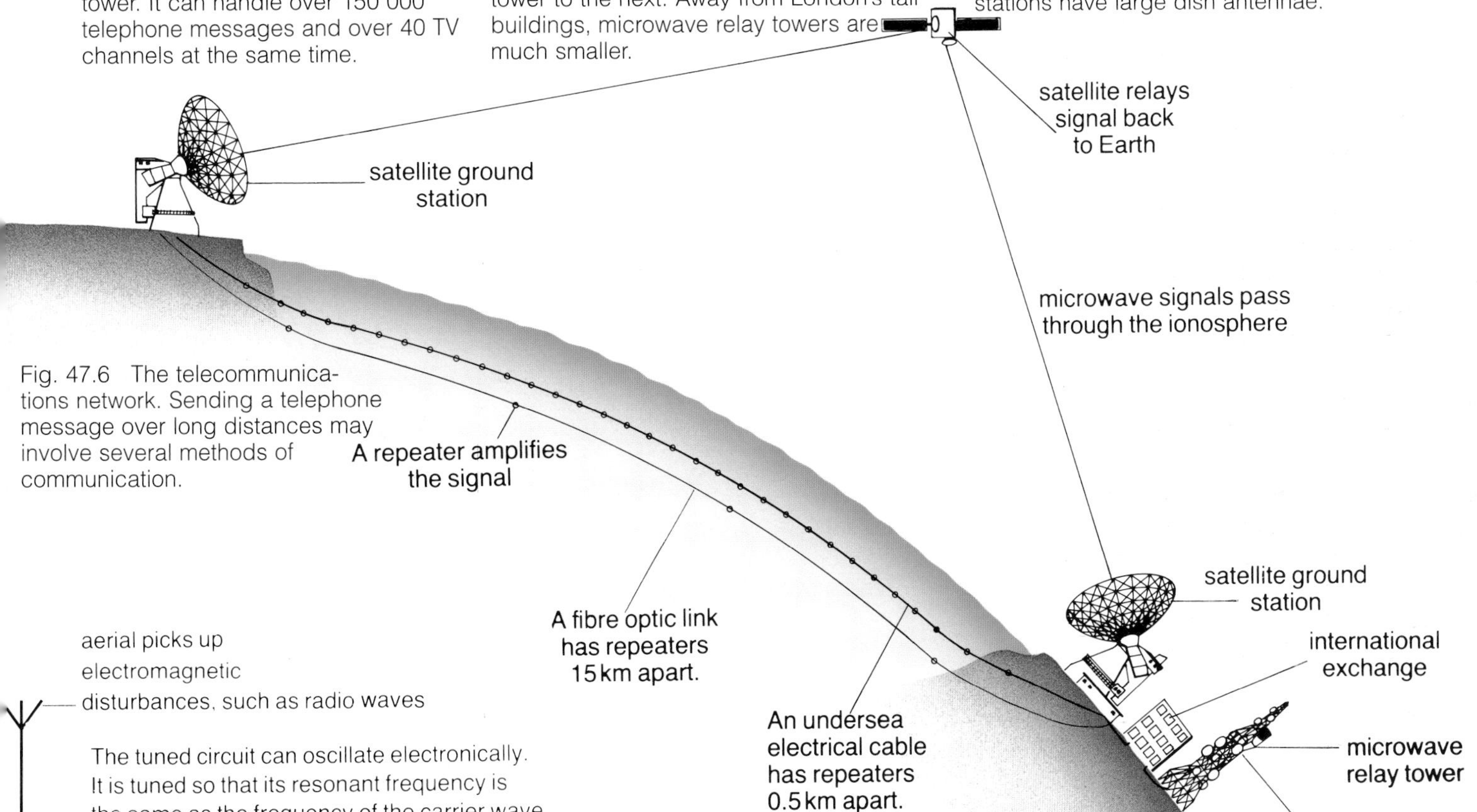

satellite relays signal back to Earth

satellite ground station

microwave signals pass through the ionosphere

A repeater amplifies the signal

A fibre optic link has repeaters 15 km apart.

An undersea electrical cable has repeaters 0.5 km apart.

satellite ground station

international exchange

microwave relay tower

microwave link, up to 80 km

microwave relay/broadcast tower

national exchange

fibre optic or electrical cable

local exchange

electrical cable

Fig. 47.6 The telecommunications network. Sending a telephone message over long distances may involve several methods of communication.

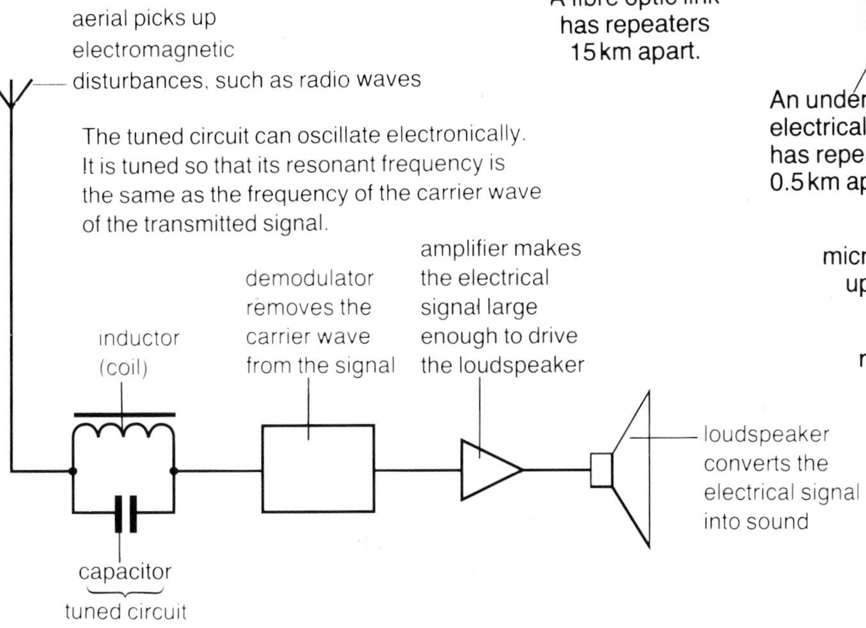

aerial picks up electromagnetic disturbances, such as radio waves

The tuned circuit can oscillate electronically. It is tuned so that its resonant frequency is the same as the frequency of the carrier wave of the transmitted signal.

inductor (coil)

demodulator removes the carrier wave from the signal

amplifier makes the electrical signal large enough to drive the loudspeaker

loudspeaker converts the electrical signal into sound

capacitor

tuned circuit

Fig. 47.7 A radio receiver converts radio signals to sound.

48 LASERS

A laser produces a beam of light in which all the waves are of the same frequency, and exactly in step with each other.

A laser produces a very intense beam of light

If you look back at Topic 8, you will see that atoms emit light when a high-energy electron falls back to a lower energy state. A laser uses ordinary light to stimulate atoms to release light in a special way. The light which they release is concentrated into a very intense beam.

The atoms which produce the laser light may be in the form of a crystal, such as ruby. Or they might be a gas, or even a liquid. If you have a laser in your school it is probably a helium/neon laser, which contains a mixture of helium and neon gas.

One way of putting energy into a laser is by means of bright flashlamps. These produce ordinary light. The light excites some of the atoms in the laser. Their electrons are raised to a higher energy level. Suddenly, an atom returns to its normal energy state. As it does so, it gives out light of a particular wavelength. This emission of light is called **stimulated emission**, because it was stimulated by the light from the flashlamps. The light from the excited atom may stimulate another atom, causing it to produce light as well. There are partly reflecting mirrors at each end of the cavity containing the gas or crystal, so the light bounces back and forth. It stimulates other atoms, so that they, too, emit light. The light can escape through the partly reflecting mirrors, and an intense flash of light emerges from the laser.

The light pulses emitted by a laser are very short – about a billionth of a second. They are released in a stream from the laser. Some lasers produce their light in pulses, while others emit light continuously. The light emitted from lasers is very special. Ordinary light contains a mixture of frequencies (colours). But laser light is all at exactly the same frequency. Secondly, the light waves produced are all in step, or **in phase**. So the waves reinforce one another, making the light very bright. Thirdly, laser light is produced in a narrow beam, which hardly spreads out at all.

The word 'laser' stands for 'Light Amplification by the Stimulated Emission of Radiation'. A laser uses ordinary light, and amplifies it by stimulating atoms to release light all together and exactly in phase.

1. Energy put into the laser excites electrons in atoms.

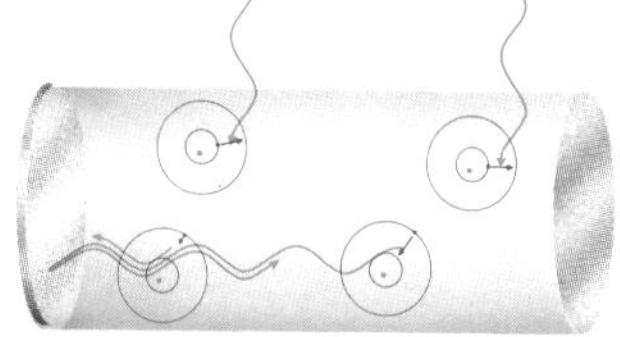

2. As an excited electron falls back to its normal energy level, it releases light.

3. The light may cause electrons in other excited atoms to fall back, releasing more light. This is stimulated emission.

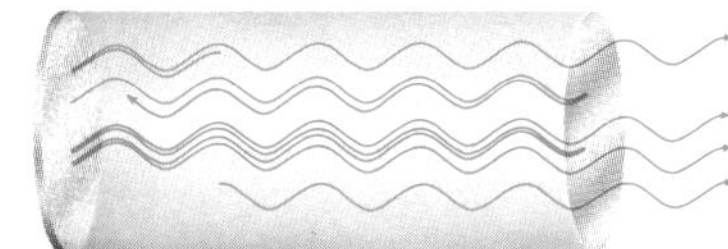

4. The light bounces back off the reflectors at each end, stimulating more and more emission from the atoms inside the laser. Some of it escapes through the partly reflecting mirrors. All the light is of the same frequency, and the waves are all perfectly in step.

Fig. 48.1 How a laser works

EXTENSION

Lasers can be used for cutting

A laser beam concentrates a very large amount of energy into a short time and space. It is very powerful. The power of a laser beam can be used for cutting. Computer controlled laser cutters can cut through forty or more layers of suit fabric at once, with great speed and accuracy.

Lasers are used in surgery. The light-sensitive layer of cells at the back of the eye, the retina, sometimes gets detached. To weld the retina back into position, a laser beam is directed into the eye. The laser passes through the cornea and lens without damaging them. When it hits the retina, its heat welds the retina back in position. The surgeon can control its narrow beam with great precision, 'spot welding' much more accurately than could ever be done with normal surgical instruments.

Laser beams are also used in surgery to cut through flesh instead of scalpels. Their heat seals blood vessels in the instant that they are cut, so there is much less bleeding. Laser beams have even been used to drill out decayed parts of teeth!

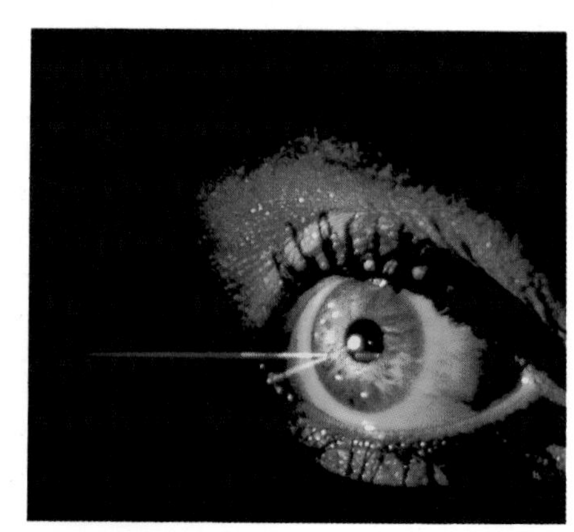

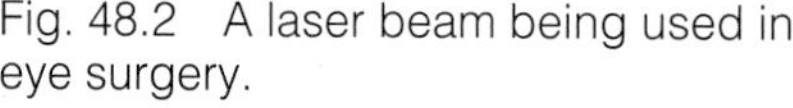

Fig. 48.2 A laser beam being used in eye surgery.

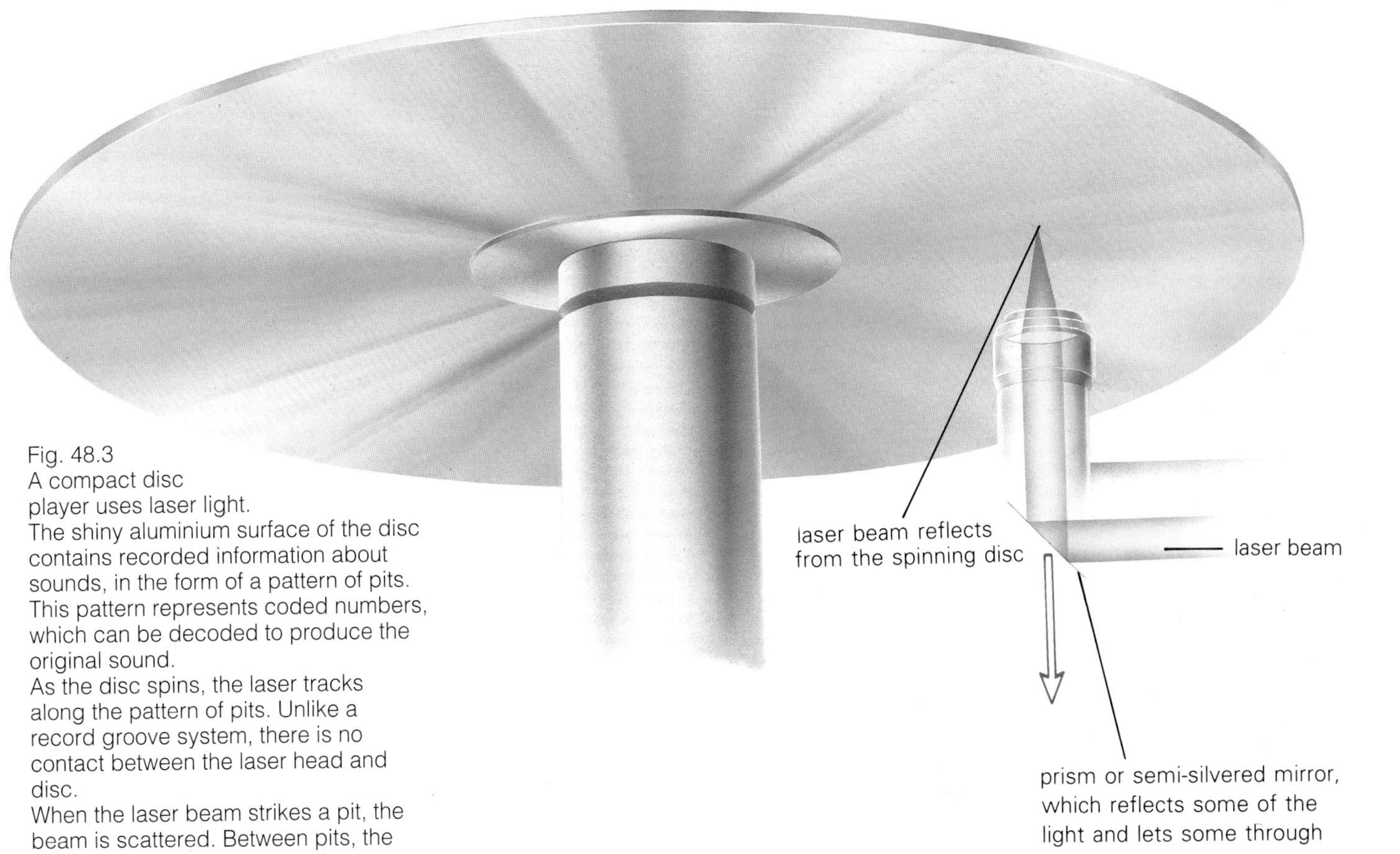

Fig. 48.3
A compact disc player uses laser light.
The shiny aluminium surface of the disc contains recorded information about sounds, in the form of a pattern of pits. This pattern represents coded numbers, which can be decoded to produce the original sound.
As the disc spins, the laser tracks along the pattern of pits. Unlike a record groove system, there is no contact between the laser head and disc.
When the laser beam strikes a pit, the beam is scattered. Between pits, the beam is reflected from the shiny surface. A detector converts the on and off flashes of the returning beam into an electrical signal. The pattern of flashes represents numbers between 0 and 65536. These are decoded to produce the sound.

Lasers can produce holograms

Perhaps the most impressive application of lasers is holography. A hologram is a way of storing a three dimensional picture. When it is reproduced, a true three dimensional image is formed. The image looks absolutely real to us, just like the original object. You can move around the hologram, and look at it from different directions – exactly like the real thing.

Apart from their entertainment value, holograms have other uses. Dentists can take holograms of their patients' mouths. They can then use them to make measurements of the teeth and their positions, without bothering the patient again. Engineers use holograms of nuclear fuel rods to inspect the inside of a rod without going near to it. The complex information contained in a hologram makes them ideal security aids. Most bank cards now carry a hologram.

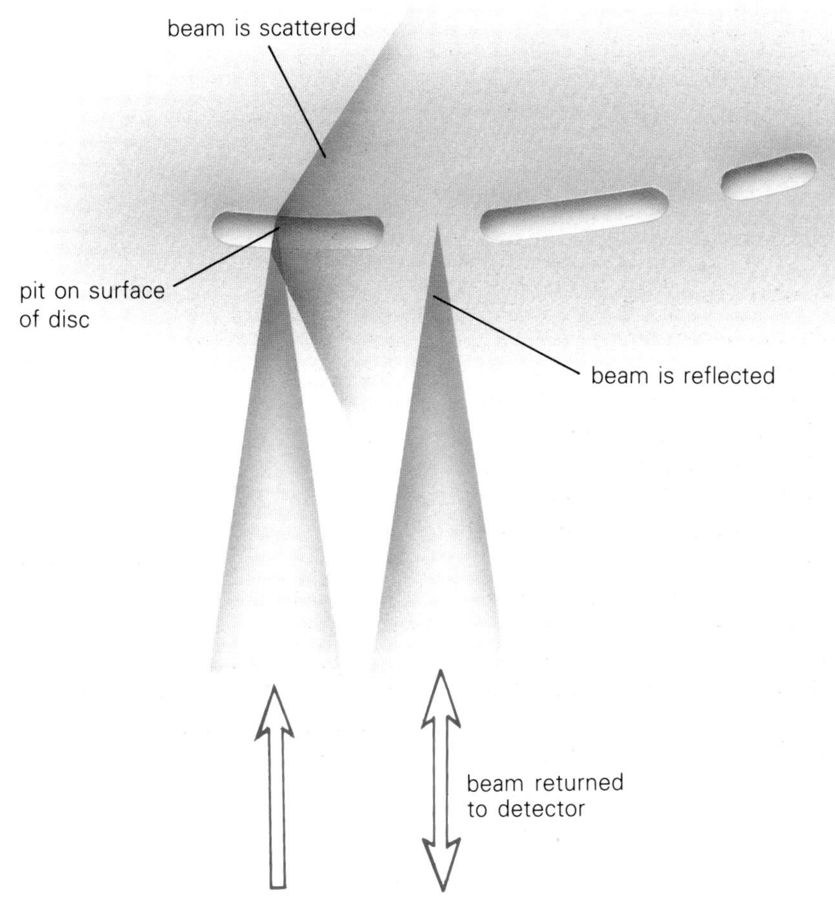

49 REFLECTION *Waves are reflected from surfaces.*

A ripple tank can be used to show how water waves are reflected

A ripple tank is a flat, shallow tank which can be partly filled with water. A vibrator at one end produces ripples, whose shadows can be seen on a screen beneath the tank. The ripples which you see are the **wavefronts**. They are at 90° to the direction in which the waves are moving.

You may be able to use a stroboscope to watch the ripples. The stroboscope produces flashes of light. If the flashes are produced at the same frequency as the ripples, then every time the light flashes on, the ripples seem to be in the same place. Although the waves are really moving, they appear to be stationary.

Figure 49.2 shows what happens if a barrier is placed in the water. The barrier **reflects** the waves.

Water waves are just one kind of wave. There are many other types, including all the different kinds of electromagnetic waves. All waves behave in a similar way. All waves can be reflected.

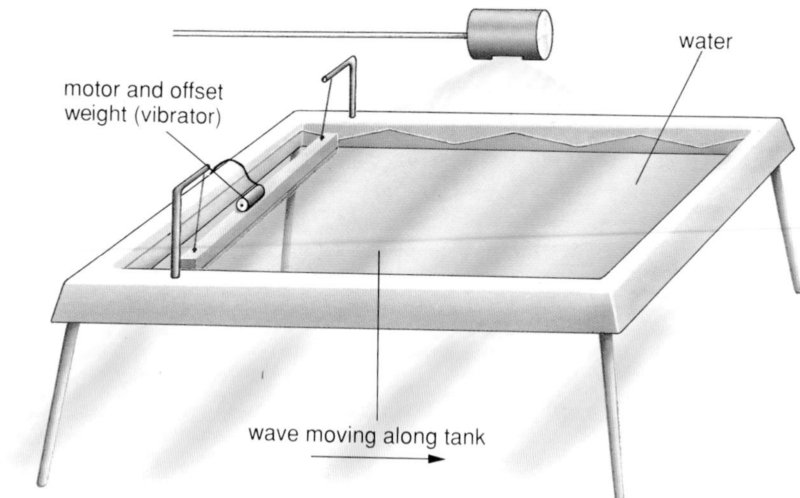

Fig. 49.1 A ripple tank

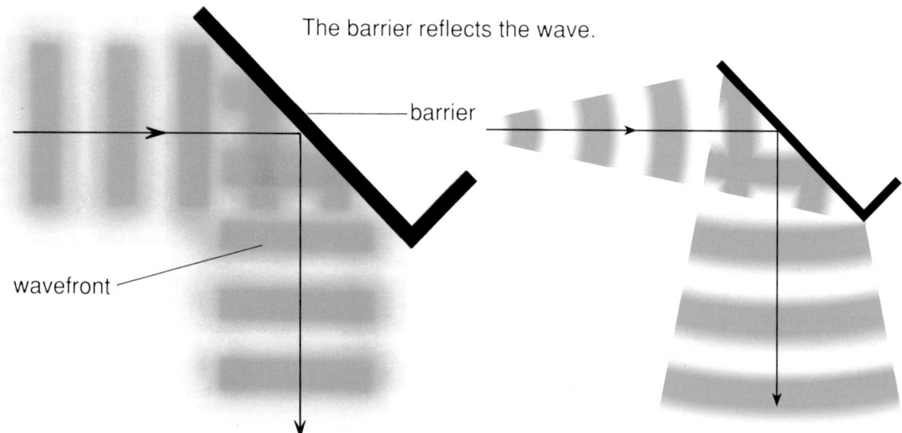

Fig 49.2a Detail showing a wave reflected in a ripple tank. The arrows show the direction in which the wave is travelling.

Fig. 49.2b Circular ripples from a point continue to spread out after reflection from a flat surface.

We see most objects by reflected light

Most objects do not produce their own light. You can see this page because light is reflected from it. The light originally came from the Sun, or from the electric lights in the room. The light rays hit the page of the book, and are reflected from it into your eyes.

Not all the light which hits an object is reflected. Some of the light is **absorbed**. The brightness of an object depends on how bright the light is which hits the object, and how much light the object reflects. Snow reflects a large proportion of the light which falls on it. If you walk in snow in bright sunlight for a long time, the brightness of the light reflected from the snow can damage your eyes. You may suffer **snow blindness**. Dark glasses will absorb some of this light before it hits your eyes.

Fig. 49.3 An Eskimo in Greenland wears dark glasses to protect his eyes from light reflected from snow.

INVESTIGATION 49.1

Reflection of light rays by a plane mirror

A **light ray** is a narrow beam of light. Figure 49.4a shows the apparatus you can use to produce a few parallel rays of light.

A **plane mirror** is a mirror with a flat surface. The mirror you use will probably be made of glass, with a silvered back. Light rays hitting the silvered surface bounce back, or reflect.

1 Set up your apparatus as in the diagram. You may need to partially black out the room. Turn the mirror around at various angles, and watch what happens to the reflected light rays.

2 The **angle of incidence** is the angle at which a light ray hits the mirror. Now make a careful record of exactly what happens to the rays at one particular angle of incidence.

a Place the mirror on a sheet of white paper. Using a pencil, draw a row of dots on the paper to mark the position of the mirror.

b In the same way, mark the position of one of the light rays as it travels to and from the mirror. If your light ray is quite wide, draw along one edge of it. Make sure you draw along the same edge all the time.

c Take your sheet of paper away from the mirror and light rays. Join up the dots, using a ruler. Draw arrows on the lines representing the light rays, to show which way they were travelling.

d Using a set-square, draw a line at right angles to the surface of the mirror, exactly where the light ray hits it. This line is called a **normal**. You should now have a diagram like Figure 49.4b

3 Repeat step 2 for several other angles of incidence, using a fresh piece of paper each time.

4 On each of your drawings, use a protractor to measure the angle of incidence and the angle of reflection.

Questions

1 What do you notice about the angle of incidence and the angle of reflection in each case?

2 Do you think this also applies to the reflection of water waves? How could you test this, using a ripple tank?

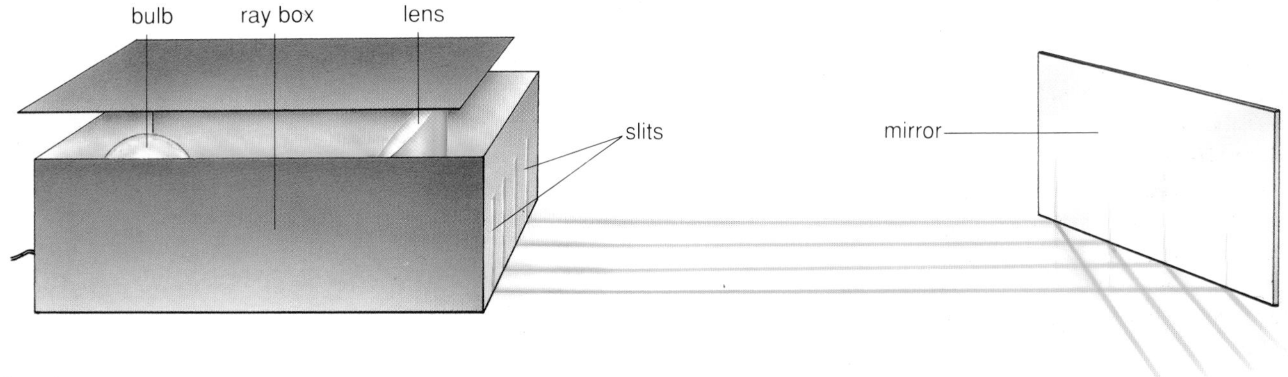

Fig. 49.4a

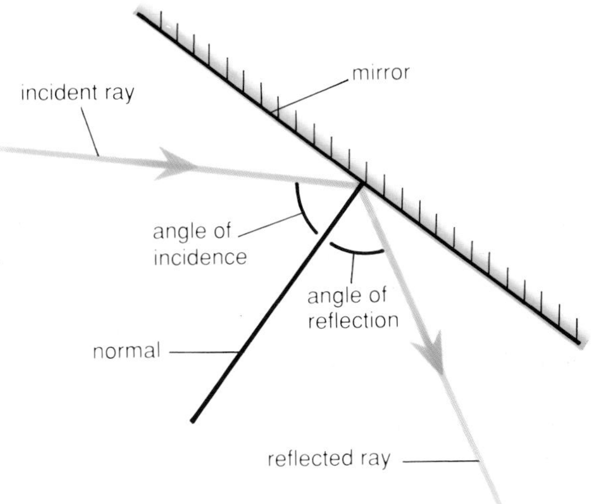

Fig. 49.4b Detail of the reflection of one ray at the mirror surface.

Fig. 49.5 Sound waves, like all waves, can be reflected from surfaces. Sound reflectors in a concert hall help to provide the best possible sound quality for the audience.

50 IMAGES IN MIRRORS

Smooth surfaces reflect light rays in a regular way forming images.

Regular reflection only happens at very smooth surfaces

A mirror has a very smooth, highly polished surface. Under a microscope, its surface might look like Figure 50.1a. Parallel light rays are all reflected to the same new direction. This is called **regular reflection**.

But most surfaces, even if they seem flat, are really quite rough. This page would look very rough under a microscope, perhaps like Figure 50.1b. Each tiny piece of the surface is angled differently. Parallel light rays falling onto the surface still obey the laws of reflection, and so are reflected to all sorts of new directions. The reflected light is scattered. This is called **diffuse reflection**.

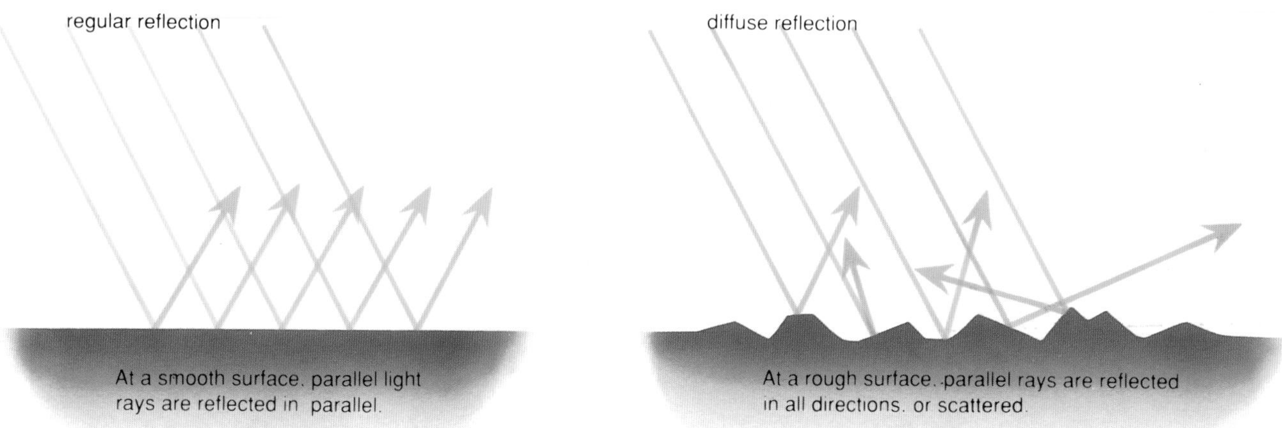

Fig. 50.1a **Regular reflection**. At a smooth surface, parallel light rays are reflected in parallel.

Fig. 50.1b **Diffuse reflection**. At a rough surface, parallel rays are reflected in all directions, or scattered.

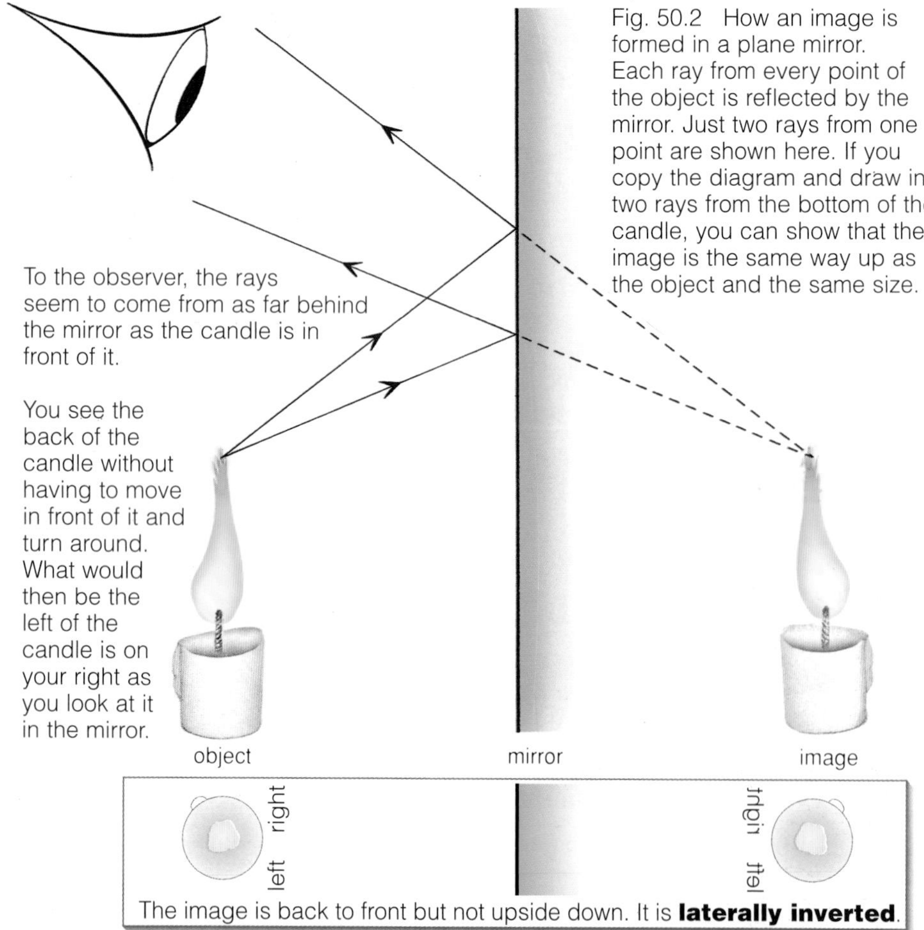

Fig. 50.2 How an image is formed in a plane mirror. Each ray from every point of the object is reflected by the mirror. Just two rays from one point are shown here. If you copy the diagram and draw in two rays from the bottom of the candle, you can show that the image is the same way up as the object and the same size.

Regular reflection can form an image

A very smooth surface reflects parallel light rays all in exactly the same direction. This is regular reflection. Regular reflection produces reflected light rays in the same arrangement as the incident light rays.

Figure 50.2 shows light rays from the tip of a candle flame being reflected by a mirror. You could draw a similar pattern for all the different points in the candle flame.

The reflected light rays go into the observer's eye. The observer's brain works out where the light rays have come from. The brain has no way of 'knowing' that the light rays have been bent, so it works out that they have come from behind the mirror. So the observer's brain sees an **image** of the candle flame behind the mirror.

If you put a screen behind the mirror, you would not see anything on it. There are not really any light rays behind the mirror. The image is not really there at all. It is called a **virtual image**.

INVESTIGATION 50.1

Images in a plane mirror

1 Place a plane mirror in the middle of a piece of white paper. Mark the position of the mirror on the paper. Don't let it move!

2 Make a cross somewhere near the end of the paper, and place a pin exactly in the cross.

3 You are now going to use a ruler as a 'sight' to find the position of the image of the pin in the mirror. Put the ruler edge-on, on the paper, pointing towards the image you can see in the mirror. Look along the ruler, and position it so that it is pointing exactly at the pin. Hold it very still, and draw along its edge. Alternatively, mark both ends of the ruler, take it away, and then draw a line between your two marked points.

4 Keeping the mirror and pin in exactly the same position, repeat step 3 for two different positions of the ruler.

5 You now have three lines drawn on the 'real pin' side of the mirror. Take away the mirror, and the pin. Carefully continue each of your three lines through to the 'back' of the mirror. If you have lined them up really well, they should all meet at the position where the image of the pin was formed. (If they don't, try again.)

Fig. 50.3

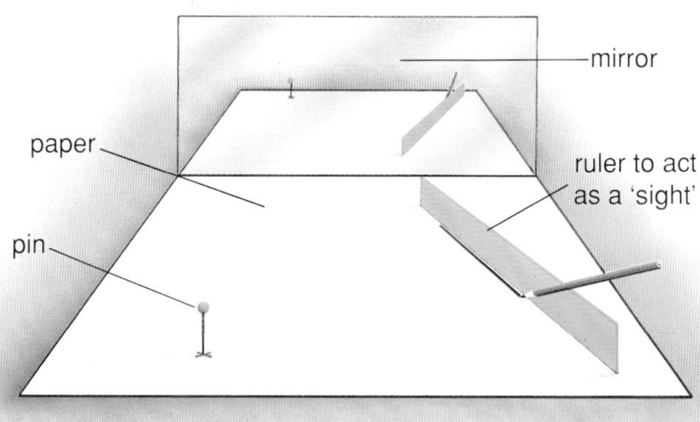

Question

1 What can you say about the position of the pin and its image? Mention both sides of the mirror in your answer.

Questions

1 a Name three objects which produce their own light.

b Name three objects which you see by their reflected light.

2 A mirror and this page both reflect light. Explain why you can see images in the mirror, but not in the page.

3 a A letter P is placed in front of a mirror. Draw a diagram showing what happens to light rays from three different points on the letter as they are reflected by the mirror.

b Extend your three rays behind the mirror, to show where the image is. Join up the three points behind the mirror to show what the image will look like.

c Is the image the same size as the original letter P?

d Is the image the same way round as the original letter P?

4 In a single lens reflex camera, the same lens is used to focus the image onto the film and for the viewfinder. A hinged mirror can direct light to your eye or allow it to reach the film (see Figure 50.4).

a In which position would the hinged mirror allow light onto the film?

b What would the eye see when the mirror was in this position?

c Some cameras have two separate lenses, one to focus an image onto the film, and one for the viewfinder. What advantages and disadvantages can you suggest between this system, and the single lens system?

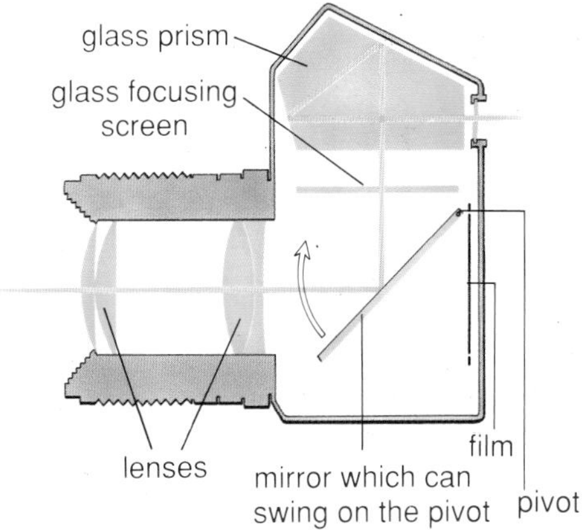

Fig. 50.4

Fig. 50.5 Emergency vehicles such as ambulances and breakdown trucks often have their name written in mirror writing, so that it is easily read by drivers looking in their rear-view mirrors.

51 CURVED MIRRORS

Curved surfaces can reflect rays inwards or outwards.

Reflection from curved surfaces

Fig. 51.1 Reflection of waves at curved surfaces

a water waves

Water waves or light rays reflected from a convex surface seem to come from a point on the other side.

Water waves or light rays reflected from a concave surface converge to a single point.

b light rays

Convex mirrors reflect rays outwards

The rays reflected from a convex mirror appear to come from a single point behind the mirror. An image is formed behind the mirror. The image is smaller than the object.

Convex mirrors can capture rays from a wide area. They are used in shops, so that an image of the whole shop can be seen from one point. Rear view mirrors on cars can also be convex mirrors. They enable drivers to see a wide area of the road behind the car.

Fig. 51.3 The convex surface of these mirrors gives a view of the whole road. The image is upright, but smaller than the object.

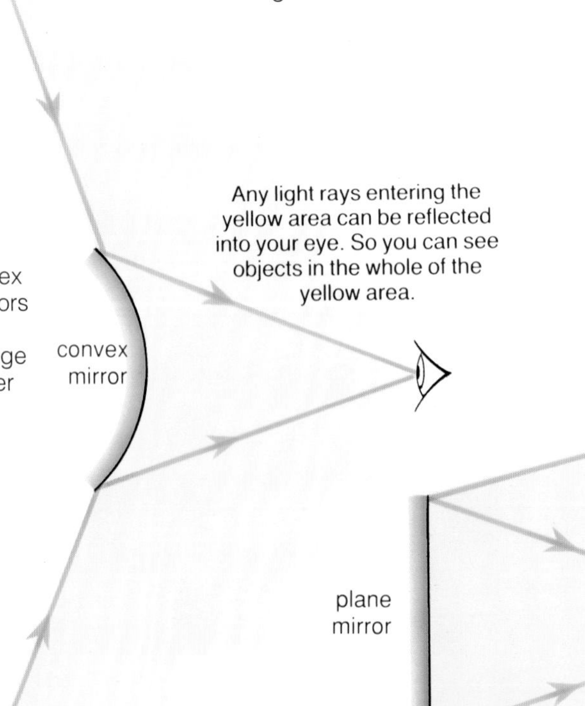

Fig. 51.2 Fields of view in convex and plane mirrors

Concave mirrors reflect light rays inwards

Concave mirrors reflect light rays inwards. The rays are brought to a focus inside the curve of the mirror. The image is larger than the object. It is a magnified image. Dentists use concave mirrors to look at the back of your teeth. The teeth appear larger than they really are.

A concave mirror which is shaped like part of a circle will only give a good focus for a very few rays. One shaped like a **parabola** is much more useful. A parabolic reflector will bring any parallel ray to the same focus. A satellite receiving dish is in the shape of a parabola. It collects radio waves transmitted by a satellite, and reflects them to a focus.

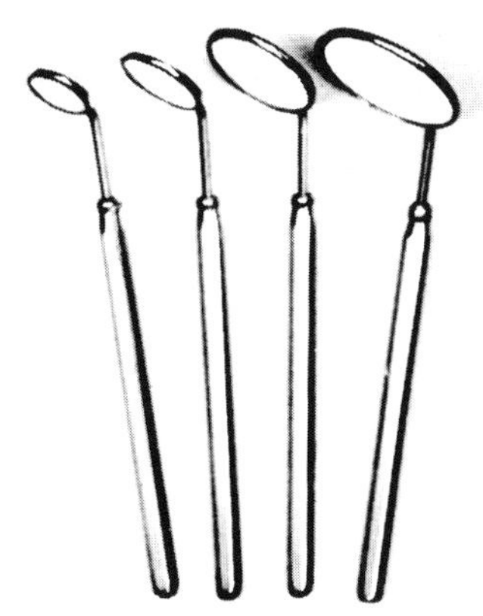

Fig. 51.4 The concave surface of a dentist's mirror forms a magnified image of your teeth.

Fig. 51.5 A parabolic satellite receiving dish.

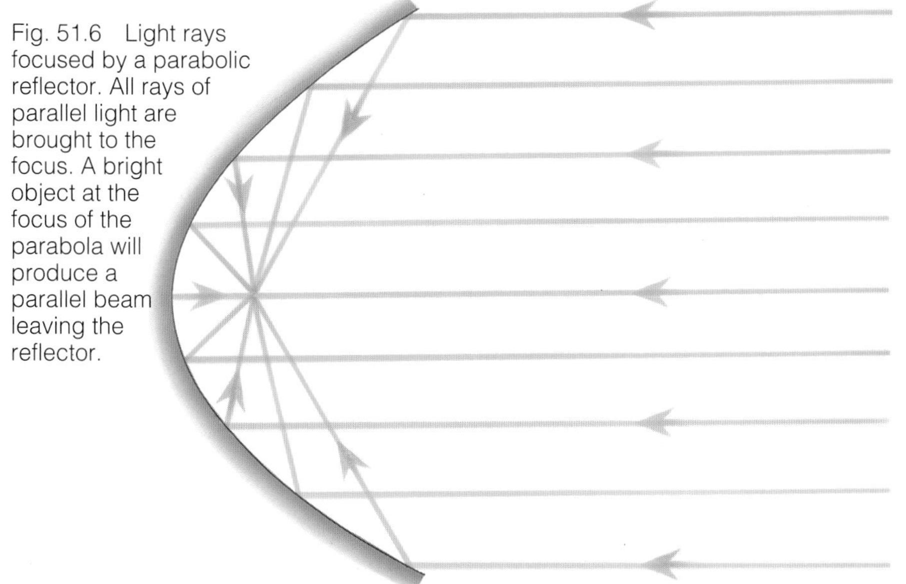

Fig. 51.6 Light rays focused by a parabolic reflector. All rays of parallel light are brought to the focus. A bright object at the focus of the parabola will produce a parallel beam leaving the reflector.

Concave mirrors may be used to spread out radiation into a beam

Waves coming from a point at the focus of a concave mirror will be reflected outwards into a beam of parallel rays. The bars of an electric fire, and the bulb of a torch, are at the focus of the parabola-shaped metal reflector behind them.

Fig. 51.7 The concave reflector of an electric fire directs infrared radiation into the room. The stretched image of the elements almost fills the whole mirror.

Questions

1 a Give three uses for each of the following:

i a plane mirror
ii a convex mirror
iii a concave mirror.

b For one of your examples for each type of mirror, explain why you would choose this type of mirror.

2 Images may be real or virtual. A real image is produced by light rays which really are in the position in which your eye sees them. A screen placed at this point would have the image on it.

A virtual image is not really there at all. You see it because your brain 'thinks' that that is where the light rays are coming from. A screen placed at the point where you see the image would not have an image on it.

Which type of image is formed by:

a a plane mirror?
b a convex mirror?
c a concave mirror?

52 REFRACTION

When a wave travels from one material to another, its speed may change. This alters the wavelength of the wave, and can make the wave change direction.

Wave speed changes in different materials

As sea waves approach the shore, the shallower water causes them to slow down. Their wavelength also changes. The wavelength becomes shorter.

You can see this happening to waves in a ripple tank. A piece of Perspex can be placed in the bottom of the tank, to make the water shallower at this point. As the waves pass over this shallower area, the wavelength becomes shorter.

If the piece of Perspex is at an angle to the direction of travel of the waves, you can see something else happening. The waves *change direction* as they pass through the shallow area. As they pass back into deeper water, they go back to their original direction of travel.

This change of direction as waves pass from one material to another is called **refraction.**

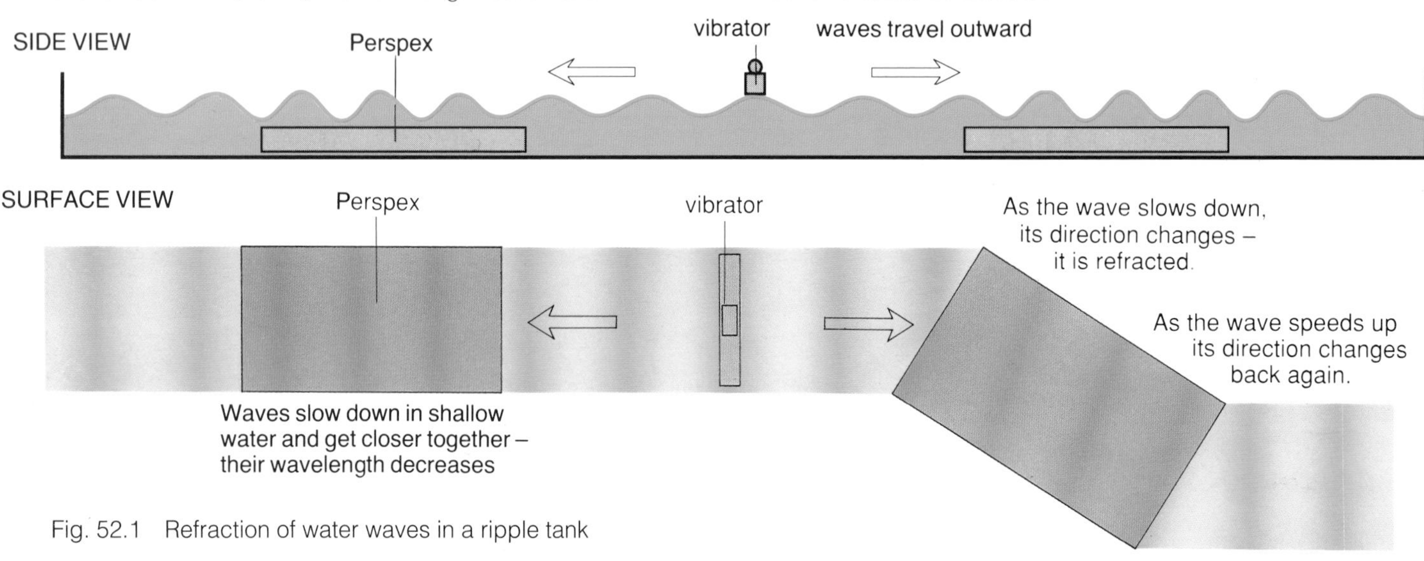

Fig. 52.1 Refraction of water waves in a ripple tank

Light rays are refracted as they pass from one material to another

Light rays passing from air into a Perspex block behave like the water waves passing from deep water into shallow water. The rays slow down. You cannot see their wavelength change, but you can see how they change direction.

Figure 52.2 shows what happens when a light ray enters and leaves a Perspex block. If it hits the face of the block at right angles, it passes straight through. But if it hits the face of the block at an angle, the ray is bent, or refracted. It is bent towards the normal.

As the ray leaves the block, it bends again. This time, it is refracted away from the normal. It ends up travelling in exactly the same direction as the one in which it began. But the ray has been displaced sideways. The ray leaving the block is parallel with the ray entering the block.

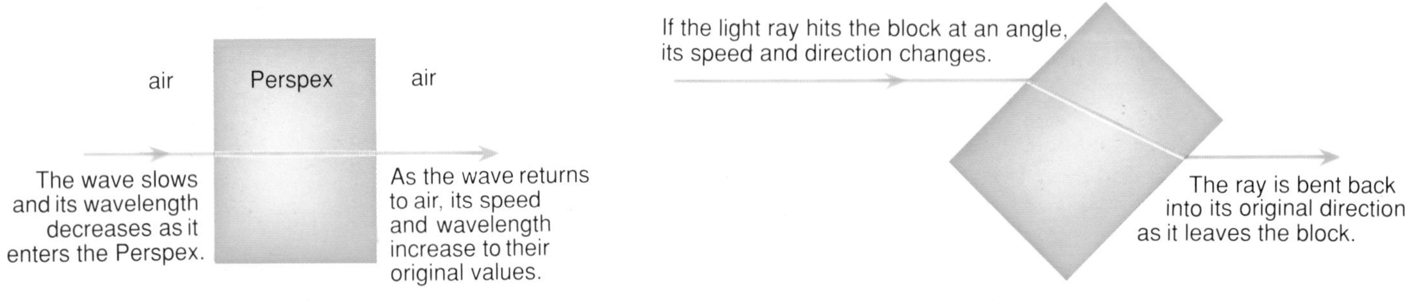

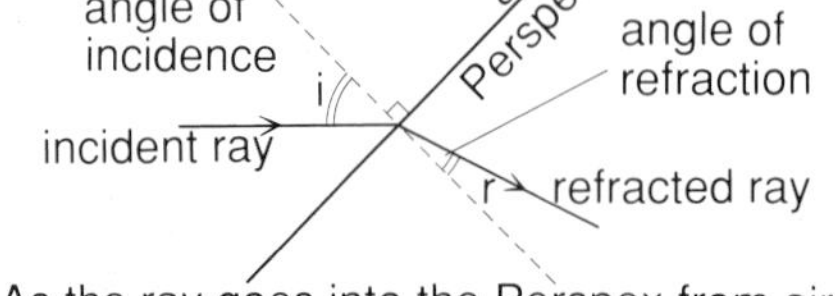

As the ray goes into the Perspex from air, it is bent *towards* the normal. The angle of refraction is *less* than the angle of incidence

Fig. 52.2 Refraction of light through a rectangular glass or Perspex block

INVESTIGATION 52.1

Refraction of light rays in a semicircular Perspex block

1 Put a Perspex block onto a sheet of white paper. Move the block around, and watch what happens to light rays as they enter and leave it.

2 Now make a careful record of what happens to a light ray with the block in one particular position. Place the block so that a light ray falls onto its straight edge. If you aim the incident ray to hit the centre of this edge, as in Figure 52.3a below, it will hit the curved face at 90°, and not be deflected. This will make your measurements easier.

Draw a diagram to show what happens to the light ray, using the same technique as for Investigation 49.1.

3 Repeat step 2 for several other positions of the block. Make sure the light ray hits the centre of the flat face each time.

4 Now turn the block around so that the light ray hits the rounded surface, as in Figure 52.3b below. The light ray will pass straight into the block without bending, but will change direction as it passes from the block back into the air. Make drawings to show what happens for several different positions of the block.

5 Measure the angles i and r for each of your drawings. Angle i is the angle of incidence. Angle r is the angle of refraction.

Fig. 52.3 Refraction of light rays through a semicircular block. In both examples, the incident ray is aimed at the centre of the flat surface.

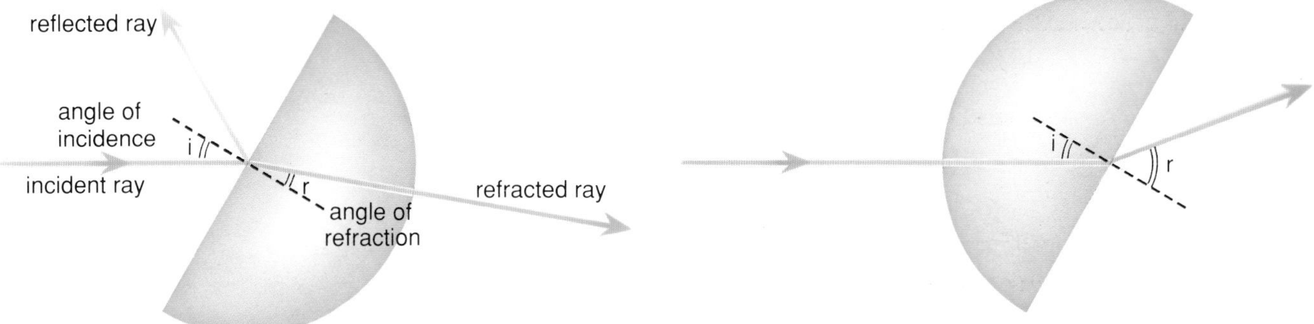

Questions

1 As light rays pass from air into Perspex, are they refracted towards or away from the normal?

2 As light rays pass from Perspex into air, are they refracted towards or away from the normal?

3 In which material do you think light rays travel faster – Perspex or air?

4 Some of the light which hits the block does not pass through it, but is reflected. What do you notice about the strength of this reflected light as the angle of incidence changes?

5 What do you notice when the angle between the normal and the light ray in the Perspex is about 42°?

Light rays are refracted as they enter and leave water

Light rays travel more slowly in water than in air. As light rays leave water, they speed up and bend away from the normal.

Light rays from a brick on the bottom of a swimming pool spread outwards as they travel up through the water. When they reach the water surface, they are refracted. Light rays hitting the surface at a large angle of incidence are refracted more than rays hitting the surface at a small angle of incidence. This makes the rays spread apart even more.

When these rays hit your eye, your brain works out where it thinks they have come from. The brick seems to be much closer to you than it really is. If the pool was 3 m deep, for example, it would look as though it was only 2.25 m deep!

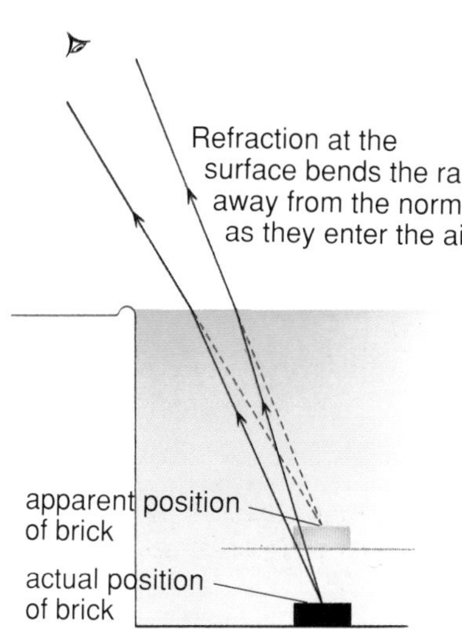

Fig. 52.4 Real and apparent depth

53 TOTAL INTERNAL REFLECTION

Light rays may be unable to escape from a dense material if they hit its boundary with a less dense material at a large angle.

Fig. 53.1 Light rays from glass or Perspex to air. As the angle of incidence increases, the refracted ray becomes weaker and the reflected ray becomes stronger. Eventually, all the light is reflected back into the glass.

Light rays may not be able to escape from a dense material

As a light ray leaves a dense material, its path is bent away from the normal. But not all the light travels along this path. Some of the light is reflected. You will have seen this happening if you investigated what happens when light rays pass through a Perspex block. Some of the light is reflected back into the block.

As the angle of incidence from the block to the air becomes larger, the reflected ray becomes brighter. If you go on increasing the angle of incidence, there comes a point where the refracted ray is very dim, and travels along the surface of the block.

If you increase the angle of incidence a little more, the refracted ray disappears altogether. All the light is reflected back into the block. This is **total internal reflection**.

The angle of incidence at which total internal reflection happens is different for different materials. For a light ray passing from glass or Perspex into air, the angle is about 42°. At angles greater than this, all the light will be reflected back into the material.

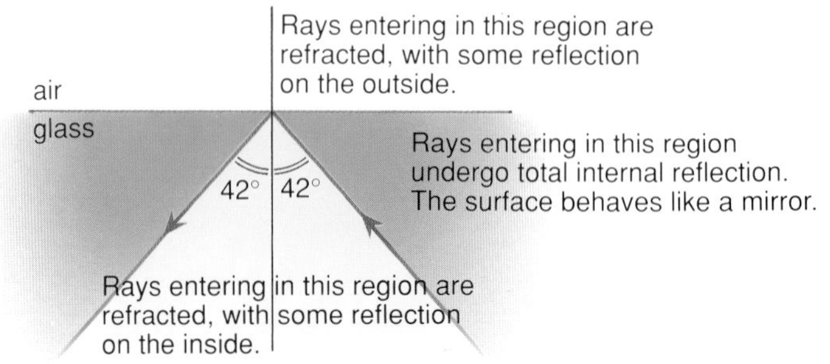

Fig. 53.2 Total internal reflection

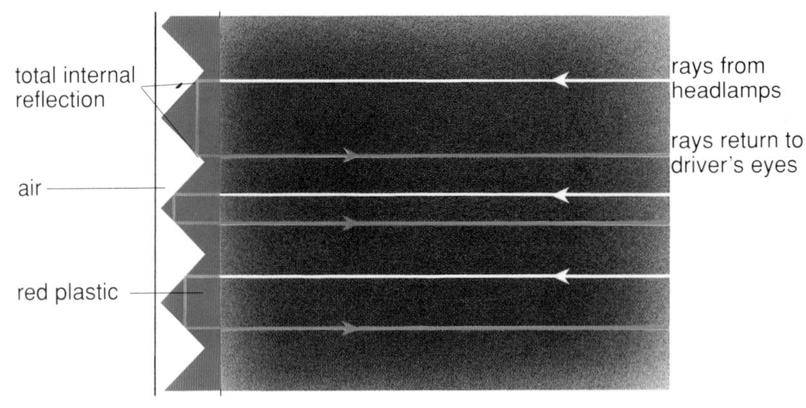

Fig. 53.3 A rear reflector on a bicycle returns light rays to their source.

Total internal reflection can replace mirrors

The red plastic reflector on the back of a bicycle uses total internal reflection.

Figure 53.3 shows what the surface of a rear reflector looks like. The plastic is shaped so that light from a car's headlights hits the front surface at a very small angle of incidence. But the back of the plastic is angled. The light hits this surface at a high angle of incidence. Total internal reflection occurs. All the light bounces back, and is returned in the direction from which it came. So car drivers see the reflection of their own headlights in the reflector.

No matter what direction the car's headlights come from, this reflector returns them to their source. A mirror only does this for rays hitting it at 90°.

This also works in three dimensions. If you construct a corner out of three mirror tiles, you can see your image in the centre of the corner from many different angles. A reflector like this was used to measure the distance to the Moon. It was placed on the Moon's surface by American astronauts. A laser beam was then sent from Earth to hit the reflector and bounce back to Earth. The time taken by the laser beam to travel to the Moon and back was used to calculate the distance between the Earth and the Moon. If a flat mirror had been used, a tiny mistake in its alignment would have made the returning beam miss the Earth completely.

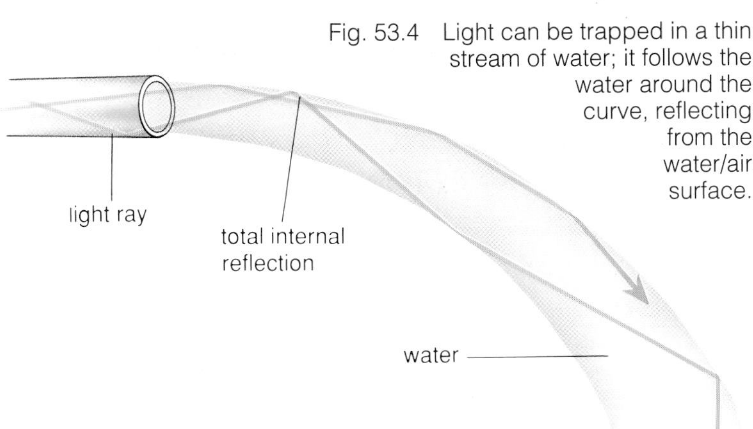

Fig. 53.4 Light can be trapped in a thin stream of water; it follows the water around the curve, reflecting from the water/air surface.

Total internal reflection is used for fibre optics

If a beam of light is sent down a thin glass rod, total internal reflection traps the light inside the rod. Light can go round corners! This technique is called **fibre optics**. The glass rods are so thin that they are called fibres. They may be only as thick as a human hair. The thinner they are, the more they can be coiled without the light 'escaping'.

Any scratches on the surface of the rod might allow a beam to pass through and escape. Optical fibres are made with an outer glass coating and a protective layer of plastic, so that this cannot happen.

Fibre optics are very important in communications, where they are replacing wires in the telephone system. Your voice is transmitted as pulses of light along such fibres. Fibre optics are also used for sending light into, and getting pictures from, inaccessible places. For example, a patient can swallow a tube containing a fine glass fibre, through which a doctor can examine the inside of their stomach without having to perform surgery. This tube is called an **endoscope**.

DID YOU KNOW?

Some hi-fi systems transmit sound between components, encoded as flashes of light in fibre optic cables.

DID YOU KNOW?

Fibre optics can be used to destroy tumours. If a tumour grows in a solid organ like the liver, it is almost impossible to remove it by surgery. If a fibre optic cable is passed into the organ, laser light can be directed along it. The laser is directed at the tumour cells, and kills them.

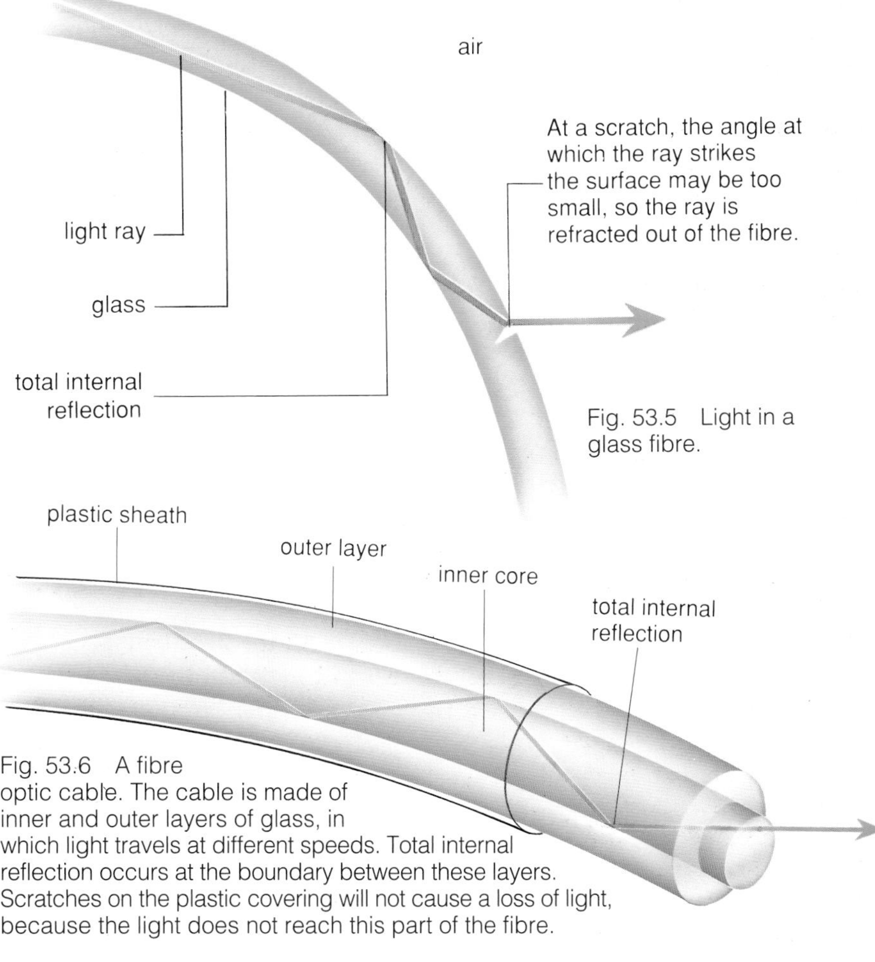

Fig. 53.5 Light in a glass fibre.

Fig. 53.6 A fibre optic cable. The cable is made of inner and outer layers of glass, in which light travels at different speeds. Total internal reflection occurs at the boundary between these layers. Scratches on the plastic covering will not cause a loss of light, because the light does not reach this part of the fibre.

54 DIFFRACTION

When waves pass the edge of an object they can spread out around the corner. This happens for sound waves and for electromagnetic radiation.

Diffraction bends waves around edges

As a wave moves forward it keeps going in a straight line. The ripples in water show the **wavefront**. The wavefront is at a right angle to the direction in which the wave is travelling. Fig 54.1 shows how the wavefront moves forward. You can think of each point on the wavefront as a new source of ripples. With no objects in the way, all the small ripples (wavelets) add together to form the new wavefront. If something gets in the way, the wavelets can't add together to make a straight wavefront. Some of the wave can then move behind the object. This process is called **diffraction**. You can see this in a ripple tank if you set up a barrier. You can also try it out with sound waves. Find a large building and see if you can stand just round the corner from someone and have a conversation with them. Experience tells us that you can. But isn't light a wave as well? If the sound can be diffracted around the corner, why can't you see the person as well as talk to them?

Fig 54.1

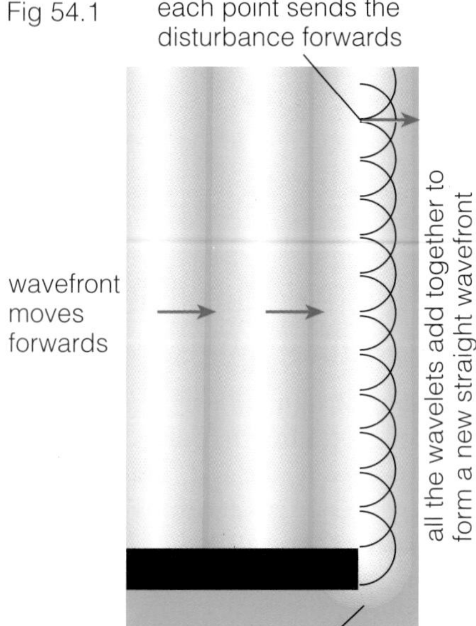

An obstruction allows the wavelets to expand into the shadow area.

When the gap is the same width as one wavelength the waves spread out completely.

Fig 54.2 The amount of diffraction depends on the size of the object or hole and the wavelength of the waves. When the size of the object is about the same as the wavelength, diffraction becomes important. If the gap is large compared to the wavelength the waves don't spread out much.

Diffraction increases with wavelength

Figure 54.2 shows two examples of waves being diffracted by a gap in a barrier. In the first diagram the gap is about eight times the wavelength. There is not much diffraction. This is like a sound wave travelling through a double garage doorway. In the second diagram the gap and wavelength are the same. The diffraction bends the wavefront completely into the area you would expect to be in shadow. Instead of making the gap smaller, you could increase the wavelength to get the same effect. Because sound waves have large wavelengths they are easily diffracted. To get the same diffraction for light you would need a hole 0.0000005 m across. This doesn't just work for holes. A small object will diffract light into the shadow region. You can see a small object distorting light waves if you try the investigation.

INVESTIGATION 54.1

Bending light

Take a sheet of paper and a pin. Use the pin to push a hole into the paper. Stand at least 2 or 3 metres from an electric light. Hold the paper at arm's length and look at the light through the pinhole. Do not look at **any** light that would be too bright to look at normally. You may be able to see a halo around the bright pinhole. Now move the pin in front of the pinhole and focus your eye on the pin – be careful not to poke your eye! With a bit of practice you can get the bright light to look as if it's shining right through the pin. Try different sizes of pinhole and widths of pin.

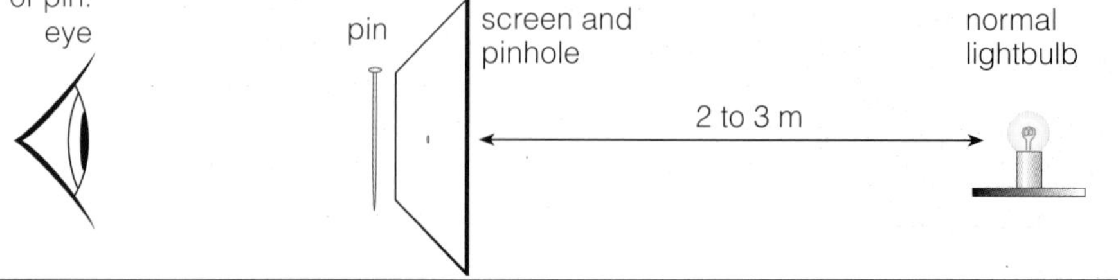

Radio waves have different wavelengths

Long wave transmissions have wavelengths around 1 km and are diffracted by geographical features like mountains. This means that wherever you are you can probably pick up long wave transmissions. FM broadcasts have wavelengths of around 3 m.

Reception is best when you have a clear view in a straight line to the transmitter – as motorists often find when they are driving around! There is more about the range of radio waves in Topic 47.

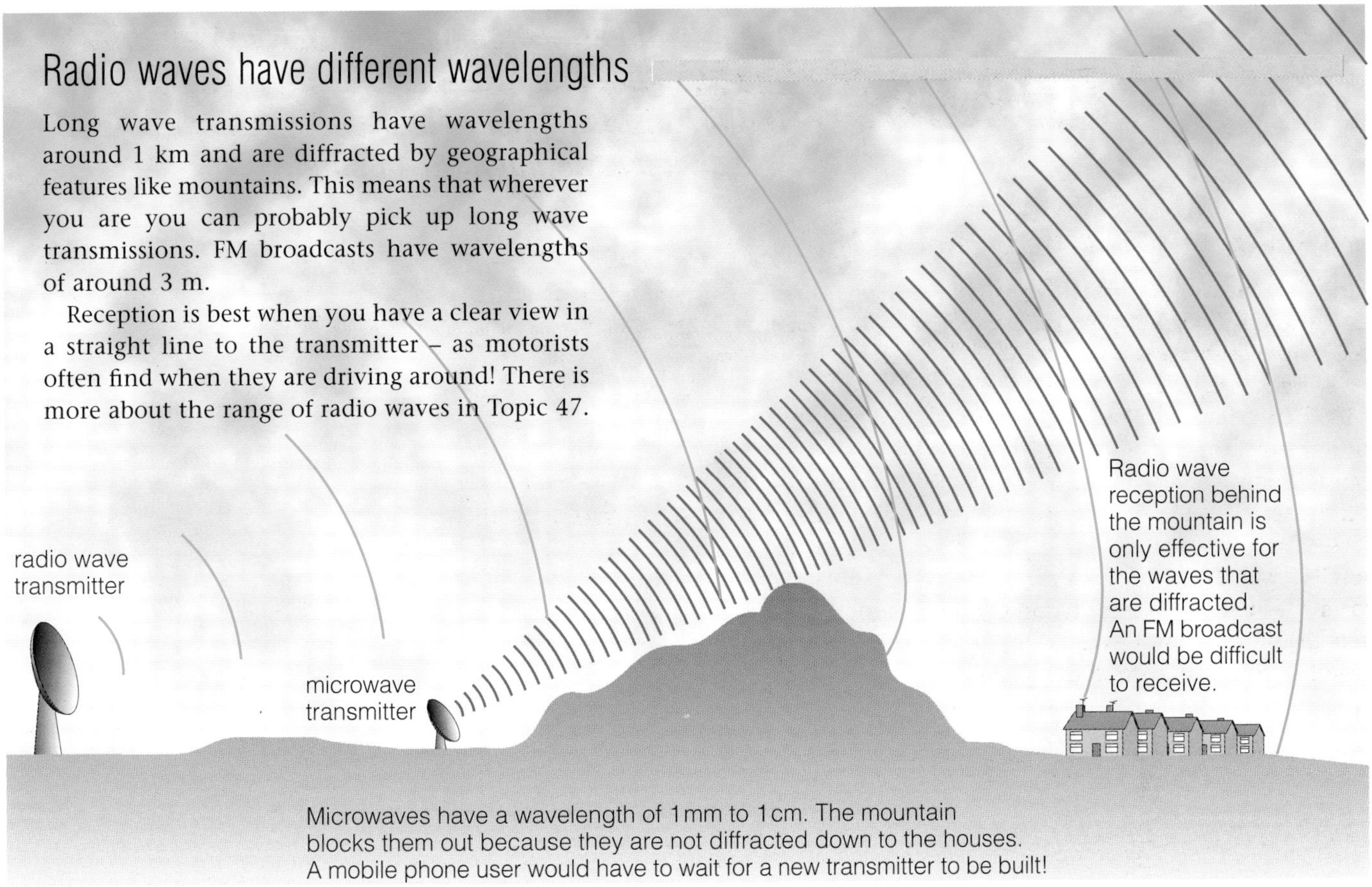

radio wave transmitter

microwave transmitter

Radio wave reception behind the mountain is only effective for the waves that are diffracted. An FM broadcast would be difficult to receive.

Microwaves have a wavelength of 1 mm to 1 cm. The mountain blocks them out because they are not diffracted down to the houses. A mobile phone user would have to wait for a new transmitter to be built!

Fig. 54.4

Diffraction happens when waves add or cancel each other

When waves meet, the two disturbances add together. You can work out the new amplitude by combining the two values. This means that if two waves are in step or **in phase** then the new wave is twice as big. If the two waves are out of phase then they will cancel each other out. This effect is called **interference**. When waves add and get bigger this is **constructive interference**. When they cancel it is **destructive interference**. Diffraction happens because in some directions the wavelets arrive in step. In other directions they don't arrive in step and cancel out. In some directions they add together and produce a disturbance where you wouldn't expect it. This means a small hole produces a pattern of light, not just a single spot. How far over you have to move before the pattern gets dark depends on how far it takes for the waves to get out of phase. This is affected by how wide the hole is and the wavelength of the light. Figure 54.6 shows the pattern you see on a screen if you shine a red laser at a small hole. The central bright spot is bigger than the hole. There are other directions in which the waves also add constructively to make the rings.

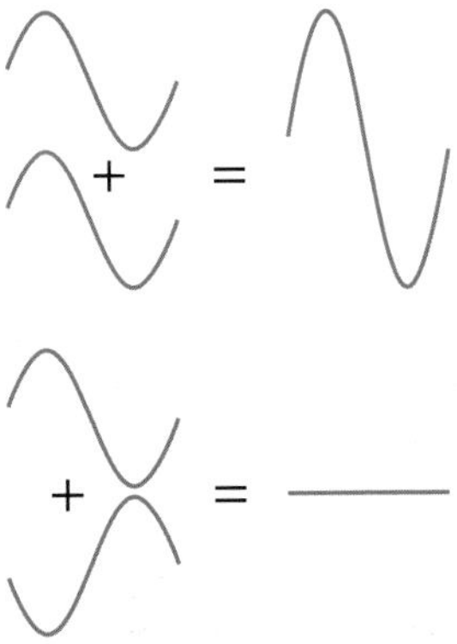

Fig. 54.5

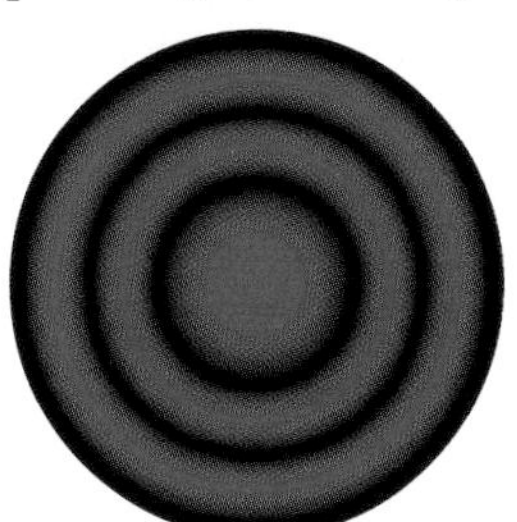

Fig. 54.6

DID YOU KNOW?

The fact that sound and light can be diffracted is very strong evidence that both travel as waves. All electromagnetic radiation can be diffracted if you can find a gap that is small enough. The gaps between atoms in crystals are used to diffract X rays. From the pattern that you get you can work out the structure of the crystal. It was an X ray diffraction picture of the DNA molecule that helped Francis Crick and James Watson to work out its structure.

Questions

1 A high pitched shriek may have a frequency of 3000 Hz, whereas a low bellow might have a frequency of only 60 Hz. For each frequency, calculate the wavelength. Use this information to explain why

a in woods it is easier to locate the direction of a scream rather than a bellow

b in cities you can often hear low traffic noise wherever you are.

2 Estimate the size of the hole needed to produce the diffraction pattern in Figure 54.6.

55 COLOUR

Light is electromagnetic radiation with wavelengths of between 0.0004 mm and 0.0007 mm. We see light of different wavelengths as different colours.

The shape of a glass block affects the way in which a ray passes through it

When a light ray passes through a Perspex block, the ray is refracted as it enters and leaves the block. If the two sides of the block are parallel, the ray emerges parallel to the direction in which it entered. But if the two sides through which the ray enters are not parallel, then the direction of the ray is changed.

Fig. 55.1

The two opposite sides of a rectangular block are parallel. A light ray passing through them is **displaced**, but its direction is not changed.

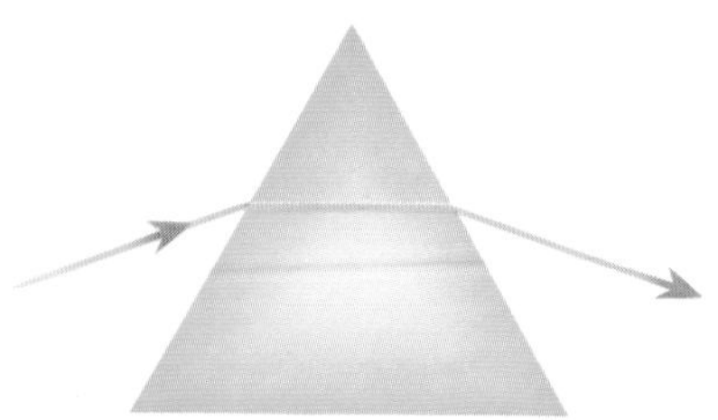

There are no parallel sides on a triangular prism. A light ray passing through it is not returned to its original direction. The ray is **deviated**.

Fig. 55.2 A rainbow is produced when sunlight is refracted by water droplets in the air.

A prism splits light into different colours

When a beam of light hits the surface of a triangular prism, it slows down. Its wavelength changes. If the light is made up of a number of different wavelengths, each wavelength is altered by a different amount, so each wavelength is bent by a different amount. The shorter the wavelength, the more it is bent as it enters the prism.

As the light leaves the prism, it is bent again, back towards its original path. But, because this face of the prism is not parallel with the first face, the light is not bent back onto its original path.

White light contains light of many different wavelengths. A prism splits up the light into all these different wavelengths. We see the different wavelengths as different colours. Each colour leaves the prism at a slightly different angle. The pattern of colours is called a **spectrum.**

Fig. 55.3 As white light passes through a triangular prism, different wavelengths are deviated through different angles. A spectrum is produced.

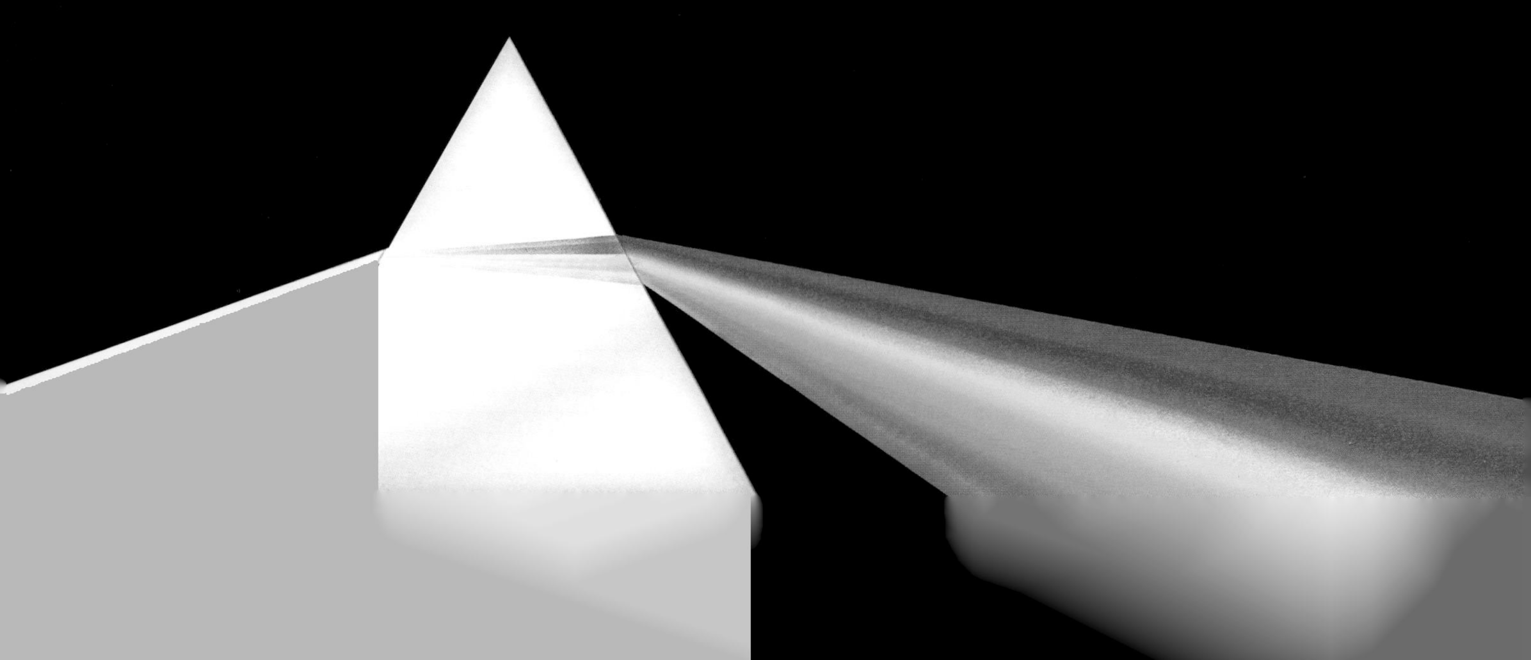

Objects absorb and reflect the light which falls onto them

Sunlight, and the light from electric lighting, is white light. White light contains most of the different wavelengths from 0.0004 mm (violet) to 0.0007 mm (red). But some of the objects around you look coloured. Why is this?

Look at something red – a book perhaps. You can see the book because light from it is going into your eyes. The light from the book is reflected light. The light has come from the Sun, or from the electric lights in the room. It is white light. When the white light hits the book, some wavelengths are absorbed by the book. The green, blue, yellow and violet wavelengths are absorbed. But the red wavelengths are reflected. This is why the book looks red. It reflects only red light into your eyes.

Objects which look white to us reflect light of all wavelengths. Objects which look black absorb light of all wavelengths.

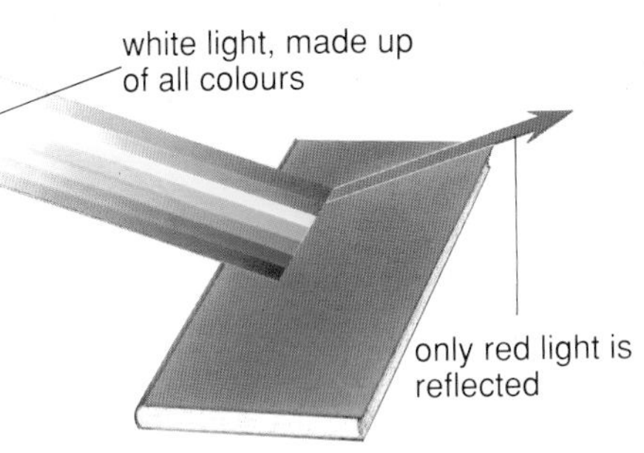

Fig. 55.4 A red book reflects red light, and absorbs all other colours.

Fig. 55.5

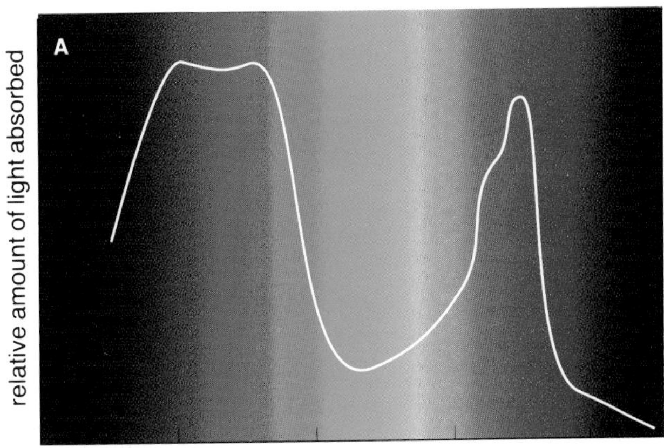

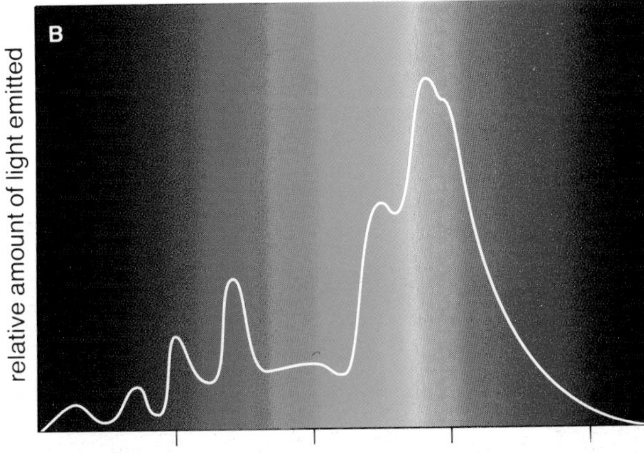

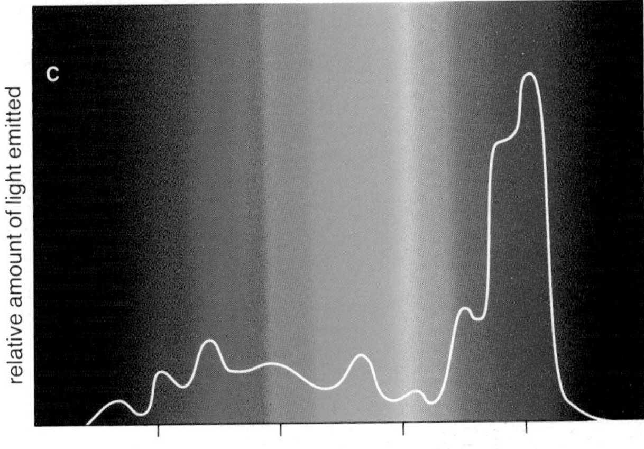

Chlorophyll does not absorb green light

Plants are green because they contain a pigment called **chlorophyll**. Chlorophyll is used in photosynthesis. Chlorophyll absorbs light, and transfers the light energy into organic molecules such as glucose.

However, chlorophyll cannot absorb all the different wavelengths in the sunlight which hits it. It can absorb red and blue light, but it cannot absorb green light. This is why chlorophyll is green. All the green light which hits it is reflected from it, or passes through it.

Some plants, such as copper beech trees, or red seaweeds, do not look green. They do have chlorophyll, and the chlorophyll reflects green light, just as in other plants. But copper beech trees and red seaweeds also contain other pigments which absorb green light and reflect red light. The mixture of green light from the chlorophyll, and red light from these other pigments, looks to us like a reddish-brown colour.

Questions

1 Look at Figure 55.5. Graph A shows the wavelengths of light which are absorbed by chlorophyll. Graph B shows the wavelengths of light which are emitted by an ordinary tungsten filament light bulb. Graph C shows the wavelengths of light which are emitted by a special type of fluorescent light.

- a What colours of light are absorbed by chlorophyll?
- b Why does chlorophyll look green?
- c Why do plants need chlorophyll?
- d Plants growing in a room lit only by tungsten filament lights will normally only survive for a few weeks. Plants growing under the special type of fluorescent light used in graph C thrive. Explain why you think this might be.

56 SEEING COLOURS

We see colour because we have cells in our eyes sensitive to different wavelengths of light. The colour we see depends on what combination of these cells is stimulated.

The human retina contains cells sensitive to different colours of light

At the back of each of your eyes is a layer of cells called the **retina.** The cells in the retina are sensitive to light. When light hits one of these cells, it sets up a tiny electrical impulse which travels along the **optic nerve** to the brain. The brain sorts out the pattern of impulses coming from all the hundreds of thousands of different cells in your retinas, and makes them into an image.

There are two types of sensitive cells in the retina. One type are called **rods.** Rods respond in the same way to all wavelengths of light. No matter what colour light falls onto them, all the rods in your eyes send the same message to the brain. So rods cannot help you to tell what colour anything is. If only your rods are working, you just see in black, white and shades of grey.

The other type of sensitive cells in the retina are called **cones**. Most people have three types of cones. One type is sensitive to red light, one type to blue light, and one type to green light. If red light falls onto a 'red-sensitive' cone, it will send an impulse to the brain. But if green light falls onto this cone, it will not send an impulse. By analysing the messages from all the cones in your retinas, your brain can work out exactly what colour light is falling on which part of the retina. It can build up a colour image of whatever you are looking at.

Cones do, however, have one big disadvantage over rods. Cones will only respond to bright light. Rods will respond to quite dim light. So cones are useless in the dark, or even at dusk. Many night-active, or **nocturnal**, animals do not have any cones at all. They just have rods. They do not have colour vision.

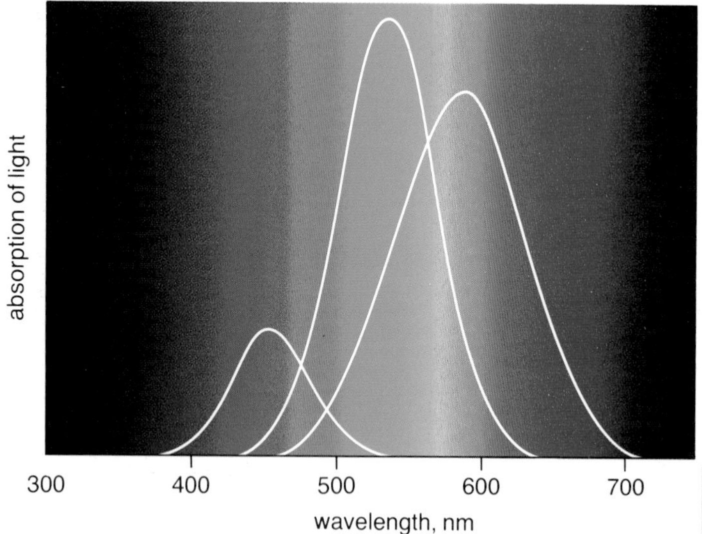

Fig. 56.1 There are three types of cone cell in the retina of the eye, each sensitive to different wavelengths (colours) of light. The three lines on the graph show the colours absorbed by the three types of cone.

Fig. 56.2 The huge eyes of a bush baby collect as much light as possible, because it hunts at night. Like many nocturnal mammals, it has few cones; the retina contains a high density of rod cells, which are sensitive even at low light intensities.

Any colour can be made from red, green and blue light

Any colour may be made by adding together red, green and blue light in the correct amounts. If a mixture of red and green light hits your eye, your red-sensitive and green-sensitive cones send impulses to your brain. Your brain interprets this as yellow light.

A colour television works in this way. The picture on the screen is made up of dots of light. The colours are made up of red, green and blue dots, in different combinations and of different intensities. If you look closely at a television screen, you can see these dots.

Red, green and blue are called the **primary colours of light.** You can make any colour from red, green and blue light. But you cannot make red, green or blue light from any other coloured light.

Colours which can be made by adding any two of the primary colours of light are called **secondary colours of light**. Figure 56.3 shows how the three secondary colours – yellow, magenta and cyan – are made.

Fig. 56.3 Mixing red, green and blue light produces white light. Which coloured lights produce cyan (turquoise), magenta and yellow?

Objects look different in different colours of light

If you shine white light onto a red book, the book looks red because it reflects only the red light into your eyes. If you look at the book in red light, it still looks red, because it reflects the red light. But if you look at the book in green light it looks black. There is no red light for it to reflect, so it does not reflect any light at all, and it looks black.

What happens if you shine yellow light onto the red book? Yellow light is a mixture of red and green light. The book will absorb the green part of the yellow light, and reflect the red part. So it still reflects red light into your eye, and still looks red.

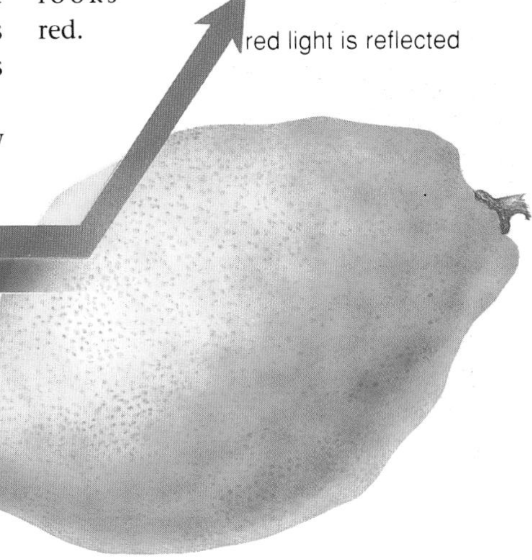

Fig. 56.4 A lemon appears red under magenta light. What colour would it appear if you used a cyan filter?

Questions

1 Pigeons can be trained to peck at a panel to make it open and allow them to reach food inside. If different patterns – for example, a circle or a square – are drawn on the panels, the pigeons can learn which pattern to peck in order to find food.

Design an experiment, using a similar method to that described above, to find out if pigeons have colour vision.

2 A car accident happened in a street lit by sodium lamps. A witness reported that a green car pulled out of a side road. It caused a red car to swerve into the path of a black car.

The following day, the three drivers were interviewed. Driver A has a blue-green car. Driver B has a blue car, and driver C has a magenta car. Could the witness' report have been accurate? Explain your answer.

3 a What colours does a magenta filter allow through?

b What colours would a cyan filter allow through?

c What colour would be produced if a floodlight producing white light had cyan and magenta filters placed together in front of it?

57 LENSES

A convex lens bends light rays inwards, and brings them to a focus, so it is a converging lens. Concave lenses are diverging lenses.

A lens can be thought of as a series of prisms

You have seen how a triangular prism changes the direction of a beam of light passing through it. Figure 57.1 shows what would happen if three rays of light passed through two triangular prisms and a rectangular block. If you used prisms with carefully chosen angles, you could get all three rays to cross at one point. You would have brought the rays to a **focus**.

A **lens** can be thought of as a series of tiny prisms. In Figure 57.1, the prisms at the edge of the lens have sharply angled edges. The prism in the middle has straight edges. Light rays can pass straight through the prism in the middle, but are sharply bent by the prisms at each end. The lens can bring the light rays to a focus.

The lens in this diagram is a **convex** lens. It bends light rays inwards, and brings them to a focus. The light rays are brought closer together, or made to **converge.** A convex lens is a **converging lens.**

Figure 57.2 shows how a **concave** lens bends light rays. The light rays are spread outwards. A concave lens is a **diverging** lens.

Fig. 57.1 A converging lens can be thought of as a series of prisms. The 'prisms' at the edge have more sharply angled sides and bend the light rays a lot. A ray passing through the centre is not deviated at all.

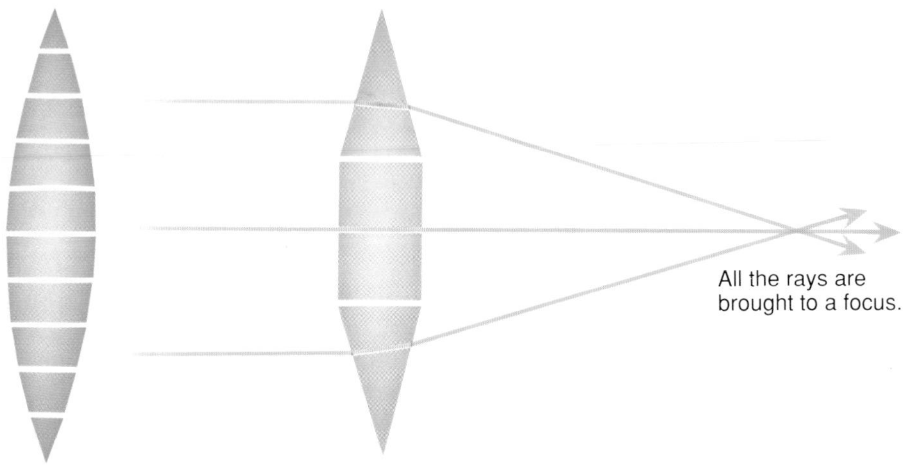

Fig. 57.2 A similar model can be used for a diverging lens. The outer parts of the lens bend the rays more than the central parts.

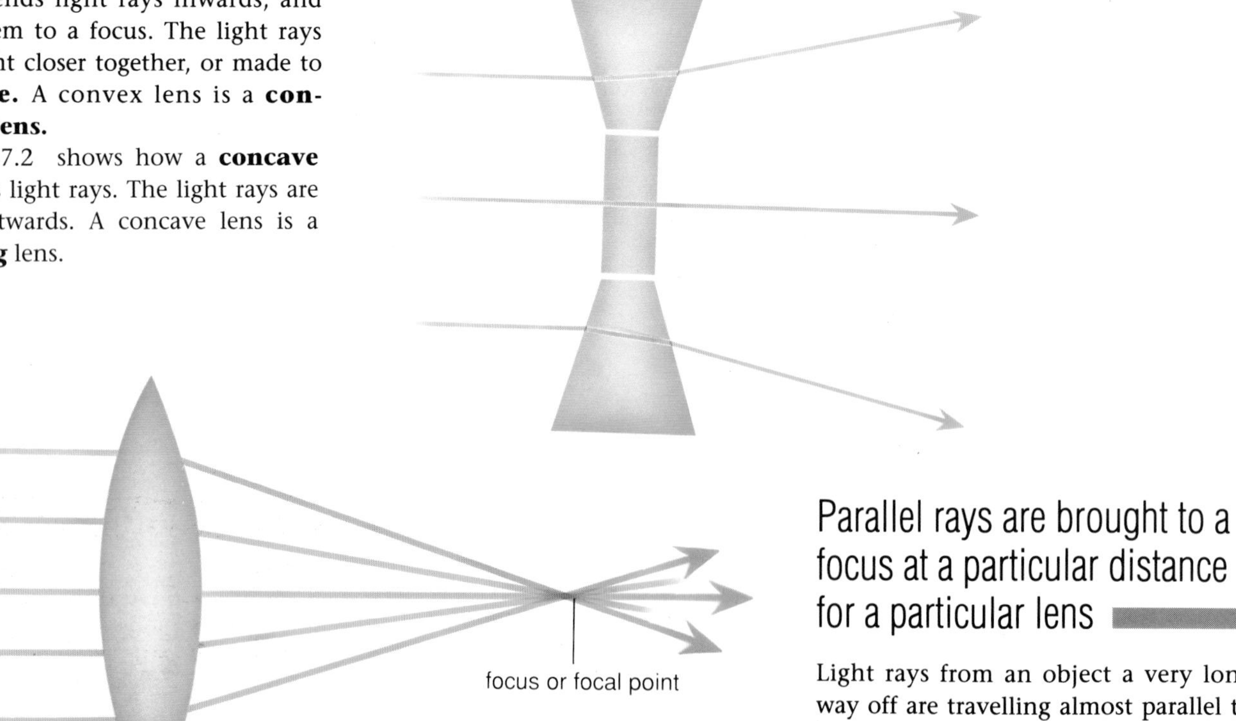

Fig. 57.3 Focal length of a convex lens.

Parallel rays are brought to a focus at a particular distance for a particular lens

Light rays from an object a very long way off are travelling almost parallel to each other when they reach you. If these parallel rays pass through a convex lens, they will be brought to a focus. The distance between this focusing point and the centre of the lens is called the **focal length** of the lens.

INVESTIGATION 57.1

Investigating a convex lens

TAKE CARE! It is dangerous to look through a lens at a bright object.

1 Find the **focal length** of your lens. Choose an object a long way away – the further away the better – such as a tree outside the window or the horizon. Hold a piece of paper (as a screen) behind the lens, and move it around until you get a sharp image. Measure the focal length.

For these experiments, a lens with a focal length of between 10 cm and 20 cm will work best. You may need to work in a darkened room.

2 Place an object (such as a candle or a lit light bulb) more than two focal lengths away from the lens. Move the screen backwards and forwards until you have a focused image.

a Measure the distance of the image from the lens.

b Which is larger – the image or the object?

c Which is larger – the image distance, or the object distance?

3 Move the object closer to the lens. Again, move the screen until you get a focused image.

a What happens to the image distance as the object distance gets smaller?

b What happens to the image size as the object distance gets smaller?

4 Place the object at a distance of exactly twice the focal length from the lens.

a Compare the image and object distances.

b Compare the image and object sizes.

5 Place the object somewhere between the focal length and twice the focal length.

a Where must the object be to produce the largest image?

b Where is this image?

6 Place the object at a distance less than the focal length of the lens.

a Can you get a focused image on the screen?

b If you are using a light bulb reduce its brightness by turning down the voltage on the power pack. Look *through* the lens. Can you see an image now? What sort of image is it? In what ways is it different from all the other images you have seen?

7 There are several patterns in the information you have collected about image and object sizes and distances. Try to summarise them.

Fig. 57.4

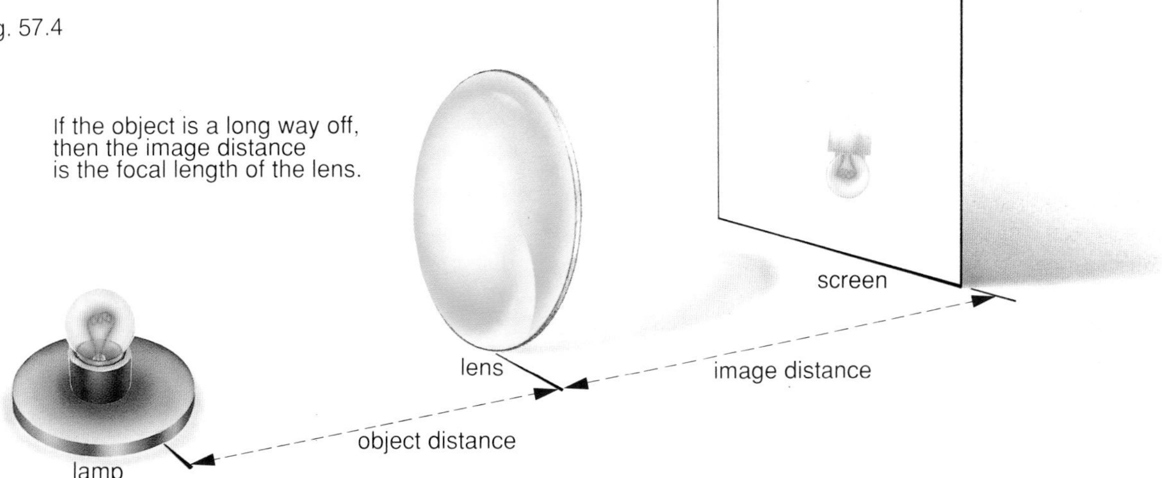

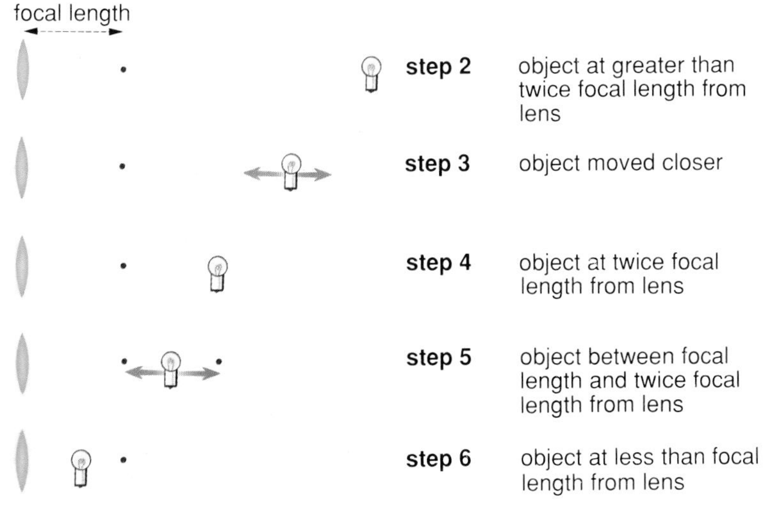

DID YOU KNOW?

Gravity can bend light. The gravity of a star could be used to focus light from stars.

58 MORE ABOUT LENSES

Diverging lenses spread light rays outwards. Ray diagrams can be used to find positions of images formed by converging or diverging lenses.

A concave lens spreads out light rays

A concave lens is thinner in the middle than at the edges. It spreads light rays outwards, or makes them **diverge.** A concave lens is a diverging lens.

If you look at the rays coming out from the lens, your brain sees them as coming from a single point behind the lens. You think that there is an object behind the lens. Really, there is nothing there. A concave lens produces a virtual image.

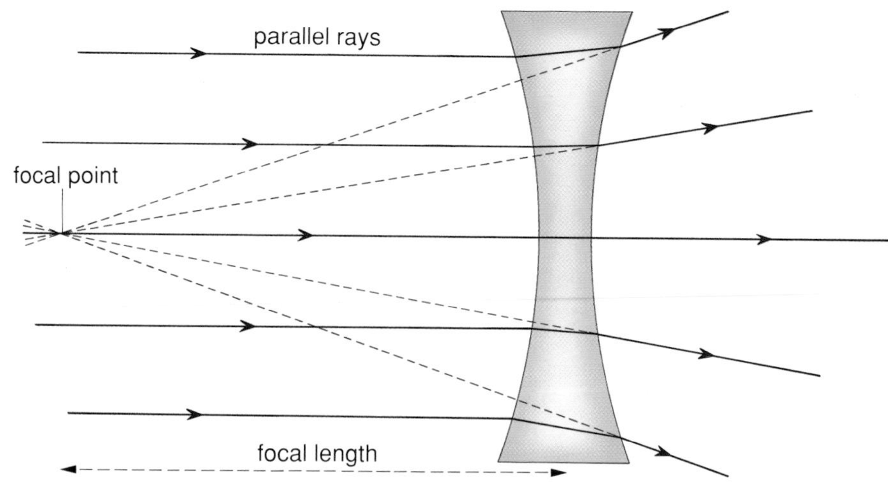

Fig. 58.1 Virtual image formation in a diverging lens. The solid lines show the paths taken by the light rays. An eye assumes the rays have travelled in straight lines, along the paths shown by the dotted lines.

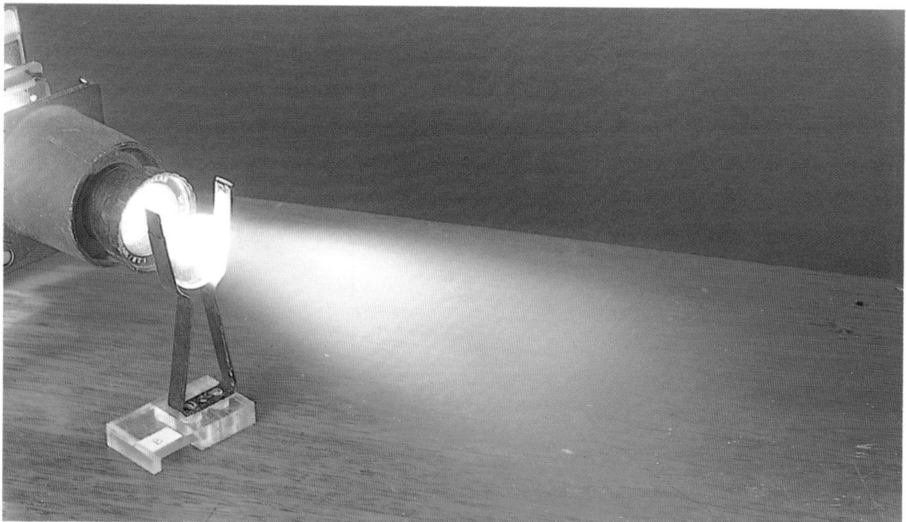

Fig. 58.2 Light diverges after passing through a concave lens.

Questions

1 A lamp is placed 10 cm from a lens of focal length 5 cm. Use graph paper to draw ray diagrams to find the position of the image if the lens is:
  a converging
  b diverging.

2 A microscope slide 22 cm from a 20 cm focal length lens forms a focused image on a wall. Draw a scale diagram (1 mm = 1 cm) to find the distance of the wall from the lens.

EXTENSION

INVESTIGATION 58.1

Finding the focal length of a diverging lens

The focal length of a diverging lens is not as easy to find as the focal length of a converging lens. When you want to find the focal length of a converging lens, you can use a screen to find where the image is. But with a diverging lens, the image is not real, so you cannot see it on a screen.

Instead, you have to trace the rays back to the focus. This is very hard to do in three dimensions! But if you use a cylindrical lens, the light is only bent in one direction, so you can work in just two dimensions.

1 Set up a ray box to provide three beams of light across a white piece of paper.

2 Place a cylindrical diverging lens in the path of the beams. Mark the position of the lens on the paper.

3 Mark crosses on the paper to show the positions of the rays entering and leaving the lens.

4 Remove the lens and continue the 'exit' lines backwards to find the focus.

5 Measure the focal length of the lens.

6 Find the focal length of a cylindrical converging lens.

7 Identify a diverging and a converging lens with the same focal length. Put the two lenses close together, and place them in the path of the light rays. What effect do they have?

Fig. 58.3 How to draw ray diagrams. A ray diagram is a drawing showing how light rays travel. Ray diagrams can be used to find the positions of images formed by lenses. Some rays are much easier to draw than others. In this figure, the following three rays have been drawn:
1 a ray of light approaching the lens, parallel to its principal axis. This ray will be bent by the lens, and will pass through the focal point of the lens.
2 a ray of light passing through the focal point of the lens, which will emerge running parallel to the principal axis of the lens.
3 a ray of light passing exactly through the centre of the lens, which will not be bent at all.
In fact, you need to draw only two of these rays to find the position of the image, but it is a good idea to draw three, to make sure you have not made a mistake.

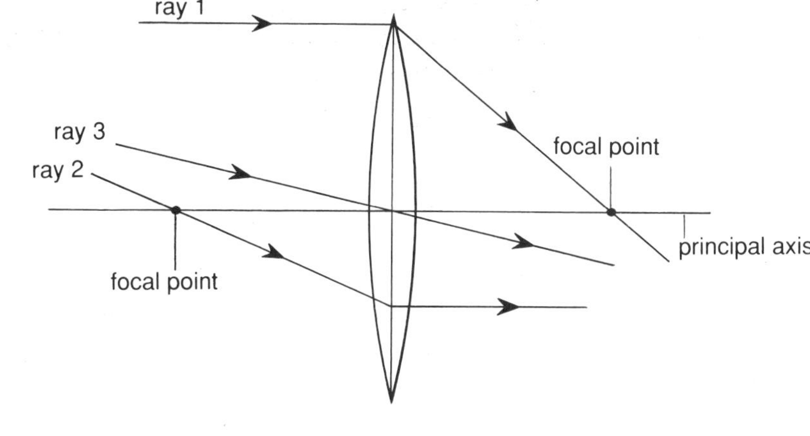

Fig. 58.4 Where is the image of a pin, placed 6 cm from a converging lens of focal length 4 cm? (This ray diagram is shown at half actual size.)
1 Draw the positions of the object, lens, and focal points on the principal axis. Notice that the size of the lens is not important, but the line marking its *position* is. Measure the distances from the centre of the lens.
2 Draw two rays from the top of the pin to locate the image. Draw a third ray to check the accuracy of your drawing. The point at which these rays cross is the image of the top of the pin.
3 In this example the image is upside-down. It is magnified and it is 12 cm from the centre of the lens.

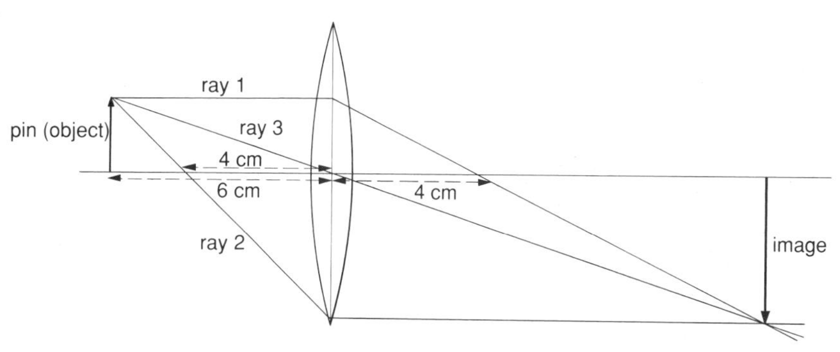

Fig. 58.5 Drawing ray diagrams for a diverging lens. Draw three rays in the same way as before.
1 A ray of light approaching the lens parallel to its principal axis. This is bent as though it had come from the focal point of the lens.
2 A ray travelling towards the focal point on the far side of the lens. This is bent to run parallel to the principal axis.
3 A ray passing straight through the centre of the lens.

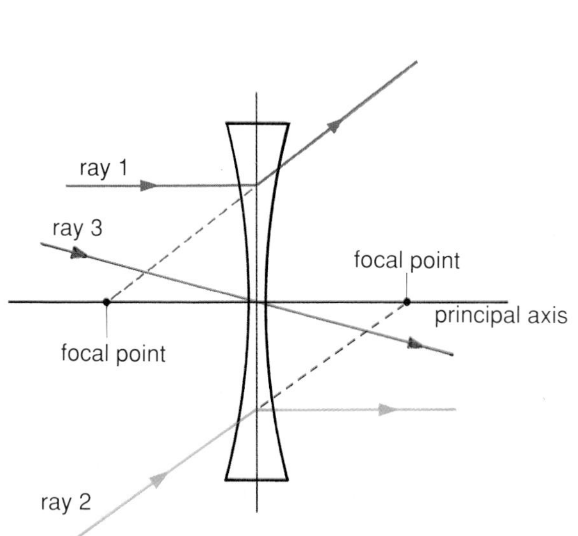

Fig. 58.6 What kind of image is formed by a diverging lens? Three rays are drawn from the top of the object. To an observer, these three rays seem to come from the point I. This is where you see the image. The image is on the same side of the lens as the object. It is the right way up and smaller than the object. It is a virtual image, and could not be focused on a screen.

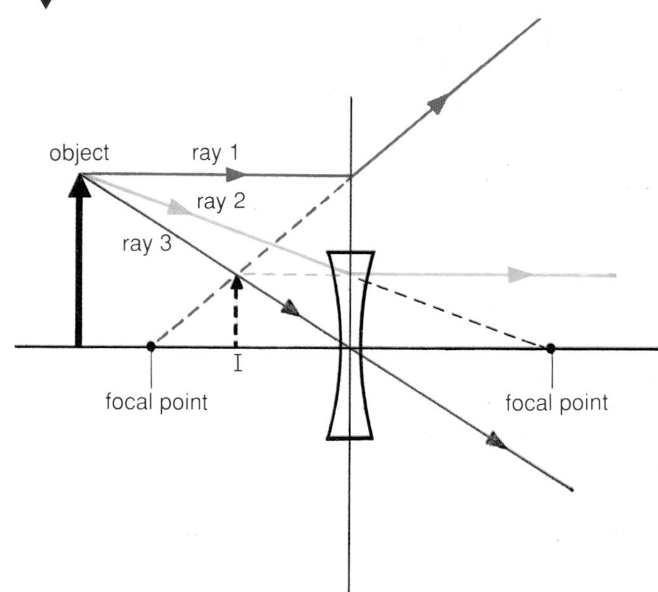

59 OPTICAL INSTRUMENTS

Optical instruments enable us to see objects which are too distant, too small, or in the wrong position for us to see with the naked eye.

Fig. 59.1 A magnifying glass is held closer to the text than its focal length. A magnified virtual image is formed. Looking through the lens, the writing appears larger.

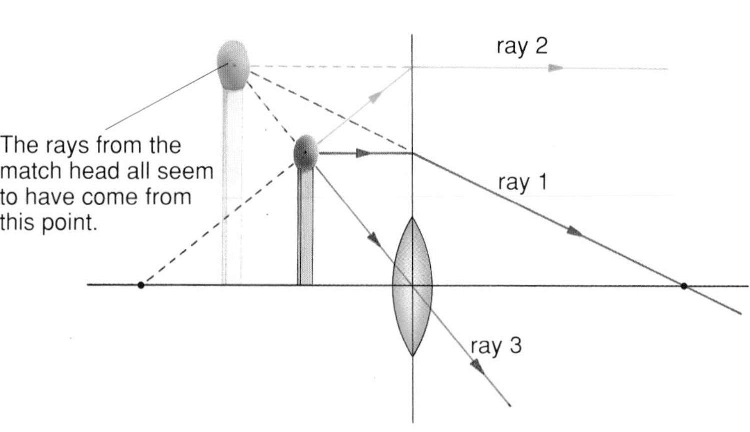

Fig. 59.2 A ray diagram shows how a magnifying glass produces an enlarged image. The object must be placed between the convex lens and its focal point. A magnified virtual image is formed on the object side of the lens. You have to look through the lens, towards the object, to see it. The image is the right way up, and can be very much larger than the object.

Fig. 59.3 An astronomer's telescope. The image formed is upside-down, which does not matter if you are looking at stars or planets.

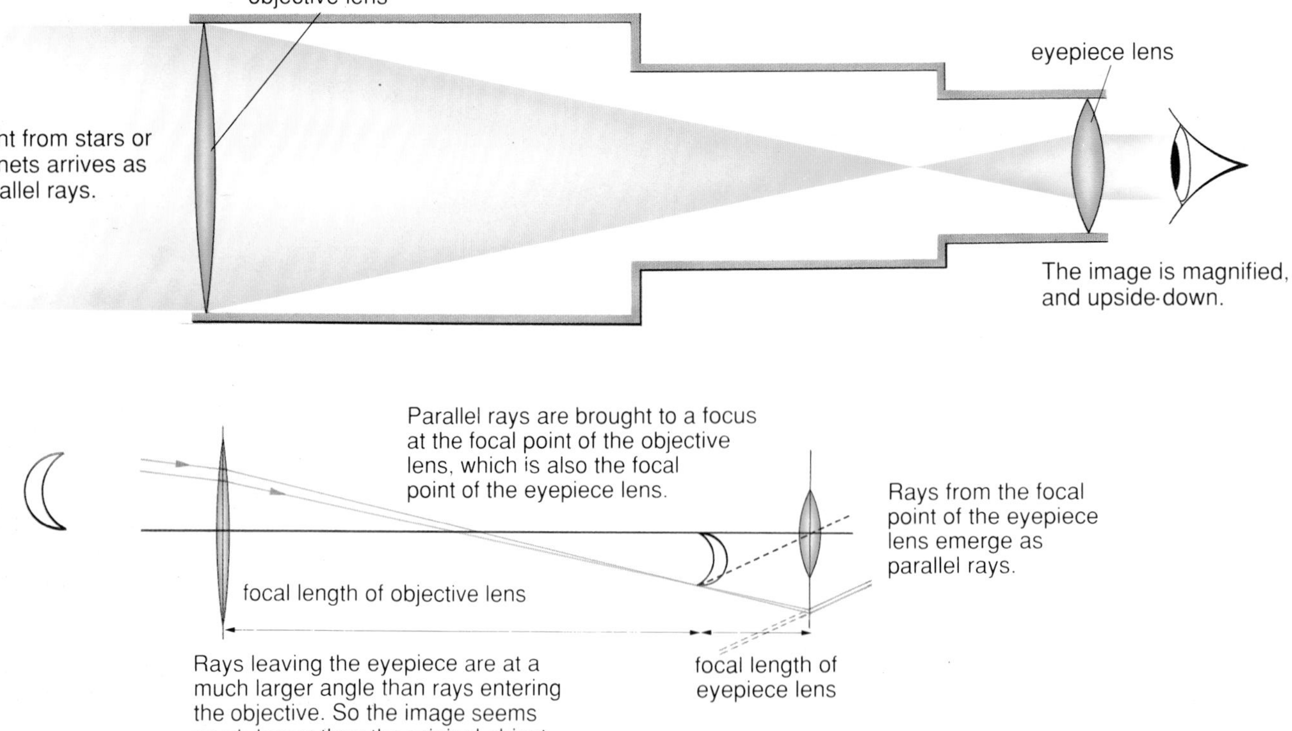

Fig. 59.4 A ray diagram for an astronomical telescope

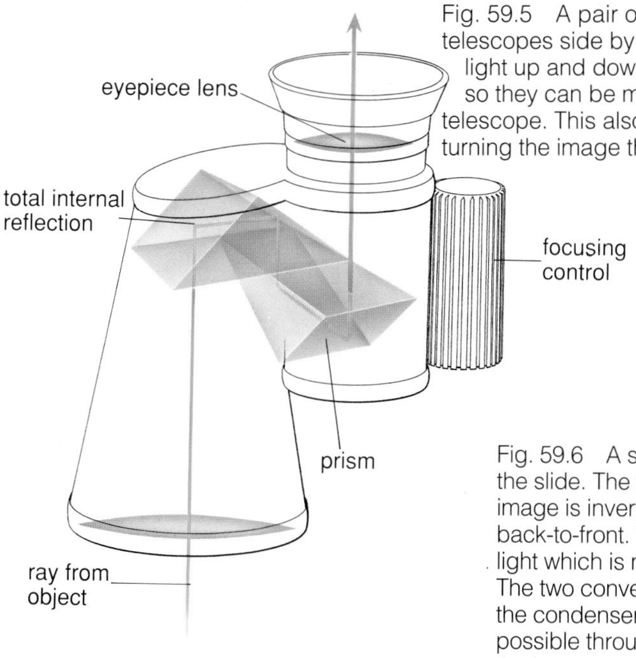

eyepiece lens
total internal reflection
focusing control
prism
ray from object

Fig. 59.5 A pair of binoculars is like two telescopes side by side. Prisms reflect the light up and down inside the binoculars, so they can be much shorter than a telescope. This also has the advantage of turning the image the right way up.

condenser
converging mirror
lamp
slide
projection lens
image on screen

Fig. 59.6 A slide projector. The mirror, lamp and condenser lenses illuminate the slide. The projection lens focuses an enlarged image onto the screen. The image is inverted, so the slide must be placed in the projector upside-down and back-to-front. The converging mirror reflects back light which is not travelling towards the slide. The two converging lenses that make up the condenser direct as much light as possible through the slide. To make the best quality image, the projection lens is often a series of lenses.

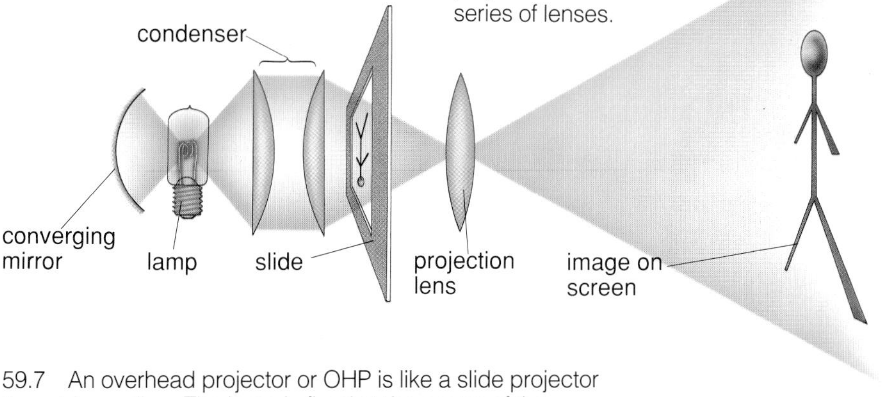

Fig. 59.7 An overhead projector or OHP is like a slide projector pointing at the ceiling. The lamp is fixed at the centre of the curvature of the bottom mirror. Rays from the lamp strike the mirror's surface at 90° and are reflected back along their path. The Fresnel lens is a carefully designed series of circular grooves and acts as a flat lens. (You can see the grooves on the lens of an OHP if you look carefully). The top mirror reflects the image towards the screen. Anything written on the transparency is focused onto the screen.

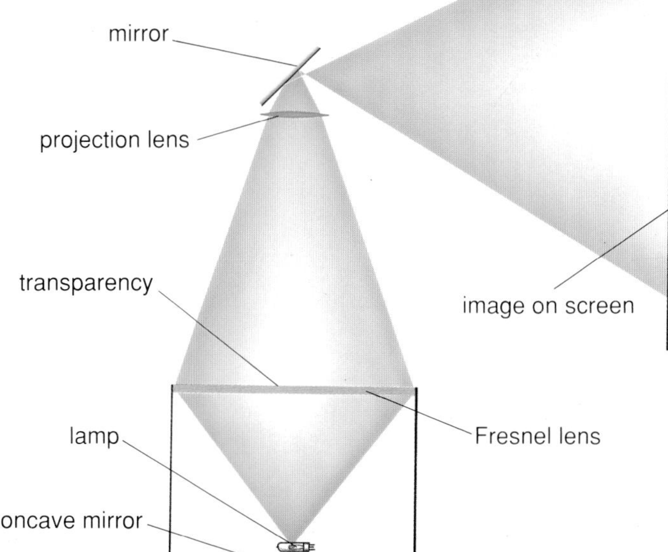

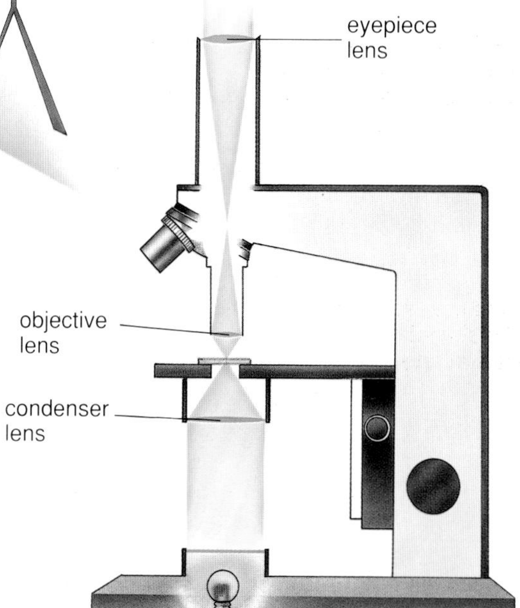

eyepiece lens
objective lens
condenser lens

Fig. 59.8 A microscope. The condenser and objective lenses behave like a projector, forming an image near the eyepiece. The eyepiece acts as a magnifying glass on this image.

DID YOU KNOW?

The first microscopes used a drop of water for the objective lens.

60 CAMERAS AND EYES

Both cameras and eyes use converging lenses to form an image on a light-sensitive layer.

INVESTIGATION 60.1

Pinhole cameras

A pinhole camera can form an image on a screen without using a lens. It works by blocking out most of the light rays falling onto the screen.

Figure 60.1 shows a pinhole camera. You can make one using cardboard, black paper, and a piece of tracing paper for the screen.

Set up your camera, using a bright light source such as a bulb to form an image on the screen. Find answers to each of the following questions.

1 Which way up is the image on the screen?

2 What happens to the size of the image as you move the camera closer to the object?

3 Make the pinhole bigger. What happens to:

a the size of the image?

b the brightness of the image?

c the sharpness (focus) of the image?

Try to explain your answers to a, b and c. Drawing ray diagrams may help.

4 Make the hole even bigger, and place a converging lens over it. How bright is the image formed on the screen? Can you focus it? How?

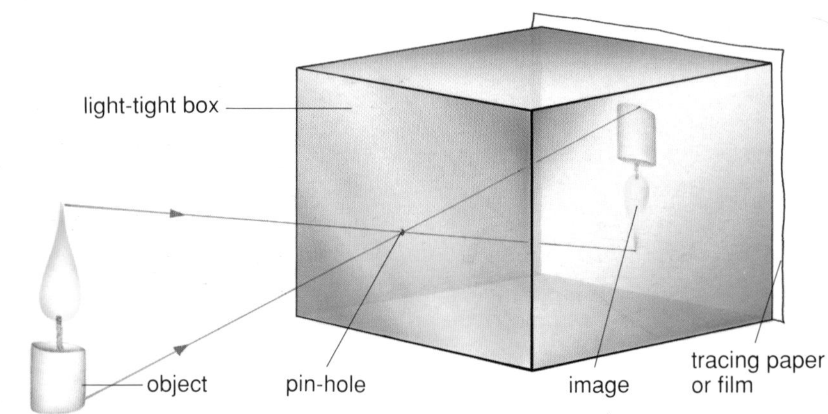

Fig. 60.1 A pinhole camera

The human eye

A human eye is a bit like a pinhole camera with two lenses. The 'pinhole' is the pupil. There are two converging lenses. One, the cornea, is at the front of the eye. The other, the lens, is in the middle of the eye. The 'screen' in the eye is the retina.

Figure 60.2 shows a vertical section through a human eye. As light hits the cornea, it is bent inwards. The cornea is a converging lens. The light rays continue through the pupil, and are bent inwards again by the lens. The rays are brought to a focus on the retina.

The retina contains light-sensitive cells, rods and cones. These send messages along the optic nerve to the brain. The brain sorts out the messages, so that you see a picture of the image formed on your retina.

Like the image on the screen of the pinhole camera, the image on the retina is upside-down. The brain automatically interprets the image the other way up.

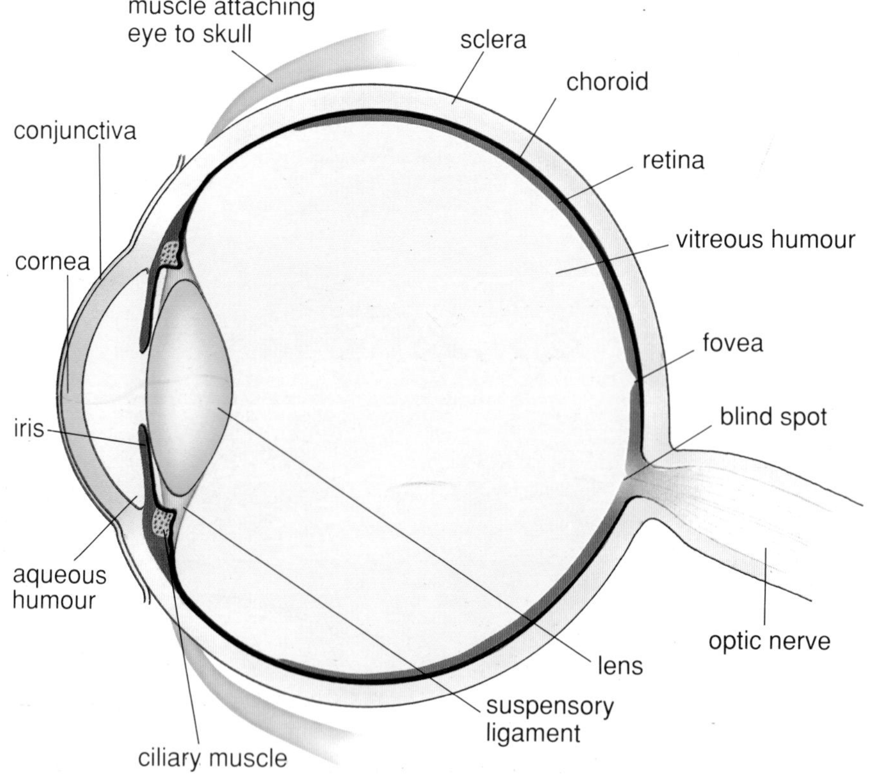

Fig. 60.2 Section through a human eye

The lens adjusts the focusing in the eye

If you did Investigation 60.1, you will have found that you could adjust the focus of the image on the screen in the pinhole camera by moving the lens backwards and forwards. Some animals use this system. Fish, for example, focus images onto the retina of their eye by moving their lens backwards and forwards.

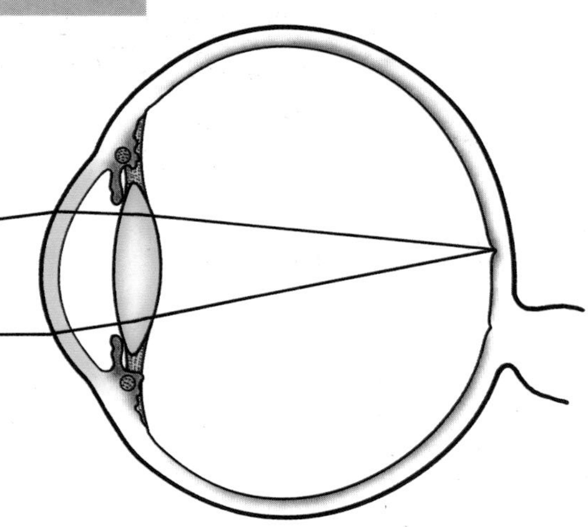

To focus on a distant object, the lens is pulled thinner, so that it bends the rays only slightly.

But mammals, such as humans, adjust the focus by changing the shape of their lens. The lens can be made thinner, which increases its focal length and makes it bend the light rays less. This enables you to focus on objects at a distance. Or it can be made fatter, which decreases its focal length. This makes it bend light rays more, and enables you to focus on nearby objects.

The lens shape is changed by a ring of muscles around it. The muscles contract to make the lens fatter, and relax to make it thinner. So when you are looking at close objects, such as writing on a page, these muscles in your eye are contracted. Some people find this makes their eyes tired, especially if they are working in dim light.

To focus on a nearby object, tension on the lens is slackened. This makes it fatter, so that it bends the rays more.

Fig. 60. 3 In the human eye, the cornea, humours and lens all act as converging lenses, bringing the light to a focus on the retina. Fine adjustments are made by changing the shape of the lens, which alters its focal length.

Fig. 60.4 A modern camera focuses by moving the lens backwards and forwards.

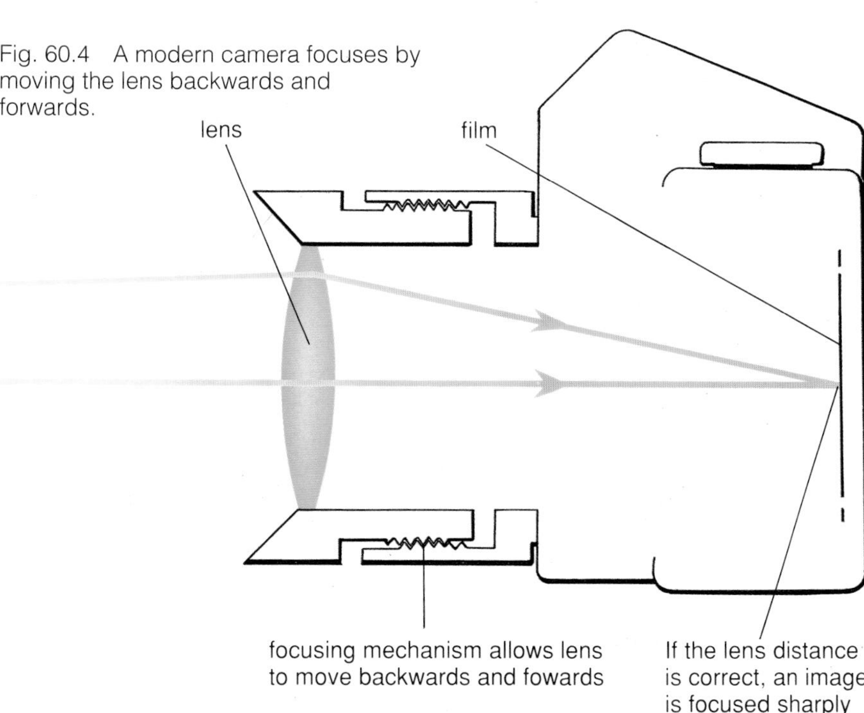

A camera focuses by moving the lens

Cameras use the same basic system as the pinhole camera and lens. A converging lens focuses an image onto a light-sensitive film. A shutter keeps light from falling onto the film until you press the button.

Most good quality cameras contain more than one lens. The lens system is moved backwards and forwards to focus the image on the film. The further away the object is, the closer the lens should be to the film. Some cameras can alter the focus automatically. They measure the distance to the object at which the camera is pointing using infrared beams, or ultrasound, and then adjust the lens position. All you have to do is decide what to point the camera at, and press the button.

61 MORE ABOUT EYES

The amount of light falling onto the light-sensitive layer must be adjusted

The retina at the back of your eye is very sensitive to light. If too much light falls onto it, particularly over a long period of time, it may be permanently damaged. The very bright light reflected from snow can cause snow blindness.

The film in a camera is also very sensitive to light. If too much light falls onto it, then the picture you get is too 'white', instead of having a good contrast between the different colours and different light and dark shades. Your picture is over-exposed.

So both cameras and eyes have systems for regulating the amount of light allowed to enter them. In dull conditions, a lot of light is let in. In bright conditions, less light is let in.

In the eye, this is done by the **iris.**

The iris is the coloured part of your eye. The colour in it absorbs light, and stops it passing through. Light can only pass through the circular hole in the middle of the iris, the **pupil.** Muscles in the iris can contract and relax to make the iris wider or narrower. The wider the iris, the smaller the pupil, and vice versa.

In a camera, the amount of light falling on the film is controlled by the width of the **aperture,** and by the time for which the shutter is open – the **shutter speed.** In very bright light conditions, you should use a small aperture and fast shutter speed. Successful photography partly depends on getting the balance between aperture size and shutter speed just right. Many cameras will do this automatically, but some professional photographers prefer to do it themselves, as it gives them the opportunity to achieve many different effects.

In dim light, the circular muscles relax while the radial muscles contract. This makes the iris narrower.

radial muscles

circular muscles

iris

pupil

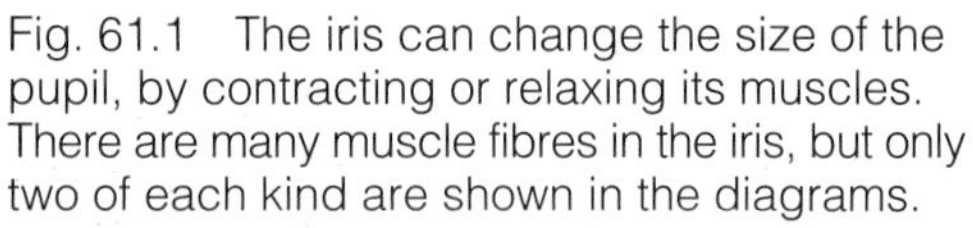

Fig. 61.1 The iris can change the size of the pupil, by contracting or relaxing its muscles. There are many muscle fibres in the iris, but only two of each kind are shown in the diagrams.

In bright light, the circular muscles contract while the radial muscles relax. This makes the iris wider.

Fig. 61.2 Several adjustments can be made to the lens of a single-lens reflex (SLR) camera. The numbers from 22 (in red) to 1.8 (in white) are f-numbers. Turning the ring with these numbers on it alters the **aperture** of the lens. The larger the number, the smaller the aperture. The yellow and white numbers on the rings nearer the front of the lens represent the **focusing distance**; this lens is focused at about 0.9 m. **Shutter speed** is usually adjusted on the body of the camera.

INVESTIGATION 61.1

Looking at a human eye

You can either look at your own eyes, using a mirror, or work with a partner. Step 3 can really only be done successfully with a partner.

1 Make a large diagram of the front view of a human eye. Using your own knowledge, and Figure 60.2, label the following: eyebrow, eyelashes, eyelid, entrance to tear duct, conjunctiva covering cornea, sclera, blood vessels, iris, pupil.

2 Briefly suggest functions for each of these structures.

3 Get a friend to shut their eyes. Make the conditions around them as dark as possible, perhaps by putting a jumper over their head. After a few minutes, remove the jumper, and ask them to open their eyes and look at a bright light.

What did their pupils look like when they opened their eyes? What happened when they looked at the light? Explain what happened to cause this change, and why.

Fig. 61.3

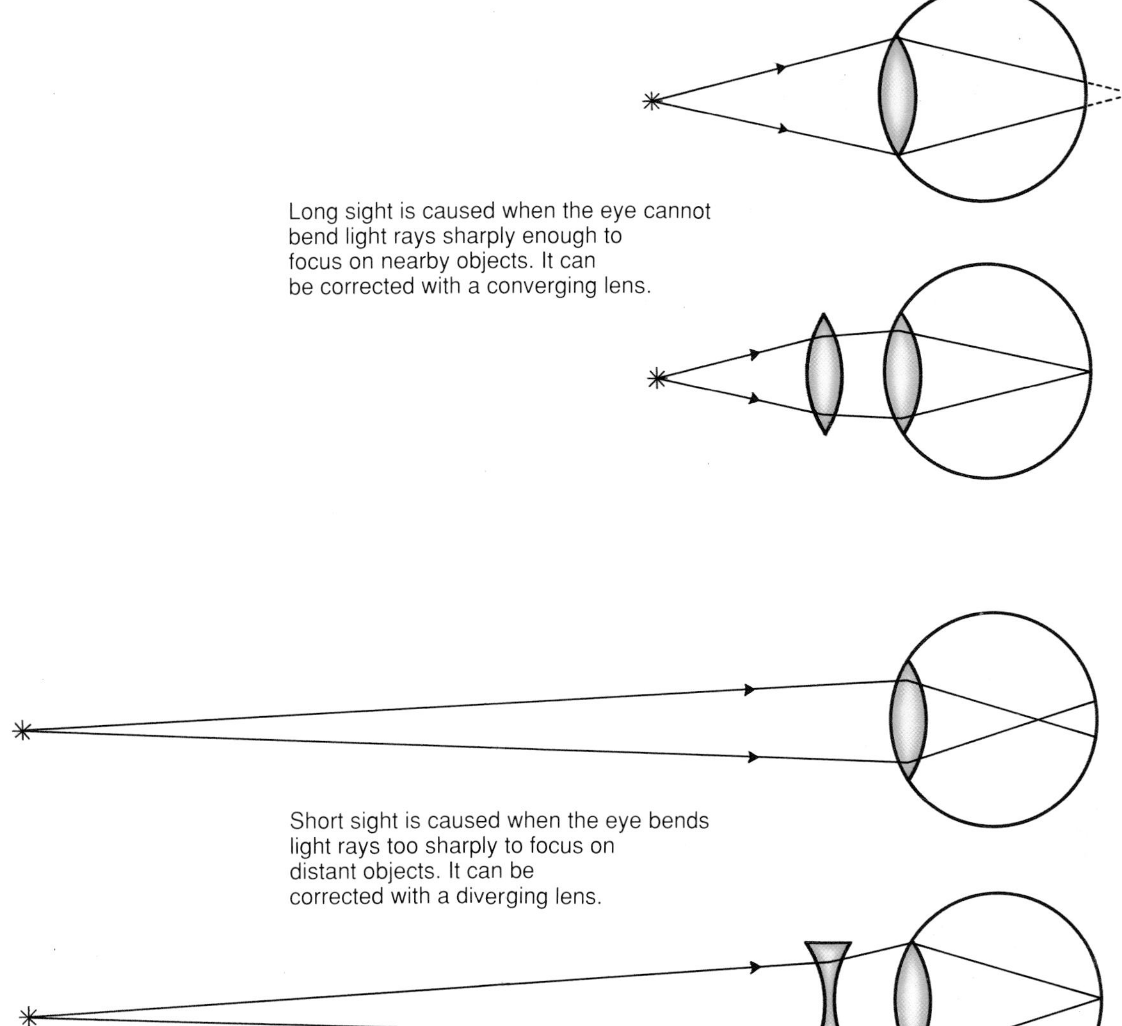

Lenses can help faulty eyes to focus

Many people have problems with focusing. The commonest problem in young people is **short sight.** You can see well close up, but cannot focus on distant objects. This is caused by having a lens which cannot be made thin enough, or an eyeball which is too long. The lens bends the rays too sharply, bringing them to a focus in front of the retina. Short sight is corrected with **diverging lenses.**

Long sight is the opposite problem. You can see well at a distance, but can't focus close up. The lens cannot be made fat enough to bring light from nearby objects to a focus on the retina. Long sight is corrected with **converging lenses.**

As people get older, their lenses become stiffer, and cannot change shape much. They may have problems with both close and distant vision. They may need two pairs of glasses – one for distant vision and one for reading. Or they may have glasses with lenses in two parts. The top part is used for distant vision, and the bottom part for reading. These are called **bifocal lenses.**

Contact lenses lie on the surface of the eye

Contact lenses are preferred to glasses by many people. They give excellent all round vision, and are not obvious to other people.

There are several different types of contact lenses. Hard lenses are made of glass or plastic. They are usually small, less than 1 cm in diameter. They are curved to fit the surface of the conjunctiva and cornea, and sit on the front of the eye over the pupil. The space between the lens and the conjunctiva fills with fluid from the tear ducts. The lens is held in position by surface tension.

Soft lenses are usually larger, and made of a softer, absorbent plastic. Some people find them more comfortable to wear than hard lenses. They are also less likely to fall out! But their absorbency may cause problems if they are not properly cleaned, as bacteria can grow on them, causing eye infections. Modern contact lenses are permeable to gases. Oxygen must be able to get through the lens to reach the cornea, which has no blood supply.

Questions

1 Your friend can read perfectly well, but cannot see the board unless she sits on the front row in class.
   a Is she short sighted or long sighted?
   b What type of lenses – converging or diverging – would an optician prescribe for her?

Questions

1 A periscope has two mirrors. It is arranged to allow you to see over high walls, or over people's heads in a crowd.

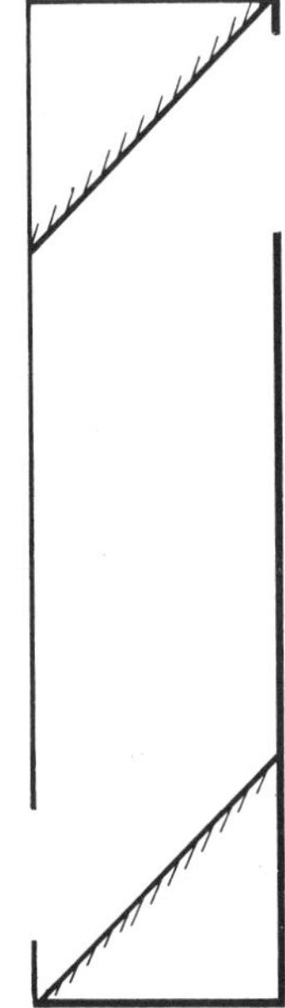

a Copy the diagram, and add an object and an eye.
b Draw in a ray of light from the top of the object, showing how this ray is reflected by the mirrors and reaches the eye. Draw a second ray from the bottom of the object.
c Is the object the right way up, or upside-down?
d Is the object the right way round, or laterally inverted?

2 The diagram shows two light rays leaving an object O and striking a mirror. Copy the diagram, draw in the reflected rays, and show where the image would be.

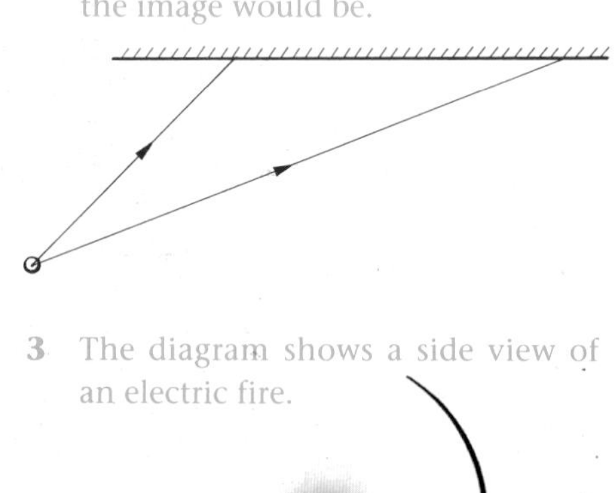

3 The diagram shows a side view of an electric fire.

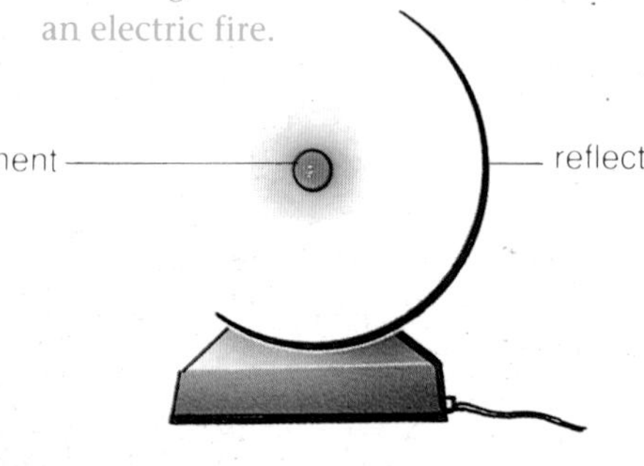

a What is the shape of the reflector?
b What would be the best shape for this reflector?
c Suggest a material from which the reflector could be made. Give reasons for your choice.
d What essential safety feature is missing from the fire?
e What types of waves will be emitted from the element of the fire?
f Draw in two rays to show how this radiation is reflected into the room.

4 The diagram shows part of the rear surface of a bicycle reflector. Copy and complete the diagram, to show what happens to each of the three rays from the different cars. (Each ray will be reflected twice.)

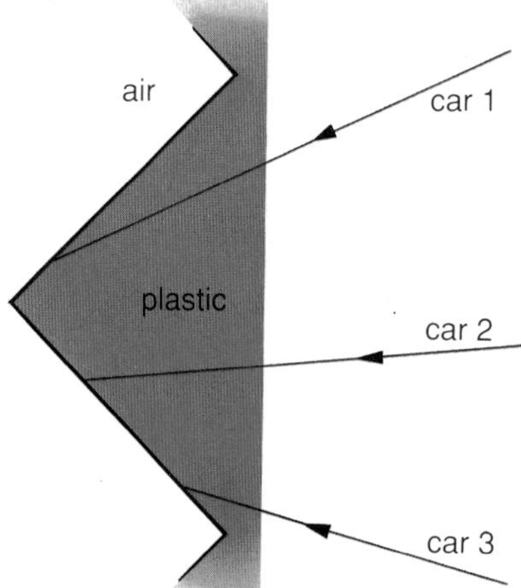

5 A man with 1 m tall waders steps into a stream which looks 90 cm deep. He gets very wet. How was he tricked by refraction?

6 The diagram shows two spotlights shining onto a stage. What colours will be seen in the regions marked A to G?

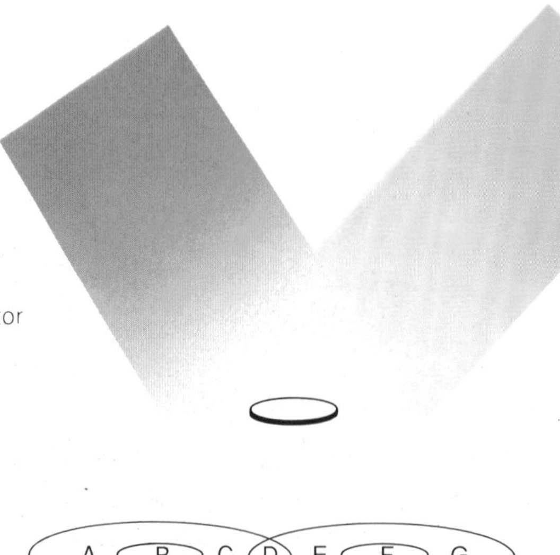

7 As sunlight travels down through deep water, different colours are gradually absorbed. The chart shows the depths to which different colours can penetrate in clear water.

a Which type of light can penetrate deepest?

If you investigate a rocky shore at low tide, you will probably find several kinds of seaweed. Green seaweeds tend to grow high up on the shore. Even when the tide comes in, they will not be covered with deep water. Red seaweeds tend to grow low down on the shore. When the tide comes in, they will be deep under water. The red and green colours of the seaweeds are caused by their light-absorbing pigments.

b Why do seaweeds need light?
c What colours of light are likely to be most available to red seaweeds when the tide is in?
d Why are the seaweeds growing low down on the shore red and not green?

MACHINES AND MOVEMENT

62 TURNING FORCES

The turning effect of a force is called a moment or a torque. It is calculated by multiplying the size of the force by the perpendicular distance between the force and the pivot.

For equilibrium, forces must be balanced

Figure 62.1a shows a rather unusual way of balancing on a see-saw. The reaction force at the pivot balances the force of the people's weight. The see-saw does not move up or down. It is in equilibrium.

In Figure 62.1b, the see-saw is also in equilibrium. It is not moving up or down, so the forces acting on it must be balanced. But this time, the forces are not all acting at the same point. Each of the weights, and the reaction of the pivot, are acting on the see-saw at different points. This produces **turning forces** on the see-saw.

The weight of person Z is tending to turn the see-saw in an anticlockwise direction. The turning force produced by person Y tends to turn the see-saw in a clockwise direction. As the see-saw is not turning in either direction, these two turning forces must be balanced.

You will probably have found out that if one heavy and one light person want to balance on a see-saw, the heavy person needs to sit closer to the pivot than the light person. This suggests that the turning forces produced by the people depend not only on their weight, but also on their distance from the pivot. In fact, the turning force is **the force in newtons multiplied by the perpendicular distance between the force and the pivot.** This turning force is often known as a **moment** or **torque**.

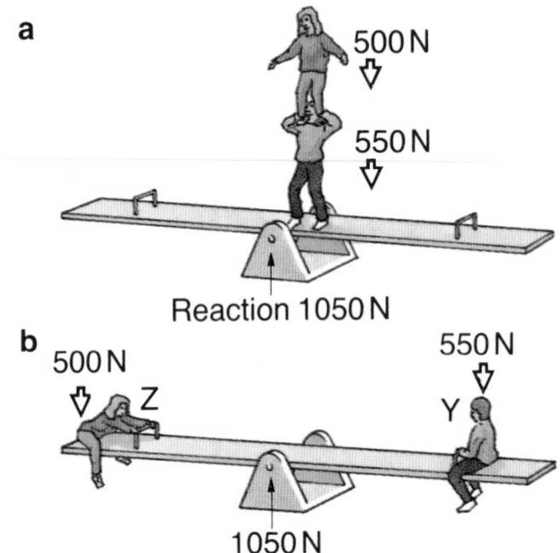

Fig. 62.1 Two ways of balancing on a see-saw

Calculating moments

Calculating turning forces, or moments, helps you to find out where the balancing positions are.

Figure 62.2 shows two forces of different sizes, acting at the same distance from the pivot. They could be the weights of two people sitting on a see-saw. Calculate the moments like this:-

clockwise moment = 550 N × 1.5 m
= 825 newton metres (Nm)

anticlockwise moment = 500 N × 1.5 m
= 750 Nm

So the clockwise moment is 75 Nm larger than the anticlockwise moment. The see-saw will swing clockwise.

For the see-saw to be in equilibrium, the clockwise moment must equal the anticlockwise moment. To balance the see-saw, one of the two people must move! If the lighter person stays where they are, where must the heavier person sit?

anticlockwise moment = 500 N × 1.5 m
= 750 Nm

clockwise moment must equal this for the see-saw to balance, so:

$$550\,\text{N} \times x\,\text{m} = 750\,\text{Nm}$$

$$\text{so:} \quad x\,\text{m} = \frac{750\,\text{Nm}}{550\,\text{N}} = \mathbf{1.36\,m}$$

The heavier person must sit 1.36 m from the pivot, to make the seesaw balance.

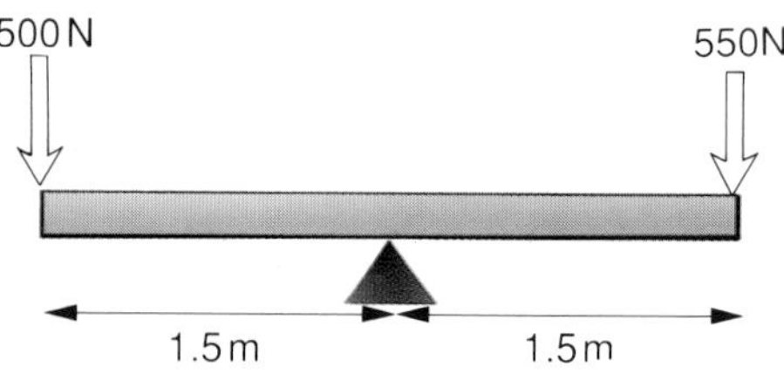

Fig. 62.2 Turning forces on a see-saw

EXTENSION

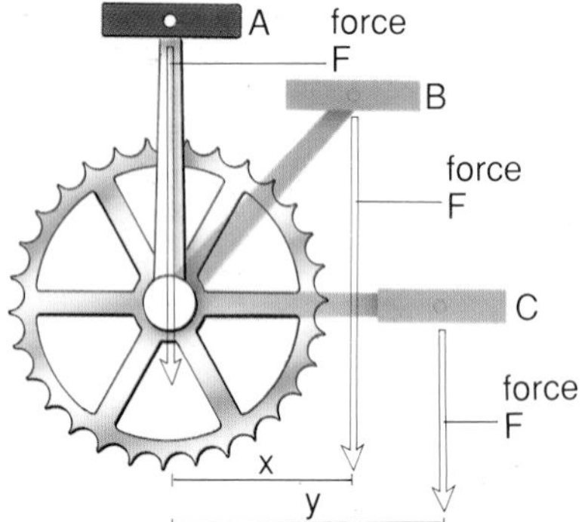

Fig. 62.3 Forces turning a bicycle pedal. A push is more effective at some positions than others.

The angle at which a force acts is also important

Figure 62.3 shows a bicycle pedal. With your foot exactly at the top of the pedal's path, you can push downwards as hard as you like without turning the pedal. The direction of the force points directly at the pivot. The line of action of the force passes through the pivot – so there is no moment. The shortest distance between the line of action of the force and the pivot is zero.

With your foot on the pedal at position B, the line of action of the force no longer passes through the pivot. The shortest distance between the line of action of the force and the pivot is *x*. The shortest distance is always perpendicular to the line of the force.

So now there *is* a turning force. It is F*x* Nm.

When your foot on the pedal arrives at position C, the perpendicular distance of the line of action of the force from the pivot is *y*. This is the length of the crank of the pedal. Now the turning force is F*y* Nm. This is the largest moment possible on the pedals. Your push is most effective at this position.

Moments of forces acting at an angle

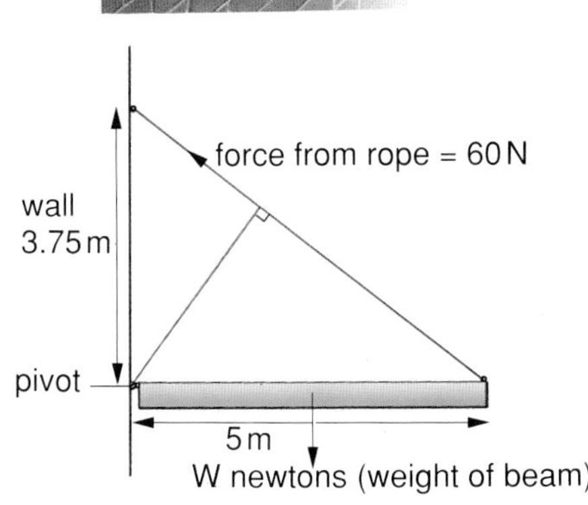

Figure 62.4 shows a horizontal beam attached to a vertical wall. The beam weighs WN. A rope is attached to the end of the beam, and is pulling upwards with a force of 60N in the direction shown. The beam is not moving. Everything is at equilibrium. Can we calculate the weight of the beam?

There are two turning forces involved here. The weight of the beam is tending to swing the beam downwards, turning clockwise about the pivot. The rope is pulling the beam upwards, turning anticlockwise about the pivot. These two turning forces must be balanced.

Begin by looking at the turning force produced by the rope. This force acts along the rope. Draw an arrow up the rope to represent the force. Keep the line going past the pivot point. You should now be able to measure the closest that the force line gets to the pivot. This distance is shown in red. The shortest distance is always this **perpendicular distance**, so you can find this by drawing or calculating the length of the line shown in red on the diagram. It is 3 m.

Fig. 62.4 You can find the shortest distance between the line of the force and the pivot from a scale diagram.

So now we know the moment of the force produced by the rope. It is:

$$60\text{N} \times 3\text{m}$$
$$= 180\text{Nm}$$

Now to the other turning force – the one produced by the weight of the beam. The weight of the beam acts at its centre of mass, half-way along it. So the perpendicular distance between the beam's weight and the pivot is 2.5m. If we call the weight of the beam W, then the moment of this force is:

$$\text{WN} \times 2.5\text{m}$$

We know that the anticlockwise turning force of the rope, and the clockwise turning force of the beam's weight balance each other. So:

$$\text{WN} \times 2.5\text{m} = 180\text{Nm}$$
$$W = \frac{180}{2.5}$$
$$= 72\text{N}$$

Questions

1 In each case, say whether or not the beam is balanced. If it is not balanced, what is the overall moment (turning force)?

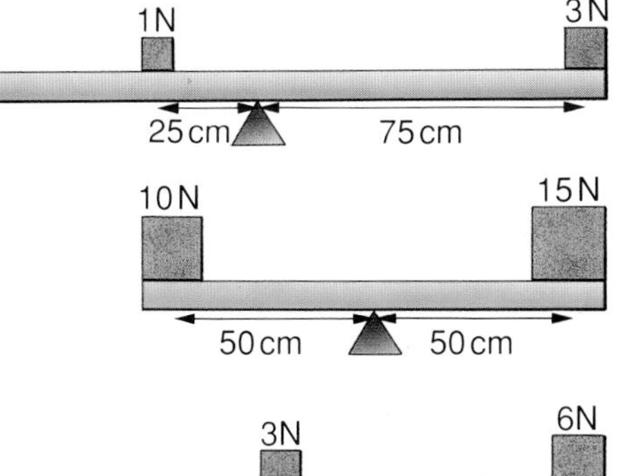

2 The diagram shows a weighing device made from a 3m long beam,with a mass of 20kg.

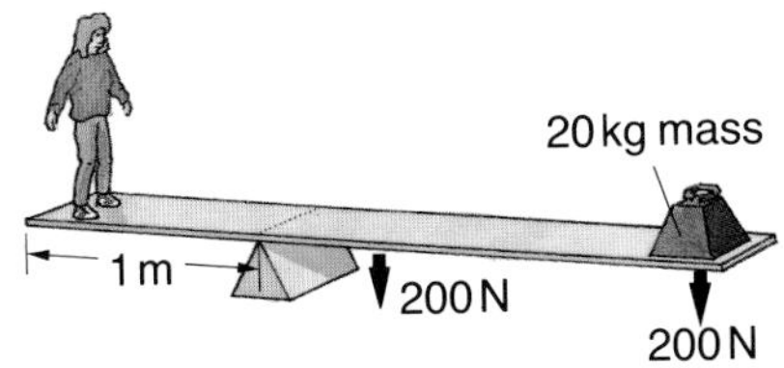

a Calculate the clockwise moments produced by:
 i the beam
 ii the 20kg mass.

b What is the total clockwise moment?

c If the beam is balanced, what is the weight of the girl?

d If the girl picks up a 5kg mass, where must the pivot be positioned to enable the beam to balance again?

3 A nut must be tightened to a torque of 70Nm.

a How hard must you pull on the end of the spanner to reach this torque?

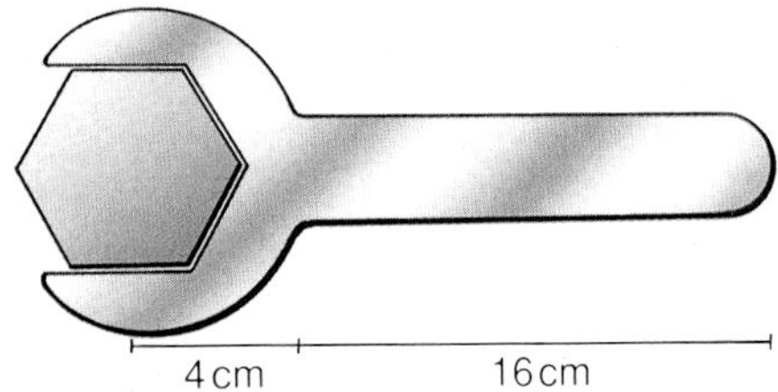

b What would be the advantage of sliding a 96cm tube over the end of the spanner, and pulling on the end of that?

4 A gardener invented an automatic watering system for a plant. A 1.2m bar, with a mass of 2kg was mounted, as shown. The empty watering can has a mass of 0.4kg. Water drips from the tap at a rate of 10g every minute.

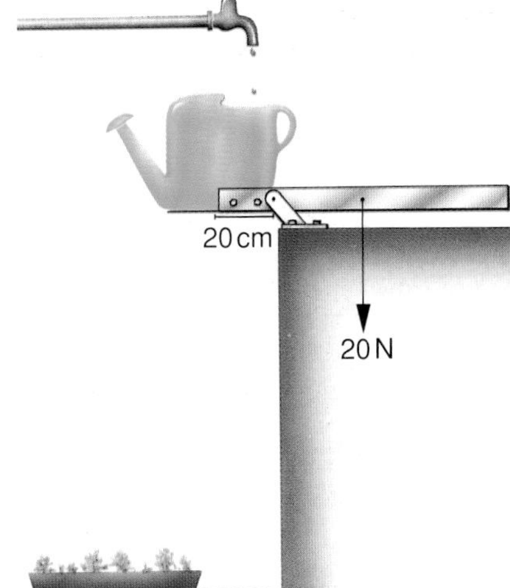

a How often does the can tip up and water the plant? (Ignore friction in the pivot.)

b Discuss whether the system would actually operate as the gardener intended.

63 MACHINES

A machine is something which makes work seem easier. It transfers energy from one point to another.

A ramp is a simple machine

Machines don't have to be complicated arrangements of clanking metal! A machine is something which makes it easier for us to do work. A lever is a machine. Your skeleton is a machine. A ramp is a machine.

In Topic 27 you looked at the energy gained by a mass as it is pushed up a slope. You will remember that work done is force x distance moved in the direction of the force. Pushing the block straight up the slope uses a small force, but covers a large distance. Pulling the block straight up uses a larger force, but covers a smaller distance. The total work done, or energy used, is the same in both cases. You don't actually save any energy by pushing the block up the slope instead of lifting it straight up. But the job is much easier. Using a ramp makes it easier to do the work as the force needed is less. So a ramp is a simple machine.

EXTENSION

Mechanical advantage tells you how much easier the machine makes your work

Figure 63.1 shows a ramp being used in the way described above. The load being lifted is a weight of 100 N. The machine lifts the load upwards by 2 m. The effort – the force you actually use – moves through a distance of 4 m. For this machine, the effort is 50 N. If no energy is lost, then:

$$\text{word done by effort} = \text{energy gained by load}$$

so:

distance moved by effort x effort force = distance moved by load x load force

Rearranging this formula gives:

$$\frac{\text{distance moved by effort}}{\text{distance moved by load}} = \frac{\text{load force}}{\text{effort force}}$$

The value of $\frac{\text{load force}}{\text{effort force}}$ is called the **mechanical advantage** of the machine. The mechanical advantage of this ramp is $\frac{4}{2} = 2$. This machine makes it twice as easy for you to get the block to the top of the slope. The effort force is only half the load force.

Friction lowers mechanical advantage

If you wanted to know how much help the ramp would be to you, without actually pushing weights up it, you could get a good idea by measuring the distances the forces would have to move. You have seen that, if no energy is lost, then:

$$\frac{\text{distance moved by effort}}{\text{distance moved by load}} = \frac{\text{load force}}{\text{effort force}}$$

So, by measuring the two distances involved, you can work out how much easier the machine will make the work.

In practice, as you pull the load up the ramp, you will also have to pull against **friction**. Some energy will be lost. As well as the 50 N needed to raise the load, extra force will be needed to overcome the frictional force.

So working out the distances moved by effort and load can give you a rough idea of how useful a machine is. But it will not give you an exact answer, because it does not take friction into account. The only way to *really* find out the advantage of a machine is to use it, and measure the effort force you need to use against a particular load force.

EXTENSION

Calculating the efficiency of a machine

The efficiency of any energy transfer is:

$$\frac{\text{useful output energy}}{\text{input energy}}$$

In practice, no machine is 100% efficient. The input energy is always more than the useful output energy. Some energy is always lost, often because work must be done against friction. The 'lost' energy is transferred as heat to the surroundings.

The useful output energy in the ramp example, in Figure 63.1, is 200 J. If the ramp is 75% efficient, then:

$$\frac{75}{100} = \frac{200}{\text{input energy}}$$

So:

$$\text{input energy} = \frac{200 \times 100}{75} = 266.7\ \text{J}$$

This energy is transferred over a distance of 4 m, so the force you would have to use would be 66.7 N.

EXTENSION

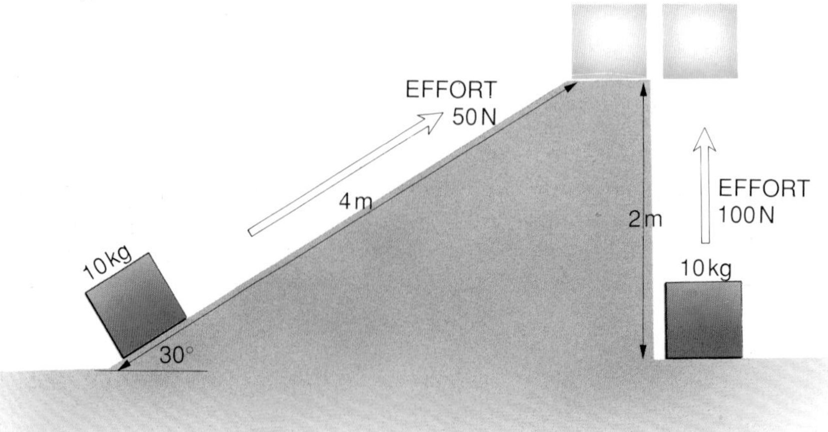

Fig. 63.1 With this ramp a 100 N weight is lifted by a 50 N force. Without the ramp, a 100 N force would be needed. Either way, 200 J of work must be done.

A screw thread is like a ramp twisted around a cylinder

A screw thread is a machine. It is a ramp twisted round and round. The distance between two adjacent levels of the ramp is called the **pitch** of the screw.

Figure 63.2 shows a car jack. Each time the handle is turned round once, the nut moves by one pitch. The nut supports the load of the car. So, by lifting the nut one pitch, the car is also lifted through this distance.

For the car jack:

$$\frac{\text{distance moved by effort}}{\text{distance moved by load}}$$

$$= \frac{\text{circumference of circle turned by handle}}{\text{pitch of screw}}$$

For a typical car jack, this is about 600. You turn the handle 600 times further than you actually lift the car! But the lifting force is not 600 times the effort force you apply to the handle. Friction means that the load force is only about 200 times the effort force. The force you have to use to lift the car is about 200 times less than the weight of the car.

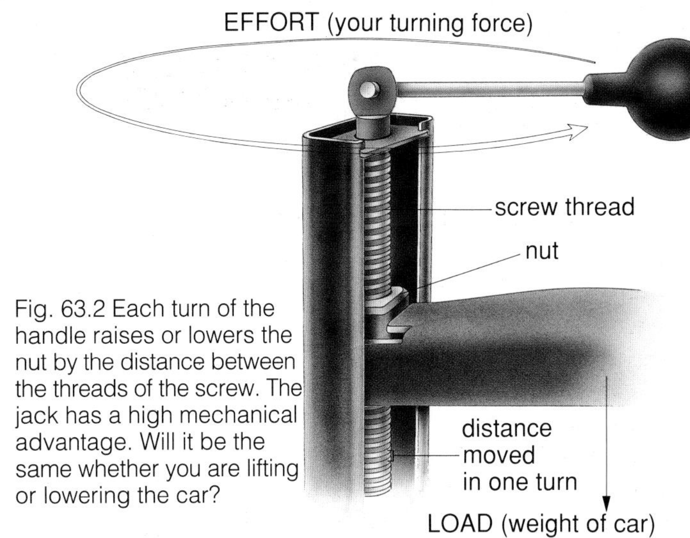

Fig. 63.2 Each turn of the handle raises or lowers the nut by the distance between the threads of the screw. The jack has a high mechanical advantage. Will it be the same whether you are lifting or lowering the car?

A lever is a machine

Levers are machines. Figure 63.3 shows a lever being used. The effort force is three times as far from the pivot as the load. If the effort force moves, the load only moves one third as much. So if there is no friction at the pivot, the effort force only needs to be one third the load force.

This lever trebles your effort force but only transfers the same energy, because the load only moves one third as far as the effort.

Fig. 63.3 The lever reduces the force needed to lift the paving slab. In this case, assume the right hand (nearer the pivot) is providing the effort force.

INVESTIGATION 63.1

Investigating levers

You will need a pivot, a long ruler or piece of wood, and a collection of masses.

1 Set up your ruler and pivot to make a lever. Place the pivot $\frac{1}{3}$ of the way along the ruler. Make a labelled diagram of the lever you have made.

2 Place a load of 100g on the shorter end of your lever. Place masses on the other end until the beam balances. Measure the effort force required to just balance the load. Record your results in a chart like the one below. Repeat for steadily increasing loads.

3 Plot a graph of efficiency against load. What shape is your graph? Can you explain its shape? Think about clockwise and anticlockwise moments with no load or effort applied.

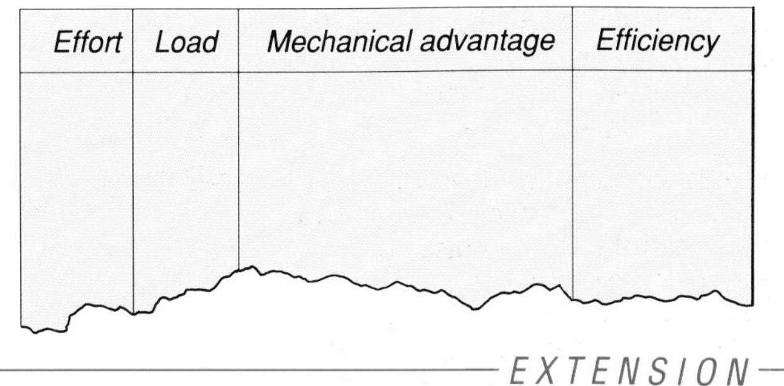

Effort	*Load*	*Mechanical advantage*	*Efficiency*

EXTENSION

There are three classes of levers

Fig. 63.4

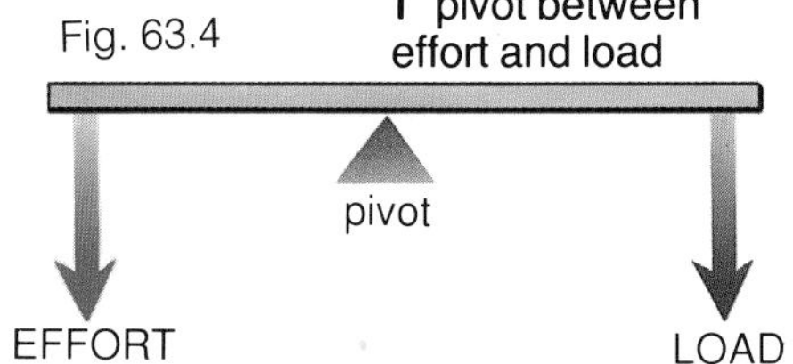

This is a class one lever. If the pivot is nearer to the load, the lever is a **force multiplier.** The effort is less than the load. If the pivot is nearer to the effort, the lever is a **distance multiplier**. The load moves more than the effort.

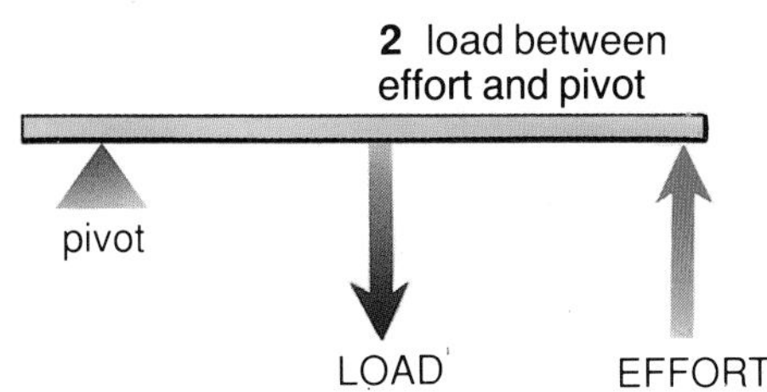

This is a class two lever. The effort always moves more than the load. This lever is a **force multiplier**. The effort is less than the load, but moves through a larger distance.

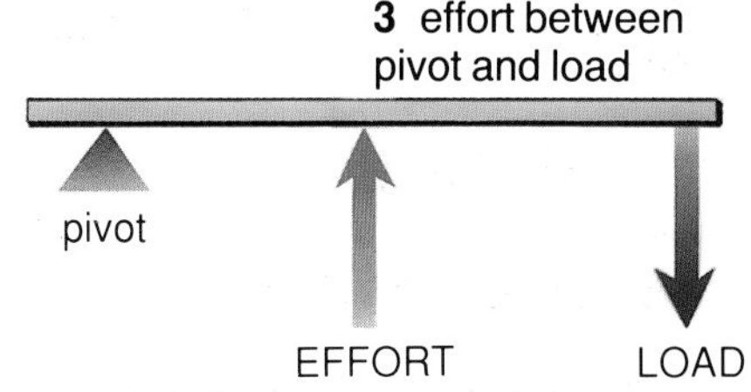

This is a class three lever. The load always moves more than the effort. The lever is a **distance multiplier**. The load force is less than the effort force.

64 VELOCITY

Velocity and displacement are vector quantities. Unlike speed and distance, they include directional information.

Average speed is distance divided by time

A car speedometer shows how quickly a car is travelling at a particular moment. It shows the **instantaneous** speed. If a speedometer reads 30 miles per hour (mph) you would cover 30 miles, if you drove for one hour at exactly this speed all the time. But this is unlikely to happen. You might reach 70 mph on some parts of your journey, and be held up at traffic lights on other parts. The thing which determines how quickly you complete your journey is your *average* speed.

You can calculate your average speed using another display on the speedometer. This is the odometer or mileometer, which shows how far the car has travelled. You also need to time your journey. If you find that you have travelled 70 miles in 2 hours, then:

$$\textbf{average speed} = \frac{\textbf{distance moved}}{\textbf{time taken}}$$

$$\frac{70 \text{ miles}}{2 \text{ hours}} = 35 \text{ mph}$$

Although we still use miles per hour in Britain, the official scientific units for speed are metres per second, or kilometres per hour. 1 m/s is 3.6 km/h, which is roughly 2.25 mph.

If you want to calculate the time taken, or the distance travelled, you can rearrange the formula above:

$$\textbf{time taken} = \frac{\textbf{distance moved}}{\textbf{average speed}}$$

$$\textbf{distance moved} = \textbf{average speed} \times \textbf{time taken}$$

Fig. 64.2 A hand-held speed checker transmits radio waves which are bounced back from a moving car. If the car is moving towards the instrument, then the wavelength of the returning radio waves is decreased. The faster the car is moving, the greater the change in wavelength. The speed checking instrument gives an instant digital read-out.

Distance and speed are scalar quantities

Distance is a measurement of length. Speed is a measurement of length per unit time. Neither gives any information about the *direction* in which length is measured. They are **scalar** quantities. Scalar quantities have a size, or magnitude, but no direction is specified.

But we often want to say in which direction a distance or speed is measured. We could say, for example, that a person has walked 1 km north. We have not only given a distance, but also a direction. This measurement is called the **displacement** of the person. We could also give their speed in this direction – say an average of 4 km/h north. This measurement is called the **velocity** of the person.

Displacement and velocity specify the direction in which the movement is taking place. They are **vector** quantities.

Speed and velocity are not always the same

Imagine you leave your house and walk 100 m down the road to the shops. You walk at an average speed of 1 m/s. You then walk back home again. You cover a total distance of 200 m. Your total journey takes you 200 s.

But what are your displacement and velocity?

Displacement = distance in a specified direction (in a straight line)

Velocity = speed in a specified direction (in a straight line)

$$\textbf{Average velocity} = \frac{\textbf{displacement}}{\textbf{time}}$$

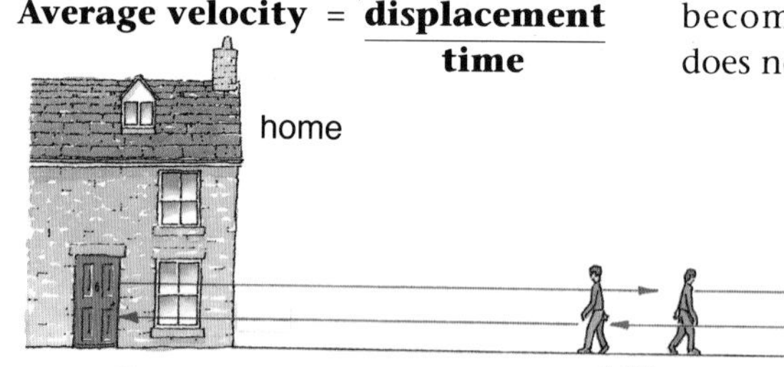

Fig. 64.1

You go 100 m one way, and then 100 m back again. You actually end up where you started – at home. So your displacement is 0!

So your average velocity is:

$$\frac{0 \text{ m}}{200 \text{ s}} = 0 \text{ m/s}$$

This is rather an unusual example. In many of the situations you meet, objects will be moving in straight lines, without changing direction. The values for speed and velocity will be the same in these situations. The difference between speed and velocity only becomes important when an object does not move in a single straight line.

Questions

Two runners race around a 400 m track. One runs steadily at 10 m/s. The second runs slowly at the start, but gets faster towards the end of the race. They both cross the finishing line at the same time.

1 What is the runners' time for the race?

2 What is the average speed of the second runner?

3 Which runner reached the highest instantaneous speed?

INVESTIGATION 64.1

Measuring reaction time

1 Using a digital stopwatch, time how long it takes for a 100g mass to fall to the ground when dropped from a height of 1 m. Get several different people to repeat this measurement. How closely do you all agree? Compare your reaction times.

2 Ask your partner to hold a 30 cm ruler vertically by the top end. Hold your hand out, so that your open fingers are at the bottom of the ruler. When your partner drops the ruler, catch it as quickly as you can. Measure the length of the ruler which passes through your hand before you catch it. You could ask several different people to repeat this experiment.

Questions

1 Which of these experiments do you think gives the better measurement of reaction time? Both experiments have their faults – can you suggest what these are? How could you make the tests as fair as possible?

2 The chart below shows the distance a 30cm ruler falls in different lengths of time. Plot a graph of distance on the y axis against time on the x axis. Then use the graph to find your own reaction time from your results to Step 2 above.

time (s)	*distance (cm)*
.045	1.0
.071	2.5
.101	5.0
.124	7.5
.143	10.0
.159	12.5
.175	15.0
.189	17.5
.202	20.0
.214	22.5
.226	25.0
.237	27.5
.247	30.0

Ticker-tape timers are used for measuring velocity

You can measure velocity by measuring a displacement and a time interval. You could, for example, use a stopwatch to time someone running 100 m. You could then work out their average velocity, by dividing 100 m by the time taken.

Your measurement of the time taken would not be very accurate, because your reaction time and the time taken to press the button on the stopwatch would delay the start and finish of the timing. Hopefully, the delays would be about the same at the beginning and the end of the race, and would cancel each other out. But if you tried to time someone running for just 2 m, your reaction time would be about the same as the time you were trying to measure. For short distances, or high speeds, you need something better.

A ticker-tape timer gets rid of any problems of reaction time. It has a vibrating arm, which puts dots onto a paper tape. Run from a 50 Hz electromagnet, 50 dots are put on the tape every second. If the tape is not moving, all the dots are put on top of each other. But if the tape is being pulled out by something moving, then the dots are spaced out.

At 50 dots per second, the time between two dots is 0.02 s. So the space between two dots represents 0.02 s. Five spaces represent 0.1 s.

If the length of five spaces on the tape is 10 cm, then it took 0.1 s for 10 cm of tape to be pulled out. The object pulling the tape travelled 10 cm in 0.1 s, or 100 cm/s.

$$\text{Average velocity} = \frac{\text{distance moved}}{\text{time taken}} = \frac{10\,\text{cm}}{0.1\,\text{s}} = 100\,\text{cm/s}$$

If you always use strips of the tape five spaces long, then each strip represents 0.1 s. You can just multiply the length of each strip by ten to find the velocity.

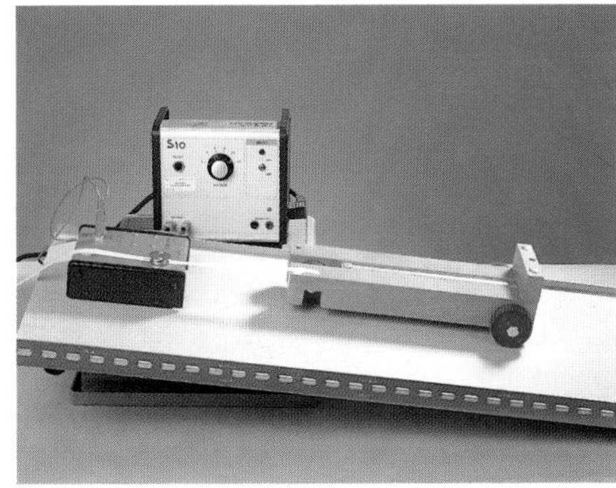

Fig. 64.3 The tape is threaded through the ticker-tape timer. As the trolley runs down the ramp it pulls the tape past a vibrating pin which leaves a series of dots. Your timer may need a carbon disc if you are not using self-marking tape.

Questions

1 A rider canters at a steady 10 m/s around a field, from A to B and then to C.

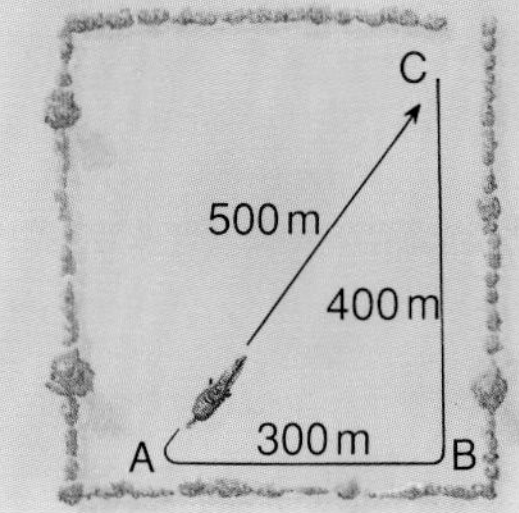

a What total distance does she cover?
b How long does this take her?
c What is her average speed?
d What is her displacement in the direction AC?
e What is her average velocity in the direction AC?

2 The diagram shows part of a ticker-tape timer strip. What was the velocity of the strip?

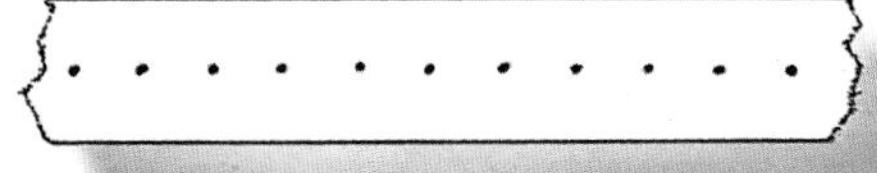

3 Suggest a method you could use to calculate the average velocity of:
a a racing car
b a toy car
c a falling feather
d a falling ping-pong ball.
Give reasons for each of your suggestions.

65 ACCELERATION

Acceleration tells you how quickly velocity is changing.

Velocity stays constant if forces are balanced

In Topic 16, Newton's First Law is stated as: 'an object keeps on going as it is, unless an unbalanced force acts on it'.

We can now state this law more precisely:

velocity is constant if forces are balanced.

The velocity of an object does not change, unless an unbalanced force acts on it. If you were to push an object to set it moving, it would carry on moving at the same speed and in the same direction for ever, if there were no unbalanced forces acting on it. In practice, though, friction slows the object down.

An air track greatly reduces friction. An object moving along an air track travels at a virtually constant velocity.

Imagine a rider A is set moving along an air track. It covers 8 m in 1 s, and another 8 m in the next second. If we plot a graph of distance covered against time taken, we get a line like the red one in Figure 65.2. It is a straight line.

The blue line is for another rider, B. This one is moving more slowly. It is travelling at 3 m/s. Like A, its velocity is constant, so the line is straight. But the slope of the line is not as steep, because the velocity of B is not as great as A.

If you used a ticker-tape timer to measure the velocity of rider A on the air track, the dots on the tape would all be the same distance apart. Strips five spaces long, each representing 0.1 s of movement, would all be the same length. For rider A, these strips would all be 80 cm long. (How long would a strip five spaces long be for rider B?) Placed side by side, these strips would give you a **velocity-time graph**. It would be a horizontal line, because velocity is constant.

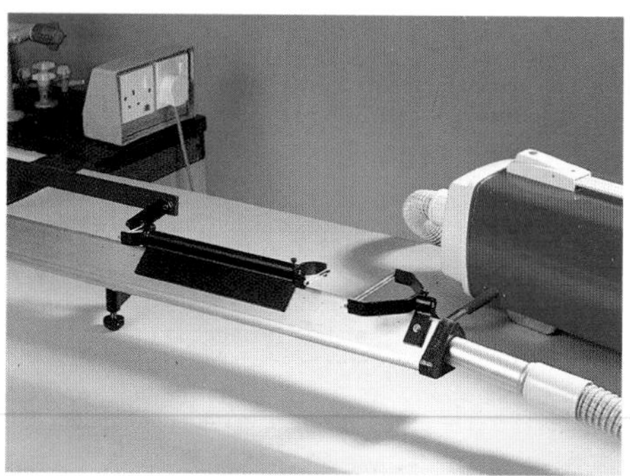

Fig. 65.1 An air track and rider. The vacuum cleaner blows air through rows of tiny holes just below the top of the track. The rider floats on a cushion of air just above the surface of the track. There is very little friction.

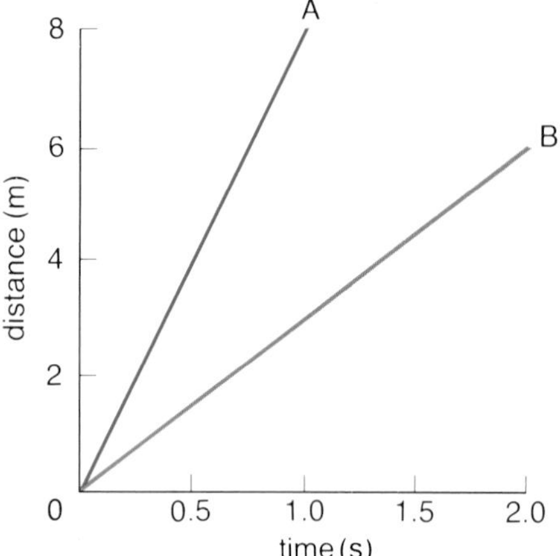

Fig. 65.2 Distance-time graphs for two different velocities.

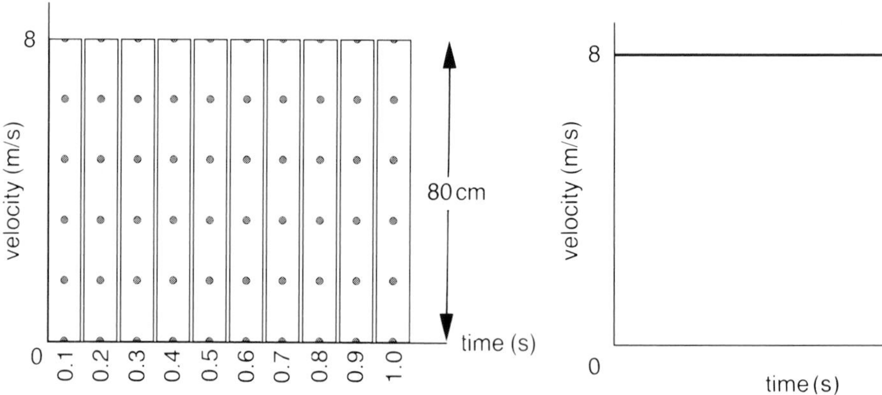

Fig. 65.3 Ticker-tapes for an object moving at a constant velocity of 8 m/s.

Fig. 65.4 Velocity-time graph for an object moving at a constant velocity of 8 m/s.

Acceleration is a change in velocity

If you try the experiment described above, you will find that your strips of ticker tape are not all the same length. They get shorter. This is because the drag of the ticker-tape slows the rider down. The velocity gradually changes. The rider is **accelerating.** In fact, this is a *negative* acceleration, or a *deceleration*. If velocity was increasing, then the acceleration would be positive.

Acceleration tells you how fast the velocity of an object is changing. If rider A starts off at 8 m/s, but has slowed down to 6 m/s after 2 s, then its velocity has changed by 2 m/s in 2 s. We say that its acceleration is:

$$\frac{\textbf{change in velocity (m/s)}}{\textbf{time taken (s)}}$$

$$= \frac{\mathbf{-2\ m/s}}{\mathbf{2\ s}} = \textbf{- 1 metre per second per second}$$

The minus sign shows that the acceleration is negative – the rider is slowing down.

'1 metre per second per second' is a very lengthy way of writing this. It can be shortened to 1 m/s^2, or 1 ms^{-2}.

If you were to collect lengths of ticker-tape five spaces long while this was happening, they would get shorter and shorter. You could make a velocity-time graph with them, as shown in Figure 65.5. The graph slopes downwards, because there is negative acceleration. If acceleration was positive – if A was speeding up – then the graph would slope upwards.

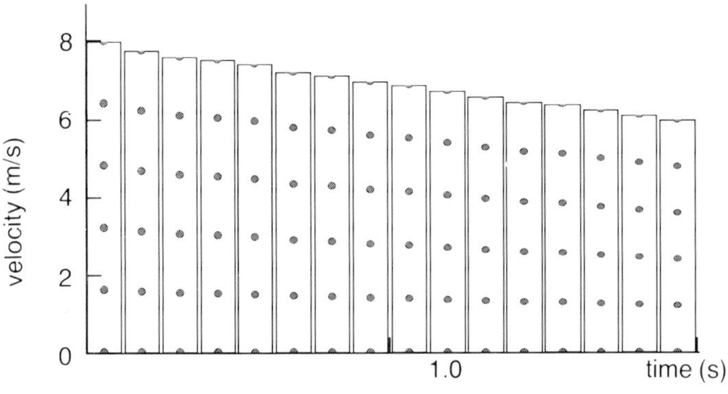

Fig. 65.5 Ticker-tapes for an object decelerating at 1 m/s²

Fig. 65.6 Velocity-time graph for an object decelerating at 1 m/s²

An object can accelerate without changing speed

You will remember that speed is a measure of how much distance is covered in a certain time. Velocity is a measure of how much distance in a particular direction is covered in a certain time. You can change velocity either by changing how *fast* you are going, or by changing the *direction* in which you are going.

Imagine a cyclist travelling along a straight track. She is moving at 10 m/s. Her speed and velocity are both constant. Her acceleration is zero.

The same cyclist now travels around a circular track, still at 10 m/s. Her speed remains constant. But her direction of travel is constantly changing. Her velocity is changing. The cyclist is accelerating. Her acceleration is at right angles to the direction of travel. For a circular track, acceleration is towards the centre of the circle. The force which causes the change in velocity towards the centre of the circle is called **centripetal force**. You can find out more about this force in Topic 68.

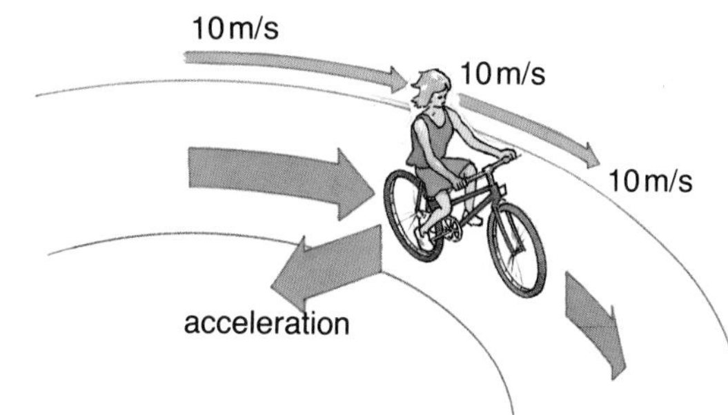

Fig. 65.7 A cyclist on a circular track is accelerating, even though she is travelling at a constant speed.

Questions

1 A ball is thrown vertically upwards, with a velocity of 20 m/s. It takes 2 s for the ball to rise to its maximum height, at which point it stops for an instant.

a What is the acceleration caused by gravity?

b In which direction does it act?

The ball falls to the ground, taking a further two seconds to do so.

c With what velocity does it hit the ground? (You can ignore air resistance in answering this question.)

2 A trolley attached to a ticker-tape timer is pushed and released down a gently sloping ramp. The ticker-tape is shown as tape 1 on the right.

a Describe the motion of the trolley.

The ramp is then tilted a little more, and the experiment repeated. The tape is shown as tape 2 below.

b What can you say about the forces acting on the trolley?

The ramp is tilted even more, and a third piece of tape, tape 3, obtained.

c How far did the trolley travel in the first 0.1 s?

d What was the average velocity in the first 0.1 s?

e What was the average velocity in the next 0.1 s?

f By how much did the velocity increase in 0.1 s?

g What was the acceleration?

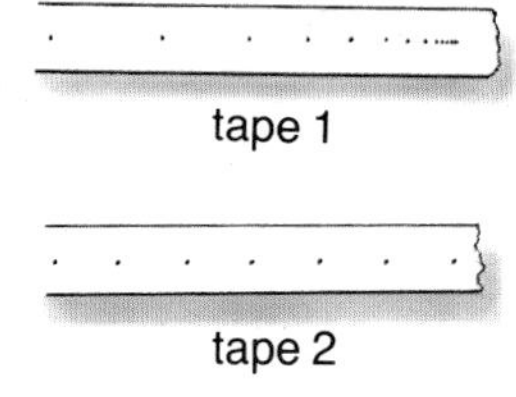

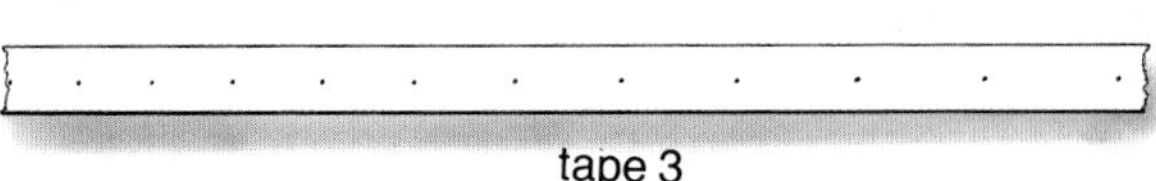

66 MORE ABOUT VELOCITY

Velocity-time graphs can be used to calculate displacement.

The area under a velocity-time graph shows the distance covered

Figure 66.1 shows a displacement-time graph for a car travelling at a steady velocity. The graph is a straight line because the velocity of the car is not changing. The slope or gradient of the graph gives the velocity of the car.

$$\textbf{Gradient} = \frac{\textbf{vertical distance}}{\textbf{horizontal distance}} = \frac{\textbf{200 m}}{\textbf{10 s}} = \textbf{20 m/s}$$

Figure 66.2 shows a velocity-time graph for the same car. It is a straight horizontal line because the velocity of the car is constant. You can use this graph to work out the total displacement of the car after a certain time.

Displacement = velocity × time
= 20 m/s × time

So after ten seconds:

Displacement = 20 m/s × 10 s = 200 m

If you look at the graph, you will see that you have worked out the area of the box formed by the velocity line, the x and y axes, and a vertical line at the time you are interested in. This always works. **The area under a velocity-time graph gives you the distance travelled.**

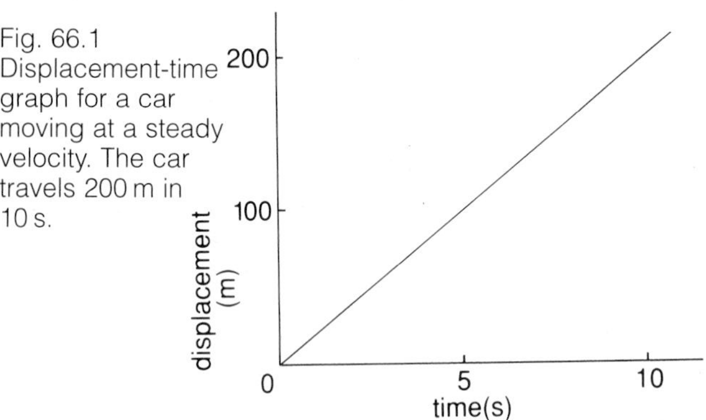

Fig. 66.1 Displacement-time graph for a car moving at a steady velocity. The car travels 200 m in 10 s.

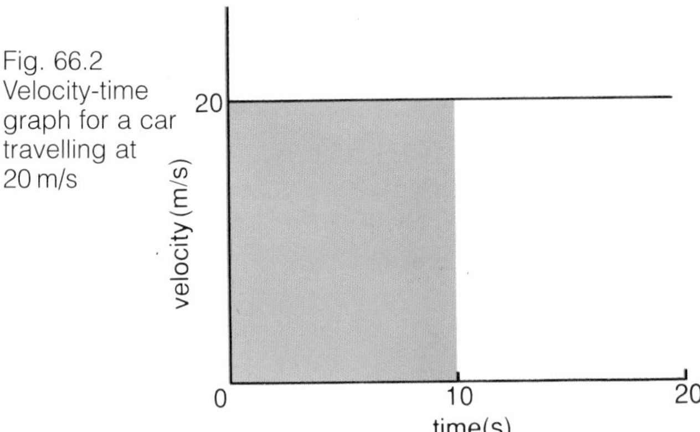

Fig. 66.2 Velocity-time graph for a car travelling at 20 m/s

When velocity changes, each section can be worked out separately

Figure 66.3 shows a velocity-time graph for a car journey. The car accelerates from a standstill to a velocity of 20 m/s. It then travels at this velocity for 5 s, and finally decelerates to a standstill. How can you work out the total distance covered?

As the car accelerates, the distance covered = average velocity × time.

The average velocity will be:

$$\frac{\text{initial velocity} + \text{final velocity}}{2} =$$

$$\frac{0\,\text{m/s} + 20\,\text{m/s}}{2} = 10\,\text{m/s}$$

So the distance covered during this first 4 s is 10 m/s × 4 s = 40 m.

Now try working out the area of the yellow triangle. It too should come to 40.

If you also work out the areas of the orange rectangle and the red triangle, and add them all together, you will have found the total distance covered by the car during its 11 s journey. You don't *have* to do it this way. You can just work out average velocities for each section of the journey and multiply by time. But working out the area under a graph is very often a much more straightforward way of doing it.

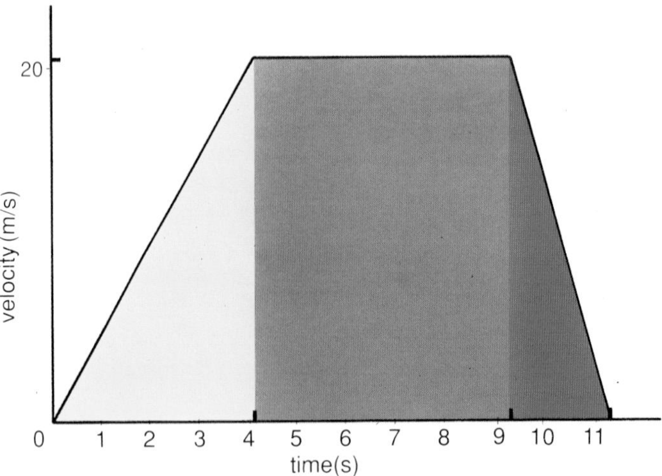

Fig. 66.3 Velocity-time graph for a car which accelerates, travels at a steady velocity, and decelerates to a stop

Displacement-time graphs for accelerating objects are curves

Figure 66.4 shows a displacement-time graph for the first part of the car's journey. As it accelerates, it covers increasingly more ground in each successive second. So the line is a curve with an increasing gradient.

What do you think the displacement-time graph would look like for the final part of the car's journey, as it is decelerating?

Fig. 66.4 Displacement-time graph for an accelerating car

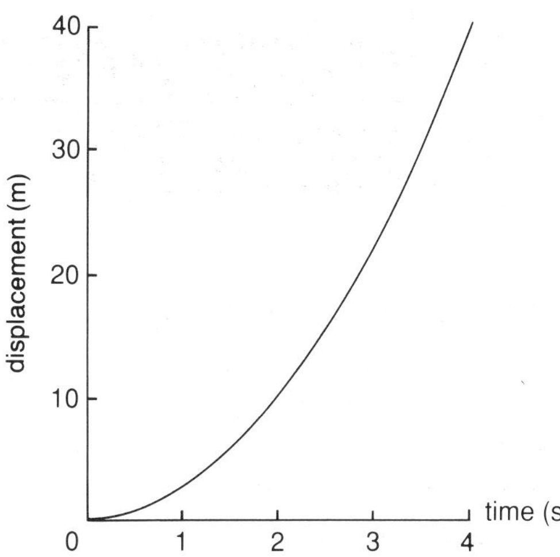

Positive and negative velocities can cancel each other out

Imagine a ball being thrown straight upwards. It has a positive upwards velocity. Gravity acting on the ball gives it a negative acceleration – the ball gradually slows down. At the top of its path it is stationary for a moment, and then begins to fall downwards. Now its upwards velocity is negative. Its acceleration is negative, as gravity pulls it downwards.

Figures 66.5 and 66.6 show this as graphs. The displacement-time graph is made up of two curves. At the beginning of the throw, the ball covers distance quickly, but as it slows down the distance covered in each second gets less and less. As it falls, it gets faster and faster, so the curve gets steeper and steeper. Finally it hits the ground. Despite its journey, it is back where it started. Its final total displacement is zero.

The velocity-time graph shows the velocity in an upwards direction. As the ball is thrown, it is started off with a positive upwards velocity. But this velocity gets less and less as the ball decelerates. Eventually the ball stops altogether for a moment, at the top of its path. At this point, the ball's upwards velocity is zero.

As the ball drops down again, its velocity gets greater and greater. But it is going downwards now so this is a negative upwards velocity. The line goes down below zero.

You can work out the total displacement in the usual way, by calculating the area under the velocity-time graph. You should find that the blue area and the green area are exactly the same size. But the green area is a negative area! When you add this negative area to the blue area, you get an answer of zero. The total displacement of the ball is zero.

Fig. 66.5 How the displacement of a vertically thrown ball varies with time.

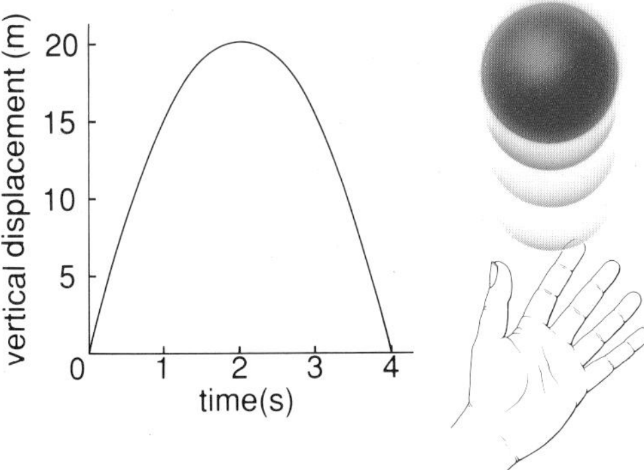

Fig. 66.6 How the velocity of a vertically thrown ball varies with time. Upwards velocity is positive.

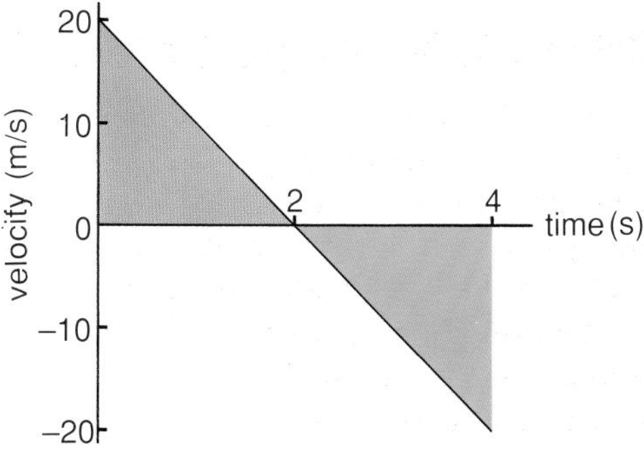

Questions

1 Two trains are travelling in the same direction, on different but parallel tracks. Train A is travelling at a constant 20 m/s. Train B is stationary, but as train A passes it train B begins to move, accelerating to 50 m/s in 5 min. It then immediately applies its brakes, and decelerates at 1 m/s^2.

a Draw velocity-time graphs for both trains. Draw both of your lines on the same pair of axes.

b When does train B overtake train A?

c When does train A overtake train B for the second time?

d How far has train A travelled when train B overtakes it?

e How far does train B travel before it stops?

2 A sports car accelerates from 0 to 60 mph in 8.6 s.

a What is a velocity of 60 mph in m/s?

b What is the acceleration of the car, in m/s^2?

c How far has the car travelled while accelerating to this velocity?

3 A ball is thrown into the air from the edge of a cliff. It falls down onto the beach below.

Without worrying about any numbers, draw curves to show the shapes of:

a the displacement-time graph, and

b the velocity-time graph for the ball, if positions above the cliff top are considered to have positive displacement.

67 FORCE AND ACCELERATION

An unbalanced force causes acceleration in the direction of the force.

INVESTIGATION 67.1

How do force and mass affect acceleration?

Figures 67.1 a and b show the apparatus used in this experiment. The ramp must be at exactly the correct angle, so that the force that accelerates the trolley down the ramp is just balanced by frictional forces. This is the angle at which, when you put the trolley on the ramp and give it a gentle push, it will travel at a constant velocity down the ramp. You will have to keep measuring the velocity of the trolley at different angles for the ramp, until you find the correct angle.

You will need a good timing method for your trolley. You could use a ticker-tape timer. When the trolley is travelling at a constant velocity, the ticker-tape dots will be equally spaced.

1 Set up your ramp at exactly the correct angle, as explained above. Attach a piece of elastic to the trolley, as shown in the photograph. Organise your timing method.

2 Put the trolley at the top of the ramp, then apply a constant force to it by pulling it down the ramp with the piece of stretched elastic. Provided you can manage to keep the piece of elastic the same length, the force will remain constant. This isn't easy! The trolley tries to catch up with the elastic, so you will need to practice first. Calculate the acceleration of the trolley.

3 Repeat step 2, with two, three and four pieces of elastic attached to the trolley, providing twice, three times and four times the original force.

4 Repeat step 2, but increase the mass of the trolley. You can do this by using masses, or by stacking several trolleys on top of one another. Do this for several different masses, and record your results.

5 Draw graphs of:

a force applied (on the x axis) against acceleration (on the y axis).

b mass of trolley (on the x axis) against acceleration (on the y axis).

Questions

1 What happens to the acceleration of the trolley when you increase the force? If the force is doubled, by how much does acceleration increase?

2 What happens to the acceleration of the trolley when its mass is increased? If its mass is doubled, what happens to its acceleration if you use the same force?

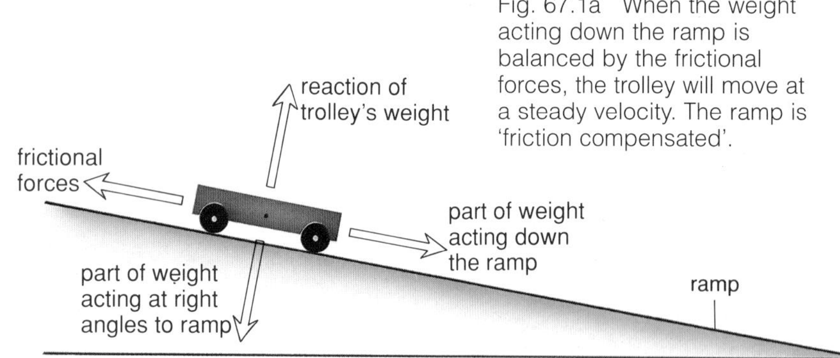

Fig. 67.1a When the weight acting down the ramp is balanced by the frictional forces, the trolley will move at a steady velocity. The ramp is 'friction compensated'.

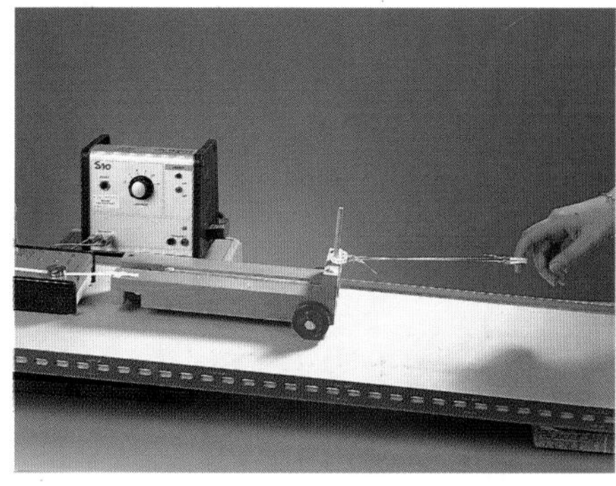

Fig. 67.1b Elastics are attached to the trolley and pulled. By keeping them at a constant length, a constant force is applied to the trolley. One, two, three or four elastics could provide different forces.

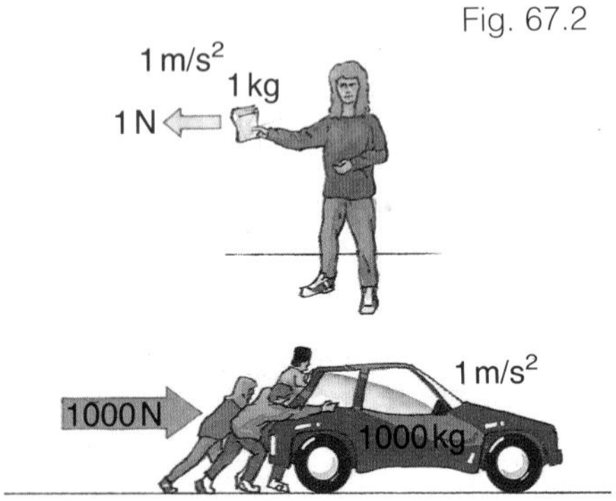

1 m/s²
1 kg
1 N
1 m/s²
1000 N
1000 kg

Fig. 67.2

Acceleration increases with force and decreases with mass

A stationary object will remain stationary until an unbalanced force acts on it. If you push the object, you provide an unbalanced force. The unbalanced force makes the object accelerate.

Common sense tells you that if you push an object harder, it goes faster. You also know that it is easier to get a light object moving fast than a heavy one. Clearly, mass, force and acceleration are linked.

The acceleration produced is greater with a large force, and smaller if a large mass is being pushed. In fact:

$$\textbf{acceleration} = \frac{\textbf{force}}{\textbf{mass}}$$

If you push on a mass of 1 kg with a force of 1 N, the mass will accelerate at 1 m/s^2. What will be the acceleration of a 2 kg mass if you push it with this same force?

Force = mass × acceleration

The equation:

$$\text{acceleration} = \frac{\text{force}}{\text{mass}}$$

is more often written:

force = mass × acceleration

or: **F = ma**.

You can use this equation to find any of these three quantities if you know the other two.

For example: *A force of 10N acts on a 1kg bag of sugar. What is the acceleration produced?*

$$F = ma$$

$$a = \frac{F}{m}$$

$$= \frac{10\,N}{1\,kg} = 10\ m/s^2$$

Another example: *A force of 10N is applied to a 60g tennis ball. What is its velocity after 0.1s?*

$$a = \frac{F}{m}$$

$$= \frac{10\,N}{0.06\,kg} = 166.7\,m/s^2$$

The ball began with a velocity of zero, so after 0.1s at an acceleration of 166.7 m/s^2 it will have reached a velocity of:

$$166.7 \times 0.1 = 16.67\,m/s.$$

(using velocity = acceleration × time)

Free falling objects all have the same acceleration

You will remember that the force pulling downwards on an object near the surface of the Earth is its weight. If the gravitational field strength (the gravitational force on 1kg) is given the symbol g, then the weight of the object is **mass × g**.

If you drop an object from your hand, it begins with a velocity of zero and accelerates towards the floor. The force producing this acceleration is caused by the weight of the object.

Imagine you drop an object of mass 1kg. If you are on Earth, then the gravitational field strength is about 10N/kg, so the weight of the object is 1 x 10N. The acceleration produced will be:

$$a = \frac{F}{m}$$

$$= \frac{1 \times 10\,N}{1\,kg} = 10\,m/s^2$$

Now imagine you drop an object of mass 5kg. Its weight (mass × g) is: 5 × 10N. So the acceleration produced will be:

$$a = \frac{F}{m} = \frac{5 \times 10}{5} = 10\,m/s^2$$

Can you see that the acceleration produced will always be 10 m/s^2? A bigger mass *increases* the force acting on it – its weight. But it *decreases* the acceleration produced by this force! The two effects exactly cancel each other out. So, no matter what the mass of an object, the acceleration due to gravity is always the same – as long as g remains the same.

We find this hard to believe because common sense tells us otherwise. If you drop a lump of lead and a feather, they do not hit the ground at the same time. In fact, this is because these calculations do not take friction into account. Friction between the feather and air – which we call **air resistance** – is a very significant force on the feather, but not a very significant force on the lump of lead. The Apollo astronauts tried dropping a feather and a hammer onto the surface of the Moon. There, where there is virtually no air, the feather and the hammer hit the ground at the same time. (Would their acceleration have been faster or slower than on Earth? Why?)

Terminal velocity

When an object falls through the air, a frictional force, air resistance, acts on it pushing it upwards. The force of gravity pulls it downwards. The two forces act in opposite directions.

As the velocity of the object increases, the air resistance also increases. Eventually, the object reaches a velocity where the frictional force balances the effects of gravity. Because the two forces are balanced, there will be no further acceleration. This is the fastest the object can fall – its **terminal velocity**.

Fig. 67.3 These free-fall parachutists spread their arms and legs to increase air resistance. This lets them control their terminal velocity. With an open parachute their terminal velocity is low enough to let them land in safety.

INVESTIGATION 67.2

Investigating terminal velocity

Devise an experiment to measure the terminal velocity of a ping-pong ball falling through air. Would you expect this to be greater or smaller than the terminal velocity of a similar sized ball of Plasticine falling through water? Test your hypothesis.

EXTENSION

Questions

1 An oil tanker has a mass of 120 000 000kg. It accelerates to 4m/s in 10 min.

a Calculate its acceleration.

b Calculate the force required to produce this acceleration.

A sailor falls overboard. The engines are thrown into reverse. The retarding (decelerating) force is twice the original accelerating force.

c How far does the tanker travel before it stops?

2 A car is driven into a brick wall at 15m/s. The mass of the car is 1000kg. The car is stopped in 0.5s.

a What is the average deceleration of the car?

b What average force does the wall exert on the car?

c What average force does the car exert on the wall?

68 CIRCULAR MOTION

If a force acts at right angles to the direction in which an object is travelling, it can make the object travel in a circle.

Objects travel in straight lines unless a force acts on them

You have probably seen the hammer event in an athletics competition. The hammer is a metal mass on a strong wire. The athlete spins the mass around in a circular path, and then suddenly releases the handle on the wire. The mass flies off – in a straight line.

You can try the same thing with a rubber bung attached to a piece of cotton. If you spin the bung around in a circle, and then let go, the bung goes off in a straight line. It goes off in whichever direction it was travelling in when you let go.

So the wire attached to the hammer, and the cotton attached to the bung, were providing a force causing the hammer and bung to travel in a circle. They provided a force pulling into the centre of the circle. This force is called **centripetal force**. Centripetal force is the force needed to make an object travel in a circle.

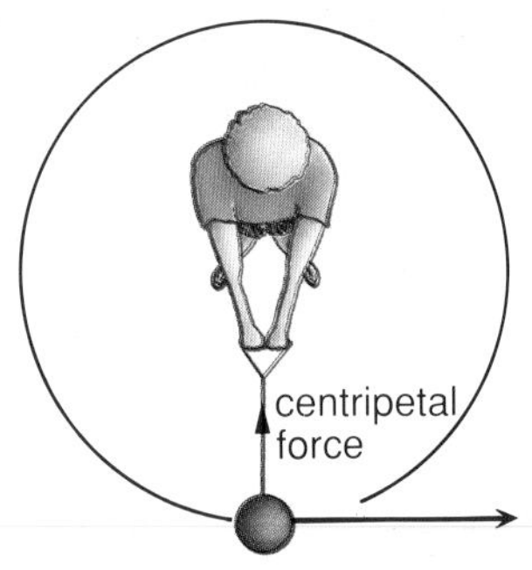

Fig. 68.1 The thrower's pull on the wire provides a centripetal force. When released, the weight carries on in a straight line.

Fig. 68.2 The faster the hammer is swung round, the greater the centripetal force needed to maintain its circular motion. Tore Gustafsson uses virtually all the muscles in his body to provide the maximum force he can, so that the hammer eventually leaves his hands at the maximum possible speed.

Centripetal force causes acceleration towards the centre of the circle

In Topic 65 you saw that an unbalanced force can produce acceleration. Acceleration is a change in velocity. Velocity is speed in a particular direction.

As the bung on the cotton spins around in a circle, its speed remains constant, but its direction is constantly changing. So its velocity is constantly changing. Even though its speed is not changing, the bung is accelerating!

It is the centripetal force which is causing this constant change of direction, and therefore constant change of velocity. The centripetal force causes the bung to accelerate towards the centre of the circle.

Friction is an important centripetal force

A car approaches a bend, travelling in a straight line. As the driver swings the wheel, the car begins to swing around the bend. As you have seen, without a centripetal force, objects tend to keep travelling in a straight line. So what is the centripetal force which pulls the car around the bend? The centripetal force in this case is friction between the car tyres and the ground. Friction provides a force which pulls the car towards the centre of a circle as it travels around the corner. As some drivers have found out, if friction is reduced, perhaps by oil or ice on the road, then it may not be great enough to provide the centripetal force. The car does not round the bend – it just carries straight on.

If you are a passenger in a car, you will also tend to carry straight on as the car corners. But friction provides a centripetal force to make your direction of travel circular too. This time, the friction is between you and the seat.

Fig. 68.3 On a wet road, frictional forces between the tyres of a car and the road are much less than on a dry surface.

Fig. 68.4 Gravitational forces between a satellite and the Earth act as a centripetal force, keeping the satellite in orbit.

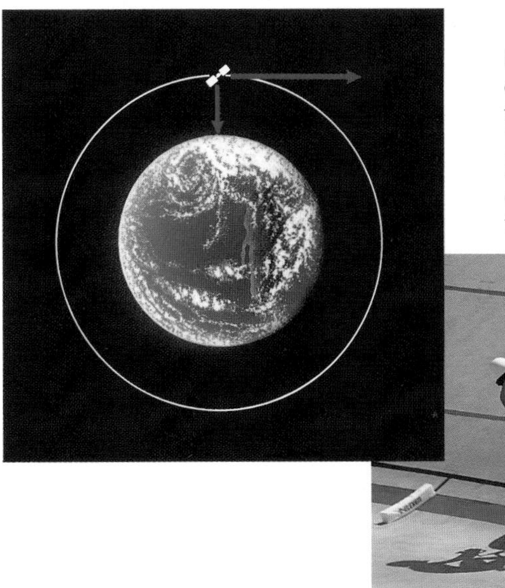

Fig. 68.5 The steep banking on a cycle track enables the cyclists to travel at much faster speeds than if it were flat. The reaction from the banked track provides some of the centripetal force, helping the cyclists to maintain a circular path.

Gravity keeps satellites in orbit

The Moon, and many artificial satellites, orbit the Earth. The Earth and Moon orbit the Sun. You have seen how a centripetal force is needed to produce circular motion. In this case, the centripetal force is **gravity**.

Gravity is a force acting between any two objects. The gravitational force on an object is its weight. The force acts towards the other object's centre of gravity.

The gravitational force between a satellite and the Earth accelerates the satellite towards the centre of the Earth. (It also accelerates the Earth towards the centre of the satellite, but the Earth is so much more massive than the satellite that the effect is too small to notice.) As the satellite orbits the Earth, gravity acts as the centripetal force which keeps it moving in a circle.

The speed of a satellite must match the height of its orbit

The gravitational force between a pair of objects decreases with distance. The further away the satellite gets from the Earth, the less is its weight. So the acceleration towards the Earth is also less.

Imagine a satellite orbiting close to the Earth's surface. Here the gravitational force is very strong. It causes rapid acceleration towards the Earth. If the satellite was travelling slowly, this rapid acceleration would cause such a large change in its velocity that it would fall out of its orbit. A satellite orbiting close to the Earth must travel very fast to stay in orbit. A satellite orbiting just above the Earth's surface would have to travel at 8000 m/s to stay in orbit.

But a satellite orbiting a long way above the Earth is not pulled so strongly by gravity. The acceleration towards the Earth is not so great. If the satellite travels very fast, the acceleration due to gravity will not be enough to keep it in orbit, and it will fly off into space. So satellites in very high orbits must travel more slowly than satellites in low orbits.

Many satellites orbit at 36 000 km above the surface of the Earth. At this distance, they must travel at 3100 m/s to stay in orbit. This speed takes them in a complete circle once every 24 hours, and this, of course, is the length of time it takes the Earth to complete one revolution. So the satellite and the Earth travel round at the same rotational speed, and the satellite stays above the same point on the Earth all the time. This is called a **geostationary orbit**.

INVESTIGATION 68.1

Spinning a bung

Figure 68.6 shows the apparatus you will need for this investigation. It is best to work with a partner. Wear goggles. Spin the bung by holding the rubber tube up, and spinning it around.

1 Spin the bung at a constant speed so that it just supports the mass. Time how long it takes to do ten revolutions.

2 Increase the length of cotton attached to the bung, so that the radius of the circle travelled by the bung is doubled. Repeat step 1. What do you notice?

3 Double the mass supported by the bung. Repeat step 1. What do you notice?

4 Continue doubling the mass until the experiment becomes impossible. Plot a graph of your results. Can you see a pattern?

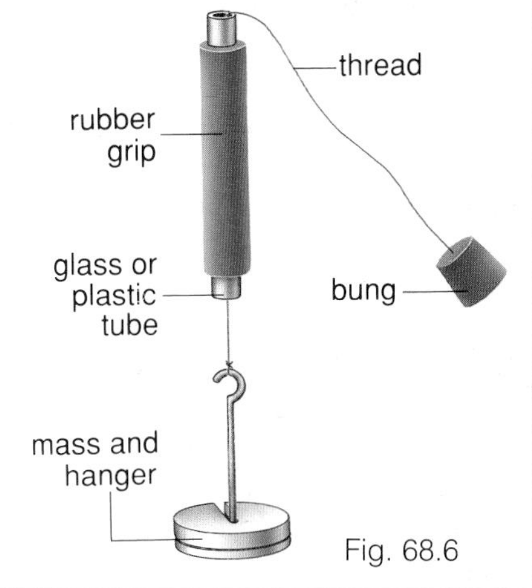

Fig. 68.6

Questions

1 Explain each of the following.

a If you swing a bung around your head on a piece of elastic, the length of the elastic changes when you change the speed of the bung.

b A roller-coaster can loop-the-loop if it is going fast enough.

c Cycle racing tracks are steeply banked, sloping towards the inside of the curve.

2 What supplies the centripetal force when:

a a train goes around a corner?

b an aircraft banks? (Think carefully about this one.)

c the Earth orbits the Sun?

69 MOMENTUM AND IMPULSE

A small force acting over a long time has the same effect as a large force acting over a short time.

Momentum is velocity × mass

In order to stop a moving object, a force must be applied to it. This force will produce a negative acceleration, or a deceleration. Obviously, a fast-moving, massive object will require more force to stop it than a slow-moving, light object.

The amount of **momentum** of an object is what makes it easy or difficult to stop. Momentum depends on the velocity of the object, and its mass. If either of these quantities increases, then the momentum increases.

momentum = mass × velocity

Momentum has units of kgm/s.

For example: *a tennis ball of mass 0.06 kg is travelling at 18.5 m/s. An air gun pellet of mass 0.005 kg is travelling at 222 m/s. Which has the greater momentum?*

Momentum of tennis ball
= mass × velocity
= 0.06 kg × 18.5 m/s
= 1.11 kgm/s

Momentum of air gun pellet
= mass × velocity
= 0.005 kg × 222 m/s
= 1.11 kgm/s

So both have the same momentum. It would take the same force to stop both of them in the same time.

Fig. 69.1

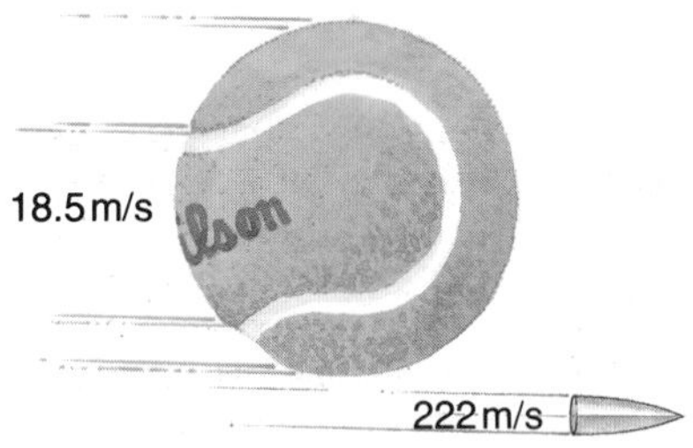

18.5 m/s

222 m/s

Impulse = force × time

Imagine a force pushing an object forwards. If the force is acting in the same direction as the movement of the object, the object will accelerate. Its velocity will increase.

But by how much does it increase? Common sense tells you that this depends on three things:

- the mass of the object,
- the size of the force acting on the object,
- the length of time for which the force acts.

A large force will speed up the object more than a small force. A force acting for a long time will speed up the object more than one acting for only a short time. Multiplying the force by the time for which it acts tells you what **impulse** is being applied to the object.

impulse = force × time

The larger the impulse, the more the object is speeded up.

Fig. 69.2 By taking his arm right through as he throws the javelin, Steve Backley keeps the forward force acting on it as long as possible. This gives the javelin a greater velocity than if the same force was applied instantaneously.

Sports men and women use the idea of impulse

The idea of impulse is an important one. The time for which a force acts can make a big difference to the effect that the force has.

Tennis players are well aware of this. If you 'follow through' with your racket when hitting the ball, you increase the time of contact between the ball and the racket. You increase the impulse. You can make the ball accelerate faster.

Making objects slow down also requires an impulse, this time acting against the direction of their movement. Imagine trying to stop a cricket ball flying towards you. The impulse to make it stop is provided by your hands. If you keep your hands absolutely still as the ball hits them, it stops almost immediately. The time for which the force acts is very small. So the force has to be very large – and it hurts your hands.

But if you pull your hands back as the ball flies into them, the time for which the force acts is increased. The force needed to provide the necessary impulse is less. The catch is much less painful.

Crumple zones lessen the force of impact

If a car crashes and stops suddenly, a large force is needed to stop it in a short time. The rapid deceleration and large forces involved can kill passengers.

Over half of all car accidents which cause injury are of this type, where the front of the car runs into another object and decelerates very rapidly. The danger of this type of accident can be reduced by weakening the front of the car. The car is designed so that the front crumples up gradually on impact. The crumple zone extends the collision time, reducing the deceleration and the size of the forces involved.

DID YOU KNOW?

Your hair acts like a crumple zone on your skull. A force of 5 N might be enough to fracture your naked cranium, but with a covering of skin and hair a force of 50 N would be needed.

Questions

1 Read the following passage, and then answer the questions which follow.

Safe car design

Modern cars are crash tested to ensure that the passenger compartment can protect its valuable contents. It is important, for example, that the engine does not get pushed into the driver's lap. If this happened on testing, the car would have to be redesigned.

The front of the car is designed to crumple up in such a way that a collision lasts as long as possible. Even with built-in crumple zones, very high rates of deceleration can occur in head-on collisions. The maximum deceleration in a 60 km/h collision can be as high as 600 m/s^2. The duration of the collision would be around 0.085 s.

Passengers are restrained by seat belts. In such a collision, even with a crumple zone, an unrestrained 65 kg passenger would hit a solid object with a force of 12750 N. This would cause serious injury, and possibly even death. But seat belts can reduce this force, because under high forces such as these they are slightly elastic. This, like the crumple zone, extends the collision time. The average deceleration on the passenger would be reduced to about 150 m/s^2. Seat belts are secured at three points. Together, these mounting points can withstand a force of about 40 000 N.

Since 1983, all front seat passengers in Britain have been required by law to wear seat belts. All new cars must now be fitted with rear seat belts. In any car, if rear seat belts are fitted then they must be used. Safe car design is wasted unless all the passengers use their seat belts.

a Why is it useful to extend collision time?

b Explain two ways in which modern car design extends collision time for head-on accidents.

c In the collision described in paragraph 2, what is the average deceleration of the car?

d What distance does the car travel during the collision?

e Apart from the features you have mentioned in your answer to part b, what other safety features are found on modern cars?

EXTENSION

Change in momentum = impulse

Figure 69.3 shows a force acting on a moving object. The object has a mass m and is travelling with a velocity u. The force acts in the same direction as the velocity. The force increases the velocity of the object, speeding it up to velocity v.

The acceleration of the object is its change in velocity divided by time:

$$a = \frac{v-u}{t}$$

We know that **F = ma**. So we can now rewrite this equation as:

$$F = m \times \frac{v-u}{t} = \frac{m(v-u)}{t} = \frac{mv-mu}{t}$$

We can rearrange this equation to get:

$$\mathbf{Ft = mv - mu}.$$

The initial momentum of the object is mu. Its final momentum is mv. So mv-mu is the change in momentum. Ft is the impulse which produces this change.

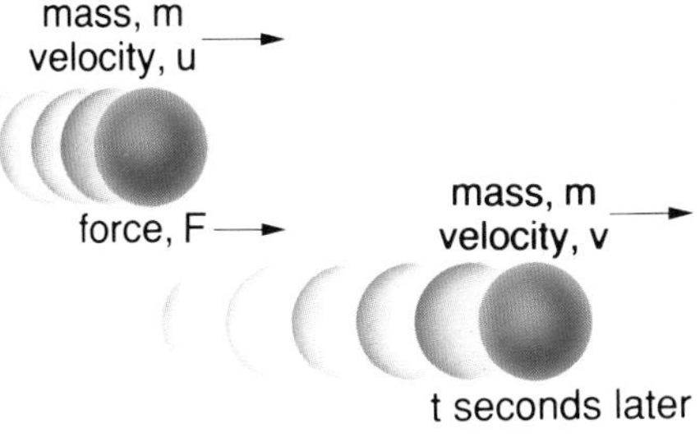

Fig. 69.3

Calculating momentum, impulse, and force

Imagine that a 1000 kg car is travelling at 15 m/s.

Its initial momentum,

$$mv = 1000\,kg \times 15\,m/s = 15000\,kgm/s.$$

If the car stops, its final momentum

$$mu = 0.$$

So the *impulse* needed to make it stop

$$= mv - mu = 15000 - 0 = 15000\,kgm/s.$$

The size of the *force* you need to stop depends on the time you have available. If you have 15 s, then:

$$\text{impulse} = \text{force} \times \text{time}$$

so:

$$\text{force} = \frac{\text{impulse}}{\text{time}} = \frac{15\,000}{15} = 1000\,N$$

So the braking force needed to stop the car in 15 s is 1000 N. This is only one tenth of the weight of the car. As long as you have plenty of time, you can stop a car with quite a small force.

But what happens if the car crashes into a wall, stopping in just $\frac{1}{100}$ of a second? Now the force is:

$$\text{force} = \frac{\text{impulse}}{\text{time}} = \frac{15000}{0.01} = 1500000\,N$$

This force is 150 times the weight of the car. The occupants would probably be killed.

2 A parachutist practises her landing technique by jumping off a table. Her mass is 65 kg. The table is 1 m high.

a With what velocity does she hit the ground?

b With what momentum does she hit the ground?

c If she keeps her legs straight, and stops in 0.01 s, what is

i the impulse on her legs?

ii the force on her legs?

d If she bends her knees and stops in 0.5 s, what force must her legs resist?

EXTENSION

70 COLLISIONS *In a collision, momentum is not lost.*

The total momentum before and after a collision remains the same

The momentum of a moving snooker ball is its mass multiplied by its velocity. If mass is m, and velocity u, then its momentum is **mu**.

What happens when a white ball hits a red ball? Think about the moment of impact. The white ball hits and pushes on the red ball, exerting a force on it. Newton's Third Law says that the reaction force will be equal and opposite. So the red ball pushes back on the white ball with the same force.

The balls can only push on one another while they are touching. They push on each other for the same time. If the force is the same on each ball, and the time is the same, then the impulse is the same. The impulse on each ball is of the same magnitude, but the impulses act in opposite directions.

In Topic 69, you saw that **impulse = momentum change**. If the impulse on each ball is the same (but the impulses act in opposite directions) then the momentum change must also be the same (but in opposite directions). Whatever momentum the white ball loses, the red ball gains.

Total momentum before and after a collision is the same. Momentum is conserved.

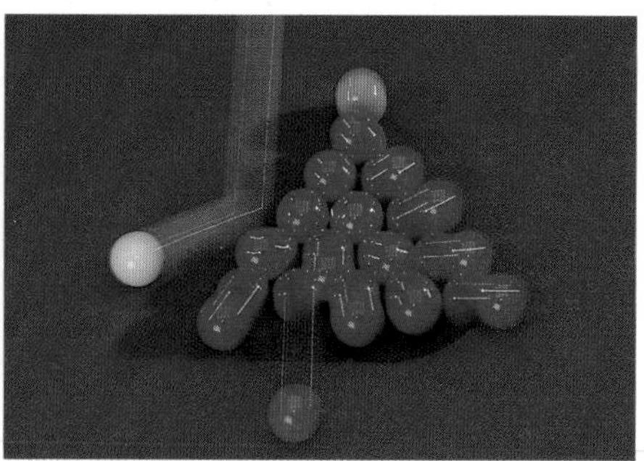

Fig. 70.1 The total momentum of all the balls is the same before and after the collision.

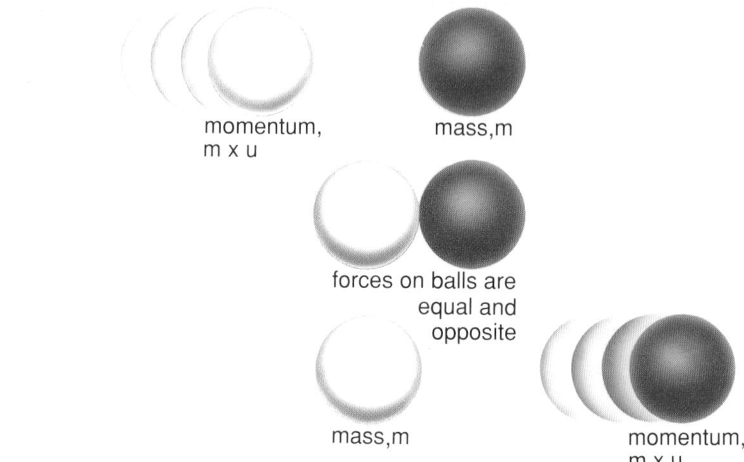

Fig. 70.2 Momentum is conserved in a collision.

INVESTIGATION 70.1

Collisions and momentum

Design and carry out an experiment to investigate the statement that: 'total momentum before a collision is the same as total momentum afterwards'.

You will need two objects which can safely collide with each other, a method of massing them, and a method of measuring their velocities before and after the collision. You could use two trolleys on a ramp, or two riders on an air track, and a ticker-tape timer.

Momentum is always conserved

If two identical cars travelling at identical velocities in opposite directions collide head on, they both stop. One has momentum in one direction, which is cancelled by the momentum of the other.

But what happens when a car runs into a tree? The car has momentum before the collision. The tree does not. After the collision, neither of them seems to have any momentum. Where has the momentum gone?

Since the tree is attached to the ground, the tree and the ground gain the momentum which is lost by the car. As the Earth is 6000000000000000000000 times more massive than the car, it is perhaps not surprising that it does not gain much velocity.

Fig. 70.3

Calculating velocities after collisions

Conservation of momentum is responsible for the recoil of a gun when it is fired. Just before firing, neither the gun nor the bullet have any momentum. If the bullet gains momentum, the gun must gain an equal and opposite momentum, so that the two cancel each other out and give a total momentum of zero. So when the gun is fired, it moves backwards. Its velocity is not as great as the velocity of the bullet, because it has a greater mass.

For example: *an air gun pellet has a mass of 0.5g, and leaves a gun at 800km/h. If the gun has a mass of 0.5kg, what would the recoil velocity be if the gun was not restrained?*

Momentum of pellet = m × v
= 0.0005kg × 222m/s
Momentum of gun = m × v
= 0.5kg × recoil velocity

Total momentum before firing is zero, so total momentum after firing must also be zero. The momentum of the pellet in one direction must exactly equal the momentum of the gun in the opposite direction.

So:

0.0005kg × 222m/s
= 0.5kg × recoil velocity

recoil velocity

$$= \frac{0.0005\,\text{kg} \times 222\,\text{m/s}}{0.5\,\text{kg}}$$

= 0.222m/s

DID YOU KNOW?

If you could throw a ball upwards with a velocity of 11km/s, it would have enough kinetic energy to leave the Earth completely.

Fig. 70.4

Using kinetic energy in calculations

In Topic 66, you saw how you could use velocity and acceleration to calculate the maximum height a ball could reach when thrown upwards. Another way of doing this calculation is to use the kinetic energy equation.

As the ball rises, its kinetic energy is transferred to potential energy (gravitational energy). At the top of its path, all its kinetic energy has been transferred to potential energy. If we ignore friction, and assume that deceleration is just due to gravity, then once the ball reaches its maximum height the potential energy gained must equal the original kinetic energy of the ball.

potential energy gained = mgh
original kinetic energy = potential energy gained

so: original kinetic energy = mgh

so: $\frac{1}{2}mv^2 = mgh$

so: $h = \frac{v^2}{2g}$

If the ball was thrown upwards with an initial velocity of 10m/s, then:

$$h = \frac{100}{2 \times 10} = 5\text{m}$$

EXTENSION

Kinetic energy is movement energy

Moving objects have energy. The energy transferred to an object because it is moving is its **kinetic energy**.

To stop a moving object, you must apply a force. The work done by this force must equal the kinetic energy of the object.

Imagine stopping your bicycle by applying the brakes. While you are applying the force, and while the bicycle is slowing down, the force is moving with the bicycle. You will remember that when a force is moved through a distance, work is done. The work you do in stopping the bicycle is the force applied multiplied by the distance travelled.

The faster the bicycle is moving, the larger the force you need to stop it, and the further it will travel whilst this force is bringing it to a halt. In fact, if the velocity of the bicycle is doubled, the force used and distance travelled are both doubled. So the work done, or energy transferred, in bringing the bicycle to a halt is four times larger. The work needed to stop a moving object depends on the square of its velocity. This is the same as its kinetic energy.

kinetic energy = $\frac{1}{2}mv^2$

So, for example, if a bicycle and rider have a combined mass of 70kg, and are travelling at 10m/s, their kinetic energy is:

$\frac{1}{2} \times 70\text{kg} \times (10\text{m/s})^2 = 3500\text{J}$

Questions

1 A ship with a mass of 100 tonnes moves with a velocity of 4m/s.
  a How fast would a 500kg car have to travel to have the same kinetic energy?
  b What is this in miles per hour (see Topic 64)?

2 A cyclist pedals as hard as she can and reaches a velocity of 10m/s after 10s.
  a What is the kinetic energy if the cyclist and the bicycle together weigh 60kg?
  b If half the cyclist's energy is lost through friction, what is her energy output during the 10s?

71 ROAD SAFETY

Road safety depends on how people drive and how quickly they can react in emergencies. The design of a car and the materials used to build it can be made to improve safety.

Stopping distance includes thinking time

The acceleration of a car or bicycle tells you how quickly its velocity is changing. At higher velocities, a greater deceleration is needed to stop the vehicle in the same time. You saw in Topic 70 how doubling the velocity would need twice the force if you were to stop in the same time. In an emergency at any velocity, most people would apply the maximum braking force. Because you can't increase this maximum braking force, you will take more time to stop from a higher velocity. The shortest possible **braking distance** is four times greater at twice the velocity. (It takes twice as long and the vehicle starts at twice the velocity – see Q1.)

To calculate the total **stopping distance**, you have to allow for the length of time it takes to start applying the brakes. An alert driver will take around 0.7 s to react to an emergency. This is the **thinking time**. (How does this compare to reaction times calculated in Topic 64? Can you explain the difference?) At 67 mph a car will travel 20 metres before the driver can even start braking. Table 71.1 shows how the stopping distance varies with speed. This assumes an alert driver with good brakes and tyres and a dry road.

Although the grooves in a tyre help to channel water out from underneath the tyre, water still reduces friction between the road and the rubber. This means the maximum stopping force that can be used is reduced. For safety in wet weather, a driver should stay at least twice as far behind other vehicles as is safe in dry weather.

Speed in mph	Shortest distances in metres		
	Thinking distance	Braking distance	Stopping distance
10	3	1.5	4.5
20	6	6	12
30	9	14	23
40	12	25	37
50	15	39	54
60	18	56	74
70	21	76	97

Table 71.1 Overall stopping distances in metres. At 70 mph the stopping distance is about 24 car lengths.

Fig. 71.1 The type of surface a tyre runs on affects the grip. On a dry surface a racing tyre doesn't need any grooves; the flat surface gives maximum contact with the track. A road tyre needs grooves to channel water out from between the rubber and the road. As the tyre wears, the tread depth decreases and its ability to stop the car in the wet is reduced. It is illegal to drive on the road if a car tyre tread is less than 1.6 mm deep across most of the centre of the tread.

A driver's reaction time affects the stopping distance

It is important that the interior of a car is designed so that the driver is not distracted from the road. Some cars even allow the driver to shut down unnecessary instruments. If the driver is not alert, it can take longer to react to emergencies. If you are tired or even have a bad cold your reaction times will increase and with it, your stopping distance. This increases the chance of having an accident. Motorists are recommended to take regular breaks when driving on motorways and should stop for a rest at least every two hours.

It is illegal to drive while under the influence of drink or drugs. Alcohol and other drugs can increase your reaction time. Many legal drugs (medicines) carry warnings about drowsiness and its affect on driving or use of machinery. As well as increasing reaction times, drugs are dangerous because they can also affect the way you feel and act. Alcohol also affects coordination, eyesight and the ability to judge speed and distance. Alcohol also increases confidence and the driver often thinks that they are driving better than they really are. At the **legal limit** (80 mg of alcohol per 100 cm^3 of blood) some drivers are 5 times as likely to have an accident. Any amount of alcohol will affect driving and the best advice is not to drink at all if you intend to drive.

In an accident the car's materials and structure must protect people

You saw in Topic 69 how a car is designed to crumple up and extend the collision time. It is just as important to a pedestrian in an accident that the front of the car crumples. This is why rigid 'bull bars' are not a good idea. The materials from which the vehicle is made should extend the collision time and absorb as much energy as possible. The three graphs in Figures 71.2, 71.3 and 71.4 show different materials being stretched. The curve for a metal shows elastic behaviour up to the elastic limit while the metal obeys **Hooke's law** (Topic 16). Beyond the elastic limit, the metal is permanently stretched. For a car, the distortion of the metal absorbs some of the energy of a collision.

An air bag in a car is designed to inflate in an accident and prevent the driver's head striking the steering wheel. The bag must not behave like a balloon, or the gas inside would be compressed when the head hit the bag. This would slow the collision time at first, but bounce the driver's head back towards the seat. An air bag can be fully inflated within 40 ms of the collision. As the driver hits the bag the gas escapes through holes and the bag deflates. This might take another 40 ms. This controlled deflation gives maximum protection to the driver.

The graph for stretching rubber shows **mechanical hysteresis**. The shape of the curve is different as you load and unload the material. Metals show this effect as well, but the difference is much smaller. The rubber does not return all of the energy used to stretch it, even though it does return to its original length. The difference raises the internal energy of the rubber. This is useful in a car because rubber mounting blocks on the engine can absorb vibrational energy and transfer it as heat. Vibrations can be an important factor in driver fatigue.

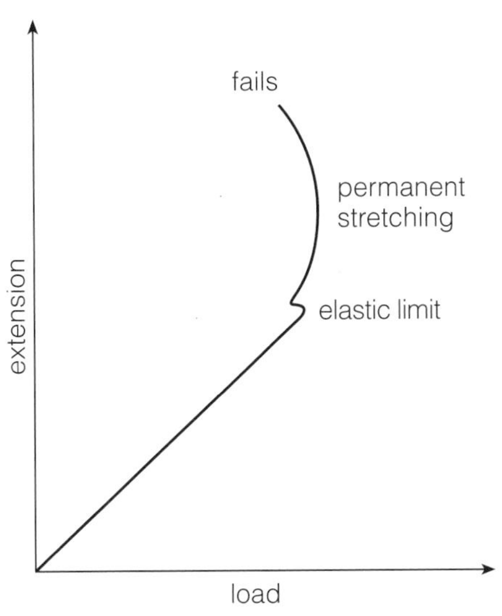

Fig. 71.2 A stretched metal follows Hooke's law up to the elastic limit. The effect is easier to measure with a spring. If stretched too far, the metal is permanently deformed and cannot return to its original length.

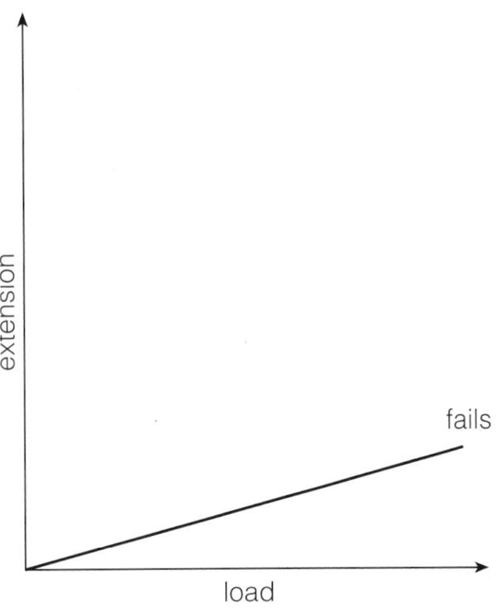

Fig. 71.3 A brittle material like glass can stretch elastically but snaps once the elastic limit is passed. The glass cannot deform much and would not absorb much energy from the collision.

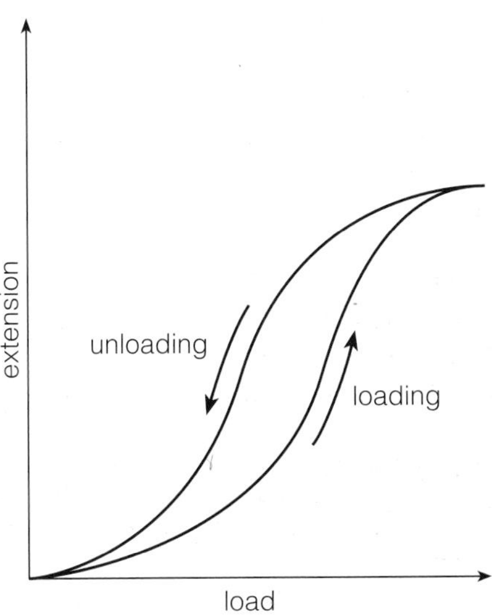

Fig. 71.4 Rubber can be stretched much more than a metal before it fails. The long molecules are able to unravel and untangle. This raises the internal energy of the rubber.

Fig. 71.5 A motorcycle does not have much bodywork to absorb the energy of a collision. An air bag system could help prevent injury.

Questions

1 A bike and rider have a mass of 100 kg. They are moving at 10 m/s. A force of 100 N brings them to a stop.

a Use $F = ma$ to calculate the deceleration.

b How long will the bike take to stop?

c How far will it travel in this time?

d Repeat the calculation for a starting speed of 5 m/s.

2 Use the information in Table 71.1 to plot a graph of speed against stopping distance. What would be the stopping distance of a car travelling at 30 m/s? (Remember to convert to mph – see Topic 64.)

1 The diagram shows a simple gearbox. The driving shaft rotates, turning the driven shaft. The driven shaft can slide backwards and forwards, to engage different gears.

a In which direction will the driven shaft rotate if:

i gears A_1 and A_2 engage?

ii gears B_1 and B_2 engage?

iii gears C_1 and C_2 engage?

b If the driving shaft rotates at a constant speed, in which gear will the driven shaft rotate fastest?

c In which gear will the driven shaft provide the greatest driving force?

d Work out the ratio between the force of the driving shaft and the force of the driven shaft for each gear.

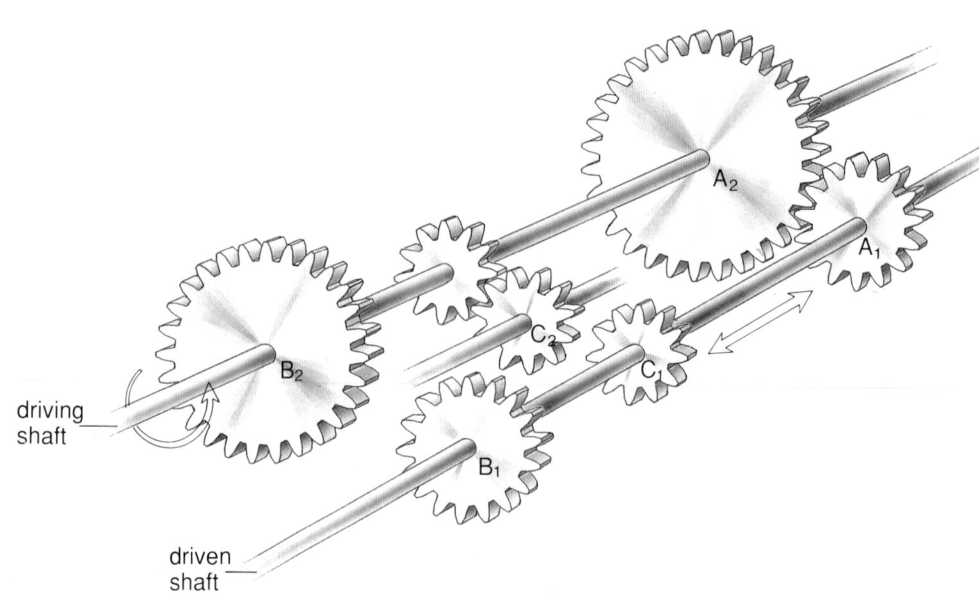

2 The diagram below shows the basic structure of the human arm. It is drawn to scale.

a Copy or trace the diagram, keeping all lengths and angles the same.

b What is the actual length of:

i the forearm?

ii the humerus?

c What is the actual distance of the biceps muscle's attachment from the elbow joint?

d Draw arrows on your diagram to show the forces acting on the bones of the forearm when:

i a weight is held in the hand (assume that the hand is at the far left of the diagram).

ii the biceps muscle contracts.

e A weight of 10 N is held in the hand. Calculate the turning force produced about the pivot (the elbow joint).

f Calculate the force which the biceps muscle must produce to balance this turning force.

g Look back at the three classes of levers, shown in Topic 63. In which class of lever is your arm? Can you suggest why this is the most suitable arrangement?

h How is friction reduced at the pivot when you bend your arm?

EXTENSION

3 A pebble was dropped from a tower. It took 8 s to hit the ground.

a If g is 10 m/s^2, what was the speed of the pebble when it hit the ground?

b Draw a velocity-time graph of the motion of the pebble.

c Use the graph to calculate the height of the tower.

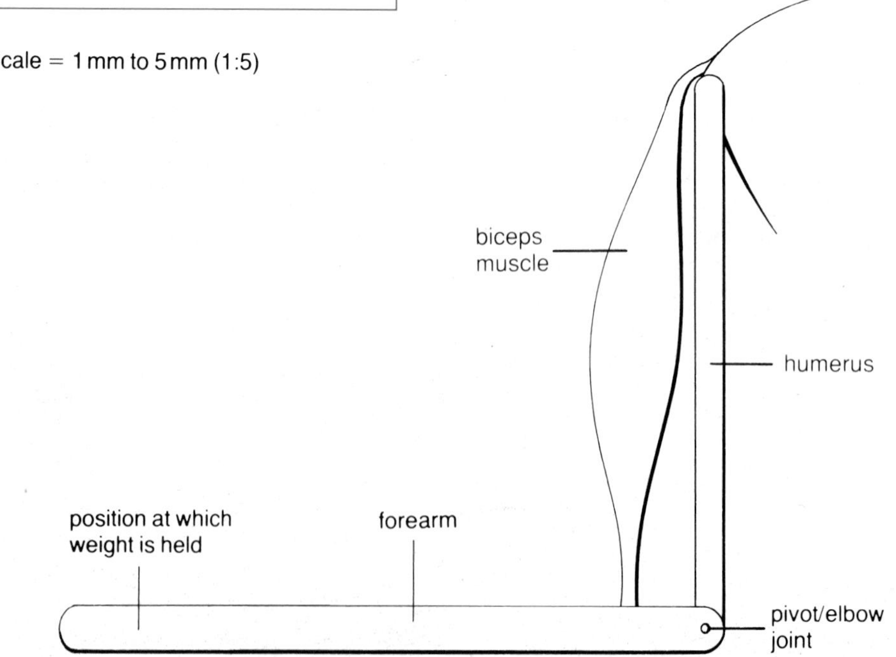

SPACE

72 THE UNIVERSE

The Universe contains millions of galaxies, each made up of millions of stars.

Distances in space are measured in light years

We live on a planet called Earth. To us it is enormous. It is our home in space. But the Earth is only a tiny part of the Universe.

If you look up at the sky on a clear night, you can see thousands of **stars**. The patterns of stars are called the **constellations**. The Sun is a star. It looks very different from the stars you see at night because it is so close to us. The Sun is about 150 000 000 km away. The next nearest star to the Earth is called Proxima Centauri. It is 40 000 000 000 000 km, or 4 x 10^{16} m, from Earth.

These distances are very large by Earth standards. The kilometre or metre is not a very useful measurement for astronomers to use. Instead, they can use **light years**. A light year is the distance that light travels in one year. Light travels through space at 300 000 000 m/s. In one year, it travels 9 500 000 000 000 km. So one light year is 9 500 000 000 000 km. Proxima Centauri is 4.2 light years from Earth. If you look at Proxima Centauri (which you would need to do with a telescope, because it is a very faint star), you see it as it was 4.2 years ago.

Fig. 72.1 The material in space tends to collect together in galaxies, with large gaps in between. The distances between galaxies are millions of times greater than between the stars in them, while stars are millions of times further apart than planets. (There is evidence to suggest that our Sun is not the only star to have planets.) This spiral galaxy is about 2 400 000 light years from our own galaxy. Its diameter is about 40 000 light years. No-one knows how many stars it contains, let alone planets. The pink patches are clouds of hydrogen gas, in which new stars are being formed. Young, hot blue stars are mostly found in the outer arms of the spiral. The yellow and red areas contain older stars.

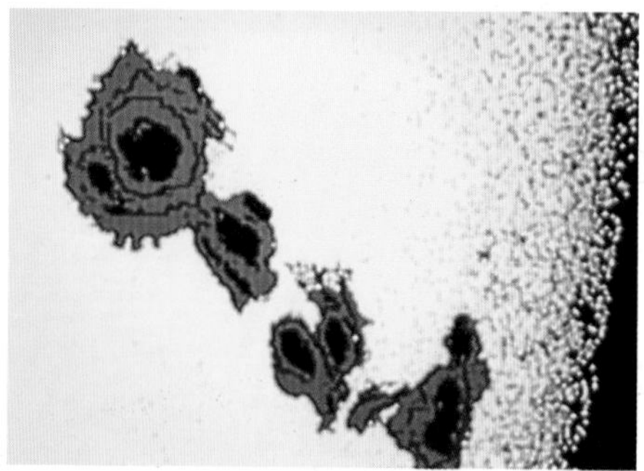

Fig. 72.2 A computer-enhanced picture of part of the Sun, showing a giant cluster of sunspots. Sunspot activity takes place in 11 year cycles, and this picture was taken in September 1989, just before the time of maximum activity. Sunspot activity is thought to affect the weather on Earth.

Stars are giant nuclear reactors

No-one knows how many stars there are. Stars exist in groups called **galaxies**. Our own star, the Sun, is part of a galaxy called the Milky Way. The Milky Way contains about 100 thousand million stars. At the present time, astronomers are aware of more than 100 thousand million galaxies. So the total number of stars in the Universe is enormous.

Because most stars are very far away, even the best telescopes show them as just spots of light. But our own Sun is much closer. Astronomers can study the Sun to find out about what happens inside stars.

The Sun is made up of gas. Most of the gas is hydrogen. The temperature at the surface of the Sun is about 6000 °C. Deep inside the Sun, the temperature is 16 000 000 °C.

Inside the Sun, the nuclei of hydrogen atoms fuse together to form helium atoms. This is called **nuclear fusion**. It releases enormous amounts of energy. Humans have also made nuclear fusion happen, using hydrogen bombs. Scientists are now trying to make nuclear fusion happen in a controlled way, so that the energy released can be used to make electricity.

The energy released from the Sun is given off as electromagnetic radiation. All kinds of electromagnetic radiation are released, ranging from X rays to radio waves. We are most aware of the visible light emitted from the Sun, and the infrared radiation, which warms the Earth. But the Sun and other stars can also be studied by observing the other kinds of radiation which they emit, especially radio waves.

DID YOU KNOW?

Each second, 600 000 000 tonnes of hydrogen are converted to helium in the Sun. For each atom that changes, a small amount of mass is lost. This mass defect is where the energy comes from.

New stars are born and old stars die

Where did all the stars come from? We know that new stars are constantly being formed. Stars are formed from clouds of gas in space. These gas clouds are called **nebulae**. Stars are born inside nebulae. The gas particles are drawn together by gravity. As these particles collapse inwards, gravitational energy is transferred to thermal energy. The particles become a **protostar**. If the gas becomes hot enough, nuclear reactions begin. The gas particles have become a star. Our Sun is such a **main sequence** star.

Stars do not shine for ever. As the energy is released, the fusion reactions convert hydrogen to helium. While the fusion reactions continue, the energy released prevents the collapse of the star under gravitational forces. Gradually, the fuel for the nuclear fusion reactions runs down. The star slowly dies. The Sun was probably formed about 4500 000 000 years ago, and it will begin to die in about 5000 000 000 years from now.

If the core starts to collapse, heating can start heavier nuclei fusing. The core of the star can go through a series of burn-outs and collapses. Each collapse starts a new heavier fusion reaction. The heating can also start fusion reactions in any hydrogen that is outside the core.

As a star like the Sun starts to run out of fuel, it becomes larger. The material outside the core expands and cools. It becomes a **red giant**. When this happens to the Sun, it will expand as far as the orbit of Mars. After a few more million years, gravity will cause it to contract into a very small, cold star, called a **white dwarf**. The density of the material in a white dwarf star is millions of times greater than material on Earth. The density could be as much as 1 tonne per cubic centimetre! The white dwarf gradually cools over billions of years. As it cools it becomes fainter and the colour changes. It becomes a **black dwarf**.

Fig. 72.3 A star exploded in a galaxy quite close to ours 160 000 years ago. The photograph shows the star before and after exploding. The pictures were taken in 1987, which was when light from the exploding star first reached us.

Fig. 72.4 Our galaxy, the Milky Way, as it would appear from space. The Sun is near the edge of one of the spiral arms.

Stars with more mass than the Sun may form supernovas or black holes

Larger stars (especially supergiants which are hundreds of times bigger than our Sun) may end their lives more spectacularly. A red giant can collapse very quickly. The huge gravitational forces within it pull the particles very close together. Heating can then start off new nuclear reactions, which can blow the core of the star apart. The explosion is called a **supernova**. Outer layers are blasted into space. The energy released in a few seconds can be as much as the star produced in its whole lifetime. The dust and gas from this explosion can contain the heavier elements that cannot be produced by nuclear fusion. The dense core of the supernova is left behind as a neutron star. The dust and gas can form new stars – **second generation** stars. The Sun and inner planets contain these heavier elements. This means that the material must have been through the life and death cycle of a star already.

In some dying stars, huge amounts of matter become compressed into a very small space. If the star is very large, then the gravitational forces between its particles may be large enough to squash even the neutrons inside the atoms into one another. The force of gravity exerted by this dense matter is so great that not even light can escape from it. The star has become a **black hole**.

73 THE DOPPLER EFFECT

Wave crests from something moving away from you are farther apart than you expect. Light from galaxies is red-shifted in this way.

A moving source of waves produces different wavelengths

You have probably noticed how the note of a car engine changes as it passes you. This is the **Doppler effect**. Christian Johann Doppler first described the effect in 1842 in a scientific paper about light from stars. Sound and light both show the effect because they are both waves.

Figure 73.1 shows a moving car, with an alarm that produces sound pulses at 1 s intervals. The sound waves travel out in opposite directions. If the car is moving at 30 m/s it will travel 30 m between each pulse. So when the car produces the next pulse it is 30 m closer to the wavefront it is following and 30 m farther from the wavefront it is leaving behind.

Each pulse travels 330 m in 1 s. After 1 pulse, the sound has travelled 330 m and the source of the sound (in the car) 30 m. The car is only 300 m from the wavefront it is chasing and 360 m from the other wavefront. The distance between waves in front of the car is made shorter; waves behind the car are further apart. This effect increases at greater speed. To someone listening to the alarm, the **frequency** of the sound appears to change.

If the source keeps producing a wave as it moves, the waves bunch up in front of it and spread out behind (Figure 73.2). In front of a moving car, the alarm sounds like it has a higher pitch. As the car passes you, the pitch drops to the normal note, then falls again to a lower pitch as the car moves away.

This effect also occurs with light. Study of the spectra (Topic 8) of stars in other galaxies shows that most spectral patterns appear at lower frequencies (longer wavelengths) than expected, so light appears shifted to the red end of the spectrum. This **red shift** means that the stars are moving away from us. By measuring the amount of red shift it is possible to calculate how quickly the galaxies are moving. It doesn't matter which way you look, in all directions galaxies are getting farther apart. By studying the distances and red shifts the astronomer Edwin Hubble discovered Hubble's law: the amount of red shift depends on distance. This means that the farther away a galaxy is, the faster it is moving away from us.

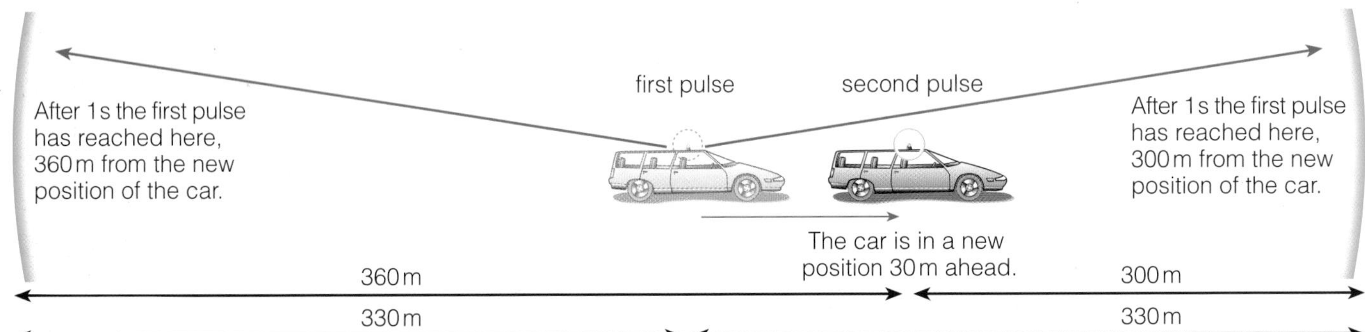

Fig. 73.1 A car travelling at 30 m/s chases the waves travelling to the right. The waves are formed closer together so wavelength is reduced in front of the car.

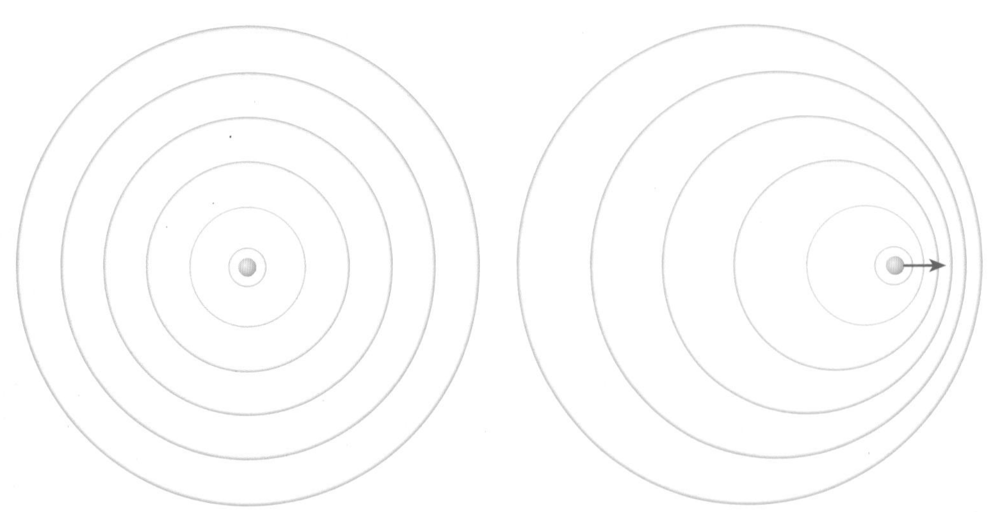

Fig. 73.2 The Doppler effect. Waves in front of a moving object are bunched together. The faster the object moves, the greater the bunching. If the object is moving away from an observer the waves have a longer wavelength. Visible light from a star moving away is red-shifted to a longer wavelength.

Fig. 73.3a The wavelengths measured in the image of any object will depend on the object's speed. If a distant object is moving away quickly, all the wavelengths will be increased. The image will appear redder than you expect. The image has a red shift – all the colours are moved to the red end of the spectrum. (The effect has been exaggerated here with a filter.) The greater the red shift, the faster the object is moving.

Fig. 73.3b With no relative motion, the image is as expected.

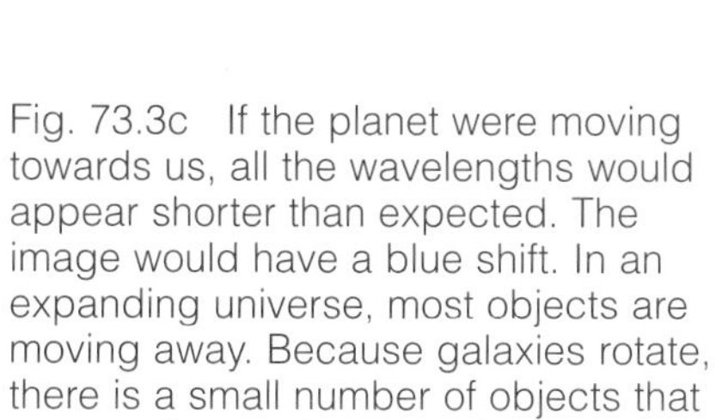

Fig. 73.3c If the planet were moving towards us, all the wavelengths would appear shorter than expected. The image would have a blue shift. In an expanding universe, most objects are moving away. Because galaxies rotate, there is a small number of objects that seem to be moving towards us.

The beginning and end of the Universe?

The Universe could be as old as 20 billion years. Stars at least 15 billion years old have been found. Astronomers using the Hubble space telescope have discovered white dwarf stars that will help them to calculate the age of the Universe. The Universe cannot be younger than the stars in it, so the rate at which the white dwarf stars cool will help to fix the minimum age. The Universe must have been around long enough to allow the white dwarf stars to cool to the temperature they have now.

Nobody knows exactly how the Universe began. One possibility is that the Universe just keeps expanding as more and more material is created. This **steady state** theory was particularly popular in the 1950s and 60s. But the most widely believed scientific theory is called the **big bang theory**. This suggests that all the matter in the Universe was suddenly created. It has expanded and cooled ever since. If this is true, space should now have cooled to a temperature of a few kelvin. At this temperature you need a radio telescope to detect the microwave radiation that the matter gives off. Wherever you look in space with a radio telescope there is a **background of radiation** representing this temperature. This is strong evidence for a big bang.

After the big bang, matter began to fly apart. It then became grouped together to form galaxies. One of the reasons that astronomers support this theory is that the Universe is still expanding. The evidence for this comes from the red shift in the spectra from these galaxies. If all the galaxies are moving apart, then this suggests that at one time they must have started out together. If we work out how quickly they are moving apart, it is possible to calculate how long ago it was they started together. This gives us the possible age for the Universe.

If, as many people believe, the Universe started with a big bang, then how will it end? This depends on how much material there is in it. If there isn't enough then the force of gravity between the particles won't be enough to stop it expanding forever and it will get cooler and cooler. If there is enough matter then the expansion could halt and the Universe could collapse in on itself again. At the moment, astronomers are still trying to find out just how much matter there is.

74 GRAVITY IN SPACE

Gravity acts within and between stars, planets and spacecraft.

Gravity acts between stars and galaxies

A gravitational force acts between all masses. The closer together two objects are, and the larger their masses, the greater the force of gravity between them. Stars are a long way from each other. But they are very massive. So the gravitational forces between them are quite strong.

You have seen that stars exist in groups, called galaxies. Galaxies, too, are grouped together. A group of galaxies is called a **cluster**. Our own galaxy, the Milky Way, is in a cluster with about 20 others. Some clusters can contain thousands of galaxies.

The galaxies which we observe from Earth all seem to be moving away from us. This is because the Universe is expanding. The spaces between the galaxy clusters are getting larger. By looking at the distances involved, and at the speed at which the clusters are moving, people have worked out that the galaxies were all in the same place somewhere between 10 000 000 000 and 20 000 000 000 years ago.

As the galaxies fly apart, gravitational forces between them tend to pull them towards each other. The outward expansion of the Universe is being slowed by gravitational forces. Will these forces ever be strong enough to make the galaxies stop, and fall back to their starting point? At the moment, it is thought that there is not quite enough mass in the Universe to make this happen. The Universe will probably go on expanding for ever.

Fig. 74.1 Two Voyager spacecraft were launched in 1977. This full-size test model was used for making electrical and countdown checks at the Kennedy Space Centre.

Gravity acts between planets

Gravity acting between a planet and the Sun provides the centripetal force which keeps the planet in orbit. A planet orbits the Sun at a speed which maintains its orbit. Planetary orbits are not perfectly circular. The Earth's orbit varies between 147 000 000 and 152 000 000 km from the Sun. Pluto's orbit varies between 4 425 000 000 and 7 400 000 000 km from the Sun.

Gravity also acts between planets themselves. As one orbiting planet approaches another, the gravitational force between the planets gets stronger. This causes changes in their orbits. Neptune and Pluto were discovered by studies of the orbits of other nearby planets.

This same effect can be used for planetary exploration. The gravitational attraction of the outer planets was used to increase Voyager 2's velocity. An alignment of the planets which only occurs every 150 years was used to send Voyager 2 to Neptune in 12 years. Without the help of gravity, we would have had to wait an extra 18 years.

Fig. 74.2 The gravitational attraction of Jupiter and Saturn helped to fling Voyager 2 out towards Uranus and Neptune.

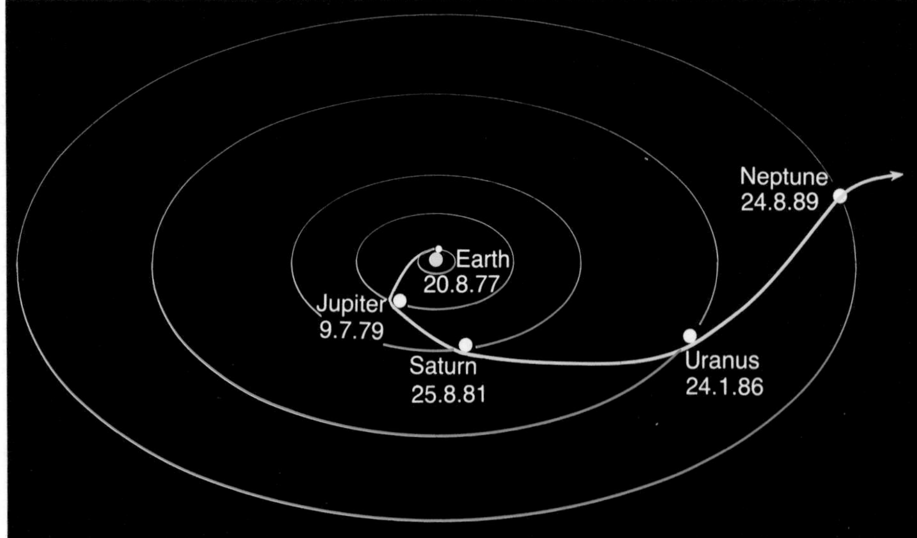

An astronaut in orbit is weightless

Weight is a force caused by gravity acting on your mass. On Earth your weight pushes down on the surface on which you are standing or sitting. If you don't exert a force on the surface, then you seem to have no weight.

Astronauts in an orbiting spacecraft exert no force on the surface on which they stand or sit. This is because both they and their spacecraft are accelerating towards the centre of the Earth. The acceleration is caused by gravity. Both the astronauts and the spacecraft accelerate towards the Earth at the same rate. So there is no noticeable force between the astronauts and their spacecraft. Both are falling freely. The astronauts seem to be weightless.

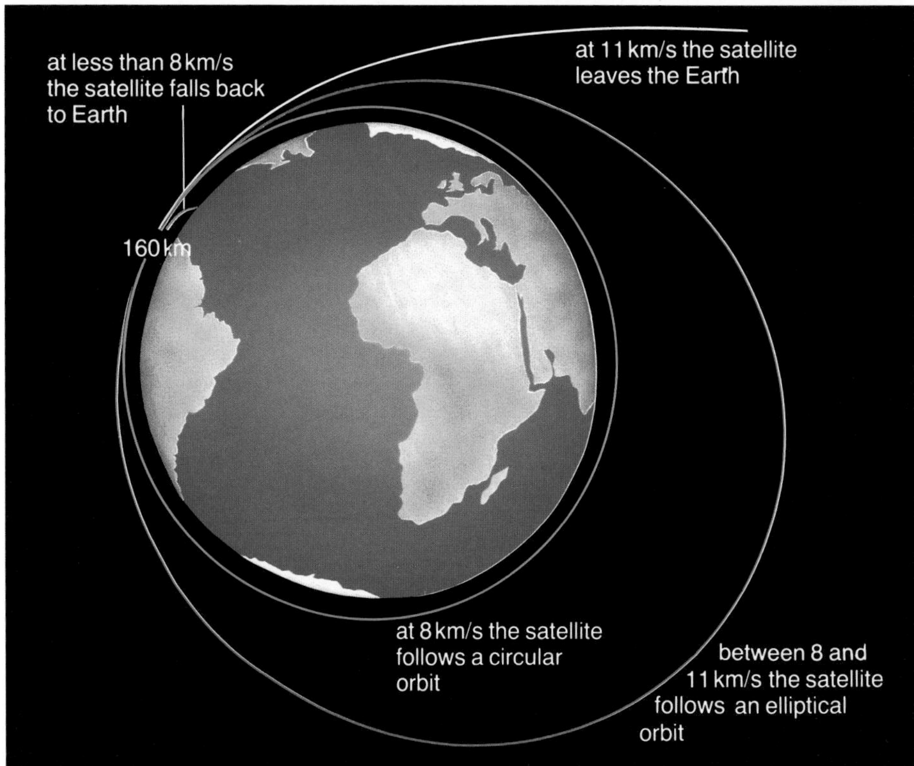

Fig. 74.3 A satellite which is to go into orbit around the Earth is lifted by a rocket to its orbital height. Chemical energy in the rocket fuel is transferred to gravitational energy in the rocket and satellite.

The satellite must then be given enough speed to maintain its orbit. Gravity provides the centripetal force which causes its circular motion.

Fig. 74.4 The launch of the space shuttle 'Atlantis', in Florida. Tremendous power is needed to lift the shuttle against gravity.

Fig. 74.5 In space, an astronaut is weightless. The picture shows two astronauts servicing the Hubble Space telescope in the cargo bay of the Shuttle Endeavour. The backdrop is the coast of Western Australia.

Satellites are used at different heights above the Earth

The height of a satellite above the Earth affects the pull of gravity on it. Gravitational force follows an **inverse square law**. That is, if you double the distance from the centre of the planet, you get a quarter of the force. The force is proportional to $1/R^2$, where R is the planet's radius.

You saw in Topic 68 how the speed of a satellite is matched to the height of its orbit. This results in two types of satellite. The first are satellites that move in low orbits around the Earth – useful if you want to cover large areas in great detail. The second are satellites at 36 000 km that stay over the same spot – geostationary, useful if you want to keep an eye on the same spot or always have the satellite in view from the Earth. Communications satellites are geostationary. They receive radio, television and telephone signals and send them on around the world. A satellite TV dish has to be pointed at a geostationary satellite – it wouldn't be much good if you could only pick up the picture as the satellite whizzed overhead for a few minutes at a time.

Satellites see weather on a large scale

Satellites high above the Earth's surface can detect electromagnetic radiation from a very large area of the Earth. They can take pictures using infra-red, light, or microwaves. These pictures give information about cloud cover and weather systems in various layers of the atmosphere.

The Meteosat satellites are geostationary satellites, staying in a fixed position over the Earth's surface. Each one monitors about 20% of the Earth's surface. The Tiros satellites follow an orbit from the North to the South Pole – they are called circumpolar satellites. Each one monitors a narrow strip around the Earth.

Fig. 74.6 Weather satellites such as Meteosat have revolutionised weather forecasting, as they can give clear pictures of cloud systems and other weather features. This picture, however, was taken by a manned spacecraft – a Soviet Soyuz craft. It shows Cyclone Rita over south-east Asia. Notice the cloud-free, quiet area in the centre, called the 'eye' of the storm.

Fig. 74.7 The Hubble space telescope. The latest measurements are helping to measure the rate of expansion of the Universe and its age.

Fig. 74.8 The Hubble space telescope produces high quality pictures because the Earth's atmosphere doesn't get in the way. Here Saturn's rings and some of its moons are clearly visible.

Question

1 For the following uses, suggest whether the satellite needs to be geostationary or not, and give reasons.

a A communications satellite.

b A TV relay satellite.

c A weather satellite.

d A Global Positioning System satellite which transmits signals to portable equipment on the ground. By measuring the length of time it takes to receive a signal from at least 3 GPS satellites, it is possible to locate your position on Earth to within a few metres.

e A Search and Rescue satellite which listens for radio distress calls.

f An astronomy satellite which avoids light from cities and all the dust, thermal and absorption effects of the Earth's atmosphere by looking at the stars from outside the Earth's atmosphere.

g An environmental monitoring satellite or a spy satellite that must see the ground in great detail.

2 In 1961, Yuri Gagarin became the first human to orbit the Earth in a spacecraft. During one orbit, the spacecraft followed an elliptical path, varying between 142 and 175 km above the Earth. The orbit took 89.1 min.

a If the Earth has a radius of 6400 km, what was the average radius of the orbit? (Give your answer to two significant figures.)

b What was the average speed in km/s?

3 On the surface of the Earth, the gravitational field strength, g, is 10 N/kg. At a height of 160 km, g is reduced to 9.5 N/kg. A satellite is launched to 160 km. It has a mass of 500 kg. Ignoring the effects of friction, answer the questions below.

a If the satellite has to be lifted against an average gravitational field strength of 9.8 N/kg, what energy would this require? (Remember that energy = force x distance.)

b If the satellite is fired from a cannon, with what velocity would it have to leave the muzzle of the cannon? (Potential energy, mgh, must be provided by the kinetic energy, $\frac{1}{2}mv^2$.)

4 Neptune is 4.5×10^9 km from the Sun. The Earth is 1.5×10^8 km from the Sun. Radio waves travel at the speed of light, 3.0×10^8 m/s.

a What delay would there have been between the transmission of a 'live' picture, from Voyager 2, in Neptune's orbit, and its reception on Earth?

b In August 1989, radio instructions were sent to Voyager 2 to cause it to adjust its course to make a closer study of Neptune's moons. What is the shortest time it could have taken for NASA to know that Voyager 2 had responded to its instructions?

75 THE SOLAR SYSTEM

The Earth is one of nine known planets orbiting the Sun. Many of these planets have their own natural satellites, or moons, orbiting them.

Nine planets orbit the Sun

The Earth is one of nine known planets that orbit the Sun. The Earth is the third planet out from the Sun.

Unlike stars, planets do not give out their own light. The planets reflect the light of the Sun. At night the planets you can see often look just like stars. You can sometimes see **Venus** just after sunset – it is often called the Evening Star.

The Sun and its planets make up the **Solar System**. The Solar System also contains other objects, such as **comets** and **asteroids**.

Jupiter
Saturn
Uranus
Neptune
Mercury
Venus
Earth
Pluto
Mars

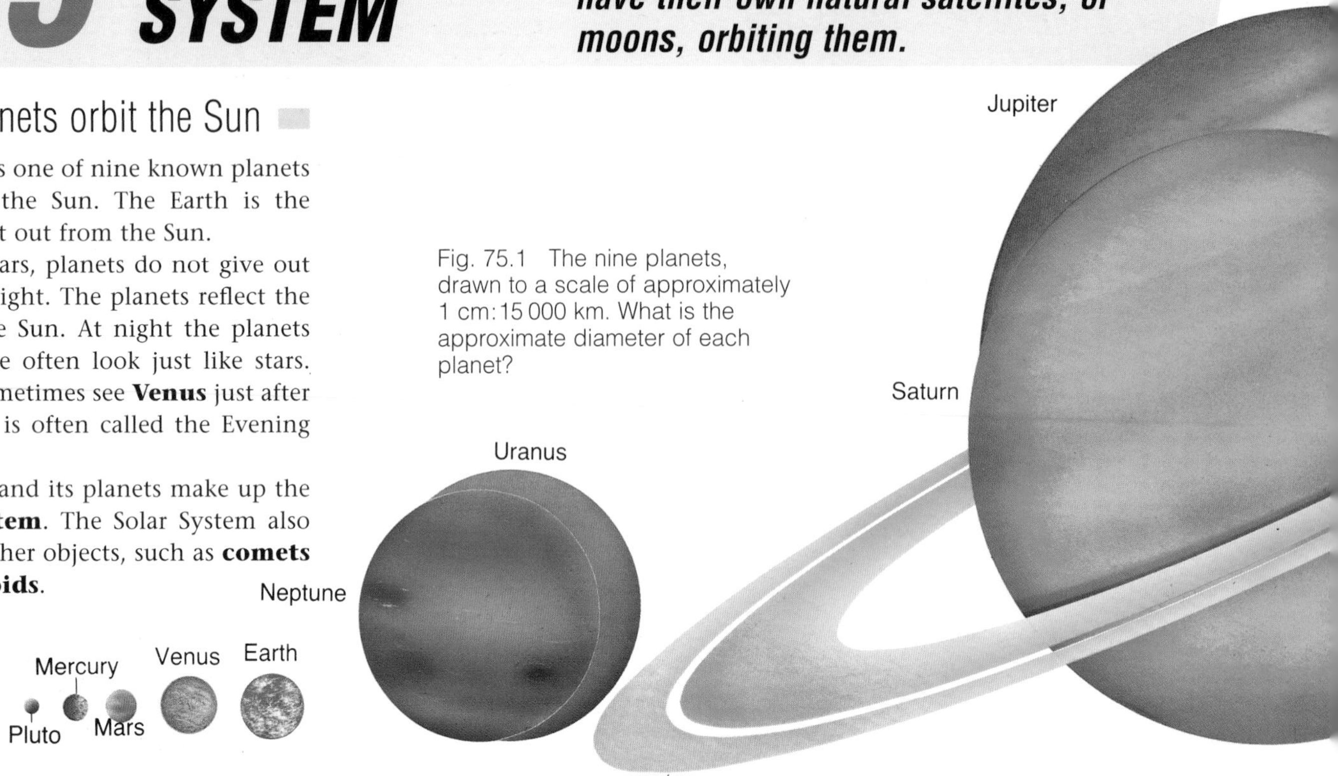

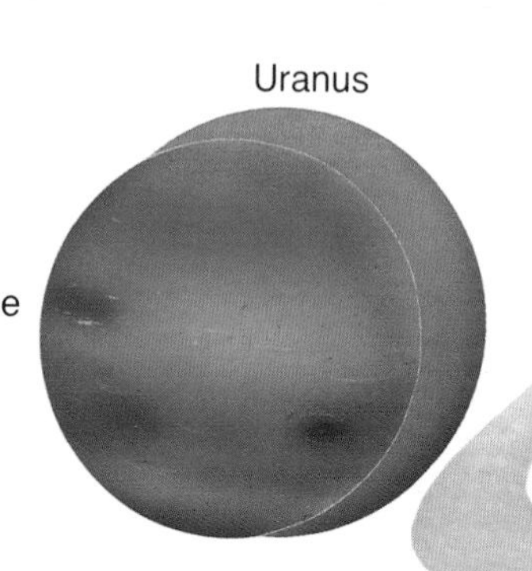

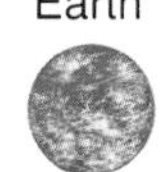

Fig. 75.1 The nine planets, drawn to a scale of approximately 1 cm: 15 000 km. What is the approximate diameter of each planet?

asteroids
Mars
Sun
Venus
Earth
Mercury
Jupiter
Saturn
Uranus
Neptune
Pluto

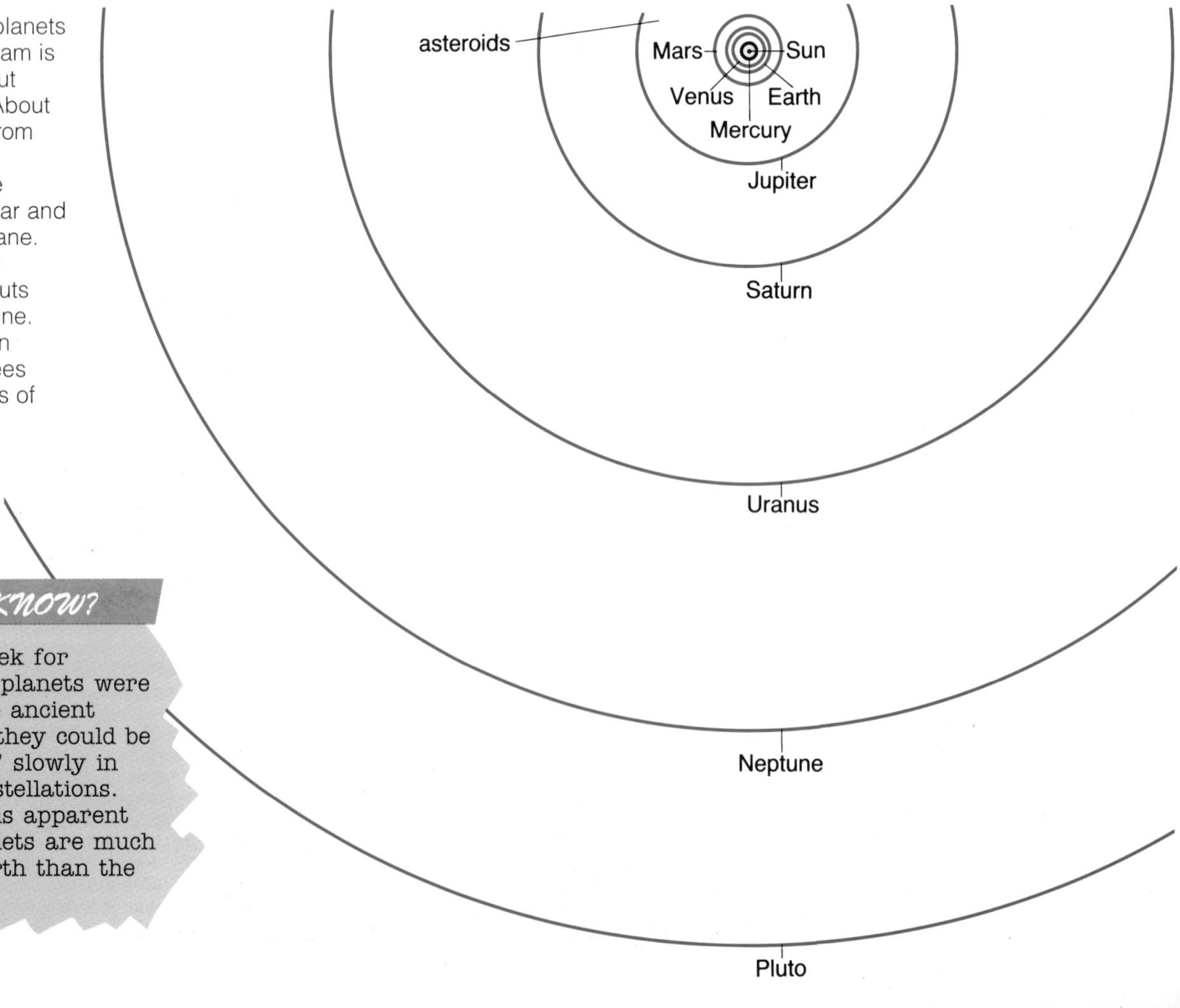

Fig. 75.2 Nine known planets orbit the Sun. This diagram is drawn to a scale of about 1 cm: 500 000 000 km. About how far is each planet from the Sun?
The orbits of most of the planets are nearly circular and lie in about the same plane. **Pluto's** orbit is the most elliptical in shape and cuts inside the orbit of Neptune. Pluto's orbit is tilted at an angle of about 17 degrees compared with the orbits of all the other planets.

DID YOU KNOW?

'Planetes' is Greek for 'wanderer'. The planets were so named by the ancient Greeks because they could be seen 'wandering' slowly in front of the constellations. This movement is apparent because the planets are much closer to the Earth than the stars.

Mercury, Venus, Earth and Mars are the inner planets

The four inner planets are all made of rock and have metallic cores. Earth is the largest of these four planets.

Fig. 75.3 Mercury, the planet closest to the Sun, has no atmosphere. It is a small planet, and its mass is not great enough to produce a strong gravitational field, so any atmospheric gases would simply drift away into space. The side of Mercury facing the Sun can reach temperatures of 430 °C, while the dark side drops to −170 °C. This picture, built up from many smaller pictures, was taken by the Mariner 10 spacecraft in 1974.

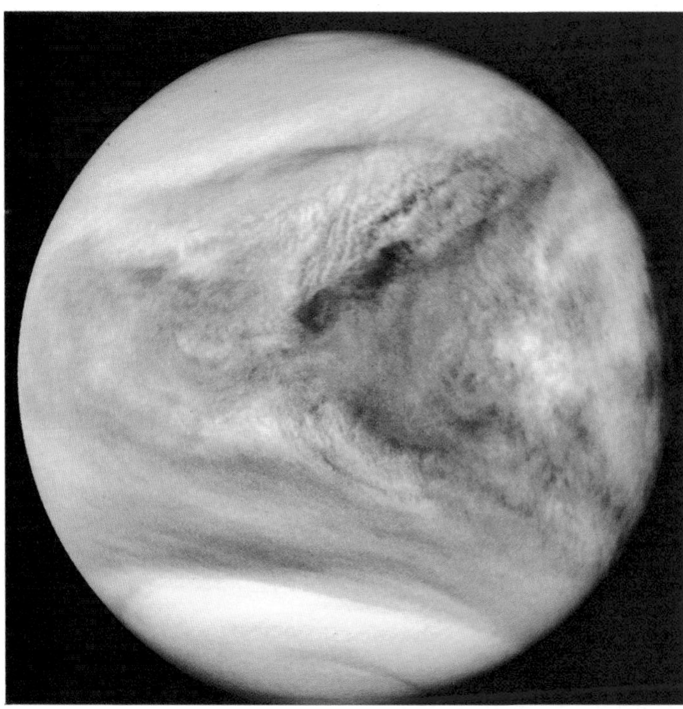

Fig. 75.4 Venus has a dense atmosphere, made up almost entirely of carbon dioxide, plus some sulphuric acid. These clouds of gas completely hide the surface of Venus. They reflect a lot of light, so Venus looks bright – we see the planet in the sky as the 'Morning Star' and the 'Evening Star'. Venus is much hotter than Earth, with surface temperatures of around 500 °C. This is partly because it is closer to the Sun than the Earth is. However, Venus' atmosphere of carbon dioxide traps solar radiation, in a kind of 'super greenhouse effect'. Without this atmosphere, Venus' temperature would be a lot lower. This picture was taken by the Pioneer Venus Orbiter, in 1980.

Fig. 75.5 The Earth looks blue from space. Like Venus, it has cloud cover, but at any one time clouds cover only about 50% of its surface. Earth is unique among the planets of the Solar System in having large quantities of liquid water on its surface. This picture was taken by a Meteosat weather satellite.

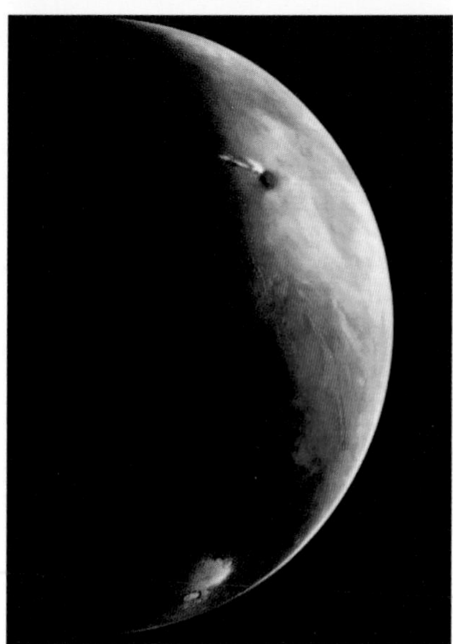

Fig. 75.6 Mars is sometimes called 'the red planet', because this is how it looks through a telescope. Of all the planets, Mars is most like Earth. It has an atmosphere containing nitrogen, oxygen, carbon dioxide, water vapour and noble gases, but the relative proportions of these gases are very different from those on Earth. The Martian atmosphere is 95% carbon dioxide.

This picture of the whole planet was taken by Viking Orbiter 2, in 1976, when it was 418 000 km away from Mars. The dark red spot is a giant volcano. The parallel 'scratches' are a great rift canyon.

Fig. 75.7 This picture of the surface of Mars was taken by Viking Lander 2 in 1979. You can see a thin coating of water ice on the rocks and soil.

The Solar System also contains comets and asteroids

As well as the planets and their moons, other kinds of objects orbit the Sun. Between Mars and Jupiter, there is an area containing several thousand lumps of rock and ice called **asteroids**. The largest ones are more than 200 km in diameter while some are only a few kilometres across.

Comets are balls of ice and dust, a few kilometres in diameter. A comet's orbit is very **eccentric**, which means that the Sun is not in the centre of it. Several hundred comets are known. Some of them reappear regularly, as their orbits pass close to Earth. The most famous one is Halley's comet, which reappears every 76 years. It was last observed in 1986. But some comets do not last very long. If their orbit is too close to the Sun, they may fall into the solar atmosphere, and be destroyed.

DID YOU KNOW?

On June 30, 1908, a tremendous explosion occurred in Siberia. It is now believed to have been caused by part of a comet colliding with the Earth. A block of ice from the comet, with a mass of 30 000 tonnes, is thought to have entered the Earth's atmosphere, and exploded several kilometres above the ground. Witnesses saw a huge fireball in the sky, and people up to 60 km away were knocked over by the shock wave.

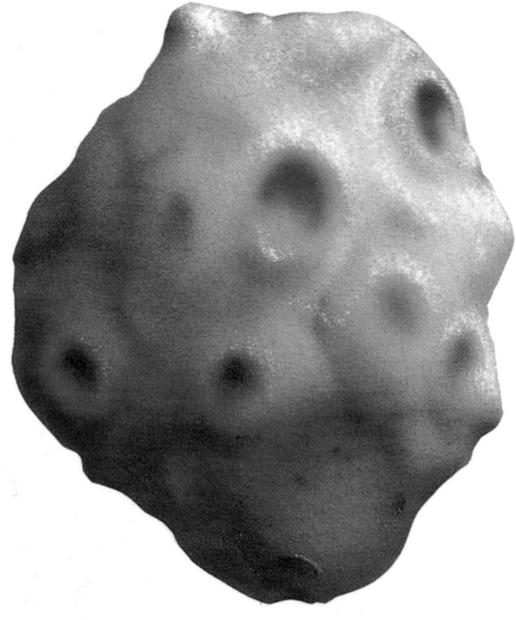

Fig. 75.8 No-one has yet had a clear view of the nucleus of a comet, but this is what it is believed to look like. It is made of ice and rock. As its orbit approaches the Sun, the ice evaporates, forming a gigantic 'tail' of gas behind the comet. The tail may be tens of millions of kilometres long.

Some planets have moons

A moon is a body which orbits around a planet. It is a natural satellite. The Earth, of course, has a moon. Neither Mercury nor Venus have moons, but Mars has two. All of the outer planets have several moons. Jupiter, for example, has at least sixteen. The largest of these is called Ganymede, and is about the same size as the planet Mercury. It is mainly made of ice. Another of Jupiter's moons, Io, has at least eight active volcanoes, and a thin atmosphere made almost entirely of sulphur dioxide. Saturn's largest moon is called Titan, and is half as big again as our Moon. Titan has an atmosphere containing mostly nitrogen, like Earth, but there is no oxygen.

Jupiter, Saturn, Uranus, Neptune and Pluto are the outer planets

The five outer planets are very different from the four inner ones. Firstly, they are much larger. Jupiter, the largest of all the planets, has a diameter ten times that of Earth. Secondly, the outer planets are mainly made of very light substances, such as hydrogen, helium, methane and ammonia. They are giant balls of gas, with relatively small solid cores.

Jupiter, Saturn, Uranus, and Neptune all have rings. The rings are made up of tiny particles orbiting the planets.

Pluto, the outermost planet, was not discovered until 1930. It is possible that there is a tenth planet which has not yet been found.

Fig. 75.9 Jupiter is the largest of the planets. This picture was taken by Voyager 1, in 1979, when it was 28 400 000 km from the planet. The bands of colour are produced by different regions in the atmosphere. The Great Red Spot is thought to be an area where the atmosphere permanently swirls around in a giant storm. You can pick out three of Jupiter's moons. Io looks reddish-orange against Jupiter's disk. Europa appears as a bright white circle on the right. Callisto is just visible as a faint circle with a tiny bright patch at the bottom left of the picture.

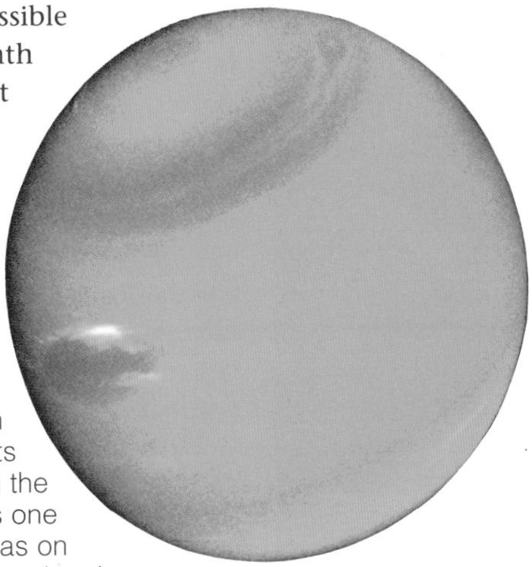

Fig. 75.10 These pictures of Saturn were taken by Voyager 2 in 1981, from a distance of 13 900 000 km. Saturn has the most striking ring system of all the outer planets. The rings are made up of tiny particles, all orbiting Saturn like miniature satellites. Saturn, like Jupiter, is made mostly of hydrogen and helium.

Fig. 75.11 Neptune can be seen only as a tiny, blue-green speck using even the most powerful telescope on Earth, because it orbits 4 500 000 000 km from the Sun, where the light is one thousandth as strong as on Earth. This picture was taken by Voyager 2, at a range of 14 800 000 km, in 1989.

Neptune is a ball of water and rock, with an atmosphere of hydrogen, helium and methane. This picture shows a huge storm in the atmosphere of Neptune, called the Great Dark Spot.

DID YOU KNOW?

Pluto is still a very mysterious planet. It has an unusual orbit, and is actually closer to the Sun than Neptune at the moment. Pluto is smaller than our own Moon. It has a moon which is almost as big as itself.

Fig. 75.12 This painting shows the flight of Voyager across the Solar System. There were two Voyager spacecraft, launched in August and September 1977.

76 THE MOON

The Moon is the Earth's natural satellite. It orbits the Earth once every 28 days, always keeping the same side facing us.

The Moon has no atmosphere

The Moon is about 384 000 km from the Earth. The Moon is much smaller than the Earth. Its mass is only 1.2% of the Earth's mass. Its diameter is 3480 km, compared with the Earth's diameter of 12 756 km.

As the mass of the Moon is much smaller than the mass of the Earth, the force of gravity is much less on the Moon. The Moon's gravity is not strong enough to hold an atmosphere. Any gases on the Moon can just drift away into space. Gravity is too weak to hold them.

Even without a telescope, you can see quite a lot of detail on the Moon's surface on a clear night. Much of the surface is covered with light areas. These are the highlands. They are covered with thousands of **craters**. The craters have been caused by **meteorites** (chunks of rock from space) hitting the Moon. Other areas of the Moon's surface look dark. They are called seas, although there is no water on the Moon. These dark areas are flat plains. They are thought to have formed from lava, which flowed from volcanoes a very long time ago. There are no active volcanoes on the Moon now.

Fig. 76.1 The Moon seen from Earth. The dark areas are the 'seas', and the light areas the highlands. The large, bright, rayed crater near the bottom is called Tycho.

Fig. 76.2 This picture of the Earth and Moon was taken by Voyager as it left the Earth at the beginning of its long journey to the outer planets.

Fig. 76.3 An Apollo 17 astronaut standing on the surface of the Moon. Most of the surface is covered with a layer of dust several metres thick.

DID YOU KNOW?

The largest crater on the Moon has a diameter of 1100 km.

Fig. 76.4 Meteor Crater, in Arizona, was formed when a huge meteor hit the Earth about 25 000 years ago. The crater is approximately 200 m deep and 800 m across.

Meteorites constantly hit the Moon and Earth

If meteorites have created so many craters on the Moon, why has this not happened on Earth?

Most of the meteorite bombardment happened between 3 000 000 000 and 4 000 000 000 years ago. Since then, weathering and other geological events have removed almost all traces of the big craters which must have formed on Earth. The Moon has no atmosphere, so weathering has not taken place. The old craters remain.

Some meteorites still bombard the Moon and Earth. Most of them are very small. Medium-sized meteorites, up to a few centimetres across, never reach the Earth's surface. As they enter the atmosphere, friction makes them so hot that they burn up. We see them as shooting stars. But on the Moon, these meteorites can get right down to the surface.

Large meteorites, up to a few tonnes, are slowed down by the Earth's atmosphere. Their outer layers burn off, but some of them still reach the ground. These would make craters on the Moon, but they do little damage on Earth. Several thousand of the meteorites which have landed on the Earth have been collected and studied. Occasionally, very large meteorites, many metres in diameter, hit the Earth. These can make huge craters, but such big meteorites are very rare.

The Moon always keeps the same face towards the Earth

The Moon orbits around the Earth once every 28 days. It always keeps the same side facing towards the Earth. Until 1959, when a spacecraft orbited the Moon, no-one had ever seen the far side.

The Moon does not produce any light of its own. We can see the Moon because light from the Sun is reflected from its surface. In the daytime, this reflected light does not seem very bright, and we may not even notice the Moon. But at night, although the light from the Moon is no brighter, it seems much more obvious in comparison with the dark night sky.

The Sun lights up half of the Moon at any one time. If the Moon is almost between the Sun and the Earth, the Sun's light is shining on the far side of the Moon. The side nearest to us gets no sunlight. So we see nothing at all, or perhaps just the edge of the Moon catching the Sun. We call this a **new moon**.

As the Moon continues to orbit around the Earth, it reaches a point where all the sunlit side is facing us. We see the whole face of the Moon, brightly lit by the Sun. This is a **full moon**.

Over a period of 28 days, our view of the Moon gradually changes. We see first a new moon, then a crescent moon, then a full moon, then a crescent moon. These changes are called the **phases of the Moon**.

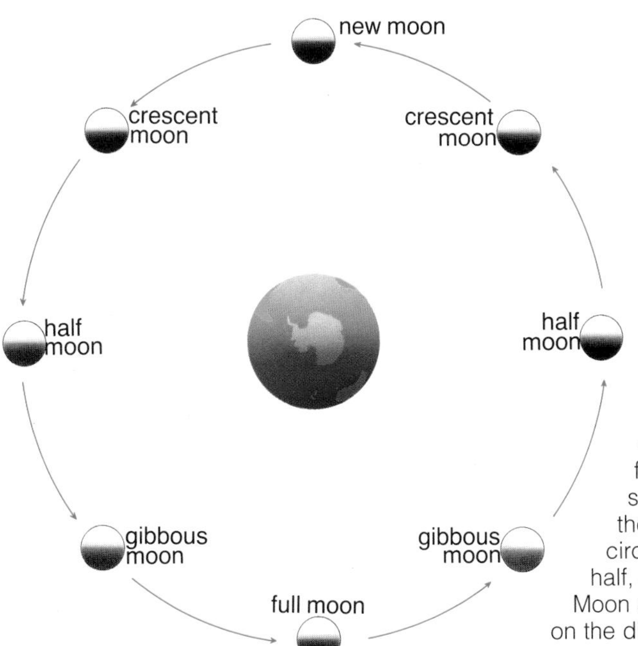

DID YOU KNOW?

The pull of the Moon does not only pull the sea up and down. This tidal effect can also distort the continents, pulling land up and down by as much as 25cm.

Fig. 76.5 The phases of the Moon. The Sun is shining from the top of the picture. When the dark face of the Moon is towards us (top), we cannot see it; this is a new moon. When the sunlit face of the Moon is fully towards us (bottom), we see a full circle; this is a full moon. In between, we see a crescent, half, or gibbous moon. Can you draw the shape of the Moon as it would appear in the sky at each position shown on the diagram?

The Moon causes tides

The Moon and the Earth are both massive objects. So they exert a large gravitational attraction on one another. The gravitational pull of the Moon on the Earth causes the tides.

The gravitational force of the Moon pulls outwards on the Earth's surface. The part of the Earth nearest to the Moon is pulled hardest. The Moon pulls the Earth's surface outwards. The water is pulled out in a bulge. This is a **high tide**. The water in the oceans rises up the shore. In some places, such as the Bay of Fundy in Canada, the water may rise as much as 12m. At the same time, there is also a high tide on the opposite side of the Earth.

In between the high tides, there are **low tides**. So, as a particular point on the Earth's surface moves round, it experiences a high tide, then a low tide, then a high tide again, and so on. It takes 24 hours for the Earth to spin round once. So there are two high tides and two low tides approximately every 24 hours.

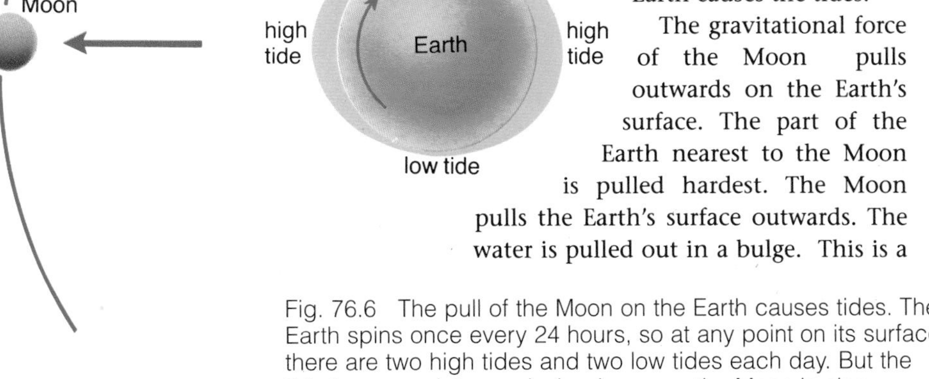

Fig. 76.6 The pull of the Moon on the Earth causes tides. The Earth spins once every 24 hours, so at any point on its surface there are two high tides and two low tides each day. But the tide becomes later each day, because the Moon is also moving, orbiting the Earth every 28 days. Can you work out how much later high tide will be each day?

77 DAYS, SEASONS AND YEARS

The regular cycles of day and night, and the seasons, are caused by the relative movements of the Earth and Sun.

Early astronomers thought that the Sun revolved around the Earth

Everyone is aware that the Sun moves across the sky in the course of a day. It rises in the east, and sinks in the west. The Moon and stars also seem to move across the sky. They too appear to move from east to west.

Early astronomers believed that the Earth was flat. They thought that the stars and planets were all the same distance from Earth, and moved around the Earth in circular orbits. Then, in about 280 BC, a Greek astronomer proved that the Earth was not flat, but a globe. But the Greek astronomers still thought that the Earth was at the centre of the Universe. They believed that the Sun, Moon, planets and stars all revolved around the Earth.

In 1543, the Polish astronomer Copernicus put forward a new and unpopular idea. He suggested that the Sun, not the Earth, was the centre of the Solar System. People found this idea very difficult to accept. Not until the middle of the seventeenth century were most astronomers sure that the Earth really did move around the Sun. Even then, many of them were afraid to say so.

Fig. 77.1 This model of the Universe was made in 1554. It shows the Earth at the centre, with the Sun, Moon and planets moving around it. This Earth-centred idea of the Universe is called the Ptolemaic system, after the Greek astronomer Ptolemy, who put forward these ideas in a book written in about 150 BC. This model still shows the old system, despite the publication of Copernicus' ideas in 1553.

Fig. 77.2 A time-exposure of the night sky shows the stars apparently moving in circular orbits. We now know that this happens because the Earth is revolving, not the stars.

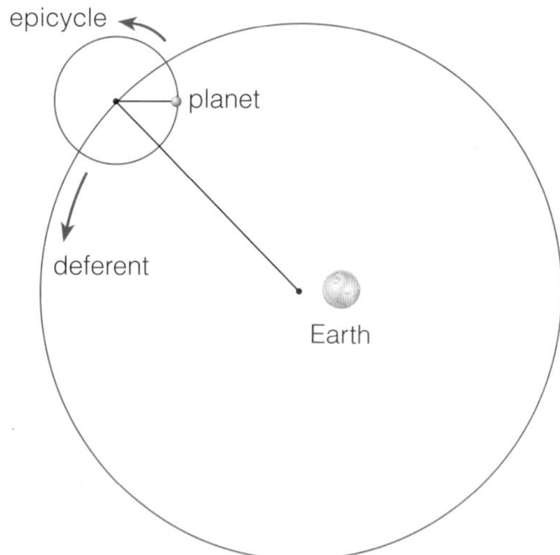

Fig. 77.3 Ptolemy's model was based on circles. Planets orbited the Earth on a large circular orbit called the deferent. Small changes in the planets' motion were explained with a second circle called the epicycle. The planets also moved around this smaller circle. This was why they seemed to wobble in the sky. This representation of planetary motion predicted the movements of the planets very accurately and was used for navigation. It was widely accepted because it agreed with observations and the religious and philosophical thinking of the time. The Earth had to be at the centre of everything (although for the model to exactly match observations it had to be placed slightly off-centre!).

Fig. 77.4 Earthrise from the Moon. This picture, taken by Apollo, shows half of the Earth bathed in sunlight, and the other half in darkness. The Earth is spinning on its axis, taking 24 hours for one complete turn, so night and day alternate within the 24 hour period. Which way is the Earth spinning in this picture?

The Earth revolves on its axis

We now know that the Sun appears to move across the sky because the Earth is revolving. The Earth spins on an axis running from the North Pole to the South Pole. It spins in an anticlockwise direction. So the Sun appears to move from east to west.

It takes 24 hours for the Earth to spin completely around. This length of time is one day. A point on the equator of the Earth faces the Sun for about half of this time. For the other half, it faces away from the Sun. So, at the equator, day and night are each about 12 hours long.

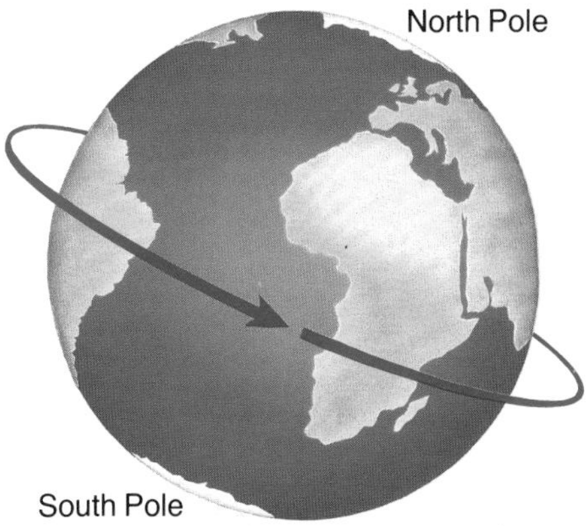

Fig. 77.5 The Earth spins on its axis once every 24 hours.

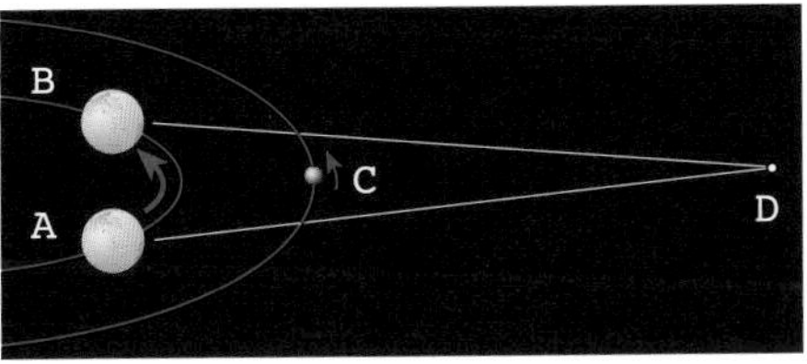

Fig. 77.6 As the Earth, at A, approaches a slower moving planet, C, the planet seems to be to the left of the star, D. The Earth overtakes the slow planet. From B, the slow planet seems to be to the right of the star. It seems to have moved backwards. This retrograde motion or wobble can be explained by a moving Earth and doesn't need Ptolemy's epicycles.

DID YOU KNOW?

Galileo did not invent the telescope. He did develop the telescope of Hans Lippershey and used it for astronomy. With 20 times magnification, Galileo observed the motion of four moons around Jupiter. Some scientists were so convinced that all things had to revolve around the Earth, they refused to look through it. Others suggested that the lenses must work differently when looking at far away objects.

A simplified model of the Solar System has the Sun at the centre

Ptolemy's model worked very well but became very complicated as it tried to match the exact positions of all the planets during a year. 1400 years later, Copernicus suggested that the same observations would be made if the Sun were at the centre and not the Earth. The apparent motion of the planets could then be explained by the fact that the Earth was moving as well as the other planets. This was a very difficult idea to accept at the time. According to religious belief, the Earth had to be at the centre of the Universe so everything had to revolve around the Earth. Copernicus' model was based on circular orbits for the planets and allowed the first estimates for the distances to the other planets to be made. The problem with his model was that the orbits of the planets are actually ellipses. Although he had the right idea, that the Sun should be at the centre of the Solar System, predictions from circular orbits don't quite match the observations. Copernicus spent many years improving his circular model, but ended up with one almost as complicated as Ptolemy's. This suited everyone who still believed that the Earth had to be at the centre of the Universe.

From Denmark, in 1576, Tycho Brahe began taking very accurate measurements of the planets and stars. After his death in 1601, his assistant Johannes Kepler continued work with his figures. Kepler supported Copernicus' model. He was able to show from the accurate observations that the planets moved in ellipses and that the planets moved faster when they were nearer the Sun. He was also able to work out that there was a link between the radius of a planet's orbit and the length of its year (time for one orbit). In Italy, Galileo Galilei supported Copernicus' ideas and produced a theory to explain the tides from the movement of the Earth. He supported Kepler's work but from 1613 his work began to be treated as heresy. In 1616 the Roman Catholic church censored books about the Copernican system and Galileo was told that he could only talk about a fixed Earth. Eventually, Galileo was sentenced to house arrest for life (the original sentence was life imprisonment). The work of Galileo and Kepler led to Newton's theories of gravitation and an explanation of why the planets move as they do.

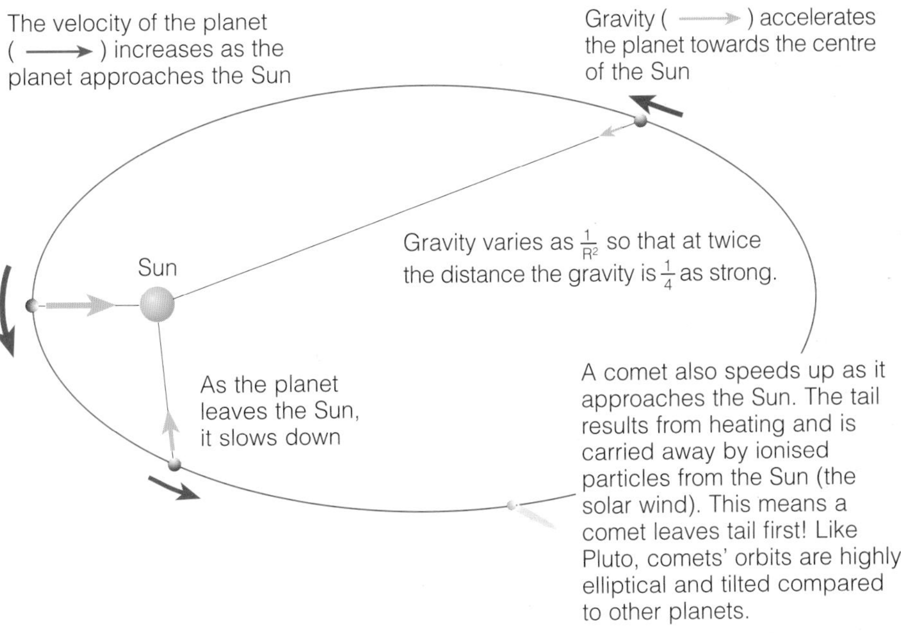

Fig. 77.7 Planets orbiting at a greater distance from the Sun have a longer year. Within their orbit, planets travel faster near the Sun. The more elliptical the orbit, the greater the change in speed.

The Earth takes 365 1/4 days to orbit the Sun

As well as spinning on its axis every 24 hours, the Earth moves around the Sun. It takes it 365 1/4 days to do this. This length of time is one year.

The north–south axis on which the Earth spins is not at right angles to the Earth's orbit around the Sun. The axis is tilted at an angle of nearly 24°. It is this tilt which causes the seasons.

Figure 77.8 shows what happens as the Earth orbits around the Sun. At position B, the Northern Hemisphere (the part of the Earth to the north of the equator) is tipped away from the Sun. Imagine what happens as the Earth spins round on its axis. The North Pole will not get any sunlight at all. It will be in permanent darkness. The South Pole will get sunlight all the time. The Sun will never set.

A country somewhere between the equator and the North Pole will get sunlight for part of the 24 hour period. But it will be for less than 12 hours. The further north you go, the shorter the days will be.

So when the Earth is in this position in its orbit around the Sun, the Northern Hemisphere has short days and long nights. The Southern Hemisphere has long days and short nights. In the Northern Hemisphere, it is winter. In the Southern Hemisphere, it is summer.

Fig. 77.8 The seasons. The Earth is tipped over at an angle of 24°. It orbits around the Sun once every 365 1/4 days. At position A, it is summer in the Northern Hemisphere and winter in the Southern Hemisphere. At position B, it is winter in the Northern Hemisphere and summer in the Southern Hemisphere.

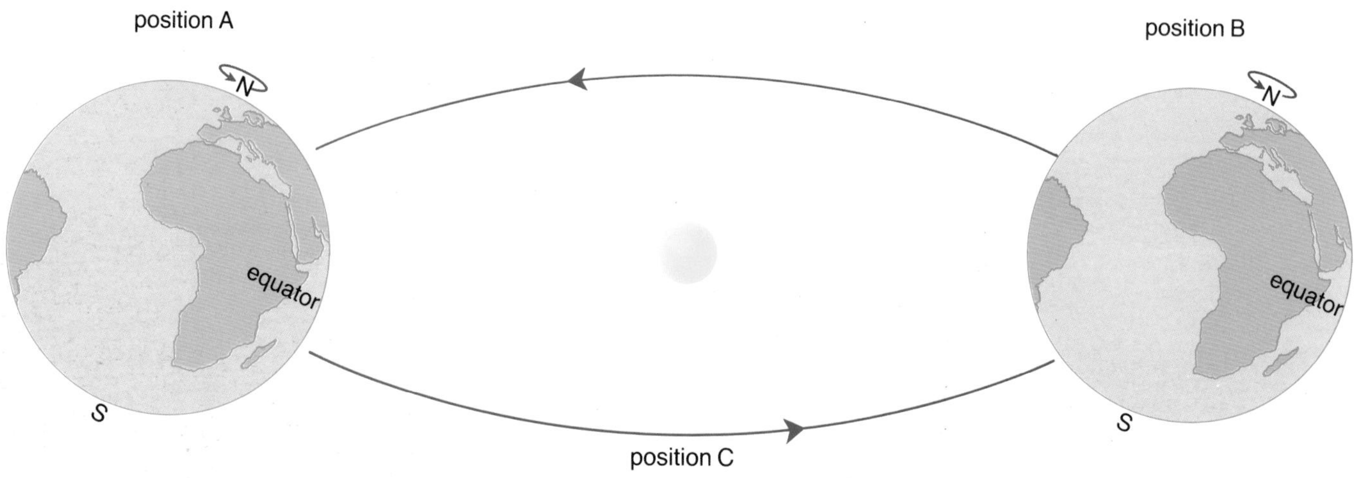

Fig. 77.9 At midnight in June, in northern Norway, the Sun is still above the horizon. In December, the Sun will not rise all day.

Questions

1 Why does the Sun appear to move across the sky from east to west?

2 The table contains some information about the movements of three planets in the Solar System.

Planet	*Time taken to rotate on axis*	*Time taken to orbit the Sun*
Mercury	59 days	88 days
Mars	24 hours	687 days
Jupiter	10 hours	4333 days

a Using this information, and your knowledge about the Earth and the Solar System, can you see any relationship between distance from the Sun, and the time taken to orbit around it?

b How long is a day on Mars?

c How long is a year on Mercury?

3 Look at Figure 77.8. When the Earth is in position C in its orbit around the Sun what season is it in:

a the Northern Hemisphere?

b the Southern Hemisphere?

c Explain your answers to parts a and b.

78 THE ORIGIN OF THE SOLAR SYSTEM

The Solar System is thought to have formed when a cloud of gas rotated and condensed.

The Earth is 4 500 000 000 years old

The problem of how the Earth was formed has puzzled people for thousands of years. When it was understood that the Earth was part of the Solar System, astronomers began to suggest theories for the origin of the Earth, the Sun and the other eight planets.

It is thought that the Sun and its nine planets all formed at the same time. This was about 4 500 000 000 years ago. They were formed from a cloud of gas called a **nebula**. The nebula rotated in space, slowly getting smaller as its own gravity pulled material in towards its centre. Gradually, parts of the cloud condensed to form the Sun in the centre, with the planets orbiting around it.

While the nebula was contracting, it became very hot. The centre of the nebula, from which the Sun was formed, was the hottest part. The outer part, from which the outer planets were formed, was the coolest part.

As the nebula slowly cooled, the gases condensed. They formed tiny particles of dust which stuck together to form larger pieces. In this way, the planets were built up.

This explanation of the origin of the Solar System is only a theory. It cannot be proved. But, at the moment, it is the best explanation which scientists can give.

DID YOU KNOW?

It is likely that the events which caused the birth of the Solar System have happened in other parts of the Universe too. So there could be other planetary systems like ours. If so, then perhaps there are other planets on which life has developed.

Fig. 78.1 The Sun and planets probably began as a huge cloud of gas (top left). Of the material in the cloud, 99% collapsed inwards to form the Sun. Over the next 100 000 000 years the remaining 1% gradually collected into larger and larger pieces, which eventually became the planets.

Questions

1 Read the following passage, and then answer the questions which follow.

The Age of the Earth

The most modern estimates of the age of the Earth suggest that it was formed about 4500000000 years ago. But only since about 1920 have most scientists come to accept this figure. Previously, people had thought that the Earth was much younger than this.

Many early civilisations believed that the Earth and Universe began at the same time. Some cultures, such as the Mayas in South America, believed that the Universe kept on being destroyed and recreated. Genesis, the first book of the Bible, tells the story according to the tradition of the Jews and Christians. In 1654, John Lightfoot used this story as the basis of his calculation that the Earth had been created at 9.00 a.m. on October 26, 4004 BC.

In the eighteenth century, people began to consider the possibility that the Earth might have been formed some time after the beginning of the Universe. In 1779, a French scientist, the Comte de Buffon, tried to work out the age of the Earth experimentally. He thought that the Earth had been very hot when it first began, and was steadily cooling. He made a small globe, and measured its rate of cooling. From this, he calculated that the Earth was 75 000 years old.

In 1862, the physicist Lord Kelvin also used the cooling idea to work out the age of the Earth. He included many factors in his calculations of which the Comte de Buffon had no knowledge, including the heat generated from gravitational contraction as the Earth formed, the rate of conduction of heat through the Earth, heating from the Sun, and tidal friction. He concluded that the Earth had been formed between 20000000 and 40000000 years ago.

Throughout the nineteenth century, ideas in other branches of science were also rapidly developing. Geologists such as Charles Lyell were beginning to understand the way in which rocks were formed, eroded, and formed again. They knew that different layers of rocks represented different periods of time. Although they had no way of working out how long it took for a layer of rock to form, they knew it must take a long time, and did not believe Lord Kelvin's ideas. They thought the Earth must be much older, or perhaps had always existed.

Biologists too were unhappy with the age suggested by Lord Kelvin. Charles Darwin's ideas on evolution were beginning to be widely supported, and biologists believed that all the different species of life on Earth would have taken much longer than 40000000 years to evolve.

As the nineteenth century drew to its close, geologists became increasingly sure that the Earth was at least 100000000 years old. But they had no really firm evidence to go on. One calculation was based on the saltiness of the sea. John Joly, in Dublin, worked out how much salt was carried into the oceans each year, and decided that it must have taken about 90000000 years for them to become as salty as they are now.

At the turn of the century, a discovery was made which was to completely change our ideas about the age of the Earth. Radioactivity was discovered by Henri Becquerel in 1896. Gradually, as researchers, like Marie Curie and Ernest Rutherford found out more and more about the way in which radioactive substances behaved, it was realised that radioactive substances in the Earth could generate heat as they decayed. Lord Kelvin's calculations had not allowed for this at all.

As it was now understood that radioactive elements decayed at a steady and predictable rate, scientists began to try to calculate the time at which the Earth was formed by looking at the amounts of different isotopes in rocks. Various methods using this idea were tried during the first part of the twentieth century. Eventually, lead isotopes were found to be the most reliable tool to use. Using this method, rocks have been found which are dated at 3800000000 years old. So we know that the Earth had a solid crust at least this long ago, and probably longer.

Meteorites which have fallen to Earth have been dated at 4500000000 years old. These are thought to have formed at the same time as the rest of the Solar System, including Earth. We now believe that the Earth was formed about 4500000000 years ago.

a What was the similarity between the Comte de Buffon's and Lord Kelvin's methods of calculating the age of the Earth?

b Why did the following not agree with Lord Kelvin's calculations:

- **i** geologists?
- **ii** biologists?

c John Joly worked out how much water ran into the oceans each year. What other quantities would he have had to estimate, or calculate, in order to make his suggestion about the age of the Earth?

d Nobody knew about radioactivity when Lord Kelvin made his first calculations. Explain how and why this lack of knowledge affected his dating of the formation of the Earth.

e What is a meteorite?

f Why is dating a meteorite likely to give an even more accurate measure of the age of the Solar System than dating the oldest known rocks on Earth?

2 Explain why:

a we see the Sun as it was 8 min ago.

b a day lasts 24 hours.

c a year lasts $365\frac{1}{4}$ days.

d we have 366 days in every fourth year – a leap year.

e in Britain we have long nights in winter and short nights in summer.

f there are two high tides and two low tides each day.

3 Find out about the contribution of some or all of the following people to the understanding of the Universe and Solar System:

a Thales and other early Greek astronomers
b Eratosthenes
c Aristarchus
d Ptolemy
e Copernicus
f Galileo
g Tycho Brahé
h Kepler
i Newton.

EXTENSION

ELECTRICITY AND RESOURCES

79 CURRENT AND SIMPLE CIRCUITS

An electric current is a flow of charge.

Current is a flow of charge

In Topic 24, you saw how a Van de Graaff generator can build up a charge on a metal dome. If the charge is caused by extra electrons, the dome has a negative charge. The dome could also be positively charged, if electrons have been removed from it.

Think about a negatively charged dome with lots of extra electrons on it. These electrons all repel one another, but they stay where they are because there is nowhere for them to go. However, if the dome is connected to earth by a wire, then the electrons have an escape route. The extra electrons flow down the wire. This movement of charge is called an **electric current**.

Fig. 79.1 A Van de Graaff generator discharges through a microammeter which registers a small current.

Current is measured in amperes

The amount of charge, such as the amount of extra electrons on the dome of the Van de Graaff generator, is measured in **coulombs**. The symbol for coulombs is **C**.

The **current** is a measure of how quickly the charge is moving. We measure electric current as the amount of charge which flows past a particular point in a particular time. If one coulomb of charge flows past in one second, then the current is one **ampere**. Ampere is usually abbreviated to **A**.

$$\text{Current in amperes} = \frac{\text{charge passing in coulombs}}{\text{time interval in seconds}}$$

So current is charge passing per second.

For example: *A total charge of 2 coulombs passes a point in a wire in 4 seconds. What is the current?*

$$\text{Current} = \frac{\text{charge}}{\text{time}} = \frac{2\,\text{C}}{4\,\text{s}}$$

= 0.5 coulombs per second, or 0.5 amperes.

Electrons move slowly

As a current passes along a wire, the electric *signal* travels at virtually the speed of light. But the *electrons* are moving much more slowly. In the experiments which you do with wires and currents, the electrons move round the circuit at about 0.1 mm/s. How can we explain this?

Think about what happens when you turn on a tap. Immediately, water starts flowing from the tap. But how long is it before water from the pumping station reaches your tap? It must be a very long time. The water which comes out of your tap is the water which was already in the pipe.

A similar thing happens when you complete an electrical circuit. Look at Figure 79.2. When you close the switch, you give the electrons at the negative end of the cell an escape route, and they begin to move around the circuit, away from the negative end of the cell and towards the positive end. If the wire connecting the cell to the bulb is 10 cm long, it will take an electron from the cell about 15 minutes to reach the bulb! You would be rather surprised if it took this long for the bulb to light up. In fact, it lights up immediately, because electrons immediately flow into it *from the wire*. The electrons which flow through the filament of the lamp during the first 15 minutes of your experiment are electrons which were already in the wire.

The metal wire, like all metals, contains some electrons which are free to move. They move around randomly. Under the influence of an electric field, provided by the cell, a force acts on these electrons. The force causes the negatively charged electrons to drift towards the positive end of the cell. Electrons leave the negative end of the cell, replacing some of the metal's electrons in the wire. At the same time, electrons from the wire are entering the positive end of the cell.

DID YOU KNOW?

0.5 amperes might sound like a small current. But one electron only carries a charge of 0.000 000 000 000 000 000 16 C, so a 0.5 A current means that 3 million million million electrons are passing each second.

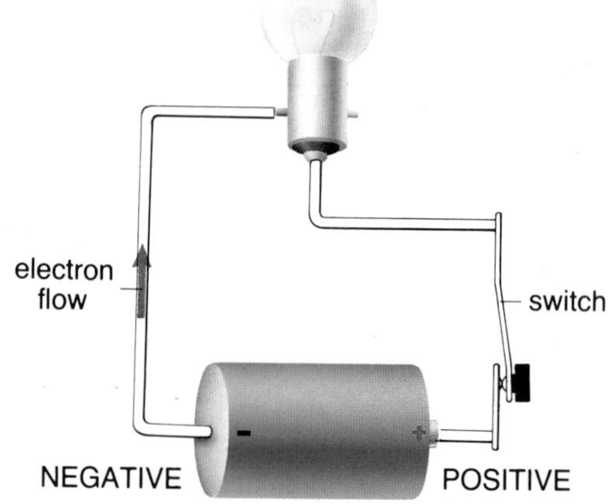

Fig. 79.2

Current is considered to flow from positive to negative

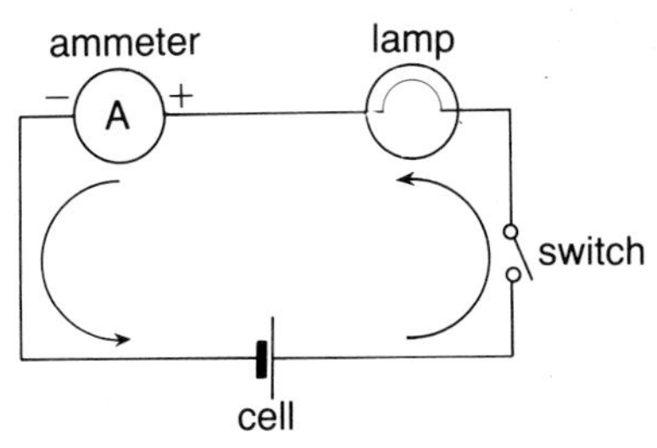

Fig. 79.3 The arrows show the conventional current flow.

When people first began to study electric current, they assumed that it was a flow of positive charge, from the positive end of a cell, around a circuit, to the negative end. It was a long time before scientists discovered that it was, in fact, negatively charged electrons which were moving! By this time, everyone had been thinking about current flowing from positive to negative for so long that it was impossible to change.

So we still consider current to flow from positive to negative. This is sometimes called 'conventional current flow'. But do remember that the real flow of electrons is in the opposite direction!

Detecting and measuring electric current

There are many different ways of detecting when an electric current is flowing in a wire. You might notice, for example, that the wire gets hot. Electric currents cause *heating*. The wire may get so hot that it glows, and gives off *light*. Or you could try holding a plotting compass near the wire, to see if it was deflected. Electric currents cause *magnetic effects*. Electric currents can also cause *chemical effects*, such as electrolysis.

To measure electric currents, we use an **ammeter**. The ammeter measures how much charge is passing through it each second, and displays this on a dial or a digital display.

You must make sure that you connect the positive terminal of the ammeter to the wire coming from the positive power supply. But it doesn't matter at all where you put the ammeter in the circuit, so long as the circuit doesn't branch anywhere. The current is the same all the way round the circuit.

But if there is a junction in the circuit, as in Figure 79.4, the electrons split up, some going one way and some the other. When the wires join up again, so do the electrons. So where there are two or more alternative routes, each alternative will carry fewer electrons per second than the main route which supplies them. The current in each alternative route will be less than in the main route. But the *total* current in the alternatives must be the same as the current in the main route.

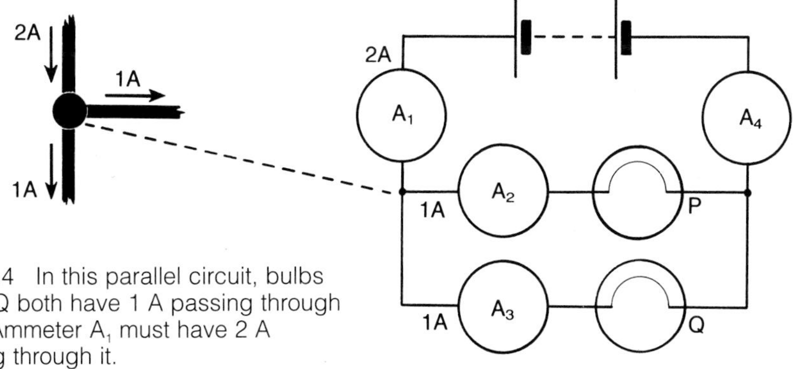

Fig. 79.4 In this parallel circuit, bulbs P and Q both have 1 A passing through them. Ammeter A_1 must have 2 A passing through it.

Questions

1 Figure 79.4 shows a parallel circuit. What would ammeter A_4 read?

2 The diagram shows a circuit. L_1, L_2 and L_3 are identical lamps.

a If A_2 measures 0.5 A, what would A_1 and A_3 measure?

b How many coulombs of charge pass through L_1 in one second?

c How long does it take for the same charge to pass through L_3?

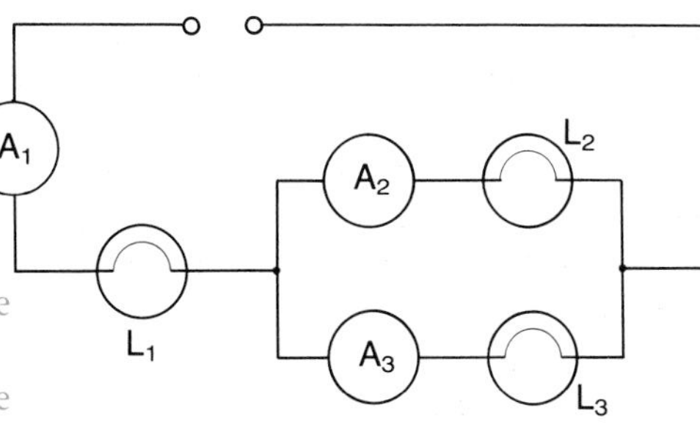

INVESTIGATION 79.1

Current in simple circuits

1 Make these circuits. In circuit 2, the lamps are connected in series. In circuit 3, they are connected in parallel.

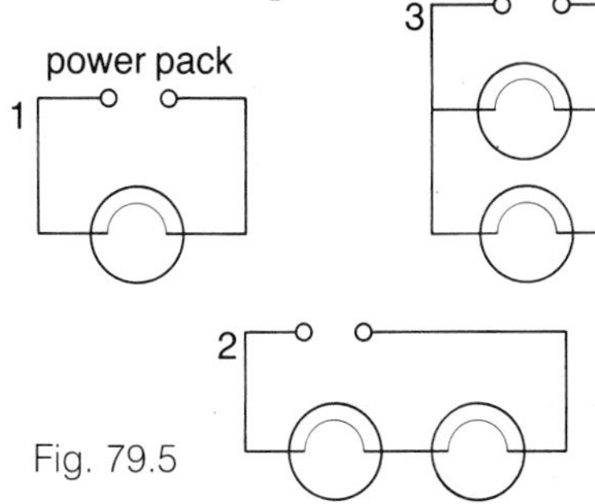

Fig. 79.5

2 In which circuit are the lamps dimmest?

3 In which circuit or circuits are the lamps of equal brightness to the lamp in circuit 1?

4 Which circuit gives out most light?

5 Add an ammeter to circuit 1. Measure the current going into the lamp.

6 Predict what current you think is going into each lamp in circuit 3. What do you think is the total current leaving the power pack in circuit 3?

7 Add an ammeter to circuit 3, in such a position as to measure:

a the current going into one lamp

b the current going into the other lamp

c the current leaving the power pack.

Do your answers match up with your predictions in step 6?

8 Repeat steps 6 and 7 for circuit 2.

9 Write a short summary describing what you have found out about current in series and parallel circuits.

80 VOLTAGE

As electrons travel round a circuit, they transfer energy.

A cell pumps electrons around a circuit

Figure 80.1 shows a simple circuit. The driving force to push the electrons around the circuit comes from the cell. The cell transfers its stored chemical energy to electrical energy. You can think of a cell as a kind of 'electron pump'.

You can measure how much energy the cell gives to the electrons by measuring the *difference* in electrical potential energy on either side of the cell. The difference in energy is called the **potential difference**, or **voltage**, and is measured in **volts**, abbreviation **V**. This is measured with a **voltmeter**. The voltmeter is connected across the cell. A potential difference of one volt across a cell means that each coulomb of charge leaving the cell is provided with an energy of one joule. So 1 volt is 1 joule per coulomb.

$$\text{voltage (in V)} = \frac{\text{energy supplied (in J)}}{\text{charge (in C)}}$$

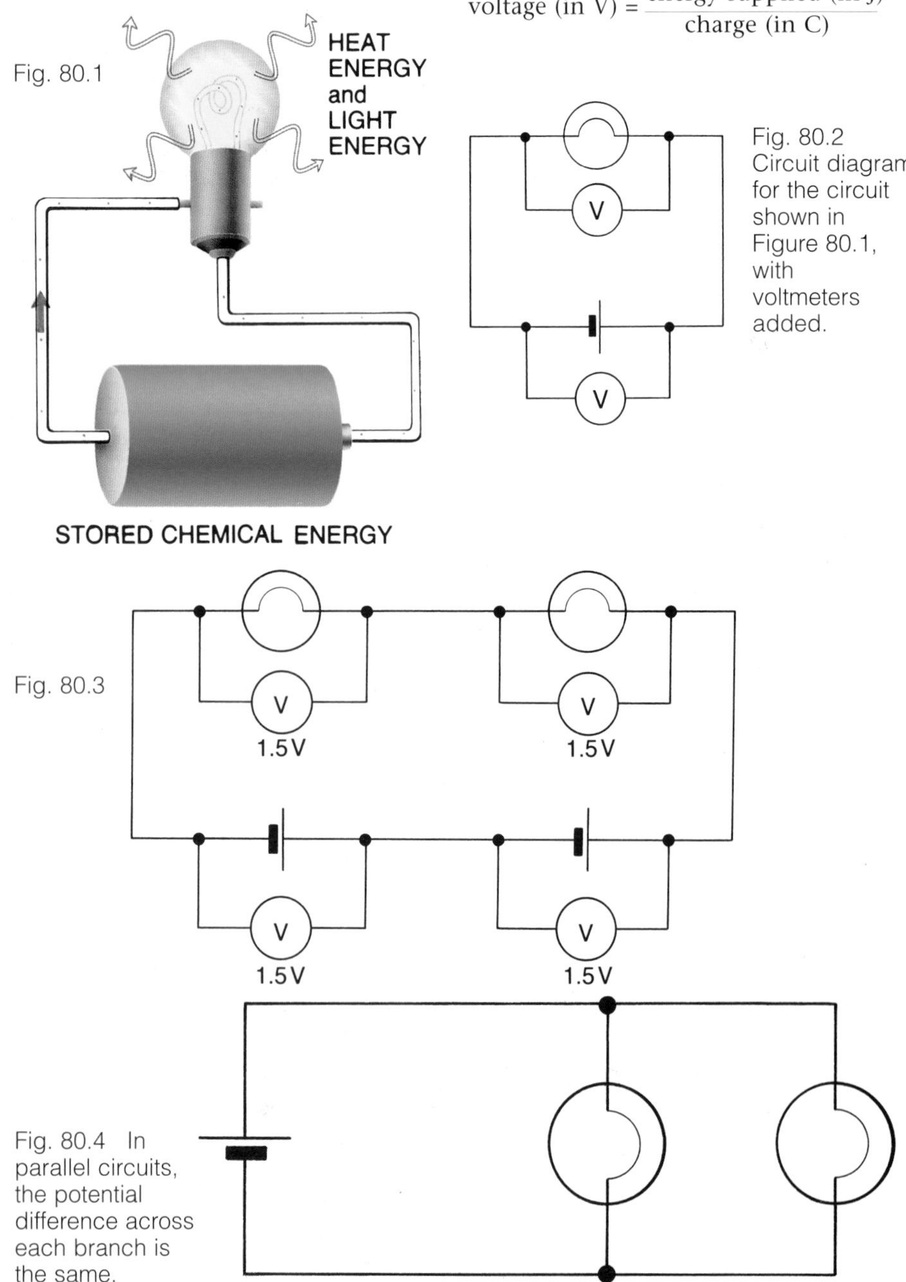

Fig. 80.1

Fig. 80.2 Circuit diagram for the circuit shown in Figure 80.1, with voltmeters added.

Fig. 80.3

Fig. 80.4 In parallel circuits, the potential difference across each branch is the same.

Energy is transferred as the electrons flow round the circuit

As the electrons flow through the lamp filament, their electrical energy is transferred to heat and light energy. They lose the energy which the cell gives them. You can measure this energy loss by connecting a voltmeter across the lamp. The voltmeter measures the potential difference across the lamp.

The total energy lost around the circuit is the same as the energy provided by the cell. So if the potential difference across the lamp is one volt, the potential difference across the cell is also one volt, provided that no energy is wasted in the wires.

Energy is shared out between the components in a circuit

In Figure 80.3, there are two cells and two lamps. Each cell has a potential difference of 1.5 V. This means that each cell is providing each coulomb of charge with 1.5 J of energy. So each coulomb of charge gets a total of 3 J of energy. In total, the potential difference provided by the two cells is 3 V. If you connected a voltmeter across the two cells, it would read 3 V.

The energy is shared out between the two lamps. If they are identical, they will take equal shares of energy. Each coulomb of charge loses half its energy in each lamp. So the potential difference across each lamp is half of 3 V, which is 1.5 V. A voltmeter connected across one of the lamps will read 1.5 V. (What would a voltmeter connected across the two lamps read?)

All electrical energy which is lost in a circuit must have been provided by the cells. So **the potential differences around a series circuit must add up to the potential difference across the cells**.

Increasing the voltage increases the current

In Topic 79, you saw that current is a measure of the *rate of flow of charge* around a circuit. One coulomb of charge passing each second is a current of one ampere.

If you increase the potential difference across your source of electrical energy – by adding an extra cell, or by turning up the voltage on the power pack – then you are increasing the electric force which is pushing electrons around the circuit. Not surprisingly, this will increase the rate of flow of charge around the circuit. It will increase the current.

At the beginning of the nineteenth century, George Ohm investigated this relationship between voltage and current. He found that, if you kept everything else constant, doubling the voltage doubled the current. To be more precise, **the current flowing through a metallic conductor is proportional to the potential difference**. This is called **Ohm's law**.

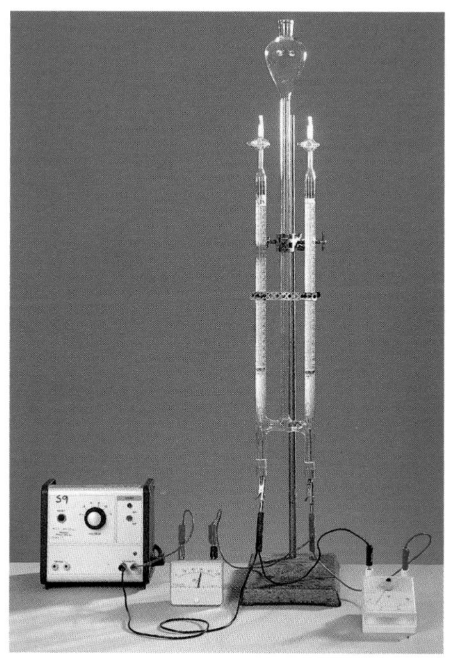

Fig. 80.7 Acidified water conducting electricity in a Hoffmann voltameter. The electrolyte does not follow Ohm's law. It is a **non-ohmic conductor**. Platinum electrodes produce hydrogen and oxygen, which you can see collecting at the top of the tubes. On which side does each gas collect?

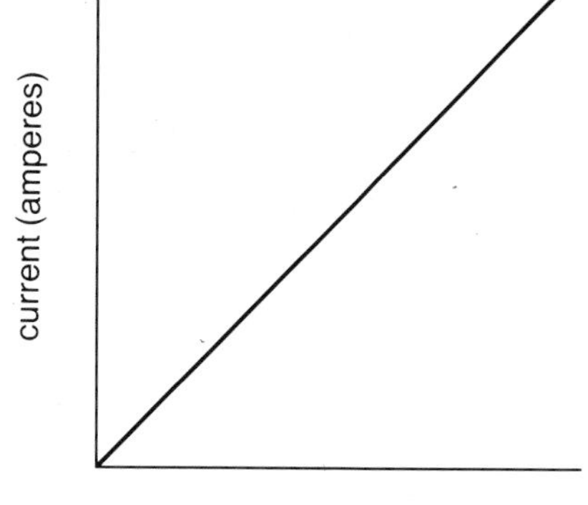

Fig. 80.5 If a conductor obeys Ohm's law, the current will increase in proportion to the potential difference. If you double the voltage, the current will also double. If the graph of current against potential difference is not a straight line, or does not pass through zero, then Ohm's law does not apply.

INVESTIGATION 80.1

Testing Ohm's law

You are going to see what happens to the current flowing through a conductor when you vary the voltage. You can try several different conductors.

1 Set up the circuit with your first material.

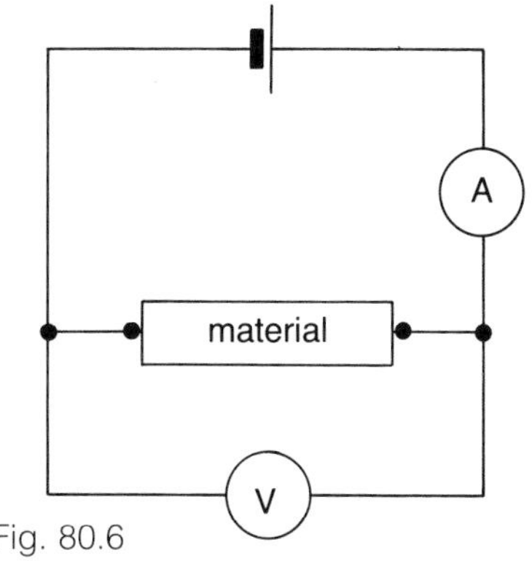

Fig. 80.6

Record the voltage, *V*, and the current, *I*. Do this for several different voltages. (You can adjust the voltage from the power pack, but you should measure it with the voltmeter.)

2 Repeat with other materials. You could try some or all of the following: graphite, lead, constantan wire, nichrome wire, a thermistor, sulphur, copper sulphate solution and a gas in a discharge tube.

3 For each material, plot a graph of *I* on the y axis against *V* on the x axis.

Questions

1 Were any of the materials you tested insulators? If so, which ones?

2 Why is it important to measure the voltage with a voltmeter, not from the power pack?

3 If a material obeys Ohm's law, then a graph of *I* against *V* should look like Figure 75.5. Did the materials you tested obey Ohm's law?

Questions

1 In the circuit below, voltmeter V_2 is reading 2 V.

a How much energy is transferred for each coulomb of charge passing between A and B?

b What is the total energy released per coulomb passing around the whole circuit?

c What energy must be released per coulomb passing through L_1?

d What will voltmeter V_1 read?

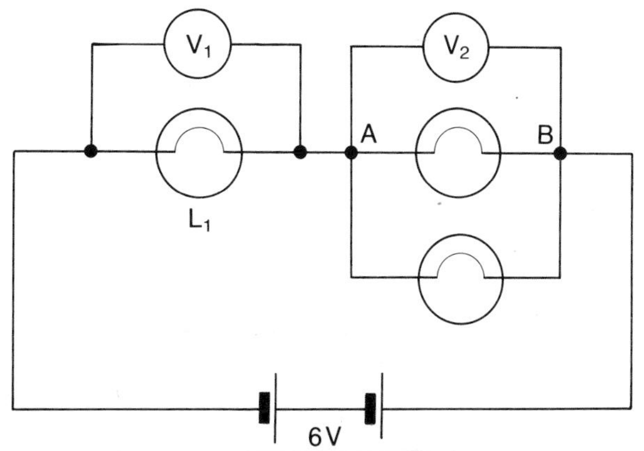

81 ELECTROLYSIS

Ionic compounds conduct electric current, and are changed by it into different substances.

Ionic compounds conduct electricity when molten or dissolved in water

If the substances that conduct electric current are investigated, there seems to be a simple rule. Metals conduct and non-metals do not – with the exception of carbon. However, there is a type of substance which will conduct electricity in some states but not in others. An example is sodium chloride.

Figure 81.1a shows sodium chloride behaving as a typical non-conductive non-metallic substance. But if the sodium chloride is heated enough to melt it, as in Figure 81.1b, a current begins to flow. Molten sodium chloride conducts an electric current well.

Sodium chloride dissolved in water will also conduct an electric current, despite the fact that neither sodium chloride nor water are good conductors when pure and separate from each other.

Many other substances behave in the same way, only conducting electricity when they are molten or dissolved in water. They include potassium bromide, sodium hydroxide, copper sulphate and zinc nitrate. All these substances are **ionic compounds**.

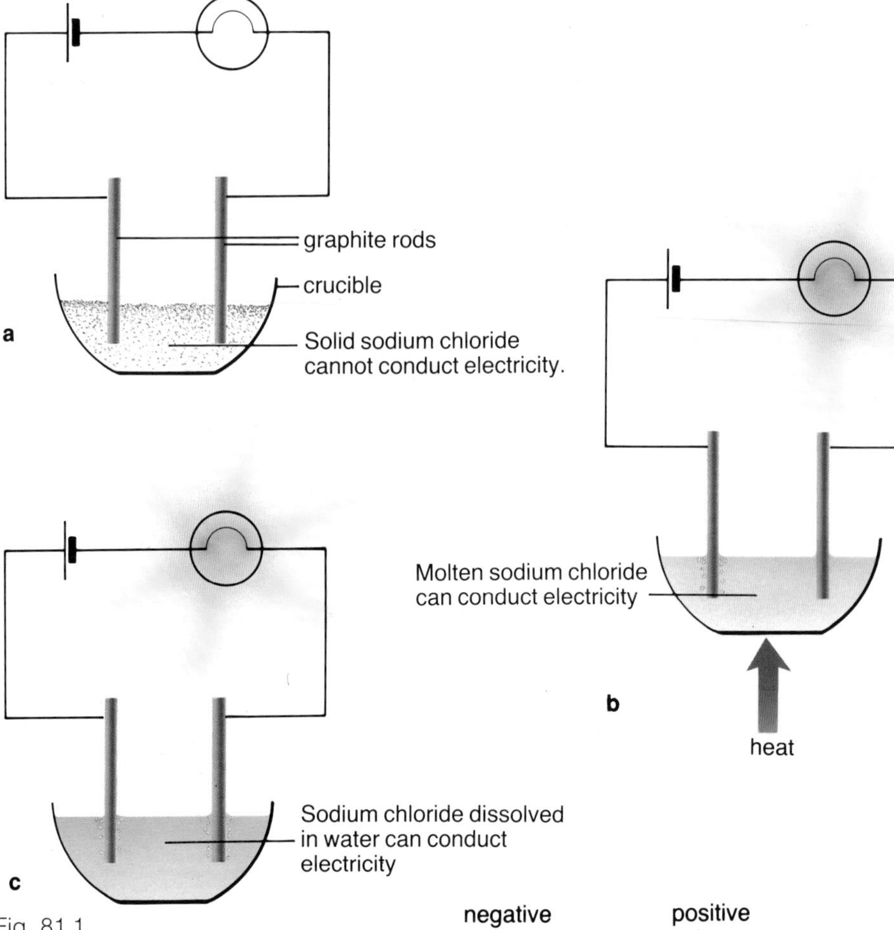

Fig. 81.1

Ions are attracted to positive and negative electrodes

How do molten or dissolved ionic substances conduct electricity? They do not have electrons which are free to move, as metals do, so the current cannot be carried as a drift of electrons. But they do contain positive and negative **ions**. Sodium chloride, for example, contains Na^+ and Cl^- ions. The movement of these ions makes up the electric current.

In Figure 81.2, the two graphite rods connected to the cell are called **electrodes**. The rod attached to the positive side of the cell becomes positively charged. It becomes a positive electrode, or **anode**. It attracts the negatively charged chloride ions, which move towards it.

The graphite rod attached to the negative side of the cell becomes negatively charged. It becomes a negative electrode, or **cathode**. It attracts the positively charged sodium ions, which move towards it.

This movement of charged particles between the electrodes is an electric current. An electric current flows between the electrodes, so the circuit is complete and the bulb lights.

Why won't solid sodium chloride conduct electricity? It does consist of Na^+ and Cl^- ions, but in the solid they are bound in one place. They are not free to move and so cannot make up an electric circuit. Molten sodium chloride, or sodium chloride dissolved in water, can conduct electricity because the ions are free to move around.

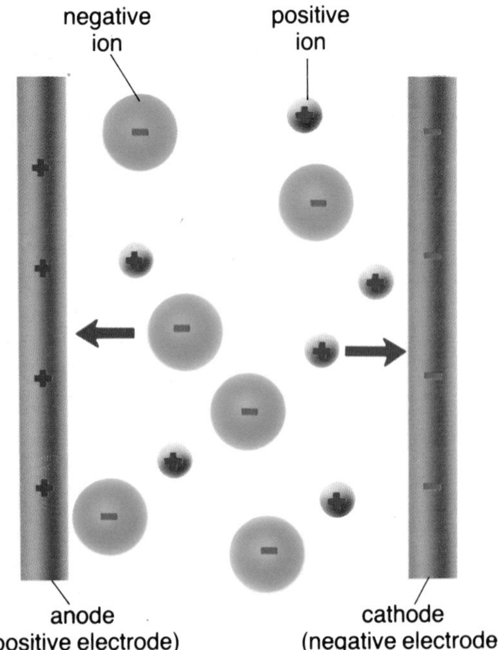

Fig. 81.2 If positive and negative ions are free to move – as they are when in solution or in a liquid state (and sometimes as a gas) – then negative ions go to the anode and positive ions go to the cathode.

Sodium chloride decomposes as a current flows through it

When an electric current flows through molten sodium chloride, bubbles are seen around the positive electrode. A choking yellow gas is produced. This gas is **chlorine**. At the negative electrode, molten **sodium metal** forms. The electric current is causing the sodium chloride to split up into the elements from which it is made.

$$2NaCl(l) \longrightarrow 2Na(l) + Cl_2(g)$$

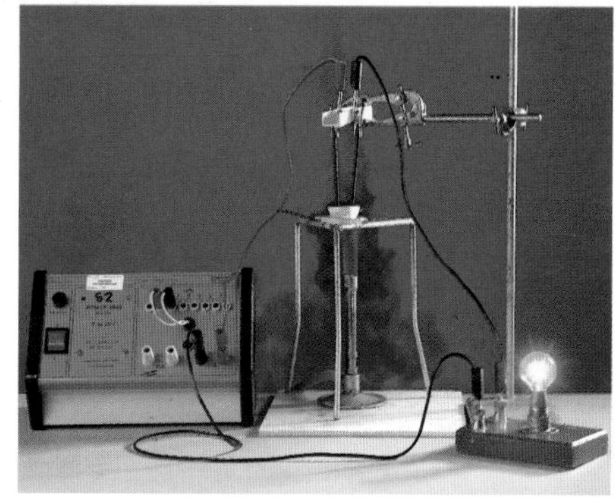

Fig. 81.3 Molten lead bromide conducts electricity. Electrolysis releases bromine gas and leaves lead in the crucible.

This is called **electrolysis**. Electrolysis is the decomposition of a compound, caused by electricity.

Sodium chloride *solution* also undergoes electrolysis as a current flows through it, but different products are formed. At the positive electrode, bubbles of **chlorine** gas form as for molten sodium chloride. But at the negative electrode, **hydrogen** gas forms, and, although you cannot see it, **sodium hydroxide** forms in solution. The products are different because the water is also involved in the electrolysis reaction.

$$2NaCl(aq) + 2H_2O(l) \rightarrow H_2(g) + Cl_2(g) + 2NaOH(aq)$$

All ionic compounds undergo similar electrolysis reactions, producing new substances when an electric current passes through them, when molten or in aqueous solution. They are known as **electrolytes**.

The mass of substance formed depends on the charge

At the anode, negative ions are attracted. They give up one or more electrons to the anode and become atoms. At the cathode, positive ions are gaining one or more electrons to become atoms. If more current flows then more electrons are being donated at the electrodes, so more atoms are being formed. More material is formed at the electrodes. Also, if the current flows for longer, then more material is formed since more electrons have been transferred.

EXTENSION

Table 81.1 Products of electrolysis of molten electrolytes

Electrolyte	*Positive ion*	*Substance at cathode*	*Negative ion*	*Substance at anode*
$Al_2O_3(l)$	Al^{3+}	aluminium	O^{2-}	oxygen
$PbBr_2(l)$	Pb^{2+}	lead	Br^-	bromine
$CaCl_2(l)$	Ca^{2+}	calcium	Cl^-	chlorine

Table 81.2 Products of electrolysis of aqueous electrolytes

Electrolyte	*Substance at cathode*	*Substance at anode*
$MgSO_4(aq)$	hydrogen	oxygen
$Zn(NO_3)_2(aq)$	hydrogen	oxygen
$KOH(aq)$	hydrogen	oxygen
$CuSO_4(aq)$	copper	oxygen
$CaCl_2(aq)$	hydrogen	chlorine
$AgNO_3(aq)$	silver	oxygen
$CuCl_2(aq)$	copper	chlorine
$H_2SO_4(aq)$	hydrogen	oxygen

What forms at each electrode?

During an electrolysis reaction, a new substance forms at each electrode. How can you predict what these new substances will be?

For *molten electrolytes*, this is quite easy. The positive metal ion is attracted to the cathode, so the metal element forms here. The negative non-metal ion is attracted to the anode, so the non-metal element forms here. Table 81.1 gives some examples.

For *electrolytes in aqueous solution*, things are a little more complicated. The substance formed at the cathode is usually hydrogen, unless the solution contains copper or silver ions. In this case, copper or silver will form at the cathode. The substance formed at the anode is usually oxygen, unless the solution contains chloride, bromide or iodide ions. In this case, chlorine, bromine or iodine will form at the anode, and may dissolve in the solution. Table 81.2 gives some examples.

Questions

1 a Why does sodium chloride conduct electricity when molten or in aqueous solution, but not when solid?

b A covalent compound like sugar will not conduct when solid, molten, or in aqueous solution. Explain why this is so.

2 Explain the terms:

a electrolysis

b electrolyte.

3 Which of the following substances are:

a conductors,

b non-conductors,

c electrolytes?

A zinc chloride (aq) **B** mercury **C** sodium hydroxide (aq) **D** sulphur **E** iron **F** water

4 What forms at each electrode when the following are electrolysed?

a $KCl(l)$ **b** $NaBr(l)$
c $MgO(l)$ **d** $PbI_2(l)$
e $Ag_2SO_4(aq)$ **f** $CuNO_3(aq)$
g $H_2SO_4(aq)$ **h** $MgCl_2(aq)$

5 Electrolysis is used extensively in the chemical industry for making such things as sodium hydroxide solution, sodium and magnesium metals, and chlorine gas. Explain how each of these could be made.

82 ELECTROCHEMICAL CELLS

An electrochemical cell is a portable electrical energy source.

A cell can be made from two metals and an electrolyte

Electrons in different metals can have different energies. If these metals are placed in a conducting liquid, or **electrolyte**, a difference in electrical potential is set up between them. A pair of different metals arranged in this way is an **electrochemical cell**. This arrangement transfers chemical energy to electrical energy.

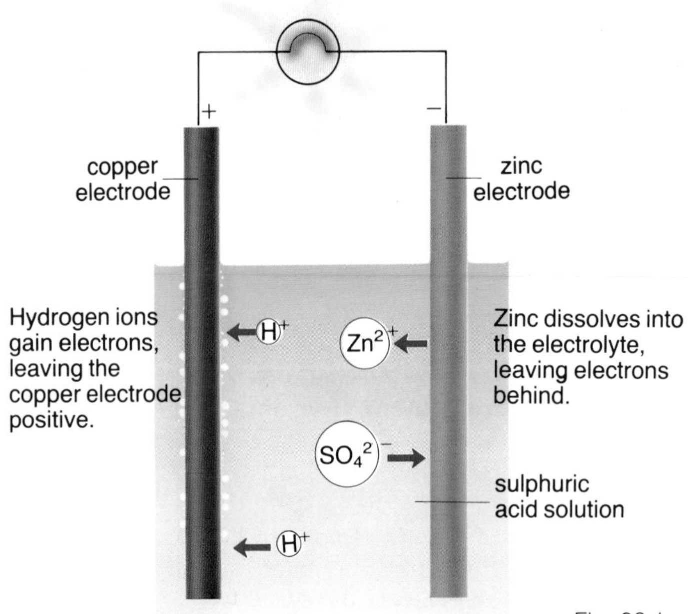

Fig. 82.1 A simple cell

INVESTIGATION 82.1

Making an electrochemical cell

Living tissues contain solutions which will conduct electricity – they are electrolytes. So you can make an electrochemical cell using tissue from plants such as lemons or potatoes.

1 Cut several slits in a potato. Into each slit push a rod of a different metal. You may be able to use some or all of the following: zinc, copper, lead, iron or nickel.

2 Using a voltmeter, measure and record the potential difference across different pairs of metals.

3 Using the pair which produces the greatest potential difference, see if you can light a bulb from them.

4 WEAR SAFETY GOGGLES. Remove this pair of metals from the potato, clean them, and put them into dilute sulphuric acid in place of the potato. Complete a circuit, and observe carefully what happens.

A dry cell uses zinc and carbon electrodes

A simple cell can be made using copper and zinc electrodes in a beaker of dilute sulphuric acid. It produces a potential difference of about 1 V. You can increase this potential difference by using a whole row of cells connected in series. This is called a **battery** of cells, or just a battery.

But this cell does not work for very long. The zinc electrode is gradually eaten away by the acid. Hydrogen bubbles collect on the copper electrode, insulating it and stopping it from working.

A modern **dry cell**, such as an ordinary torch battery, uses electrodes of zinc and carbon. The electrolyte is not a liquid, but a paste of ammonium chloride. The zinc electrode doubles as the outside case of the battery.

Like the simple cell, this one would soon stop working as hydrogen bubbles built up on the carbon electrode. But in the dry cell, manganese dioxide is packed around the carbon electrode. The manganese dioxide oxidises the hydrogen as soon as it forms, converting the hydrogen to water. So this cell works for much longer than the simple cell.

But even this dry cell will not last for ever. Gradually, the zinc electrode will be used up. As the zinc electrode is also the outside case of the cell, the cell could begin to leak. Eventually, the cell will become useless. This sort of cell, which can only be used once, is called a **primary cell**.

Despite their fairly short life, dry cells like this are still very widely used because they are cheap. They produce a potential difference of about 1.5 V.

Fig. 82.2 The cells on the left are all 1.5 V cells. They are all primary cells and can be used only once. The cells on the right are 1.2 V rechargeable cells, except for the rectangular one which is a battery containing seven 1.2 V cells. The small mercury battery in the centre provides 5.6 V and might be used in photographic equipment or in a calculator.

Alkaline cells are more expensive, but last longer

Alkaline cells, like dry cells, have electrodes of zinc and carbon. But they contain potassium hydroxide, not ammonium chloride, as the electrolyte. As potassium hydroxide is a strong alkali, it is very important that these cells should not leak. So each cell is surrounded by a strong leakproof steel case. The steel case does not take part in the reaction.

A typical alkaline cell provides a potential difference of 1.5 V. It lasts about six times longer than an ordinary dry cell. Alkaline cells are currently the most popular type on the market.

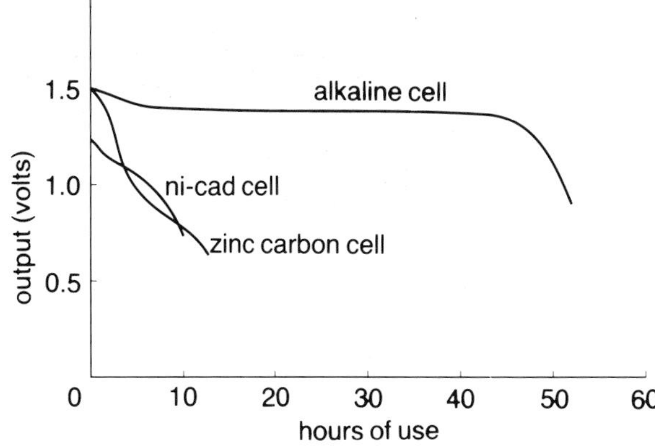

Fig. 82.3 The approximate life-span of three types of 1.5 V cell, with similar conditions of use.

INVESTIGATION 82.2

Making a lead–acid cell

This experiment will probably be demonstrated for you. You should wear safety goggles if you are anywhere near the apparatus.

1 Dip two lead plates into sulphuric acid. Connect a voltmeter to the plates. Connect a power pack to the plates, and apply 4 volts across them. Observe what happens. Look for any differences in the two plates.

2 Disconnect the power pack, but leave the voltmeter in position. What happens?

You have made a simple rechargeable cell. It transfers electrical energy to chemical energy, then back again.

3 Try lighting a lamp from your lead–acid cell. Does the cell's energy storage improve or get worse after a few charge/discharge cycles?

Secondary cells are rechargeable

The lead–acid cell in Investigation 82.2, like the cells already described in this topic, transfers chemical energy to electrical energy. But it can do something which the other cells cannot. It can transfer electrical energy to chemical energy. It can be **recharged**.

Cells which can be recharged are called **secondary cells**. A car battery contains a collection of lead–acid cells, which are recharged using electrical energy generated by the engine when the car is running.

But the lead in a car battery makes it very heavy, and the sulphuric acid is very corrosive. A more practical, portable and rechargeable cell is the **nickel–cadmium** or **ni-cad cell**. These cells can be recharged up to 700 times so, even though they are more expensive than alkaline cells, they soon pay for themselves. Ni-cad cells use nickel as the negative electrode, cadmium as the positive electrode, and potassium hydroxide as the electrolyte.

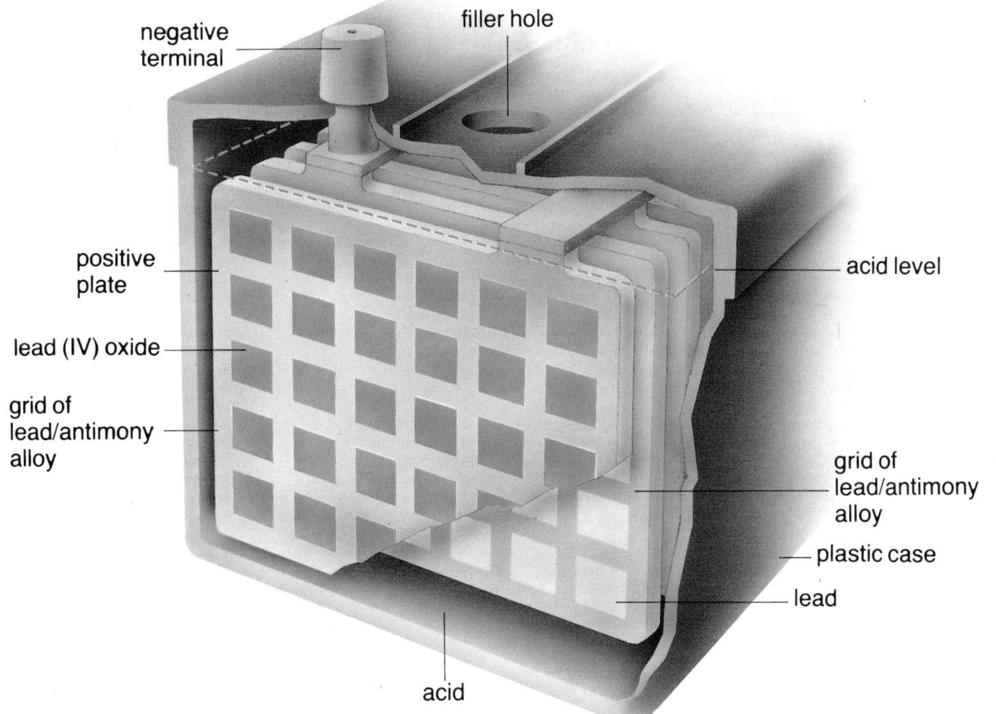

Fig. 82.4 A car battery

Questions

1 Suppose an alkaline cell costs 40p. The same size ni-cad cell costs £1.20. A recharger for four ni-cad cells costs £8.00.

a If the ni-cads can be recharged 600 times, how much money can be saved by buying a set of four ni-cads and a recharger instead of alkaline cells? (Assume that a single charge provides one third of the energy of an alkaline cell.)

b What are the disadvantages of having a single set of ni-cads?

2 Using the information in Figure 82.3, suggest which type of cell you would buy and use for each of the following purposes. Give reasons for your choice. Choose from zinc/carbon, alkaline or ni-cad cells.

a a torch you are taking on a camping trip

b a model aircraft

c a personal stereo

83 RESISTANCE

The movement of electrons through a circuit is resisted by the atoms of the materials through which they pass.

A high voltage produces only a low current if resistance is large

If there is a potential difference, or voltage, across the ends of a conductor, a current flows through the conductor. But, for the same voltage, you do not always get the same current. Some conductors will allow a large current to flow, while others will only allow a small current to flow.

The current you get for a particular voltage depends on a property of the conductor called **resistance**. A conductor with a high resistance 'resists' the current, and only a small current flows. A low resistance allows a higher current for a particular voltage. The equation linking current, voltage and resistance is:

voltage = current x **resistance**

V = I x **R**

Resistance is measured in units called **ohms**. The symbol for ohms is Ω.

A resistance of one ohm carries a current of one ampere if there is a potential difference of one volt across it.

You can work out the resistance of a conductor by measuring voltage and current, and then rearranging the above equation:

$$\text{resistance} = \frac{\text{potential difference (voltage)}}{\text{current}}$$

This equation is a definition of resistance. You can use this equation even if the conductor you are using does not obey Ohm's law.

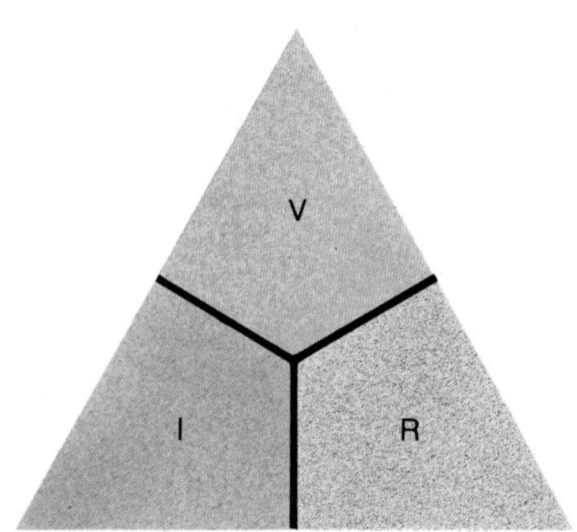

Fig. 83.1 Formula triangle for V = IR. Cover up what you want to find. For example, if you cover I you are left with $\frac{V}{R}$.

So $I = \frac{V}{R}$.

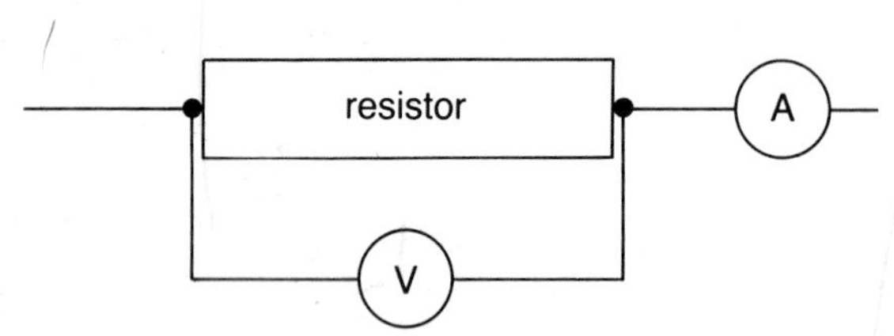

Fig. 83.2 If the ammeter reads 2 A and the voltmeter 12 V, the resistance is 12 V divided by 2 A, which is 6 Ω .

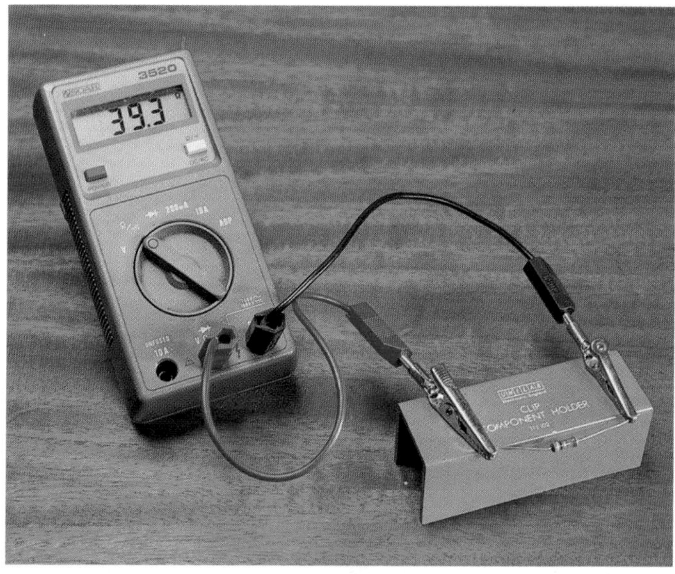

Fig. 83.3 A multimeter is used to measure directly the resistance of this resistor. It reads 39.3 Ω .

INVESTIGATION 83.1

Investigating resistance

A conductor with a high resistance is sometimes called a **resistor**. Nichrome wire, often used in heating elements, is a conductor with a high resistance.

1 Take a piece of nichrome wire and cut it into three equal lengths. Make a suitable circuit and find the resistance of each length. Draw your circuit, and record your results.

2 Using the same circuit, join the three pieces of wire in series, as in Figure 83.4a. What is their resistance? How does resistance vary with length?

3 Test your answer to step 2 by using a different length of nichrome wire. How can you calculate the total resistance of resistors in series?

4 Now make another circuit, this time with your three original pieces of nichrome wire in parallel, as in Figure 83.4b. What is the resistance now?

5 How does the cross-sectional area of three wires in parallel compare to the cross-sectional area of a single wire? How does resistance vary with the cross-sectional area of a wire?

6 Can you find a rule which enables you to work out the total resistance when resistors are arranged in parallel? (The answer is on this page – but don't look yet!)

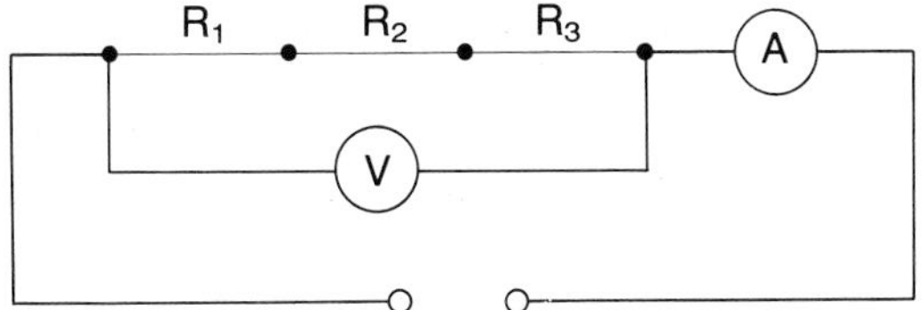

Fig. 83.4a Three resistors in series

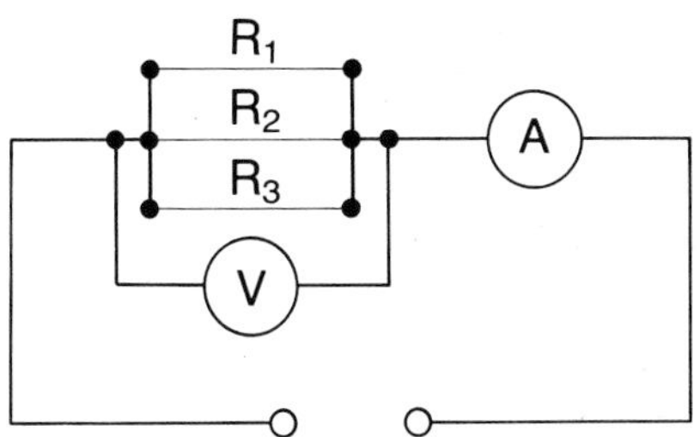

Fig. 83.4b Three resistors in parallel

Resistors in series and parallel

In a series circuit, resistance increases as more resistors are added. Each one restricts the flow more, and the resistances add together. In a *series* circuit:

total resistance = $R_1 + R_2 + R_3$ and so on.

In a parallel circuit, each resistor provides an alternative route for the current. The more resistors there are, the more alternative routes there are.

Having two resistors in parallel is rather like having a small side road in parallel to a main road. Even if the side road is narrow and difficult to get along, it can increase the traffic flow. A similar thing happens with resistors. When two or more resistors are arranged in parallel, the overall resistance is *reduced*. The total resistance will always be *less* than that of any individual resistor.

In fact, when resistors are arranged in *parallel*:

$$\frac{1}{\text{total resistance}} = \frac{1}{R_1} + \frac{1}{R_2} + \frac{1}{R_3} \text{ and so on.}$$

EXTENSION

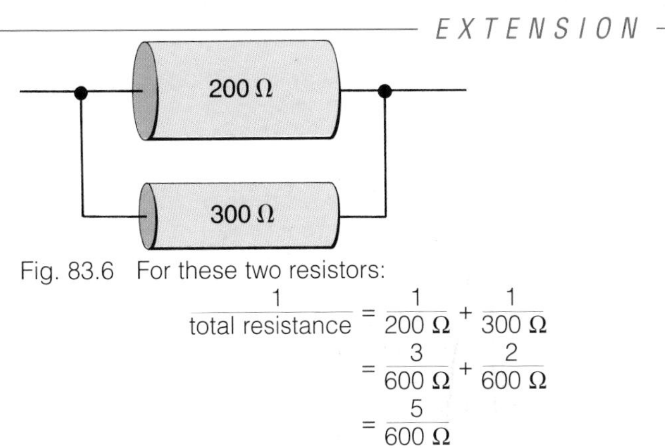

Fig. 83.6 For these two resistors:

$$\frac{1}{\text{total resistance}} = \frac{1}{200\ \Omega} + \frac{1}{300\ \Omega}$$
$$= \frac{3}{600\ \Omega} + \frac{2}{600\ \Omega}$$
$$= \frac{5}{600\ \Omega}$$
$$= \frac{1}{120\ \Omega}$$

So the resistance of the combination is 120 Ω. It is important to remember to take the reciprocal ($\frac{1}{x}$) of the final addition.

A rheostat is a variable resistor

A rheostat is a conductor whose resistance can be varied. It is a variable resistor. A slider moves along a coiled resistance wire. This increases or decreases the resistance.

A rheostat in series with a lamp or motor can be used to control the current going through it. The larger the resistance, the smaller the current.

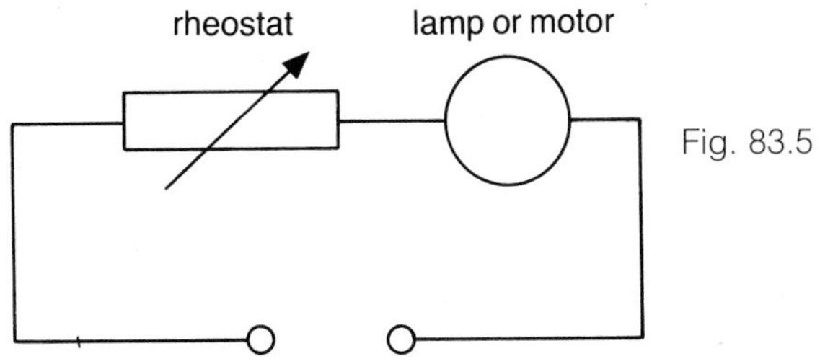

Fig. 83.5

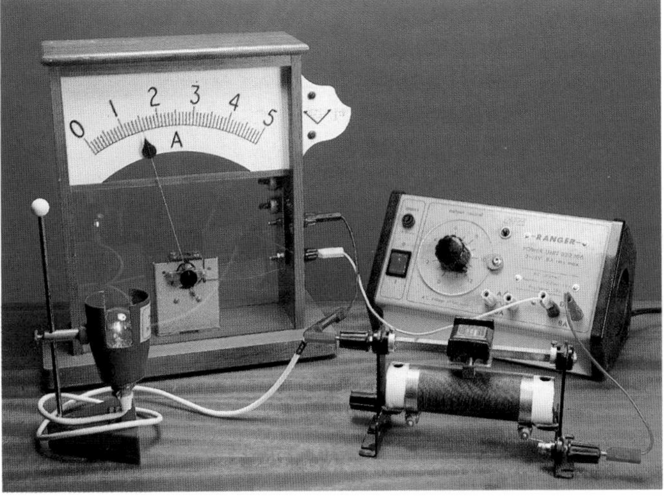

Fig. 83.7 A rheostat can be used to control the current passing through a lamp.

A change in the physical conditions can change resistance

Ohm's law applies to metals if the physical conditions do not change. If the wire gets hot or its length changes, the resistance will change. A graph of current against voltage will only be a straight line if the resistance stays the same. The steepness or **gradient** of the line shows if the resistance is changing. If current is plotted on the y axis a **steep** gradient shows a **low** resistance (Figure 83.8a). This is why you often see current–voltage graphs plotted the other way round (Figure 83.8b) – so the gradient shows what the resistance is doing! Notice that the graphs are symmetrical, showing that it does not matter which way the current is flowing through the resistor. For either graph, if the resistance changes, the straight line becomes a curve. If you use the apparatus of Figure 80.6 to investigate a light bulb, you will get a graph like Figure 83.9. As the voltage increases, the graph gets shallower and the resistance increases. This is because the wire in the filament gets hotter. The atoms vibrate more and it is harder for the electrons to move through the metal. When a light bulb is cold it has a lower resistance and draws more current. The heating effect causes the filament to glow and its resistance to rise.

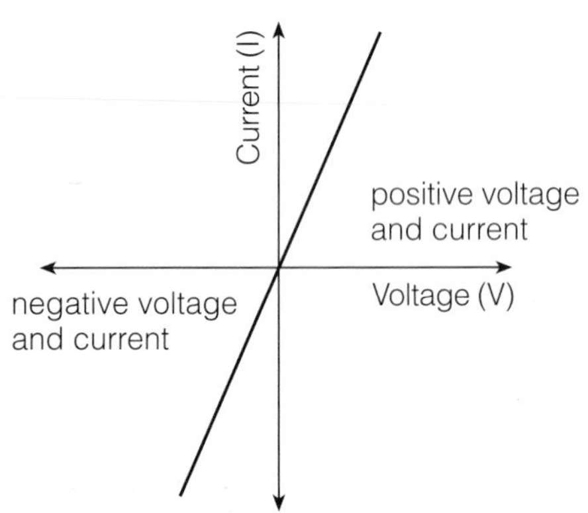

Fig. 83.8a The graph of current against voltage for a resistor is a straight line if the resistor does not get hot. A steep line shows a high current for a small voltage – a low resistance.

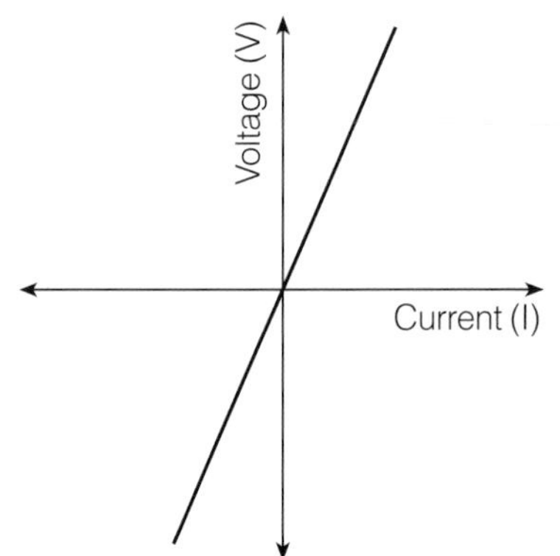

Fig. 83.8b The graph of voltage against current. A steep gradient (voltage/current) means a high resistance.

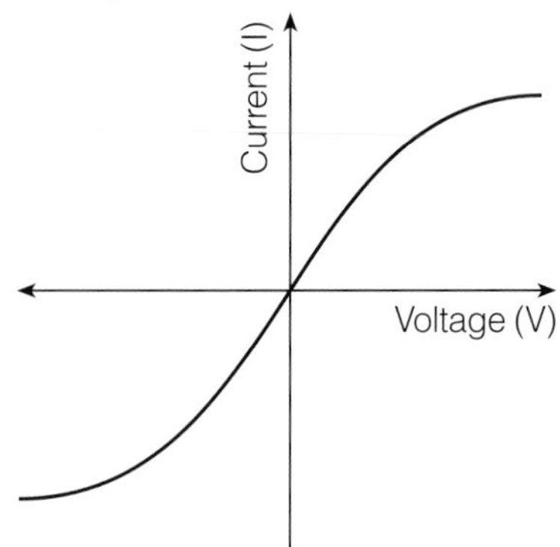

Fig. 83.9 The current–voltage graph for a filament lamp shows the resistance increasing.

Some resistors can act as sensors

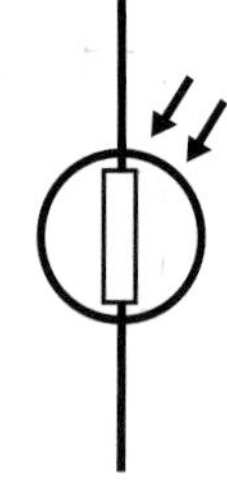

Fig. 83.10 Two special resistors. The one on the green board is a light-dependent resistor, and the stripey one is a thermistor.

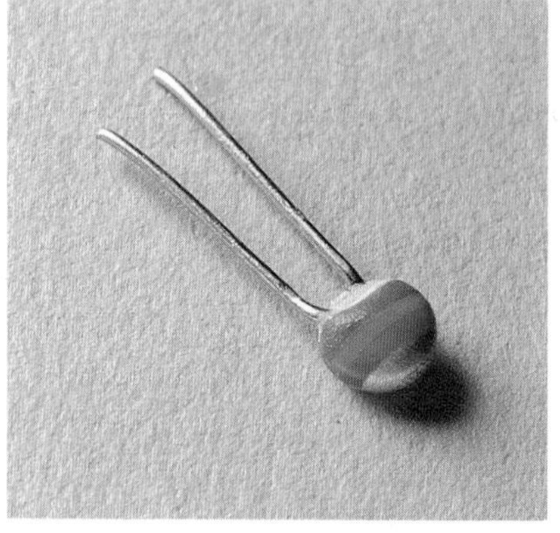

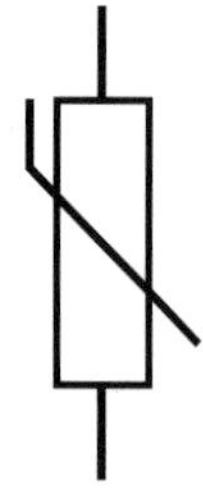

The light-dependent resistor (LDR) and the thermistor are special types of resistor. The LDR is sensitive to light. As the light intensity increases, its resistance falls. This can be used to control circuits for automatic lights or street lamps. The thermistor is sensitive to temperature. Unlike a metal, a thermistor can be made so that its resistance falls as the temperature increases. A thermistor can be used to measure temperature, and is often used to control the heat production in a heating system.

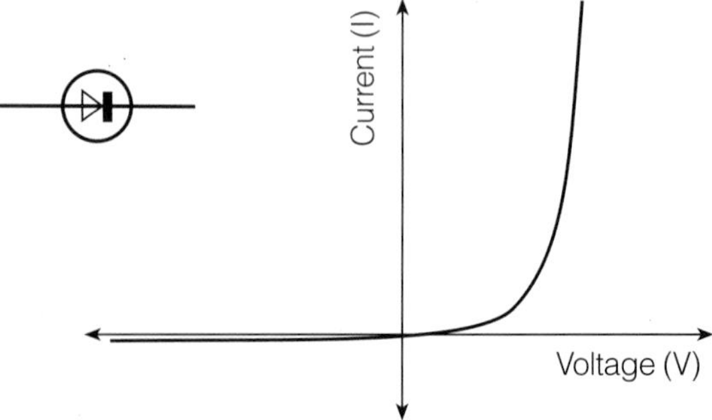

Fig. 83.11 A diode conducts in one direction, but not the other. The direction of **conventional current** flow is shown by the arrow on the symbol. As the diode only lets current go one way, it converts a.c. to a type of d.c. (Topic 87).

INVESTIGATION 83.2

Voltage–current characteristics of a silicon diode

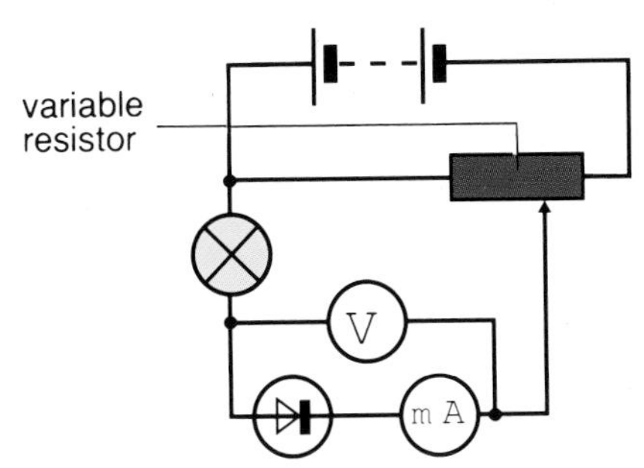

Fig. 83.12

1 Set up the circuit as shown in Figure 83.12. The lamp stops the diode passing too much current, which could overheat the diode or short-out the power pack.

2 Adjust the voltage across the diode and measure the current. Display your results in a suitable way.

3 When would you say the diode 'switches on'?

Questions

1 A lamp is run from the mains, which provides a voltage of 230 V. The lamp draws a current of 1.3 A. What is its resistance?

2 A kettle has a resistance of 23 Ω.

a If it is connected to the mains, what current does it draw?

b How many joules does each coulomb of charge transfer?

c Into what form of energy is this electrical energy transferred?

3 The resistors below are all made of the same material.

a Which has the highest resistance?

b Which has the lowest resistance?

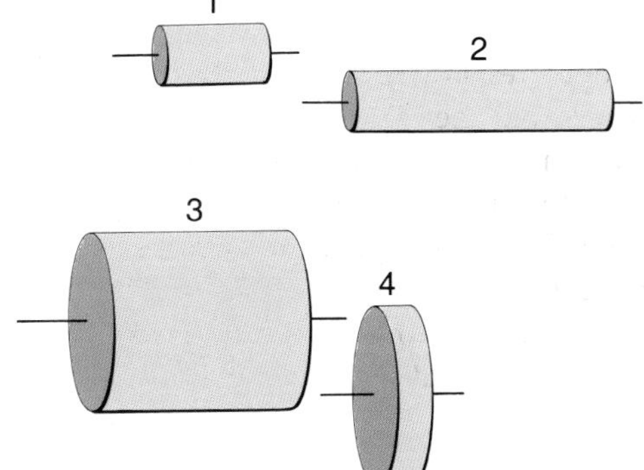

4 A 60 W light bulb draws a current of about 0.26 A from the 230 V mains.

a What is the resistance of the filament?

A cold filament has a resistance of 16 Ω.

b What current flows in the filament at the instant the light is switched on?

5 If you are provided with three resistors of 1 Ω, 2 Ω and 3 Ω, what different values of resistance can you get by making up different series and parallel circuits?

6 LED is short for light-emitting diode. LEDs are used as indicator lights, e.g. on a video recorder, and in some kinds of digital displays. The chart shows voltages and currents for an LED.

V (volts)	0	1.0	1.5	2.0	3.0	4.0	5.0
I (milliamps)	0	0.0	0.3	10.0	61.0	125.0	236.0

a Plot a graph of voltage against current.

b Does an LED obey Ohm's law?

c What happens to the slope of the graph with increasing voltage or current? What happens to the resistance?

d Because the current rises so quickly, an LED must be protected with a series resistor.

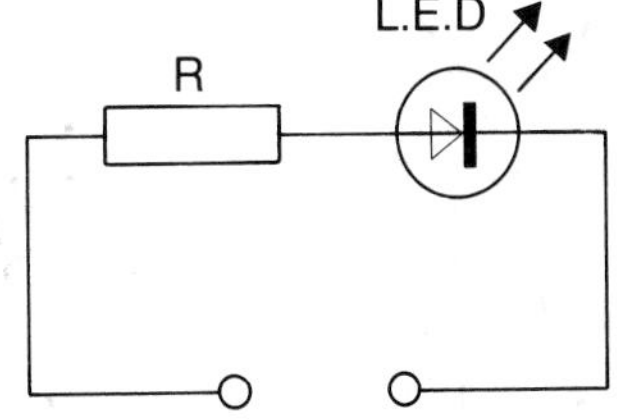

A circuit designer wishes to restrict the current to 20 mA. What potential difference does this correspond to?

e If the supply voltage is 9 V, what is the excess voltage? (How much bigger is the supply than your answer to part d?)

f If the potential difference across the series resistance equals this excess then the current through the whole circuit will be 20 mA. What value of resistor produces this potential difference for a current of 20 mA?

EXTENSION

84 ELECTRICAL POWER

The amount of energy transferred depends on current, voltage and time. The electrical power of a device is the rate at which this energy transfer takes place.

Resistance in a circuit always causes a conversion to heat

As electrons pass through a wire, they transfer some of their energy to the atoms in the metal. This causes heating. As a current flows through a resistor, the resistor gets very hot.

Electric heaters, kettles, toasters, hair driers and light bulbs all use this heating effect of an electric current. So do **fuses**.

A fuse is a built-in 'weak link' in a circuit. If a fault occurs in a circuit, too much current may flow, which could cause damage or even start a fire. So a piece of thin, tin-plated copper wire is included in the circuit. If too much current flows, this fuse heats and melts, breaking the circuit.

Electrical power isn't only transferred as heat. Motors and loudspeakers produce movement and sound. Microwave ovens and radios produce electromagnetic energy.

INVESTIGATION 84.1

Resistance and heating

1 Make this circuit.
2 Measure and record the voltage across the light bulb as you vary the current which passes through it.
3 Plot a graph of voltage against current. Does the filament obey Ohm's law?
4 Plot a graph of resistance against current.
5 What is the resistance of the hot filament?
6 What is the resistance of the cold filament?
7 Into what form of energy is the electrical energy transferred?

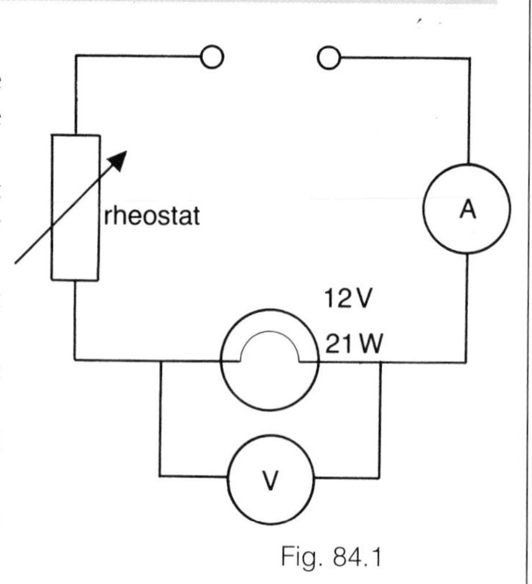

Fig. 84.1

Energy transferred = potential difference x current x time

In Topic 80, you saw that potential difference is a difference in electrical energy between two points. A more complete definition of potential difference is:
the potential difference between two points is the energy transferred by one coulomb of charge moved by the electric field between these two points.

If charge moves through a potential difference, energy is transferred. You can calculate the amount of energy transferred using the equation:

energy transferred	=	**potential difference**	x	**charge**
(in joules)		(in volts)		(in coulombs)
E	=	***V***	x	***Q***

Charge is difficult to measure. It is much easier to measure current. The charge passing a point is current multiplied by time:

charge = current x time

$Q = I \times$ time

So **E** = **potential difference** x **current** x **time**

For example, if 0.25 A flows through a bulb connected to a 12 V power supply for 2 s, then the energy transferred is:

energy released = 12 x 0.25 x 2 = **6 J**.

So the rate of energy transfer is **3 J per second** or **3 W**.

This bulb must be a 12 V, 3 W bulb. If you look at a selection of bulbs, you will see that most of them are labelled with their voltage and wattage.

Fig. 84.2 Both of these bulbs give the same light output. The electronic bulb on the right transfers 11 J of electrical energy per second. The filament bulb on the left transfers an extra 49 J per second, and has an average life of 1000 hours, which is eight times shorter than the electronic bulb.

Power = potential difference x current

In Topic 28, you saw that:

$$\textbf{power} = \frac{\textbf{energy transferred}}{\textbf{time}}$$

We now know that, in an electrical circuit:

energy transferred = p.d. x **current** x **time**

where p.d. stands for potential difference. If we substitute this into the 'power' equation:

$$\textbf{power} = \frac{\textbf{p.d} \times \textbf{current} \times \textbf{time}}{\textbf{time}}$$

So **power**	=	**p.d.**	x	**current**
(in watts)		(in volts)		(in amperes)
Power	=	***V***	x	***I***

For example, if a light bulb carrying 0.25 A is connected to a 240 V supply, it would have a power of 240 V x 0.25 A = **60 W**. Notice that this is much more than a 12 V bulb carrying the same current.

You could also calculate how much energy your light bulb uses over a certain period of time. From the above equations.

energy transferred = power x **time** (in seconds)

So if you left your 60 W light bulb switched on for 6 hours, all evening, the energy you have used is:

60 W × 6 × 60 × 60 = 1 296 000 J.

Quite a lot of energy!

Questions

1 The two kettles below both have a 2.4 kW element. The water in them needs to be heated by 90 °C. It requires 4.2 J to heat 1 g by 1 °C. Each kettle holds 1700 g of water.

a What current does one of these elements carry when plugged in?

b What resistance does the element have?

c The element in the jug kettle is shorter than the other element. What does this suggest about the thickness of the wire inside?

d What energy is required to heat the water in either kettle?

e How long would it take to provide this energy?

f In practice, it takes a little longer. Suggest why this is.

g It is unsafe to operate a kettle with its element exposed. Why is this?

h A jug kettle's element can be covered using less water than the conventional kettle. Explain why this would save energy.

EXTENSION

Other methods of calculating power

Since:
power = $V \times I$ and $V = I \times R$
then:
power = $I \times I \times R = I^2 R$

Can you show that:
power = $\frac{V^2}{R}$?

These equations enable you to calculate power if you know resistance and either current or voltage.

EXTENSION

2 In a heating experiment, a heater runs at 12 V and a current of 3 A is measured. The experiment runs for 35 minutes. This increases the temperature of 1 kg of water by 18°C.

a How much energy is transferred per second?

b How much energy is transferred in 35 minutes?

c If this energy produces a rise of 18°C, how much energy would be needed to increase the temperature of 1 kg of water by 1°C?

d If the voltage was increased to 24 V, what temperature rise would you expect?

3 A 6 V motor lifts a 15 N weight through 1 m.

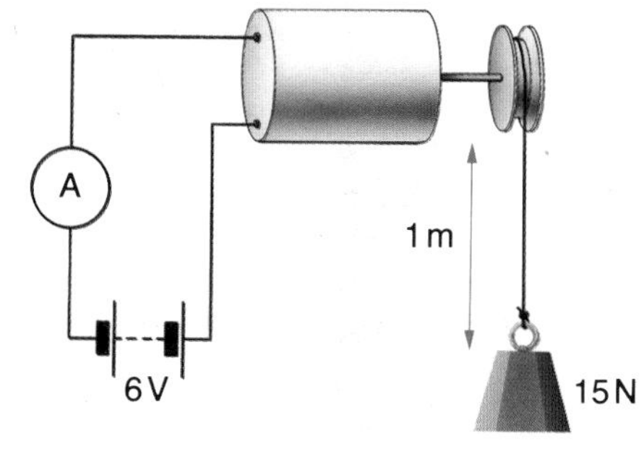

a What work is done?

b If the ammeter reads an average of 0.3 A, what is the power of the motor?

c The motor takes 10 s to lift the mass. What electrical energy is used?

d How efficient is the motor?

e Into what forms is the wasted energy transferred?

4 The chart below shows how rated current varies with diameter of fuse wire. The rated current is the current the fuse wire can carry without deterioration.

a The fuse blows at approximately 1.75 times the rated current. Plot a graph of current which will blow the fuse, against diameter of fuse wire.

b What thickness of wire is needed for

i a 3 A fuse,

ii a 13 A fuse?

Rated current (A)	5	15	30	60	100
Diameter of tinned copper wire (mm)	0.2	0.5	0.9	1.4	2.0

INVESTIGATION 84.2

Energetic elements

You work in the research and design department of an electrical company which makes electrical heating elements. You are asked to design a mini immersion heater which can be used in a car, to fit into a mug and heat water for hot drinks. The diagram shows the kind of heater to be used.

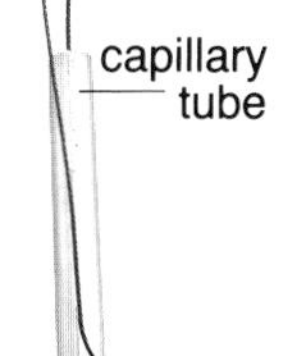

Fig. 84.3

Here is some information you will need in designing your heater.

- The heating element is to be used at 12 V.
- It takes 4.2 J to heat 1 g of water by 1°C.
- When water is heated, the amount of energy it gains is mass × 4.2 × temperature rise.

1 Make a prototype heater. Use it to heat some water, and measure the temperature rise for a particular time. Calculate the energy used and the power rating of your heater. Present your results in a suitable way.

2 Your company's main competitor makes a similar product, rated at 50 W. How much energy does this transfer each second? Your company decides that their product will be rated at 60 W. Why would this heat water faster than their rival's heater?

EXTENSION

3 Now work on improving your heating element. Try changing its length. What effect does this have? Design an element which will use 60 W. How long will it take to boil a mug of water?

85 ELECTROMAGNETISM

Electrons moving around a circuit produce a magnetic field, which can be switched on and off.

A current in a wire produces a magnetic field

In 1820, Hans Oersted noticed that a wire carrying a current placed above a compass caused a deflection (movement) of the compass needle. We now know that the electrons moving along the wire produce a magnetic field. The field is circular, around the wire.

Fig. 85.1 Iron filings scattered around a wire carrying a current show the circular pattern of the magnetic field.

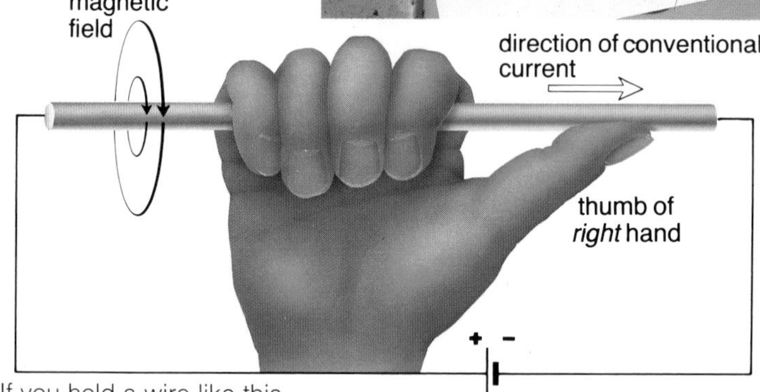

Fig. 85.2 If you hold a wire like this, with your right thumb pointing in the direction of the conventional current – that is, from positive to negative – then your fingers point along the direction of the magnetic field lines. If the current is reversed then the magnetic field is reversed. If the current is increased then the magnetic field is increased.

INVESTIGATION 85.1

Magnetic field around a solenoid

1 Make a long thin coil – a solenoid – by winding wire around a pencil. Pass a current of a few amperes through your solenoid. You will need a rheostat or a 12V lamp in your circuit, to restrict the current.

2 Use a plotting compass to plot the magnetic field around the solenoid. Record your results as a diagram.

3 Replace the pencil with an iron nail. Is the magnetic field stronger, weaker or the same as with the pencil? How can you test it, using a plotting compass?

4 Find out how the strength of the magnetic field varies with the current flowing through the solenoid.

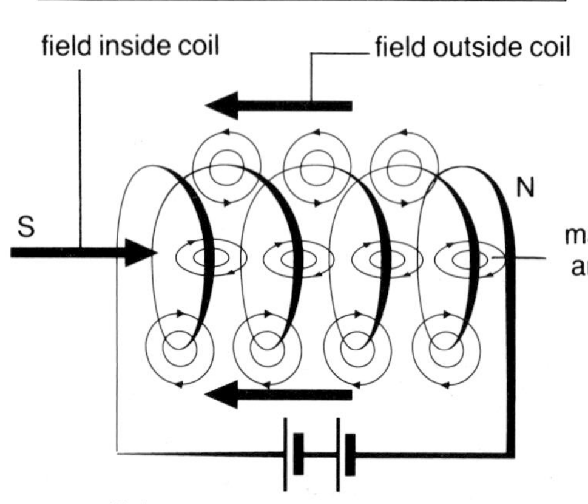

Fig. 85.3 The magnetic field around a coil carrying a current. The field is increased by: more turns more current an iron core.

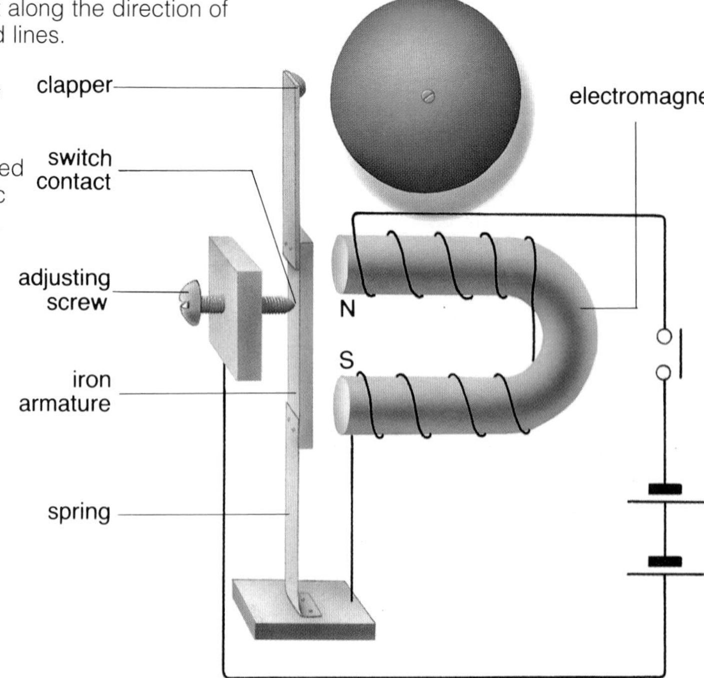

Fig. 85.4 An electric bell uses an electromagnet to pull the clapper onto the bell. When a current flows in the circuit, the magnetism induced in the coil attracts the armature towards the electromagnet. This breaks the circuit, so that no current flows through the electromagnet. The armature is no longer attracted to the electromagnet, and falls back. This remakes the circuit, and the armature is attracted again.

A relay is an electromagnetic switch

Figure 85.4 shows how a bell works. The circuit contains a coil, an armature and a switch contact. These are connected so that the circuit keeps switching itself on and off. The same idea can be used to switch a *different* circuit on and off. This is called a **relay**.

Figure 85.5 shows a relay circuit. When switch A is closed, a current flows in coil C. This attracts the armature, closing the switch contacts, D. So the lamp will light up. Switch A switches on the lamp, even though there is no electrical contact between them.

What advantage does this arrangement have? You could use it if the circuit you wanted to switch on or off was working at a *high* voltage and you wanted your switch circuit to be at a *lower* voltage. In the example shown in the diagram, the switch circuit could be battery operated, while the lamp could be a mains lamp supplied with 230 V. Or you might want to switch on the pump for a bathroom shower, which operates off the mains. It could be dangerous to do this directly with wet hands, but a relay circuit at a low voltage could be used to close contacts in the mains circuit outside the bathroom, switching the mains circuit on safely.

A car starter motor is also switched on and off using a relay. The starter motor has to be connected to the battery with cables nearly 1 cm thick, as up to 400 A can flow through the cables when it is switched on. It would be awkward to have the ignition switch in this circuit, because these thick cables would have to run out to the steering column, where the ignition switch is usually placed. So the ignition switch is made to be part of a relay circuit, running on a much smaller current and using much thinner wires. When the ignition key is turned, the relay circuit is closed, the electromagnet closes the contacts and starts the motor.

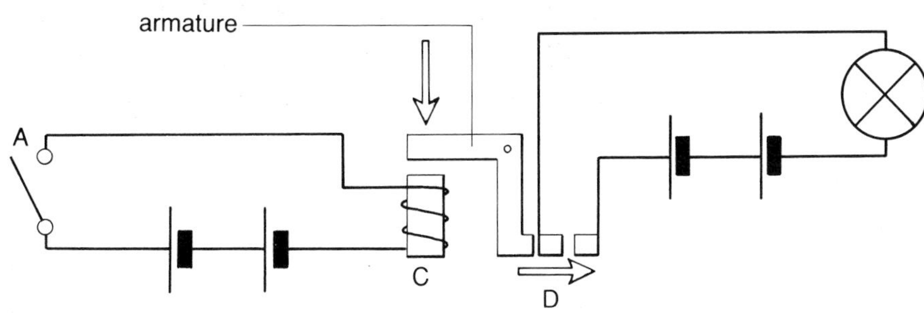

Fig. 85.5 A relay circuit

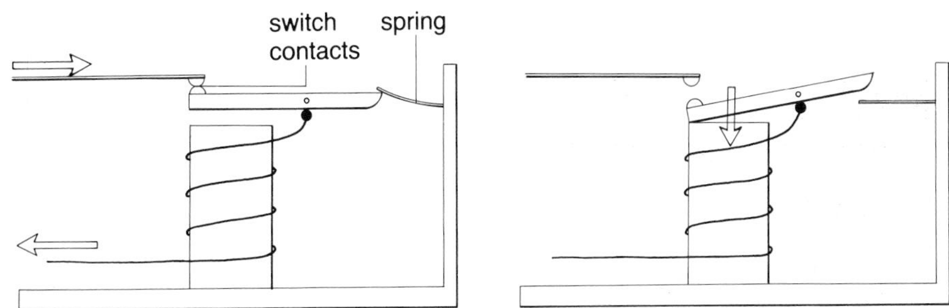

Fig. 85.6 A simple circuit breaker. If the current in the coil is too large, the switch is opened. Some circuit breakers combine the electromagnetic coil with a heating coil that warms either a bi-metallic strip or wax to open contacts. Other circuit breakers may rely on the heating effect alone.

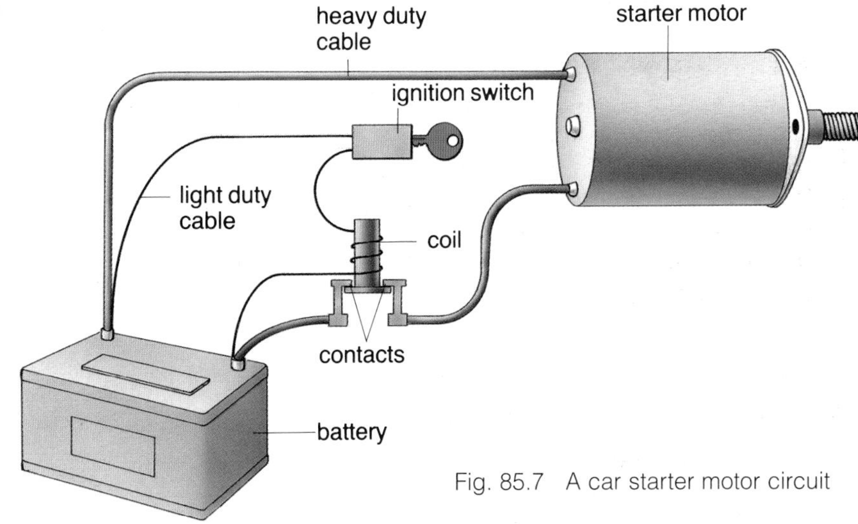

Fig. 85.7 A car starter motor circuit

Questions

1 Draw a circuit diagram to show how the relay in Figure 85.5 could be wired up to produce:

a a buzzer,

b a 'latch' that keeps itself switched on once a switch has been triggered, even if the switch is released.

2 A technology student wires up a pair of relays as shown on the right.

a What happens when the switch is closed?

b Draw a circuit diagram of this arrangement.

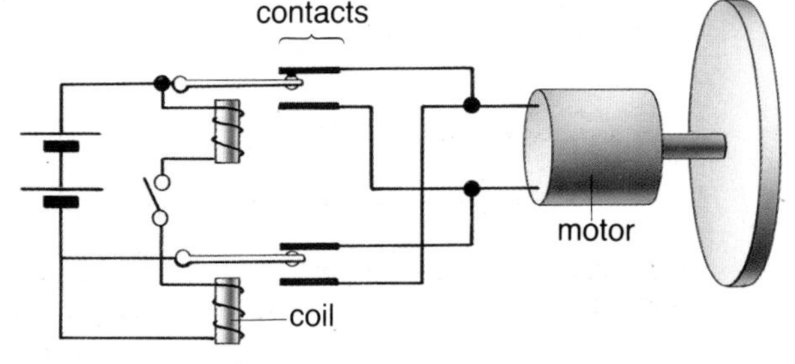

86 MOTORS

A motor is an energy converter. The interaction of current in wires and magnetic fields produces motion.

A current in a magnetic field can produce motion

When two magnetic poles are brought together, a force acts. When two magnetic fields interact, a force may act between them.

A current in a wire produces a magnetic field. If a current in a wire flows through a region of magnetic field, there are *two* fields. These two fields may interact. A force is produced. The greatest force is produced when the current flows at *right angles* to the field lines.

If you know the direction of the current and the direction of the field lines produced by the magnet, then you can work out the direction of the force which is produced. It is *at right angles to both of them*. Figure 86.2 shows how you can use your fingers – with a bit of contortion – to show the direction of the force.

Fig. 86.1 The foil carries a current of 2.75 A at 90° to the magnetic field. The foil experiences a vertical force which lifts it above the magnet.

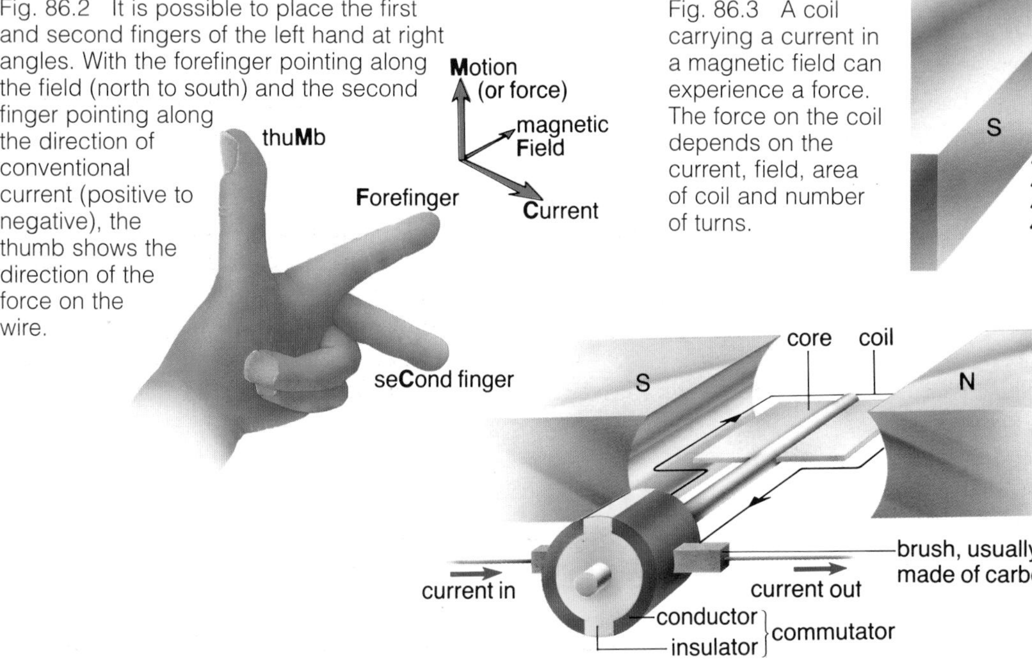

Fig. 86.2 It is possible to place the first and second fingers of the left hand at right angles. With the forefinger pointing along the field (north to south) and the second finger pointing along the direction of conventional current (positive to negative), the thumb shows the direction of the force on the wire.

Fig. 86.3 A coil carrying a current in a magnetic field can experience a force. The force on the coil depends on the current, field, area of coil and number of turns.

Fig. 86.4 A commutator and brushes provide connections to the coil.

A coil will turn in a magnetic field

Figure 86.3 shows a coil of wire between a pair of magnets. The magnets are arranged with opposite poles facing one another. The field lines between these two magnets run straight from one to the other.

If a current is passed through the coil of wire, a magnetic field is produced around it. This field interacts with the field between the two magnets. As the current flows in opposite directions on each side of the coil, the forces produced on each side are also in opposite directions. So the coil is pulled upwards on one side and downwards on the other. It turns. The turning force is called a **couple**.

No force acts on sides C and D. Here, the current is flowing along the direction of the magnetic field lines, not at right angles to them. So no force is produced.

Can you see what will happen as the coil turns through 180°? When side A gets round to where side B was, the current nearest the N pole is now running in the opposite direction. So the force is reversed. The coil will turn back to its first position.

This isn't much use! To make a useful motor, you want the coil to spin round and round in one direction. This can be done by using a commutator and brushes, as shown in Figure 86.4. These provide a connection to the coil which doesn't get twisted as the coil spins round and round. They also reverse the connections each half turn, so the couple always acts in the same direction.

But even this arrangement may produce a jerky movement as the coil spins. This is because the size of the turning force is greatest when the coil is horizontal. When it is vertical, there is no connection and no couple. If you have a second coil mounted at 90° to the first, and a second set of contacts, then the forces are more evenly spaced out as the coil spins and the motor will turn more smoothly.

Larger motors usually have electromagnets instead of permanent magnets. Can you suggest why?

INVESTIGATION 86.1

Making a motor

1 Figure 86.5 shows the parts you will need to make an electrical motor. Check that you have them all.

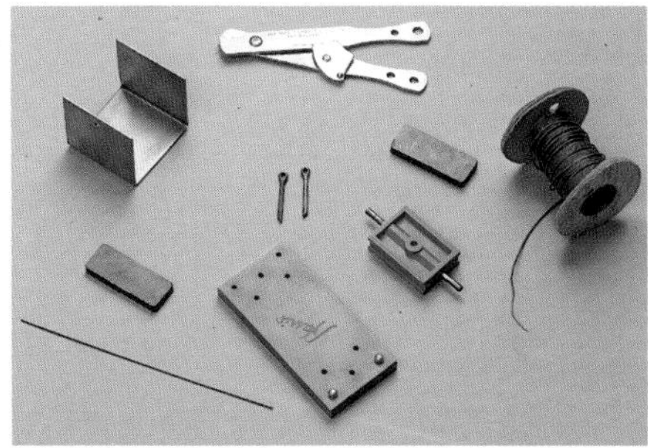

Fig. 86.5 Parts for making a motor

2 Insulate one end of the axle tube with insulating tape as in Figure 86.6.

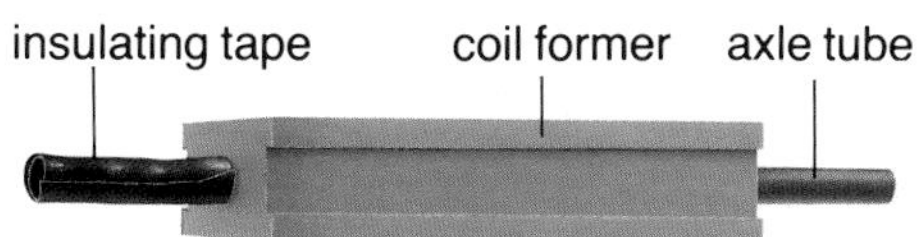

Fig. 86.6

3 Remove 2 cm of insulation from one end of your length of wire. Wind the wire round and round the former. Start and finish at the insulated end of the axle tube. You will need about 10 turns altogether. Leave about 2 cm of wire free when you finish, and remove its insulation.

bared wire lying along the *sides* of the insulated axle

wire coil

Fig. 86.7

4 Now fold the two ends of wire back on themselves. Arrange them neatly against the *sides* of the axle tube, and secure them with a rubber band or tape. Make sure they don't touch each other.

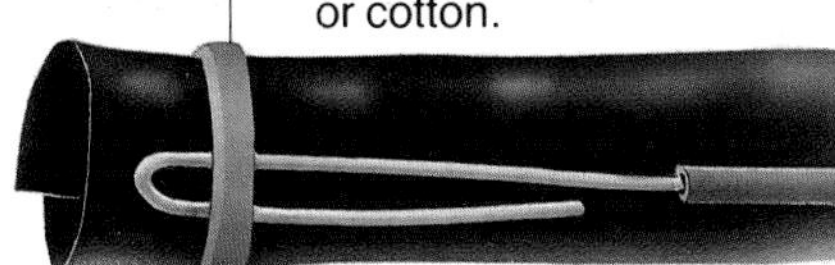

Fig. 86.8

5 Take two fresh pieces of wire. Remove about 3 cm of insulation from one end of each of them. Remove enough insulation from the other ends to allow you to connect them to a power pack. Use the long ends to make brushes. To do this, look at the diagram of the finished motor (Figure 86.9).

6 Push the split pins into the base unit, and hold the coil unit between them. Insert the axle rod through the split pins and the axle tube. Make sure the coil unit can spin freely.

7 Now line up the brushes with the bare wire which is looped against the axle tube. The brushes should push tightly against these loops, but must not touch each other.

8 Stand your unit in the yoke, and put the magnets on either side. The magnets must have opposite poles facing each other. Check that they attract each other.

9 Finally, connect your motor to a 3–6 V power supply. Give it a flick to get it going. If it doesn't work check:

- the magnets have opposite poles facing each other.
- the brushes are making a good connection with the bare wire loops.
- the brushes are not making a connection with each other.
- the motor can spin freely without rubbing against anything.
- the bare wire loops are not making a connection with each other.

A good motor will spin very quickly and will run at a lower voltage, compared with a poorly made one.

Try these investigations with your motor. Describe what happens each time.

a Remove one of the magnets.

b Put the magnet back, and add an extra one on each side, on the outside of the yoke.

c Rewind the coil, using fewer turns. What is the smallest number of turns your motor will run on?

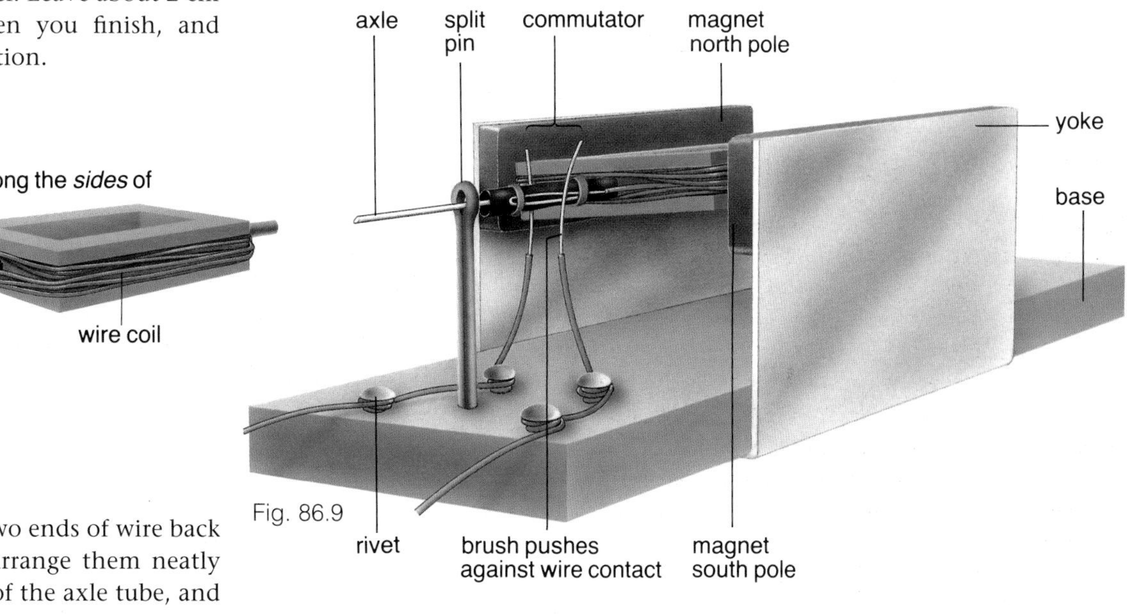

Fig. 86.9

87 GENERATORS

A generator uses motion in a magnetic field to produce an electrical current.

INVESTIGATION 87.1

Testing a simple generator

For this investigation, use the motor you made in Investigation 86.1.

1 Connect your motor to a milliammeter as shown in Figure 87.1.

2 Spin the coil. Does it produce a current? If so, when does it do this?

3 Find out the effect of:

a increasing the number of turns of wire in the coil.

b increasing the magnetic field (you could add more magnets).

You have turned your motor into a **generator** or **dynamo**. It has transferred the movement energy into electrical energy.

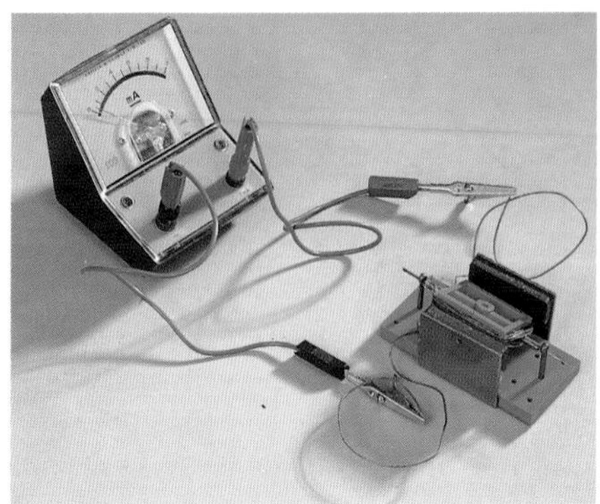

Fig. 87.1

INVESTIGATION 87.2

Voltage and current in a motor

1 Connect a motor to a power pack. Measure the voltage across the motor, and the current passing through it.

2 Reduce the voltage until the motor is just spinning. Measure the current. Keep increasing the voltage in small steps and measure the current each time. Record your results in a table.

3 Plot a graph of voltage against current.

Questions

1 When does the largest current pass through the motor?

2 Comment on the shape of your graph.

3 Does the motor obey Ohm's law?

4 What does this experiment have to do with generators?

EXTENSION

Movement in a magnetic field can produce current

If you did Investigation 87.1, you will have found that moving a coil between the two magnets causes a current to flow in the wires. You can generate electricity by moving a wire in a magnetic field.

If a wire is moved in a magnetic field, the electrons in it experience a force. This produces a potential difference across the ends of the wires. Electrons flow along the wire.

You have to do work to move the wire. The current flowing in it produces a field, which interacts with the magnetic field to produce a force. The force resists the movement of the wire. Your work against this force is the source of the energy which produces the electric current.

When a motor is used like this, it is called a **generator**. The same piece of equipment can be used to transfer electrical energy to movement energy, or to transfer movement energy to electrical energy. The **magnetic flux** tells you how concentrated the magnetic field is. If the wires move through more flux, then more electrical energy is transferred.

Generators can produce alternating or direct current

If you did Investigation 87.1, when you spun your motor you probably found that the milliammeter reading was not steady. It flickered as the coil spun round. The largest current is produced when the coil is horizontal. No current is produced when the coil is vertical, because the sides of the coil are moving *along* the field lines, not across them. So the current is produced in a series of pulses, as in Figure 87.2.

You saw in Topic 86 that this arrangement of brushes reverses the connections each half turn. This means that the current always flows in the same direction around the circuit. It is called **direct current**, abbreviation **d.c.** Batteries also produce direct current. But the current from a battery stays at a fairly steady level, whereas the current from your generator swings from high to low to high again as the coil spins round.

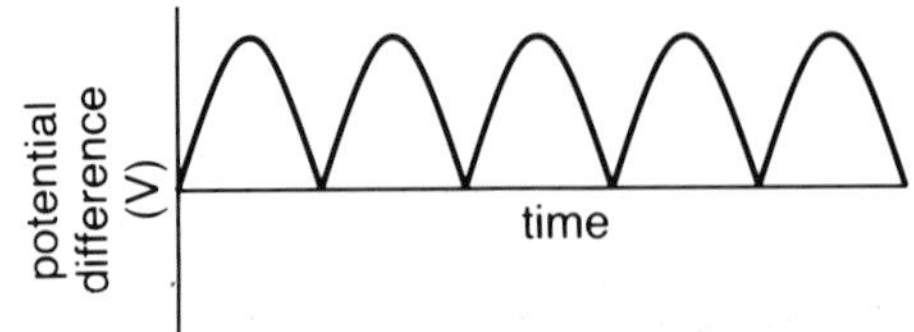

Fig. 87.2 The output from a d.c. generator is a series of pulses. The current always flows in the same direction.

Figure 87.4 shows a different design of generator. It has continuous rings touching the brushes. With this arrangement, the coil connections are not reversed each half turn. As the coil turns round, it moves up through the field on the left hand side and then down through the field on the right hand side. So the direction of current reverses as the coil turns. On one complete turn, it flows first one way and then the other. This is called **alternating current**, abbreviation **a.c.** A generator which produces alternating current is called an **alternator**.

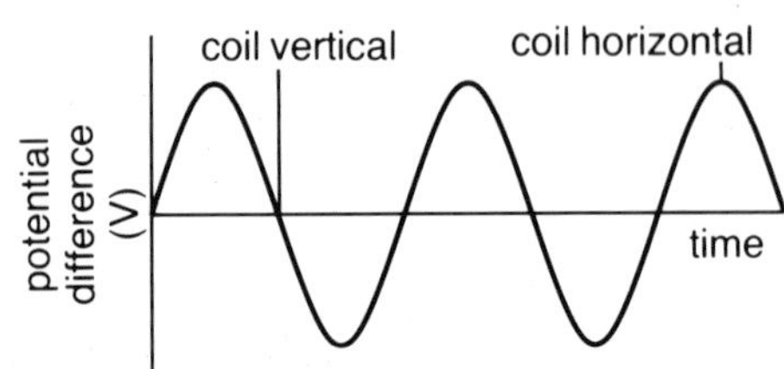

Fig. 87.3 The output from an a.c. generator (like the generator shown in Figure 87.4) swings from positive to negative with each pulse.

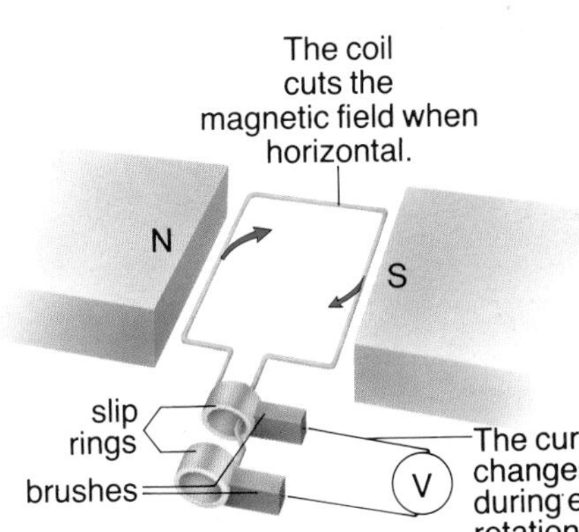

Fig. 87.4 An alternating current generator or alternator

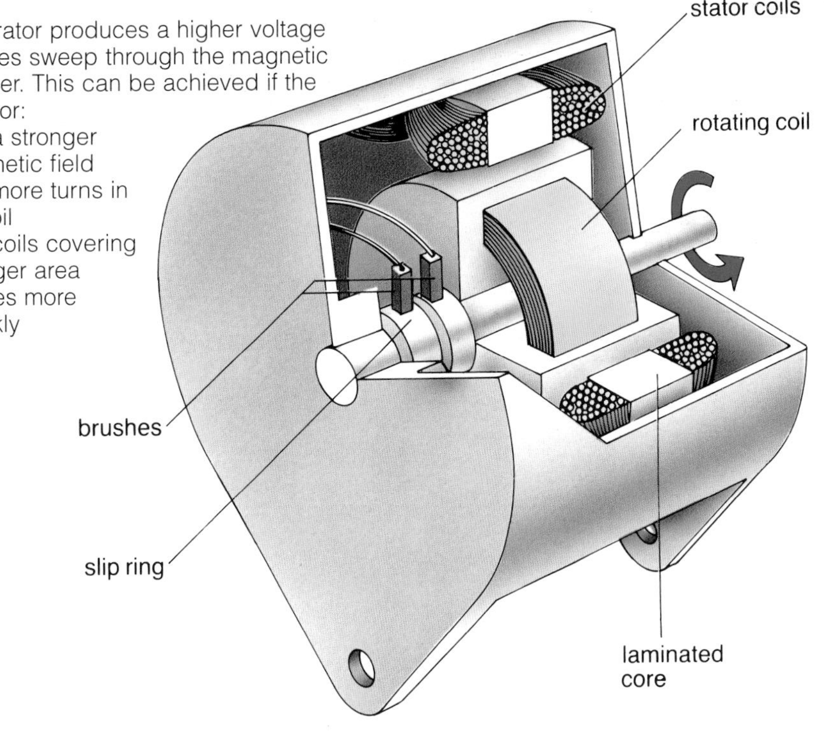

Fig. 87.5 A car alternator produces an a.c. current in the stator coils. This is rectified by diodes, so the actual output is a d.c. current. The principle of having fixed coils and a rotating electromagnet is the same as for the power station generator. Only a small d.c. current has to be fed into the slip rings to supply the electromagnet. The larger output currents from the stator coils run through fixed connections.

Bicycle dynamos spin a magnet inside a coil

If you have a bicycle, it may have a dynamo to back up your battery-powered lamps. The dynamo is a generator, producing electricity from the movement energy of your legs as you turn the pedals.

Figure 87.6 shows a bicycle dynamo. It looks very different from the other generators you have met, but it works on the same principle. But, instead of having a coil turning inside a magnetic field, the coil is held still while the magnet turns inside it as you turn the pedals. This arrangement means that no slip rings or brushes are needed because the wires aren't moving round.

A dynamo can save you money on batteries for your bicycle lights. But it would not be safe to have lights powered *only* by a dynamo, and not by batteries. Why is this?

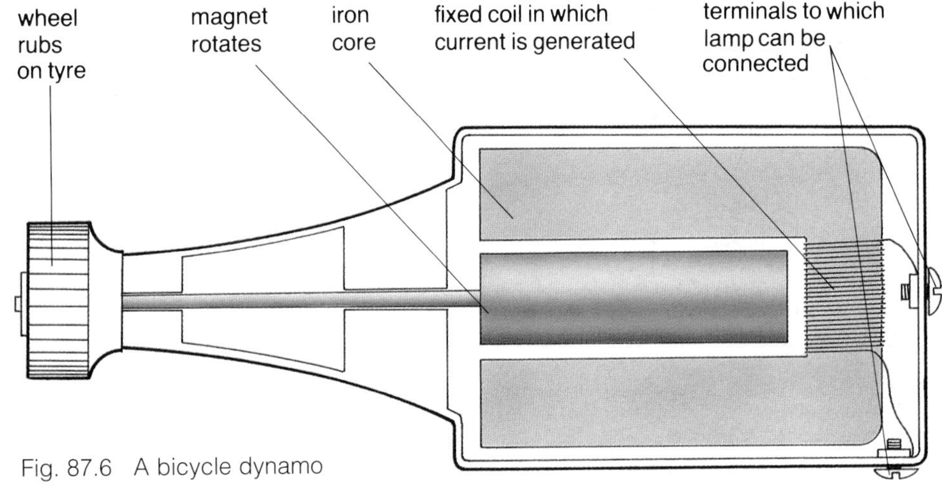

Fig. 87.6 A bicycle dynamo

Questions

1 A dynamo and generator are connected together, as shown in the diagram.

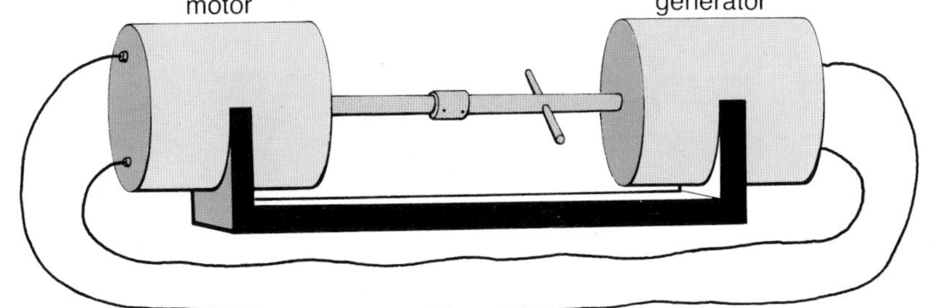

a What energy transfers take place when the shaft is spun and released?

b Would this system keep going for ever? Explain your answer.

2 a Draw a circuit diagram to show how you would connect a rheostat to control the speed of a motor. (The symbol for a motor is -Ⓜ-.)

b How could you use this, together with some other laboratory apparatus, to find the resistance of a running motor? Would you expect the resistance to be the same when the motor was stationary?

88 TRANSFORMERS

A transformer changes electrical energy from one voltage to a different voltage.

A voltage can be induced by a changing current in a nearby coil

In Topic 87, you saw that you can induce a voltage in a coil by moving the coil in a magnetic field. You can get the same effect by moving the magnetic field or by changing the magnetic field. A changing magnetic field induces a voltage in a coil.

Figure 88.1 shows two coils close together. If a current flows through the left hand coil, it produces a magnetic field. If this field changes, then it will induce a voltage in the right hand coil. One way of making this happen is to pass an alternating current through the left hand coil. The alternating current produces a changing magnetic field. It induces a voltage in the right hand coil. So a current flows in the right hand coil if it is connected up to a circuit. It will be an alternating current.

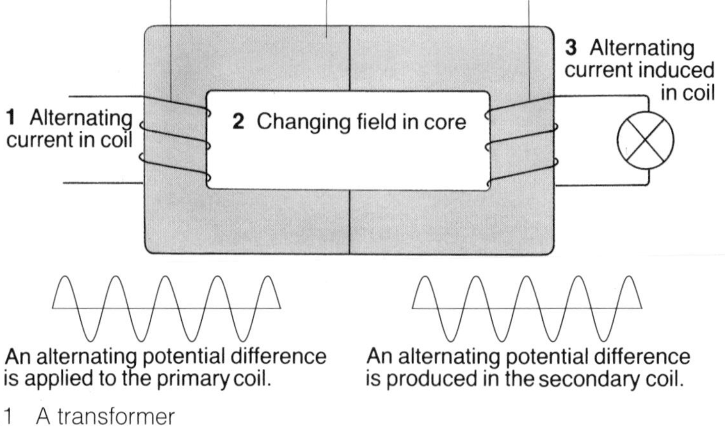

Fig. 88.1 A transformer

The size of the induced voltage depends on the number of turns in the two coils

If you try Investigation 88.1, you will find that changing the number of turns in either of the coils changes the size of the induced voltage. The size of the induced voltage depends on the ratio between the number of turns in the two coils, and on the size of the voltage in the first coil.

$$\frac{\textbf{input voltage}}{\textbf{output voltage}} = \frac{\textbf{turns on input coil}}{\textbf{turns on output coil}}$$

So $$\textbf{output voltage} = \textbf{input voltage} \times \frac{\textbf{turns on output coil}}{\textbf{turns on input coil}}$$

If you want your transformer to produce a *larger* voltage than the one in the input coil, then you need *more* turns on your output coil. This would be called a **step-up transformer**. It transforms a small voltage into a large voltage.

Transformers can also transform a large voltage into a smaller one. This kind is called a **step-down transformer**. On which coil would you need most turns to produce a step-down transformer?

Step-up transformers are used in televisions. They transform the 230 V mains voltage into almost 25 000 V. Step-down transformers are used in laboratory power packs. They transform the mains voltage into a much smaller and safer voltage, which is less likely to damage you or the equipment you use. However, a transformer produces a.c. current. Before battery operated equipment can use the power from a transformer, it must be converted to d.c. One or more diodes can be used to make the current flow one way only. The pulses of d.c. can then be smoothed out with capacitors.

Fig. 88.3 A high voltage power pack has many sets of coils. Some are used to step down the mains for the control circuits. Some are used to step up the voltage to high levels, around 5 kV.

INVESTIGATION 88.1

Making a transformer

1 Wind twenty turns of wire around one side of an iron core. Using a different wire, wind twenty turns around the other side.

2 Connect the wires from one side to the a.c. terminals of a power pack. Connect the wires from the other side to a bulb. What happens? Explain why.

3 Add some extra turns to the 'bulb side' of the core. What effect does this have?

4 Add some extra turns to the 'power pack side' of the core. What effect does this have?

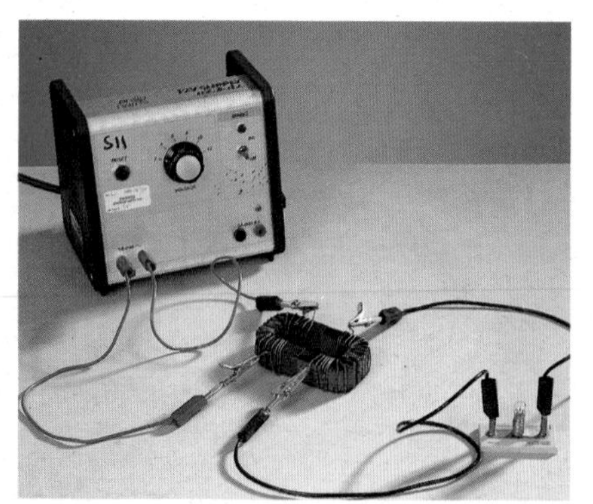

Fig. 88.2

The National Grid uses step-up and step-down transformers

Electrical power is distributed around the country on a network of cables called the **National Grid**. Many power stations are connected to the grid. If one area needs extra power, power stations in different areas can provide it.

A power station can provide 2000 MW of electrical power. The output can be around 23.5 kV. At this voltage, the current flowing through the cables of the grid would be 85 000 A. This is a very large current and would need heavy and expensive cables.

So power stations use step-up transformers to increase the voltage to 400 kV. The higher the voltage, the lower the current which runs in the cables. The 2000 MW of power can then be supplied using a current of 5000 A. This means that lighter cables can be used. It also reduces the heating effect in the cables, which would otherwise lose a lot of energy.

As 400 kV is a high voltage, it would be dangerous to supply this in people's homes. So, near its destination, the voltage in the power lines is stepped down, often in several stages using several transformers. The final step down to 230 V is done in local electricity substations, some of which supply only a few houses. Your local step-down transformer could have 11 000 V across its input coils. This is why substations are dangerous. At high voltages, the electrical current can jump across an air gap of a metre or more.

DID YOU KNOW?

If electrical power was sent all the way from a power station at only 230 V, the cables of the National Grid would carry 8 000 000 A for each power station.
A generator spins at a fixed frequency. If the generator speeds up, the a.c. frequency increases. If the generator rotates at 3000 rpm then the voltage will oscillate at 50 Hz.

Fig. 88.4 Although aluminium is not the best conducting metal, it is often used in power cables because it has a low density, which reduces the weight of the cable and increases the possible distance between the supports. Some of the cables shown in this photograph are signal cables, and have a layer of aluminium around them to screen out interference.

Fig. 88.5 The 400 kV transformer at a power station. The tall insulating columns have to be carefully designed so that they work even in the rain. Without them the current would flow to earth through the supports.

Questions

1 List ten uses of a transformer. For each one, say whether it is a step-up or step-down transformer.

2 A welder's transformer is rated at 13 A, and runs from the mains. If the output is 40 V, what is the output current? (Assume the transformer is 100% efficient.)

3 The mains voltage is 230 V, a.c. A transformer for a computer gives 9 V at 0.2 A.

a What electrical power does the transformer provide at its output?

b If the transformer draws 9 mA from the mains, how efficient is it? Where does the 'lost' energy go?

c Why couldn't a transformer work on direct current?

EXTENSION

89 POWER STATIONS

Most of our electrical energy comes from rotors spinning in the alternators of power stations.

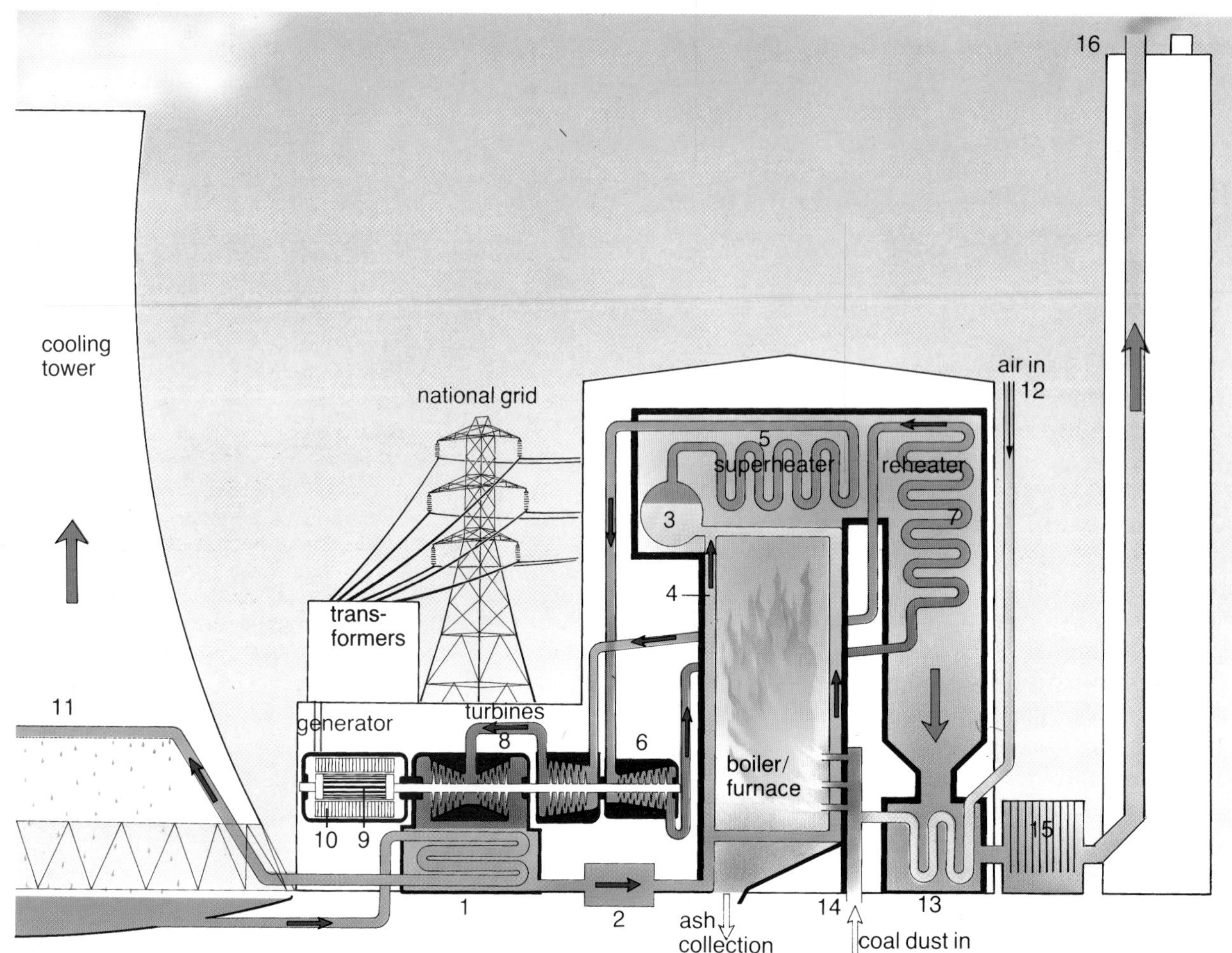

Fig. 89.1 A coal-powered electricity generating station.

Steam from the turbines (6) and (8) is cooled to water in the condenser (1). After preheating (2), which includes passing through the hot exhaust gases, the water passes to the steam drum (3) and circulates through many kilometres of piping in the boiler (4). Steam from the drum is heated at the top of the boiler (5). The superheated steam passes to the high pressure turbine (6) for the first transfer of heat energy to kinetic energy. The steam is then reheated (7) before driving the intermediate and low pressure turbines (8). The three turbines drive the rotor (9) – an electromagnet inside the stator coils (10). Kinetic energy is transferred to electrical energy. The transformers raise the voltage from 235 kV to 400 kV for transmission across the grid. Water from the cooling tower (11) keeps the condenser cool, and the cycle repeats itself. Cooling air circulates through the cooling tower and water from the condenser is sprayed into this draught to cool it.

Air is drawn into the furnace (12) through an air heater (13) which preheats the air with the hot flue gases. The heated air is blown into the furnace, and is also used to blow in pulverised coal dust (14). The dust and air mixture burns like a gas. As the flue gases leave the furnace they reheat the steam and preheat the air and water. The gases then pass through the precipitator (15), where ash is removed electrostatically (see page 67), and finally go out through the chimney (16).

Most power stations in Britain burn fossil fuel

The majority of power stations in Britain use coal as their energy source. Chemical energy stored in the coal is released as the coal is burnt. The energy is used to heat water, producing steam which turns giant fans, or **turbines**. The turbines turn electromagnets, called **rotors**, inside a stationary coil, which generates electricity. The generator is an **alternator**, producing alternating current.

This large-scale burning of coal and other fossil fuels creates all sorts of problems. The carbon dioxide produced contributes to the greenhouse effect. Sulphur oxides can cause acid rain, although many power stations now remove these pollutants before releasing waste gases into the air. There is a limited supply of the fossil fuels themselves – all of them will eventually run out. It is essential that we look at other methods of generating electricity.

DID YOU KNOW?

The average coal-powered station releases more radiation from its chimney than a nuclear power station.

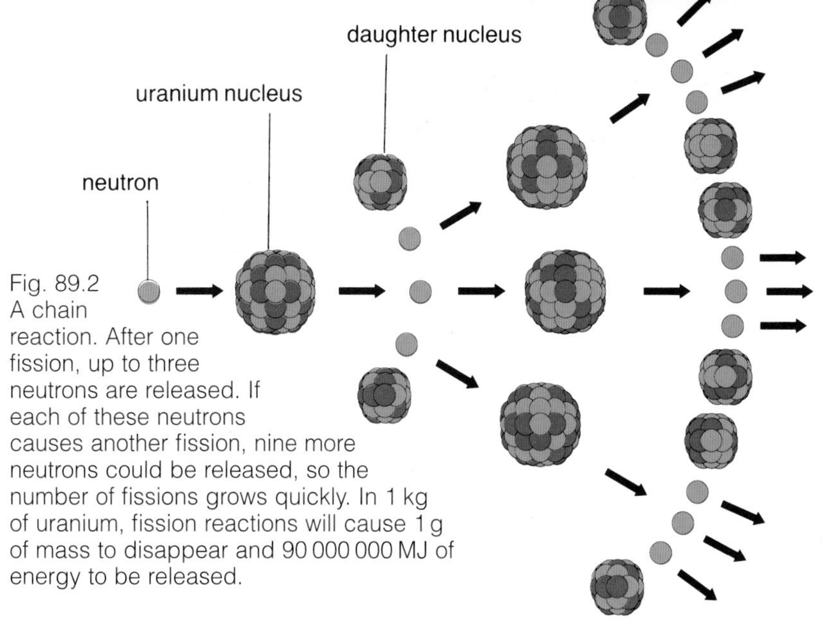

Fig. 89.2 A chain reaction. After one fission, up to three neutrons are released. If each of these neutrons causes another fission, nine more neutrons could be released, so the number of fissions grows quickly. In 1 kg of uranium, fission reactions will cause 1 g of mass to disappear and 90 000 000 MJ of energy to be released.

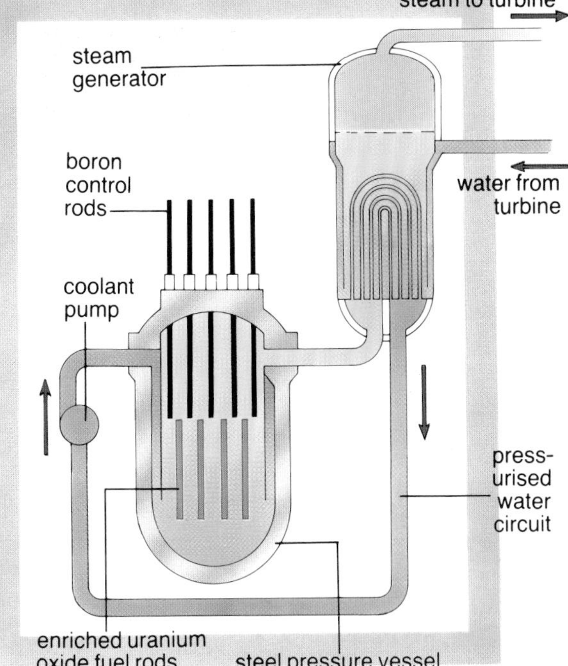

Fig. 89.3 A pressurised water reactor, or PWR. Water is used both as the moderator and as the reactor coolant. Sizewell B in Suffolk is a 1100 MW PWR reactor. Other types of reactor used in Britain are Magnox and advanced gas cooled reactors.

Nuclear power uses heat from radioactive decay to drive turbines

About one fifth of the electricity generated in Britain comes from nuclear power stations. These use heat generated from the radioactive decay of uranium 235 to heat water, producing steam to turn turbines.

At the heart of a nuclear power station is the **reactor**. Here, rods of uranium undergo **nuclear fission**. 'Fission' means 'splitting'. The uranium 235 atoms split apart, releasing high energy neutrons. The neutrons can collide with other uranium nuclei, so that they also split up and release more high energy neutrons. A chain reaction is set up. A large amount of heat energy is released, which heats water around the fuel rods.

The uranium rods are surrounded by a **moderator**. This slows the neutrons down, making sure that they do not escape from the reactor core before they have split another uranium nucleus. So the chain reaction keeps going. In a pressurised water reactor, the moderator is water. Other types of reactor may use heavy water (which contains deuterium instead of hydrogen) or graphite as moderators.

To stop or slow down the chain reaction, **control rods** can be lowered between the rods of uranium. These are made of boron steel. They absorb the neutrons, stopping them from continuing the chain reaction. If the control rods are lowered right down, the reaction stops completely.

Penalties of nuclear power

Nuclear power stations have some big advantages over coal-burning power stations. Firstly, they do not produce carbon dioxide or sulphur oxides, so they do not contribute to the greenhouse effect or acid rain. Secondly, their fuel, uranium, will not run out until long after we have used up all the available fossil fuels. Some nuclear reactors, called **breeder reactors**, actually create nuclear fuel as they run.

But, for many people, these advantages are outweighed by the disadvantages.

- **Nuclear waste** Nuclear power generation produces waste materials which are radioactive. They will remain radioactive for a long time and it is difficult to dispose of them safely.
- **Risk of accidents** If a nuclear reactor runs out of control, large amounts of radiation may be released into the air. This happened at Chernobyl, in Russia, in 1986. Radioactive materials were carried huge distances, contaminating land as far away as Western Britain. In 1991, some farmers in Britain were still not able to sell their lambs for meat because of radioactive contamination of the soil from the Chernobyl accident.
- **Expense** It is more expensive to produce electricity from nuclear reactors than from coal-burning power stations.

Questions

1 a Each of the four alternators at Didcot power station transfers 507 megajoules of energy to 500 megajoules of electrical energy each second. How efficient are the alternators?

b If the 2000 MW station transfers 5000 MJ of chemical energy from the coal every second, how efficient is the power station overall?

2 Draw a simple block diagram to show the stages in the transfer of chemical energy to electrical energy in a coal-burning power station. Annotate your diagram to explain the energy transfers which take place.

3 a What are the similarities between a nuclear and a fossil-fuel power station?

b What are the differences?

c What is done to ensure that the chain reaction in a nuclear reactor does not get out of hand and cause a nuclear explosion?

d Do you think that nuclear reactors are safer than fossil fuel reactors? Give reasons for your answer.

e Discuss the environmental problems associated with each of these two types of power station.

90 RESOURCES

The Earth contains huge numbers of resources which we use to release energy or to make objects. Some of these resources are running out.

Resources may be renewable or non-renewable

All of our many manufactured articles are made from the Earth's natural resources. We obtain all our materials, and many of the resources which we use to provide energy, from the Earth.

Some resources are being constantly produced on the Earth. They are called **renewable** resources. Others are not being replaced. They are called **non-renewable** resources.

Fig. 90.1 A cotton field in Louisiana, USA. The cotton fibres are part of the seed heads, or bolls, of the cotton plants.

Renewable resources include solar energy and plants

Many things which we obtain from plants and animals can be considered renewable resources. Such resources include cotton, wool and leather for clothing, and wood for timber and paper.

Cotton is obtained from plants which are grown just so that cotton can be obtained from them. When the plants have been used, new ones are grown in their place. The supply of cotton will never run out. But much of the wood which is used for building, or making paper, comes from trees which are cut down and not replanted. If we do not take care, this resource may be in short supply in the future.

Some sources of energy are renewable resources. Solar power, hydroelectric power and wind power will never run out.

Before the industrial revolution, renewable resources were much more important than non-renewable ones. People wore clothing made from natural fibres, such as cotton, linen, wool or animal skins. Water-mills, windmills and firewood were the chief sources of energy.

Fig. 90.2 People in many parts of the world still use only renewable resources. This irrigation system uses mud, wood and leather as construction materials, and animal food as fuel.

Non-renewable resources include fossil fuels and minerals

The Earth contains many resources which are not being replaced. These include **minerals** buried in the Earth's crust. Some of these minerals are important sources of metals. They are called **ores**. As we dig them up, the supply in the ground decreases.

Fossil fuels such as oil, coal and natural gas are very important sources of energy and chemicals in our modern industrial society. They were produced many millions of years ago, and they are not being replaced.

With many of our non-renewable resources, however, there is no real problem. **Silicon**, for example, is an element used in the manufacture of electronic chips. It can be obtained from sand. But the world's consumption of silicon is tiny compared with the amounts of sand available. Similarly, the extraction of **sodium chloride** from sea water will not make the sea any less salty!

But many non-renewable resources are in real danger of running out. The prices of many metals have gone up in recent years, as ore reserves become depleted. The rate at which we are using oil makes it a real possibility that it will be in very short supply during the next century.

Fig. 90.3 Oil is an important natural resource. Britain's largest oil field lies beneath the North Sea. This offshore production platform is called Brent Charlie, where drilling for, and extraction of, oil and natural gas take place.

Non-renewable resources must be used more efficiently

The problem of future shortages of some of our important resources must be faced. The answer to this problem will probably be a combination of four approaches.

- **Relying more heavily on renewable resources.** If a non-renewable resource becomes scarce, its price goes up. This can result in an alternative renewable resource becoming cheaper than the non-renewable resource, so the renewable resource will be used instead.
- **Increasing product lifetime.** We must try to make products made from non-renewable resources last longer. For example, most cars are made of steel, which contains large amounts of iron. The iron rusts. If every car could be made to last longer, then less iron would be needed by the motor industry.
- **Recycling.** Much of what we throw away could be reused. Glass, for example, can be crushed, remelted and reused. Glass made in this way requires much less energy than glass made from scratch. Many people already take their empty glass bottles to bottle banks. If more and more people were encouraged to do this, the amount of resources needed to make new glass could be greatly reduced.
- **Opening up new sources.** Improved technology is continually allowing resources which were previously unavailable to be extracted from the Earth.

Fig. 90.4 Quite a high proportion of glass in Britain is now recycled. It would be even better if the bottles themselves could be re-used.

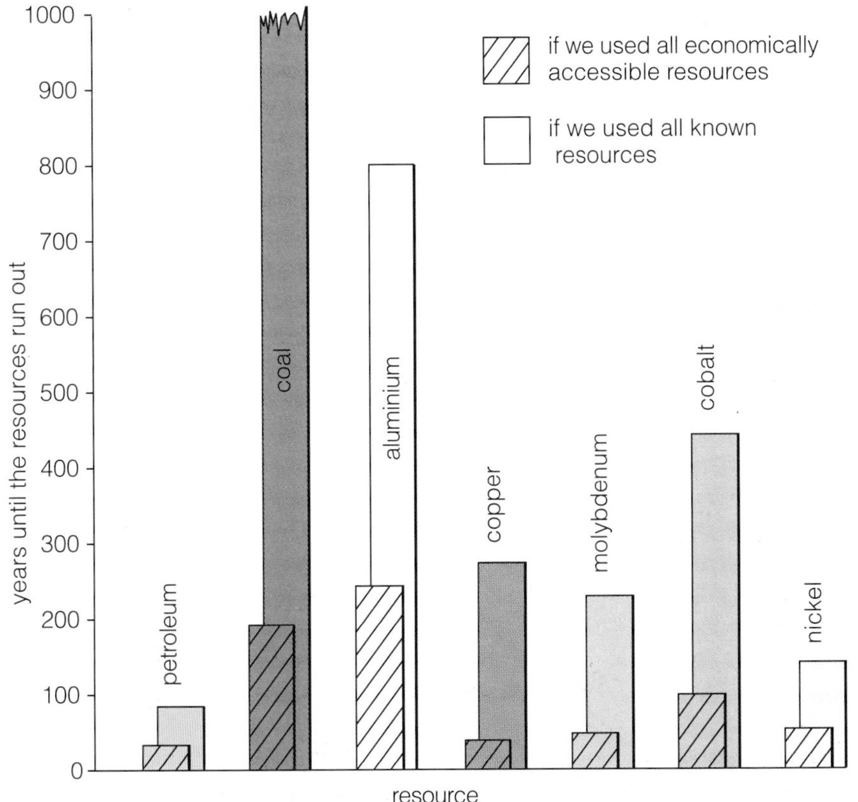

Fig. 90.5 Lifetimes of some important resources. These estimates assume that we will continue to use these resources at the same rate as we are doing now.

Questions

1 a List the problems associated with renewable and non-renewable resources.

b Explain why our exploitation of non-renewable resources could be termed 'short-sighted'.

2 Glass and paper are two materials which can be recycled.

a What resource is conserved when glass is recyled?

b What resource is conserved when paper is recycled?

c Discuss the reasons for the relatively small amounts of glass and paper which are recycled in Britain.

d What can be done to increase the amounts of glass and paper which are recycled?

3 Figure 90.5 shows the estimated lifetimes of some important resources.

a Are the resources shown in this graph renewable or non-renewable resources?

b Which are fossil fuels?

c Which of these resources will run out first?

d Which has the greatest total reserves?

e Calculate the percentage of each resource which it is currently uneconomic to extract.

f Will these reserves always be uneconomic to extract? Explain your answer.

EXTENSION

91 FOSSIL FUELS

Fossil fuels were formed from the remains of living organisms. They are important energy resources and also sources of many chemicals.

Coal, oil and natural gas are important energy sources

Amongst our most important non-renewable resources are the three fossil fuels – coal, oil (petroleum) and natural gas (methane). They are major energy sources. All three are used in the power stations which generate over half of Britain's electricity. All three are used for space heating in homes. Most of our road vehicles use oil products like petrol and diesel.

These three fossil fuels are also important sources of industrial chemicals. Coal is used to make coal tar. Coal tar is used to make nylon. Coal itself is used as a form of carbon for smelting iron. Petroleum is a source of a wide range of chemicals, including many plastics. Methane is the source of hydrogen used for making ammonia, which is used to make fertilisers.

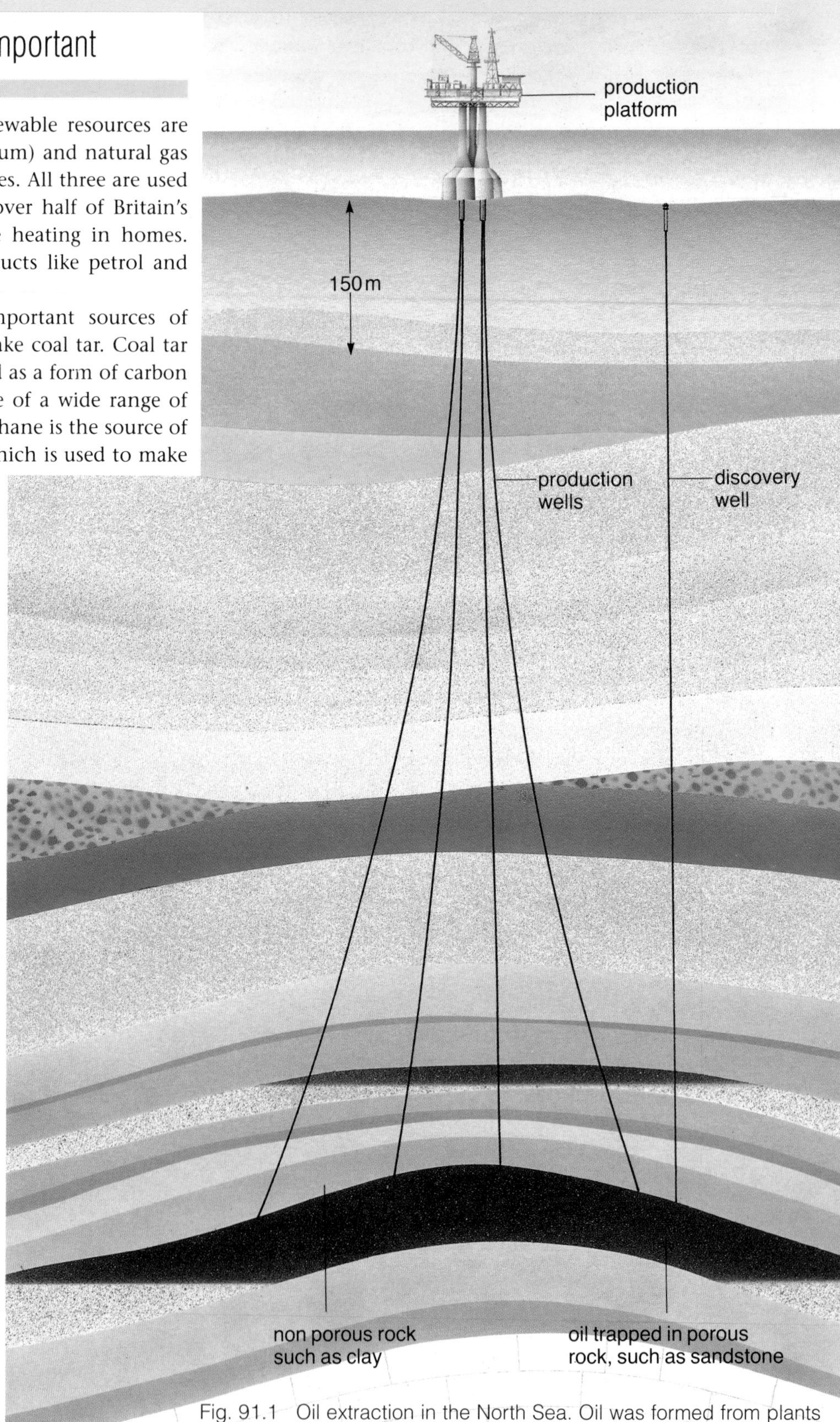

Fig. 91.1 Oil extraction in the North Sea. Oil was formed from plants and microorganisms which died millions of years ago. The oil can seep into rocks with tiny spaces in them (porous rocks). If there is a non-porous rock above, then the oil is trapped. Folded rocks form traps where oil may collect at the top of the fold.

Fossil fuels were formed millions of years ago

About 300 000 000 years ago, in the Carboniferous period, much of the Earth's surface was covered with dense forests and swamps. As trees and other plants died and fell, they did not rot away completely. The wet, airless mud made it difficult for decay bacteria to live. So the half-rotted trees gradually sank into the mud.

More and more dead vegetation and sediments collected on top of them. The half-rotted trees were crushed and flattened. They formed **coal**.

Oil formed during the same period. Oil formed under the seas. Tiny plants, animals and bacteria sank to the bottom of the sea when they died, mixing with the sand and silt on the sea bed. Their bodies did not rot away completely, but were crushed by the weight of sediments falling on top of them. Their remains became a mixture of carbon compounds – petroleum or crude oil.

Gas is found in the same rocks as coal and oil. It, too, was formed from the half-decayed remains of plants, animals and bacteria. Gas is often only found in small amounts, because it can easily leak away through tiny spaces in rocks.

Fig. 91.2 Coal was formed from trees and other plants. It sometimes contains fossils, such as this fern frond.

Coal is dug out of mines

We get coal by digging it out of the ground. Coal was formed in horizontal layers, called **seams**. In between the seams are layers of other rocks. A mine shaft is dug down through these other layers to reach a coal seam. Horizontal tunnels or galleries are then dug into the coal.

Sometimes the rocks will have been folded and twisted since they were formed. This can bring the coal close to the surface. The coal can then be dug out in an **open-cast mine**, rather like a quarry.

Rock movements or erosion by rivers may form a valley, cutting down through rock layers. A coal seam might then be exposed on the sides of the valley. Miners can dig straight into the valley side. This is called a **drift mine**.

DID YOU KNOW?

Between 1937 and 1988, world consumption of fossil fuel increased by a factor of 4.5. Consumption of coal doubled, that of oil increased by a factor of 10, while consumption of natural gas increased by a factor of 13. Despite the introduction of nuclear power, the world is still largely dependent on fossil fuels for energy supplies.

Fig. 91.3 An open-cast mine

Oil is pumped out of porous rocks

Oil does not form underground 'lakes'. Oil moves through porous rocks underground, until it gets trapped by non-porous rocks above it. It is held in the porous rocks like water in a giant sponge. To get at the oil, drills cut down through the non-porous rocks into the porous ones.

The oil may be under pressure, perhaps because there is gas trapped in the same place. If this happens, then the oil will surge up out of the drilled shaft. But often the oil has to be pumped out. Sometimes, a detergent solution is pumped into the oil-bearing rocks. The detergent dissolves the oil, and the mixture of oil and detergent is then pumped out.

Natural gas does not need to be pumped out of the ground. It will come out under its own pressure, once a shaft has been drilled down to it.

DID YOU KNOW?

In 1956, people drilling for oil in Iran struck oil deposits under such pressure that the oil gushed out in the world's biggest 'wildcat'. The oil shot to a height of 52m, at a rate of 120 thousand barrels a day. It took 90 days to bring the gusher under control.

Questions

1 a Why are coal, oil and gas called 'fossil fuels'?

b What are the two main uses of fossil fuels?

c Why are large amounts of fossil fuels no longer being formed?

d Where would you look to see if coal was still being formed?

e Where would you look to see if oil was still being formed?

f Coal is not explosive, but many mining disasters have involved explosions. What caused these explosions?

EXTENSION

2 Britain's main oil field is under the North Sea. What problems does this give to the companies trying to extract the oil? Try to find out how some of these problems have been solved.

92 CHEMICALS FROM FOSSIL FUELS

All three fossil fuels are used for making chemicals.

Coal is used to make coke, ammonia and coal tar

At the present time, well over half of the coal mined in Britain is burnt in power stations. But coal can also be used as a source of chemicals. In the past, a lot of coal was used in this way. It is now cheaper to obtain these chemicals from oil. But as oil and gas supplies begin to run out, we may soon need to turn to coal again.

Coal is heated in the absence of air. (If air was present, the coal would burn.) Gases and tarry products are driven off from the coal, leaving **coke**. Coke is an excellent smokeless fuel. The fumes from the heated coal are passed through water, where some components dissolve. One of these soluble components is **ammonia, NH_3**, from which fertilisers can be made. Other substances in the fumes form an oily layer on the surface of water. This layer is called **coal tar**. Coal tar contains many useful substances, including some which can be used for making plastics.

The rest of the fumes pass through the water unchanged. They are called **coal gas**. Coal gas is a good fuel.

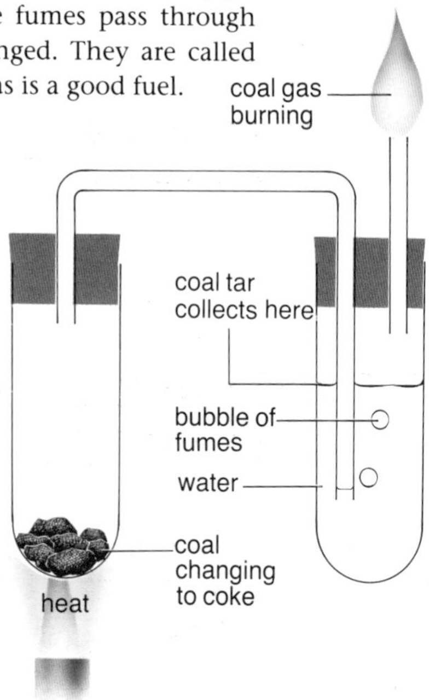

Fig. 92.1 A laboratory scale demonstration of coal as a natural resource.

Fig. 92.2 If the coke burning here is pure carbon, what are the products of this chemical reaction?

Natural gas is used to make ammonia

Natural gas is mostly composed of **methane, CH_4**. It can be used as fuel. Its other main use is as a source of **hydrogen**. Methane is mixed with steam, and passed over a nickel catalyst where a reaction takes place.

$$CH_4(g) + 2H_2O(g) \rightarrow CO_2(g) + 4H_2(g)$$

The carbon dioxide is removed. The hydrogen is mixed with nitrogen which has been extracted from the air. The hydrogen and nitrogen are reacted together to make **ammonia**. Methane, water and air have replaced coal as the world's main source of ammonia.

Oil is refined by fractional distillation

Oil is a mixture of so many valuable chemicals that it has been nick-named 'black gold'. Many of these chemicals are liquids, but others are solids and gases dissolved in the liquid. The mixture of chemicals is separated or **refined** using **fractional distillation**. This process works in the same way as the process for separating a mixture of alcohol and water. The different components separate because they have different boiling points.

Fig. 92.3 A crude oil fractionating column at Pulau Bukom, Singapore.

The untreated, or crude, oil is heated and injected into the bottom of a **fractionating tower**. The tower is very hot near its base, so most of the oil boils and the vapour rises up to the next level. The parts of the oil which do not boil include wax and tar. These parts, or **fractions**, of the oil are collected from the base of the tower.

The next level up, where the vapours go, is a little less hot than the base of the tower. So part of the vapour, including components such as lubricating oils, condenses here and can be collected. The rest of the oil, still in the form of vapour, rises up to the next level, which is a little less hot, and so on. The many levels of the fractionating tower separate the oil into its many fractions.

Questions

1 a Why will the exhaustion of oil and gas supplies affect our use of coal? What changes will take place?

b Why is coal rarely used now as a source of chemicals?

2 a What is the job of an oil refinery?

b What is the main device used in refining oil?

c What is meant by a crude oil 'fraction'?

d Which crude oil fraction is used to power:

i ships? **iii** jet aircraft?

ii cars? **iv** lorries?

e Which crude oil product may be found in a medicine cupboard?

3 a In the reaction in which hydrogen is obtained from methane, what does the nickel catalyst do?

b How could you remove the carbon dioxide from a mixture of carbon dioxide and hydrogen?

c Methane can also react with steam to give carbon monoxide and hydrogen. Write a balanced chemical equation for this reaction.

d How might nitrogen be extracted from the air?

EXTENSION

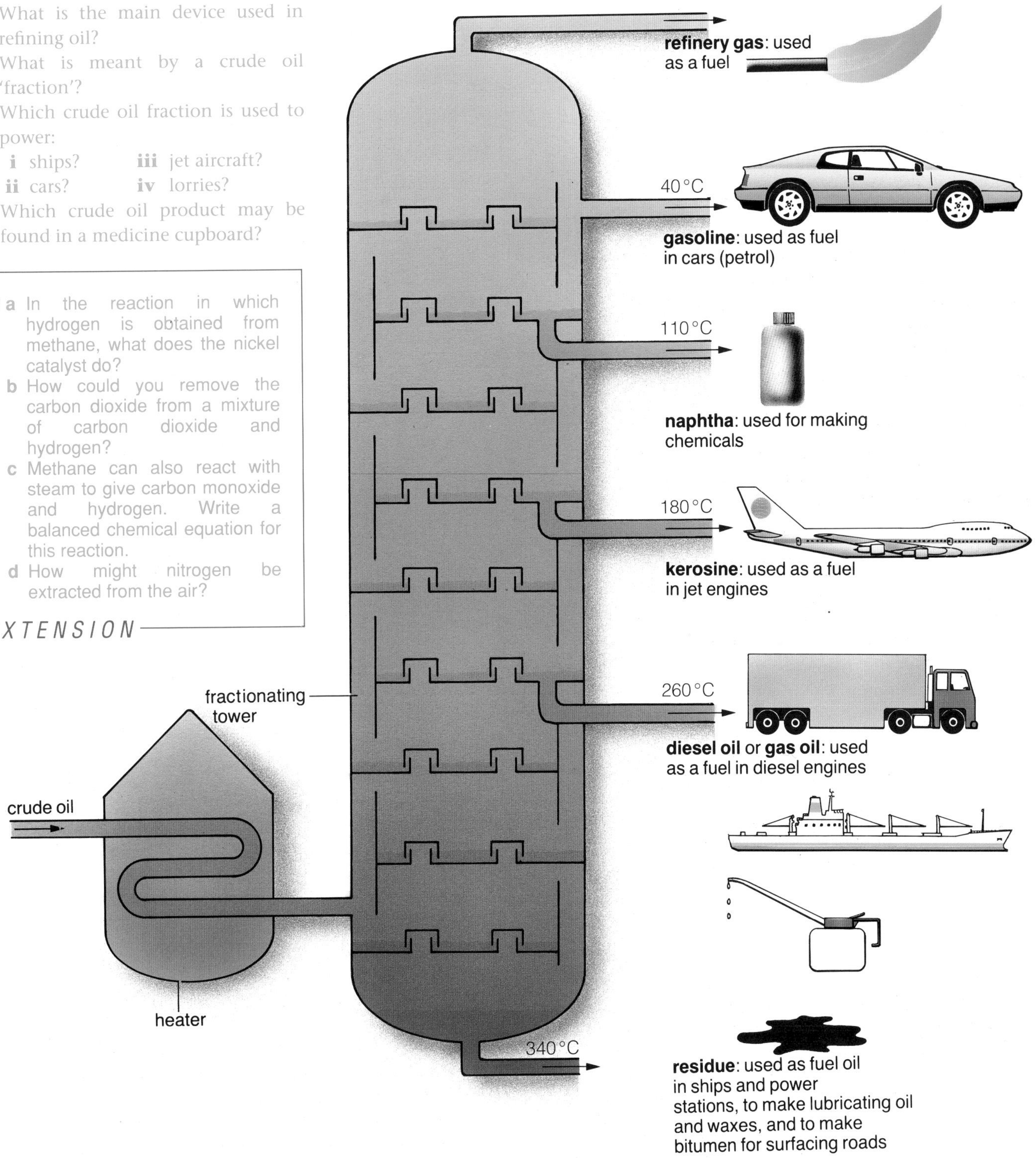

refinery gas: used as a fuel

40 °C

gasoline: used as fuel in cars (petrol)

110 °C

naphtha: used for making chemicals

180 °C

kerosine: used as a fuel in jet engines

260 °C

diesel oil or **gas oil**: used as a fuel in diesel engines

fractionating tower

crude oil

heater

340 °C

residue: used as fuel oil in ships and power stations, to make lubricating oil and waxes, and to make bitumen for surfacing roads

Fig. 92.4 Fractional distillation of oil. The hot gases rise up the tower, cooling gradually. As each component cools below its boiling point, it condenses onto the trays. The liquids run off, and are collected.

93 BURNING FUELS

Fuels are a useful way of storing energy. Fuels are usually burned in oxygen. Incomplete burning can waste fuel and produce a poisonous gas called carbon monoxide.

Many reactions give out heat

Most chemical reactions give out heat to the surroundings. Reactions that give out heat are called **exothermic** reactions. All the reactions we call 'burning' are exothermic reactions. Some examples include:

coal burning: $C(s) + O_2(g) \longrightarrow CO_2(g)$

propane gas (used in portable blow lamps) burning:

$$C_3H_8(g) + 5O_2(g) \longrightarrow 3CO_2(g) + 4H_2O(g)$$

butane gas (main part of camping gas) burning:

$$2C_4H_{10}(g) + 13O_2(g) \longrightarrow 8CO_2(g) + 10H_2O(g)$$

What these reactions also have in common is that something is combining with oxygen to release heat, carbon dioxide and water. These chemicals (coal, propane and butane) are all used as **fuels**. A fuel is a chemical that reacts with an oxidising agent to release useful energy. Most fuels we use are reacted with oxygen. Most of our fuels contain carbon, so carbon dioxide is released. Possibly the cleanest fuel is hydrogen. Burning hydrogen just produces water.

$$2H_2(g) + O_2(g) \longrightarrow 2H_2O(g)$$

Unfortunately, the manufacture of hydrogen often involves the production of carbon dioxide!

Most fuel burning systems take their oxygen from the air around them. Rockets must take their oxidiser with them either as liquid oxygen, ammonium perchlorate, hydrogen peroxide or nitric acid.

Combustion of fuels

When a fuel burns, it gains oxygen – it is oxidised. Energy is released. Natural gas (methane, CH_4) is a good example.

$$CH_4(g) + 2O_2(g) \longrightarrow CO_2(g) + 2H_2O(g)$$

However, this only shows how a fuel burns under ideal conditions. You can see from the oil flare picture (Figure 93.1) that the products of combustion are not always just carbon dioxide and water. Incomplete combustion usually happens when there is not enough oxygen available. This can happen if a boiler, fire or engine is not properly serviced or if the flue is blocked. Apart from wasting fuel, incomplete combustion can be very dangerous. Instead of producing carbon dioxide, carbon monoxide can be formed. This is a very dangerous gas. It is odourless and colourless. It combines with haemoglobin in red blood cells, and this stops the haemoglobin from carrying oxygen. Early symptoms of carbon monoxide poisoning are headaches, dizziness, sickness and tiredness or flu-like symptoms. The victim often falls asleep or is too confused to do anything about it. Carbon monoxide poisoning is fatal and even if rescued in time, the after-effects can be permanent. Warning signs to look for on appliances are yellow rather than blue flames on boilers (the yellow is from unburnt carbon) and any signs of staining, soot or burns on the outside above the burners. If someone often complains of drowsiness or sickness when a fire is on, it should be investigated by a professional. With energy efficiency in mind, many people block up the vents that are supposed to allow fresh air and oxygen into the room. Oxygen that is used up is not replaced fast enough and this encourages the production of carbon monoxide. It is important that systems are designed and installed properly. Carbon monoxide detectors can be used to give warnings of problems.

You can write an equation for carbon monoxide production from methane, although most appliances produce a mixture of carbon monoxide and carbon dioxide. A well-maintained car engine may produce 1% carbon monoxide in its emissions.

$$2CH_4(g) + 3O_2(g) \longrightarrow 2CO(g) + 4H_2O(g)$$

Carbon monoxide is also produced when unburnt carbon reacts with carbon dioxide.

$$C(s) + CO_2(g) \longrightarrow 2CO(g)$$

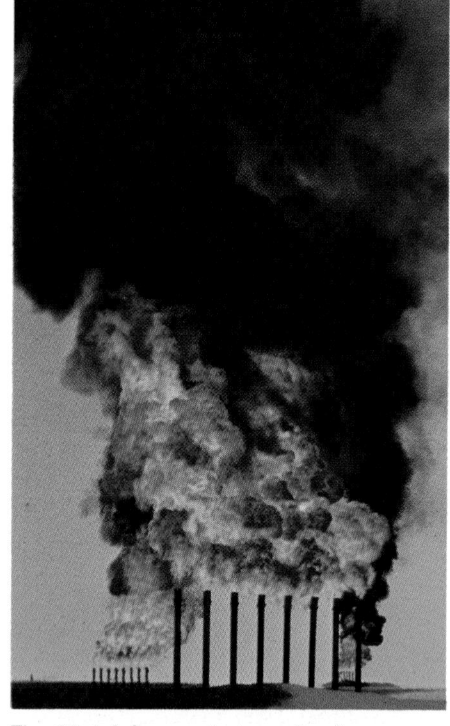

Fig. 93.1 A flare-out at an oil refinery

Fig. 93.2 A carbon monoxide detector can be placed near a fire or boiler. The alarm warns of high levels or continuous low levels of carbon monoxide.

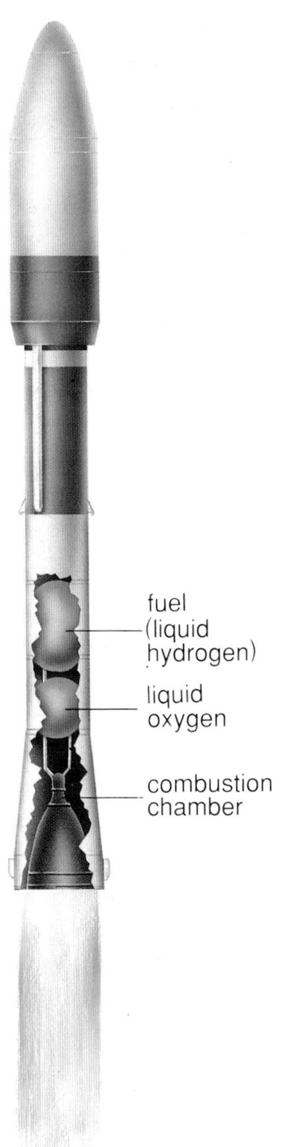

Fig. 93.3 Fuel and oxygen mix in the combustion chamber. Hot gases from their combustion leave the chamber at a very high velocity. The gain in momentum of the gases equals the gain in momentum of the rocket. The gas and rocket push against each other, and move in opposite directions.

Fig. 93.4 The space shuttle Atlantis must take its oxidiser with it. The brown cylinder is the shuttle's main fuel tank. This contains liquid oxygen and liquid hydrogen. Attached to each side of this are two white chemical booster rockets. These burn solid fuel, a mixture of fuel and oxidiser. Each of these booster rockets has a mass of more than 500 000 kg. It was a leak in one of the rubber seals of a booster rocket that caused the explosion of the space shuttle Challenger. Hot burning gases leaked out. These cut through the booster supports and caused the explosion of the main fuel tank.

Question

1 Read the following passage, and then answer the questions which follow.

Pollution from exhaust fumes

The chart on the right shows the number of licensed vehicles on the roads in Britain since 1950. This large number of cars and other vehicles is causing a major pollution problem.

Unleaded petrol does greatly reduce the output of lead compounds. But it does nothing to help with the oxides of carbon and nitrogen present in car exhaust fumes.

There are two approaches to solving this problem. In Britain, some manufacturers have developed 'lean burn' engines. These burn a fuel/air mixture which has less fuel and more air. Less pollution results. Another approach, favoured in the United States and parts of Europe is the catalytic converter. This is a ceramic honeycomb, coated with precious metals, which is placed in the exhaust system. The surface area of the honeycomb is about the same as a football pitch. The exhaust gases react on the hot surface of the converter, producing less-harmful products. These converters can only be used with unleaded petrol.

Governments are beginning to provide incentives to drivers to use unleaded petrol and catalytic converters. In Britain, tax is reduced on unleaded petrol, so that it is considerably cheaper than leaded. In Germany, there are tax incentives for drivers who buy cars with catalytic converters.

Year	*Millions of vehicles*
1950	4.4
1960	9.4
1970	13.0
1980	19.2
1986	21.7

Over the period 1950–1986, the population of Britain increased by 12%.

a Describe how car ownership must have changed during this time.

b Can you predict the number of cars on the road in Britain in the year 2000? (The best way to do this is to plot a graph.)

c The population in 1986 was 55 200 000. How realistic is your answer to b?

d Why is the metal in a catalytic converter spread over a large area?

e A new small car might cost around £7000. The cost of a catalytic converter on this car would be around £400. The life expectancy of the converter is about five years, by which time the value of the car would be about £3000. Can you explain why even environmentally-conscious people may be reluctant to fit catalytic converters to their cars? What could the government do to increase the use of catalytic converters?

94 RENEWABLE ENERGY RESOURCES

Renewable energy resources can be replaced or renew themselves.

We cannot use fossil fuels for ever

There are many reasons for looking at alternative ways of producing usable energy. Fossil fuels are being used up far more quickly than they are formed. They also cause pollution problems. Sources of uranium are limited and will eventually run out. So it is essential that we look at other ways of producing electricity, using renewable energy sources. In 1989, the British government announced that the electricity industry should be producing 600 MW of power from renewable sources by the year 2000.

DID YOU KNOW?

More coal has been used since 1945 than was used in the whole of history before that.

Fig. 94.1 Part of a wind farm in California. The farm is in a pass in the mountains through which the wind is naturally channelled, turning hundreds of turbines.

Wind power

Energy from the Sun heats the atmosphere and powers the Earth's winds. The kinetic energy of the wind can be transferred to electrical energy using a windmill and generator.

We will never run out of wind power, and there is no pollution. But there are major difficulties in producing large amounts of electricity in this way. For large-scale power generation, a 'wind farm', with a hundred or more wind turbines, is needed. This covers large areas of land. The turbines must be sited in windy areas, which are often some of the most attractive parts of the landscape. The turbines are big and noisy.

Fig. 94.2 The wind has been used as a renewable energy source for a long time. The large sails on this windmill are turned by the wind, to turn stones for grinding grain. The smaller sails at the back keep the larger ones pointing into the wind. The sails turn too slowly to generate electricity.

Wave power

If we could use all the energy in the waves in the sea around Britain, we could replace 60 large power stations. But we could not surround all of Britain with wave power generators! Some of the most suitable conditions for electricity generation from wave power are in the north west of Scotland. Here, wave power could be practical, particularly for supplying small communities on islands.

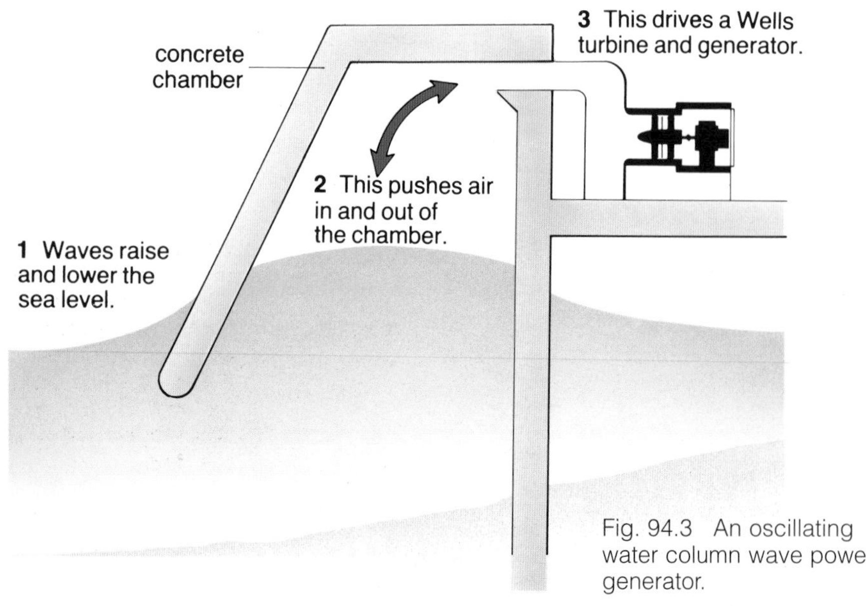

Fig. 94.3 An oscillating water column wave power generator.

Fig. 94.4 This prototype wave power generator is at Islay Island in Scotland. You can see the concrete wall, and the narrow cove into which the waves are channelled.

Tidal power

The energy of the tides results from the gravitational forces between the Earth, Sun and Moon. If the rising tide is allowed to fill a reservoir, the water can be released later to drive turbines and generate electricity. This only works well where the tide is naturally funnelled into an estuary. In Britain, the most suitable area is the Severn estuary, where a barrage could be built across the estuary to capture and hold back the water, and then release it in a controlled way to turn turbines. This could produce 10% of the electricity we need. Some people are concerned, however, that this would alter the landscape, destroying mud flats where many birds feed. Others think it might actually improve the environment, as not so much mud would flow out to sea. The water would become clearer, allowing marine plants and phytoplankton to photosynthesise, producing more food for animals.

Fig. 94.5 The barrage across the Rance river in Dinan, in France, contains large turbines. When the tide comes in, the water is trapped behind the barrage. It can be allowed to flow out later at a controlled speed. As the water flows through the barrage, it turns turbines and generates electricity.

Fig. 94.6 The Severn Bore is a fast-travelling wave which moves up the Severn river. It is caused by the rising tide being funnelled from the Bristol Channel into the narrowing mouth of the river. Some of this energy could be harnessed to generate electricity if a barrage was built.

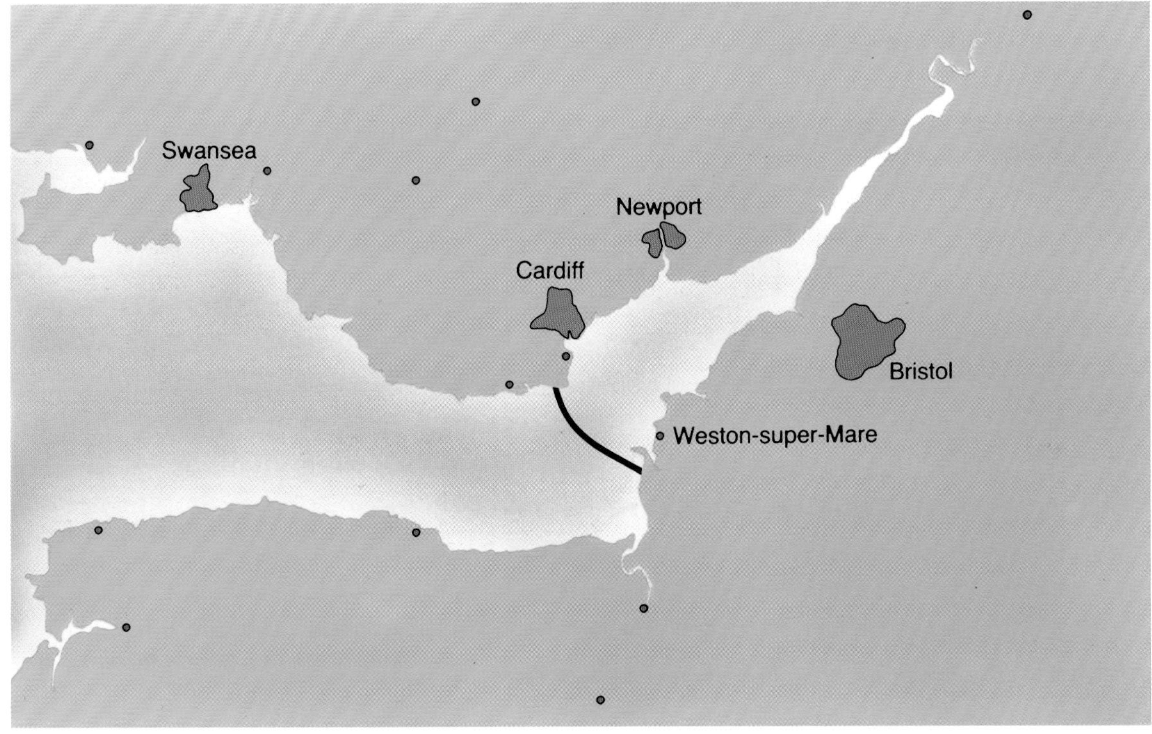

Fig. 94.7 The proposed position for a tidal barrage to be built in the Severn estuary. The shape of the estuary increases the average spring tidal range to 10 m at this point.

Hydroelectric power

Water falling from high ground transfers large amounts of energy. Approximately 4.9 kJ of energy are transferred by 1 kg of water falling 500 m. Rain collected in a reservoir high up a mountain can be released to provide energy when required. The falling water turns turbines, generating electricity.

The demand for electricity from the National Grid varies widely at different times of year and different times of day. One big disadvantage of wind, wave and tidal power is that the wind, waves and tide do not occur all the time – you cannot guarantee a steady production of electricity from them, and you certainly cannot boost up the production to meet a sudden peak in demand. Hydroelectric power stations can help to solve this problem. When demand is low, excess power generated from other stations can be used to pump water back up into the high reservoir. When a peak demand occurs, some of the water can be released to generate extra electricity. This is called a **pumped storage scheme**. At Dinorwic, in Wales, the turbines can be set running in eight seconds to meet peaks in demand.

Hydroelectric power stations do not create pollution and they do not use up non-renewable energy resources. But they can cause major problems all of their own. To create the reservoirs, large areas of upland valleys must be flooded. This can destroy important habitats for wildlife, often in beautiful countryside.

Fig. 94.8 This reservoir is the lower of the two reservoirs of a pumped storage hydroelectric power station at Ffestiniog in Wales. The building is the power station.

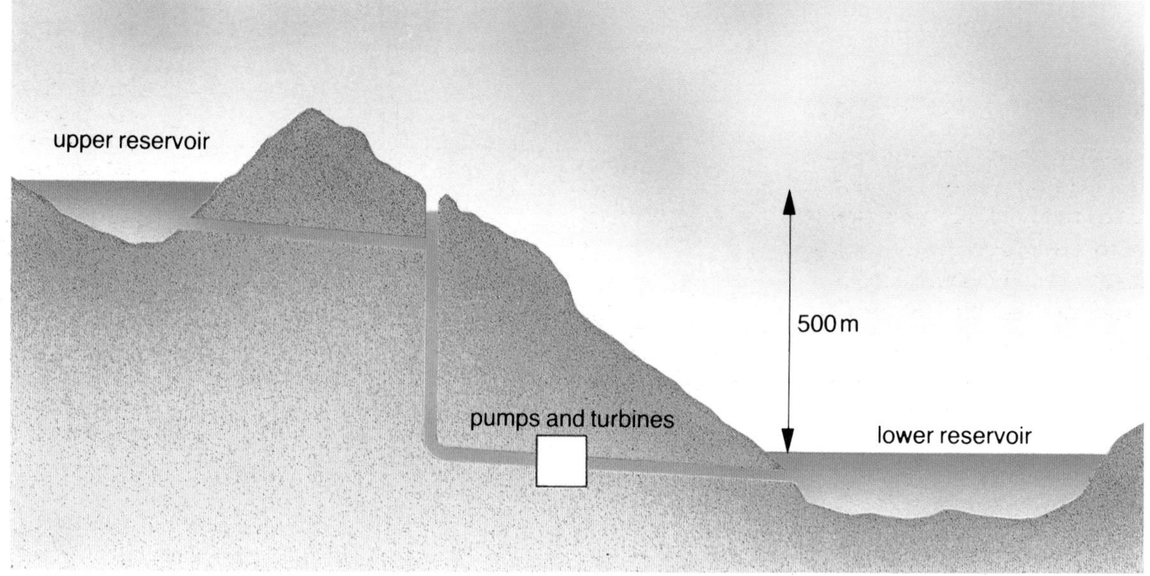

Fig. 94.9 The Dinorwic hydroelectric power and pumped storage scheme in North Wales.

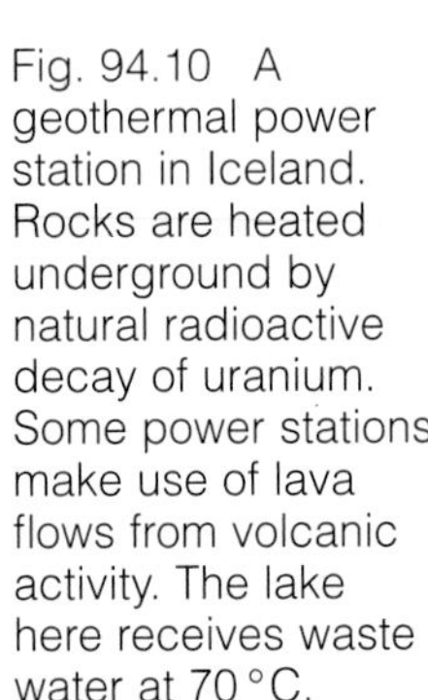

Fig. 94.10 A geothermal power station in Iceland. Rocks are heated underground by natural radioactive decay of uranium. Some power stations make use of lava flows from volcanic activity. The lake here receives waste water at 70 °C.

Geothermal energy

Underground rocks are hot. If water is pumped several kilometres underground, it returns as steam. The steam can be used to drive turbines or for direct heating. In some parts of the world, such as Iceland, hot water comes naturally to the surface. This heat energy from rocks, or **geothermal energy**, is used for power generation in Iceland, New Zealand and some parts of America.

Not all areas are suitable for the production of electricity in this way. It all depends on the rock structures. Apart from this, there are also problems associated with the noise and costs of drilling so deeply into the Earth.

Solar energy

Nearly all our energy comes from the Sun. On a sunny summer day in Britain, a 1 m^2 solar panel can have 1 kW of solar power falling on it. This can be used to heat water or be converted to electricity. In many countries, there is enough solar energy available to meet all heating needs.

You may have a solar powered calculator. Solar cells convert solar energy to electrical energy. They are expensive to produce, but last a long time and have low running costs.

Fig. 94.11 The house in the foreground has three solar panels on its south-facing roof. In the background is Sizewell A nuclear power station.

Fig. 94.12 A merry-go-round powered by solar cells. Solar cells are expensive and are usually only used when supplying electricity in other ways is difficult. Examples of things that use solar cells are satellites, remote ground-based weather stations and rainforest communication systems.

Biomass energy

Plants photosynthesise and store solar energy as chemical energy. If burnt, plants such as trees provide a renewable alternative to fossil fuels. However, this creates many of the same environmental problems as the burning of fossil fuels. The burning of plants releases carbon dioxide, which contributes to the greenhouse effect. We must also take care to grow the trees as a crop, replanting them as we use them. Cutting down forests to burn for fuel can create more problems than it solves. Care must also be taken in choosing suitable areas for planting the trees, so that important habitats are not destroyed.

Another way in which living things can be used to provide energy is by using decomposers, such as bacteria. These can break down organic wastes, such as sewage and waste foods on rubbish dumps, producing fuels such as methane. This happens naturally in many landfill waste sites. The methane produced seeps up through the ground. It can be a hazard, building up in houses near the site and causing explosions. But if the gas is trapped, it can be used as a fuel. However, burning the methane does release carbon dioxide, contributing to the greenhouse effect.

Fig. 94.13 The landfill gas recovery facility in Puente Hills, California, collects methane gas from rotting rubbish. The gas is burnt to fuel a steam turbine and generate electricity. The plant has an output of 46.5 MW and can supply 70 thousand homes. Without the facility the gas would have to be burnt off or released straight into the atmosphere.

Questions

1 Look at the following information about a wind farm.
Number of turbines 29
Power of each turbine 225 kW
Building costs £4 000 000
Payment to landowners for use of land £100 000
Additional cost of loan (based on 20 years' payment) £3 900 000

- **a** What is the total cost of the wind farm over 20 years?
- **b** What is the generating capacity of the site?
- **c** What is the cost per kW of generating capacity?

The farm generates 16 million units of electrical energy per year. The running costs are 0.5p per unit.

- **d** What are the running costs for 20 years?
- **e** What is the total cost over 20 years (including building costs etc.)?
- **f** What is the total cost per unit for the first 20 years?
- **g** Assuming the cost per unit of electricity is similar to a nuclear power station, what are the advantages and disadvantages of each method of electricity generation?

2 Describe the energy transfers in a pumped storage scheme.

3 A large coal-fired power station produces 2000 MW of electrical energy. A wind turbine with 33 m blades can produce 300 kW.

- **a** How many turbines would be needed to replace the power station?
- **b** Why, in practice, couldn't this number actually replace a coal-fired power station?

95 CONSERVING ENERGY

The best answer to the problem of dwindling energy reserves is to use them up more slowly.

Energy efficient housing can reduce energy wastage

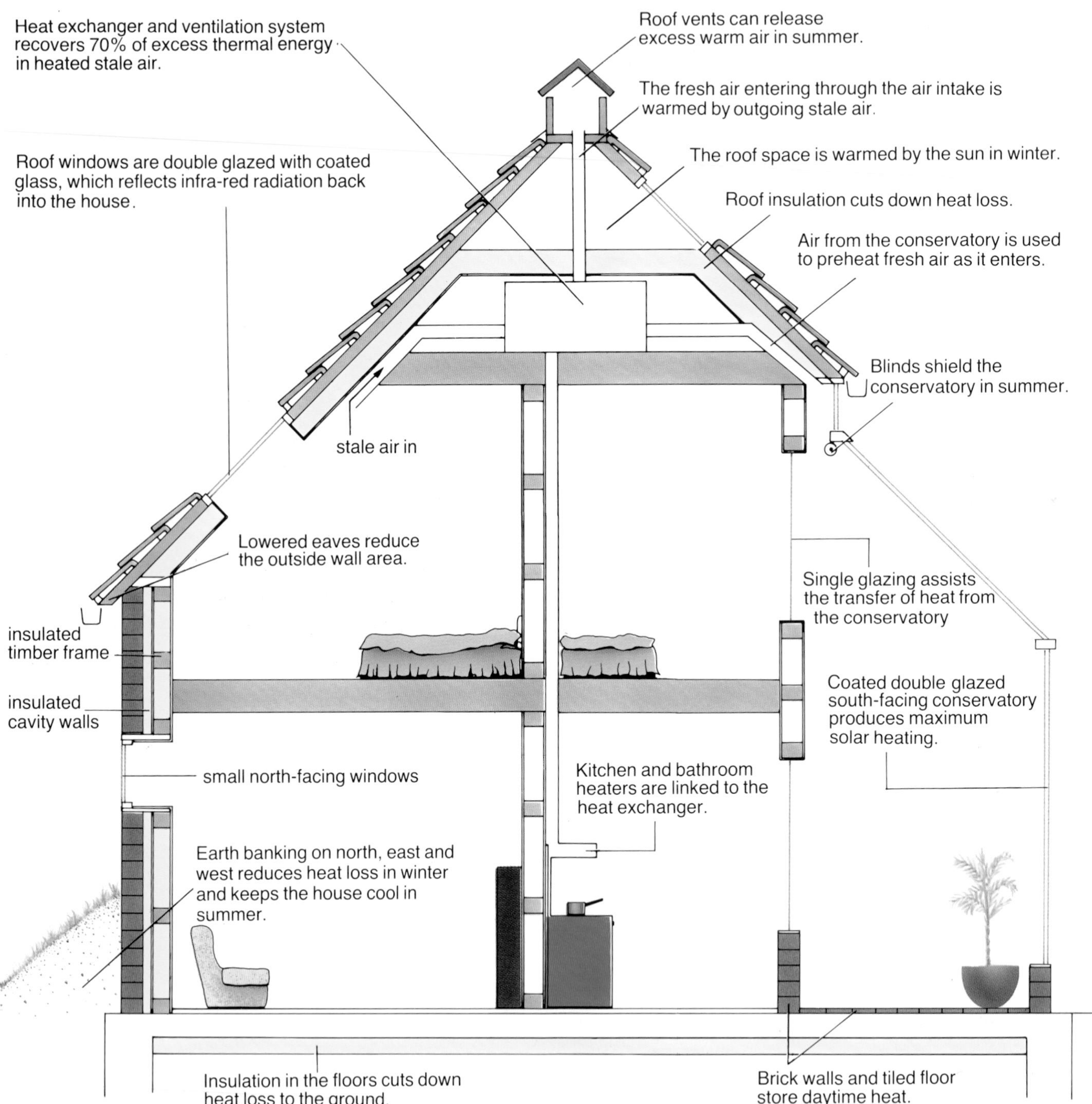

Fig. 95.1 An energy-efficient house

Power stations waste a lot of heat energy

A traditional coal-fired power station wastes most of the chemical energy in the coal. Several methods are now being used to try to reduce this wastage.

The coal can be burned more efficiently in a **fluidised bed**. A bed of red-hot sand is kept fluid by blowing air through it. Coal mixed with the sand burns, and keeps the bed hot. Pipes in the sand carry water, which turns to steam. The steam is used to turn a turbine.

As well as wasting less energy, this type of boiler has the advantage that limestone can be added to the sand. The limestone absorbs 95% of the sulphur dioxide produced by the burning coal. But 50% of the energy from the coal still goes up the chimney and into the cooling water, as wasted heat.

In a **combined heat and power station**, this heat can be used for direct heating. The hot water or steam is piped to offices and factories. A combined heat and power station is not quite as efficient at transferring chemical energy to electrical energy, but because it does not waste as much heat energy its overall efficiency can be as high as 85%. This system only works where the power station is near to the buildings which it supplies, so if we used combined heat and power stations more, they would have to be built in cities.

DID YOU KNOW?

In Sheffield, a power station burns rubbish to heat two housing estates. An extra 20 000 tonnes of rubbish per year would enable it to heat all the major buildings in the city centre and also produce 10 MW of electrical power.

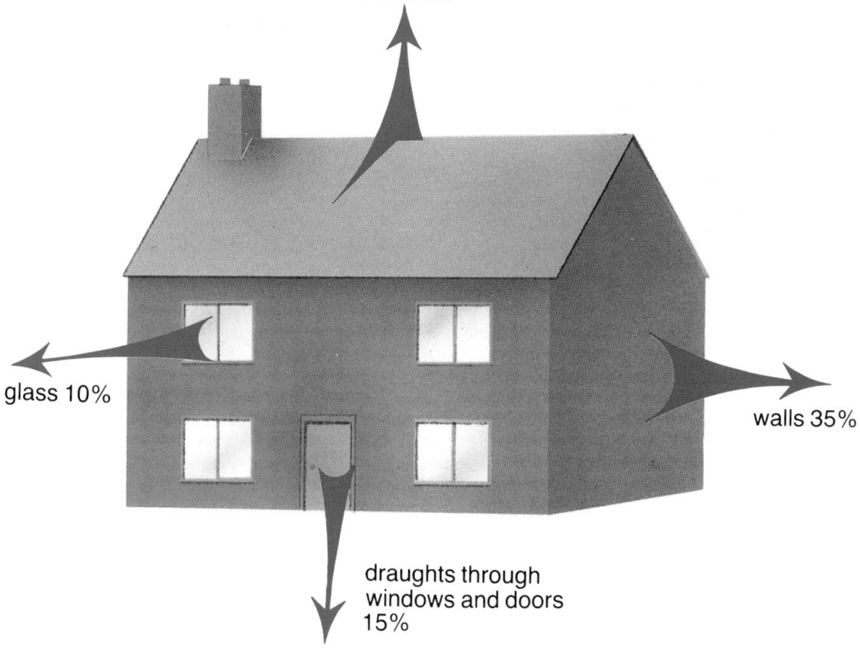

roof 25%

glass 10%

walls 35%

draughts through windows and doors 15%

DID YOU KNOW?

Much of the environmental damage caused by cars is in their manufacture. Half the homes in Wolfsburg in Germany, are heated by 'waste' heat from the Volkswagen car plant. This helps to reduce some of the pollution effects of the car plant and also saves other fuels.

Questions

1 The table shows the time in which home improvements can pay for themselves in terms of energy saved.

Home improvement	*Payback time (years)*
Draughtproof doors and windows	1
Loft insulation, 80 mm thick	2
Loft insulation, 100 mm thick	3
Double glazing	85
Insulating cavity walls	10
Lining solid walls internally, 25 mm thick	20
Lining solid walls internally, 50 mm thick	24
Lining solid walls externally, 50 mm thick	43

The diagram on the left shows the approximate percentage of heat energy lost through different parts of a house with no insulation. The total amount of heat lost is 35 kW.

a What is the most cost-effective energy saving improvement to a house?

b Where is the greatest heat loss from the house?

c How many joules of heat energy pass through the roof every second?

d Double glazing will reduce losses through window glass, and draughts. If you allow for heat gained by solar heating through the glass, south facing windows using specially coated glass (which reflects heat back into the room) reduce heat losses to one sixtieth. Good loft insulation reduces heat loss through the roof by four fifths.

A double glazing salesman uses this argument to persuade you that double glazing is a much more effective way of insulating your home. What hasn't he included in his argument?

96 PAYING FOR ELECTRICITY

The amount of energy used can be calculated by multiplying power by time. The kilowatt hour is a unit of electrical energy.

Energy used = power × time

Electricity is sold in units of one kilowatt hour, or kWh. If one kilowatt is used for one hour, the energy used is power × time (in seconds)

= 1000 W × 60 x 60 s = 3 600 000 J

So if a one bar 1 kW electric fire is switched on for one hour, it transfers 3 600 000 J, or 1 kWh, or one unit of energy. One unit will run a 100 W light bulb for 10 hours. To calculate the number of units you have used, you multiply the power of the appliance by the number of hours for which it was switched on.

number of units used
= number of kWh
= power × time
(in kW) (in hours)

In 1990, the electricity boards charged about 5p for one unit. This is much more convenient than charging per joule of energy you use. The cost would be about 0.0000014p per joule!

A meter records how many units you use

The electricity cables entering your house pass the current through a meter. The meter records the electrical energy passing through it.

Modern meters have digital displays which you can read directly. Older style meters have dials and hands for each number. If you have one of these, they are more difficult to read. You will see that each dial is numbered in the opposite direction to its neighbours. Each hand turns at one tenth the speed of its neighbour. This is done with gears – each hand has ten times as many teeth on its gear as the one which drives it, and rotates in the opposite direction.

If you want to find out how much electrical energy you have used in a certain time read the meter twice, and work out the difference. This tells you the number of units you have used. If you know the price per unit, you can work out the cost.

Electricity is cheaper at night

The demand for electricity varies in a 24 hour period. People use a lot of electricity first thing in the morning, and when they get home from work in the evening. Demand is much less during the night.

It is not easy for the electricity boards to switch their power stations on and off to meet these peaks in demand! It can take several days to get a coal-fired or nuclear power station running at full power, so these **base load** stations are kept running all the time. Hydroelectric and gas turbine stations, though, can be brought into operation more quickly. They can be brought into full operation when there is a surge in the demand for electricity.

At night, when the demand for electricity is low, there is spare electricity being produced by the base load stations. Some of this is used to pump water up to high reservoirs of pumped storage schemes. To encourage people to use this night-time power, the electricity boards sell electricity at a cheaper rate during a seven-hour night-time period. Cheap rate off-peak electricity is sold at nearly one third of the price of peak period electricity. You can use cheap-rate electricity to heat water to use later in the day, or for storage heaters. If you have a time switch, you can set appliances such as washing machines and dishwashers to run at night while you are asleep.

If you belong to an Economy 7 scheme, then your house will have two meters to record the electricity you use at the two different rates. The meters are switched in and out by a clock or by a radio signal sent by the electricity board.

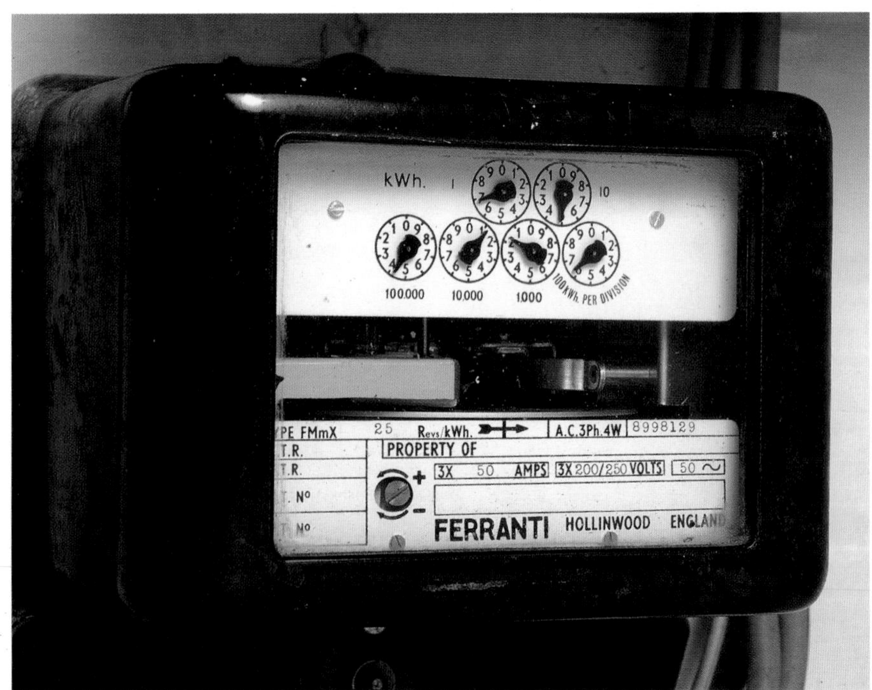

Fig. 96.1 An old electricity meter has dials which go round in opposite directions. You read the number the pointer has just passed, even if it has nearly reached the next one. This meter reads 411646 kWh.

Fig. 96.2 A modern electricity meter. This one records the off–peak units at the top, and the daytime units at the bottom. The off-peak reading is 7166.62 kWh.

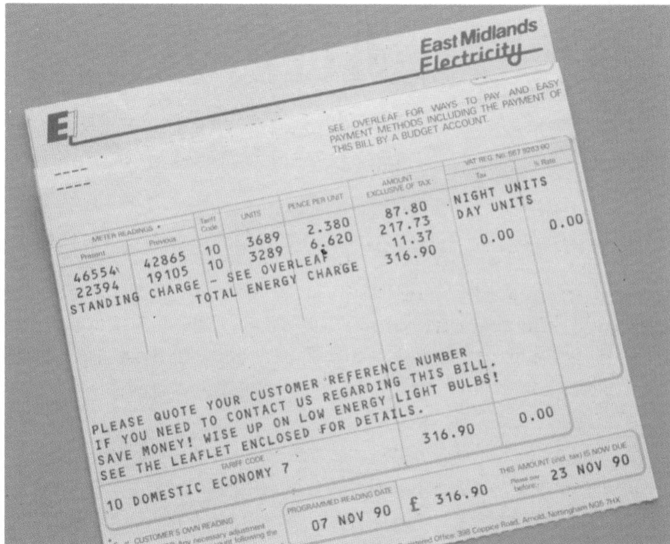
East Midlands Electricity

Present	Previous	Tariff Code	Units	Pence per unit	Amount exclusive of tax		
46554	42865	10	3689	2.380	87.80	NIGHT UNITS	
22394	19105	10	3289	6.620	217.73	DAY UNITS	
STANDING CHARGE			- SEE OVERLEAF		11.37		
			TOTAL ENERGY CHARGE		316.90	0.00	0.00

PLEASE QUOTE YOUR CUSTOMER REFERENCE NUMBER IF YOU NEED TO CONTACT US REGARDING THIS BILL.
SAVE MONEY! WISE UP ON LOW ENERGY LIGHT BULBS!
SEE THE LEAFLET ENCLOSED FOR DETAILS.

316.90 0.00

10 DOMESTIC ECONOMY 7

07 NOV 90 £ 316.90 23 NOV 90

Fig. 96.3 The first row on this electricity bill shows the number of off-peak units recorded for present and previous readings of the meter. The number of units used is the difference between these readings. The second row shows the daytime electricity use. This consumer uses overnight storage heating, and so has used more electricity during the seven hour off-peak period than during the rest of the day.

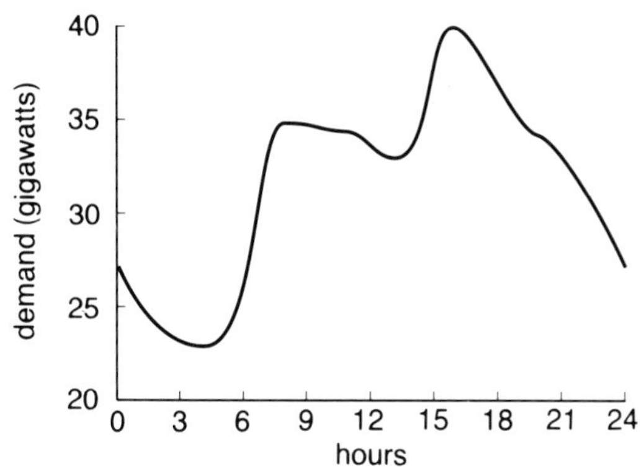

Fig. 96.4 Demand for electricity over a 24 hour period

DID YOU KNOW?

A gas meter records the number of cubic feet of gas passing through it. The cubic feet are converted to therms, which represents the energy content of the gas you have used.

Questions

1 A 150 W television is used for seven hours. How many units of electricity have been used?

2 You receive an electricity bill:

Present	Previous	Units	Pence per unit	Amount	
01685E	01511	174	2.070	3.60	NIGHT
03777E	03151	626	5.770	36.12	DAY
STANDING CHARGE				9.92	
TOTAL				49.64	

The letter E means that your meter has not been read, and the amount of electricity you used has been estimated. After your last bill, you have changed your habits and now do all your washing at night and leave fewer lights on. Your meters actually read:

night time	01859
daytime	03507

By how much have you been overcharged?

3 a Your television is rated at 200 W. You watch television for five hours in the evening. What does this cost you?

b If, on average, your family watches three hours of television each night, what does the electricity for this cost per year?

4 For security, you switch on an energy efficient porch light from 7:00 p.m. to 8:00 a.m. each night. The light bulb uses 18 W.

a What does this cost, charged at peak rate?

b If you switch to Economy 7, this period will include seven hours at the cheap rate. How much will you save?

97 HOME DISTRIBUTION SYSTEMS

A house has at least two different circuits to provide light and power. Although most of the house wiring is in parallel, switches, fuses and Christmas lights are in series.

The electricity supply system in a house

The electricity supply to the home is 230 V a.c. The supply oscillates at 50 Hz. The live wire is oscillating at about 325 V positive and negative compared to the neutral wire, giving power equivalent to 230 V d.c. The neutral wire is nearly at the same voltage as the earth connection.

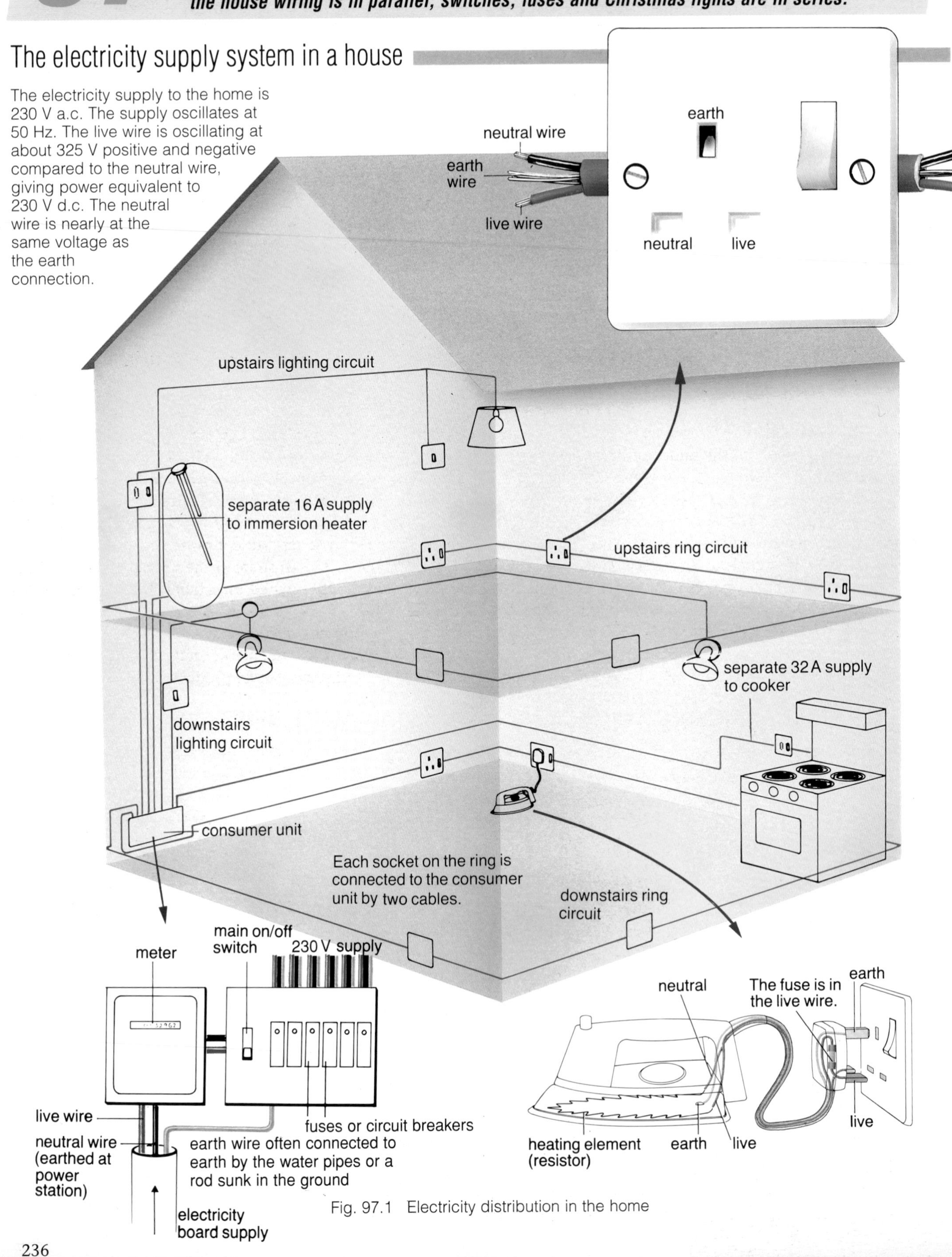

Fig. 97.1 Electricity distribution in the home

The earth wire protects the user from electrocution

The live wire of a mains supply circuit is at a high voltage compared with the ground. A person in contact with the mains can carry enough current through their body to kill them. The charge flows through the body to earth. The conducting path is improved by moisture, so electrical safety is especially important in the kitchen or bathroom. If the iron in Figure 97.1 developed a fault, such as a loose wire or damaged cable, it might be possible for the metal plate to become connected to the mains. If the iron wasn't earthed, anyone touching the plate would get an electric shock. The earth wire is there to carry the current safely to earth. The resistance of the circuit from the live wire to earth is small so a large current flows. This will blow the fuse in the live wire. This is why it is very important to make sure the live and neutral wires in a plug are the right way round. If they are reversed the appliance will still work, but you wouldn't be protected. The fuse is also there to prevent too large a current setting fire to the cable if a fault occurs. If an appliance has no metal parts on the outside that could become connected to the mains, then it doesn't need earthing. This kind of appliance is called a **double-insulated** appliance, and there are only two wires in the cable – live and neutral.

Extra safety protection can be provided by an **earth leakage**, or **residual current**, circuit breaker. This is often in the form of an extra adapter placed in the socket before the plug is inserted, although it can form part of the house circuit. The ELCB or RCCB compares the current leaving the socket through the live wire with the current returning down the neutral wire. Any difference would suggest that current was going where it shouldn't – possibly through a person. When using electrical equipment outside you must always use an ELCB. School laboratories usually have a circuit breaker that switches off all the sockets if a small current imbalance of 30 mA is detected. New fuse boxes are usually fitted with resettable circuit breakers. These activate if the current is too large (Figure 85.6).

Most house circuits are wired in parallel but appliances often have series circuits

The lighting and sockets in a house are set up as parallel circuits. Each socket or light is connected across the live and neutral wires. Each appliance takes its share of the current, but they are all connected to the same voltage. If the circuits were in series then it would not be possible to switch anything off without stopping everything else from working. The switch and fuse for an appliance have to be wired in series with it so they can break the circuit. At school you may find a dark room or chemical store has the interior light wired in series with an external bulb. If the internal light is on, the external bulb is on as well, so that you know there is someone inside or that the light has been left on. Also, if either bulb fails the circuit stops working.

Christmas tree lights are often wired in series. If each bulb is 11.5 V then 20 bulbs in series each take their share of 230 V. However, it only takes one loose bulb to stop the whole circuit from working. These circuits are not very safe because it is still possible to get a 230 V shock, even though each bulb only works from 11.5 V. More modern lights use a combination of series and parallel circuits. An 80 light set uses a transformer to convert 230 V to a safer 23 V. Ten 2.3 V bulbs are wired in series and connected to the transformer. Each bulb takes a $^1/_{10}$ th share of the voltage. Eight of these series circuits are then wired in parallel. This has the added advantage that if one bulb is faulty, only 10 bulbs stop working and you only need to check ten bulbs. If each series circuit can be switched on and off on its own by a controller, attractive light displays can be produced.

What fuse should you use

The power of an appliance can be used to calculate the fuse needed.

$$\text{power} = \text{voltage} \times \text{current}$$

$$\text{so } \mathbf{current} = \frac{\mathbf{power}}{\mathbf{voltage}}$$

For example, a 60 W, 12 V car headlamp draws $\frac{60}{12}$ = 5 A.

So a 5 A fuse would just carry the current without blowing. When the bulb is switched on, it carries a higher current and would blow the fuse.

A 2.5 kW electric fire running off the mains draws $\frac{2500\text{ W}}{230\text{ V}}$ = 10.86 A.

This fire would be protected by a 13 A fuse.

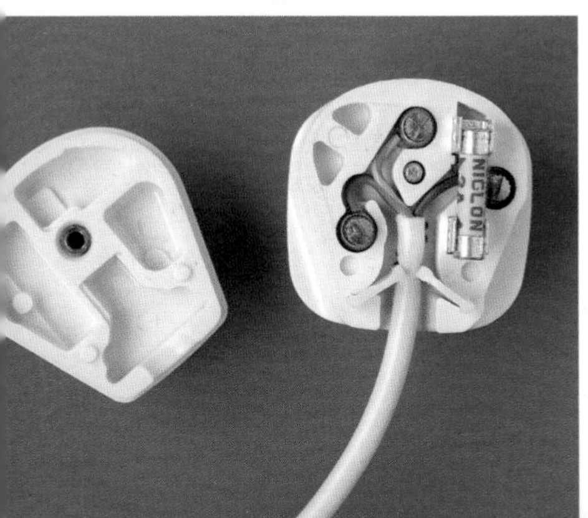

Fig. 97.3 A correctly wired plug. The cable clamp grips the outer insulation. The inner insulation of each wire just reaches to the terminals, so no wire is exposed inside the plug. This means there is little risk of a short circuit. The brown wire is live, blue is neutral, and green and yellow is the earth wire.

A 3 A fuse has been placed in the fuse holder. It is always worth checking that you have put a suitable fuse into the plug, depending on the appliance to which you have fitted it – don't just assume that it is safe to use the fuse supplied with the plug.

Question

1 The diagram below shows an electrically heated hot water tank.

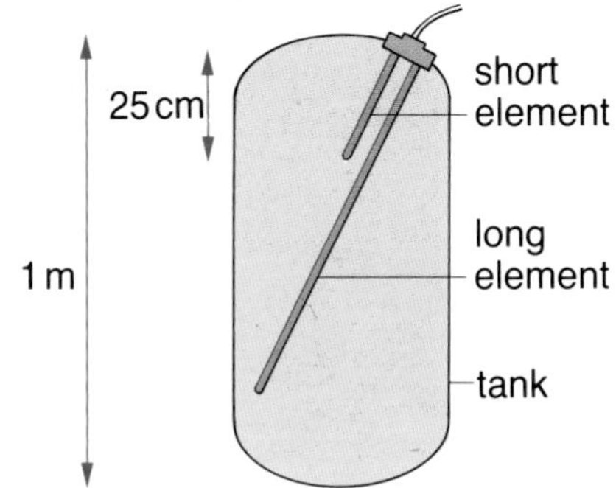

The short element uses peak rate electricity. The long element can only be used during off-peak hours.

a How does the long element heat the whole tank of water?

b What fraction of the water will the short element heat?

c This tank saves you money only if it is well insulated. Why?

Questions

1 a In circuit A, the ammeter reads 0.1 A. How many coulombs per second pass through the bulb?

b What is the resistance of the bulb in circuit A?

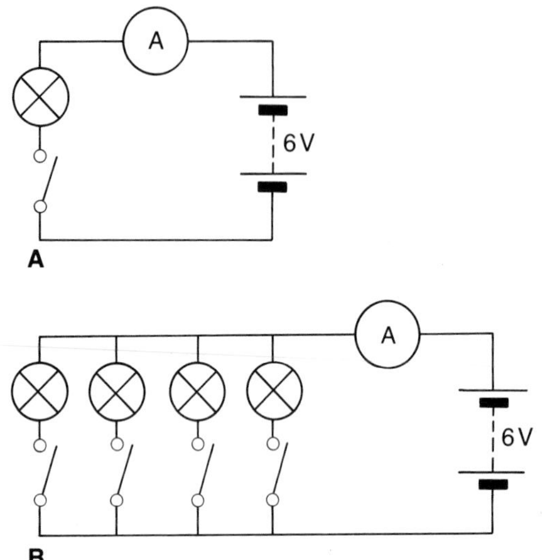

c What will the ammeter read in circuit B if all the switches are closed?

d What will be the voltage across each bulb in circuit B if all the switches are closed?

e What is the wattage of one bulb?

f How much electrical energy is transferred to light and heat per second by all the bulbs in circuit B together?

g In what ways is circuit B like the lighting circuit in a house?

h How does circuit B differ from a lighting circuit in a house?

2 Examine some electrical appliances at home. Find the voltage and power ratings for each one. Calculate the fuse needed for each appliance. How many have the right fuse?

3 The photograph below shows the inside of a fuse box. Each fuse protects a particular circuit in the house. A white fuse is 6 A, blue 16 A, yellow 20 A, and red 32 A.

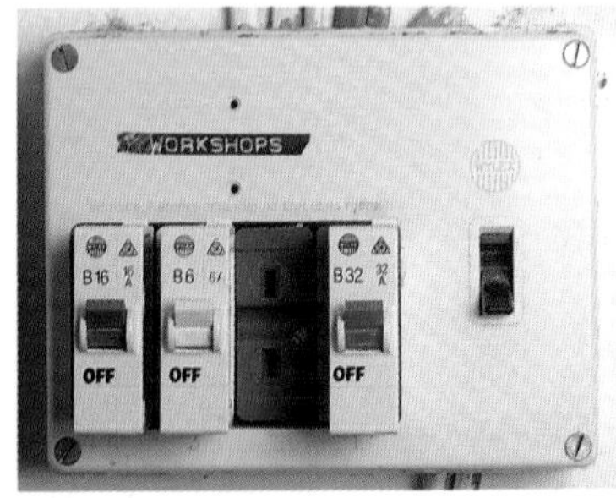

a What is the total current the fuses in the photograph could carry together?

b If a yellow fuse was inserted into the empty socket, what would the total possible current be?

c If the cable carrying this current to the house can carry 120 A, is this a safe system?

d Why does the electricity board fit a 100 A fuse in series with your fuse box?

4 a Describe how an electric bell works. A diagram will help you to do this.

b Show how you could connect two switches and a battery to the bell, so that the front door switch rings the bell continuously, but the back door switch produces a single 'ding'.

5 a An electric kettle takes $5^1/_2$ min to boil 1.7 dm^3 of water. The element is rated at 2.4 kW. The initial temperature of the water was 10 °C.
How much electrical energy does the kettle use?

b If 1 kWh costs 6p, how many joules do you get for 1p?

c How much does it cost to boil the water?

d What is the temperature rise of the water?

e If it takes 4200 J to raise the temperature of 1 kg of water by 1 °C, how many joules has the water gained?

f How efficient is the kettle?

6 The flow diagram shows some components of a power station.

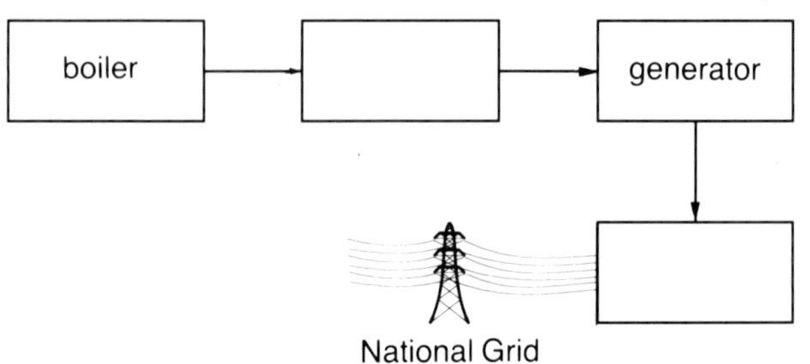

a Name the two unlabelled components.

b What are the energy transfers taking place in these two components?

c Name three possible sources of energy for the boiler, apart from coal.

d What is the main type of pollution caused by each source you have named in part c?

e Are any of these sources renewable?

f In a coal-fired power station, which energy transfer is least efficient?

g How could this energy transfer be made more efficient?

7 A wind turbine has the following outputs under different conditions.

Wind speed (km/h)	*Power output (kW)*
3.6	3
7.2	25
11.0	85
14.5	200
18.0	390

a What wind speed is required to produce an output of 100 kW?

b The wind speed 12 m above the ground is 1.5 times greater than at 1.5 m above the ground. If a turbine produces 25 kW at head height, what will it produce at 12 m above the ground?

c What other reason is there for using tall towers for wind turbines?

USEFUL FORMULAE + CIRCUIT SYMBOLS

Useful formulae

moment = force x perpendicular distance from pivot

$$\text{mechanical advantage} = \frac{\text{load force}}{\text{effort force}}$$

$$\text{efficiency} = \frac{\text{useful output energy}}{\text{input energy}}$$

$$\text{average speed} = \frac{\text{distance moved}}{\text{time taken}}$$

$$\text{acceleration (m/s}^2\text{)} = \frac{\text{change in velocity (m/s)}}{\text{time taken (s)}}$$

displacement = velocity x time

$$\text{acceleration} = \frac{\text{force}}{\text{mass}}$$

momentum = mass x velocity

impulse = change in momentum

$$\text{kinetic energy} = \frac{1}{2}\ \text{mass} \times \text{velocity}^2$$

Electricity

$$\text{current} = \frac{\text{charge passing}}{\text{time}}$$

energy = velocity x charge

potential difference (voltage) = current x resistance

$$\text{resistance} = \frac{\text{potential difference (voltage)}}{\text{current}}$$

total resistance in series = $R_1 + R_2 + R_3 + \ldots\ldots\ldots$

$$\frac{1}{\text{total resistance in parallel}} = \frac{1}{R_1} + \frac{1}{R_2} + \frac{1}{R_3} + \ldots\ldots\ldots\ldots$$

power = potential difference x current

energy transferred = potential difference x current x time

$$\text{power} = \frac{\text{voltage}^2}{\text{resistance}}$$

power = resistance x current^2

$$\frac{\text{input voltage}}{\text{output voltage}} = \frac{\text{turns on input coil}}{\text{turns on output coil}}$$

number of electricity units used = power (in kW) x time (in hours)

Circuit symbols

connection

switch

push switch

relay

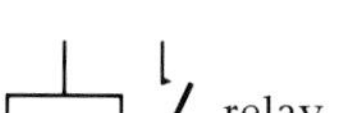

battery

cell

power supply (connections)

a.c. supply

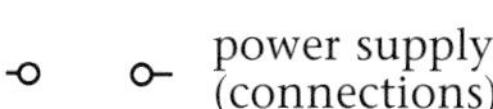

lamp

lamp

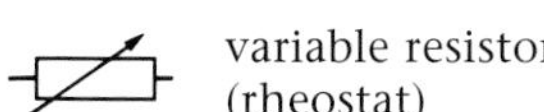

resistor

variable resistor (rheostat)

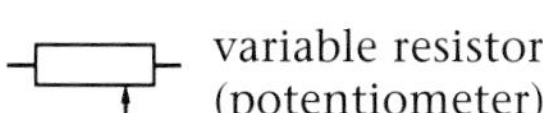

variable resistor (potentiometer)

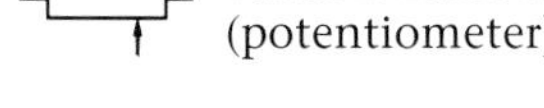

thermistor

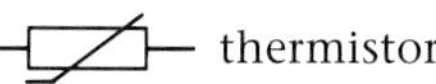

capacitor

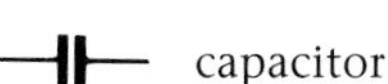

capacitor (electrolytic)

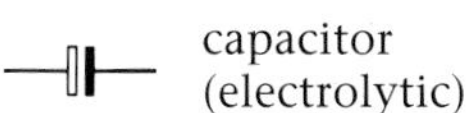

ammeter

voltmeter

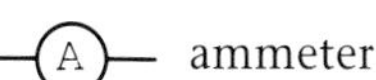

motor

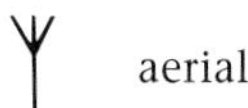

galvanometer

aerial

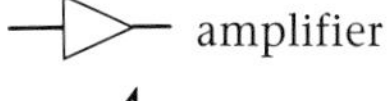

amplifier

loudspeaker

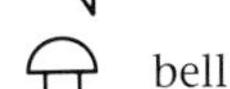

bell

diode

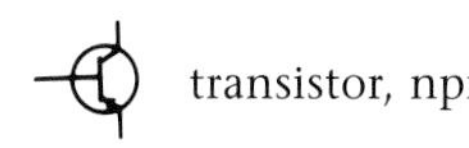

transistor, npn

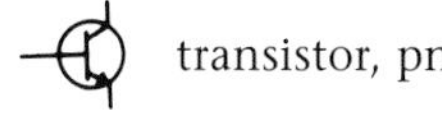

transistor, pnp

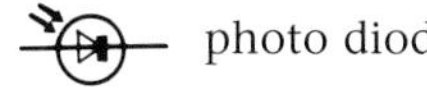

photo diode

LED

LDR

photo voltaic cell

inductor

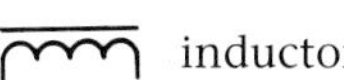

OR gate

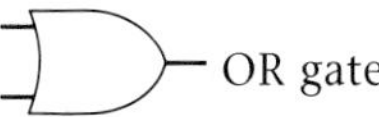

NOR gate

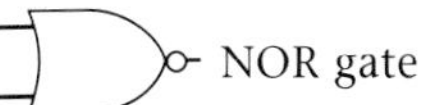

AND gate

NAND gate

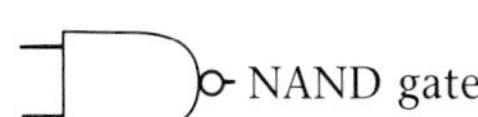

NOT gate

APPARATUS LISTS

Quantities given are those needed per group if the experiment is performed by students, or the quantity needed to perform a demonstration.

It is expected that teachers will provide safety goggles whenever students are handling potentially dangerous materials, or heating substances.

Teachers should also carry out their own risk assessments, bearing in mind the nature of the equipment, chemicals, environment and people involved.

1.1 Using a smoke cell to see Brownian motion

smoke cell (including light source, lens, cell and cover slip)
power pack to suit bulb leads
microscope; check that there is sufficient clearance between stage and objectives to accommodate smoke cell
waxed paper straw or string to make smoke

3.1 How quickly do scent molecules move?

Students will ask for their own apparatus, but are likely to need:
perfume - any will do
stopclock
metre ruler or tape

3.2 Diffusion of gases

The apparatus is shown in the diagram on page 13. Concentrated hydrochloric acid and ammonia solution give the best results, but care must be taken not to expose students to fumes at close quarters, or for very long. This is especially important for students with asthma. A small amount of each liquid can be poured into a watch glass in a **fume cupboard**, and a piece of cotton wool (held with forceps) dipped into each. If the soaked cotton wool is quickly pushed into the tube ends, and then immediately held in position with a bung, only a relatively mild smell will be noticed by students. (Consider carrying out the whole demonstration in a fume cupboard where practical.)

3.3 How small is a potassium permanganate particle?

10 test tubes in rack
a few crystals of potassium permanganate
syringe or pipette to measure 1 cm^3
access to water

5.1 The effect of evaporation on temperature

5 boiling tubes and single hole bungs to take thermometers
cotton wool
clamps and stands
small quantities of ethanol
stopwatches
N.B. If datalogging equipment is available, this is an ideal experiment as the cooling curve can be acquired directly.

10.1 Investigating the radiation levels from a gamma source

Students must not handle radioactive sources.
scalar/counter or ratemeter, and Geiger-Müller tube
tongs for handling gamma source
gamma source (mounted in such a way that students do not handle it)
ruler
clamp or similar so that GM tube can be 'held' remotely or moved by the teacher according to student instruction.
The gamma source should not be handled by students, or pointed directly at anyone.
Students could also plan investigations into the penetration of aluminium/lead by gamma rays; or compare the penetration of gamma rays with that of alpha and beta radiation.
Datalogging equipment could be used for this investigation.

10.2 The effect of radiation on living organisms

Students will ask for their own apparatus, but are likely to need:
barley seeds, normal and irradiated, about 10 of each
containers for growing them, e.g. margarine tubs with drainage holes
compost
labels
The seeds will germinate and grow faster if kept in warm conditions.

13.1 Using cubes to simulate radioactive decay

At least 100 cubes, each with one face marked differently from the others.

16.1 Measuring the extension of a spring

spring, masses and hanger, masses up to 40 g should be sufficient
retort stand, boss and clamp
A similar experiment could be performed with elastic bands, and a comparison made between them and a spring. Careful measurements should show hysteresis (page 173) with the rubber band.
Elastic limit can also be investigated. This should be attempted with care, and safety goggles must be worn. If the bottom spring loop gives way, the spring can fly up.
Students could also try making their own springs from copper wire and investigating how the size of wire and the size of the spring affects its strength.

18.1 Finding centres of gravity

card shapes
cotton
pins
retort stand, boss and clamp
weight or piece of plasticine

19.1 Equilibrium in animals

plasticine
cocktail sticks

21.1 Finding the density of an object

object
thread
balance to give mass or weight, newton balances
Either:
beaker
measuring cylinder
container to catch water
Or:
displacement can
beaker
measuring cylinder

21.2 Finding the density of sand

measuring cylinder
beaker
balance
dry 'silver' sand
access to water

23.1 Plotting magnetic fields

bar and horseshoe magnets
plotting compass
sheet of paper
pencil
Students could also try plotting fields in three dimensions or use a flux meter to investigate the strength of the field.

23.2 Comparing the strength and permanence of iron and steel magnets

iron wire
steel wire, e.g. paper-clips
bar magnet
iron filings
Students could also investigate methods for demagnetising magnets, using a magnetised paper-clip – for example, heat, shock, another magnet etc.

28.1 Calculating power output
stairs or exercise bicycle – it makes a good comparison if students try both and think about the energy wasted in each case.
scales for weighing students
ruler
newton meter
stopwatch

33.1 Penguins
Students will ask for their own apparatus, but are likely to require:
test tubes
beakers
access to hot water – almost boiling water from a kettle is best
thermometers
stopwatches
fan
paper or card
Datalogging equipment can be used for this investigation.

37.1 Investigating a pendulum
bob, string and support
ruler
stopwatch
Some types of position sensor can be connected to a pendulum and used with a datalogger to record the motion of the pendulum.

38.1 Standing waves
apparatus as shown in Figure 38.7 using a signal generator and vibrator. The masses and pulleys should be arranged to ensure that there is no sideways force on the vibrator shaft.
ruler to measure string
various types of string – thick, thin, and of different materials
assorted masses – enough to maintain the balance on each side as they are changed

41.1 Measuring the speed of sound in air
Long tape for measuring length of school field – the longer the distance which can be used, the more accurate the results.
A distance of 100 m will give a delay of 0.3 s.
starting pistol (banging blocks and/or blown whistles co-ordinated with waved arms are generally less satisfactory, but can yield surprisingly accurate readings if averaged over ten or more 'timers' and multiple timings)
stop watch

42.1 How is the speed of a wave affected by the depth of water through which it travels?
tray – the type which is used for storage in many schools is ideal (a long length of square guttering is a useful alternative if the experiment can be performed outside)
ruler to measure mm
stopwatch

43.1 Investigating oscilloscope traces of different types of sound
oscilloscope and microphone
various sources of pure sounds – tuning forks, radio, musical instruments, electronic keyboard etc.
A fast response datalogger and sound meter can be used to capture sound traces.

43.2 The range of human hearing
oscillator and loudspeaker (a good quality loudspeaker is needed so that the test is of hearing and not the frequency response of the loudspeaker)

45.1 Building a loudspeaker
thin cardboard sheet, at least A4 size (cereal boxes are ideal)
cardboard coil-former
sticky tape
scissors
thin insulated wire
commercial loudspeaker to study
signal generator or other 'sound' producing system (for example a radio and amplifier) (an a.c. power pack can produce a convincing hum)
4 Ω resistor to protect amplifier from short circuit
bar magnet
leads and crocodile clips
hole punch and rubber bands to mount the cone between lab stands

49.1 Reflection of light rays by a plane mirror
ray box set up as in diagram
plane mirror and supports
partial blackout
white paper
ruler
set square, protractor

50.1 Images in a plane mirror
white paper
plane mirror and supports
pin with a large head
ruler

52.1 Refraction of light rays in a semicircular Perspex block
semicircular Perspex block
white paper
ray box producing a single ray (as 49.1 with single slit)
partial blackout
ruler, protractor

54.1 Bending light
optical pin (the end of which is best pushed in to piece of cork)
card to make screen
light bulb and power source

57.1 Investigating a convex lens
partial blackout, but access to a window
convex lens with a focal length of between 10 and 20 cm
piece of white paper and support to act as a screen
light source to use as an object
metre rule and shorter rule
If graph paper is used as the screen, the image size can be measured and magnification can be investigated.

58.1 Finding the focal length of a diverging lens
partial blackout
ray box providing three parallel rays (as 49.1 with triple slit)
white paper
cylindrical diverging and converging lenses of similar focal lengths
ruler

60.1 Pinhole cameras
partial blackout
pinhole camera, or material for making one – cardboard, sticky tape, glue, black paper, tracing paper, pin (to make the pinhole)
light source to use as an object (candles or large filament lamps are most impressive)
converging lens with a focal length about the same as the box length

61.1 Looking at a human eye
mirror
something with which to cover eyes
bright light

63.1 Investigating levers
triangular wooden pivot
beam – a metre ruler works well
a selection of 10, 20, 50 and 100 g masses, allowing combinations up to 500 g
graph paper

64.1 Measuring reaction time
stopwatch
100 g mass
metre ruler
30 cm ruler
The time taken for the 100 g mass to reach the ground when dropped from a height of 1 m will be 0.45 s.
Students may ask for this information in order to estimate reaction times.
Light gates or sensors and datalogging equipment can be used to extend this investigation.

67.1 How do force and mass affect acceleration?
ramp
dynamics trolley and elastics
ticker tape timer
power pack and leads
ticker tape (self-marking tape is the easiest to use)
extra trolleys or masses
balance to mass trolleys
graph paper
It is not necessary to measure the actual force applied. If the force with one elastic is xN, then the force with two elastics is 2xN, and so on. Less able students may however feel happier if they have numbers to deal with, instead of unknowns.
Datalogging equipment with position/speed sensors can be used in this experiment.

67.2 Investigating terminal velocity
Students will ask for their own apparatus, but are likely to need:
ping-pong balls
stopwatch
ticker tape timers and associated equipment
metre ruler
Plasticine
balance to mass objects
tall measuring cylinders or clear tubes sealed at one end, through which Plasticine balls can be dropped through water
access to water

68.1 Spinning a bung
mass and hanger
plastic tube and rubber grip is safest (a glass tube could be used in demonstrations taking care that it could not shatter)
cotton thread
rubber bung
a selection of different masses
hanger for masses
ruler
graph paper
Set up the apparatus as shown in Figure 68.6

70.1 Collisions and momentum
Students will ask for their own apparatus, but are likely to need:
ramp
trolleys
ticker tape timer
power pack and leads
ticker tape (self-marking tape is the easiest to use)
stopwatch
ruler
air track and riders (if available)
balance to mass objects used
speed/distance computer or suitable datalogging equipment

79.1 Current in simple circuits
power pack
bulbs (all of the same type : voltage in V and current rating in A or wattage in W)
ammeter – 6 V MES type bulbs will require 1 A; 12 V raybox type bulbs a 5 A meter
leads and crocodile clips

80.1 Testing Ohm's law
power pack
voltmeter
ammeter or milliammeter (students should try the ammeter first)
samples as listed in step 2
The gas in a discharge tube, for example neon, will need voltages above 90 V, and must be shown as a demonstration only.

82.1 Making an electrochemical cell
potatoes, lemons or other vegetables or fruit
samples of copper, zinc, lead, iron and nickel
voltmeter
leads and crocodile clips
1.25 V (2 V) bulbs
beaker
dilute sulphuric acid
Students should wear **safety goggles**.

82.2 Making a lead–acid cell
lead plates
leads and crocodile clips
dilute sulphuric acid
safety screen
power pack
voltmeter
1.25 V or 2.5 V bulbs and holder
Students should wear **safety goggles**.

83.1 Investigating resistance
nichrome wire 30–36 swg
ammeter
voltmeter
leads and crocodile clips
power pack
heatproof mats
N.B. it is possible to heat the wire to beyond 'orange heat' and melt it – goggles should be worn and fingers kept clear.

83.2 Voltage–current characteristics of a silicon diode
power pack
rheostat
bulb (12 V or 6 V)
bulb holder
leads and crocodile clips
voltmeter
milliammeter
silicon diode, e.g. 1N4001

84.1 Resistance and heating
rheostat
leads and crocodile clips
ammeter
voltmeter
12 V 21 W bulb (ray box lamps are expensive; car indicator bulbs are much cheaper)
power pack capable of at least 3 A

84.2 Energetic elements
glass beaker
thermometer
power pack
capillary tube
36 swg nichrome wire (about 20 cm)
crocodile clips
stop watch or other means of timing
access to water
ability to mass the water e.g. balance
If the capillary tubing is too narrow, and becomes blocked at one end by the wire, water boiling in it can spit from its end if it is not submerged.
Students should therefore wear **safety goggles**.

85.1 Magnetic field around a solenoid
insulated wire
power pack
12 V 21/36 W bulb, or rheostat (without this a 4 A power pack will quickly trip)
plotting compass
iron nails (6″ steel nails will work well)

86.1 Making a motor
motor kit as illustrated: insulating tape, axle tube and coil former, wire, rubber band or tape, wire strippers, two split pins, axle, base and rivets, yoke
power pack
four magnets

87.1 Testing a simple generator
Motor made in Investigation 86.1 (a commercial motor could be used)
milliammeter or microammeter
extra magnets
extra wire
leads and crocodile clips

87.2 Voltage and current in a motor
d.c. motor
power pack with adjustable voltage
ammeter
voltmeter
leads and crocodile clips
Datalogging equipment can be used to investigate variation of current and voltage with load.

88.1 Making a transformer
iron C cores
crocodile clips
insulated wire
6 V bulbs
power pack providing 6 V a.c. and at least 4 A (4 A power packs can be quickly tripped)
N.B. the output voltage depends on the turns ratio. If the secondary has more than four times as many turns as the primary, the output could **peak** at 34 V from a 6 V power pack. (Although C cores make rather inefficient transformers.)
Students should not be exposed to voltages above 25 V so it is sensible to limit the turns ratio to 3.

ANSWERS TO QUESTIONS

Topic	*Question*	
4	**4**	273 K
6	**2b**	1, 3, 92
7	**1**	10
9	**2a**	12
	2b	12
	2c	24
	2d	14
	2f	^{24}Mg
	3a	144 525 protons and neutrons
	3b	59 885 protons and neutrons
	3c	204.4 protons and neutrons
	3d	204.4
	4a	29
	4b	34 and 36 neutrons
	4c	63.6
13	**1**	4 510 000 000 or 713 000 000 years
	3a	${}^{226}_{88}\text{Ra} \longrightarrow {}^{222}_{86}\text{Ra} + {}^{4}_{2}\text{He}$
		${}^{222}_{86}\text{Rn} \longrightarrow {}^{218}_{84}\text{Po} + {}^{4}_{2}\text{He}$
		${}^{234}_{90}\text{Th} \longrightarrow {}^{234}_{91}\text{Pa} + {}^{0}_{-1}\text{e}$
	4a	15 m^3
	4b	300 Bq
	5	7.65 days
15	**4f**	5600 years
End of topic		
	5b	110.5
	5c	40.5 if background remains constant
	7b	12.5 min
	7c	12.5 min
	7d	12.5 min
	7e	49 min from the start or an extra 9 min
	8	${}^{235}_{92}\text{U}+{}^{1}_{0}\text{n} \longrightarrow {}^{144}_{56}\text{Ba}+{}^{90}_{36}\text{Kr}+2{}^{1}_{0}\text{n}$ only two neutrons are released
	9	${}^{60}_{27}\text{Co} \longrightarrow {}^{60}_{28}\text{Ni} + {}^{0}_{-1}\text{e}$
		${}^{60}_{28}\text{Ni} \longrightarrow {}^{60}_{28}\text{Ni} + \gamma$
16	**2a**	6 cm
	2b	No – the spring would probably have passed its elastic limit.
	3a	1500 N
	3b	3000 N
	4	8 cm
	5a	6.67 mm
	5b	The scales would no longer show an accurate reading.
17	**1**	20 N, 46 N, 8.5 kg
	2a	97 000 kg
	2b	970 000 N
	2c	970 000 N
	3	Earth: weight = 10 N Jupiter: mass = 1 kg, g = 24.9 N / kg Earth: mass = 25 kg, g = 10 N / kg Sun: weight = 274 N Moon: 3340 N

Topic	*Question*	
19	**3**	35°
20	**1a**	10 000 N
	1b	3000 N
	2a	hydrogen
	2b	salt water
	2c	the same each time
21	**1**	540 g
	2	888.9 cm^3
	3a	7 g / cm^3
	3b	450 g
	4	17.04 g
	5a	2000 N
	5b	200 kg
	5c	0.2 m^3
	6a	100 g
	6b	125 cm^3
	6c	125 cm^3
	6d	500 g
End of topic (page 40)		
	2a	650 N
	4b	1.67 N/kg
	4c	The 1.8 kg mass on Earth
	4d	The 10 kg mass
	8a	4 000 000N
	8b	4 000 000N
	8c	400 kg / m^3
	8e	more
	8f	less
27	**1**	125 N
	3a	600 N
	3b	1500 J
	3c	About 6000 J but allow a wide range
	4	294 000 J
	5a	300 J
	5c	No
28	**1a**	person A 105 W, person B 300 W
	1b	person A
	2a	1800 J
	2c	280 W
	2d	1.8 s
	2e	The conveyor, as the builder does not also have to be lifted
	3a	44.9 kW or 44 900 W
	3b	1750 N
29	**1a**	5.1 MJ or 5 100 000 J
	1b	About half as much
	2a	0.6°C
	2b	25 200 J
	2c	4.2 J / g °C
	3a	10 g
	3b	52.5 g
	3c	210 cm^3
30	**2a**	2000 J
	2c	25 MJ or 25 000 000 J every second
	2d	25 MW or 25 000 000 W
31	**1**	(light bulbs) 20 %
	2	80 %
	1a	(kettles) 240 kJ
	1b	95 %
	2a	(gas fire) 60.6 %

Topic	*Question*	
	3a	74 074 J
	3b	13 888.9 J
	4a	5 revs per second
	4b	314 cm
	4c	300 W
	4d	300 J
	4e	95.5 N
	5	Engine 40 % efficient,generator 75 % efficient, motor 80 % efficient, so total 24 % efficient
34	**2a**	0.2 J
	2b	0.4 W
35	**2a**	30 000 N / m^2 or Pa
	2b	20 000 000 N / m^2 or Pa
	3a	6 000 000 Pa
	3b	6 000 000 Pa
	3c	2400 N
36	**1b**	136.5 kPa
	1c	0 °C or 273 K
	1d	melting ice
	2	15 MPa Force of 1500 N so probably no
	4a	40 000 N
	4b	4000 kg
	6	250 ml
	7	10 mm^3
	8	Volume is 60.1 litres PV = 6 010 000 Pa 60.1MPa 45.1 MN
	9	237 kPa
End of topic (page 96)		
	3c	12 m^2
	4a	100 kJ or 100 000 J
	4c	90 000 J
	4d	50 N
	5b	125° hotter
	6a	20 800 MJ
	6b	52 800 MJ
37	**1**	1 Hz
	2	approx 25 cm
page 99	**1a**	4 Hz
	1b	0.25 s
	2a	50 times
	2b	1/300 or 0.0033 s
39	**1a**	125 km
40	**1b**	approx $^1/3500$ or 0.03 %
41	**1a**	3 s
	2a	3 m
	3	375 000 km
	4a	Fish at 3.3 m stationary. Killer whale at 330 m and moving away
	4b	sea bed
42	**1a**	275.5 m; 909.1 kHz; 300 105 000; 299 970 000; 300 000 000; 3.25 m
	2a	17 m and 17 mm
	2b	0.2 and 200
45	**3a**	4 ms
	3b	250 Hz
	3c	20 ms
	3e	50 Hz

Topic	Question	Answer
47	**2a**	4950 m
	2b	0.0008 %
	2a	3 W
	2b	20 W
	2c	20 %
	3c	falls to $^1/_{32}$
	4b	£525
	4c	£165 if 1 tube for every 3 lights
54	**1**	11 cm and 5.6 m
	2	0.0000006 m or 0.0006 mm
58	**1a**	10 cm from other side of lens
	1b	3.3 cm from same side of lens
	2	2.2 m from lens
62	**1a**	2 Nm clockwise
	1b	2.5 Nm clockwise
	1c	2.25 Nm clockwise
	2ai	100 Nm
	2aii	400 Nm
	2b	500 Nm
	2c	500 N
	2d	94.7 cm
	3a	350 N
	3b	a force of only 70 N would be needed to tighten the nut
	4a	every 6 hours
64	**1**	40 s
	2	10 m/s
Page 159	**1a**	700 m
	1b	70 s
	1c	10 m/s
	1d	500 m
	1e	7.1 m/s
	2	25 cm/s or 0.25 m/s
65	**1a**	$10 m/s^2$
	1c	20 m/s
	2c	28 mm
	2d	28 cm/s
	2e	40 cm/s
	2f	12 cm/s
	2g	$120 cm/s^2$
66	**1b**	after 240 s
	1c	after 437.5 s
	1d	4800 m
	1e	8750 m
	2a	26.67 m/s
	2b	$3.1 m/s^2$
	2c	114.6 m
67	**1a**	$0.0067 m/s^2$
	1b	800 000 N
	1c	1.2 km
	2a	$30 m/s^2$
	2b	30 000 N
	2c	30 000 N
69	**1c**	$196 m/s^2$
	1d	70 cm
	2a	4.47 m/s
	2b	290.55 kgm/s
	2ci	290.55 kgm/s
	2cii	29055 N
	2d	581.1 N
70	**1a**	56.6 m/s
	1b	127.3 mph
	2a	3000 J
	2b	6000 J
	2c	600 W
71	**1a**	$1 m/s^2$
	1b	10 s
	1c	50 m
	1d	5 s, 12.5 m
	2	90 m

Topic	Question	Answer
End of topic (page 174)		
	1	74
	1b	A gear
	1c	C gear
	1d	2:1, 1:1 and 17:27
	2bi	45 cm
	2bii	38.5 cm
	2c	5 cm
	2d	3.85 Nm
	2e	77 N
	3a	80 m/s
	3c	320 m
74	**2a**	6600 km
	1b	7.7 km/s
	2a	784 MJ
	2b	1.8 km/s
	3a	4 hours
	3b	8 hours
77	**2a**	59 Earth days
	2b	88 Earth days
79	**1a**	2 A
	2a	A1=1 A; A2=0.5 A
	2b	1 coulomb
	2c	2 s
80	**1a**	2 J
	1b	6 J
	1c	4 J
	1d	4 V
82	**1a**	£307.20
83	**1**	177 ohms
	2a	10 A
	2b	230 J
	3a	2
	3b	4
	4a	885 ohms
	4b	14.4 A
	5	3 ohms, 5 ohms, 4 ohms, 6 ohms, $^2/_3$ ohms, $^{11}/_5$ ohm, $^3/_4$ ohm, $^6/_{11}$ ohm
	6d	2.25 V
	6e	6.75 V
	6f	337.5 ohms
84	**1a**	10.4 A
	1b	22 ohms
	1c	it's thinner
	1d	642.6 kJ
	1e	267.75 s
	2a	36 J
	2b	75.6 kJ
	2c	4200 J
	2d	72 °C
	3a	15 J
	3b	1.8 W
	3c	18 J
	3d	83.3 %
	4bi	0.14 mm
	4bii	0.45 mm
88	**2**	74.75 A
	3a	1.8W
	3b	87 %
89	**1a**	98.6 %
	1b	40 %
90	**3e**	approximately: petroleum 65 %, coal >80 %, aluminium 70 %, copper 85 %, molybdenum 85 %, cobalt 80 %, nickel 60 %

Topic	Question	Answer
94	**1a**	£8 000 000
	1b	6525 kW
	1c	£1226 per kW
	1d	£1 600 000
	1e	£9 600000
	1f	3p per unit
	3a	6667 turbines
95	**1c**	8750 J
96	**1**	1.05 units
	2	£11.98
	3a	5.77p
	3b	£12.68
	4a	£4.93 per year
	4b	£1.70
End of topic (page 238)		
	1a	0.1 coulombs per second
	1b	60 ohms
	1c	0.4 A
	1d	6 V
	1e	0.6 W
	1f	2.4 J
	3a	54 A
	3b	74 A
	3c	No
	5a	792 kJ
	5b	600 kJ
	5c	1.32p
	5d	90 °C
	5e	642.6 kJ
	7a	11.7 km/h
	7b	80 kW

INDEX